Software Product Lines

T0189812

Timo Käkölä · Juan Carlos Dueñas (Eds.)

Software Product Lines

Research Issues in Engineering and Management

With 251 Figures and 62 Tables

 Springer

Editors

Timo Käkölä
Dept. Computer Science and
Information Systems
University of Jyväskylä
P.O. Box 35
40014 Jyväskylä, Finland
timokk@cc.jyu.fi

Juan Carlos Dueñas
Dept. Telematic Systems Engineering
Technical University of Madrid
Ciudad Universitaria
28040 Madrid, Spain
jcduenas@dit.upm.es

ISBN 978-3-642-06986-4   e-ISBN 978-3-540-33253-4

This work is subject to copyright. All rights are reserved, whether the whole or part of the material is concerned, specifically the rights of translation, reprinting, reuse of illustrations, recitation, broadcasting, reproduction on microfilm or in any other way, and storage in data banks. Duplication of this publication or parts thereof is permitted only under the provisions of the German Copyright Law of September 9, 1965, in its current version, and permission for use must always be obtained from Springer. Violations are liable for prosecution under the German Copyright Law.

Springer is a part of Springer Science+Business Media
springer.com
© Springer-Verlag Berlin Heidelberg 2010

The use of general descriptive names, registered names, trademarks, etc. in this publication does not imply, even in the absence of a specific statement, that such names are exempt from the relevant protective laws and regulations and therefore free for general use.

Cover design: KünkelLopka, Heidelberg

Foreword by John D. McGregor

Software Product Lines: Research Issues in Engineering and Management comes at an opportune time in the maturation of software product line engineering. The product line strategy has reached the point of being noticed by the "Early Majority" technology adopters. Many basic issues have been resolved and standard practices have begun to emerge. This volume furthers our understanding of product line engineering by reporting the results of a number of applied research studies that will serve to direct future practice.

The software product line strategy has allowed many organizations to significantly improve productivity, reduce the time required to produce a new product, and address niche markets that were previously not viable. The strategy has proven successful in a variety of settings, including large and small organizations in business, industry, and governmental sectors, and across a variety of domains. In particular, the strategy provides a framework within which organizations can target and achieve specific goals through analytic product selection from the pool of potential products as defined by the common and variable features, design for architectural qualities, and appropriate production techniques.

The product line strategy does not fit into the development plans of every organization. Markets that are changing too much too rapidly to permit payback, products that are too diverse, and domains whose futures are uncertain pose great risk to the success of a product line organization. Unlike one-at-a-time product development, a product line organization must anticipate changes that will occur over the full time horizon of its planned product producing lifetime. Economic modeling of a proposed product line is one technique I have used to evaluate these risks. Wesselius presents an economic modeling technique that accounts for risk by using scenarios to address the uncertainty of the future. A comprehensive model of the product line aids in decision making by classifying costs and benefits. This makes tradeoff analyses less complex and more accurate.

The product line approach to software development is the result of integrating many threads including Parnas' notion of product families, the software architecture-centric development approach of Bass, Clements, and Kazman, and the production planning techniques of companies such as Toyota. The product line organization benefits from the experience in each of these separate areas but the synergy of their integration enables even more powerful opportunities such as the ability to provide highly customized products and the agility to address new opportunities rapidly.

The topics covered in this book reflect some of the most important practices in a product line organization. You will find a number of investigations into front-end activities, including requirements representation, architecture evolution, and modeling. Bühne et al. address the issue of developing product specifications from the product line requirements. They provide a conceptual tool that assists the application requirement engineer in traversing the various combinations of variability values made possible by the domain engineer. The theme of developing product-specific assets from the product line assets, usually by resolving variabilities, is seldom discussed. Most of the variability literature focuses on recognizing and representing variability choices in the various assets instead of when actual choices of variants are made. This important issue is addressed in several chapters.

Product line engineering has been successful because it has broadened the scope of assets which we consider reusing. The code reuse techniques of the 1990s' consistently produced 10–15% savings for their users. By including the front-end activities and by considering the interactions of technical activities with management activities, product line engineering organizations routinely achieve a return on investment of over 100% after just three products. Product line organizations use the architecture as leverage for reuse of many assets. The architecture is the driving force behind many product line practices. Immonen presents a method for predicting reliability and availability from architectural information. That method is one of a growing number of practices that use a detailed architectural model to make decisions earlier in the development process than can be done with vague, high-level architectures. Other chapters provide investigations into active use of the architecture. Hallsteinsen et al. describe how to manage architectural variation. Fægri et al. describe a security architecture that cuts across the product line architecture.

The success of the product line strategy is directly related to the interactions among the software engineering, technical management, and organizational management practices that constitute the strategy. These synergies support the coordination needed to exploit the commonalities among products and to control their variations. Traditional approaches to software reuse have missed these essential interactions and, as a result, failed to deliver substantial benefits. Mansell addresses the interaction of managerial and technical concerns by examining the concerns of organizations implementing systematic reuse programs.

I have participated in several projects where the similarity among a set of products had been recognized and the projects scheduled with the intention of exploiting the commonality. In some cases, a separate "platform" team was formed to facilitate sharing of the common behavior among products. In the 1980s and 1990s these attempts often ended in failure when technical problems combined with insufficient, or short sighted, managerial planning prevented the use of artifacts across multiple products from happening. The software product line community has developed approaches that more closely coordinate the business planning and product implementation techniques for producing multiple products so that these opportunities are not lost.

Many product line organizations separate the role of producing product parts and the role of assembling products from those parts into different teams. This division allows each role to focus more clearly and precisely on their specific responsibilities. The group creating product parts focuses on enabling sufficient breadth of variation in those parts to accommodate the entire product portfolio. The group assembling products focuses on selecting the appropriate feature variations for their product. The two groups must collaborate. The assets produced by parts developers must be of use to the product builders. The product builders must provide feedback to the parts developers where assets are not sufficient. Oldevik et al. discuss the evaluation of product line engineering tools that will enable this coordination and collaboration.

The successful product line organization achieves strategic levels of reuse of assets across the products in the product line. These assets are not limited to code. The assets include the requirements, software architecture, and testing assets. This strategic level of reuse results in savings of production costs and time. These savings only take place if the organization has discipline in planning, process, and execution. Several of the chapters in this book present interesting perspectives on these assets, how they are created, managed, and evolved. Isabel John, for example, investigates bootstrapping a new product line by mining requirements from user documentation of legacy products. Rommes and America consider using scenarios to create architectures.

Assets evolve over the life of the product line. They do not all evolve at the same rate or even in the same direction. The product line organization needs techniques for managing evolution of all the assets, including the goals of the product line itself. Arciniegas et al. describe a holistic approach to managing the evolution of assets through the architecture. Engelsma addresses evolution of individual assets and presents a technique for coordinating the evolution of sets of assets that interact.

The similarity among the products in the product line reduces the cost of developing certain assets such as tools that automate development tasks. Developing generators for producing product-specific assets such as documentation becomes a cost-effective solution. Bertolino et al. take advantage of product line requirements to derive test cases to be reused for the products of the line, while Nebut et al. take advantage of the strategic levels of reuse to offer a comprehensive test strategy that includes automatic generation of test assets.

The roles of building product parts and building products can be viewed from the perspective of specifying variability options in the assets and resolving variabilities in the products. A variety of modeling approaches have been proposed for capturing variability in a software design. This is a difficult problem since there is a broad range of variability mechanisms that are applied at a variety of binding times. Bayer et al provide a comprehensive description and evaluation of a number of modeling approaches and provide a metamodel for variability modeling. In product line organizations the specification of variation often begins with developing scenarios that describe product situations. Reuys et al. illustrate this technique as they discuss how to define and then use generic test cases. As with many product line activities, their generic test cases begin with use cases and their scenarios, the identification of variation points in the scenarios, and then developing test cases with corresponding decision points.

Producing products is the ultimate goal of any product line organization and the focus of much of my recent work. I have found that much of the product line literature focuses on issues about the assets that will be used to produce products. Less attention is given to actually producing the products on the grounds that we have been doing this for a long time. The problem is, in a product line, product production is different from previous practices. Ziadi et al. report on an investigation into model transformations that can be used to derive products from a description of the product line.

The chapters of this book contribute to the evolution of the product line strategy. In particular, they provide descriptions of hypothesized theories for new practice which are supported by industry-based studies. The practical nature of these studies greatly enhances the value of this book. The constraints on validation and the decisions necessary to fit the studies into an industrial context are useful examples of how research can be conducted in industrial settings.

This volume is a valuable resource for researchers wishing to move the product line strategy forward and for those charged with translating state-of-the-art ideas into state-of-the-art practice processes and activities. Those interested in the product line strategy should be familiar with the results presented here and consider how the results can be applied to their product lines.

John D. McGregor
Clemson University
Clemson, South Carolina 29634-0974, USA
johnmc@cs.clemson.edu

Foreword by Frank van der Linden

Introduction

Between July 1999 and June 2005 a group of European companies, research institutes, and universities executed the EUREKA-ITEA projects ESAPS, CAFÉ, and FAMILIES on the topic of product line engineering. The projects originated from the need of the industry to improve software engineering performance by organizing product development in product lines. The results obtained within the projects have been implemented in several large industries (e.g., automotive, e-business, medical systems, and mobile phones). They involve a radical shift in software construction and production. The most important research results of the projects are collected in this book.

Product line engineering was already applied within industry in the 1980s and presumably earlier. In the 1980s, good architects in many telecommunications companies based their architectures on the ideas of David Parnas, who published on the subject of "program families". They were facilitated by the CHILL language widely used by the telecommunications companies. This language deploys the same modularity principles as the Modula programming language family. Modularity is a crucial ingredient for implementing systems with a component-based architecture. Being able to compose the products of components is an important mechanism in all product line architectures.

In the 1990s, the product line ideas started to gain ground in other industries. Around 1995, the company experiences reached the academia and since then people in companies and academia have collaborated widely on this subject. The ESAPS, CAFÉ, and FAMILIES projects manifest an institutionalized form of this collaboration.

As the project leader I was very happy with the excellent collaboration spirit within the three projects. Although initially we needed some time to get acquainted with, for example, the varying terminologies and aims of partners from numerous countries, the level of mutual understanding between project partners got better and better throughout the projects. People from all partners in the projects participated in regular meetings and learned good and not-so-good practices from each other. Academia obtained research ideas and presented the results within the projects, often leading to improved insights within the companies. Several bilateral collaborations with companies and academia started in this way.

As can be seen from this book, the research results were not obtained just within academia and research institutes. In fact, because of the working collaboration, people in industry found ways to introduce their ideas into research leading to new approaches that could not have been obtained within industry or academia alone. This means that the research results are based on company experiences founded, in turn, by the results.

The series of collaboration projects ended in 2005 because the basic knowledge base in the field was available to be applied in practice and further developed in academia and there was no need to continue collaborating in such a broad scope any more. Instead, new initiatives have been and will be started, which focus on more narrow issues like the ones addressed by individual chapters in this book.

Software product line engineering has shown to be an important way to improve the development of software by introducing managed reuse, supported by managed variability. It enables the companies to focus more on new features, leading, for example, to a shorter time-to-market. Legacy software still needs attention and maintenance, but large parts of legacy systems find their way as parts of other products in the product line. Therefore the time spent on maintaining legacy software is still valuable for the companies.

Companies still feel the increasing demand for having even more software functionality available at even shorter times to market. The improvements brought by software product line engineering have not got to an end. Further improvements need to be made, partially by automating activities needed during software product line engineering. But automation only gives reliable results if it is based on good theory. This book presents the early steps in the theory development needed to achieve an ever more extensive, reliable, and comprehensible software product line engineering environment in future.

As the demand for software is growing fast, companies are increasingly dependent on software developed by third parties. This is a challenge for companies leveraging software product line engineering, since that is a well-managed way of producing software. Software obtained from third parties cannot be controlled as well as own software. The situation that large parts of the software are beyond full control can only be dealt with effectively if software product line engineering is a well-understood discipline easily deployable by third parties as well. This book provides research results to be used to provide and acquire such an understanding.

Quality Assurance

This book has been designed to meet the highest quality criteria with respect to both new scientific knowledge validated using rigorous research methods and practical relevance. Only chapter submissions with careful scientific validation and interesting, new, and enduring contributions to the knowledge base in the software product line field have been incorporated in this book by the editors. All chapters have been reviewed and revised several times, some even more than 10 times. The revisions have typically taken several months of exhaustive work. The reviewers of the chapters, some of whom have been external to the three projects that have lead to this book, have worked enthusiastically and hard. They are acknowledged in the acknowledgment sections of the chapters. And the authors have really made the difference in this book. They delivered the best results of their research but did not know when they submitted the first drafts how much work would lay ahead of them. They have successfully met all the requirements of the editors and reviewers due to their willingness and ability to deliver an exceptionally high-quality book.

The editors have invested two years in designing and implementing the review and consolidation process. The results of this effort are well worth the time spent: the stakeholders involved have had a unique learning experience, the results of which have been consolidated into a coherent set of chapters. I expect this book to set the frontier of scientific knowledge for product line engineering research, upon which the communities of research and practice can pursue further research.

To ensure maximum coherence and cross-referencing across the chapters, Timo Käkölä, the editor-in-chief, has reviewed all chapters several times; participated in the writing of chapters when authors have needed extensive guidance in revisions; managed the review process so the authors have been able to evaluate, take into account, and participate in the development of all related chapters; written the preface, part introductions, and the glossary and index of this book in collaboration with the authors and other key stake-holders; and coordinated the publication process with the publisher. Juan Carlos Dueñas, the associate editor, has also reviewed most chapters many times. Without the enthusiasm and diligent work of the editors the quality objectives could not have been met.

Frank van der Linden
Philips Medical Systems
Postbus 10.000, 5680 DA, Best, The Netherlands
Frank.van.der.Linden@philips.com

Preface

Introduction

Are you interested in producing differentiated software products or software-intensive systems at lower costs, in shorter time, and with higher quality? Or are you interested in researching or teaching these issues? If so, this is the book for you.

Software product line engineering is an industrially validated methodology for developing software products and software-intensive systems faster, at lower costs, and with better quality.

This book is the second in the series of three software product line engineering books based on the European Eureka-ITEA projects ESAPS (1999–2001), CAFÉ (2001–2003), and FAMILIES (2003–2005) and published by Springer. It is for systems and software engineering researchers, lecturers, students, and professionals alike.

In this book, we use the term "software product line" or "product line" as identical to what is also commonly known as "software product family" or "system family." We have also aligned the terminology to the maximum possible extent with the first book of the series: *Software Product Line Engineering – Foundations, Principles, and Techniques* by Klaus Pohl, Günter Böckle, and Frank van der Linden. The first book is primarily targeted for educational purposes, thus leveraging the most widely adopted results of the three projects, while this book presents research results, most of which have already been experimented in the industrial arena, but have not been put into the mainstream yet.

Software product line engineering differs from single system development in two primary ways:

1. It needs two distinct development processes: domain engineering and application engineering. Domain engineering defines and realizes the commonality and variability of the software product line, thus establishing the common software platform for developing high-quality applications rapidly within the line. Application engineering derives specific applications by exploiting the variability of the line.

2. It needs to explicitly define and manage variability. During domain engineering, variability is introduced in all domain artifacts such as requirements, architectural models, components, and test cases. It is exploited during application engineering to derive applications tailored to the needs of different customers.

This book provides experience-based knowledge about the two distinct development processes, the modeling and management of variability, and the design and use of tools to support the management of product line related knowledge and to automate tasks. It holistically covers the interacting domain and application engineering life-cycles from initial product line planning through requirements engineering, reference architecture design, system design, component design and implementation, and testing to delivering products to markets and, to some extent, revising the product line and the products based on feedback from the markets. The book has thus been divided into five parts corresponding to the main areas of software product line engineering and management research:

1. Product line management
2. Product line requirements engineering
3. Product line architecture
4. Product line testing
5. Specific product line engineering issues

It should be noted that only a few chapters in this book address certain aspects of product line realization, a complete process to

- design in detail and implement reusable software assets with adequate variability during domain engineering based on the product line reference architecture and
- implement applications during application engineering by designing and implementing application-specific components and interfaces and configuring them with the right variants of the reusable assets into applications.

Product line realization relies upon mature detailed design and implementation processes during application engineering. However, little research has been performed on it. Since product line realization is not completely covered in this book, we have decided not to include a separate part for it. Such a part would be valuable between Parts 3 and 4 to cover the product line engineering life-cycle even more fully.

Product line engineering research has mostly focused on domain engineering that has been less developed and known than application engineering. While the concept of application engineering appears in all the parts of the book, specific techniques and tools for creating and deriving products within a product line are described in Part 5.

Why This Book?

The ESAPS, CAFÉ, and FAMILIES projects produced numerous results usable for companies leveraging or planning to adopt software product line engineering. These large and ambitious projects were executed during 6 years in nine European countries (Austria, Finland, France, Germany, Italy, the Netherlands, Norway, Spain, and Sweden) with more than 100 million euros of European public money. It is thus the duty and the privilege of the projects to publish coherently to the European community and to the world as many high-quality results as possible. The three books lay down three views on the experience obtained in the projects.

The other two books deal with validated organizational and technical knowledge related to the practical organizational and process enactment and improvement within the industry. This book deals with research results that have the potential to improve the practices within the industry even further. It is a basis for future research and improvement and, expectedly, for a better fundamental understanding of the issues touched upon in the other two books.

This book is a valuable resource for researchers and lecturers in universities and research institutes. It is equivalently useful for software and systems engineers and project, product, and quality managers in industry who face problems in their daily work in software product line engineering. Although the research results may not always be immediately applicable, they give ample insights in the causes of the problems and how the problems can eventually be tackled. The book probes the different phases in product line engineering, and its five-part structure is aligned with the traditional generic system development phases relevant to product line engineering as well.

The book recognizes that substantial organizational learning and investments are typically needed to fully leverage the product line strategy by establishing the common set of domain artifacts, building products from it, and having supportive processes and organizational structures in place. The book is thus useful for technology managers and R&D-technology policy makers who play central roles in steering and resourcing the organizational learning, adoption, and execution of product line practices so that the benefits afforded by the strategy can truly be achieved.

Which Questions are Answered by This Book?

The primary questions addressed by the five parts of this book are discussed next. Part 1 provides answers to the following questions:
- How should long-term and short-term business needs be balanced when designing and evaluating product line architectures?
- Why should the expected economic values of alternative product line architectures be evaluated? How can a business decision be made on when and how much to invest in domain engineering in order to realize the product line benefits (e.g., reductions in time-to-market, increased development efficiency, and improved quality) that outweigh the investments when economic criteria are applied?
- What are the primary organizational and managerial problems in introducing the software product line culture and practices in an organization and what are the ways to overcome these bottlenecks?

Part 2 provides answers to the following questions:
- How can a product line be built from legacy products by extracting commonality and variability information (e.g., requirements and features) from the documentation of the legacy products and transforming this information into requirements specifications and other product line models?
- How can application requirements engineers be made aware of the capabilities of the product line so they can systematically and consistently reuse or adapt the product line requirements during application requirements engineering?
- Which information elements compose a consolidated metamodel for software product line variability that can be used for all artifacts across all product line engineering phases to facilitate (a) the standardization of variability modeling with respect to terminology, representation, and concepts and (b) the creation of effective model-driven product line engineering tools?

Part 3 provides answers to the following questions:
- How can architectural variations in product line reference architectures be modeled when the product line members have substantial variations in architecturally significant requirements and how can the models preserve the support for product derivation (a complete process of building products from the product line) normally associated with more focused product lines?
- Is it viable to represent architectural security knowledge in a reference architecture? If so, is such a reference architecture useful for designing software product line architectures that effectively deal with security?
- How can product line evolution be supported by leveraging architectural recovery and conformance methods, techniques, and tools to meet nonfunctional architectural security requirements for distributed system environments?
- How can critical quality attributes such as reliability and availability of the product line architecture be analyzed prior to implementing the architecture, when changes are easier and cheaper to perform and the proper design decisions can still be made?

Part 4 provides answers to the following questions:
- How can the textual use cases notation be extended and modified to
  a) model common and variable product line requirements from an external point of view?
  b) guarantee the conformance of the derived products with respect to the product line requirements?
  c) derive (1) domain test plans for testing the common features across the product line and (2) application test case scenarios for validating that the derived products satisfy the user requirements?
- How can the generation of application system tests, for any chosen product, from product line requirements be automated?
- How can generic test artifacts for system and integration testing be systematically designed and reused?

Part 5 provides answers to the following questions:
- How can the domain engineering organization synchronize the work products from all areas of expertise engaged in developing the components so that increments for components can be efficiently integrated and tested before delivery to the application engineering organization?
- How can product derivation be formalized using a UML model transformation in the context of product line engineering?
- What are the generic requirements for product line engineering tools and how to evaluate such tools to partially automate tasks such as system modeling, variability modeling, model analysis, model transformation, system derivation, code generation, and model traceability?

All five parts have introductions to provide the chapters in this book with proper contexts that let readers understand how the chapters interrelate and how they fit within the big

picture of software product line engineering. In addition, we provide at the end of the book:
- A glossary for software product line engineering
- The index

Acknowledgments

Timo Käkölä is grateful to Günter Böckle from Siemens Corporate Technology and Frank van der Linden from Philips Medical Systems, who invited him to serve as the editor-in-chief of this book, and Nokia, TEKES (the Finnish Funding Agency for Technology and Innovation), the University of Jyväskylä, and the University of Oulu for supporting this work.

Juan C. Dueñas is grateful to Frank van der Linden for inviting him to participate in the Eureka-ITEA projects on product lines from the very beginning; the Ministerio of Educación y Ciencia of Spain, which supported his work under the reference TIC2002-12426-E; and the Spanish company Telvent and Universidad Politécnica de Madrid for supporting this work. Special thanks go to Timo Käkölä for his enthusiastic dedication to the book.

We thank Eureka-ITEA and all the other national public authorities for funding the projects ESAPS (1999–2001), CAFÉ (2001–2003), and FAMILIES (2003–2005). Most of the results presented in this book have been achieved in these projects.

We thank Ralf Gerstner and Ulrike Stricker from Springer-Verlag, Heidelberg, and Shylaja Gattupalli from SPi, Pondicherry, for their support in getting this book to market.

Finally, our thanks go to our collaborators within academia and industry who directly or indirectly were involved in creating this book.

Timo Käkölä   University of Jyväskylä, Finland
Juan Carlos Dueñas   Universidad Politécnica de Madrid, Spain

July 2006

Contents

Part 5: Specific Product Line Engineering Issues

List of Contributors

Pierre America
Philips Research
Prof. Holstlaan 4
5656 AA Eindhoven, The Netherlands
pierre.america@philips.com

Jose L. Arciniegas
Departamento de Ingeniería de Sistemas Telemáticos
Universidad Politécnica de Madrid, ETSI Telecomunicación
Ciudad Universitaria s/n
E-28040 Madrid, Spain
jlarci@dit.upm.es

Joachim Bayer
Fraunhofer IESE, Germany
Fraunhofer Platz 1
67663 Kaiserslautern, Germany
bayer@iese.fhg.de

Jesus Bermejo
Telvent
Tamarguillo 29
E-41006 Seville, Spain
jesus.bermejo@telvent.abengoa.com

Antonia Bertolino
Istituto di Scienza e Tecnologie dell'Informazione del C.N.R.
Via G. Moruzzi 1
I-56124 Pisa, Italy
antonia.bertolino@isti.cnr.it

Gert Jan Boot
Philips Medical Systems
Postbus 10.000
5680 DA, Best, The Netherlands
g.j.boot@philips.com

Stan Bühne
Software Systems Engineering, University of Duisburg-Essen
Schützenbahn 70
45117 Essen, Germany
buehne@sse.uni-due.de

Rodrigo Ceron
Departamento de Ingeniería de Sistemas Telemáticos
Universidad Politécnica de Madrid, ETSI Telecomunicación
Ciudad Universitaria s/n
E-28040 Madrid, Spain
ceron@dit.upm.es

Juan C. Dueñas
Departamento de Ingeniería de Sistemas Telemáticos
Universidad Politécnica de Madrid, ETSI Telecomunicación
Ciudad Universitaria s/n
E-28040 Madrid, Spain
jcduenas@dit.upm.es

Erwin Engelsma
Philips Medical Systems
Postbus 10.000
5680 DA, Best, The Netherlands
erwin.engelsma@philips.com

Alessandro Fantechi
Dip. di Sistemi e Informatica
Università di Firenze
Via S. Marta 3
I-50139 Firenze, Italy
fantechi@dsi.unifi.it

Tor Erlend Fægri
SINTEF ICT
N-7465 Trondheim, Norway
tor.e.fegri@sintef.no

Sebastien Gerard
CEA-List / L-LSP
Saclay
91191 Gif-sur-Yvette Cedex, France
sebastien.gerard@cea.fr

Stefania Gnesi
Istituto di Scienza e Tecnologie dell'Informazione del C.N.R.
Via G. Moruzzi 1
I-56124 Pisa, Italy
gnesi@isti.cnr.it

Günter Halmans
Software Systems Engineering, University of Duisburg-Essen
Schützenbahn 70
45117 Essen, Germany
halmans@sse.uni-due.de

Svein Hallsteinsen
SINTEF ICT
N-7465 Trondheim, Norway
svein.hallsteinsen@sintef.no

Øystein Haugen
Department of Informatics, University of Oslo
P.O. Box 1080 Blindern
N-0316 Oslo, Norway
oysteinh@ifi.uio.no

Anne Immonen
VTT Technical Research Centre of Finland
P.O. Box 1100
FIN-90571 Oulu, Finland
anne.immonen@vtt.fi

Jean-Marc Jézéquel
Institut de Recherche en Informatique et Systèmes Aléatoires (IRISA) &
University of Rennes 1
Campus de Beaulieu
F-35042 Rennes Cedex, France
jezequel@irisa.fr

Isabel John
Fraunhofer IESE
Fraunhofer Platz 1
67663 Kaiserslautern, Germany
john@iese.fraunhofer.de

Erik Kamsties
Software Systems Engineering, University of Duisburg-Essen
Schützenbahn 70
45117 Essen, Germany
erik.kamsties@imail.de

Timo Käkölä
Department of Computer Science and Information Systems
University of Jyväskylä
FIN-40014 Jyväskylän Yliopisto, Finland
timokk@cc.jyu.fi

Giuseppe Lami
Istituto di Scienza e Tecnologie dell'Informazione del C.N.R.
Via G. Moruzzi 1
I-56124 Pisa, Italy
giuseppe.lami@isti.cnr.it

Yves Le Traon
France Télécom R&D/MAPS Lannion France
yves.letraon@rd.francetelecom.com

Kim Lauenroth
Software Systems Engineering, University of Duisburg-Essen
Schützenbahn 70
45117 Essen, Germany
lauenroth@sse.uni-due.de

Jason Mansell
European Software Institute (ESI)
Parque Tecnológico de Bizkaia #204
E-48170 Zamudio, Bizkaia, Spain
jason.mansell@esi.es

Birger Møller-Pedersen
Department of Informatics, University of Oslo
P.O. Box 1080 Blindern
N-0316 Oslo, Norway
birger@ifi.uio.no

Clémentine Nebut
LIRMM (Laboratoire d'Informatique, de Robotique et
de Microélectronique de Montpellier)
161 rue Ada
34392 Montpellier Cedex 5, France
clementine.nebut@lirmm.fr

Jon Oldevik
SINTEF ICT
P.O. Box 124
Blindern
N-0314 Oslo, Norway
jon.oldevik@sintef.no

Miguel A. Oltra
Telvent
Tamarguillo 29
E-41006 Seville, Spain
miguel.oltra@telvent.abengoa.com

Klaus Pohl
Software Systems Engineering, University of Duisburg-Essen
Schützenbahn 70
45117 Essen, Germany
pohl@sse.uni-due.de

Sacha Reis
Software Systems Engineering, University of Duisburg-Essen
Schützenbahn 70
45117 Essen, Germany
reis@sse.uni-due.de

Andreas Reuys
Software Systems Engineering, University of Duisburg-Essen
Schützenbahn 70
45117 Essen, Germany
andreas.reuys@sqs.de

Eelco Rommes
Philips Research
Prof. Holstlaan 4
5656 AA, Eindhoven, The Netherlands
eelco.rommes@philips.com

Jose L. Ruiz
Departamento de Ingeniería de Sistemas Telemáticos
Universidad Politécnica de Madrid
ETSI Telecomunicación, Ciudad Universitaria s/n
E-28040 Madrid, Spain
jlruiz@dit.upm.es

Gerard Schouten
Philips Medical Systems
Postbus 10.000
5680 DA, Best, The Netherlands
g.schouten@philips.com

Arnor Solberg
SINTEF ICT
P.O. Box 124 Blindern
N-0314 Oslo, Norway
arnor.solberg@sintef.no

Patrick Tessier
CEA-List / L-LSP
Saclay
91191 Gif-sur-Yvette Cedex, France
patrick.tessier@cea.fr

Jean-Philippe Thibault
IRISA & Institut National de Recherche en Informatique et Automatique (INRIA)
Campus de Beaulieu
F-35042 Rennes Cedex, France

Jacco Wesselius
Philips Medical Systems
Postbus 10.000
5680 DA Best, The Netherlands
jacco.wesselius@philips.com

Tanya Widen
Nokia Research Center
P.O. Box 407
FIN-00045 NOKIA GROUP, Finland
tanya.widen@nokia.com

Tewfik Ziadi
LIP6 & University of Paris 6
8, rue du Capitaine Scott
F-75015 Paris, France
tewfik.ziadi@lip6.fr

Part 1: Product Line Management

Introduction

Part 1 deals with product line management, which covers the fuzzy front end of creating a product line during which software-intensive product companies need to build product roadmaps that initially define the intended set of products and targeted markets for the line, the intended commonalities and variability for the products, a schedule for bringing the products to the markets, and legacy systems and other artifacts to be considered when defining software product line requirements. Product line management also covers the management of the organizational change process where product line engineering and management culture is institutionalized in organizations.

Part 1 consists of three chapters:

Chapter 1. A Scenario-Based Method for Software Product Line Architecting

Chapter 2. Strategic Scenario-Based Valuation of Product Line Roadmaps

Chapter 3. Experiences and Expectations Regarding the Introduction of Systematic Reuse in Small- and Medium-Sized Companies

Software product line engineering implies making a long-term investment in a common software product line architecture to support the derivation of potentially many generations of products in the line. Short-term and long-term business considerations should be well balanced when defining and evolving software product line architectures. Established methods for architecting lack support for doing this in an efficient manner.

Chapter 1 presents a scenario-based architecting method to address this problem. The method uses various types of scenarios to ensure that the long-term future is taken into account and to enable the efficient description, evaluation, and comparison of multiple candidate architectures in parallel. Chapter 1 also serves as an excellent introduction to this book as it takes a holistic view on product line engineering and management to an extent seldom seen in academic product line literature. Its perspectives range from considering market needs and business strategic issues to product line implementation using available technologies. Only product line testing is strictly outside the scope of the chapter.

The business case for the long-term investments in developing the architecture, setting up the organization, and developing engineering and managerial skills has to show that the expected outcomes ranging from reductions in time-to-market to increased development efficiency and improved quality outweigh the investments when economical criteria are applied. Models exist for evaluating the impact of product line engineering on development cost. But revenues, lifecycle costs, time, and uncertainty must also be accounted for in assessing the economical value. More comprehensive economical models are thus needed to base product line roadmap decisions on valid assessments of the expected economical outcomes.

Chapter 2 complements the scenario-based architecting method by introducing a general model for evaluating the value of investments made in product line engineering to evaluate the expected economical values of scenarios for product line architecture development. To address assumptions and expectations about the future, the model uses strategic scenarios and assigns each of them a probability. Chapter 2 also combines the general model and previously available models into a single comprehensive framework covering all factors in the equation of economical value for product line engineering.

All software reuse initiatives have encountered similar organizational, managerial, and knowledge-related problems in the organizational implementation of software reuse techniques. Organizations thus need effective solutions to face these problems. Chapter 3 provides insights into what are the reuse opportunities and the problems organizations confront when implementing systematic reuse initiatives. It addresses organizations that are considering implementing a systematic software reuse initiative and wish to have an idea of what other organizations have undergone, how they have resolved problems encountered, and what is the expected evolution of the initiative.

The chapters of Part 1 complement each other in many ways. Most importantly, they recognize that, from the technical viewpoint, the maturity of the techniques and mechanisms for implementing systematic software reuse is considerable but the software product line initiatives often fail due to managerial, economical, and organizational challenges. Solutions to these challenges are scarcely available in the literature. Yet, they are critical to successfully launch software product lines in industrial settings. Therefore, the managerial and economical perspectives of software product line engineering taken in Part 1 are especially justified. All chapters rely on empirical experiences from the industry.

1 A Scenario-Based Method for Software Product Line Architecting

E. Rommes and P. America

Abstract

Software product line engineering implies making a long-term investment in a common architecture. This architecture must support the derivation of potentially many generations of products in the line. Short-term and long-term business considerations should be well balanced when defining and evolving software product line architectures. Established methods for architecting lack support for doing this in an efficient manner. We present a scenario-based architecting method that addresses this problem. The method uses various types of scenario to ensure that the long-term future is taken into account, and to enable the efficient description, evaluation and comparison of multiple candidate architectures in parallel.

1.1 Introduction

Architecting is at the core of software product line engineering. The architecture of a product line determines how products are derived efficiently from the core assets. To allow the derivation of several different products, a product line architecture has to deal with variation. The architecture's support for variation determines the scope of the product line. Overly complex variation will make the architecture itself overly complicated, and therefore expensive to design, implement, and maintain. On the other hand, support for too little variation will result in a limited scope and may mean losing out on business opportunities.

To complicate matters further, the optimal scope of a product line is not fixed in time. Over time, the needs of a business change, and hence the demands made on its products. New features will be introduced, redundant ones will be removed, neighboring domains may be entered or new products may be added to well-known domains. In addition, advances in technology may offer opportunities to enhance the product line. These are just a few examples of changes that lead to new requirements for the architecture to support. The architecture must evolve to support the efficient derivation of new or improved products.

Evolving an architecture can be challenging, and implementing a change can be costly, especially in cases where the change was unforeseen and the architecture is therefore probably not suited. Changes made to the architecture to meet today's needs may prove to be obstacles to the changes that need to be made next week. There is a point at which it becomes cheaper to throw away the architecture and start a new product line than to adapt the existing architecture.

To take a product line well into the future, system derivation in the right scope must remain efficient. The architecture must be flexible in terms of what is likely to be required in the near future, and must evolve in a direction that will keep it flexible in the long-term. Architects designing or evolving a product line architecture need to balance the short-term and long-term business needs.

From what we have seen in practice, architects carry out such balancing exercises implicitly. For each factor requiring change, there will be numerous possible ways of adapting the architecture. Each of these will have its own specific short-term and long-term consequences. An architect will use his experience and intuition to dismiss the majority of options without hesitation, and will choose just a handful to pursue. However, intuition and experience are not always correct, nor are they easy to communicate to other stake-holders. An explicit overview of available options and their implications can help architects to arrive at and document decisions that will suit both the short-term and the long-term business goals.

1.1.1 Research Questions

Based on the above problems, we define the following research questions:

1. How can the long-term future be taken into account systematically during the design and evolution of product line architectures?
2. How can multiple candidate architectures for a product line be described, evaluated, and compared efficiently?

1.1.2 Existing Architecting Methods

Many architecting methods have been proposed. We take a closer look at four of them: PuLSE-DSSA [12], Bosch [7], ADD [4] and Visual Architecting [8,31]. A comparison of four other architecting methods aimed specifically at product lines is presented by Matinlassi [32].

PuLSE-DSSA (Product Line Software Engineering – Domain Specific Software Architecture) is a framework for developing product line reference software architectures. The design of a reference architecture is driven by a set of scenarios that describe the functional and nonfunctional requirements. The scenarios are sorted according to architectural significance. A subset is used to create an initial architecture, which is then improved by applying the rest of the scenarios one by one.

Bosch [7] starts by designing an initial architecture based on functional requirements. This initial architecture is input to an iterative process, where quality scenarios drive the evaluation and improvement of the architecture.

The ADD (Attribute Driven Design) [4] method takes quality requirements into account right from the start. A set of system-specific quality scenarios is used to guide the design of the architecture. Starting from a single element representing the whole system, the architecture is recursively decomposed into more specialized design elements.

The Visual Architecting Process [8,31] iterates over three steps: requirements, specification and validation. In the requirements step, a subset of architecturally relevant system requirements is selected and refined. A study is also made of the business objectives for the architecture and the future products for which use of the architecture is intended. The specification step entails creating artifacts that describe the architecture, such as component and interface descriptions. During the validation step, the quality properties of the architecture are evaluated.

None of these methods offers explicit support for long-term requirements or the consideration of a wide range of architecting options in parallel.

We propose Scenario-Based Architecting (SBA), which builds upon these and other architecting methods and improves them in two respects:

1. *SBA supports the design and evaluation of multiple candidate architectures in parallel in an efficient way.* Taking a family of candidate architectures into account allows architects to make better-informed decisions. Most architecting methods entail the repeated improvement and evaluation of a single candidate architecture. PuLSE-DSSA allows a number of architectures to be designed and evaluated in parallel, but only as an exceptional case, and the method offers no further support in this situation.
2. *SBA takes future business requirements into account during the design and evaluation of candidate architectures.* While the Visual Architecting Process deals with future requirements explicitly in that it takes future products into account, SBA takes a much broader future into account by means of strategic scenarios that describe not only products but also the entire business domain. Candidate architectures can thus be designed with future business requirements in mind, and can be evaluated in terms of how well they fit certain future scenarios.

1.1.3 The Use of Scenarios in Architecting

Scenarios are widely used in software architecting for describing requirements. SBA introduces two new types of scenarios to the architecting process. We identify three types of scenarios that are useful in architecting:

- *Usage scenarios* focus on particular instances of a system's use to describe system requirements. Clements et al. define this type of scenario as: "a short statement describing an interaction of one of the stakeholders with the system." [10] (p. 33)

  Usage scenarios are a fairly common element of system architecting methods. Such scenarios are used in SBA and other methods to evaluate the functional and quality properties of candidate architectures.
- *Strategic scenarios* are plausible stories regarding the long-term future. Schwartz defines this type of scenario as: "a tool for ordering one's perceptions about alternative future environments in which one's decisions might be played out." [37] (p. 4)

  Strategic scenarios are a tool for making decisions that have a long-lasting effect. They are most commonly used in the field of business management. In SBA they are used to add strategic business information to the design and evaluation process.
- *Architecture scenarios* are a new type of scenarios. An architecture scenario describes a coherent set of design choices within a single view. Architecture scenarios can be linked to form candidate architectures.

  In SBA, architecture scenarios are used to deal efficiently with many different candidate architectures at the same time.

1.1.4 Applicability of Scenario-Based Architecting

Within Philips, we have applied SBA to the evolution of an architecture for a product line of software-intensive medical imaging systems. The method was designed to be more generally applicable, however, and our assumption is that it can also be applied in other domains and other companies.

It is easier to apply SBA using an existing architecture as a basis, because deltas to the current architecture can be considered instead of entirely new candidate architectures. Still, nothing prohibits an architect from using the SBA method to design a completely new architecture. Much of the commercial information should be available from the start, unless a good business model is lacking. Legacy systems could be mined for technical elements of the new architecture. From there, a top-down approach would be advisable. The main decomposition should be defined early. Further details relating to individual subsystems can then be added as needed.

Since SBA incorporates long-term requirements into the architecture design process, it makes sense to apply it to architectures that are intended to be long living. Product line architectures certainly represent a long-term investment, but SBA can be applied equally well to single-system architectures.

While *architecture* scenarios are a useful tool in general, in situations where the support of long-term requirements is not an issue, SBA's use of *strategic* scenarios is too much. It should be noted that the definition of "long-term" very much depends on the application domain. In the case of medical imaging, the long-term future is 10 years away. For mobile phones, the long-term future may start four years from now. In the world of e-commerce, long-term may mean next month.

1.1.5 Structure of This Chapter

The remainder of this chapter describes the scenario-based architecting method. Section 1.2 outlines our research approach. A high-level overview of the method is given in Sect. 1.3. In Sect. 1.4, we present a detailed description of the method, using a medical imaging case study as a running example. Our conclusions can be found in Sect. 1.5.

1.2 Research Method

We used two case studies over a two-year period as our primary research strategy for developing SBA. In these case studies, we iteratively designed a part of the method, applied it to a real-world problem and evaluated the application and its results. We then moved on to designing the next part. This incremental and iterative approach is in line with Hevner et al. [20]: "Because design is inherently an iterative and incremental activity, the evaluation phase provides essential feedback to the construction phase as to the quality of the design process and the design product under development." (p. 85)

Robson advocates the applicability of the case study method in real world research [36]. Although he focuses on social sciences, much of his work is applicable in other domains as well, including information systems research. According to Robson, "the purpose of an evaluation is to assess the effects and effectiveness of something, typically some innovation, intervention, policy, practice or service." (p. 201) and *"formative evaluation* is intended to help in the *development* of the program, innovation or whatever is the focus of the evaluation." (p. 207) We used the case study method as a means of formative evaluation of SBA.

Robson defines case study as "a strategy for doing research which involves an empirical investigation of a particular contemporary phenomenon within its real life context using multiple sources of evidence." (p. 177)

The *real-life context* of our case studies was the department of Philips Medical Systems responsible for the product line of medical imaging systems under study. Both case studies entailed the extension of the architecture of this product line to support new or enhanced products. Stakeholders of the product line helped us to define the scope of these case studies in such a way that they were realistic and useful. Both cases were designed to include problems that Philips expected to encounter within two years.

Our studies were *empirical:* We gathered evidence on the method results and its application in workshops and from our own studies. The *contemporary phenomenon* we investigated was the application of SBA to a product line of medical imaging systems.

We used *multiple sources of evidence*: documents, interviews, reviews, presentations, and workshops. We held 20 interviews with 15 different people. Topics included marketing, application and the architecture of existing and future products in the product line. We used multiple types of documents, such as business scenario studies, architecture descriptions, requirements specifications, product manuals and presentations by business, application and technical experts.

We regularly asked experts from the field to evaluate the method results. Philips architects reviewed most of the mature results for completeness, soundness and usefulness. The end results, i.e., architecture descriptions, were reviewed by the product line's architects and found to be realistic and useful. In this way, we could be certain that we were working on a realistic problem and that the method could be used to produce useful solutions to real-world problems.

The SBA method itself was also applied and evaluated by practitioners. To this end, we held six workshops, which were visited by 34 different people. We invited experts in marketing, architecture, application domain and management. Not all those invited were stakeholders of the product line on which our case studies were based. We also invited experts from other parts of Philips, to make sure that the method was general enough to be applied elsewhere too. The average number of participants per workshop was 14.

The general format of the workshops was as follows:

- We presented the current version of the method and the current results of the case study.
- Experts from Philips Medical Systems presented topics relevant to the case study at that point, for example architecture issues, domain trends or requirements.
- Participants worked in subgroups to apply (part of) the method. They extended or enhanced existing artifacts or created new artifacts (scenarios, variation models, etc.).
- The subgroups' results were presented and evaluated in a plenary session, and the method was discussed. The feedback from these discussions was used as input for the further improvement of the method.

1.3 Method Overview

This section presents an overview of the SBA method. We introduce the CAFCR model of architecture views in Sect. 1.3.1. An overview of the SBA process is given in Sect. 1.3.2.

1.3.1 The Views

An architecture cannot be developed and described from a single viewpoint. As Clements et al. argue: "a software architecture is a complex entity that cannot be described in a simple one-dimensional fashion." [9] (p. 13) Instead, a set of views must be chosen in order to describe the many different aspects of the architecture. We chose to use the CAFCR (Customer Application, Functional, Conceptual, Realization) [33] set of views in SBA, see Fig. 1.1. We shall first explore each view in detail, and then discuss alternative view sets and the reasons for choosing CAFCR.

CAFCR

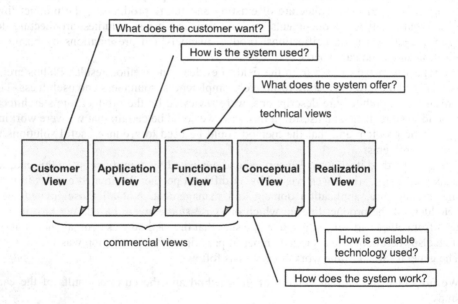

Fig. 1.1. Overview of the CAFCR views

The Customer View
The customer view captures information on the customer. We define the customer as the party that makes the final decision to buy the system. This may be a person, or a group of persons. The customer may or may not be a user of the system under design.

These are the major questions that are addressed in the customer view:

- Who is the customer? Who are the major stakeholders who influence the customer's decision to buy a product? What are their objectives, needs, and wishes?
- What is the customer's context? What external forces influence the customer?
- What is the essential value that the system offers to the customer?

The Application View
The application view describes how the system can be used to fulfill the customer's needs.
The major questions addressed in the application view are:

- How do the system's stakeholders apply the system to achieve their objectives?
- Which stakeholders will use the system? In what ways? How does this usage fit their way of working?
- In what context must the system operate? What other systems are in use?

The Functional View
This view is used to describe the desired externally perceivable properties of the system under development, in a concise way. Where such a property indicates the presence of a certain piece of functionality, we typically call it a feature. Other properties are usually called qualities.

The description of the functional view aims to be as independent as reasonably possible from the way the system is used or the way it is implemented. In this respect, the functional view can be seen as an interface between the customer and application views on the one hand and the conceptual and realization views on the other hand.

These are the major questions that are addressed in the functional view:

- What is the behavior of the system?
- What features and what qualities does it offer?

In answering these questions, commercial considerations play an important role.

The Conceptual View
The goal of this view is to describe the essential concepts that govern how the system works.

Some of the major questions addressed in the conceptual view are:

- What are the components that comprise the architecture? How do these components collaborate?
- What styles and principles are used to guide the product line design?
  An architecture style "[defines] a *vocabulary* of components and connector types, and a set of *constraints* on how they can be combined." [38] (p. 20)

A principle is "a specific approach to the (architectural) design process that leads to good designs." [45] (p. 9)

The Realization View
The realization view describes how the system is realized using available technologies.
The major questions that are addressed in the realization view is:

- What technology is used to implement the system?
- What are the consequences of this use?

Alternative View Sets

The 4+1 model contains five views [29]. The *logical* view primarily supports the functional requirements. It contains a set of key abstractions (classes and objects) taken mainly from the problem domain. The *process* view addresses concurrency and distribution: the way in which processes are distributed across a set of hardware resources. The *development* view focuses on the organization of the actual software modules in the software-development environment. In the *physical* view, the various elements identified in the other views are mapped onto the system's processing nodes. The *scenarios* view contains a small set of important functional scenarios to show that the elements of the four views work together seamlessly.

Soni et al. propose the Siemens Four View model [40]. The *conceptual* view describes the system in terms of its major design elements and the relationships between them. The *module interconnection* view encompasses two orthogonal structures: functional decomposition and layers. The *execution* view describes the dynamic structure of a system. The *code* view describes how the source code, binaries, and libraries are organized in the development environment.

These and most other view sets focus on the technical side of architecture. Business aspects are not included in the architecture description. In addition to CAFCR, at least one other view set explicitly takes business aspects into account:

The Visual Architecting Process (VAP) [8,31] uses three technical views, one meta-view and a requirements view. Although views are referred to as "architectures" in VAP, the general concept is the same. The *conceptual* architecture describes the structure of a system in terms of components, their responsibilities and collaborations. The *logical* architecture comprises detailed component and interface specifications. The *execution* architecture is a description of the distribution of components on processes and nodes. The *meta-architecture* contains rules that guide architecture decisions. Functional and non-functional requirements are considered in the *architectural requirements*. Business concerns are also taken into account here: "The business objectives for the system, and the architecture in particular, are important to ensure that the architecture is aligned with the business agenda." [31]

The views used to describe an architecture determine the ways in which the architecture can be evaluated: "Different views also expose different quality attributes to different degrees. Therefore, the quality attributes that are of most concern to you and the other stakeholders in the system's development will affect the choice of what views to document." (Clements et al. [9] p. 14) Some of the most important stakeholders of a product line are the future customers and users of the systems. CAFCR addresses these stakeholders directly. This allows the evaluation of an architecture's commercial properties, such as usability and product value, as well as its technical properties, such as performance. This is the main reason behind our decision to choose this set of views.

In theory, views are orthogonal to the method, and SBA can be applied using any set of views suitable to describe the architecture under consideration. We have not tested this hypothesis, but we expect that it will be harder to relate candidate architectures to strategic scenarios and business goals when a purely technical set of views is used. This is a topic for further research.

1.3.2 The Process

Scenario-based architecting is an iterative process. An iteration consists of three core steps: explore variation, create architecture scenarios, and evaluate candidate architectures, cf. Fig. 1.2. The five architecture views are involved in each of these steps. Typically, more time and effort is spent on the commercial views in early iterations, with the focus shifting to the technical views in later iterations. In a way, this is analogous to the process from capturing requirements to doing design. It can be useful to start with coarse-grained decisions, exploring many options while paying less attention to details. In later iterations, the number of serious candidate architectures will decrease and the remaining options can be studied in more depth, if desired.

The details of the process are given in the example in Sect. 1.4. Here is a brief overview, to give some insight into the basic steps and their mutual relationships. In our description of the method, we have kept the steps within an iteration strictly separated for the sake of clarity. In practice, the boundaries are less clear. Architects may move from one step to the next without even thinking about it, or go back to do some more work in the previous step to remove an obstacle that is blocking progress. When iterating is complete and the evaluation shows satisfactory results, the last step is to select a candidate architecture and document it appropriately.

Strategic Scenarios

Strategic scenarios are stories about plausible long-term futures in the world at large. They are typically the result of a multi-disciplinary study into the business domain, taking business, technical, application and organization trends into account. Strategic scenarios are tools used to make decisions that have long-lasting implications.

The creation and use of strategic scenarios in management and business planning is described among others by Schwartz [37] and Van der Heijden [19]. According to Schwartz [37]: "Scenarios are not about predicting the future, rather they are about perceiving futures in the present." (p. 36) Ionita et al., have extended the use of strategic scenarios in architecting with an approach to estimate the market share, sales, and profit of future products [23]. Ionita's SODA (Strategic Options Design and Assessment) method [22] is closely related to SBA, and is based in part on the results of our case studies. A major difference between SODA and SBA is the latter's use of candidate architectures to handle multiple architectures in parallel. Chapter 2 describes how product line roadmaps can be evaluated for their economic benefits.

In SBA, strategic scenarios are used as input to the iterations. They are a source of inspiration when seeking out architecture choices, and are used to evaluate candidate architectures. If strategic scenarios are not available, one option is for the architect to write them himself. Architects should have a thorough insight into the technical aspects of their domain. They can gather additional information by consulting experts from other fields, such as marketing and research. In principle, this information can be applied directly as input for the method but bundling it into a set of scenarios carries with it the advantage that the information becomes available to many stakeholders. Using the scenarios they can provide valuable feedback and highlight flaws or gaps in knowledge that would otherwise have gone unnoticed. Furthermore, the scenarios provide a set of coherent visions and are easier to use and discuss than a pile of loosely related documents, let alone a pile of the architect's personal memories.

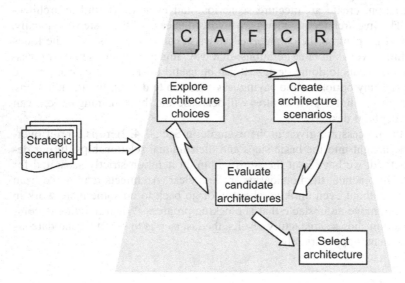

Fig. 1.2. The scenario-based architecting process

Explore Architecture Choices

The first step of an SBA iteration is to explore architectural options. This is done by modeling variation in all five CAFCR views [3]. The resulting variation models outline plausible architecture choices. They guide further decision-making and document the options that were considered.

Techniques for variation modeling have been well investigated in the software product line community. Most existing approaches concentrate on the modeling of diversity in the *features* of the systems. Examples are Feature-Oriented Domain Analysis (FODA) [28], and the work by Ferber et al. [14]. A meta-model of such modeling languages can be found in Chap. 6. Chapter 5 describes a scenario-based approached to functional variation modeling.

Feature models belong to the functional view in CAFCR. However, SBA uses variation modeling as a tool to describe possible architecture choices, not just features. We have therefore extended existing feature modeling techniques by adding support for multiple architecture views and their relations [2,3].

Create Architecture Scenarios

In the next step, the variation models are used to create a set of architecture scenarios. Each scenario describes a plausible architecture in a single CAFCR view. There are three to five scenarios per view. This step results in a family of related candidate architectures. Individual candidate architectures can be created by selecting one architecture scenario in each view and linking them together. We first described architecture scenarios in 2004 [2]. Now, we add the combination of architecture scenarios to form a family of candidate architectures.

Evaluate Candidate Architectures

The final step of an iteration is to evaluate the candidate architecture. We distinguish between functional, quality, and strategic evaluation. During functional evaluation, a candidate architecture is assessed for its support of functional requirements. Quality evaluations result in estimations of values for quality attributes of candidate architectures. Strategic scenarios are used to evaluate how well a candidate architecture fits a certain business strategy.

Completion of this step results in a set of plausible candidates for the product line architecture, plus evaluation results showing their properties in respect of a number of quality attributes and how well they fit a set of possible futures.

A wide range of architecture evaluation methods exist. Some evaluation methods focus on a single or few quality attributes, e.g., performance [39] or reliability and availability (see Chap. 10). Others are more general: Bosch describes a framework for architecture assessment (Chap. 5 in [7]). Clements et al. [10] describe and compare three methods: the Architecture Trade-off Analysis Method (ATAM), the Software Architecture Analysis Method (SAAM), and Active Reviews for Intermediate Designs (ARID). The Family Architecture Assessment Method (FAAM) addresses the interoperability and extensibility of families of information systems [13]. An overview of scenario-based software architecture evaluation methods is given by Ionita et al. [26]. Ionita also defines SQUASH (Systematic Quantitative Analysis of Scenarios' Heuristics), a method that focuses on the evaluation of architecture scenarios [22].

Each of these methods has its strengths and weaknesses. There is no single method that is most appropriate in all circumstances. What they have in common is that they are designed to evaluate one architecture at a time. To compare the results of multiple architectures, the method must be repeated. In contrast, SBA allows the efficient parallel evaluation of several candidate architectures. The primary units for evaluation are the architecture scenarios. Information on all the candidate architectures that use a particular scenario is obtained by assessing the properties of that one architecture scenario.

It is the way that candidate architectures are described in SBA that makes this possible, and not the evaluation method. In fact, any evaluation method can be used in combination with SBA. We evaluated architecture scenarios for a diverse range of qualities, including usability, performance, product value, risk, and cost of use [2,24,25], using various approaches.

If a product line architecture already exists, it can be a good idea to start with the evaluation step. This helps the stakeholders of the updated architecture to set its scope and to reach agreement on the most important (quality) requirements.

Select Candidate Architecture

The last step is to select a product line architecture and document it according to our needs. The candidate architectures and their evaluation provide some input in this context, but additional documentation is usually needed. Section 1.4.7 gives an overview of the artifacts used for this purpose in SBA.

1.4 Scenario-Based Architecting Applied

Below is a detailed explanation of scenario-based architecting. We illustrate the method with a running example. Although the example is based on our case studies, it is not a complete description of a single case: elements of the two cases have been mixed, simplified and adapted for the purposes of this publication. We introduce the resulting example in Sect. 1.4.1. Section 1.4.2 deals with strategic scenarios. Each of the subsequent sections deals with a single step in the method: explore architecture options, create architecture scenarios, evaluate candidate architectures, and select architecture. Finally, Sect. 1.4.7 explains the supporting artifacts used in SBA that were not explained previously.

1.4.1 Running Example: The 3D Cathlab

The catheterization laboratory (cathlab) is a hospital room used for the diagnosis and treatment of patients with vascular disease (Fig. 1.3). One of the most common forms of such diseases occurs when an artery is narrowed by plaque.

The plaque limits the blood flow through the artery, causing part of the body to be deprived of access to fresh blood. This situation may result in a heart attack if the artery leads to the heart, or a stroke if it supplies the brain. These and related diseases can be diagnosed and treated in the cathlab. The physician inserts a catheter into an artery near the patient's groin, and moves it gently through the arteries to the desired location. The tip of the catheter can hold various instruments to treat the disease.

The cathlab houses various forms of equipment used to support such catheterization procedures. A central role in the cathlab is fulfilled by a cardiovascular X-ray system. This system is used to visualize the patient's vessel structure and the exact location of the catheter. High quality images can be used to carry out measurements relating to the vessel blockages, such as the blood flow through the blockage, its length, and its width.

In other applications, catheters interact directly with the heart itself, rather than with vessels. Children require special treatment, as they have smaller blood circulation systems and faster heartbeats. To minimize the amount of contrast fluid and scattered radiation that a child is exposed to, two detectors may be used simultaneously. Different members of the product line address these and other variations.

Other devices used in the cathlab include monitoring devices for electrocardiograms (ECG) and blood flow (hemodynamics), as well as reporting and archiving applications. Sometimes special imaging systems are used to visualize the inside walls of an artery.

Another way of obtaining extra information is the use of three-dimensional images. These images can either be created on the spot or taken from diagnostic procedures that the patient has undergone earlier, for example using magnetic resonance imaging. These are referred to as *multi-modality* procedures, because information from different types of imaging systems is combined in a single procedure. The creation of three-dimensional models from two-dimensional X-ray images is achieved via an application known as three-dimensional rotational angiography (3DRA). Several images are created from different angles, and then combined into a single three-dimensional model.

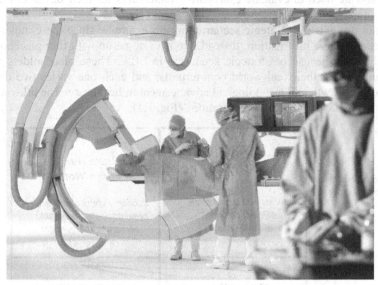

Fig. 1.3. The cathlab

1.4.2 Strategic Scenarios

One of the goals of the scenario-based architecting method is to make architectures more resilient to future changes. Effecting architecture changes in the implementation is a major task. These changes must therefore be chosen carefully.

Future changes in requirements are, by nature, very uncertain. A number of different scenarios are therefore considered, each of which describes possible future global developments, along the lines of the work carried out by Schwartz [37]. These scenarios focus on the relevant field of business, which in our example is the area of healthcare for cardiovascular patients. Such scenarios form a good basis for business decisions and are therefore referred to as *strategic scenarios*.

Strategic scenarios are usually created by a multi-disciplinary team of experts. The team's expertise should cover business strategy, the application domain, the technical domain, and company management.

A common pitfall to be avoided when reasoning about the future is the choice of a single "official future." This may be the result of wishful thinking, or of the simple extrapolation of observed trends. Choosing a single scenario is unwise, since it means that all opportunities and threats that happen to fall outside this official vision are neglected. To mitigate this risk, multiple strategic scenarios should be used as input. Four seems to be an effective number: two scenarios are not enough to span a wide range of possibilities, and creating three scenarios carries the risk of creating a "low," "middle" and "high" scenario, with the result that the middle one tends to be thought of, at least implicitly, as the "official future."

In SBA, strategic scenarios are used as input to the architecting process. They provide the knowledge of business context needed to create both variation models and architecture scenarios, and are used to evaluate candidate architectures for their business value in the long-term future.

We do not use existing strategic scenarios in this example, since these inevitably contain business-sensitive information. Instead, we have come up with four placeholders that serve to illustrate the use of strategic scenarios in SBA. These placeholders are much more simplistic than their real-world counterparts, and each one varies two dimensions only: economic growth and technological advancement in healthcare. The titles were based on publicly available commercial presentations (Fig. 1.4).

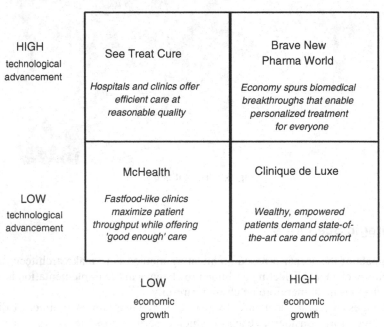

HIGH technological advancement	See Treat Cure *Hospitals and clinics offer efficient care at reasonable quality*	Brave New Pharma World *Economy spurs biomedical breakthroughs that enable personalized treatment for everyone*
LOW technological advancement	McHealth *Fastfood-like clinics maximize patient throughput while offering 'good enough' care*	Clinique de Luxe *Wealthy, empowered patients demand state-of-the-art care and comfort*
	LOW economic growth	HIGH economic growth

Fig. 1.4. Strategic scenarios

A useful means of communicating these scenarios is via *cover stories*: fake magazine articles that use natural language to describe the future world depicted in the scenario (Fig. 1.5).

Fig. 1.5. Cover stories

1.4.3 Explore Architecture Choices

The goal of this step is to explore the space of possible architectural choices. To do this, the construction of a model can be of help in several ways:

1. *To structurally explore the variation space in and across the various views.* By modeling the variation space, one soon gets a feel for the complexity of and the main issues in the domain. It is relatively easy to spot gaps in a model, ensuring that the variation space will be explored thoroughly. The disadvantage is that models tend to get very large. It is therefore essential to be practical, and not to try to include everything in the domain.
2. *To guide and document both the choices made and the options that were rejected.* The resulting models can be used to guide decisions. Which core features will the system architecture support? What kinds of application? In the next step, the models will be used to incorporate such choices into scenarios. The original models contain the full range of possibilities that were considered *and* the options that were not chosen. This helps to avoid the endless reconsideration of the same options.
3. *To enhance communication and raise awareness about these choices among the architecture's stakeholders.* The actual creation of the models demands an adeptness at working with abstract models. In our experience, however, the resulting models can be understood by people without a background in modeling. This allows stakeholders other than the architect to contribute to the models by reviewing, or in some cases even co-creating them. For example, marketers or sales people could be co-authors of the customer variation model. At least, they will be able to read the model to verify that their input was interpreted correctly.

Sources of input for this step are the strategic scenarios, roadmaps, design documents, requirements and, of course, the knowledge of (company) experts. The exploration step results in a variation model covering all views. It allows the architect to explore a wide range of possible architectures simultaneously without pinning down definite choices.

Notation

The technique we used for variation modeling is based on a publication by Ferber et al. [14]. We chose this technique because it is simple, expressive enough for our purposes and easy to extend. An alternative notation is FODA [28], but it has no support for multiplicity which can result in more complex models. Some other notations are more expressive, but are also more complex and harder to extend (for example Gomaa and Webber [18] and Geyer [17]).

The notation itself is almost exactly the same as the original one (Fig. 1.6). We added the use of letters in the upper right hand corner to indicate which view an element belongs to (C for Customer, A for Application, etc. The difference between Customer and Conceptual can usually be seen from the element name and its context. Otherwise, Co and Cu may be used instead). This is useful, since models can contain elements from multiple views. The model name indicates the main view, which is also the view of those elements without letters in their upper right hand corners.

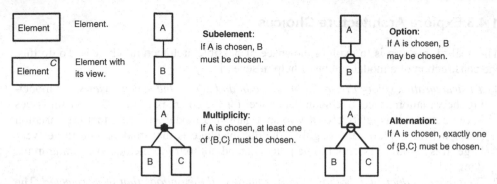

Fig. 1.6. Notation for variation modeling

Ferber et al. describe two types of models:

> One [type] shows hierarchical refinement of features similar to common feature modeling approaches in a feature tree. The second [...] describes what kind of dependencies and interactions there are between various features. [14]

The reason for introducing this second model lies in complexity:

> In real life context, relations between features often become very complex without a clear way to model features with different dimensions or aspects leading to a very complex graph of features. [14]

This is certainly true for feature models, which are intended to describe *all* the features and their relations in a product line. The purpose of variation models in SBA is different. The architect is only interested in *a small subset* of features, namely those that affect the product line architecture. SBA uses a single directed, acyclic graph per view. Each graph expresses both the view's elements and their dependencies. If a model becomes too complex to understand, this can be taken as a clear sign that the architect is trying to do too much at once and needs to rethink the scope and abstraction level of the design. Although not all the possible dependencies between features or other elements can be captured in this way without cluttering up the diagram, the notation does allow the modeler to capture many of them in a single diagram in a straightforward manner.

For practical reasons, we have opted to present a separate model for each of the CAFCR views, but in reality these diagrams form a single variation model covering all views. Elements from one view can relate to elements in adjacent views. Customer view elements can relate to application view elements, which can relate to functional view elements, and so on.

Customer Variation Model

At its most basic level, a customer variation model should express the basic market segmentation that underlies the design of the product portfolio. Other differences among the customers may also be useful, especially if these may have implications for the product line architecture. Figure 1.7 shows a customer variation model for the cathlab.

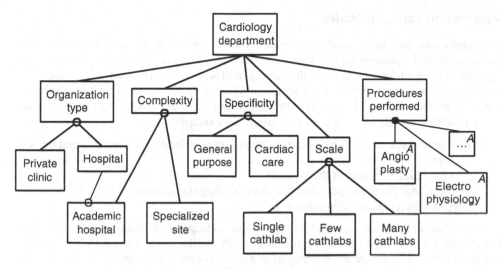

Fig. 1.7. Customer variation model

Cardiology departments are the customers. A cardiology department is part of a larger *organization*, which may be either a *private clinic*, a *hospital* or an *academic hospital*. The latter gives an indication of the *complexity* of procedures performed by the department. Typically, academic hospitals treat the "interesting" cases, whereas *specialized sites* focus on the most common treatments. *Specificity* indicates the range of cardiovascular procedures performed. Here we distinguish between *general-purpose* departments and those specialized in *cardiac care*. *Scale* determines the number of cathlabs that the department has available. The notation does not allow the easy specification of the precise number. This is not a problem, as an indication of the scale expressed as *single*, *few* or *many cathlabs* will do.

The element *procedures performed* refers to elements from the application view. Procedures are a form of action, and therefore they belong in the application view. *Angioplasty* is the balloon procedure briefly described in Sect. 1.4.1. This procedure is the focus of the application view's variation model. *Electrophysiology* is a family of procedures that have to do with the electrical pulses that make the heart beat. There are other procedures that are left unspecified in this example.

The resulting model should describe current customers, but should also cover the typical customers in the strategic scenarios. The typical McHealth customer will be a private clinic, constituting a high-volume site with many cathlabs and relatively little variation in procedures. A Clinique de Luxe would be a specialized cardiac care clinic with a small number of well-equipped cathlabs. Brave New Pharma World hospitals offer personalized care to a wide variety of patients. Large and medium-sized general-purpose hospitals offer the complexity of procedures currently found in academic hospitals. In a See Treat Cure future, a typical hospital would be general purpose with a large number of cathlabs, performing a wide range of procedures.

Application Variation Model

The application variation model captures activities performed by a user in interaction with the systems in the product line. A moderately complex but well-engineered system can be applied in many different ways and the variety of procedures performed in a cathlab is very large. An attempt to model the variation allowed by a number of architectural variants of a product line may lead to models with thousands of elements. This variation stems from a number of different sources of variation, for example:

– Properties such as supported features among the candidate architectures and derived systems
– The (technical) context of the systems
– The business goals and practical purposes of using the systems
– Personal preferences among users

Capturing all these variations in a single model is impossible in anything but the most trivial cases. In our experience, it is useful to build smaller models around the issues that are most difficult to decide on, starting from a small number of use cases that describe the issue, and to then build the variation model around them.

It should be noted that an application variation model is not the same as a workflow model. Although both types of models capture activities and their relations, a workflow model focuses on the temporal order and dependencies of these activities, whereas an application variation model does not contain timing information. It shows a hierarchy of activities, i.e., which activities are (optional) parts of other activities.

The application variation model can be hard to understand without domain knowledge. We shall therefore give a general description of the angioplasty procedure before explaining the model.

Angioplasty is a catheterization procedure that aims to open up a blocked artery. A catheter is inserted into a vessel and then navigated towards the blocked artery. The cardiologist pushes the catheter manually through the blood flow system towards the correct spot. X-ray is used to visualize the patient's vessels and the location of the catheter. To this end, contrast fluid is inserted through the catheter and into the patient's blood flow. The contrast fluid scatters the X-rays and allows the visualization of the arteries.

The tip of the catheter holds a tiny balloon, which is inflated at the correct position to push the blocked artery open. A wire mesh tube called a *stent* may be placed inside the artery to prevent the artery from closing again. The stent is unfolded as the balloon expands and it stays behind in the vessel once the balloon is deflated again. The length and diameter of the balloon and stent to be used must be determined beforehand by measuring the length of the blockage and the diameter of the artery.

Finding the optimal position for the balloon to be inflated can be difficult. It can therefore be useful to have a three-dimensional map of the local vessel structure available. Such a map can be reused from an earlier diagnostic procedure, but it can also be generated on the spot with a technique called three-dimensional rotational angiography (3DRA).

After the blockage has been treated, the results of the treatment can be assessed. This requires the visualization of the arteries to see if the blockage has been removed and the blood flow restored.

The variation model in Fig. 1.8 captures the main angioplasty activities and their relationships. At the top of the model is the element *procedures performed*, which belongs to the customer view. The *angioplasty* procedure as a whole is an activity and is therefore an element of the application view.

A *balloon is inflated* to open a blocked artery. The balloon must be placed in the correct position. To *find this position*, the *arteries are visualized*. This may be done by *performing 3DRA*. In any case, the *insertion of contrast fluid* is required. To this end, the *catheter must be navigated* to deliver the contrast fluid to the right spot. For precise navigation, a *3D roadmap* can be used. This can be a *3DRA roadmap* obtained earlier, or a *non-X-ray roadmap* created by a different type of imaging system.

Optionally, a *stent can be placed* as part of the balloon inflation activity. In that case, *measurements* must be done to determine the artery's diameter and the length of the blockage. In order to measure an artery, it must be *visualized*.

Part of the angioplasty procedure is to *assess the post-intervention situation*. This entails checking to see whether the blockage has been removed, by *visualizing* the arteries.

Mapping this variation model to the strategic scenarios shows that a McHealth procedure would not require 3DRA and 3D roadmaps unless they greatly enhanced procedure efficiency. The Clinique de Luxe cardiologists, on the other hand, would need the full repertoire of actions to satisfy their very demanding patients. In a See Treat Cure world, technological advancements would have made imaging processing so cheap that 3D would be standard. A Brave New Pharma World would need far more advanced systems to be able to deliver highly personalized care, but this model would constitute a step in the right direction.

Functional Variation Model

The functional variation model is what is commonly called a *feature model* in software product line engineering. It shows the possible features of the 3D cathlab and their dependencies (Fig. 1.9). The graph shows activities taken from the application variation model and the features that support these activities. To *use a 3D roadmap*, the system must *support 3D viewing*. To manipulate 3D models, a specialized user interface is required. It can be a *Graphical User Interface (GUI)*, a *Non-Graphical User Interface (NGUI)*, or both. The images can be a *3DRA roadmap* or a *non-X-ray roadmap*. In the latter case, the system must *support multi-modality* images created via other types of systems.

The system must *support 3DRA* for the user to *perform* or *use* it. This can either be done as *remote 3DRA*, meaning that a separate workstation implements this functionality, or as *local 3DRA* if it is integrated into the main system. The *auto 3DRA-reconstruction* feature (a workflow enhancement) is an optional extra.

With respect to the strategic scenarios, it is clear that customers in the low economic growth scenarios would consider price very important when selecting a cathlab. This means that McHealth clinics would only want to pay for basic functionality. In the case of See Treat Cure, technological advancements would make it possible to realize the more advanced features in an affordable way. In the cases of the Clinique de Luxe and Brave New Pharma World scenarios, price is less of an issue. More important is the availability of a wide range of features. Brave New Pharma World in particular would demand support for multi-modality procedures, in order to deliver its highly personalized care.

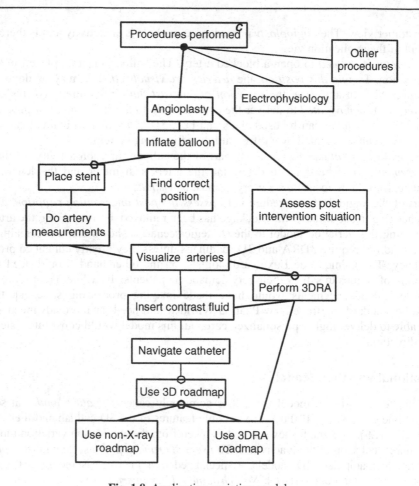

Fig. 1.8. Application variation model

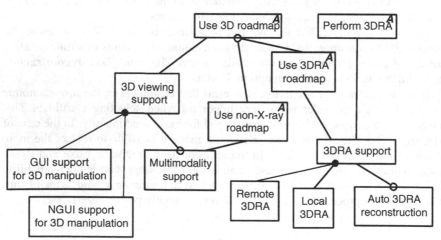

Fig. 1.9. Functional variation model

Conceptual Variation Model

The conceptual variation model explores possible concepts of the product line architecture. Elements from the functional variation model are included, to show which features are supported by which concepts (Fig. 1.10).

Support for multi-modality images can be implemented in two ways: via a *native 3D viewer* or by *hosting a 3D viewer*. A native viewer is a software component that is dedicated to the cathlab environment. It needs a *3D renderer* to visualize the 3D images, as well as *3D navigation controls* to enable the user to manipulate the models. In turn, these controls could be implemented as software in a *GUI* or in hardware as an *NGUI*. These controls are actually conceptual implementations of the GUI and NGUI support features from the functional view. We have omitted these features here to keep the example model simple.

An existing *3D viewer* can be *hosted* as an alternative to developing a specialized, *native viewer*. Such general viewers are commercially available. They have their own GUI controls, and a *non-graphical interface* can be provided as an optional extra.

For *remote 3DRA*, all that is needed is a separate *3DRA workstation* that is connected to the system. To implement the feature *local 3DRA*, a *3DRA reconstructor* is needed. A reconstructor combines a vast quantity of two-dimensional image data into a single three-dimensional model. This can be a *real-time reconstructor*, specialized for this type of X-ray equipment, or a slower but *portable reconstructor*.

In the conceptual and realization views, the focus lies on the technological aspects of the strategic scenarios. In the high technological advancement scenarios, concepts that are currently complex and expensive will be easier and cheaper to realize in the future. It can

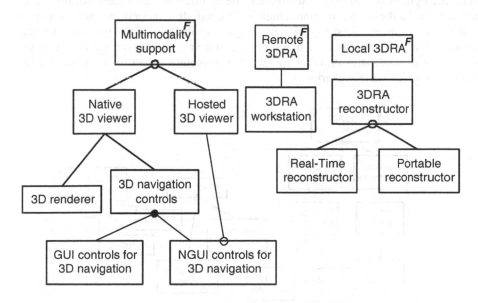

Fig. 1.10. Conceptual variation model

be worthwhile to consider what will happen when the boundaries of Moore's law are reached and faster, smaller, cheaper hardware ceases to be available. In such a situation, best illustrated by the McHealth and Clinique de Luxe scenarios, the system would have to make do with what is state-of-the-art at the time.

Realization Variation Model

The realization variation model explores different ways of mapping architectural concepts onto available technology (Fig. 1.11).

The *3DRA reconstructor* can be either *portable* or *real-time*. A portable reconstructor runs on the *default processor* of the system, or a *multi-processor* for improved performance. A real-time constructor should be implemented on a *dedicated processor*, for which there is a choice between an *ASIC* (Application Specific Integrated Circuit) and a *COTS* (commercial off-the-shelf) *processor*. Although we stop detailing at this level to keep the example model simple, it could include more details, such as the specific types of processors.

The model shows two possible ways of implementing the *3D renderer* concept: via a *default graphics card* that is already present in the system, or via a *specialized 3D graphics card*.

Non-graphical controls can take the form of a *trackball*, a *joystick*, some form of *proprietary hardware*, or any combination of these.

1.4.4 Create Architecture Scenarios

Once the options for adapting the product line architecture have been explored, the next step is to make these options more tangible. The variation models themselves do not provide sufficient information to make an adequate evaluation of the possible architectural choices. The implications of a single choice in a variation model cannot be evaluated because of dependencies on other choices. It is therefore necessary to consider a limited number of architecture scenarios.

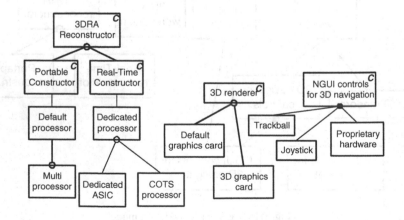

Fig. 1.11. Realization variation model

While the variation models describe the variation space, the scenarios define individual points in that space. Each architecture scenario describes an architecture in a single view. An architecture scenario consists of a single set of choices in that view's variation model. For example, an architecture scenario in the customer view will typically describe a market segment or a type of customer, whereas scenarios in the conceptual view will document possible conceptual designs for the product line architecture.

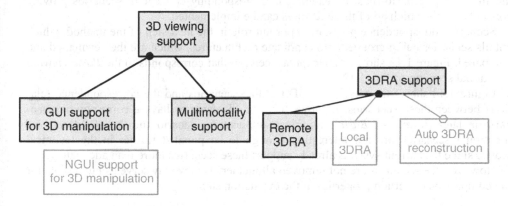

Fig. 1.12. Functional scenario: "Basic viewing"

As an example, we present the functional scenario *Basic viewing* (Fig. 1.12). The system it describes supports basic 3D viewing and a simple 3DRA implementation. It has a graphical user interface for handling three-dimensional images, and can show images from other modalities besides X-ray.

Architecture scenarios must satisfy the following criteria:

- The set of choices that defines the scenario must be *consistent* with the variation model semantics.
- A scenario must be *reasonable*, meaning that the set of choices as a whole must show a certain balance. It would not be reasonable to omit a basic feature from a high-end system, even though this is technically possible.
- A scenario should be *interesting*. The next step will be to evaluate the scenarios, and it makes no sense to put effort into scenarios that will be disregarded anyway.
- The total set of scenarios should *span* a large enough part of *the variation space*. This means that they should be sufficiently different from each other. In our experience, about three to five architecture scenarios per view are sufficient.

Scenario Correspondence

We now look for *correspondence* between pairs of scenarios in different views, at the points at which they describe choices that are consistent across the views, according to the cross-view relationships of the variation models. This rule is used as the basis for selecting pairs of corresponding scenarios.

The correspondence between application and customer scenarios, for example, helps guide our reasoning in respect of the way a given customer would perform the angioplasty procedure that was modeled in the application view. An academic hospital is likely to use more advanced functionality, whereas a high-volume production site will favor the more basic features.

To find conceptual scenarios that correspond to a functional scenario, the features of the functional scenario must be examined. Corresponding conceptual scenarios provide concepts within which all of these features can be implemented.

Scenario correspondence plays an important role in the next step of the method, which entails scenarios being grouped into candidate architectures, which are then evaluated and compared. Figure 1.13 shows a conceptual scenario that corresponds to the *Basic viewing* functional scenario of Fig. 1.12.

Figure 1.14 shows the total set of 3D Cathlab scenarios and the correspondence relations between those scenarios. It shows that not all scenarios have a corresponding scenario in later views. The *Basic angioplasty* application scenario and the *3DRA enabled* functional scenarios are not interesting enough to be pursued further in the technical views, since the current systems already support these scenarios more than adequately.

However, the scenarios are not removed altogether, as they may serve as null points for the comparison of certain properties in the evaluation step.

Candidate Architectures

The total set of scenarios forms a family of candidate architectures. The correspondence relations can be used to derive the particular instantiations of this family. A candidate architecture consists of a set of five corresponding scenarios that together describe the architecture using the CAFCR views. In the graph of scenarios listed in Fig. 1.14, there are 18 complete paths from customer to realization scenarios. Each of these paths represents a single unique candidate architecture.

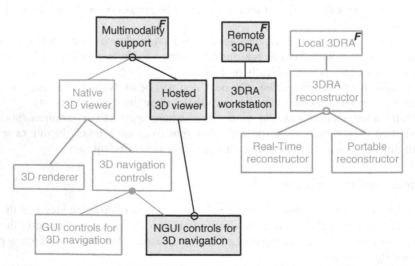

Fig. 1.13. Conceptual scenario "Alt-Tab Viewing" corresponds to scenario "Basic Viewing"

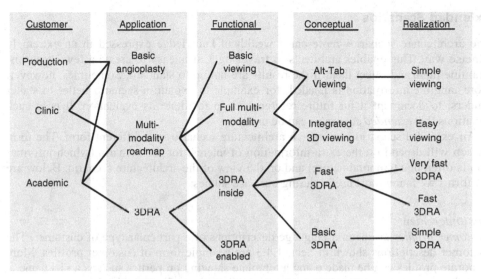

Fig. 1.14. Corresponding scenarios for the 3D cathlab

Candidate architectures that differ in their commercial scenarios but share the same conceptual and realization scenarios actually represent different systems that can be derived from a single product line architecture.

We identify two candidate architectures (cf. Fig. 1.15) and examine them in more detail in the rest of this chapter.

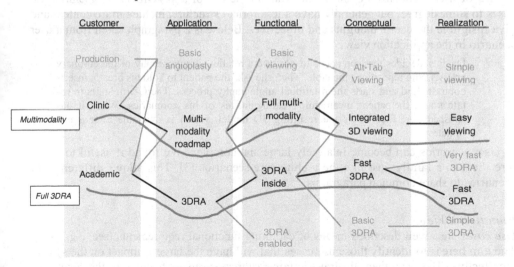

Fig. 1.15. Two candidate architectures

The *Multimodality* candidate architecture supports both the generation of 3D images in the cathlab and the use of 3D images created on other types of systems. The *Full 3DRA* scenario focuses on the tight integration of 3DRA in the cathlab, but does not support non-X-ray images.

Extended Scenarios

The architecture scenarios represent a wealth of knowledge expressed in an extremely concise way. This enables architects to travel light: it is easy to create a few scenarios, examine them and reject them if the results are not up to standard. Sometimes, however, more tangible information is needed, for example to explain a scenario better to stakeholders, to document it for future reference or to facilitate its evaluation. It is in such situations that *extended scenarios* can be used.

An extended scenario captures an architecture scenario in a different form. The form chosen will depend on the extra information of interest for the scenario (which information is often of a temporal nature) and on the view of the architecture scenario. Below are the forms we found most useful during our case studies:

Customer View
Customer profiles are natural language descriptions of a particular type of customer. The customer descriptions shown in Sect. 1.4.3 are a simple form of customer profiles. More elaborate profiles can be made using a template showing properties such as a nickname, a brief description, business strategy, and goals. Similar profiles can also be made for other types of stakeholders, such as patients and clinicians. Such stakeholder profiles can be used as a tool for relating strategic and customer scenarios, and as background information for the application view.

Application View
Stories or *user scenarios* are short stories about the use of a system. They resemble use cases to some degree, but generally have a less formal structure, include more context and give insight in the user's thoughts and objectives. Below is a paragraph taken from a user scenario in the application view:

> Dr. Eter decides that she needs to perform a rotational angiography of the coronary arteries. She repositions the table. Then she asks the patient to hold his breath, inserts contrast fluid and starts the rotational angiography process. The C-arm starts to rotate around the patient, meanwhile creating images of his coronaries. When it has finished, Dr. Eter views the resulting 3D model, which is available after a few minutes.

User scenarios can become relatively large and complex. We found it useful to structure them in a family, just like the architecture scenarios [3]. This allows different user scenarios to share common paragraphs.

Functional View
Use cases are a well described means of capturing functional requirements (see, e.g., [11]). The aim here is to identify those use cases that will have the largest impact on the system architecture. They can then illustrate certain features or sets of features in the functional scenarios.

Conceptual View
Collaboration diagrams and *sequence diagrams* describe how components interact to achieve a goal. Both types of diagrams are a part of the UML [6]. They can be coupled to

a use case to describe how the components implement it. The advantage of collaboration diagrams is that they can show the underlying component structure in the same view.

Realization View
Collaboration estimates are used to find out whether a collaboration that implements a certain use case is likely to satisfy all the relevant quality requirements. A rough estimate can be made based on specific technology choices. Such estimates can never be relied on completely, since there may still be bottlenecks that have not been considered, but they can help identify certain problems at an early stage.

1.4.5 Evaluate Candidate Architectures

The last step of an iteration is to evaluate the candidate architectures that have been created. The goal is to assess several plausible architectures at once in an efficient way. The evaluation produces information about the expected quality properties of the architectures. It can also ensure that the architecture is able to handle the desired functionality, and may bring shortcomings to light. The evaluation results are used either to enhance the architecture scenarios in another iteration or to select a suitable candidate architecture if the results prove satisfactory.

Functional Evaluation

Functional assessment entails the architect checking whether or not the architectures support the required functionality. Several types of extended scenarios can be used to carry out functional evaluations. Use cases can be employed to describe those functional requirements that are of interest. Each use case is coupled to the functional scenarios that support it. The architect can take the scenarios as a starting point to trace back to the application view to identify the applications in which the feature is used, and further back to the customer view to see what types of customers are likely to be interested in performing these applications. In the other direction, extended conceptual and realization scenarios can be used to test the candidate architectures. Each response by the system in a use case must be supported by its concepts. A collaboration diagram shows how the system concepts collaborate to achieve these steps. This process is similar to the *use case realization analyses* applied in the Unified Process [27] (p. 46).

As an example, we present the reconstruction of a three-dimensional model from two-dimensional, rotational data. The *3DRA support* feature (Fig. 1.9) is augmented with a use case that describes the user-system interaction leading to the creation of a 3D model. This feature is present in the functional scenarios *3DRA inside* and *3DRA enabled*. As Fig. 1.14 shows, the *3DRA enabled* scenario was disregarded as uninteresting and will not be pursued any further. *3DRA inside* corresponds to three conceptual scenarios: *Integrated 3D viewing, Fast 3DRA,* and *Basic 3DRA*. A single collaboration diagram will suffice for all three, since they share all the components involved in this collaboration.

Figure 1.16 shows the reconstruction of a 3D model from rotational angiography data. The detector generates data, which is stored and sent to an image processor for image enhancement. The resulting two-dimensional data is then displayed directly, while the system continues to gather new data. Concurrently, the repository sends the acquired data to a 3D reconstructor, which creates a model and sends it to the image enhancer to display.

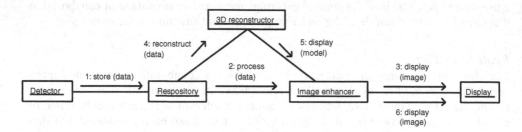

Fig. 1.16. UML collaboration diagram "3DRA reconstruction"

This single collaboration diagram captures information about three distinct conceptual scenarios and about 12 of the 18 possible candidate architectures (i.e., all candidate architectures that contain the functional scenario *3DRA inside*).

Reasoning back from the functional view, we see (cf. Fig. 1.14) that the *3DRA* and *Multimodality roadmap* application scenarios both use this feature. The *academic* and *clinic* types of customers perform these particular applications. The same checking procedure can be applied to each use case.

Finding Qualities of Interest

The qualities of interest must be identified before a system architecture can be evaluated. A helpful tool is to create a key driver diagram. In this context, a key driver is defined as a motivating factor for a particular stakeholder. In other words, it is something that the stakeholder really wants or really does not want.

Muller writes: "The essence of the objectives of the customers can be captured in terms of customer key drivers. The key drivers provide direction to capture requirements and to focus the development." [33] (p. 59). In most instances, a large number of drivers will play a role, and said drivers are often causally related. Ultimately, our own customer's drivers are most important, but these are often related to our customer's customers (sometimes across several links in a value chain) and other stakeholders.

These relationships can be expressed using an extended form of *influence diagrams*. Weinberg originally described influence diagrams [42] and Beck used them to describe small patterns in software development [5] (e.g. p. 124). According to Beck, "the purpose of an influence diagram is to see how the elements of a system affect one another." (pp. 207–210) Influence diagrams contain three elements: activities, positive connections, and negative connections. We have adapted them to suit our purpose of understanding the relation between stakeholders and their drivers. Our notation for key driver diagrams includes stakeholders, key drivers, and derived drivers instead of activities. Derived drivers may be connected to other derived drivers or key drivers to show influence. Key drivers may be connected to one or more stakeholders to express that these stakeholders have an interest in the key driver. Stakeholders are connected to derived drivers in cases where they influence these drivers.

The diagram in Fig. 1.17 shows key drivers for three types of stakeholders: The *heads of cardiology departments* were identified as the customers, *cardiologists* as the most important users, and *patients* as the customers of the customers. Below is an explanation of the derived and key drivers in this diagram for each of these stakeholders.

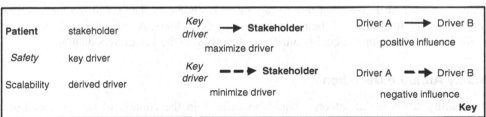

Fig. 1.17. Key driver diagram

The *patient satisfaction* rate and the availability of *state of the art equipment* in a department both influence its *reputation*. A solid reputation is important when it comes to attracting a large *number of patients* and especially *well-insured patients* who can afford more expensive treatment. Both factors influence the *department returns*. A department's *returns* and *costs* determine its *revenues*, which form the major responsibility of the *head of a cardiology department*.

The *length of patient's stay* negatively influences the department's patient throughput and therefore the *number of patients*. The *cardiologist's efficiency* influences the *department efficiency* and the *lengths of procedures*, both of which can reduce a patient's stay. *Ease of use* is one means of enhancing a cardiologist's efficiency. Another influencing factor is the ease with which *patients* can be *handled* during a procedure. A patient who is *comfortable* will generally be more relaxed and cooperative.

An important cost factor for cardiology departments is the *cost of owning* cathlab equipment. *Cathlab purchase costs* can be considerable. Cathlabs should therefore have an optimal *lifespan,* to avoid having to buy a new cathlab too early. A longer lifespan obviously influences the *price* of the product.

A *cardiologist* routinely works with X-ray emitting equipment, which can damage his *health* if the necessary precautions are not taken. The *radiation dose* used during a procedure negatively influences the safety of both cardiologist and patient. In other words, it affects both the *doctor's health* and the *quality of care.* On the other hand, higher radiation doses lead to better *image quality,* which improves the *intervention outcome* and reduces the risk of *medical errors.* In the end, this leads to improved quality of care. This is an example of how influence diagrams can help make conflicting requirements explicit. Such conflicts of interests force the architect to give careful consideration to what really matters. (In this case, the conflict is resolved by delegating the decision: the system allows adjustment of the radiation dose by its users.)

The key driver diagram gives starting points for finding the important quality attributes. Quality attributes can be linked to stakeholders using a second influence diagram. Figure 1.18 shows the six quality attributes used during this example and their relation to stakeholders (a definition for each attribute can be found in Tab. 1.1).

Treatment selection represents how well patients are treated based on the information created and presented by the cathlab. *Frequency of use* deals with the number of times that new features are used. It is directly influenced by the *performance* of the new features. *Ease of use* was already mentioned in the key drivers diagram. *Patient accessibility* means how well the doctor can reach and handle the patient: pieces of equipment should not get in the way. *Cost* here means the cost price of a complete cathlab system.

Each quality attribute is linked to one or more derived drivers, which are in turn related to one or more key drivers and stakeholders. The paths from derived drivers to stakeholders are taken from the key drivers diagram and condensed. The result is a clear overview of quality attributes and their relations with stakeholders. A more detailed view can be obtained by inserting the quality attributes directly into the key drivers diagram.

Quality Attribute Definition

The quality attributes of interest should be defined in the context of the product line with the greatest feasible precision. As Clements et al. argue: "Quality attributes form the basis for architectural evaluation, but simply naming the attributes by themselves is not a sufficient basis on which to judge an architecture for suitability. [...] Without elaboration, each of these [quality attributes] is subject to interpretation and misunderstanding. What you think of as robust, your customer might consider barely adequate – or vice versa." [10] (p. 32).

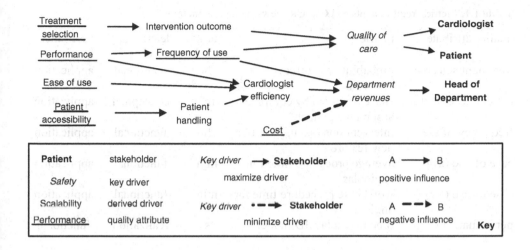

Fig. 1.18. From quality attributes to stakeholders

Quality attribute definitions are used to express both the quality requirements for the system and the estimated quality properties of the architecture. It is beneficial to define the metrics in a precise, quantitative way whenever possible, even if their values are based on experience or expert intuition alone. The main advantage is that it forces one to be as precise as possible in defining quality metrics. This can prevent misunderstanding and disagreement among stakeholders on what is meant by a certain quality. Another advantage is that the results of the assessment can be compared to experiments on real systems.

An inherent risk lies in the fact that although metrics seldom fully reflect their underlying quality attributes, they become goals in their own right. This may lead organizations to aspire for suboptimal results from the original quality attribute viewpoint. The key driver diagram serves as a reminder of what is really important to the stakeholders.

With their definition, the relevant architectural views for the evaluation of each metric are determined. Two views can generally be distinguished, which may or may not be the same:

– The *determining view:* This is the view where the architectural decisions are made that determine the quality property of the system.
– The *assessment view:* This is the view where the quality properties can be assessed in their context.

Table 1.1 gives metrics and associated views for the quality attributes in this example.

Quality Requirements
Quality requirements can be expressed as values for the quality attribute metrics. Such requirements are often expressed as the *threshold* that is required. For example:"a 3D model should be available within three minutes or faster." It makes sense however to include a reasonable *optimal* value too. Evaluations can then show how close the system property is to its optimum. Table 1.2 shows threshold and optimum values for each metric, with their evaluation results.

Table 1.1. Metrics, requirements and CAFCR views for quality metrics

quality attribute	metric	unit	determining view	assessment view
treatment selection	probability of correct diagnosis	%	functional	application
patient accessibility	space occupied by equipment around the patient	m^3	conceptual	application
frequency of use	interventions making use of a new feature	%	functional	application
ease of use (avg)	average procedure time for angioplasty	min	functional	application
ease of use (wc)	worst case procedure time for angioplasty	min	functional	application
performance	time to display 3D model	s	realization	functional
cost	added cost per system	k$	realization conceptual	functional

Multi-view Quality Evaluation

The candidate architectures can now be evaluated for their properties relating to the quality attributes of interest. As an example, we describe the performance of the candidate architectures when creating a 3D model from two-dimensional input:

> The time it takes to display a complete 3D model to the user once the 3DRA function has been activated.

In this example, the determining view is the realization view. However, the assessment view is the functional view, since we need to establish how much time the execution of a single *feature* takes. Somehow, we need to use information from the realization scenarios to obtain information about the functional scenarios. Figure 1.19 illustrates this 'view hopping.'

First, we find the corresponding scenarios for the functional scenarios that we are interested in. In this case, we consider the *3DRA inside* scenario only, as the other scenarios either do not include the 3DRA feature or do not have corresponding conceptual scenarios. Moving to the application and customer views, we can then deduce which procedures use this feature, and which types of customers perform such procedures.

To find a value for the performance metric, information from the implementation side is needed: the conceptual and realization views. There will be four such values, as there are four candidate architectures that offer this feature. These values will not all be different, since some of the architectures share concepts and implementations for the feature. The architecture scenarios and variation models hold the necessary information.

The values for the metric can be calculated as follows: First, a use case is created in the functional view. The use case describes the precise steps taken by the user and the system. Moving to the right, collaboration diagrams are created for each corresponding conceptual scenario. The collaboration diagrams show which components are involved in the realization of the use case. Architecture scenarios that have common concepts to implement this

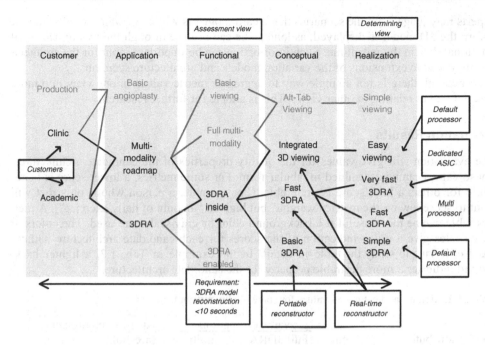

Fig. 1.19. View hopping for performance assessment

particular feature will share diagrams. The diagrams can be seen as formulas to calculate the values for the metric. The input for these formulas comes from the realization view. We may include such information as the algorithms used, the hardware setup, the size of the data and the speed of hardware buses. The detail of the information in the realization view determines the precision of the resulting metric values. The point in time at which each component is activated and how long it takes to process the data can be calculated by mapping this information to the conceptual diagrams. We have now moved from the realization view back to the conceptual view. The next step is to use the information acquired to calculate the amount of time the use case takes to complete. At this point, we are back in the functional view where the results of the evaluation can be compared.

As a second example, we look at the frequency of use of 3DRA:

The percentage of interventions that use 3DRA.

The assessment view is the application view, because it contains information about the interventions that the product line supports. The functional view determines whether 3DRA is available or not. In this case, getting from the determining to the assessment view is straightforward: we take the functional scenarios that offer the 3DRA feature and find the corresponding application views. User scenarios describe procedures with and without 3DRA, and can serve as input to help experts determine the values for the metric.

The frequency of use attribute is more complex than this evaluation suggests. It depends on many other qualities such as ease of use and performance. User scenarios are a good tool for exploring such dependencies and their consequences. For example, the experts may judge from the scenarios that a cardiologist is willing to wait for half a minute before the 3D model is displayed, as long as he can browse through the two-dimensional rotational data in the meantime. Such information can be important input for the architect, and may lead to extensions of the variation models and architecture scenarios.

In general, there is not a single way to aggregate metric values in one view into more abstract values relating to other views. This is a topic for further research.

Evaluation Results

The evaluation will give values for the quality properties of the candidate architectures. These values can be assembled in tabular form. For some metrics, a lower score is better while for others a high score is preferable. (For example, a person who is on a diet will want to score low on the metric "weight," but high on "amount of daily exercise"). A metrics table can be more useful if a background color or gray scales are used. The colors or gray scales give a quick indication of the scores for each candidate architecture without the user having to study the table in detail. In the example in Tab. 1.2, a lighter background indicates a more desirable property for the candidate architecture.

Table 1.2. Metrics, and estimated values for some quality atttributes

quality attribute	unit	value estimations		quality requirements	
		Full 3DRA	multi-modality	threshold	optimum
treatment selection	%	81	93	75	95
patient accessibility	m^3	0.6	0	1	0
frequency of use	%	40	30	20	50
ease of use (avg)	min	55	42	60	30
ease of use (wc)	min	60	71	90	30
performance	s	28	120	180	20
cost	k$	60	40	70	10

Strategic Evaluation

It is unlikely that any one of the candidate architectures will be completely right for every strategic scenario. Strategic scenarios represent possible distant futures, whereas the architectures are designed with relatively short-term requirements in mind. However, projecting candidate architectures into the future does give feedback about the direction in which the architecture is evolving, and about the potential of the architecture to adapt to different futures. Previously obtained evaluation results can be reused, and additional evaluations may be performed if necessary.

When assessing for the present, current business needs are used to determine what properties are desirable for the product line and its architecture. When assessing for the future, something similar can be done. A quality profile is created for each strategic scenario, describing the demands of that specific future. The quality profiles share a single set of quality attributes. Experts assign weights to each attribute according to its importance in a strategic scenario. Marketing and architecture expertise can often complement each other in this step. Table 1.3 shows the quality profiles for the cathlab.

Table 1.3. Quality profiles for strategic scenarios

quality attribute	Brave New Pharma World	McHealth	Clinique de Luxe	See Treat Cure
treatment selection	0.5		0.5	0.2
patient accessibility			0.2	
frequency of use		0.2		0.15
ease of use (avg)	0.25	0.3	0.05	0.15
ease of use (wc)	0.25		0.05	0.1
performance		0.1	0.2	0.2
cost		0.4		0.2

The weights can be used to calculate a single score for each candidate architecture in each strategic scenario. The estimated values of the quality attributes are combined with their weights in each quality profile and added up to arrive at a single end value, generally expressed as a percentage. To this end, the quality attribute values must first be normalized to relative scores, for example percentages of their optimal value. This can be done by a simple linear function that maps the threshold value to 0% and the optimum to 100%. This leads to the function:

$$relative\_score = 100 \times \frac{absolute\_score - threshold}{optimum - threshold}.$$

Such a normalization function can be assigned to each of the attribute values, as shown in Tab. 1.4.

Table 1.4. Worst and optimal values can be used to calculate normalized values for quality attributes

quality attribute	unit	value estimations		quality requirements			normalized values	
		full 3DRA	multi-modality	threshold	optimum	unit	Full 3DRA	multi-modality
treatment selection	%	81	93	75	95	%	30	90
patient accessibility	m³	0.6	0	1	0	%	40	100
frequency of use	%	40	30	20	50	%	67	33
ease of use (avg)	min	55	42	60	30	%	17	60
ease of use (wc)	min	60	71	90	30	%	50	32
performance	s	28	120	180	20	%	95	38
cost	k$	60	40	70	10	%	17	50

Multiplying these relative scores with their associated weights leads to a single percentage for each candidate architecture for each strategic scenario. This percentage indicates how well the candidate architecture fits the strategic scenario, given the quality profiles.

Table 1.5. Weighted scores for quality attributes of candidate architecture *Full 3DRA* per strategic scenario

quality attribute	Candidate architecure *Full 3DRA*			
	Brave New Pharma World	McHealth	Clinique de Luxe	See Treat Cure
treatment selection	15	0	15	6
patient accessibility	0	0	8	0
frequency of use	0	13	0	10
ease of use (avg)	4	5	1	3
ease of use (wc)	13	0	3	5
performance	0	10	18	19
cost	0	7	0	3
weighted score	32	35	45	46

Tables 1.5 and 1.6 show that the *multimodality* architecture is a better long-term prospect. It scores especially well in the Brave New Pharma World and Clinique de Luxe strategic scenarios. The *Full 3DRA* architecture performs less well, with scores below 50% for each strategic scenario. Figure 1.20 shows these results in the form of *radar charts*.

Table 1.6. Weighted scores for quality attributes of candidate architecture *Multimodality* per strategic scenario

quality attribute	Candidate architecure *multimodality*			
	Brave New Pharma World	McHealth	Clinique de Luxe	See Treat Cure
treatment selection	45	0	44	18
patient accessibility	0	0	20	0
frequency of use	0	7	0	5
ease of use (avg)	15	17	3	9
ease of use (wc)	8	0	2	3
performance	0	4	8	8
cost	0	20	0	10
weighted score	68	48	77	53

The side-effects of the strategic evaluation process are at least as important as the end results. The process forces stakeholders to discuss the product line in the light of the future. Such discussions can raise awareness of long-term issues and reveal hidden assumptions. They can be especially useful in cases where stakeholders with different backgrounds are involved: not just architects, but also marketers, application experts, and management.

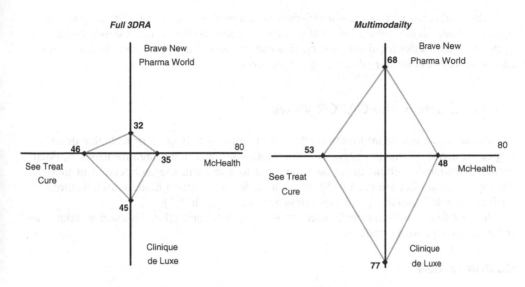

Fig. 1.20. Weighted scores per strategic scenario for two candidate architectures, as radar charts

1.4.6 Select Architecture

If the evaluation shows satisfying results, the most suitable candidate architecture is selected. This will not necessarily be the architecture with the highest evaluation scores. There are many subtle factors that play a role in this decision that cannot be automated. However, during the execution of the SBA method the architects and the other stakeholders will have become familiar with the candidate architectures and the choices they represent. Their knowledge helps them to make a final choice and to understand the implications of that choice. The reasoning behind the selection made should be documented concisely, referring to the most important considerations. The candidate architecture itself must also be further documented, so that it can be deployed in the product line organization.

The precise way in which the architecture is documented varies from situation to situation, and depends on the needs and preferences of the architect and other stakeholders of the architecture: "To choose the appropriate set of views, you must identify the stakeholders that depend on software architecture documentation. You must also understand each stakeholder's information needs. The set of stakeholders will vary, depending on the organization and the project." (Clements et al. [9], p. 290).

Some of the documentation has already been carried out. The variation models, key drivers diagram, architecture scenarios, extended scenarios and evaluation results that were created during the process can all be included in the final architecture documentation. Additional forms of documentation will probably also need to be added to suit the needs of all the stakeholders. More information on documenting architectures can be found in various sources, especially Clements et al. [9] and IEEE 1471-2000 [21].

If the evaluation results are not satisfactory, a new iteration can be started by returning to the *explore architecture choices* step. The variation models can be extended with new options so that better architecture scenarios can be created or specific areas of the models can be worked out in more detail to get more precise assessment results.

1.4.7 Artifacts in the CAFCR Views

An artifact is a piece of information, often in the form of a diagram or table that describes a specific aspect of the architecture. Artifacts are used to guide design decisions, to document the rationale behind those decisions and to document the architecture in general. Five types of artifact are used in SBA: strategic input, variation models, architecture scenarios, extended scenarios, and supporting artifacts (cf. Tab. 1.7).

The first four types have been described in Sects. 1.1.3 and 1.1.4. This section addresses the topic of supporting artifacts.

Customer View

Key drivers have been discussed in Sect. 1.4.5. The other supporting artifacts in the customer view are described below.

Table 1.7. Artifacts in the CAFCR views

artifact type	customer	application	functional	conceptual	realization
strategic input			strategic scenarios cover stories quality profiles		
scenario	architecture scenarios	architecture scenarios	architecture scenarios	architecture scenarios	architecture scenarios
			candidate architectures		
extended scenario	customer profiles	user scenarios	use cases	collaborations	collaboration estimates
supporting artifact	key drivers	system context	quality attribute definitions	principles	technology mapping
	value proposition	workflow context	quality requirements	styles	conventions
	PESTLE	domain model	quality property estimates	system decomposition	
	customer context			information models	

Value Proposition

A value proposition is a management tool used to describe the added value of a business or business proposal. According to O'Dell and Grayson, a value proposition is "the unique added value an organization offers customers through their operations" [35]. Value propositions are a useful means of explicitly relating architecture requirements to customer needs.

In the customer view, value propositions are closely related to the customer key drivers diagram (Fig. 1.17). They describe the benefits that a product line architecture brings to the major stakeholders. Table 1.8 holds value propositions for the two candidate architectures.

Table 1.8. Value propositions for candidate architectures *Full 3DRA* and *Multimodality*

stakeholder	Full 3DRA	multimodality
patient	3DRA information leads to better diagnosis and treatment	3DRA and other multimodality information leads to better diagnosis and treatment enables less invasive diagnostic procedures (MR, CT): may render cathlab appointment unnecessary use of diagnostic roadmaps leads to lower X-ray dose
cardiologist	3DRA information leads to better diagnosis and treatment	3DRA and other multimodality information leads to better diagnosis and treatment use of diagnostic roadmaps leads to lower X-ray dose
head of department	patient satisfaction and state-of-the-art equipment are good for department reputation	patient satisfaction and state-of-the-art equipment are good for department reputation use of non-cathlab diagnostic procedures results in more efficient use of cathlab

PESTLE Analysis

PESTLE (Politics, Economics, Society, Technology, Legal, Environment) is a categorization of driving forces used in, e.g., marketing and business analysis. Schwartz argues that: "As individuals, or even as companies, we have little control over driving forces. Our leverage for dealing with them comes from recognizing them, and understanding their effect." [37] (p. 107).

In architecting, PESTLE can be used as a tool to gain insight into external influences that may affect the system's use, the context in which it is used or the architecture itself.

- *Politics.* Demographic trends show an increase in the political influence being exerted by elderly people. Not only is the number of elderly voters increasing, but more and more elderly people are starting to occupy influential positions in society.
- *Economics.* The aging population of western countries is leading to pressure to reduce the costs of healthcare.
- *Society.* The widespread use and acceptance of the internet and other digital media has led to patients being very well informed about their disease and the benefits and risks of possible treatments.

– *Technology.* Technologies that matured in other domains are now entering the health-care domain. Hospitals are introducing more and more information technology in an effort to become paperless and filmless.
– *Legal.* Privacy and quality regulations such as the 1996 Health Insurance Portability and Accountability Act (HIPAA) [41] are impacting healthcare.
– *Environment.* The increasing public perception of ecological harm is an influence fac-tor. The use of throwaways like catheters and contrast agent in hospitals is important here, as is the energy used by hospital equipment.

Customer Context Diagram

A customer context diagram (Fig. 1.21) shows the relations between the customer and the customer's environment. It can be seen as a special form of the system context diagram used in requirements engineering (e.g. [43] pp. 208–211) and can be created using the same notation.

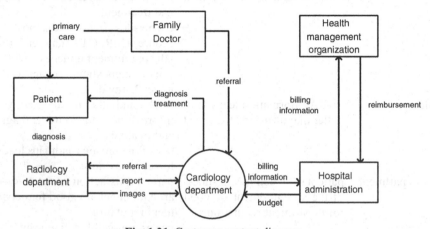

Fig. 1.21. Customer context diagram

Patients receive *primary care* from their *family doctor*. If necessary, they are *referred* to *cardiology departments* for specialized *diagnosis* and *treatment*. In turn, the cardiology department may *refer* a patient to a *radiology department* for *diagnosis*. The resulting *report* and *images* can be used for treatment planning and during interventions.

The department sends its billing information to the hospital administration department, which collects it and sends it to the appropriate health management organization. In return, the hospital receives reimbursement for the care provided, which is used to help set the budget for the cardiology department.

Application View

System Context Diagram

A system context diagram gives an overview of the environment in which the system is to function. The system itself is considered as a single entity in this type of diagram. Wieringa describes the system context diagram as follows: "A data flow diagram that represents the entire system by one data transformation is called the context diagram or level zero diagram of the system." ([43] pp. 208–211). Such context diagrams focus on the exchange of data between the system and its users.

Clements et al. state that "a context diagram shows what is in and what is out of the system under construction and the external entities with which it interacts." [9] (p. 196) They refer to UML use case diagrams, UML class diagrams and informal notations as candidate notations for context diagrams (pp. 198–200). They argue that "because context diagrams are often used to explain systems to people who know more about the externals of the application than the internals, [informal] diagrams can be quite elaborate and use all sorts of idiomatic symbols for the entities in the environment." (p. 198). Fowler calls such diagrams "informal cartoons" [16] (p. 145). Figure 1.22 shows an example of an informal cartoon for the cathlab.

The *cardiologist* may interact with the system using *hand* or *foot control*. The cathlab's user interface includes a foot pedal to start and stop image acquisition. This leaves both hands free to deal with the patient, and with catheters and other instruments.

Information about the *patient*, such as *echocardiograms (ECG)* and other *hemodynamic information (hemo)* like blood pressure, is collected by the cathlab and displayed to its users.

A *power* supply is needed for the system to function at all.

Cathlab systems in the field are actively maintained over many years, either on the spot or remotely. The former approach entails a service engineer bringing a *field service laptop computer* to the cathlab and accessing it using a standard *ethernet* connection. In the latter case, a *Virtual Private Network (VPN)* connection is made from a *remote service computer* over a *modem*.

The cathlab is connected to the hospital *ethernet* network to enable access to *archive servers* and access by *network computers*. Data can also be burned onto *DVD* and carried to a *non-networked computer*.

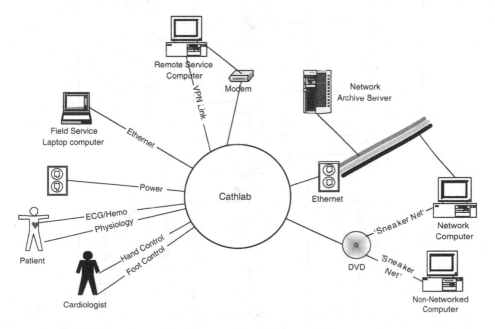

Fig. 1.22. Context diagram

Workflow Context

A workflow context model shows the customer's business process and where the system fits in. The use of the system is therefore modeled as a single activity. Workflows can be modeled in many ways. An overview is given by Van der Aalst and Van Hee [1] (pp. 293–303). In Fig. 1.23, we have used UML activity diagrams [16] (pp. 129–140) because they show activities and their relations with the actor performing them.

Before the procedure, the cardiologist *reviews the patient record*. Meanwhile, an assistant *prepares the cathlab* for the procedure, and a nurse *prepares the patient* and *brings him to the cathlab*.

During the *procedure*, the assistant *logs* all medical events such as the use of catheters, the placing of stents and the measurements performed. Afterwards, this information is used by the cardiologist to create a *report* on the procedure, and by the assistant to *create a bill*. The patient is *taken to the recovery area*, or *to intensive care* in case of an emergency.

Domain Model

Larman [30] points out that the term "domain model" has two common meanings: It can either refer to a domain layer of software objects or to a description of the domain concepts in a domain of interest. The latter, also called a *conceptual model*, is what we are talking about here.

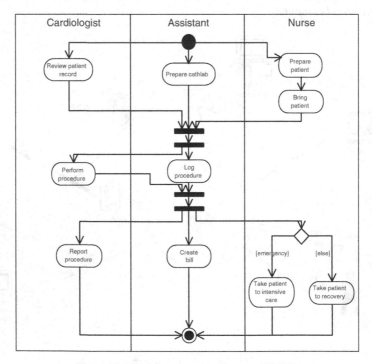

Fig. 1.23. Workflow context diagram (UML)

A domain model shows the most important concepts in the problem domain, and their relations. Fowler argues that a domain model is "a mental model that allows one to understand and simplify the problem." ([15] p. 2)

The UML class diagram ([16] pp. 49–65) is the de facto standard for domain modeling. The example in Fig. 1.24 shows the part of the cathlab domain that deals with clinical information.

The *cardiologist* controls the *X-ray system* to support the *acquisition* of *images*. These images are shown on the cathlab's *monitors* along with *hemo signals*, like *blood pressure* and *echocardiograms (ECG)*. These signals are produced by a *hemodynamics monitoring system*. Images can be the result of normal two-dimensional acquisition, or they can be rendered *3D models*. The cathlab can produce such images itself, using the *three-dimensional rotational angiography (3DRA)* type of acquisition. Alternatively, the models can be produced by *diagnostic modalities* like *magnetic resonance imaging (MR)* or *computed tomography (CT)*.

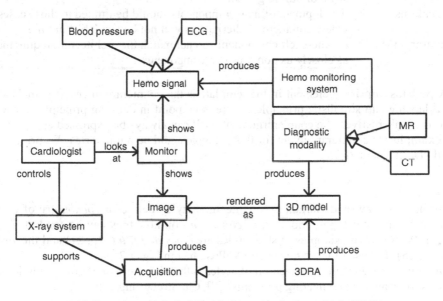

Fig. 1.24. Domain model of clinical information in the cathlab (UML)

Functional view

The supporting artifacts in the functional view (namely quality attribute definitions, quality requirements and quality property estimates) are discussed in Sect. 1.4.5.

Conceptual view

Principles
Witt et al. describe a principle as "a rule of behavior that leads to good things; by a principle of [architecture] we mean a specific approach to the [architectural] design process that leads to good designs." ([45], p. 9)

The Visual Architecting Process uses principles as part of its meta-architecture: "principles can be used both to justify or refute architectural options" ([8], Ch. "Structuring 1", p. 6). The example in Tab. 1.9 uses the Visual Architecting Process template for principles (p. 9).

Table 1.9. Example of a principle

name	use more COTS
description	home-grown solutions and components should be replaced by commercial off-the-shelf (COTS) alternatives whenever this is feasible
rationale	the use of standard hardware and software often leads to cheaper and faster development. The cathlab market is small, in terms of the number of systems sold. Development costs dominate component costs and it may, therefore, be worthwhile to buy components instead of building them
implications	development of new components should be limited to those cases where commercial alternatives will not be available on time
counterargument	off-the-shelf components do not match the architecture requirements as closely as home-grown components

A perhaps surprising element in the template is the counterargument. It is included to avoid lapsing into simplistic principles: there is no point in defining principles for which there is no alternative. The counterargument itself can always be expressed as a principle. For example, the counterargument for this example could be put in terms of a principle labeled "Do It Yourself".

Styles

According to Shaw and Garlan, an architectural style "defines a *vocabulary* of components and connector types, and a set of *constraints* on how they can be combined" [38] (p. 20). Well-known examples of such styles are *pipes and filters* (p. 21) and the *layered* style (p. 25). The use of these two styles is illustrated in Fig. 1.25.

Bredemeyer argues that one benefit of styles is that they "provide proven solution approaches to identified architecting problems" [8], Ch. Structuring 1, p. 13).

System Decomposition

The system decomposition shows the major subsystems and their components. The styles used in the architecture should be readily recognizable in the system decomposition diagram. In Fig. 1.25, the *layered* style has been used to organize the components of the host subsystem, and the *pipes and filters* style has been used in the imaging pipeline subsystem.

The cathlab system has two major subsystems – the *host* and the *imaging pipeline*– connected by a system bus.

The imaging pipeline creates, stores and processes X-ray images before sending them to the live monitor for display. The live monitor shows images as they are being acquired in real-time.

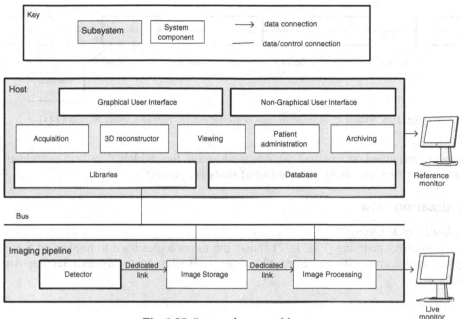

Fig. 1.25. System decomposition

The host components are structured in three layers: a user interface layer, an application layer, and an infrastructure layer. Components in a higher layer may use components in the lower layers. The reference monitor can display information such as previously acquired images and measurements.

Information Models
An information model defines the structure and meaning of information that is stored in the system and shared between its components. As Wijnstra argues: "[C]oncepts that are relevant at several places in the architecture [...] are captured in a so-called 'information model'. An information model captures relevant concepts from the domain, and is independent of the underlying technology." [44] Such information may be exchanged via interfaces that are specific to a given particular information model (comparable to static typing in programming languages) or via generic interfaces. In the latter case in particular, the information model is an essential part of the architecture description, since it cannot be derived from the interface definition.

As an example, Fig. 1.26 shows part of the image information model, based on the Digital Imaging and Communications in Medicine (DICOM) standard [34]. The image concept is important when images are displayed on a screen, stored on a medium such as DVD or shared with other systems over a network.

Each *image* is part of a *series* of images. A *presentation state* contains information on how to display images. Each series may contain zero or more images, and is part of an *examination*. An example of an examination is the angioplasty procedure described in Sect. 1.4.3. A *study* contains zero or more examinations. If, for example, a diagnostic procedure

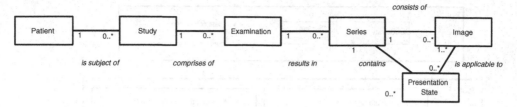

Fig. 1.26. Example of an information model (UML, redrawn from Wijnstra [44])

has been performed on a patient prior to treatment in the cathlab, then both examinations form part of the same study. The subject of study is a *patient*.

Realization view

Technology Mapping
The technology mapping (Fig. 1.27) shows the technologies used to implement the conceptual architecture. It can be visualized as an overlay on the system decomposition diagram.

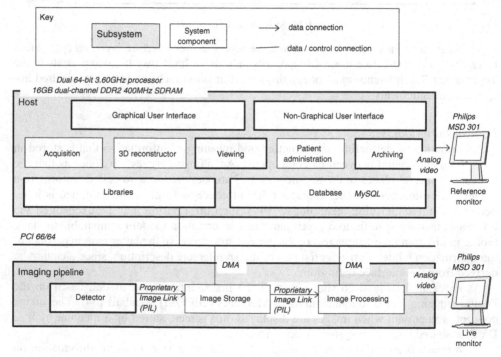

Fig. 1.27. Technology mapping

Although the technology mapping duplicates the information contained in the system decomposition, it cannot replace it. In general, an overlay is intended for short-term use ([9] p. 201). The system decomposition is a much more stable part of the architecture, likely to survive many changes in the technology that implements it. For example, the Peripheral Component Interconnect (PCI) bus could be replaced by a faster successor (like PCI X or PCI Express) without affecting the main system decomposition.

Different members of the product line may share the same conceptual architecture but have different technology mappings. Different members may have different types of monitors, or the speed and number of processors may vary. In such cases, the technology mapping should show the common technology used across the product line. Separate diagrams can be used to show the variation for different product line members.

Conventions

Conventions are rules to be followed during the implementation of the system. They serve to streamline the development process or to achieve certain quality properties. The result of conventions may or may not be observable in the end product. An example of a performance-related convention is not to use malloc statements in inner loops. Standard coding conventions can be used to facilitate the reviewing and maintenance of code in a team of programmers.

1.5 Conclusions and Future Research

A product line architecture represents a significant long-term investment. The ease with which the architecture can deal with changes such as new features, new products, and better quality properties will have a significant impact on the success of the product line. The design and subsequent evolution of the product line architecture determines its ability to adapt to new requirements. It is crucial that both long-term and short-term requirements are taken into account when designing a product line architecture.

Designing an architecture involves many trade-off decisions. Many of these decisions are taken implicitly, drawing on the experience, talent, and intuition of the architect. One problem is that this may lead to a tendency to follow well-trodden paths. Also, implicit decisions are difficult to communicate to other stakeholders of the architecture.

We have presented scenario-based architecting, a method that supports the design and evolution of product line architectures. SBA takes long-term future requirements into account through the use of strategic scenarios during design and evaluation of architectures. Variation modeling in all architecture views and architecture scenarios are used as means of exploring and comparing design options and documenting design decisions. The method was evaluated in two industrial case studies involving a product line of medical imaging systems. We have used an example based on these case studies to explain the method.

The evaluation of the method has so far been limited to a single domain (medical imaging systems), a single organization (Philips Medical Systems) and a single product line (cathlabs). Application of the method in other domains, organizations, and system families could help to further identify its weaknesses and strengths.

Following SBA can be a laborious process. Tool support is one possible way of reducing this problem, in that it helps to limit the time spent keeping track of scenarios, quality attributes and evaluation results. An automation tool could take the form of a spreadsheet extension, possibly coupled to a database. The most effective way to limit the effort involved in SBA without loosing its rewards, however, is to work iteratively and incrementally. By modeling and evaluating small parts of the architecture at a time, dead ends can be spotted quickly and time and effort can be invested in the most crucial parts. Further research is needed to come up with heuristics and guidelines on how to do this.

Scenario correspondence is a topic that deserves more attention. Here, we have used a simple one-one relationship to indicate that one scenario supports the requirements of another scenario. In our experience, this simple approach is good enough for the *commercial* views of CAFCR. In the *technical* views however, it soon leads to many scenarios that have considerable overlap. It could be beneficial to find a way of combining smaller scenarios into larger ones and developing candidate architectures from these. An obvious candidate approach is to extend the multi-view variation modeling technique to support scenarios and candidate architectures as well.

The use of SBA with view sets other than CAFCR is another topic of future research. Such research should focus on the new elements of SBA: multi-view variation modeling, architecture scenarios and the use of strategic scenarios. We expect that it will be harder to relate candidate architectures to strategic scenarios and business goals when using a purely technical set of views. The relationship between view sets and quality attribute evaluation also merits further investigation.

Transferring and combining metric values from one view to another as a general problem has not been solved. This is another topic for further research.

Acknowledgments

We wish to thank our colleagues in the SBA project: Henk Obbink, Eugene Ivanov, Cristian Huiban, as well as Mugur Ionita and Dieter Hammer of the Technical University Eindhoven, and the people at Philips Research and Philips Medical Systems that have contributed to the project in any way, especially Jacco Wesselius. Our Philips Research colleagues Rik Willems and Erwin Bonsma, and Jason Mansell of the European Software Institute read draft versions of this chapter and gave valuable feedback. Finally we want to thank Timo Käkölä, who has spent a lot of time and energy on this text. His comments and insights were very helpful.

References

1.   van der Aalst, W., van Hee, K.: *Workflow Management* (MIT, Cambridge 2002)
2.   America, P., Hammer, D., Ionita, M.T., Obbink, H., Rommes, E.: Scenario-based decision making for architectural variability in product families. In: SPLC-2004: 3rd Software Product Line Conference, Boston, MA, USA, ed by Nord, R.L. (Springer, Berlin Heidelberg New York 2004)
3.   America, P., Obbink, H., Rommes, E.: Multi-view variation modeling for scenario analysis. In: PFE-5: 5th International Workshop on Product Family Engineering, Siena, Italy, ed by van der Linden, F. (Springer, Berlin Heidelberg New York 2003)
4.   Bass, L., Klein, M., Bachmann, F.: Quality attribute design primitives and the attribute driven design method. 4th International Workshop on Product Family Engineering, Bilbao, Spain, 2004
5.   Beck, K.: *Test-Driven Development: By Example* (Addison-Wesley, Reading, MA 2003)
6.   Booch, G., Rumbaugh, J., Jacobson, I.: *The Unified Modeling Language User Guide* (Addison-Wesley, Reading, MA 1998)

7. Bosch, J.: *Design and Use of Software Architectures: Adopting and Evolving a Product-Line Approach* (Addison-Wesley, Reading, MA 2000)

8. Bredemeyer, D.: Software architecture workshop. http://www.bredemeyer.com/ (2002)

9. Clements, P., Bachmann, F., Bass, L., Garlan, D., Ivers, J., Little, R., Nord, R., Stafford, J.: *Documenting Software Architectures – Views and Beyond* (Addison-Wesley, Reading, MA 2003)

10. Clements, P., Kazman, R., Klein, M.: *Evaluating Software Architectures – Methods and Case Studies* (Addison-Wesley, Reading, MA 2002)

11. Cockburn, A.: *Writing Effective Use Cases* (Addison-Wesley, Reading, MA 2001)

12. DeBaud, J.-M., Flege, O., Knauber, P.: PuLSE-DSSA – a method for the development of software reference architectures. Proceedings of the 3rd International Workshop on Software Architecture (ISAW3) (ACM, New York 1998)

13. Dolan, T.J.: Architecture assessment of information-system families. Ph.D. thesis (Technical University Eindhoven 2002)

14. Ferber, S., Haag, J., Savolainen, J.: Feature interaction and dependencies: modeling features for reengineering a legacy product line. In: Software Product Lines: 2nd International Conference (SPLC2), ed by Chastek, G.J. (Springer, Berlin Heidelberg New York 2002)

15. Fowler, M.: *Analysis Patterns – Reusable Object Models* (Addison-Wesley, Reading, MA 1997)

16. Fowler, M., Scott, K.: *UML Distilled* (Addison-Wesley, Reading, MA 1997)

17. Geyer, L.: *Feature Modelling Using Design Spaces. 1. Deutscher Produktlinien Workshop* (Kaiserslautern, Germany 2000)

18. Gomaa, H., Webber, D.: Modeling adaptive and evolvable software product lines using the variation point model. Proceedings of the 37th Hawaii International Conference on System Sciences (HICSS-37) (IEEE, Edinburgh 2004)

19. Heijden, K.V.Q.: *Scenarios: The Art of Strategic Conversation* (Wiley, New York 1996)

20. Hevner, A.R., March, S.T., Park, J., Ram, S.: Design science in information systems research. MIS Q **28**(1), 75–105 (2004)

21. IEEE Architecture Working Group: *IEEE Recommended Practice for Architectural Description of Software-Intensive Systems* (IEEE, Edinburgh 2000)

22. Ionita, M.T.: Scenario-Based System Architecting. Ph.D. thesis (Technical University Eindhoven 2005)

23. Ionita, M.T., America, P., Hammer, D.: A method for strategic scenario-based architecting. Proceedings of the 37th Hawaii International Conference on System Sciences (HICSS-37) (IEEE, Edinburgh 2005)

24. Ionita, M.T., America, P., Hammer, D., Obbink, H., Trienekes, J.J.M.: A scenario-driven approach for value, risk and cost analysis in system architecting for innovation. WICSA 2004: 4th Working IEEE/IFIP Conference on Software Architecture (IEEE, Edinburgh 2004)

25. Ionita, M.T., America, P., Obbink, H., Hammer, D.: Quantitative architecture usability assessment with Scenarios. In: *Closing the Gaps: Software Engineering and Human--Computer Interaction*, ed by Harning, M.B. Workshop at Interact 2003, Zürich, Switzerland (2003)

26. Ionita, M.T., Hammer, D., Obbink, H.: Scenario-based software architecture evaluation methods: an overview. Software Architecture Review and Assessment Workshop Proceedings (SARA) (ACM, New York 2002)

27. Jacobson, I., Booch, G., Rumbaugh, J.: *The Unified Software Development Process* (Addison-Wesley, Reading, MA 1998)

28. Kang, C., Cohen, S., Hess, J., Novak, W., Peterson, A.S.: *Feature-Oriented Domain Analysis (FODA) Feasibility Study* (Software Engineering Institute, Pittsburgh 1990)

29. Kruchten, P.: The 4+1 view model of architecture. IEEE Softw. **12**: 42–50 (1995)

30. Larman, C., Wiki Wiki Community: DomainModel. http://www.c2.com/cgi/wiki?DomainModel (2005)

31. Malan, R., Bredemeyer, D.: The visual architecting process. http://www.bredemeyer.com/pdf_files/WhitePapers/VisualArchitectingProcess.PDF (2005)

32. Matinlassi, M.: Comparison of software product line architecture design methods: COPA, FAST, FORM, KobrA and QADA. Proceedings of the 26th International Conference on Software Engineering (ICSE'04) (IEEE, Edinburgh 2004)

33. Muller, G.: CAFCR: a multi-view method for embedded systems architecting; balancing genericity and specificity. Ph.D. thesis (Technical University Delft 2004)

34. National Electric Manufacturers Association (NEMA): DICOM homepage. http://medical.nema.org/ (2005)

35. O'Dell, C., Grayson, C.J.: *If Only We Knew What We Know: The Transfer of Internal Knowledge and Best Practice* (Simon & Schuster, New York 1998)

36. Robson, C.: *Real World Research*, 2nd edn (Blackwell, Oxford 2002)

37. Schwartz, P.: *The Art of the Long View*. (Doubleday, Broadway 1996)

38. Shaw, M., Garlan, D.: *Software Architecture – Perspectives on an Emerging Discipline* (Prentice-Hall, Englewood Cliffs, NJ 1996)

39. Smith, C.U.: *Performance Engineering of Software Systems* (Addison-Wesley, Reading, MA 1990)

40. Soni, D., Nord, R., Hofmeister, C.: Software architecture in industrial applications. Proceedings of the 17th International Conference on Software Engineering (ICSE'95) (ACM, New York 1995)

41. United States Department of Health and Human Services: Office for Civil Rights – HIPAA. http://www.hhs.gov/ocr/hipaa/ (2005)

42. Weinberg, G.: *Systems Thinking* (Dorset, New York 1992)

43. Wieringa, R.: *Requirements Engineering -- Frameworks for Understanding* (Wiley, New York 1995)

44. Wijnstra, J.G.: Components, interfaces and information models within a platform architecture. 3rd International Conference on Generative and Component-Based Software Engineering (GCSE'01), Erfurt, Germany (Springer, Berlin Heidelberg New York 2001)

45. Witt, B., Baker, T., Merritt, E.: *Software Architecture and Design: Principles, Models and Methods* (Van Nostrand Reinhold, New York 1994)

2 Strategic Scenario-Based Valuation of Product Line Roadmaps

J.H. Wesselius

Abstract

Developing a product line requires investments in developing the core assets, setting up the organization and developing skills for engineers and managers. These investments are made because of the expected outcome, which may range from reductions in time-to-market to increased engineering efficiency and improved quality. The business case for investments in product line engineering has to show that the expected outcome will outweigh the investments when economical criteria are applied.

In literature, models for evaluating the impact of product line engineering on development cost can be found. Development cost is only one factor in the equation of economical value however. Other factors are: revenues, life cycle cost, time and uncertainty. Due to their limited scope, the models found in literature do not result in an estimation of "expected economical value." As a result, decision-making relying solely on the existing models during product line roadmapping cannot be based on valid assessments of the expected economical outcomes of the investments.

In this chapter, a more general model for evaluating the value of investments made in product line engineering will be introduced to evaluate the expected economical value of scenarios for product line (architecture) development. To address uncertainty about the future, this model will use strategic scenarios and assign them a probability to capture assumptions and expectations about the future. The chapter will also indicate how this model and the other models can be combined into a single comprehensive framework covering all factors in the equation of economical value for product line engineering.

2.1 Introduction

Developing a product line is a major undertaking, which requires investments in asset development, setting up the organization and developing skills for engineers and managers. When all of this is done properly, the assets, organization and skills can be employed to develop a series of products reusing a set of common assets. A large volume of literature is available providing guidelines for starting product line engineering (see for instance [8, 19] for a comprehensive overview of product line engineering best practices, guidelines and theory). An essential element in successful product line engineering is developing the business case. The business case has to convince the organization's business management that investments in asset, organization and skill development will be outweighed by the expected benefits of more efficient product development.

The business case for product line architecture development is based on *future* benefits: Investments made today are expected to result in benefits in the future. The business case should take into account that not all investments have to be made at the very beginning: An evolutionary or iterative approach can be used. The business case must put the investments and the expected benefits on a timeline answering questions like:

– What products are expected to be released at what moment?
– What assets are needed for those products?
– What investments in assets are needed at what moment in time?
– What benefits are expected? At what moment?

The answers to these questions constitute the product line roadmap. This roadmap should be driven by the integral value being created. As Barry Boehm argues in [7], the results from value-driven evaluation of investments will be different from the results of cost-driven evaluations. Many of the approaches to product line economics focus on minimizing cost. They do not address the full scope of maximizing value. In this chapter, our focus will be on value: A business case should optimize value for money.

Since a positive business case is based on *expected* costs and benefits, the product line roadmap is always made in the context of expectations and assumptions relating to future developments. This is something that should be kept in mind: A roadmap is not made in hindsight. In hindsight it is relatively simple to assess whether investments have been optimal because all uncertainty is gone and facts have taken the place of expectations.

When developing the roadmap and business case for product line engineering the uncertainty should be explicitly addressed. In [22], we introduced an approach for dealing with uncertainty and time to judge the value of investments in product line engineering. In this chapter we take this approach to show how it addresses some of the well-known pitfalls and benefits in product line engineering. Furthermore, a case inspired by reality will be discussed to show how the value estimation approach deals with various business aspects. But first of all an overview of the value estimation approach will be given, and existing product line cost models will be discussed.

2.2 Research Question

This work was done primarily in an industrial context. On the basis of observations in industrial practice the following question was addressed: *How can we deal with the economical justification for the investments needed for product line engineering in an industrial/commercial environment?*

The relevance of this question stems from the following observations:

– To justify investments in product line engineering, expectations regarding the expected benefits are often set too high.
– Often the expected benefits are not made explicit: "time-to-market," "quality improvement," etc. are used as magic words that do not allow proper debate. Who can argue against "time-to-market reduction"? Making the true value of "time-to-market reduction" tangible is essential for a proper business discussion.
– Depending on the type of business and the size of the platform to be developed, the expected benefits may be achieved only after a relatively long period of making

investments. The business case is often based on assumptions about the future; only when those assumptions become reality the benefits will be achieved. When assumptions are made about the mid/long-term future, the chances are relatively high that the "actual future" will prove to be different from the "assumed future." This means that justifications for making the initial investments are often relatively weak.

2.3 Research Method

We have looked at several cases in our industrial practice, asking the following questions:

- Was there a valid business case for the investments in product line engineering?
- Were assumptions underlying the business case made explicit?
- What factors influenced the economical success or failure of the product line?

We also performed a literature survey to find out what methods for developing product line engineering business cases were available. In this survey we noticed that the available methods do not address all economical factors; they focus primarily on development costs.

On the basis of this observation and the case studies we have proposed a framework for building a product line business case. This framework was inspired by the scenario-based architecting approach [2] (see also Chap. 1) and the ATAM method for architecture evaluation [9].

The framework was validated by applying it on:

- Some trivial cases to determine whether our extensions to existing methods actually make a difference (some of these trivial cases can be found in this chapter).
- A case inspired by a true project (executed at Philips Medical Systems in the period 1997–2001) to see how the framework would have performed in a practical case. Some results of this study can be found in Sect. 2.7 of this chapter.

These case studies were executed in a relatively informal manner during an iterative process for developing the framework.

Considering the results of our work from a scientific point of view, it is important to realize that we do not claim that our proposal is the ultimate method for building product line engineering business cases. We claim that our work shows that:

- Existing methods need to be extended for building a proper business case.
- Existing methods can be well combined into a single framework.
- The scenario-based approach we propose in this chapter offers a tool for building business case that captures more economical factors than just development cost.

We do not claim that the application of our method results in the *ultimate* business case for various reasons:

- The concept of the *ultimate* business case is undefined.

– The *ultimate* business case may not even exist, as what is assumed to be an optimum business case depends on an organization's business strategy: Some organizations may choose to avoid risks, whereas others may decide to accept (or even seek) risks on the basis of a potentially higher outcome. (see Chap. 3 for a brief discussion of the relation between an organization's attitude to risk and the return on investment the organization needs to expect to make a risky investment).

The quality of a business case cannot be expressed in a single objective value. It is my strong conviction that *quality* can never be judged objectively (see [21]) and cannot be expressed in a single value as too many factors are involved, and too many conditions change over time. So seeking a method for arriving at the ultimate business case is fruitless. The research method applied in this work does therefore not focus on proving claims regarding the absolute quality of our approach, or the absolute quality of business cases derived by applying the approach. The results of our work are intended to provide a stepping-stone for future work focusing on the development of more sophisticated methods. By discussing cases, and showing how our approach extends existing methods, we claim to have chosen a promising route.

2.4 Overview of Our Value Evaluation Approach

Many approaches for identifying business opportunities are available in marketing literature (e.g., [12] and many others). A central theme is how to explicitly quantify the expected profit, investments and risks. By numerically or graphically comparing various scenarios (e.g., profit-versus-cost and investment-versus-risk grids, etc.) insight is gained into the characteristics of investment scenarios. In cases in which a financial result will not fully capture the value of investments, other results of the investments are quantified and valued too (see for instance [3] for business parameters in non-profit organizations).

In this section our approach to estimating the expected economical value of investments in product line engineering will be presented (we first presented it on the Software Product Line Conference 2005 [22]). Our approach is also based on a quantitative approach to evaluating investments: costs and benefits need to be quantified. In judging the economical value of investments two aspects are to be taken into account:

– Cash flow generated today is worth more than cash flow generated in the future.
– The future is uncertain.

It is clear that these two aspects are especially critical in businesses with a long product (platform) life cycle. In businesses with a very short product (platform) life cycle, the impact of time on value will be far less, and uncertainty about future developments will be less when development times are short. When building capital equipment (like medical equipment), these factors should not be ignored.

We propose an approach to judging the value of investments in product line engineering taking these two aspects into account:

– Net Present Value calculations can be used to compensate for the effect of time on value.
– Uncertainty about the future is made explicit by describing strategic scenarios and by estimating the likelihood of their occurrence.

2.4.1 Net Present Value Calculations

Net Present Value (NPV) calculation is a commonly used method for evaluating the value of future income relative to the value of the investments to be made to generate that income (see Chap. 3 for an example of the application of NPV for analyzing the economical value of reuse). NPV calculations use the following formula to compensate for the effect of time on the value of cash flow:

$$NPV = \frac{cashflow}{(1+discount\ rate)^{time}}$$

In NPV calculations, the value of a future cash flow is discounted to compensate for the effect of time: By using a proper discount rate the value of a future income is converted to the cash flow of equivalent value generated today. A minimum value to be used for the discount rate is the expected interest rate: If I were to have €1,000 today and the interest would be 4%, it will be worth €1,480 in 10 years from now. Therefore, if I would expect to receive €1,480 in ten years from now, its value would be equivalent to the €1,000 I have today. Making a risky investment of €1,000 today with the promise of getting €1,480 in 10 years from now is therefore not a sensible investment.

2.4.2 Scenario-Based Value Evaluation

To compensate for risk and uncertainty, a simple approach would be to use a significantly higher discount rate for future cash flow with a high-risk profile. This is a relatively implicit approach, which only addresses the fact that cash flow expected to be generated in the near future is more certain than cash flow expected to be generated in the distant future. Inspired by the scenario-based architecting approach (see for instance [2] and Chap. 1) our approach is based on making assumptions and expectations about the future explicit by drawing up a set of relevant scenarios for the future and estimating their likelihood.

Two central notions in our approach are:

1. *Architectural scenarios*. An architectural scenario represents a series of investments in the product line. In fact, an architectural scenario is a potential product line architecture roadmap. For making the value estimation, each investment has two properties: the required investment (i.e., cost) and the moment in time at which the investment is made.
2. *Strategic scenarios*. A strategic scenario represents a series of events in "the market" that have an influence on the value of the product line. Various types of events are conceivable

    - The market demands a certain product (or it no longer does).
    - New technology becomes available (or affordable) enabling new products or architectures.
    - The organization is restructured (e.g., from central development to distributed development or development work is outsourced).

In fact, each of the views in the BAPO/CAFCR framework (see [15,18]) can result in strategic scenarios:

- Business scenarios identify changes in the business model
- Process scenarios identify changes in processes for development, manufacturing, service, etc.
- Organizational scenarios identify changes in the way (development) organization is organized
- Scenarios in the Customer Value, Application and Functional view identify changes in functionality that future products will be required to realize
- Realization Scenarios identify changes in the available technology

Scenarios in the conceptual view of the CAFCR-views come closest to the architectural scenarios whose value is to be estimated.

The value of an architectural scenario will differ for different strategic scenarios:

- If an architectural scenario creates value by enabling easy development of certain features, the value of the architectural scenario will be high in strategic scenarios that predict a high business value for those features.
- If the enabled features prove to have no business value in another strategic scenario, the value of the architectural scenario will prove low in that strategic scenario.

There is of course a continuum between these two options. Furthermore, an architectural scenario will support multiple features; some of which may have a declining value and some may have a rising value. All these factors need to be dealt with when estimating the value of architectural scenarios.

The value of architectural investment scenarios is never 100% certain, because the future is not certain. We therefore speak of the *expected* NPV. The expected NPV can be evaluated in the context of a set of strategic scenarios that make assumptions and expectations about the future explicit. Using these strategic scenarios, the expected value of architectural scenarios can be estimated in four steps:

1. Draw up the architectural scenarios
2. Draw up the most important strategic scenarios and quantify the probability that the scenario will become reality
3. Estimate the cash flow for the architectural scenarios in combination with the strategic scenarios (a) estimate the investments needed to realize the architectural scenarios, (b) estimate the expected income for the architectural scenario if combined with the strategic scenario
4. Calculate the *expected* NPV as follows:

$$NPV_{Expected}(\text{Arch Scenario, Strat Scenario}[1..n]) =$$

$$\sum_{i=1}^{n} NPV(\text{Arch Scenario, Strat Scenario}[i]) * probability(\text{Strat Scenario}[i])$$

This approach makes explicit what factors contribute to the economical justification of investments in architectural features of the product line:

1. A high *probability* of actually creating value on the basis of the architectural investments
2. A *short time interval* between making the architectural investment and realizing the benefits of the investment

The higher the uncertainty, the higher the NPV of the expected benefits should be (see Chap. 3 for a brief discussion of the relation between an organization's attitude to risk and the return on investment the organization needs to expect to make a risky investment). The example we discussed in [22] showed that it really does make a difference if the effect of NPV and strategic scenario probability are taken into account. In our example we proposed three architectural scenarios. When only the costs or NPV are considered, the architectural scenario, which proposes first to build the complete platform, would be most profitable. This was based on the assumption that a product line of three products would be built in a period of three years. When taking into account that this is not a fact, but only an assumption, the outcome becomes different.

Three strategic scenarios were defined:

- SS_1: the three products will be developed in the coming three years
- SS_2: the first product will be developed immediately, and the second and third product will be developed later (i.e., not within three years, but in a period of 5 years)
- SS_3: the first product will be developed immediately, but the second and third product will never be built

By varying the probability of the strategic scenarios it becomes clear that the option of building the entire platform upfront is probably not a wise decision. Although the example is artificial, it does give an indication of how an architectural reasoning process can change when assumptions and expectations are made explicit. More examples can be found in Sects. 2.6 and 2.7.

Since it is not feasible to define and evaluate a complete set of strategic and architectural scenarios, the process will be an explorative process: Starting with a limited set of scenarios, new scenarios will be added and scenarios which prove to be irrelevant will be dropped. The four steps will typically be performed iteratively as sketched in Fig. 2.1, finally resulting in the selection of the architectural scenario which is in view of the assumptions about the future (made explicit in scenarios) expected to yield the highest value. From that moment on this scenario will be the architectural roadmap of the product line.

2.5 Existing (Product Line) Cost and Value Models

Several models for dealing with product line cost and value estimation can be found in the literature. Some of the better-known approaches will be discussed briefly in the sections below. The main questions in these sections will be:

- How do the models fit in the approach discussed in the previous section?
- What does our approach add to the existing models?

Our conclusion will be that the various models do not compete with one another. The question "which of these methods is the best" is not a valid question; different models will prove to address different pieces of the puzzle: from project cost estimation to product line cost estimation, to expected value estimation for product line investments.

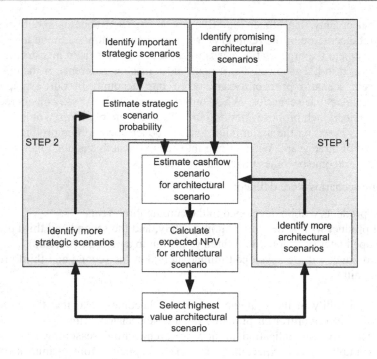

Fig. 2.1. The iterative roadmap optimization process

The following sections should therefore not be seen as an attempt to show that our approach outperforms the other methods. The questions is: where do they overlap and where do they complement one another? The various approaches (including the one we presented in the previous section) will be combined into a single picture, which will form a comprehensive framework for product line cost/value evaluation.

2.5.1 COCOMO II and Function Points

Two well-known methods for software development cost estimation are COCOMO II [5, 6] and Function Point Analysis [1,13]. Both methods characterize the software to be developed in a specific way:

– Function point analysis takes the specification of the software and counts the inputs, outputs, internal data and interactions with external systems to estimate the size of the software to be developed. The development effort can be estimated on the basis of the number of function points and characteristics of the development project.
– COCOMO is based on size estimates (e.g., by using Function Point Analysis) and a set of cost multipliers ranging from complexity to team capacity, process maturity (CMM score) and application experience. One factor which is explicitly taken into account is the *required reuse cost driver* (RUSE), which is defined in such a way that two well-known

phenomena are accounted for (i) reuse is never for free, and (ii) making small modifications in a component to be reused is relatively expensive.

Both methods use large industry-based databases to convert the size estimates into cost. They have proven to be useful in practice, but the models do not explicitly address product line cost factors (except for the RUSE factor in COCOMO II).

2.5.2 Breakdown of Product Line Cost

In [11,23] a cost model is presented that explicitly focuses on product line engineering. A formula is used to calculate the cost of developing a series of products on the basis of a product line architecture. The formula identifies the cost elements for developing a product line:

- The cost of setting up the *organization* for product line engineering
- The cost of developing the *core asset base* of the product line (reusable building blocks of any nature: requirements, architecture, design)
- The cost of building *components which are specific* to one member of the product line (building blocks that are not reusable, and therefore not considered a core asset)
- *The cost of reusing the core assets.* The formula explicitly expresses that the cost of reusing components should not be ignored. From both theory and practical experience it is clear that reusing components can become a major cost factor: finding the components to be reused, changing the design of the rest of the software in order to be able to reuse the component, slightly modifying the reusable components, organizational overhead needed to coordinate the life cycle of the reused components if changes are made in it or bugs are fixed, etc.

When these factors are combined, the formula below gives the total cost of developing a product line consisting of the products $P_1...P_n$.

$$C_{org} + C_{cab} + \sum_{i=1}^{n}(C_{unique}(P_i) + C_{reuse}(P_i))$$

C_{org}	Organizational cost to adopt product line engineering
C_{cab}	Development cost of core asset base suited to support the product line being developed
$C_{unique}(P)$	The cost of developing unique software for product P (software that is not based on the product line platform)
$C_{reuse}(P)$	The development cost to reuse core assets for the development of product P

In [4] this formula is made more specific for a set of implementation scenarios.

This model requires other methods for estimating the basic cost parameters found in the formula. The cost modeling approaches discussed in Sect. 4.1 could be used to model the cost of developing the core asset base and the costs of specific components.

In [11,23], the formula is used to evaluate the effectiveness of product line engineering for some specific cases. The formula clearly identifies the cost factors to be considered. The approach is useful as some costs are easily forgotten (preparing the organization and the cost of reuse), but it is limited in three aspects:

- Only one aspect of the effectiveness of product line engineering is taken into account: Do investments in setting up a product line effectively reduce the overall development cost? This is not the only factor that has to be considered when building a business case for product line engineering: In addition to development costs, all other life cycle costs should be considered.

  Life Cycle Costs are all costs during a product's entire life cycle. Life cycle costs are for instance: cost of creating bug fixes, cost of developing product upgrades, cost of adapting the product when hardware or operating systems have become obsolete, cost of keeping spare parts in stock, etc. Especially in the case of products with a relatively long life time (capital goods, for instance medical equipment) life cycle costs may become very significant. If the architecture has been designed well, selling life cycle services can be very profitable. When the number of distinct configurations in the field becomes too large, the life cycle costs can become so high that profitable life cycle services can no longer be offered. Product line engineering can help to reduce the number of different configurations in the field.
- Apart from costs, income effects of developing a product line must also be taken into account (like enhanced profitability thanks to a reduction in the time-to-market).
- The formula does not take the effect of time into account. Not all costs are made at the same moment in time. As discussed above, NPV calculations should be used to compensate for this. Especially because in product line engineering many costs are made up-front (preparing the organization and developing the core asset base) this effect should not be ignored.
- It is not clear how this model deals with uncertainty. It is not addressed explicitly in the publications. Knowing that much of the SEI work on architecture evaluation is based on defining scenarios, this will probably also be their approach to dealing with uncertainty in the case of evaluating the value of investments in product line engineering.

In [10] and on the associated web-site http://simple.sei.cmu.edu, the most recent version of the model is presented. In these publications, two factors have been added to the model (i) in addition to the cost-factors, a benefits-factor is introduced; (ii) the factor *time* is addressed by adding a parameter t to the cost and benefits factors. The model does not prescribe how to deal with the factor time itself. This is considered to be part of the models for estimating the cost and benefits factors.

2.5.3 Product Line Engineering Cost Reduction Model

The model discussed in the section earlier defines the main types of cost in product line engineering, but it does not indicate how those values should be determined. A model that makes an attempt to translate characteristics of a product line into a value for cost reduction in terms of the effort to be spent on developing a complete product line can be found in [18]. In this section, a formula is introduced for calculating a cost reduction factor for a single common component:

$$\Delta S = \left[1 - \frac{1}{(1 + \delta p)\,(1 + (N\lambda - 1)\,\omega)}\right] \tilde{S} \qquad \text{(reduce cost version)}$$

N The number of products using the common component

δp The relative change (positive or negative) in productivity is expressed as a percentage.

     If for instance δp = +25%, this indicates that the same group of people can develop 25% more functionality in the same time. Negative values of δp can be used to indicate a productivity drop. This can be used to capture the cost of reuse, which was modelled explicitly in the model presented in Sect. 2.5.2.

ω The commonality in requirements should be interpreted:

- if the products are built as a common component + extensions for the various products which contain the product-specific requirements,
- the commonality is reflected in the relative size of the common component and the total software developed for the N products, i.e.,

$$\omega = \frac{\text{size(common component)}}{\text{size(common component)} + \Sigma\,\text{size(extension)}}$$

λ The "leverage by the product groups" parameter is used to express that the product groups will not use all functionality built into the component by the component development group. This means that if the functionality needed by the component groups would require 1,000 SLOC, the component developed by the component development group will count 1,500 SLOC if λ = 66%.

$\hat{S}$ The development staff size needed to develop the functionality of the component for the entire product range consisting of the N products when no reuse is applied.

ΔS The reduction in the staff size required for developing the functionality of the component for the entire product range consisting of the N products when reuse is applied.

For a given set of parameters, Fig. 2.2 (taken from [18]) gives the cost reduction factor for a varying commonality. To understand the results, assume that:

N = 3

δp = 0

ω = 70%

λ = 66%

$\hat{S}$ = 3,000 → the size of the implementation in the event of no reuse

In that case, the cost reduction would be 41% according to the formula. This can be explained as follows:

- The functionality requires an investment of 1,000 per product (on average).
- A common component will be developed, which requires an effort of 1,246.
- Of this common component, only 66% will actually be used by the product groups, which means that the common component represents only 66% of 1,246 of functionality to the product groups = 822.

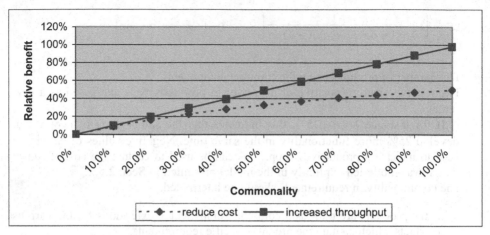

Fig. 2.2. Relative cost avoidance benefits for selected parameters

– To ensure the full functionality, each product group would (on average) have to spend 1,000 – 822 = 178.
– The overall result would be:

Common component	1,246
Product 1 Extension	178
Product 2 Extension	178
Product 3 Extension	178
Total	1,780 = 3,000 * (1 – 41%) → cost reduction factor
	1,780 * 70% = 1,246 → commonality

On the basis of the cost reduction factor, the paper presents a formula for determining the throughput improvement of an organization if product line engineering is deployed. This formula can easily be expressed as:

$$\text{Factor}_{\text{throughput improvement}} = \frac{\text{Factor}_{\text{cost reduction}}}{1 - \text{Factor}_{\text{cost reduction}}}$$

where Factor $_{\text{cost reduction}}$ equals the result of the first formula.

In the example given above, a cost reduction factor of 41% corresponds to a throughput improvement of 69%, which means that the same group of engineers would be able to achieve 69% more output if product line engineering were to be deployed (at the given parameter values).

Since the formula is applicable to a single component, it would have to be applied to each individual component that is suitable for reuse in the product line. Or, as done in the case presented in the second part of [17], an average value for the parameters can be used for a larger group of components.

After presenting this formula an analysis of the economical cost and value of investments in a transition to software product line based development is presented. The analysis consists of:

– An overview of cost elements, cost drivers and time drivers
– An overview of the relations between cost elements and cost/time drivers
– The definition of a software product line introduction scenario which provides information on the timing of the costs and benefits
– A calculation of NPV, internal rate of return and payback time for the introduction scenario. Furthermore, the results of a sensitivity analysis are presented

The section's conclusion is that timing of the investments is crucial in building a business case. The business case should not only provide an answer to the question *whether* a company should start product line engineering, but it should also provide insight into the *timing* of investments: Should all investments be made upfront? Or should an incremental approach be chosen? Which elements should be built first? There is no general answer to these questions; the answer will be very much case-dependent.

2.5.4 NPV-Based Product Line Adoption Modeling

In the models discussed in the previous section, product line engineering costs are estimated independently of the timing of investments. In [20], an analysis is made of product line adaptation. With a focus on modularity, an analysis is given of the total cost (and cost saving) involved in introducing variability mechanisms in the software. The question analyzed in this paper is: When should investments in implementing/designing variation points be made?

A series of formulas for calculating the cost of implementing variation points are introduced for this analysis. Without going into detail about all the parameters and formulas, the results of the analysis (for a specific set of parameters) are given in Fig. 2.3. The chart should be understood as follows:

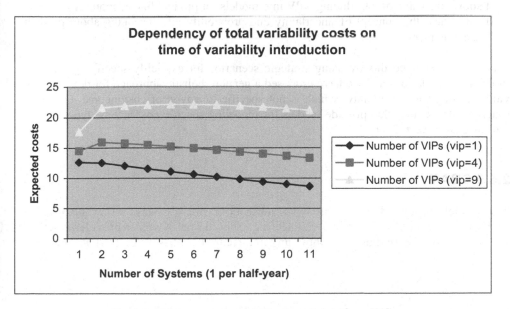

Fig. 2.3. Total expected variability costs (taken from [20])

- VIP = Variation Impact Point. This denotes a place in the software where a variation point takes effect.
- The chart indicates the total cost involved in implementing a variation point for a given number of VIPs (e.g., for the number of VIPs = 9, introduction of the variation point will have an impact on 9 places in the software) at a given moment in time. This moment is denoted by the product in which the variation point is first implemented, assuming that 10 products will be developed over a period of 5 years (with 6 months between the product releases).

From the chart it can be concluded that if the number of VIPs is high, it is worthwhile to implement the variation point at the very beginning. The chart also shows that if the number of VIPs is low, implementing the variation point later may be cheaper. This cost reduction is caused by the fact that the NPV is taken into account in the formulas. When looking at the results of this analysis, the conclusion could be that implementing a variation point at the very beginning is the preferred strategy, but this actually to a large extent depends on the parameters chosen in the analysis. Regardless of the specific model being used, this analysis shows the potential effect of considering the effect of time in NPV-based calculations.

As a next step, the section addresses *uncertainty*: Implementing a variation point is only useful when the likelihood of using the variation point is sufficiently high. The analysis shows that delayed implementation of a variation point is only useful when the probability of using the variation point is relatively low. On the basis of the results of the analysis, decisions can be made regarding the introduction strategy for variation points.

The paper presents a rather abstract analysis for modeling the cost (saving) associated with variation points. The analysis addresses only one specific aspect. The contribution of the work to the framework presented in this paper is primarily that:

- It shows the value of introducing NPV into models for product line economics
- It introduces the concept of uncertainty and probability into reasoning about product line economics

We have generalized this by using strategic scenarios for explicitly specifying assumptions and expectations and we have proposed a general, holistic approach for dealing with value, timing and uncertainty, which is not specific to a type of cost/income. Our approach needs methods that provide models for modeling specific cost/income types, as we will discuss in Sect. 2.5.6.

2.5.5 CBAM

The models discussed in the previous subsections provide ways of evaluating the cost/value impact of product line engineering. They do not however provide a method for systematically finding the optimum architectural scenario. In [14] an iterative method for finding the optimum scenario is proposed. This method (called *CBAM*, which is short for Cost Benefit Analysis Method) is based on a sequence of steps that are executed iteratively to optimize the architectural scenario with respect to the generated value. The method is not specifically designed for product line engineering; it addresses the more general issue of how to reason about system/software architecture when economical factors are to be considered.

The method is (like the ATAM method [9]) based on the definition of architectural scenarios that represent potential ways of shaping a product (line) architecture. After the impact of the architectural scenario on some key features of the product (quality attributes) has been evaluated, the business value of the architectural scenario is expressed in a single value using a QFD-like approach. For each of the architectural scenarios a cost estimate is made, which can be used to calculate the *return on investment*[1] as the total value generated by the architectural scenario divided by the total cost of the scenario.

The method does not really translate value into financial terms like NPV, but it makes two contributions:

- It provides an interactive sequence of steps that can be executed in a structured way to optimize the architectural scenario selection process. In this process, the performance indicator proposed by the CBAM (benefit/cost) can easily be replaced by evaluating the economical value.
- It addresses the notion of *uncertainty* in a very specific way: The values assigned to scenarios may vary when different stakeholders are asked about them. The method proposes a way of dealing with this in a statistical way. This approach may or may not be reusable when reasoning about economical value in combination with strategic scenarios as we propose in our method, but either way it constitutes clear support for our choice of making uncertainty a core element in our value estimation approach.

2.5.6 Combining the Models

Having studied various models for product line cost estimation, we can make the following observations:

- COCOMO II and Function Point Analysis offer a method for estimating the cost of development efforts on a project-by-project basis, but it does not directly address the cost of product line engineering, which is a combination of the costs involved in multiple development projects.
- The formula based on the product line cost factors (discussed in Sect. 2.5.2) quantifies the cost of building a product line without providing any clues how to estimate the cost of individual development activities.
- The NPV-based approach discussed in Sect. 2.5.3 additionally uses NPV calculations to compensate for the effect of time, but it does not explicitly address all cost components. Furthermore, it introduces the notion of uncertainty by estimating the probability of actually using variation points.

---

[1] Note: the term *Return on Investment* is not used in the conventional way in [14]. What is meant is basically *value for money*.

- None of the methods make assumptions about the future explicit as we propose doing by defining strategic scenarios and their probabilities.
- None of the methods discussed above explicitly address life cycle costs and income benefits (although in [4] this is mentioned as one of the topics for future extension of the model).

When looking at the models discussed in this section, we concluded that they do not conflict. What's more, we concluded that each model could be considered an essential step in building a value estimation framework for product line development. In Fig. 2.4, we sketched how we would combine the various types of models into a framework.

1. On the basis of estimates of project costs, the development costs of a product line can be estimated using the formula discussed in Sect. 2.5.2
2. If the model is completed by:

   - Putting the costs on a time line (when do we develop which assets → architectural scenario/roadmap)
   - Defining strategic scenarios for which expected income and life cycle cost saving can be estimated
   - Estimating the probabilities of the strategic scenarios
   - The expected NPV for an architectural scenario can be estimated (NPV and multiplication with strategic scenario probability as discussed in Sect. 2.4.2)

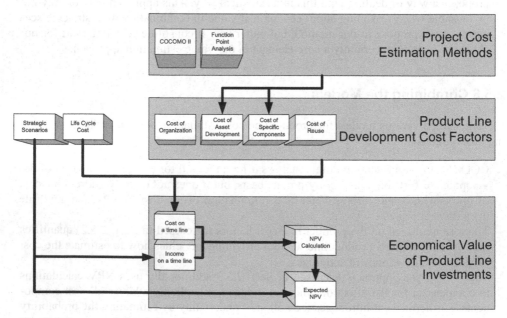

Fig. 2.4. Framework for evaluating the expected value of investments in product line engineering

2.6 Product Line Pitfalls and Benefits

To justify the approach we are proposing (as introduced in the previous section and in Sect. 2.4.2 of this chapter), we will in this section look at some well-known pitfalls and potential benefits of product line engineering. The questions we will try to answer are:

- Does the approach satisfactorily explain the pitfalls and benefits? Does it provide ways of optimizing the benefits and avoiding the pitfalls?
- Does the introduction of strategic scenarios and NPV calculations add something to the existing methods discussed in the previous section?

In the next section we will use a case study inspired by reality to validate the approach in a more practical way.

2.6.1 Pitfall: Platform Over-Design and Perfectionism

"Perfectionism" is a major pitfall. Building "the perfect and complete product line architecture" from the beginning will require major initial investments. This will result in a long development period for the product line platform. The first product will consequently become available only after a long initial development period. The economical payback of the investments will start later than might have been possible if another approach would have been taken. This will significantly limit the return on investment. Quick introduction on the market and incremental implementation of the architecture might in many cases be a more attractive approach.

Another penalty of implementing the product line architecture completely from the beginning is that many architectural features might never be used in products. This is clearly a waste of time and money.

It is important to realize that a company can't afford to be prepared for everything. What's more, since the future is unknown, it is *impossible* to be prepared for everything; by the time a complete and perfect product line architecture has been implemented, market values will have changed, rendering the architecture imperfect after all.

One of the defences against *perfectionism* is to "quantify the economics." By quantifying the value of investments, economically unjustified investments can be avoided. The perfection-pitfall will be addressed by identifying investments that do not realize return on investment in the following two ways:

- The NPV calculations if return on investment is to be expected only in the distant future
- The strategic scenario probability if the return on investment will only be achieved in strategic scenarios with a relatively low probability

The following example may clarify this:

1. Suppose a company is considering the development of two products P_1 and P_2
2. Suppose that P_1 is needed next year and P_2 might be needed in 6 years from now
3. Suppose that the development of P_1 would cost €300,000 if no investments are made in the product line
4. Suppose that the development of P_2 would cost €500,000 if no investments are made in the product line

5. Suppose that the investment in the product line needed to make it perfectly suitable for the development of P_2 would cost €200,000 in addition to the cost of developing P_1 and that the development of P_2 would cost only €100,000 if those investments in product line engineering would have been made

6. Two architectural scenarios are defined:

   – AS_1: fully prepare the platform for P_2
   – AS_2: ignore P_2, just build P_1 and develop P_2 when the need arises

7. Suppose that the strategic scenario SS_1 which says P_2 will be needed in 6 years from now has a probability of $X\%$ and that the probability of a scenario SS_2 in which P_2 will never be developed is $100 - X\%$.

The expected values of the architectural scenarios based on these parameters are given in the top chart in Fig. 2.5 (calculated with the formula which can be found in Sect. 2.4.2, using an NPV discount rate of 7%). The chart only shows the expected NPV of the development costs. The conclusion that can be drawn from this chart is that architectural scenario AS_1 will be beneficial only when the likelihood of P_2 development is more than 75%.

When the NPV and strategic scenarios are ignored, the conclusion might be different:

1. The total cost of AS_1 would be €600,000 (for P_1 and P_2 together)
2. The total cost of AS_2 would be €800,000

This would lead to the conclusion that fully preparing the platform would be justified. It could be argued that no company will make an investment decision based on just cost calculations, but in conjunction with the cost model presented in Sect. 2.5.2, studies have been performed to look into the economical justification of product line engineering solely on the basis of cost comparisons [4,11].

When the NPV is taken into account, but strategic scenarios are ignored, the same conclusion is reached: the NPV for developing P_1 and P_2

1. Based on AS_1 would be -€566,634
2. Based on AS_2 would be -€633,171

This example shows how our approach helps to avoid the "perfection pitfall": While the other models discussed in Sect. 2.5 would justify full platform preparation, our approach indicates that this is only justified when the likelihood of developing both products is sufficiently high.

The charts in Fig. 2.5 also indicate the effect of expected timing. If the second assumption in the case description is changed into: Suppose that P_1 is needed next year and P_2 might be needed one year later.

The expected NPV will change as indicated in the bottom chart in Fig. 2.5. In that case preparing the platform for P_2 will become justified already when the likelihood of the strategic scenario is 55%. Since the uncertainty will typically be less when a product is scheduled for introduction in the near future, preparing the platform for P_2 will probably be justified in this case. This phenomenon will remain unobserved if NPV and strategic scenario probability are not taken into account.

2.6.2 Pitfall: Short-Term Focus

This pitfall is rather obvious: When the time horizon is set too near, investment decisions will not be optimum because opportunities for positive cash flow will be ignored. On the other hand, future costs (life cycle costs) may also be ignored. Since investments in product line engineering need sufficient time to be profitable, care should be taken to ensure that the planning horizon is set to a reasonable minimum.

An organization may be inclined to set a planning horizon too close after bad experiences with investments in building platforms. When investments can only be justified by income in the relatively distant future, the risk of not realizing the payback will be high. To avoid this risk, the organization may choose to set the planning horizon close: "Do not make assumptions about any income from the platform in more than two years from now."

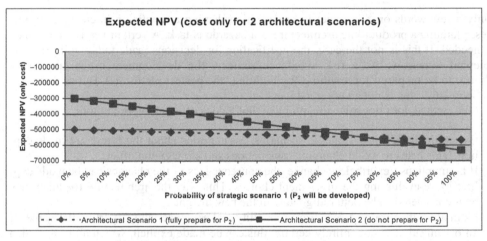

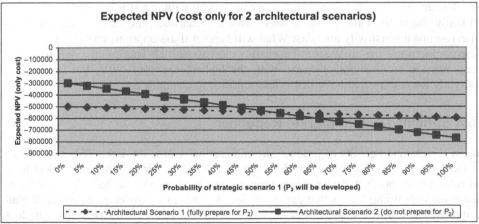

Fig. 2.5. Expected NPV (cost only) for two architectural scenarios (*top*: assuming P_2 in 2001, *bottom*: assuming P_2 in 2006)

Does the approach to making value judgments we propose help to avoid this pitfall?

- No, it does not: An organization that is sceptical about platform development and that has chosen not to consider benefits in the relatively distant future will simply not define the strategic scenarios that will result in future income.
- But by challenging the organization to make its assumptions explicit, and by challenging it to define scenarios, and by allowing it to give very low probability estimates, the process of thinking about the future can be catalyzed.
- Furthermore, a sceptical organization will appreciate the effect of using NPV calculations instead of plain cost calculations in the business case, since the effect of NPV will reduce the value of income expected in the distant future. NPV calculations are such a common tool that sceptical organizations will certainly reject approaches that do not use them to take the effect of time into account.

2.6.3 Pitfall: Lack of Vision and Clear Decision Making (No Constancy)

Only a few words on this issue: In organizations having a reputation in changing priorities, planning a product line architecture is a hazardous task. A certain level of constancy is needed. If this is not the case, the justification for decisions made today will prove irrelevant tomorrow. As a risk avoidance strategy, the development organization may choose to be prepared for anything (by building "the perfect platform"). But as discussed in Sect. 2.6.1, this is not a very good idea!

Our method does not solve this problem, but it does offer an important tool:

- By explicitly defining strategic scenarios, assumptions about the future are made explicit. This helps to avoid changing assumptions and strategy too often.
- If assumptions nevertheless change, the consequences of the changes can be made explicit by re-evaluating the investment choices. This way the architecture roadmap may be reconsidered to be better aligned with the new insights.
- Estimating the strategic scenario probability makes "uncertainty" part of the game. If an organization is not entirely certain, this can be made explicit, which all of a sudden makes uncertainty a "normal thing" that can be dealt with in a structured way.
- Finally, the method allows one to play "what-if scenarios." This can be very helpful in performing a sensitivity analysis: What will happen if assumptions change? For which assumptions are the architectural scenarios most sensitive? This could result in selecting not the architectural scenario with the highest expected NPV, but one with a slightly lower expected NPV that is less sensitive to changing assumptions.

2.6.4 Benefit: Time-to-Market Reduction

One of the clearest benefits of product line engineering is time-to-market reduction: When the market demands for a new product, the time between identifying the market need and releasing the product can be reduced significantly if a platform has been developed containing major building blocks that can be reused. An effect that enhances the value of platform reuse is the typical market price development of innovative products: When a product is introduced, the market is willing to pay a premium price, but after some time (when similar or improved products have entered the market) the price will drop. This means that the highest margins are to be expected in the first years of a product's lifetime. Having a product in the market in those early years can therefore be very profitable. If the development of a product line platform will help to market a product at an early stage, this can be a very positive business case for investments in product line engineering.

But there may also be a penalty to product line engineering: If a product line platform must be developed in its entirety before a first product can be launched, some time will be lost at the beginning. This may mean that the expected high income in the first couple of years will not be realized (while a company is busy building its platform, competitors may introduce new products on the market).

To assess the effect, consider the following example:

1. Suppose that the development of a product platform will take 3 years, and will require an investment of €500,000 per year.
2. Suppose that developing a product without reuse will take 2 years and cost €200,000 per year.
3. Suppose that developing a product on the basis of the platform will take 1 year and cost €100,000
4. Suppose that a new product is expected to be demanded by the market every 2 years:

   $-$ P_{2005} in 2005
   $-$ P_{2007} in 2007
   $-$ P_{2009} in 2009, etc.

5. Suppose that the products have a commercial life of 4 years and that the income generated by those products may be:

$-$ 1st year	€1,000,000
$-$ 2nd year	€750,000
$-$ 3rd year	€250,000
$-$ 4th year	€100,000

6. Assume two architectural scenarios:

   $-$ AS_1: do not build the platform, just build the products one by one
   $-$ AS_2: build the platform first

To enable comparison of the two scenarios, we have made sure that the cumulative investments in both scenarios will be roughly the same in the period 2005-2014 (€2,000,000 for AS_1 and €1,900,000 for AS_2).

Note that in AS_2 the platform will not be ready in 2005, and therefore the high income expected for P_{2005} will be lost. As from 2007 (P_{2007}), the platform will allow the introduction of a product at the most profitable time (i.e., generating the expected €1,000,000 income).

As is to be expected, the NPV for AS_1 would be better than the NPV of AS_2 in the first years. But the NPV of AS_2 will become better as new products are launched at lower costs, and with a shorter time-to-market. But since the future is never certain, consider two strategic scenarios:

- SS_1: products will be demanded that can be developed on the basis of the platform until at least 2013
- SS_2: products will be demanded that can be developed on the basis of the platform until 2009. From 2011 onwards, the products will require features that require an entirely different platform.

It will be clear that AS_2 will be most profitable in combination with SS_1. The NPVs of the architectural and strategic scenarios are shown in Fig. 2.6. The effect of taking the probability of the two strategic scenarios into account is shown in Fig. 2.7: Depending on the probability of SS_1 (and SS_2, which is set to 100%-probability(SS_1)), either AS_1 or AS_2 may be the preferred architectural scenario (calculated using the formula introduced in Sect. 2.4.2)

When the risk of SS_2 being realized is ignored, the business case for building the platform would be positive in the example shown in Fig. 2.6. in 2011 the NPV of AS_2 would be higher than the NPV of AS_1 (this is rather long in true business cases, but that doesn't make any difference for the sake of the discussion of this example). When only cash flow is taken into account (and the effect of NPV is ignored), this would be the case in 2009 already.

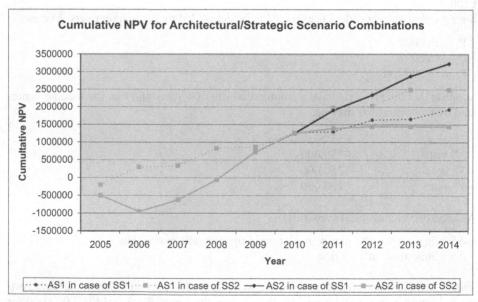

Fig. 2.6. Expected NPV for architectural scenarios AS_1 and AS_2 and strategic scenarios SS_1 and SS_2

The outcome of the product line investment decision might be different on the basis of the results from the simplified scenario analysis: The business case will only be positive when the probability of SS_1 is more than 50%. How sure can an organization be about market demands in 2011?

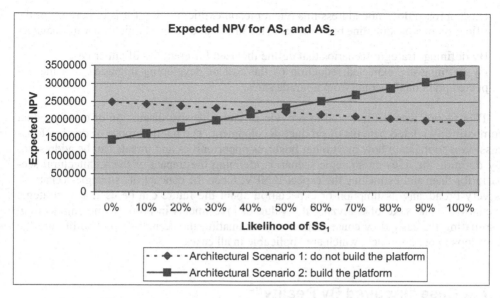

Fig. 2.7. The effect of platform development on expected NPV: impact of time-to-market

The example shows that time-to-market can be a major selling point for investments in product line engineering, but the effect of the initial investments should be accounted for in two ways:

– Money spent early has a greater value than money spent in later years: The investments in developing the platform upfront have a major impact on the business case in the given example.
– If an investment is justified only on the basis of the assumption that the market will demand a complete range of future products, allowance should be made for the risk of the platform proving to be unsuitable for developing those products. In that case, the return on investment of the platform development may never be realized.

2.6.5 Benefit: Cross-Product Compatibility

Without going into too much detail, we will now devote a few words to this potential benefit of product line engineering. When products with a relatively long lifetime are sold, selling upgrades of those products may be very lucrative. There are several types of possible upgrades (i) problem-solving upgrades (Service Packs, Patches, etc.) and (ii) upgrades with new functionality/improved performance. These two types are typically dealt with in different ways: Problem-solving upgrades are commonly distributed free of charge, while upgrades with new functionality will in most cases generate income.

When products are built on a shared platform, one of the potential benefits is that upgrades need to be built only once. Or even better, as a new product is being developed, upgrades for the existing installed base may become available at very low development costs. When products in the installed base do not share the same platform, this spin-off will not be available, and neither will the associated income of upgrade sales be generated.

Our approach does not address this phenomenon explicitly, but if it is important for the justification of a product line business case, it can be handled in a straightforward manner:

- By defining strategic scenarios that define the need for upgrades of either type
- By defining the expected reduction of the cost of developing upgrades, and the expected additional income from upgrade sales.

This section was not intended to provide a comprehensive discussion of cross-product compatibility related benefits of product development. The main purpose of this brief discussion is to indicate how most other business opportunities and threats can be addressed: By defining the relevant strategic scenarios, defining the impact of the architectural scenario for them and estimating the expected NPV. Since the concept of "strategic scenarios" is very broad, any assumption or expectation about the future can be used as a strategic scenario for the sake of analyzing the value of investments in product line engineering. Estimating the cash flow consequences and estimating the scenario's probability are the key steps in our approach, which are applicable in all cases.

2.7 A Case "Inspired By Reality"[2]

In the period 1996–2001, Philips Medical Systems developed a product line of CT scanners. The relevance of considering strategic scenario probability and time will be discussed in this section on the basis of experiences gained in this project. First a brief description will be given of the nature of the product line. In the remainder of this section, several strategic scenarios will be discussed. The impact of the probability of each scenario on the product line architecture will be discussed in order to show the relevance of explicitly taking the strategic scenario and its probability into account.

2.7.1 Description of the Case

A CT scanner is a medical modality for acquiring diagnostic information with the aid of X-rays. In a CT scanner, the X-ray tube and an X-ray detector are rotated around the patient at a high speed (in those days 0.7 s per rotation). During the rotation the X-ray detector acquires data representing the X-ray absorption. Typically, 1,440 views are acquired during each rotation (4 views per degree rotation). From the acquired views a 3D voxel (= a pixel in 3D) space can be reconstructed. The value of each voxel corresponds to the X-ray absorption at the position of the voxel in the human body. In a CT scanner, the voxel value can be directly related to the tissue type.

---

[2] The case described in this section is based on actual events, but for the sake of making the example concise and to illustrate the effects of considering the consequence of time and strategic scenario probability in architectural decision-making in the following sections, I took the liberty to simplify things and to change the facts a little bit. In practice, many more aspects play a role. These have been ignored in the case description. The case description should not create the impression that things are completely straightforward in industrial practice.

The scanner can be logically split into two main subsystems:

- the Front End (FE), which consists of the scanner gantry (X-ray tube, X-ray detector, High Voltage, Cooling Units, etc.)
- the Back End (BE), which is the operator console that is used for planning scans, starting and stopping scans, reviewing the scanned images and integration with the hospital IT infrastructure

The Front End is placed in a lead-shielded room and the Back End is outside this room to avoid the risk of the clinical staff being exposed to the X-rays (Fig. 2.8).

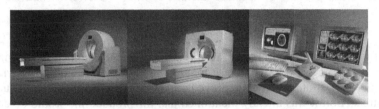

Fig. 2.8. The CT-Scanner Product Line (mid-end FE, high-end FE, and Back End)

For various reasons it was decided that the product line of CT scanners would be developed in close cooperation with two companies:

- A US partner would build a Front End for the mid-range of the market.
- A Japanese partner would build a Front End for the high-end of the market.
- Philips would build the Back End so that it would be usable with both the US and the Japanese Front Ends. The Back End would be usable for both the high-end and the mid-end of the market, since features of the Front End made real market segment differentiation. The Back End was primarily a differentiator for the product's attractiveness within the market segment targeted by the specification of the Front End.

Without going into detail about the specific functions and features of the CT scanner product line, we will focus on the design of the interface between the FE and BE. Which variants were considered, and what would the impact of considering strategic scenario probability have been?

2.7.2 Strategic Scenario 1: Level of Alignment of Business Goals

The first approach in building the product line would be to minimize the interface software; the highest level of reuse would be achieved if the FE–BE interface would be the same for both FEs. In that case, a completely reusable BE could be built as shown in Fig. 2.9.

In this architectural scenario, the cost would probably be minimal. Of course, the cost of defining the common interface should not be ignored, but if it is assumed that this can be done relatively easily, this will probably be outweighed by the reduced cost of building and maintaining the software for the FE–BE interface on the BE-side.

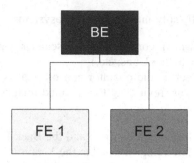

Fig. 2.9. Architectural Scenario 1: minimize interface software – one FE–BE interface for both scanners

But what if it should prove to be not so simple to define the common FE–BE interface? What if this should prove to be not a task requiring a major effort, but a task with a very long lead-time? This strategic scenario proved important when building the product line.

In the introduction it was already mentioned that the product line would be developed by three partners on three different continents. This is not a typical case for fast and easy communication. If the intention was moreover for the Japanese partner to reuse the FE for its own systems for the Japanese market (on the basis of its own BE), the situation would suddenly become a bit more complex (see Fig. 2.10):

- The Japanese partner would not be as flexible as one would hope, because it would also be building a BE with a specific architecture.
- The Japanese partner would have its own requirements for the interface because it would have its own commercial strategy for introducing a CT-scanner on its home market.
- The Japanese partner may also have plans to develop a mid-range or low-range scanner for its home market for which it would want to reuse the BE it had developed for the high-range scanner. Such plans may not yet be concrete and may not be shared with the other two partners.

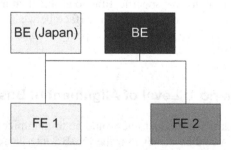

Fig. 2.10. Architectural scenario 1 in combination with the strategic scenario: The Japanese partner also uses FE 1 for the Japanese market with its own back end

The fact that the three partners did not have a completely aligned strategy due to the "home market concern" of one of the FE builders has a major impact on the likelihood of the three partners being able to define a common FE–BE interface. It decreases the likelihood of this being done in a very short time. This would have serious time-to-market consequences.

In the value estimation of this architectural scenario, the consequences of the strategic scenario based on one partner building an entire system for its home market should be taken into account: It has consequences for the likelihood of the interface being quickly defined.

Besides the time-to-market consequences, other phenomena should be taken into account, too:

- Since the FE–BE interface would also be used for the Japanese system, the interface cannot be easily changed if necessary. The consequences for the Japanese system would always have to be taken into account, resulting in complex (frustrating) discussions, as it may be completely unclear to the other two partners why the Japanese partner would reject certain change proposals for the FE–BE interface definition.
- The timing of the development of FE 1 and FE 2 would be coupled to that of the development of the Japanese BE, because once the interface has been implemented in the Japanese BE, that implementation will become a de facto standard for the interface: If the interface definition is not 100% complete and unambiguous, the Japanese interpretation of the interface definition may become the standard definition (if they were to use this interpretation for both their BE and their FE, they would have a working system that could be marketed).

Therefore, a second architectural scenario may be necessary to completely decouple the interface discussions between Philips and the two FE partners. Philips would have separate discussions with each of them and would define a FE-API in the BE to abstract from the exact FE–BE protocol. For Philips the challenge would be to make sure that one FE-API could be designed to cover the characteristics of both FE–BE interfaces. The design would then be as shown in Fig. 2.11.

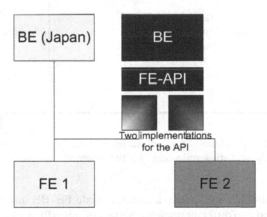

Fig. 2.11. Architectural scenario 2: Two different FE–BE interface definitions under one FE-API

The cost of the second scenario would be higher:

- Two FE–BE interface definitions would have to be made
- The FE-API would have to be designed
- Two implementations of the API would have to be built
- At least part of the functionality of the sub-system of the BE would have to be tested twice

If the likelihood of defining one common FE–BE interface with both partners in a short time would be judged to be rather small, this approach could still be beneficial.

To study how our approach would address this issue, we considered the following expected value calculation[3]:

- Assume that the investment needed to make the common interface definition would amount to €10k per year.
- Assume that implementing the common interface would cost €100k.
- Assume that the income generated by the sale of the product would decrease every year.
- Figure 2.12 shows the cash flow for developing the interface for a range of scenarios: Each scenario is based on an assumption about the time needed to develop the interface.

The above assumptions would result in the expected NPV calculation given in Fig. 2.12. The calculation was made using the formula given in Sect. 2.4.2 with an NPV discount rate of 10%. It indicates that the NPV expected for this architectural scenario for six strategic scenarios reflecting the uncertainty regarding the time needed to develop the interface, for which the likelihood of occurrence has been estimated, is €382k.

Years to define Interface	Cash Flow (per year)								Total NPV	likelihood	Expected NPV
	2005	2006	2007	2008	2009	2010	2011	2012			
1	−10	−100	500	400	300	200	100	50			
2	−10	−10	−100	400	300	200	100	50			
3	−10	−10	−10	−100	300	200	100	50			
4	−10	−10	−10	−10	−100	200	100	50			
5	−10	−10	−10	−10	−10	−100	100	50			
6	−10	−10	−10	−10	−10	−10	−100	50			
				Net Present Value							
1	−10	−91	413	301	205	124	56	26	1024	10%	102
2	−10	−9	−83	301	205	124	56	26	610	25%	152
3	−10	−9	−8	−75	205	124	56	26	309	30%	93
4	−10	−9	−8	−8	−68	124	56	26	103	20%	21
5	−10	−9	−8	−8	−7	−62	56	26	−22	10%	−2
6	−10	−9	−8	−8	−7	−6	−56	26	−79	5%	−4
									Total		362

Fig. 2.12. Expected NPV calculations for architectural scenario 1: Build one common FE–BE interface for six strategic scenarios reflecting the time needed to develop the shared interface definition

Now take the second architectural scenario: two separate FE–BE interfaces are defined, a FE-API is developed and two different implementations of this API are made. Assume that:

- Defining the interface takes twice the effort (though it is more realistic to assume that it will be less): €20k per year.
- Designing the API and building two implementations for the API costs €500k (again a lower sum would be more realistic, since this is 5 times the effort needed to build the shared interface).

---

[3] The numbers used in the example are artificial. They have been chosen to clarify the approach. They are not representative for the real investments made in the projects. The outcome of the evaluation cannot be used to evaluate decisions made in the project.

– Estimate the likelihood of two interface definitions being developed (one for each partner). The likelihood of this being done quickly is much higher than in the previous case.

An example expected NPV calculation based on these assumptions is shown in Fig. 2.13.
This example shows an expected NPV of €404k, which is higher than the expected NPV of
architectural scenario 1. It would not be fair to claim that the preferred architectural scenario
can be chosen on the basis of this calculation because many more factors will be involved in
practice. But the example does show how our approach can help to make the assumptions
explicit and to calculate the expected NPV on the basis of these assumptions. It is worthwhile
to note that a straightforward cost calculation (also taking NPV into account) would have
resulted in a preference for architectural scenario 1: The total cost of defining and implementing the interface would in this scenario be less than in the second architectural scenario.

Years to define Interface	Cash Flow (per year)								Total NPV	likelihood	Expected NPV
	2005	2006	2007	2008	2009	2010	2011	2012			
1	−20	−500	500	400	300	200	100	50			
2	−20	-20	−500	400	300	200	100	50			
3	−20	−20	−20	−500	300	200	100	50			
4	−20	−20	−20	−20	−500	200	100	50			
				Net Present Value							
1	−20	−455	413	301	205	124	56	26	650	50%	325
2	−20	−18	−413	301	205	124	56	26	260	35%	91
3	−20	−18	−17	−376	205	124	56	26	−19	10%	−2
4	−20	−18	−17	−15	−342	124	56	26	−205	5%	−10
									Total		404

Fig. 2.13. Expected NPV calculations for architectural scenario 2: Define two FE–BE interfaces for
four strategic scenarios reflecting the time needed to develop the two interface definitions

In reality, the project was started on the basis of the first architectural scenario, but when
reaching a common FE–BE interface definition proved cumbersome, it was decided to restart
the interface definition activities separately. This still proved to be cumbersome, but in the
end the two interfaces were defined and the API was implemented, resulting in the release of
two CT scanners. To facilitate the work of our BE software engineers, even a third implementation of the FE–BE interface was made, which could be run without a FE connected to
the BE. This FE simulator served as the test bench for the application software running on
top of the FE-API.

2.7.3 Strategic Scenario 2: Similarity of Functionality

The architectural scenario shown in Fig. 2.11 is based on the assumption that one FE-API
will be defined, covering the complete functionality of the FEs. If this is the case, one
piece of application software can be built that uses the FE-API to access the full FE functionality. A set of strategic scenarios could be defined to study the effect of diverging
functionality: What if one FE is expected to offer more functionality than the other?

    If one FE offers a function that the other FE does not offer, this can of course be handled
with a common API. If a function is made part of the API that returns the availability of a
function, it is not so hard to disable a function and remove its UI from the BE when it is

not available at the connected FE. In such cases, the architecture shown in Fig. 2.11 works just fine. But what if functions that need a very specific interface become available in both systems? Or what if functions are needed in the BE with a user interface that is very specific to the FE? Is it still worthwhile to define one common API for that?

In this specific case, everything went just fine, apart from the FE-diagnostic functions; a separate application was developed for diagnosing and calibrating the system (called the "service application" in the remainder). At first, our intention was to build one service application to be used for both systems. This application would contain the full BE application discussed in the previous subsection for normal operation of the system during system calibration and diagnostics. In addition to the functions for normal usage, the service application would provide a set of calibration and diagnostics functions. A separate API (FE-SVC-API) would be defined for the service application that would contain functions that were only available to the service application and not to the clinical application.

This architectural scenario was chosen on the basis of the assumption that a common FE-SVC-API could be defined for both FEs. The outcome of the system design activities was that the two FEs were based on entirely different designs: The entire diagnostics and calibration package for one of the FEs would be built by the FE supplier and in the other case the FE would offer a set of interfaces for calibrating and diagnosing the FE and Philips would build the user interface needed to use those functions. Again, it would technically have been possible to build a common service application, but nontechnical circumstances made it impossible to reach a common service approach for both FEs. And again our initial focus was primary on reuse and code size/cost reduction. If we had considered the likelihood of the scenario of the three partners not being able to arrive at a common approach, we would probably have chosen the approach outlined in Fig. 2.14 from the beginning.

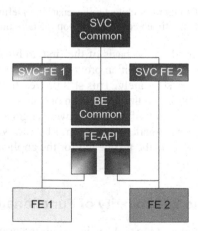

Fig. 2.14. Architectural scenario 3: FE specific service extensions to the common service application

2.7.4 Strategic Scenario 3: Evolving System Functionality

When defining the FE–BE interface, one of the questions was: What is the functional level of the interface? Let's consider two options:

- A relatively high level, with the BE sending a request to the FE to perform a complete function, for example: perform a scout scan, perform a volume scan, move the table to a certain position, reconstruct images and transfer them, etc.
- A relatively low level, with the BE sending commands to individual components of the FE; not necessarily at the lowest level of motion controllers, but at least at such a level that the BE development group can program new scan sequences, e.g., to build a sequence such as: Start low-dose X-ray and image reconstruction, keep the table at a certain position for some time until the contrast agent has passed the scanning position, then move to high-dose scanning, and start moving the table in the direction of the blood flow, stop scanning when a certain position is reached, etc.
- In the former design, with high-level interfaces, building new scan sequences is hard, and involves re-negotiating the FE–BE interface with (both?) FE partners. In the latter design, Philips would have been able to build new scan sequences on the BE.

But there's a drawback to the second interface design: It requires far more detailed understanding of the internals of the FE to be considered when building the BE. What's more, as the two FEs differ substantially in terms of their architecture, it may prove difficult to actually develop a single common BE. In view of time-to-market considerations for the first scanners, it would probably be wise to take the high-level interface approach.

For a good analysis of the values and costs of the two architectural scenarios, strategic scenarios would have to be developed indicating:

- The functionality expected to be developed in the coming 5 years (for instance based on clinical roadmaps) and their business value
- The value of reducing time-to-market for the first systems

One way of doing that this using our approach would be as follows:

1. Architectural scenario 1: building the initial product using a high-level interface:

    Assume that building the initial system(s) would cost €100k
    - Assume that the initial system(s) can be built in one year
    - Assume that the income from selling these systems will start at €500k per year and will after that decrease every year
    - Assume that building a feature requiring changes to the high-level interface costs €100k in total, and has a lead time of 2 years (due to interface negotiations with the FE supplier)
    - Assume that a new feature will generate an income of €400k in the first year and that this will then decrease every year

The cash flow and NPV for this scenario can be summarized as follows:

Architectural Scenario 1	2005	2006	2007	2008	2009	2010	Total
			Cash Flow				
Initial Product	−100	500	250	125	60	0	
New Feature in 2006		−50	−50	300	200	100	
New Feature in 2007			−50	−50	300	200	
New Feature in 2008				−50	−50	300	
			NPV				**Total**
Initial Product	−100	455	207	94	41	0	696
New Feature in 2006		−45	−41	225	137	62	337
New Feature in 2007			−41	−38	205	124	250
New Feature in 2008				−38	−34	186	115

2. Architectural scenario 2: build the product(s) using the low-level interface:

- Assume that building the initial system(s) would cost €200k and would involve a lead time of 2 years.
- Assume that the features that would require changes to the high-level interface would cost only €50k that can be implemented in one year in the second architectural scenario, since no interface changes would have to be negotiated with the FE supplier.

The cash flow and NPV for this scenario can be summarized as follows:

Architectural Scenario 2	2005	2006	2007	2008	2009	2010	
			Cash Flow				
Initial Product	−100	−100	250	125	60	0	
New Feature in 2006		−50	400	300	200	100	
New Feature in 2007			−50	400	300	200	
New Feature in 2008				−50	400	300	
			NPV			**Total**	
Initial Product	−100	−91	207	94	41	0	151
New Feature in 2006		−45	331	225	137	62	709
New Feature in 2007			−41	301	205	124	588
New Feature in 2008				−38	273	186	422

From the cash flow and NPV summary it can be easily inferred that the first scenario is preferable when it is unlikely that features will be developed in the future that require changes to the high-level FE interface since the initial costs are much lower. It will however also be clear that the NPV of additional features involving changes to the high-level interface will be much higher in the second architectural scenario.
To compare the effect, assume the following:

- N new features will be developed every year
- For each the likelihood of a change to the high-level interface being needed is p
- Then the expected number of features requiring high-level interface changes is $n*p$
- The expected NPV can now be calculated for given values of N and p, as:

NPV (initial product) $+ n * p * ($NPV (feature 2006) $+$ NPV (feature 2007) $+$ NPV (feature 2008))

The expected NPV for both architectural scenarios is given for $N=3$ in Fig. 2.15. This figure shows that for this value of N, the crossover point is at 20%. So, the question is how likely is it that changes to the high-level interface will be necessary?
Of course, many factors have been ignored in this example that should be considered when making a full-scoped analysis of the two architectural scenarios, e.g.,

- Apart from the $n*p$ features per year that would require modifications to the high-level interface, $n*(1-p)$ features that will not involve modifications to the interface are expected

to be developed each year. It is reasonable to assume that developing these features will cost less effort using the high-level interface than using the low-level interface.
- It would make sense to explicitly name the features in order to (i) give an effort estimate per feature and (ii) estimate the expected impact on income for each feature individually.

The aim of the example is not to give a detailed analysis of the two architectural scenarios, but to provide an indication of how this question could be addressed using our approach. When the full scope of the analysis is considered it however becomes evident that a complete analysis would result in an explosion of scenarios. The number of cash flow estimates to be made for a full analysis would be overwhelming. Therefore, striving for completeness should be avoided. It is important to realize that the business case will never be the "formal proof" of the justification of making investments. The business case should provide the *rational*; assumptions and value assessments should be made explicit. The most relevant scenarios (both architectural and strategic) should be selected on the basis of business and architectural insights to provide a solid foundation for making business decisions.

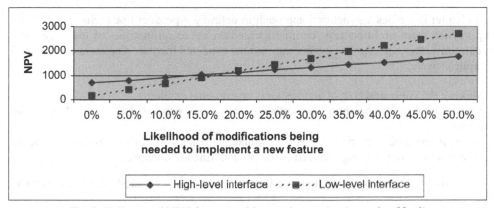

Fig. 2.15. Expected NPV for two architectural scenarios (assuming $N = 3$)

2.7.5 Summary

On the basis of the preceding sections, we can draw one conclusion from the strategic scenarios discussed in this section: The optimum design of the FE–BE interface of this CT scanner product line cannot be determined by just looking at the expected size or cost of the (interface) software. Software size (i.e., cost) is a sure concern, but it is not the only concern. If great amounts of time would be wasted in harmonizing an interface among several cooperating companies, factors such as time-to-market and straightforward code size minimization may have to be weighed up against one another. The likelihood of such harmonization being reached and maintained for the future is a parameter that needs to be considered in the architecture selection process.

The views in the BAPO/CAFCR framework [15,16] (see also Chap. 1) provide excellent starting points for finding factors that will have to be considered in assessing the value of architectural scenarios:

- Business considerations: will business values change? Are the business goals of all partners well aligned? etc.
- Architectural considerations: changes in the CAFCR-views: changes of Customer vaues, changes in Application scenarios, changes in Functionality, changes in technology (technical Concept and Realization view).
- Process considerations: will development processes, manufacturing processes, service processes, etc. change?
- Organizational considerations: will the organization change, e.g., will partners be involved? Will multi-site development be needed? etc.

2.8 Conclusions and Future Research

This chapter describes a structured approach to defining a product line architecture roadmap (which is an architectural roadmap) based on value estimations of the necessary investments, the expected life cycle costs and the expected income. The main elements of the approach are:

- Making the value and cost of architectural investments explicit.
- Value generated in the future is worth less than value generated today (NPV calculations).
- A set of strategic scenarios is used to evaluate the likelihood of the potential value of investments actually being realized in the product line architecture.

A set of simple formulas shows how the value calculations associated with this approach could be done.

An important warning is not to be tempted to think that spreadsheets and charts provide the ultimate answers. Estimating the values and probabilities is difficult. It is not uncommon for estimates to prove to be wrong by an order of magnitude (as experienced in practice and supported by the literature [12], page 32 *The Dark Side to the Financial Approaches to Project Evaluation*). This means that the analyses discussed in this chapter constitute a starting point for business discussions. In the end, it boils down to business managers making business decisions. Formulas and charts are means for helping them reason about profitability, costs and risks. So one should not be surprised or frustrated if their business choices should prove to differ from the outcome of the analysis. If business managers have used the analysis to clarify their assumptions and to substantiate their choices, the analytical effort will have been useful.

This chapter offers a framework identifying the aspects that are to be considered in product line architecture roadmapping. *Complete* implementation of this approach will prove impractical because of the overwhelming number of conceivable scenarios and the explosive number of scenario combinations to be considered. The "art of roadmapping" consist of reducing the number of scenarios: only consider those that will have the greatest business impact. In practice, the execution of the roadmapping process will be neither linear, nor complete, nor completely rational.

In this respect, creating an architecture roadmap is no different from designing software or a system. The recommendations made by Parnas and Clements in [17] for a design process also apply to the architecture roadmapping process: Having a rational process in mind will steer the process by identifying the issues to be considered and their dependencies. As such, it will improve the execution of the roadmapping activities in practice, and define a framework for structuring the deliverables.

The work presented in this chapter shows the main mechanisms involved in reasoning about product line roadmaps from an economical point of view. Although the mechanisms are relatively straightforward from a theoretical point of view, many issues remain for further academic and industrial work:

- Executing the process is cumbersome, too many scenarios may seem relevant and it is not clear how to decide when enough scenarios have been considered. How to end the process?
- Determining the probability of scenarios is difficult. It is difficult to objectively assess whether probabilities have been reasonably assigned. Can criteria be defined to check the consistency of the assigned probabilities?
- Similarly, many of the cash flow estimates are relatively arbitrary. It is not necessary to judge the absolute correctness of estimates, but it is important to assure their consistency. Can this be done in a structured way?
- From the case study it is evident that a thorough analysis of the value of architectural scenarios is complex. Many factors have to be considered and many scenarios need to be studied. The process is information-intensive: Many attributes of the scenarios have to be managed, and since this will be an iterative process, many of the evaluations have to be repeated several times as new scenarios are added. Although the calculations are trivial, having to repeat them numerously will completely frustrate the process. As long as simple cases are being considered, a simple spreadsheet will do the job, but when tackling cases involving more than three or four strategic and architectural scenarios, a spreadsheet-based approach will be sure to fail.
- This does not mean that the approach itself is too complex; the complexity mirrors the complexity of the problem we are trying to solve.
- Future work needs to be done to develop tools that support the process by structuring the information to be supplied in a scenario database and by automating the computations to be done. Furthermore, the tool should provide means for graphically representing the results of the evaluations.
- We have chosen a relatively simple approach for dealing with the probability of strategic scenarios. Better results can probably be obtained by using probability distributions. One reason for using probability distributions is that it is often difficult to assess architectural scenario probability. Answering a question like "what is the likelihood of some event occurring two years from now?" is rather difficult. It may be more convenient to say that the event is expected to occur two years from now with a certain bandwidth of uncertainty. In fact, the way we handled the duration of the FE–BE interface definition activities in Sect. 2.7.2 of the CT scanner case description was an initial attempt at using a probability distribution.
- And finally, the cost models discussed in Sect. 2.5 are of great value for doing the basic cost estimates. Can these models be extended to cover life cycle costs, too? Or can similar models be developed which specifically address the life cycle costs? Can models be

used to quantify the benefits of product line engineering in economical terms to get away from the relatively arbitrary cash flow estimates?

Although there are a lot of issues that could be subject to future research, the basic message of our approach is relevant in industrial practice: Strategic scenarios can be used to make assumptions and expectations explicit and to serve as foundation for evaluating the value of architectural scenarios. Especially in businesses with long product line life cycles, and long development times this will serve as a means to deal with the consequences of uncertainty and time on value.

Acknowledgments

I wish to thank Klaus Schmid and John McGregor for reviewing this chapter and providing me with useful comments. I also wish to thank Timo Käkölä for reviewing all the versions, including the very first ones, of this chapter. His comments (and those of reviewers of [22]) made me rewrite this chapter completely resulting in very significant improvements.

References

1. Albrecht, A.J.: Measuring application development productivity. Proceedings of the Joint SHARE, GUIDE and IBM Application Development Symposium, October 1979
2. America, P., Hammer, D., Ionita, M.T., Obbink, H., Rommes, E.: Scenario-based decision making for architectural variability in product families. In: *Software Product Lines*, ed by Nord, R.L., Proceedings of 3rd International Conference, SPLC 2004, Boston, MA, USA, 30 August–2 September 2004. Lectures Notes in Computer Science, vol 3154 (Springer, Berlin Heidelberg New York 2004) pp 283–303
3. Andreasen, A.R., Kotler, P.: *Strategic Marketing for Nonprofit Organizations*, 6th edn (Pearson Educational International 2003)
4. Böckle, G., Clements, P., McGregor, J.D., Muthig, D., Schmid, K.: Calculating ROI for software product lines. IEEE Softw. **21**(3), 23–31 (2004)
5. Boehm, B.W.: *Software Engineering Economics* (Prentice-Hall, Englewood Cliffs, NJ 1981)
6. Boehm, B.W.: *Software Cost Estimation with COCOMO II* (Prentice Hall, Englewood Cliffs, NJ 2000)
7. Boehm, B.W.: Value-based software engineering: overview and agenda. In: *Value-Based Software Engineering*, ed by Biffl, S., Aurum, A., Boehm, B., Erdogmus, H., Grünbacher, P. (Springer, Berlin Heidelberg New York 2006)
8. Clements, P.C., Northrop, L.: Software Product Lines – Practices and Patterns. *The SEI Series in Software Engineering* (Addison-Wesley, Reading, MA 2002)
9. Clements, P.C., Kazman, R., Klein, M.: Evaluating Software Architectures – Methods and Case Studies. *The SEI Series in Software Engineering* (Addison-Wesley, Reading, MA 2002)
10. Clements, P.C., McGregor, J.D., Cohen, S.G.: The structured intuitive model for product line economics (SIMPLE). Technical report, CMU/SEI-2005-TR003 (The Software Engineering Institute/Carnegie Mellon University). http://www.sei.cmu.edu/publications/documents/05.reports/05tr003.html
11. Cohen, S.: Predicting when product line investments pays. Technical note, CMU/SEI-2003-TN-017 (The Software Engineering Institute/Carnegie Mellon University). http://www.sei.cmu.edu/publications/documents/03.reports/03tn017.html
12. Cooper, R.G., Edget, S.J., Kleinschmidt, E.J.: *Portfolio Management for New Products* (Addison-Wesley, Reading, MA 1998)
13. Jones, C.: *Applied Software Measurement – Assuring Productivity and Quality*, 2nd edn (McGraw Hill, New York 1996)

14. Kazman, R., Asundi, J., Klein, M.: Making architecture design decisions: an economic approach. Technical report, CMU/SEI-2002-TR-35 (The Software Engineering Institute/Carnegie Mellon University September2002). http://www.sei.cmu.edu/publications /documents/02.reports/02tr035.html

15. Muller, G., Müller, J.,Wijnstra, J.G.: Multi-view architecting. http://www.extra.research.philips.com/natlab/ sysarch/IntegratingCAFCRPaper.pdf

16. Muller, G.: CAFCR: a multi-view method for embedded systems architecting; balancing genericity and specificity. Ph.D. thesis (Delft University of Technology 2004). http://www.GaudiSite.nl/ThesisBook.pdf

17. Parnas, D.L., Clements, P.C.: A rational design process: how and why to fake it. IEEE Trans. Softw. Eng. 19(2), 251–257 (February 2003)

18. Peterson, D.: Economics of software product lines. In: PFE-5: 5th International Workshop on Product line Engineering, Siena, Italy, 4–6 November 2003, ed by van der Linden, F. Lecture Notes in Computer Science, vol 3014 (Springer, Berlin Heidelberg New York 2003) pp 381–402. http://www.convergys.com/ pdf/whitepapers/ econ_spl.pdf

19. Pohl, K., Böckle G., van der Linden, F.: *Software Product Line Engineering – Foundations, Principles, and Techniques* (Springer, Berlin Heidelberg New York 2005)

20. Schmid, K.: A quantitative model of the value of architecture in product line adoption. In: PFE-5: 5th International Workshop on Product line Engineering, Siena, Italy, 4–6 November 2003, ed by van der Linden, F. Lecture Notes in Computer Science, vol 3014 (Springer, Berlin Heidelberg New York 2003) pp 32–43

21. Wesselius, J.H.: Software quality control & software requirements specification. Ph.D. thesis (Delft University of Technology April 1993). http://home.planet.nl/~jacco.wesselius/phd-thesis.pdf

22. Wesselius, J.H.: Modelling architectural value: cash flow, time and uncertainty. In: SPLC 2005, ed by Obbink, H., Pohl, K. Lecture Notes in Computer Science, vol 3714 (Springer, Berlin Heidelberg New York 2005) pp 89–95. DOI: 10.1007/11554844_10

23. Economics of Software Product Lines: http://www.sei.cmu.edu/productlines/economics_spl.html

3 Experiences and Expectations Regarding the Introduction of Systematic Reuse in Small- and Medium-Sized Companies

J. Mansell

Abstract

Though systematic reuse promises several large business benefits, it is not optimally leveraged in the industry. Small- and medium-sized organizations especially often face big hurdles in adopting systematic reuse practices. The literature on systematic reuse tends to focus on large sized organizations and lacks case studies dealing with small- and medium-sized organizations. It does not help these companies decide whether systematic reuse would be an adequate approach for them. In order to ease the decision making for adopting systematic reuse by small- and medium-sized companies, the European Software Institute (ESI) performed a study of the risks and opportunities of reuse within a group of software development organizations in the Basque Country. This chapter provides an overview of the most relevant findings in the study, which will enable small- and medium-sized organizations foresee issues that have to be adequately addressed when adopting systematic reuse.

3.1 Introduction

The development of software has always been concerned with reusing previous developments in order to provide solutions to new problems emerging from the market. In most organizations the systematic reuse initiative is initially led by an expert or by a process improvement team, which is asked by management to provide evidence that the investment required will have an adequate return on investment. In many cases the initiative leader is not capable of providing adequate facts and figures that management is asking for because of lack of knowledge of economics, the lack of expertise on quantifying the business value of the initiative because such quantification has never been done before, or other reasons. Even though the maturity of the techniques and mechanisms for implementing systematic reuse is considerable, additional problems are faced when adapting these practices to a specific organizational context.

In order to provide an insight into what are the reuse opportunities and the problems an organization faces when implementing a systematic reuse initiative, the European Software Institute (ESI) performed a study of the risks and opportunities of reuse within a group of software development organizations in the Basque Country (a heavily industrialized area, with many small- and medium-sized software-related companies). This study addresses organizations that are considering implementing a systematic software reuse initiative and wish to have an idea of what other organizations have undergone, how they have resolved problems encountered and what is the expected evolution of the initiative. At the same time this study provides a means to decide on economic grounds whether adopting systematic reuse is beneficial in an identified organizational business domain.

The study was undertaken by the ESI in eight companies with the purpose of providing an overview of the market interest on software reuse and identifying the benefits of implementing a systematic reuse initiative in these organizations and the reuse practices already carried out by the organizations. At the same time, the study was useful in identifying the practices in small- and medium-sized companies starting out with reuse.

In many small- and medium-sized organizations driven by hectic every day work, reuse is undertaken on an ad hoc basis depending on individuals' initiatives and knowledge. There is usually little organizational and managerial support for these practices. Even though these practices may provide benefits in the short term, this is only true if the time spent identifying what to reuse is less than that one would have spent developing from scratch [1].

This study provides an outline of the reuse possibilities identified in this group of organizations, the current reuse practices in these organizations as well as the infrastructure and resources provided to favor reuse in the long term.

Moreover, the knowledge captured in this research will allow practitioners to identify how the organizations that have participated in the case study have addressed problems encountered in the introduction of systematic reuse practices.

Special focus is given to the analysis of the following aspects:

- Areas within the organizations most likely to adopt reuse as a mechanism to support the development of software applications.
- Benefits that the organizations gain in these specific analyzed areas of the organization by implementing reuse.
- Risks identified in the organizations that can negatively influence the success of implementing a reuse initiative, analizing factors related to personnel, processes, products and organization.
- The organizations' attitudes towards risk with respect to the investment required for achieving the expected benefits of implementing reuse.
- State of the infrastructure (technology, tools, etc.) and support (assigned resources, training, etc.) within the organizations in order to allow for reuse and the effective use of reuse techniques and practices in the projects.

For this purpose, two levels of analytic techniques have been used: Reuse–Check and Reuse–Invest. As shown later, the results of the analysis performed must not be understood solely from the viewpoint of their statistical significance but also as views on the actual situations in many organizations and as a guideline for practical implementation of systematic reuse strategies.

The chapter is divided into several sections: Section 3.2 provides an overview of the methods used to carry out the study, Sect. 3.3 provides the overall results and findings of the experiments carried out, Sect. 3.4 provides the Reuse–Invest specific results, Sect. 3.5 provides the Reuse–Check specific results and finally Sect. 3.6 provides a set of conclusions based on the analysis performed.

3.2 Method and Sample of the Study

3.2.1 Method of the Study

The diagnosis and evaluations consisted of the execution of two different analysis methods developed by the European Software Institute: Reuse–Invest [2,21] and Reuse–Check. These are carried out within the target organizations by means of interviews and joint meetings with the different stakeholders in the analyzed domains. While Reuse–Invest allows the identification of whether it is economically beneficial to introduce systematic reuse within a specific domain, Reuse–Check provides the means to introduce reuse practices within the organization.

Reuse–Invest allows us to make a quick analysis of the risks versus benefits for determining the adequacy of introducing reuse practices within a specific domain.

The major objective of Reuse–Invest is to analyze reuse potential for candidate domains in order to make an economically justified selection. The selection of the domain in which reuse efforts should be devoted is one of the most important decisions to increase the overall success of a reuse institutionalization program.

Reuse–Invest guides the analysis of the reuse opportunities within a domain (in terms of estimated economic benefits that reuse allows to achieve) and the evaluation of the ability of the organization to exploit these opportunities (in terms of the readiness of the organization to adopt reuse practices). By combining reuse opportunities and organizational ability with organizational preferences, Reuse–Invest provides valuable data and recommendations so that the domain selection is performed systematically. Important to notice that in this context, "domain" refers to "organizational domain," considered as an area in the organization where a specific kind of systems are developed for specific needs or markets.

Reuse–Invest can be applied to more than one domain to make a comparison among them and to select the most appropriate one. However, the methodology described here considers only one domain. To apply Reuse–Invest to several domains some steps of the methodology need to be performed multiple times.

Reuse–Invest allows the organization to:

- Attain a deeper knowledge of the reuse opportunities in the organization.
- Identify the aspects of the organization that are not ready for adopting reuse practices.
- Identify the domains that are adequate for introducing reuse practices.
- Make an informed selection and prioritization of reuse investments.
- Adequate reuse strategy to the specific characteristics of the organization.
- Establish a baseline to be used as a starting point of a systematic monitoring of progress achieved.

As a result of the performing Reuse–Invest, the organization is provided with all the estimation data gathered during the analysis, an aggregation of the estimations to facilitate domain selection and recommendations for the introduction of reuse practices. The information provided is the following:

- *Economic information.* This information includes the estimations of investments, savings and expenses to be made by the organization and the economic indicator that is determined from these estimations, the benefits that the reuse program would obtain in the domain. Related information can be found in [18].
- *Risk information.* This information includes a risk profile that collects the estimations made by the organization and the risk level that determines from these estimations the readiness of the domain for starting a reuse program.
- *Organizational attitude towards risk* [19]. This information includes a way of rellating both the economic information and risk information to help taking the final decision. The organization should decide if the expected return is enough to make the transition feasible in assuming the risks or if, on the contrary, the risk is too high given the expected return.
- *Reuse potential graphic.* This graphic summarizes all the information collected during the analysis in order to help in the selection of an adequate domain for reuse investment. If more than one domain takes part in the analysis, this graphic helps the organization to prioritize those domains and select the most appropriate one [2].
- *Recommendations.* This information includes actions that could be taken within the domain in order to prepare it for reuse introduction, issues that require special atttention when performing the transition, etc.

On the other hand, once a domain for reuse is selected, or ad hoc reuse initiatives are in place, the second method Reuse–Check is used. Reuse–Check's main objective is to analyze the software reuse practices already deployed in a specific domain of the organization as the first step for introducing organization-wide systematic reuse practices. The process framework used in this assessment is the R-SPICE model [17], which provides a refinement of the reuse organizational process category, ORG.6, from SPICE [9], which explicitly addresses reuse based product-lines.

In general terms, this analysis provides the basis for starting an initiative for systematic reuse in an organization. The analysis is performed through group sessions at the customer site where information about the reuse activities and reuse initiatives is captured. Group sessions involving several individuals are included to collect different perspectives on the problem and promote discussion. Then, this information is structured, processed and analyzed with the staff organization to identify improvement actions to support current reuse practices and ensure a proper infrastructure for reuse adoption. Improvement actions derived from this work will keep the organization aligned with principles of systematic reuse.

Thus Reuse–Check allows the organization to:

Take the first steps in systematic reuse adoption with a small effort and a short analysis period.

- Understand the current situation of the organization with respect to software reuse, be aware of the current initiatives undertaken towards software reuse in the organization and the expectations that staff have. This way the organization will be able to determine reuse objectives that satisfy those expectations.

– Obtain the basis from which to prepare a reuse adoption plan by identifying the main actions and areas where the organization should focus to enable transitioning to systematic reuse according to the defined objectives.

As a result of using Reuse–Check the organization is provided with:

– A description of the current situation of the organization in relation to reuse processes. It contains initiatives detected and their correspondence with reuse infrastructure and reuse based development, identifying good practices and weaknesses found during the analysis. It will also describe the expectations and current barriers for reuse that staff that participated in the analysis has identified.
– A description of a sequence of actions to be undertaken in order to support good current reuse practices and to work towards the implementation of systematic reuse within the organization.

3.2.2 Sample of the Study

The sample of the study involves eight organizations. These companies were selected out of one hundred organizations which were informed of the possibility of participating in the study. From this initial list thirty organizations were selected based on organization characteristics, which made these organizations more reliable for implementing reuse practices.

The criteria followed for this filtering and reasoning are the following:

– Small and medium-sized organizations from 5 to 500 people in the development area. The main idea behind selecting this kind of organizations is that these methods are intended to provide quick and low cost analysis methods. These methods can also be used in large organizations.
– Organizations in specific domains in which the dedication and experience was high, implying that they may already have considered reuse as a choice.

From the thirty organizations contacted by phone, twelve showed interest in participating in the study. From these twelve, eight committed to participate in the study. The other four, even though they were interested in participating, could not take part due to a lack of time and resources required for the analysis.

The organizations that showed interest in participating, received a detailed description of the two types of analysis (R-Invest and R-Check) and the relationship between the two analyses. Based on this information provided, each organization selected the analysis they were interested in, five Reuse–Invest analyses were performed and four Reuse–Check analyses. Fig. 3.1 provides an overview of the organizations interest in participating in the study.

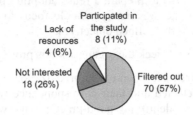

Fig. 3.1. General overview of organizations interested in participating in the study

For a correct understanding and interpretation of this report it has to be considered that the organizations in which the analyses have been carried out are organizations interested in systematic reuse, that were interested in identifying and predicting the benefits of introducing reuse and understanding how to adapt or complete their current reuse practices in order to implement systematic reuse more effectively. Moreover most of the organizations analyzed already implemented reuse and a reuse culture was present. "A reuse culture is one that encourages and encourages developers to reuse code and to assemble systems rather than writing everything from scratch" [15].

3.2.3 Overview of Participating Organizations

This section provides a brief overview of the type of organizations that have participated in the study. The organizations have been identified by a letter in order to maintain the privacy of the organizations participating in the study.

Organization A

Organization A is the application development department of over 400 people that have to develop internally commercial management tools both for the purchasing department as well as for the organization's sales department. Each time a new product is added, a semi-manual update is required in both departments. Also, each time a new sales centre is built the required software is also deployed and the adequate tests are performed. Every time a new sales centre is deployed there is a full time person dedicated to maintenance work for a period of three months.

The organization is interested in providing a stable deployment architecture which captures all the known and foreseen variability in order to reduce maintenance effort once the sales centre is deployed and at the same time reducing the deployment time and effort. In order to address this change they are interested in identifying the cost introducing reuse will have and the return on investment of this cost. The analyzed domain is the internal development department on business software.

Organization B

This organization is a public owned organization of over 200 employees which is mainly focused in providing the solutions the government requires to provide their services to the citizens. The main problem addressed is the need for an Internet centralized solution to provide all the services the government needs to offer the citizens online. This organization has to deal with a huge number of change requests and update requests due to a great amount of errors encountered when dealing with a high degree of legacy systems which in many cases are not interoperable.

The main reason for participating in the study was to identify whether the organization is at a stage in which it can deal with addressing new methods such as reuse-based ones and at the same time identify whether the economical implications of the reuse approach will really provide a return on investment. The analyzed domain is the Internet service deployment department.

Organization C

This organization is a small one just over 20 employees and its main focus is in the development of project and software management applications. At the same time they provide full support for their products once they have been deployed. Currently the most costly activity they perform is maintenance at customer's site.

Their main interest is in identifying whether reuse is the right choice in order to reduce the maintenance costs as well as a considerably reduce their development times. The analyzed domain is the development of software projects and maintenance department.

Organization D

This organization provides full integrated organization management solutions. This organization consists of 40 employees. Their main focus is in providing updated version of their ERP system every year. The current status is that most of the system is unstable and needs to be retuned for each release. The main purpose of this department is single product development.

Their interest in the study is identifying whether reuse could help them in producing a standard architecture of their system which is stable and therefore reduce the cost of releasing new versions of their solution.

Organization E

Organization E deals with the provision of internal support tools for application development on windows. The department of organization E that is interested in the study provides internal solutions for helping the applications developers in the development of windows based applications. The organization consists of 31 employees from whom 5 are involved in the department studied. The main purpose of this department is the provision of internal software libraries to the development department. The main problem that currently needs to be addressed is that being a small organization they need to identify in economic terms if really spending a single day in a reuse initiative will provide benefits in the short term.

3.3 State of Practice of Systematic Reuse in the Case Study

In order to describe the state of practice about reuse in the analyzed organizations, we must take into account that the analysis undertaken in these organizations was of two types and therefore the information obtained is presented in the following manner:

- Objectives which are to be achieved in the organizations by introducing reuse.
- Barriers detected that hinder an adequate implementation of a systematic reuse approach.
- Type of domains analyzed within the organizations.
- Existing expectations for the development of future work in the field of systematic reuse within the organization.

Common Aspects for All the Organizations

Even though Reuse–Invest and Reuse–Check have different objectives and use different mechanisms, they partially share similar information. This section contains the common aspects identified from both types of analysis.

Reuse Objectives

Any organization when addressing a reuse initiative has certain objectives. These are understood as the expectations reuse creates in the organizations. The most relevant objectives identified from both analyses are:

- Reduction in the development cost and time for new developments.
- Increase and ensure the quality and reliability of the developed software products.
- Increase coherence in the way software is coded as well as the user interfaces provided by the different applications developed within an organization.
- Share specific complex knowledge and solutions to similar problems. In this way the knowledge and experience of the people involved in software development will be transformed into business knowledge of the organization.
- Reduce and ease maintenance of final systems deployed in the customer.

Identified Barriers when Considering Reuse

When an organization addresses any change, in this case reuse, there are certain barriers that must be considered. The barriers identified in the companies which were analyzed are classified as follows:

Staff related:

- Initial skepticism of the usefulness and success of the reuse initiative. People in the organization do not understand the need to change the current practices of software development and the benefits that can be obtained. This makes it difficult to implement a reuse initiative which is continuously being criticized if it does not provide the expected positive results.

- Lack of personnel and training culture. Systematic reuse requires a change in the way of understanding the application development process and at the same time requires a training effort in order to understand and undertake new reuse concepts.

Organization:

- Lack of communication. For a correct implementation of a reuse initiative there is a need for fluent communication among the personnel in the organization. This is especially critical in organizations, which have subcontracted personnel, high staff rotation, or given their business are distributed in customer offices.
- Lack of time and resources required for the initial investment required for starting implementing reuse and the required steps for identifying and defining reusable assets, creation of reusable assets and maintenance. Project-based organizations do not have the time required to face developments which in order to be more generic, require more effort. In most cases dedicating additional effort for future reuse is not considered useful.
- Lack of discipline in development and configuration management. Software reuse requires a certain level of management maturity at different levels regarding application development management as well as configuration management of the different products involved in the development life cycle. These practices are not always well implemented in the organizations with an adequate level of rewarding discipline.
- Lack of a well defined and documented process. Often, the knowledge regarding the development process relies in the personnel. This makes it difficult to study the current process, for defining what activities to include or modify in the development process in order to introduce reuse.

Management:

- No management commitment. It is not an easy task to gain management commitment in any change process, which in the case of implementing reuse is a necessary condition. In order to undergo a reuse implementation initiative it is necessary to obtain the support of the management and for doing so it is required to provide arguments and benefits the initiative will provide to an organization.

Market conditions:

- Existence of software and/or products confidentiality/property rights agreements. In specific cases the customer may require an exclusive ownership of developed software for different issues, which does not allow for reuse.
- Technological evolution. The reusable assets developed can become obsolete if technology evolves. In many cases organizations consider that the technology being used for the development of applications is in an unstable situation, since in specific development environments the market is dynamic and the development alternatives increase. Instability may lead to situations in which it is not worth to perform technological long-term investments.
- The set of running projects is too diverse. In the developments foreseen within the organization, there are not enough similarities which can be shared between them and therefore the benefits of reuse in the organization can not be obtained.

Types of Analyzed Domains

The evaluated domains mainly include horizontal domains, where the main objective of the reusable assets is sharing technological solutions among several projects that work on the specific development environment. This includes assets developed for communications, error management, file management, and so on. To a lower degree, additional initiatives on vertical domains have been identified, focused on providing business or functional solutions, which provide a complete or partial solution to a customer [17].

The main reason for this circumstance is that horizontal domain assets can be directly reused with no major adaptation effort to make them reusable, while in the case of the vertical domain assets, these require more effort in making the common part usable by all stakeholders while at the same time identifying every variable issue and at the same time identifying how to implement this within a reusable asset.

Plans for Future Work on Systematic Reuse in the Organizations

Several of the analyzed organizations are already undergoing initiatives organizing for reuse or improving their reuse initiatives. As a result of the different analyses performed, some organizations have committed to perform specific activities in order to implement systematic reuse in the organization. The following list is the summary of the most relevant issues:

- Once the reuse opportunities and benefits within a domain are identified, several strategies are to be considered in order to identify the most adequate in order to maximize the potential of the organization with respect to reuse. Prior to these activities a market analysis must be undertaken in order to obtain an overview of the future of the domain and based on this picture initiate the most adequate reuse plan.
- Once the reuse initiative within an organization has been evaluated with the analyses, and the validity of the reuse actions has been determined, a decision must be made to continue with the existing initiative by formalizing the reuse and support group, already defined by the organization.
- Once the usefulness of reuse has been validated and other areas in the organization in which reuse is not formally performed have been analyzed, if high expectations regarding reuse initiative are perceived, the reuse initiative will extend to other areas of the organization.

Even though these initiatives have a common objective they must be defined in more detail (in several cases these were defined after performing the analysis) and the definition, design and implementation should be managed as any other project, where the group responsible for reuse within the software development department is responsible for its management.

3.4 Reuse–Invest Specific Results

The Reuse–Invest analysis was undertaken by five organizations; in four of them one potential domain was identified, while in the other, three potential domains were identified.

The following data are the results of these analyses, where in some cases the information is related to the organization and in others to the domain.

The analysis in each organization includes:

– Identification of the risks an organization must face during the implementation of a reuse program. The risk analysis method used is based on previous work on software reuse suchand [11,12,13].
– Attitude to risk within the organizations. This work is based on previous work by [19].
– Economic analysis of the investment, costs and savings when implementing a reuse program. This economic analysis is based on previous work in the reuse field such as in [14,19].
– Reuse potential analysis of a domain. This analysis is based on the usability theory that studies the measurement and representation of preferences [7].

3.4.1 Risk Analysis

The risks of each organization have been analyzed using the risk model included in the Reuse–Invest method [2]. The model is summarized in Tab. 3.1.

Table 3.1. Reuse–Invest factors analyzed in an evaluation

Factor Description	Attributes Groups and related attributes:
The factor organization addresses risks associated with the maturity of leadership, resources allocated to reuse, organizational structure and communications	COM: Management commitment COM.1 Management considers reuse to be a means of reaching business objectives COM.2 All levels of management are committed to developing and implementing reuse strategies RES: Resource allocation RES.1 Management allocates the necessary resources to reuse RES.2 The group in charge of the reuse transition has enough knowledge to carry it out RES.3 The reuse transition group is independent of other development units and has the authority to decide on and implement reuse actions STR: Organizational structure STR.1 Organizational structure can be easily adapted to reuse requirements STR.2 Good communication mechanisms and authority lines exist across the domain
The factor Personnel addresses risks associated with the ability to develop applications within the domain and carry out a reuse transition	EXP: Experience in the domain EXP.1 There are individuals among the staff who are experts in the business EXP.2 There are individuals among the staff who have experience in building applications within the domain ATT: Attitude to the improvement ATT.1 Personnel believes reuse will make them more productive ATT.2 Personnel is not reluctant to change from current practices

The factor process addresses risks associated with the lack of certain processes in the domain that are important when transitioning to reuse	DEV: Development process DEV.1 Development process can be adapted to reuse requirements MAN: Management processes MAN.1 Project management is performed within the domain MAN.2 Mechanisms for configuration management of work products, documents and processes are in place and can be adapted to reuse requirements MAN.3 Mechanisms to identify, prevent and mitigate risks are in place for projects in the domain MAN.4 Mechanisms for quality management of work-products, documents and processes are in place and can be adapted to reuse requirements
The factor products addresses risks associated with the lack of legacy products, low rate of variability or non-manageable variability within the domain	LEG: Legacy products. By legacy we mean any asset available at the organization before any reuse initiative. LEG.1 There are legacy products available covering all the phases of the development cycle (requirements, design, code, test data and documentation.) LEG.2 Existing legacy products can easily be used in the development of new products VAR: Variability and Commonality VAR.1 Products share a high proportion of similarities VAR.2 Variable requirements can be managed VAR.3 Product requirements are known or trends can be predicted VAR.4 Variability can be negotiated with the customer TEC: Technology TEC.1 Technology used in applications development is stable or trends can be predicted

The risk analysis is performed by focusing on groups of risks. Figure 3.2 provides a graphical overview of the identified average risk presence by risk group which is calculated as the sum of all the attributes of the group divided by the number of attributes (data obtained from the analysis and the surveys made available to the organizations).

In Fig. 3.2 the risks related to management process (MAN), existence of legacy products (LEG) and resource allocation (RES) are the most common risks identified in the organizations analyzed when considering introducing systematic reuse. The risks which have been identified as less common are the experience of the personnel (EXP) and the attitude towards improvement and change (ATT). The main idea behind Figs. 3.2 and 3.3 is that for example, in the group COM there is a 35% change that the whole initiative fails due to this group of risks.

Figure 3.3 provides an overview of the Averages of the risks per attributes of each of the groups presented in Fig. 3.2.

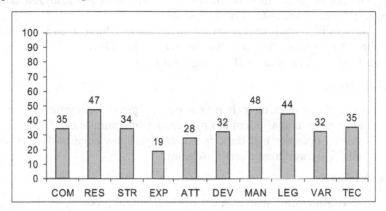

Fig. 3.2. Average of risk factors by group of risks

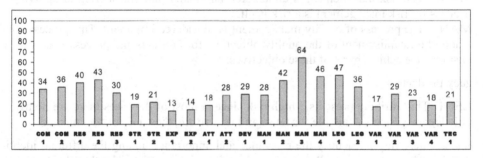

Fig. 3.3. Percentages of presence of risks per attribute

In Fig. 3.3 the attributes in which a low risk has been identified are:

Organizational structure:

– STR1: In most of the organizations the organizational structure required for reuse is already in place and no major problems are foreseen if any improvement program is undertaken.

Experience in the domain:

– EXP1: The organizations consider that there is expert personnel within the organization for the business the organization is involved in.
– EXP2: The organization has proven experience in the development of applications in the analyzed domain; therefore this is not considered as a major risk.

Attitude to the improvement:

– ATT1: This risk is low since the personnel within the organization consider reuse as a minimal additional effort necessary for improving the development process.

Variability and commonality:

- VAR1: The results show that the developed products in the analyzed domain have similarities; therefore the risk is considered low.
- VAR4: The specific requirements for all the customers, have been identified as negotiable with the customers, therefore the risk is considered low.

On the other hand the factors that exhibit higher risks are:

Resource allocation:

- RES1: Personnel consider there is a lack of management commitment, in many improvement initiatives management has proven lack of commitment.
- RES2: Personnel consider that there is not enough knowledge on how to implement, organize and drive a systematic reuse program.

Management Process:

- MAN2: The configuration management of the different products generated among the software development projects is not addressed adequately and presents a high risk.
- MAN3: The risk management is undertaken informally, not considering or applying a process for risk management is a risk itself.
- MAN4: The process of quality management is considered important. This process considers the establishment of the quality objectives for products and processes as well as ensuring the achievement of these objectives.

Legacy products:

- LEG1: This attribute presents a high risk since in most of the cases there are no available legacy systems available for reuse and if there are, they are not documented.

It is also interesting to identify the relevance and importance among the different identified risks. This importance allows us to classify which are the risks that the organizations consider most relevant when implementing a reuse program.

Figure 3.4 presents the relevance that the organizations have assigned to each of the risks. The relevance is depicted based on the impact a risk factor has in the success of implementing a systematic reuse program in the organization. The importance values for each attribute are in a scale of 1 (lower importance) to 3 (higher importance).

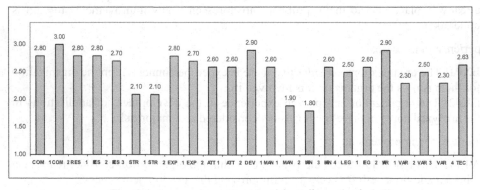

Fig. 3.4. Average importance by risk attributes (scale 1–3)

The risk attributes that the analyzed organizations consider have a higher importance in the success of a reuse initiative are:

- COM2: That the different levels of personnel within an organization with decision making responsibilities adopt a compromise with reuse, is considered a critical aspect for any activity performed towards improving the current state of the art in the organization. Any lack of compromise in any management level can by itself make the reuse initiative fail.
- DEV1: If the current software development process does not allow for the adaptation required for a reuse program, this is considered a major risk.
- VAR1: The importance given to this attribute is justified since reuse will only have an impact when there are commonalities among the products developed in that domain, allowing to obtain benefits from reuse in future developments in different projects.

While the following attributes are less important:

- STR1: This attribute is considered of low importance since the organizational structure is not considered a major problem and will not interfere in the creation of new roles and the definition of their interrelationships.
- STR2: Same as previous case applied to the existence of communication channels and authority.
- MAN2: Configuration management of the development cycle products is not considered a vital risk attribute.
- MAN3: Risk management is not considered as something that can determine the success or failure of a reuse program.

There are risks that are considered important and relevant for ensuring the success of a reuse implementation program within an organization and present a high risk for the organizations, since those attributes are not currently present. These risks have to be analyzed carefully, such as:

- COM2: Not all management levels are committed to develop and implement the reuse strategies and this itself is a high risk.
- RES1: As a result of the lack of management commitment, in many cases the required resources for implementing the reuse strategy are not allocated, which represents high risk.
- RES2: The existence of adequate reuse knowledge within an organization is a must in order to implement a reuse program, which currently is not the case in many organizations.
- MAN4: The lack of quality management mechanisms for products, documents and processes and the adaptation of these to the reuse requirements is also a high risk which must be taken care.

Additional attributes such as MAN2 and MAN3 related to configuration and risk management have also been identified, but in these cases even though they present a high risk in the initial evaluation, the organizations consider these to have low or even no importance. Therefore in the overall estimation they are not considered relevant and do not have an impact on the final estimations.

3.4.2 The Organization's Attitude to Risk

When considering an organization's attitude to risk we consider there to be three possible attitudes; described as follows [14]:

- Risk averse: An organization will not consider investing if the chances of success are not clear, even though the benefits can be high. The risk taking has a higher importance than the benefits to be obtained.
- Risk indifferent: This approach gives the same importance to the chance of obtaining a greater benefit and assuming greater risks in a reuse investment. The minimum benefits expected from this approach are lower than the risk adverse case. Two organizations analyzed were of this type.
- Risk taker: This approach is identified when the importance is given to the benefits to be obtained over the risks being taken. The benefits are more important than the risks, because an improvement justifies the risk to be taken.

This attribute is used to establish the starting point from which an organization is ready to assume risks related to the return on investment expected. It represents the minimal return on investment (ROI) [4] a company expects for a given risk level.

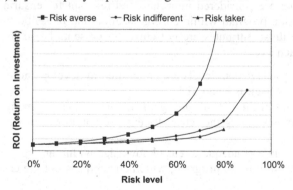

Fig. 3.5. Attitude to risk graphical representation

In Fig. 3.5 the exponential line represents basically the relationship among the risk that an organization is able to assume for a given expectation of its return on investment. In a risk averse organization, for assuming more risks, the return of investment expected must increase exponentially; and in a risk taker organization, the assumption of greater levels of risk can be taken without expecting huge increases in the return on investment expected.

3.4.3 Economic Analysis of the Investment on Systematic Reuse

The economic analyses have been determined based on the investment required to implement a reuse program, the cost required for the maintenance due to reuse and an estimation of the overall savings expected from the reuse program.

This economic analysis considers that when asking an organization to estimate the effort required for doing something that they have never done before, there is some kind of level of uncertainty. Therefore this analysis, as an initial step, identifies what this level of uncertainty is, based on the current knowledge and situation with respect to reuse of the organization. This level of uncertainty is used to calculate both the optimistic and the pessimistic cases. The optimistic case is calculated by increasing the results of the analysis by the percentage of level of uncertainty, while the pessimistic is calculated by reducing the results by applying the level of uncertainty. For example if the level of uncertainty is 10% and the economic results are of € 100, then the optimistic case would be 100 + (100/10) = € 110 while the pessimistic will be 100 + (100/10) = € 90.

Based on these estimations several economic indicators for each organization have been calculated. They are provided in the Fig. 3.6 and expressed in thousands of euros and absolute values.

- *Investment:* Investment includes the activities necessary to develop the domain infrastructure. These activities include transition management activities, domain definition activities, engineering activities, and application development support activities.
- *Expenses.* Cost of the required activities for maintaining the domain: asset maintenance as well as activities for providing support for the use and development of assets.
- *Savings.* Cost savings include the reduction in effort, money and time as a consequence of developing applications within the domain. These cost savings are calculated as the difference between the costs of the applications before reuse was introduced and the costs of the new applications within the domain. The activities considered in calculating the cost savings are the customer activities, management activities and engineering activities.
- *Benefits.* The result of subtracting the costs and investments from the savings considering the number of applications to be implemented during the economical analysis period.
- Net Present Value (NPV): The NPV of an investment is the difference between the sum of the discounted cash flows which are expected from the investment and the amount which is initially invested. NPV is calculated by estimating the cash flows (often per year) that result out of the investment, discounting for the cost of capital (an interest rate to adjust for time and risk). If the NPV is greater than zero, the investment in the domain is economically justified. The following formula is used to determine the NPV, where *"n"* is the number of periods within which the analysis is being performed, Cashflow$_i$ = Savings$_i$ - expenses$_i$ - investments$_i$ and DiscountRate is greater or equal to the interest rate of a risk free bank account:

$$NPV = \sum_{i=1}^{n} \frac{Cashflow_i}{\left[DiscountRate + 1\right]^i}$$

Equation 1: NPV calculation

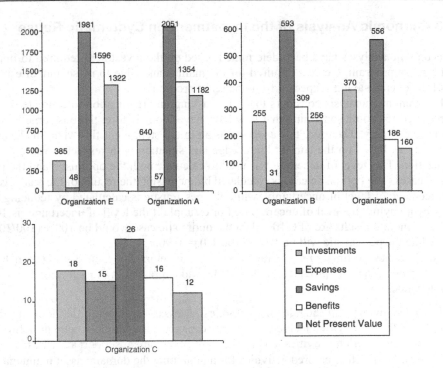

Fig. 3.6. Organizations economical information

These economical estimations consider reuse programs of three to five years duration. At the same time the Internal Rate of Return (i.e., the true interest yield expected from a re-use investment that equals the discount rate resulting in the NPV of zero for a series of future cash flows) has varied between 4% and 6%. Based on the collected data from the organizations participating in the analysis, the average estimate of the ROI in systematic reuse is 3.07, calculated using the following formula:

$$ROI= \frac{Benefits}{Investments}$$

Equation 2: Return On Investment calculation

The average estimate of the profitability index (PI) is 2.94, which means that the organizations will recover 2.94 times the investment on average. This is calculated using the following formula:

$$PI= \sum_{i=1}^{n} \frac{\dfrac{NPV}{Investment_i}}{\left[DiscountRate +1 \right]^i}$$

Equation 3: Profitability Index calculation

The savings have been estimated based on the number of applications that will be developed using reusable assets, during the analyzed period. The number of applications foreseen by the organizations may be too optimistic. Therefore, even though this analysis provides information estimated by the organizations, it is likely that the overall results at the level of savings and therefore benefits, return on investment, net present value and profitability index, require a correction which decreases the figures. In any case the margin is sufficient so as to conclude that the investments are expected to be beneficial in economical terms.

As shown in Fig. 3.7 the variation among the investment, costs and savings in the different organizations is considerably high in some cases.

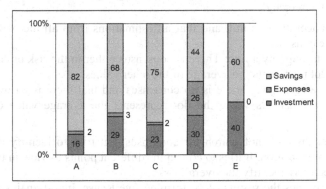

Fig. 3.7. Organizations economical percentage information

The case of organization D, where the expenses have a greater relevance, is due to these expenses mainly being derived from the estimation of the maintenance needs of the reusable assets and because the cost for support in the creation and use of these reusable assets is considered high.

In organization E, the investment is more relevant and the cost is considered null since the organization's focus will make all the effort required for implementing systematic reuse in the initial investments stage, the major efforts are centered on creating the reuse infrastructure, therefore, the support and maintenance costs are considered minimal in the period established for the economical analysis.

We can conclude that on all the analyzed cases the investment is expected to become a greater benefit for the organization than a risk free interest yielding bank account.

3.4.4 Reuse Potential Analysis

In order to take the decision on investment in systematic reuse in the analyzed domains, the organizations have to consider the economical aspects (benefits, investment, costs, and NPV), the risks encountered and the attitude to risk must be taken into account. Based on this set of analyses, a set of figures is provided, which is used in an initial phase for determining whether or not an organization should implement a reuse program.

The graphics in Fig. 3.8 represent in the X-axis the risk level identified in the organization. The Y-axis plots the ROI that an organization can obtain from the investment. The continuous line of exponential character represents the attitude to risk of the organization. This line divides the graphic into two sections; the upper section represents an area where the investment is beneficial and the lower section represents an area where there is no return on investment.

At the same time the domain analyzed is represented within the graphics. The position of the analyzed domains can be represented by a box both in terms of (minimum and maximum) risk, and return of investment (minimum and maximum), whose width and height are determined by the uncertainty level. The average values have been represented as a dot within the rectangle.

– A dot: The uncertainty is null and that all estimations from all the participants in the analysis have consensus.
– A dot struck through by a line: There is consensus either in the risk or economic analysis, and the dot represents the average of the other values,
– A dot within a rectangle: There is no consensus and that there is an overall rectangle representing all answers while the dot represents the average value of the answers received.

The risk analysis does not search for consensus, but tries to identify the presence of risks within an organization. It tries to collect the different points of view in the organization in order to objectively identify the overall risks.

Figure 3.8 provides the results of performing five Reuse–Invest analysis on six different domains. These graphics are not to be compared among each other, but only provide an overview of the adequacy and the percentage of risk the organization is assuming when addressing each of these domains [2].

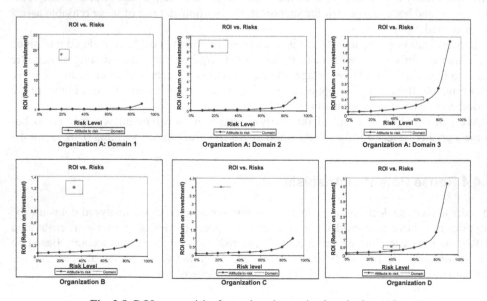

Fig. 3.8. ROI versus risks for analyzed organizations in the study

In Organization A, three domains were analyzed. In Domain 1, uncertainties both at economical estimations and risk aspects are present. Given the high return on investment resulting from the economical analysis, the investment is considered beneficial based on the estimations of investment, costs and savings expected. In Domain 2, the situation is similar to the previous, even though the uncertainty on risks is very high. Once again the ROI is much more than the minimum expected, therefore the investment is beneficial if the estimations are met. Finally, Domain 3 is characterized by a high uncertainty at the risk level. This risk analysis within the organization was performed in two different groups which provided a more clear view of the overall organizational risks. In order to obtain a greater compromise on the risks in the domain, joint meetings between both groups could be necessary and careful attention must be given to the areas that have shown greater risk in order to ensure the success of the reuse program.

In Organization B even though the risk is between 25 and 40%, the investment is expected to be beneficial given the high return on investment.

When analyzing the potential of the Organization C, the economic estimation does not present major uncertainty, while there is a risk uncertainty of 15–30%. The ROI estimated is much greater than the expected minimum ROI defined by the organization; therefore, based on these estimations, the reuse program can be beneficial to the organization.

In Organization D the analyzed domain presents high risk and, in the worst case, the domain coincides with the line dividing the areas in favor of investing and those against investing. In this case the organization should review their estimations in more detail and in the case of deciding on investing in systematic reuse, keep a close control of the risks of greater presence and importance in order to ensure the success of the reuse initiative.

In all the cases analyzed, the investment on systematic reuse is favored, this is, the domains analyzed are in the upper area of the graphic. In those cases where the domain is close to the Attitude to risk line (organization D), special focus and attention must be given to tracking the identified risks when implementing a reuse program.

Based on the estimations related to the number of applications developed using the reusable assets, the depreciation of the value of money overtime, the risk that can impact negatively on the implementation of reuse program and based on the attitude to risk of these organizations, it can be concluded that the domains analyzed are in an advantaged position for investment.

3.5 Reuse–Check Analysis Results

In those organizations in which a reuse activity was already taking place the state of reuse, the infrastructure and practices that favor reuse were analyzed.

The results of these analyses are presented by the following schema:

- A first general description of the state of practice on each organization.
- A second, more detailed description of the different types of reuse approaches identified as well as a description of the reusable assets.
- A description of the detected faults in the different organizations and the strengths of the approaches in these organizations.
- Description of the proposed situations to the organizations as objective situations for reuse.

3.5.1 Identified Reuse Situations Description

As a starting point for presenting the results of the analysis performed in four organizations, each of the identified situations is detailed next:

Case 1 – Organization A

The analysis performed within this organization made a differentiation between knowledge reuse and software reuse. The knowledge reuse is due to the importance given within the organization to know-how, both business and technical. This knowledge is shared at offer negotiation time. In this case the reusable assets make reference to the information collected from previous projects, which includes offers, customer requirements and many more.

The current state of practice in the organization is depicted in Fig. 3.9. The need for reuse is identified during the launching phase and development of the projects, were the opportunities for reusing results from other projects is considered. Among the most reused components the following can be found: routines, modules, products, configuration scripts, DB designs.

The way to develop applications starts by using a common platform, parameterize and finally the ad hoc reuse, as a strategy for reducing costs and at the same time providing the same product quality, and the ability to be competitive.

The identification of reusable potential knowledge assets is driven by people, in this case: project leaders and responsible areas.

The assets are modeled under predefined structures and the users know of their existence and location. Since there is a quality culture and management mechanism in place, the know-how assets are fed in a formal and systematic manner.

The reuse identification opportunities depend on the project participants. The reusable elements do not have the same mechanisms as the knowledge reuse: only the knowledge of the existence and the location of assets are shared. Criteria for managing and maintaining the reusable software assets are not in place.

It is worth mentioning that the reuse is not limited to the development phase, but it also includes other products of the life cycle (offers, documentation and design) and the reuse

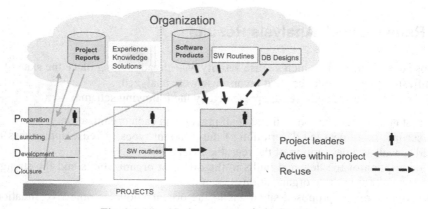

Fig. 3.9. Identified reuse scenario in Case 1

is supported by the infrastructure in place for the quality system and by the culture of evolvement and improvement present in the improvement groups created. The reuse is clearly centralized in the people not in the organization which identifies clearly the organizational dependence on people.

Case 2 – Organization B

The domain is defined by applications that are developed in client/server environments using several technologies. A reuse focus is already undertaken by a technological approach, in which an application is developed by reusing a common base application, formed by templates and program skeletons that cover basic functionalities. The same approach needs to be applied for different target technologies, therefore the main idea is to analyze current improvements for the reuse base already in place and analyze the state of practice in order to have an overall picture of the problem. At the same time the host development environment has been analyzed in order to identify the benefit for the whole organization.

The current state of practice in the organization is depicted in Fig. 3.10. The reuse in some cases is performed by calls to functions within the base application and in other cases by derivation of the base application. At the same time there is also ad hoc reuse of elements from other projects and even from the base application.

There is an administration role responsible for the maintenance and improvement of the base application, but no person has been assigned to that role due to a lack of resources. This responsibility is shared among the base application development environment group therefore this role can be easily forgotten. Another issue identified is that even though the communication is favored by the size of the group, there is a lack of mechanisms to formalize this communication. Therefore issues addressed via this communication channel are never recorded and in some cases are lost.

The reuse potential is identified by the people, not the projects. The development cost of building a reusable asset is made within the projects. The maintenance effort is made by the administrator and the criteria for generalizing an asset are dependent on the administrator or the project that has developed the asset.

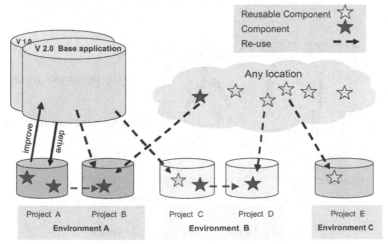

Fig. 3.10. Identified reuse scenario in Case 2

The identification of reuse opportunities within a project is made by the people within the project, which is not included within the development methodology used, although the guides of how to reuse are actually included in the current methodology.

Case 3 – Organization D

As a result of the analysis, an organizational infrastructure was identified. This infrastructure collects technological assets that are then used in the application development. The contribution of assets to this infrastructure is an initiative that emerges from the projects and requires for the creators of the assets to assume the responsibility of its quality and maintenance. This implies that the contribution to this infrastructure is carefully analyzed and at the same time it is necessary that the asset undergoes certain level of use within an established number of projects, prior to sharing them as a means to validate its quality and avoid errors. The current state of practice in the organization is depicted in Fig. 3.11.

In this case reuse is favored by the technological character that is in place. The development environment allows reusing assets and managing them as a library. At the same time there is a configuration management tool that allows organizing the library at different levels, allowing the development of a corporative library where only assets that comply with certain quality criteria are published. There is also a group responsible for managing the library, which is responsible for notifying the existence of new assets to all participants in the development group.

There is also an exchange of assets among projects which is not controlled by the group responsible for the library. It cannot be considered as a systematic reuse approach because is based on a copy and paste basis, incurring a major maintenance problem. In specific cases, cooperation among projects in order to share resources and cost for the development of general purpose assets has also been identified.

The expectations with respect to reuse are positive and benefits are expected from this way of systematic reuse. The improvement areas are aligned into an improvement in the correct structuring of responsibilities, avoiding the situation in which the projects take this role, by creating a technical office responsible for the maintenance of assets and assume the asset creator role of maintenance, in order to encourage the development of reusable assets.

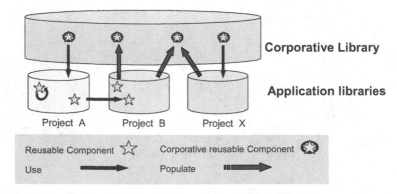

Fig. 3.11. Identified reuse scenario in Case 3

The analyzed organization is driven by project base reuse, where the projects are responsible for reuse activities, but it is not performed in a systematic way. This is due to the lack of processes explaining how to reuse and develop reusable assets; there is no certainty that all identified potential assets for reuse are really developed as such; and the major problem detected is that the reusable asset creator is responsible for its maintenance, which discourages the creation of reusable assets.

The proposed improvement actions are aimed at driving the efforts towards domain engineering, by defining and creating a group which will guide and manage reuse. The activities proposed for doing so are:

- Increase the number of people involved in the technical office by incorporating personnel currently working on projects, with previous reuse experience in projects.
- Allocate the maintenance of the reusable assets to the technical office.
- Allocate the responsibility of developing assets among the technical office and the projects.
- Identify and define metrics in order to be able to manage the evolution of the reuse initiative and identify whether the reuse initiative is providing the expected results.
- Define guidelines to ensure the correctness and ease of use of the asset catalogue.
- Define asset quality criteria for introduction of assets in the library.

The proposed actions consolidate the project based reuse in place and at the same time enhance the systematic development of assets by the technical office.

Case 4 – Organization E

In this case, two reuse potential cases have been analyzed: a generic domain which provides support to the rest of the domains in the organization, which can be identified in Fig. 3.12.

The first case, Case 4a is a library which contains specific functionality used to develop projects related to "material behavior." It has evolved and migrated to a number of technologies that form the basis for new development projects. For this domain there is a reuse group that is responsible for:

- Maintaining the library functions (migrations to new technological environments)
- Providing support on the use of the library by the projects
- Creating new reusable functions based on the projects results

The communication of the existence of reusable functions is done informally on a project need basis. The reuse initiative depends on the people involved in the project and there is no formal way to verify if functionality is already within the library.

There is no systematic process defined for the inclusion of a function within the library, nor there is validation or quality criteria established to verify the assets. Then, the identified improvement actions are:

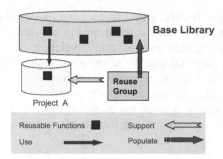

Fig. 3.12. Identified reuse scenario in Case 4a

– Formalize and define the roles and responsibilities of the reuse group: identifying reuse opportunities, maintaining the assets and the management of the library.
– Standardize the mechanism and requirements for introducing an asset within the library.
– Improve the documentation of both the library and the assets: Currently it is not easy to use the library since the documentation provided is too technical and lacks a general description on the use of the reusable assets.

The second domain is a specific software development which centers on machine and vehicle simulators. The development in this environment uses the asset based development approach. The organization of reuse is the responsibility of the people involved in the projects within the domain. The communication and knowledge sharing among personnel is fluent since the number of people involved in the domain is low. There is no specific technical office.

The identified reuse strategy within this domain is a project based reuse, but due to the maturity of the domain it is possible to evolve towards domain driven reuse. Basically the product family for the simulation environment is composed by a number of predefined assets for developing any simulation, and some more flexible assets that adjust to specific project needs. In this case it is recommended that an in - depth investment analysis is undertaken to identify whether the organization can undergo such a change and whether it is economically feasible.

3.5.2 Current State of Reuse Practice Analysis

This section includes a description of the reuse practices that the organizations undertake, the types of reuse being implemented, the kind of assets most often used, the infrastructures put in place, the current state and the potential improvements.

The following two types of reuse have been identified:

– Ad hoc reuse: This kind of reuse basically consists of extracting a piece of code from a development base, adapting it to the application requirements and including it within the development. This kind of reuse requires adaptation of the piece of code for every implementation it is used in [20].

– Systematic reuse by reusable asset integration: This kind of reuse is based on the availability of reusable assets that can be used in the development of new applications with no major adaptation effort.

In most cases, the reuse applied is the ad hoc reuse. We must take into account that in most cases this kind of reuse is performed in routines which require little effort in adaptation for the target environment and in which the maintenance effort is low. At the same time, due to the topology of the organizations analyzed, the applications are installed at the customer who in most of the cases does not share software assets and, thus, the installations are performed independently.

The software elements identified as reused within the analyzed organizations are shown in Tab. 3.2.

Table 3.2. Software elements reused in the context of the analysis

finding	Types of reusable items
software routines	– error control routines – utilities and access and maintenance routines – SAP access routines – security routines (users and access)
software functions	– specific menu and control functions – functions of the organization methodology – searching, bar code reading functions – user maintenance functions – communication functions
C++ classes	– basic classes (C++ objects) – data access classes
application and software modules	– e-mail server – base application for the development of applications – whole product
other (documentation, templates, designs, analysis)	– function and procedures base structures – interfaces – relational data bases – data base procedures – graphical window assets (used as templates) – screen and reports formats – documentation models – variables and code definition rules – tool configurations

3.5.3 Identified Strengths and Major Problems

The major aspects identified within the organizations which favor reuse are the following:

1. Reuse techniques are in place and the new developments are already reusing assets; this provides a time and effort reduction in the projects.
2. A reuse infrastructure is in place
   - An organizational structure (a person/role or group) responsible for repository management and maintenance is available.
   - A repository/library containing the reusable assets as well as the documentation for its use is in place.
3. People in the organization are in favor of both reusing and developing reusable assets. Reuse is considered a mechanism to improve the current organizational results.
4. Quality management system is in place, which provides support for reuse. When an organization has already a methodology, procedures and rules for developing code as well as documentation procedures, this favors and eases the introduction of systematic reuse.
5. An improvement group in charge of the continuous process improvement in the organization is in place. This group is also responsible for the reuse activities, since they are improvement activities. This group provides a current state of practice of the organization as a whole.
6. Organization performs reuse not only of code, but also other life cycle products (documentation, design, and analysis). The reuse methodology itself can also be reused.
7. Reuse opportunities are considered at initial steps of a project which increases reuse possibilities and impact. All possible project stakeholders are involved in the project definition and planning.

At the same time, the organizations have also presented some difficulties which are:

1. In most cases the person responsible for the maintenance and providing support for a reusable asset is the developer of the reusable asset. The major drawback is that this reduces the motivation of the personnel, since if someone develops a reusable asset this implies assuming new responsibilities which are not really considered as such by the organization.
2. There are no criteria to decide whether something is common to all applications or specific to a single application. The project leader has to identify reusability among the project results, which may result in investing effort in assets not useful for the domain or some functionality common to all developments, may not be identified.
3. There is no overall view of the benefits of reuse in the organizational results, which does not allow for the reuse evolving within the organization. An organization will not provide resources and effort to an area in which the benefits are not proven.
4. The use of the library is not correctly extended throughout the organization; often this is due to, the interface provided for the use of the library is not easy to use and no guidelines are provided.
5. There is a dependency between the reusable assets and the developer of the asset.
6. There are no rules or guidelines for the development of reusable assets.

7. In many cases there is no centralized effort in which all the reusable assets can be efficiently accessed which reduces the reuse opportunities.
8. Reuse is considered as a mechanism to be used in specific cases but has not been considered as an institutional issue.
9. The reuse performed is on an ad hoc basis, which results in many different versions of the same asset, which increases maintenance costs. A defect encountered within an asset must be corrected in all the different places were it has been copied and adapted, so if there is no traceability mechanism in place this process can be too effort consuming. For further information on these issues refer to [5].

The general reuse infrastructure detected in the organizations follows the following schema as shown in Fig. 3.13.

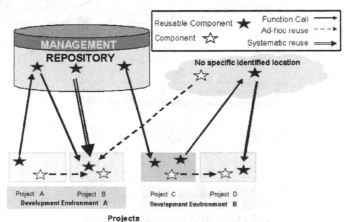

Fig. 3.13. Identified common reuse scenario schema

Fig. 3.13 provides a view of the allocation of the assets:

– Repository: Representing an asset catalogue or library of reusable assets which is established within the organization in order to favor reuse.
– No specific identified location: Implies that although the assets are physically located within the organization there are no mechanism in place which helps in the location and use of the assets.

The Management element included above the repository in Fig. 3.13 is related to the group responsible for managing and evolving the reuse infrastructure.

3.5.4 Improvement Actions Reported to the Organizations

The objective scenarios for reuse that have been identified in the organizations vary depending on the context and current state of reuse in each one, but all the cases fit to the following schema, representing the desirable situation as depicted Fig. 3.14.

In this sense the proposed improvements are intended to consolidate the current situation and drive the organization to adopt a systematic reuse approach, in which domain engineering plays a relevant role. The basic ideas proposed to achieve this new scenario are:

- Establishment of a management group (Domain Engineering) which is responsible for identifying reuse opportunities in the domain, the maintenance of the assets and the management of the reuse infrastructure.
- The development of reusable assets can be a shared responsibility among the projects and domain engineering, depending on the resource availability of domain engineering.
- Introduction of reuse metrics and mechanisms which will help the organization identify the evolution and benefits of the reuse initiative. The kind of metrics proposed are related to the use of assets, quality of assets, effort reduction and other benefits in projects using assets.

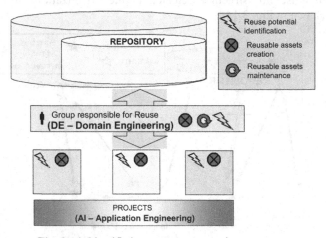

Fig. 3.14. Identified target reuse scenario

- Improvements in the documentation provided for the use of the reuse infrastructure and the assets, in order to motivate the application of the assets.
- Establishment and standardization of quality requirements in order to include a new asset in the catalogue/library.
- The initial proposal is to concentrate the reuse effort on a specific domain in the organization as an initial state in order to validate the approach, and once results are obtained, extend the reuse program to additional domains.

These improvement suggestions have been made based on an overall schema of systematic reuse which is characterized by the separation of the development lifecycle into two main processes with clearly distinct objectives: Domain Engineering (DE) and Application Engineering (AE).

Domain engineering focuses on the development of a common infrastructure of reusable assets and streamlined processes for a given application domain. Application engineering is aimed at deriving a single product or application from the common infrastructure to meet specific user requirements.

Domain engineering is not done once only. Instead, it is an iterative process that uses the domain knowledge in the organization to incrementally build the infrastructure for the domain. Domain engineering includes the following processes:

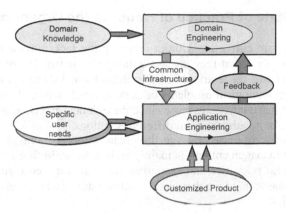

Fig. 3.15. Systematic reuse overview

- *Manage the domain.* Involves the organization and planning of the domain efforts to achieve business objectives. It includes the development of domain plans, the definition of roles, the assignment of resources and the evolution of the domain.
- *Analyze the domain.* Defines the focus and scope of the domain. It establishes both the similarities among the potential products of the domain and how they differ from each other.
- *Engineer the domain products.* Includes the specification, design, implementation and maintenance of the domain assets. These assets include all kinds of software development work-products: requirement documents, designs, architectures, source code, test cases, etc.
- *Engineer the domain process.* Covers the standardization and development of the processes definitions and process support to produce applications. The results include procedures, guidelines, templates, examples and tools such as repositories or generators to support and guide the application developer.
- *Provide project support.* Ensures that the domain meets the business needs. This is achieved by supporting the application engineers in using the common infrastructure and collecting the feedback from its usage as an input for the evolution of the domain.

The structure represented in Fig. 3.15 provides the overall organization for any systematic reuse approach, also addressed for in literature as product line engineering. A similar framework for software product line engineering is fully dealt for in [6]. The methods and tools for undertaking this approach can be found at [3] that collects within a catalogue all methods, techniques and tools that have been developed in Europe in the last 6 years within a set of European projects: ESAPS, CAFÉ and FAMILIES.

3.6 Conclusions and Future Research

Based on the analysis performed and the results obtained, the following conclusions provide an overview of the analyzed situations and their characteristics. It must be pointed out that these conclusions are based on the analyses performed in small to medium-sized companies in which systematic reuse practices are in early stages.

3.6.1 Current State of Practice of Reuse in the Organizations

Many organizations are currently, without realizing the fact, introducing reuse practices and putting them in place, but they are not gaining all the benefits of a systematic reuse approach. In many cases reuse arises initially in horizontal domains, as a mechanism to share solutions to technological problems or generic functionality. This is the first step an organization takes when confronting reuse since the technical assets, in most cases, are used as they require little or no adaptation to different solutions.

In other cases software reuse arises in the organizations bottom-up, as an opportunity, it is not defined by management and is mainly ad hoc reuse. In those companies in which reuse receives special relevance and resources are available, reuse strategies are in line with the idea of systematic reuse that clearly defines domain engineering and application engineering activities.

Most of the times, reuse is performed by many organizations, not only for code, but also for templates, requirement and documents; this strategy has a great impact in the software development life cycle.

It is in the organizations which already have quality and improvement management in place, were the state of reuse practices is more easily identified and were the current improvement actions can be updated to include systematic reuse practices. These organizations are better fit to address and manage change.

3.6.2 Reuse Analysis as an Investment

Based on the economical results presented in Sect. 3.4, software reuse can be seen as an investment mechanism by the organizations, in spite of the identified risks. The average economical analysis results indicate that there is expected profitability index of 2.94.

The benefits of reuse are derived from the savings that are determined based on the number of applications expected to be developed from the reuse infrastructure. The number of expected applications as provided by the organizations during the analyses may be optimistic. Therefore a reduction of the average benefits may be more than expected.

3.6.3 Current Situation Characterization

The organizations already involved in reuse practice consider that the current situation can be improved and that systematic reuse – in the way it has been addressed – provides a logical organizational approach, which is required to obtain maximum benefits. This idea is shared when addressing aspects such as:

– Identifying, centralizing and assigning responsibilities related to the creation and maintenance of reusable assets, to a specific working group dedicated to such activities.
– Establishing a mechanism that allows keeping a traceability of the efforts dedicated to implement and improve reuse in the organization and the results obtained, this could range from a centralized document where every effort is annotated to complex information systems.
– Establishing criteria and mechanisms that allow for the inclusion of new assets in the common reuse infrastructure.

The domain in which the reuse initiative will take place must be carefully defined. The organizations must not apply reuse to everything that could be subject to reuse. Since the return on investment will not be sufficient in all cases, it is necessary to identify and define carefully a domain or area in which the reuse efforts provide the most substantial benefits.

One of the main critical issues when introducing systematic reuse is the commitment of the organization, as well as the commitment at the different levels of management in providing the required resources and time for getting the initiative running. Another issue which clearly impacts in the capability for systematic reuse in an organization is the range of different technologies used. Organizations that have customers which share few common technological aspects present a handicap for obtaining benefits from systematic reuse. Even though the technology is very unstable, the organizations consider that once the reuse culture is in place the migration between technologies is better undertaken and should be performed using a systematic reuse approach.

Based on the results of the analysis made in these organizations, we can deduce that within these organizations systematic reuse has been shown to be a beneficial approach towards improved software development efficiency. In the organizations which already have reuse practices in place, there are many similarities. For example, they have a similar schema of reuse organized among projects in which the initial step to consolidate a systematic reuse is the creation of a group responsible for reuse. This does not in any case imply that by defining a reuse group systematic reuse is achieved, but it is one of the pillars on which success stands. The organization must commit to provide the time and resources so that this group is created and is made responsible for making a success of the systematic reuse approach.

The main hurdle for any systematic reuse initiative in small and medium-sized organizations is the lack of resources. The proposed tools, reuse–Invest and Reuse–Check, provide an adequate starting point for any organization interested in adopting a systematic reuse approach, by identifying whether it is economically beneficial to do so. At the same time these tools provide means to identify which are the weakest areas in which specific systematic reuse practices should be institutionalized as well as what risks can be found and solved. Similar approaches and studies exist such as [8,22].

If the domain for investment and risks are identified, and the means for mitigating these risks are put in place, systematic reuse can be a reality for any small and medium-sized organization. In many cases the selection of a target domain for which systematic reuse is not an adequate approach results in the failure of the systematic reuse initiative. In those cases, systematic reuse will probably never be considered in the future by the same management body. Those small and medium-sized organizations in the case studies that applied Reuse-Invest clearly identified the domain where adopting systematic reuse would have the highest return on investment. This clearly benefited the organizations since it allowed them to introduce systematic reuse successfully. Those organizations that applied R-Check had a clear view of the risks to be addressed and where major effort should be spent to implement a systematic reuse initiative successfully.

3.6.4 Future Research

Organizations need to analyze the economical impacts of new technologies such as systematic reuse and product line engineering before introducing such technologies. Future research is needed to analyze the use of the proposed approach in big enterprises which have to deal with emerging technologies such as Model Driven Development, Service-Oriented Architecture, and Aspect-Oriented Software Development in order to leverage product line engineering. The approach also needs to be further developed to provide the industry with an adequate mechanism to decide whether or not adopting such technologies will enable organizations to maintain and possibly improve their market positions while adopting new technologies.

Acknowledgments

I would like to thank Pablo Ferrer who was directly involved in the development of both the assessments and the conclusions, for his effort in the successful completion of this case study. I gratefully acknowledge the extensive reviews of Juan Carlos Dueñas, Timo Käkölä, Eelco Rommes, Alberto Berreteaga and Jacco Wesselius that significantly improved the quality of this chapter.

References

1. Amar L., Coffey J., Measuring the Benefits of Software Reuse, 9 may 2005, http://www.ddj.com/184406111
2. Bandinelli, S., Mendieta, G.S.: Domain potential analysis: calling the attention on business issues of product-lines, software architectures for product families. International Workshop IW-SAPF-3 (March 2000)
3. Böckle, G., Wittmann, M.: Catalogue of methods and processes for system-family engineering. FAMILIES Catalogue 2005. http://www.esi.es/Families/E1.4b-Method-Catalogue/Start_SFE_Catalogue.htm
4. Böckle, G. et al: Calculating ROI for software product lines. IEEE Softw. 21(3), 23–31 (May/June 2004)
5. Brown, W.J., Malveau, R.C. et al: *AntiPatterns: Refactoring Software, Architectures, and Projects in Crisis* (Wiley, New York 1998)
6. Clements, P., Northrop, L.: *Software Product Lines: Practices and Patterns* (Addison-Wesley, Boston 2001)
7. http://cognet.mit.edu/library/erefs/mitecs/ (MIT Encyclopedia of Cognitive Sciences)
8. IEEE: Product line engineering: the state of the practice. IEEE Softw. 20(6), 52–60 (November 2003)
9. ISO/IEC 15504: 1998, Information technology – software process assessment. Technical report type 2 (International Standards Organisation 1998) (approved for publication)
10. Jacobson, I., Griss, M., Johnsson, P.: *Software Reuse; Architecture, Process and Organisation for Business Success* (ACM, New York 1997)
11. Karlsson, E.-A.: *Software Reuse: A Holistic Approach* (Wiley, New York 1995)
12. Lim, W.C.: *Managing Software Reuse* (Prentice-Hall, Englewood Cliffs, NJ 1998)
13. McClure, C.: *Software Reuse Techniques* (Prentice-Hall, Englewood Cliffs, NJ 1997)
14. Pike, R., Neale, B.: *Corporate Finance and Investments* (Prentice-Hall, Englewood Cliffs, NJ 1996)
15. Plummer, D.: Unconventional wisdom: staffing an integrative policy group for SOA governance. Business Integ. J (June 2005)
16. Pohl, K., Böckle, G., van der Linden, F.: *Software Product Line Engineering, Foundations, Principles and Techniques* (Springer, Berlin Heidelberg New York, 2005)
17. R-SPICE described in system family process frameworks. http://www.esi.es/esaps/publicResults.html (September 2001)
18. Schmid, K., Verlage, M.: The economic impact of product line adoption and evolution. IEEE Softw. 19(4), 50–57 (July 2002)
19. Sprandlin, T.: *A Lexicon of Decision Making* (March 1997)
20. Sullivan, K., Chalasani, P., Jha, S., Sazawal, V.: Software design as an investment activity: a real options perspective. In: *Real Options and Business Strategy: Applications to Decision Making* (Risk Books 1999)
21. System Family Transition Economy in Public Results Section. http://www.esi.es/Families/ (October 2005)
22. Verlage, M., Kiesgen, T.: Five years of product line engineering in a small company. Proceedings of the 27th International Conference on Software Engineering, 15–21 May 2005, St. Louis, MO, USA

Part 2: Product Line Requirements Engineering

Introduction

Part 2 deals with product line modeling and requirements engineering. The purpose of product line requirements engineering is to identify and document common and variable requirements and features for the product line and draw upon them in developing the applications of the product line.

Part 2 consists of three chapters:

Chapter 4. Capturing Product Line Information from Legacy User Documentation

Chapter 5. Scenario-Based Application Requirements Engineering

Chapter 6. Consolidated Product Line Variability Modeling

The three chapters are grouped together in Part 2 as they present complementary approaches to variability modeling both from conceptual and language viewpoints and the viewpoint of methodologies for creating effective variability models. The first two chapters present complementary approaches to derive product line requirements in domain requirements engineering and draw upon the requirements in application requirements engineering.

The development of a software product line is seldom a green field task. Legacy systems exist that serve as information sources or that should be integrated into a product line. The information needed for this task is usually elicited interactively with high involvement by the domain experts of the application domain. As domain experts have a high workload and are often unavailable, relying primarily on high expert involvement is a risk for the successful introduction of a product line engineering approach into an organization.

Chapter 4 presents an approach for extracting requirements from existing user documentation and transforming this information (e.g., commonalities and variabilities among different existing products) into product line models. It is directly linked with product line management discussed in Part 1 because product line requirements can only be created effectively by drawing upon both product roadmapping and existing legacy systems and other available artifacts. It describes the metamodel that is the basis of the approach, the extraction patterns that are derived from the metamodel, and the process that guides the application of the patterns and the derivation of information relevant for building a product line. The initial validation of the approach shows that, with the help of this information, a product line model with the product line requirements can be built much faster and the workload of the domain experts is significantly reduced.

A number of partly overlapping methods for describing software product lines have been defined. They diverge with respect to terminology, representation, and concepts. Software product line engineering would benefit from a more unified approach that facilitates interoperability of tools and increased collaboration. Chapters 5 and 6 present two complementary modeling approaches for this purpose: orthogonal and consolidated variability modeling. To avoid misinterpretations concerning the terminologies used in Chaps. 5 and 6 and facilitate future research on variability modeling, Chapter 5 compares the metamodels of the orthogonal and consolidated variability modeling approaches.

In product line engineering the application requirements engineers have to assure both a high degree of reuse and the satisfaction of the application stakeholders' needs. The vast number of possible variant combinations and the influences of the selection of one variant to different requirements models present a challenge for the consistent reuse or adaptation of product line requirements. Only if the engineers are aware of the product line capabilities, can they decide whether a stakeholder requirement can be satisfied by the product line or not. Chapter 5 presents an approach for the development of application requirements specifications that uses the orthogonal variability model and scenarios to support the engineers during the elicitation, negotiation, documentation and validation of requirements and tackles the challenges of application requirements engineering by iteratively employing the orthogonal variability model and the product line scenarios.

Chapter 6 presents the consolidated metamodel for modeling software product line variability that aims to be the starting point for the standardization of variability modeling and the creation of commercial and open source tools better suited to product line engineering than the ones available in the market (some of which are evaluated in Chapter 16). It describes a prototype tool that uses the metamodel as its foundation to validate the metamodel, to show how the metamodel can be successfully drawn upon to design supporting tools, and to encourage the software industry and open source community to develop such tools. It also presents approaches for capturing variability using standard languages, exemplified by UML 2.0, annotations to standard languages, and domain-specific languages.

It should be noted that variability modeling, being a critically important research area in product line engineering, is also addressed in Chaps. 1, 7, 11, 12, 13, and 15. Both the orthogonal and consolidated variability modeling approaches provide excellent support for modeling and designing product line reference architectures discussed in Part 3. Chapters 4 and 11 are also complementary as the requirements derived using the approach described in Chap. 4 can be analyzed and tested further using the approach proposed by Chap. 11.

4 Capturing Product Line Information from Legacy User Documentation

I. John

Abstract

The development of a software product line is seldom a green field task. Legacy systems exist that serve as an information source or that should be integrated into a product line. The information needed is usually elicited interactively with high involvement by the domain experts of the application domain. As domain experts have a high workload and are often unavailable, relying primarily on high expert involvement is a risk for the successful introduction of a product line engineering approach into an organization. This chapter presents an approach for the extraction of requirements from user documentation, which gives guidance on how to elicit knowledge from existing user documentation and how to transform information from this documentation into product line models. This approach is called the PuLSE-CaVE-approach (Commonality and Variability Extraction) and is part of the PuLSE-Framework for product line engineering. We describe the metamodel that is the basis of the approach, the extraction patterns that are derived from the metamodel, and the process that guides the application of the patterns and the derivation of information relevant for building a product line. This information can be features of legacy products, parts of use cases that can be used for product line analysis, different kinds of requirements and, most important for product line engineering, commonalities and variabilities among existing products. With the help of this information, a product line model with the product line requirements can be built much faster and the workload of the domain experts is significantly reduced. We performed an initial validation of the approach in industrial case studies and in a controlled experiment.

4.1 Introduction

The goal of product line engineering is to achieve planned domain-specific reuse by building a family of applications. Unlike in single system software development there are two life cycles, domain engineering and application engineering [47]. In domain engineering, the reusable asset base is built and in application engineering, this asset base is used to build the planned products.

In existing product line engineering and domain analysis approaches, the information needed to build a product line or domain model is elicited interactively from domain experts. As domain experts have a high workload and are often unavailable, this high expert load is a risk for the successful introduction of product line engineering into an organization. Reducing the expert load and thus reducing the risk of failure can allow product line introduction in a planned and controlled way. Reducing the expert load by systematically collecting information from existing documents and thus decreasing the amount of time that has to be spent by the domain experts on the product line introduction is the main goal of our work.

When introducing a product line engineering approach in a new context, a large amount of information on the domain of the planned product line and on the planned and existing products of the product line has to be collected. The commonalities and variabilities of products in the domain and subdomains in focus have to be captured, modeled, and later implemented and stored in an asset base. Constructing such a reusable asset base for specific products in a domain is an intellectually more sophisticated task than the development of assets for a single system because several products with their commonalities and variabilities have to be considered. This implies that planning and scoping, elicitation, analysis, modeling and realization are more complex than for single systems. So, all tasks that are known from single system engineering have to be done, but in a more sophisticated way, by thinking about several products and realizing solutions in a generic way. Figure 4.1 shows the principal information gathering process during scoping and modeling of product lines.

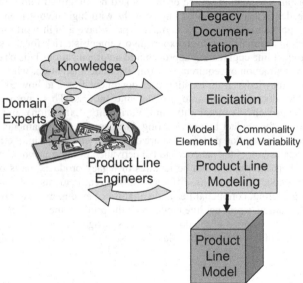

Fig. 4.1. The principal elicitation and modeling process

Usually, before starting to develop a product line, one or more systems in the domain were already built. The information from those systems is a valuable source for building the reusable assets. For the domain analysis phase, general textual information on the existing systems is a very valuable source, as textual artifacts that are built using older textual information are built in these early phases.

The approach we introduce in this chapter focuses on the analysis and integration of information of user manuals and similar textual documentation, as in practice, natural language documents are the most common assets during the requirements phase [2,26,36]. A document-based approach can decrease the effort the domain experts have to spend on workshops, interviews, and meetings, and therefore leads to a high expert load reduction.

Our goal is to extract the information from documents semiautomatically so that the experts can concentrate on innovative functionality.

Our main research hypothesis is thus that the workload of experts can be reduced by extracting requirements from user documentation with a structured extraction approach. The goal of our work is to develop and validate an approach that efficiently supports the introduction of product line engineering by systematically using existing documentation to gather information on the products and the product line and thus reduce expert load.

Our secondary research hypothesis is that an approach that extracts partial requirements elements from user manuals produces results that are more correct and complete than unguided and ad hoc extraction of requirements in different forms.

4.1.1 Outline

In this chapter, we describe the scientific approach we developed and its validation. We describe the product line related problem that we solve with our approach in Sect. 4.2 and give a classification of related work in Sect. 4.3. The metamodel and the patterns that are the basis of our approach are described in Sect. 4.4. In Sect. 4.5, we describe the method and process of how to apply the patterns and find useful information in user documentation, and in Sect. 4.6, we show how we validated our approach in a controlled experiment and in an industrial case study.

4.1.2 Research Approach

The research approach we chose is separated into two phases: First, a phase with action research [40], a research paradigm that uses an iterative process, which alternates between action and critical reflection, and second an experimentation phase [5], where we perform case studies and an experiment to validate the approach.

First, we analyzed the related literature on requirements engineering, information extraction, domain engineering and product line requirements engineering for useful techniques in the context of requirements extraction for product lines. Then we followed the action research paradigm and applied those techniques and some new techniques in two initial explorative studies, see [24]. We built a first version of our approach and a metamodel underlying our approach in parallel in short improvement cycles when performing the studies. After stabilizing this first version, we went over to the experimental phase. We conducted a controlled experiment and showed external validity in an industrial case study. In the last phase, the phase that we are currently in, we will finalize the approach, perform further case studies, and package the results in different kinds of publications.

By combining action research and experimental software engineering, we also comply with the guidelines given by design research as described in [21]:

- *Design as an artifact.* In our case, the extraction approach serves as the purposeful and useful artifact. The extraction approach described in Sect. 4.5 is described in such a way that it can be applied by others and helps to construct product line models.
- *Problem relevance.* By solving or at least minimizing the problem of expert load, a technology-based solution to a well known practical problem is given.

- *Design evaluation.* The evaluation of the approach is done through a controlled experiment and industrial case studies.
- *Research contributions.* As the main contribution described here is the extraction approach described in Sect. 4.5 (with the basis in the metamodel and patterns described in Sect. 4.4), our contribution is mainly in the area of design artifacts. As described in [21]: "The artifact must enable the solution of heretofore unsolved problems." The approach described here partially solves the problem of information gathering for product lines.
- *Research rigor.* An explicit survey on related work and the use of the well known and established research methods action research and experimentation give a stable basis for the approach and the research done.
- *Design as a search.* By taking into account current product line modeling methods, the outcome of the method is aligned with the problem environment.

By following this combination of action research and experimentation, we can perform well-founded research that is applicable to different contexts in practice.

4.2 Problem

When starting a product line in an organization there are normally legacy systems that have been built in the product line domain. Legacy systems of the organization can be old systems that have already been completed or systems currently under development and not integrated into the product line yet. The integration of those existing systems into a planned product line to be built can happen on different levels, like analysis and integration of code, analysis and integration of the architecture, reuse and integration of knowledge and expertise, and analysis and integration of documentation. As also discussed in Chap. 9, approaches or methods exist for the code and architecture analysis and integration like Architecture Recovery methods or reengineering methods [8]. But for the transfer and integration of less formal or even tacit knowledge like requirements or expertise, no method exists that supports this integration.

Knowledge or expertise that exists in the organization is owned by the stakeholders within the development organization. This knowledge can be used for the transition of the legacy systems and for modeling and development of the product line.

Legacy assets should not only be used for reverse engineering [11], which in the product line case can mean for finding a product line architecture from legacy code [8], and documentation, but also for (Re-)modeling a product line. There is information in legacy documents which is useful for domain requirements engineering and for increasing completeness. By analyzing the documents and integrating their information into the product line, knowledge and requirements can be reused for domain requirements engineering like code can be reused by transformation through reengineering.

4.2.1 Product Line Engineering

Product line engineering is an approach that aims at exploiting reuse potential between products developed in an organization by identifying the commonalities between the products and systematizing the variabilities. In Product line engineering, variabilities have to be identified, modeled, stored, resolved, instantiated, and changed.

This requires a comprehensive approach to the management of variability that can be applied throughout the various life-cycle stages, their artifacts, and their accompanying notations in a universal manner. Additionally, domain understanding has been identified as one of the key practices for successful product line engineering [12].

Moreover, in order to enable a smooth transition to product line development for an organization that so far only performed single system development, it is necessary to keep as much of the existing notations and approaches in place as possible. For this reason, we developed a customizable approach to variability management that can be used as a full lifecycle approach [41] but is also applicable for product line modeling. This allows us to practically apply the approach in a wide range of industrial settings. This is particularly motivated by our industrial projects using the PuLSE approach [19,30], as there we needed an approach that enables us to homogeneously manage variability, independent of the specific notation. Therefore an extraction approach for product lines has to be accompanied by explicit variability management in order to integrate and manage the extracted artifacts at the right stage and at the right place into the product line model.

4.2.2 Product Line Modeling

There are many approaches to product line modeling or product line requirements engineering like PuLSE-CDA7, Foda [28], ODM [43], Commonality analysis within FAST [50] or Synthesis [29]. Most of them use similar notations. Notations and artifacts that are state of the practice in product line modeling are features (see, e.g., [10,15,31]). Also quite often, extensions of Use Cases are used (see, e.g., [15,20,27,48]). In addition to these specific artifacts, general textual artifacts like functional requirements, nonfunctional requirements, glossaries, etc. are in use. Until now, the information needed to build a product line model has been elicited interactively with high expert involvement. As domain experts have a high workload and are often unavailable, this high expert involvement is a risk for the successful introduction of a product line engineering approach into an organization. in this chapter, we present an approach for extraction that overcomes the following problems:

- Domain experts have a high workload and are hardly available, so we need to relieve the experts by eliciting product line related information from documents.
- There is a lack of guidance on how to integrate legacy information found in documents into product line models.
- There is no extraction approach that is general enough to integrate all kinds of artifacts into a product line model.
- Single system elicitation methods cannot be taken as they are because multiple documentations have to be compared, commonalities and variabilities have to be elicited, and additional concepts (e.g., abstractions, decisions) are needed.

4.2.3 User Documentation as Information Source

In the case of integrating requirements by reusing and integrating knowledge about legacy systems, documents play an important role. The understanding of the domain as far as it was recorded by the development organization in earlier projects can be found in documents. Thus those documents are a valuable source for domain understanding and domain analysis.

By documents or documentation assets we mean the written representation of information concerning the legacy system. Documents that are developed during system or software development are more or less structured.

User manuals are often less structured and normally less formal than the other documentation assets. They provide an external or user view on the system and can also vary strongly in size. They can be expected to exist for almost any system that has a certain amount of user interaction. User Manuals can therefore be a rich source for increasing domain understanding. They describe domain concepts from a user perspective and can thus provide valuable input for domain analysis. Sometimes user manuals do not describe the system as it is but as it should be. But for use as a source for domain analysis, this is rather an advantage than a disadvantage because the systems in the product line should be realized in a more ideal way than the legacy systems. So information about the legacy system as it should be is a good input for product line modeling.

When introducing product lines with PuLSE [8] we found especially in small and medium enterprises [30] that there are almost no requirements specifications or design documents, and if there are any, they are outdated. As described above, user manuals describe the legacy systems from a perspective that is relevant for domain requirements engineering. For document processing it is therefore reasonable to concentrate on the analysis of user manuals of all systems the development organization has built in the domain of the product line.

According to [44] there are different types of user documentation: functional descriptions, installation documents, introductory manuals, reference manuals and administrator's manuals. All those kinds of user manuals can serve as input for product line engineering. Figure 4.2 shows how the different parts of a user manual can correspond to different use case elements that can be used for product line modeling. The relation of use cases to product lines is further elaborated in Chap. 11.

So the problem that we solve with our approach is: How can product line engineering be efficiently supported by systematically using user documentation from existing systems?

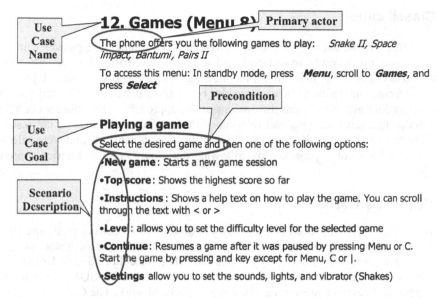

Fig. 4.2. Correspondence between user manual parts and use case elements (from [15])

4.3 Related Work

The area of fields and techniques that can contribute to the elicitation of information that is useful for the early phases of product engineering is rather large. Techniques from requirements elicitation and requirements analysis as well as knowledge engineering or information retrieval techniques can contribute to our research question of how to find information that is relevant for domain engineering and thus helps to reduce expert load. The techniques can range from interview techniques via reading techniques to code based techniques from reengineering.

To restrict the amount of related work, we built a classification of factors that can help solve our research question and explicitly searched for literature that contributes to the main dimensions of our classification. In the remainder of this section we will describe this classification and give the classification for related work from the fields that we investigated.

In our classification, we will only focus on textual information since analyzing existing textual information reduces the expert load most effectively. This can best be realized by analyzing existing textual information that is available [32,36]. Interview techniques can support structured elicitation but they require strong expert involvement and thus do not help in reducing expert load.

4.3.1 Classification

In the classification and survey we performed our goal was, compare approaches that can contribute to solving the problem of how to elicit textual information for the early phases of product line engineering and domain engineering. As this is a new research problem, with a new focus, the approaches we consider come from different areas and are only comparable by looking at different dimensions of the approaches. Therefore a classification is needed to enable viewing the relation of the chosen approaches to the research question. In this section we will describe the classification dimensions that were selected for the differentiation of approaches by following the Goal Question Metrics approach (GQM) [4].

Classification Derivation

According to the GQM approach [4], a study can be refined by setting goals specific to needs in terms of purpose, perspective and environment, by refining the goals into questions that are traceable and by deducing metrics and data to be collected in order to answer the questions. The here introduced classification is the result of a GQM Analysis, that should support our research question and classify the related work. The Goal of the survey can be decomposed as follows:

– *Object* (process or product under study). "All approaches that contribute to the extraction of common and variable information from existing textual software documentation that is relevant for product line modeling and requirements engineering."
– *Purpose* (motivation behind the measurement goal). Characterization of the approaches and extraction of useful techniques.
– *Focus* (quality attribute of the object under study). Usefulness of the approach/techniques for product line engineering.
– *Environment* (context in which the analysis shall be performed). Applied research in product line engineering.

When applying GQM, questions are defined that refine the goal, are traceable and can lead to concrete metrics. These questions can be derived from the object, the environment and the focus. Several questions were identified and metrics, which in our case are the classification dimensions for the classification, were derived. We derived the questions and metrics, respectively, the classification dimensions as follows (the dimensions are described in detail in [24]):

– *Question 1.* Is the approach suitable for knowledge recovery for the early phases of Product line engineering?
  Classification Dimensions: Area, Legacy, Product Line Relation
– *Question 2.* Is the approach well founded?
  Classification Dimensions: Metamodel, Conceptualization
– *Question 3.* Does the approach contain useful techniques for analyzing textual requirements information?
  Classification Dimensions: Focus, Artifacts, Constructiveness

We identified one of those classification dimensions, namely product line relation, as the main dimension, since the approach we are looking for has to support product line introduction.

Primary Classification Dimension

As the goal of the classification is to find information useful for product line modeling, the product line relation is the main classification dimension. Since the information to be searched has to be used in a product line engineering environment, the approach has to have some relation to finding commonality, variability, or both. The primary dimension *Product Line Relation* can be described as follows:

This classification dimension describes whether the approach has a direct relation to product line engineering, which means that the approach addresses commonality and variability of products or common and variable information entities. Approaches with a strong product line relation are better suitable for our goal than those with a weak or no product line relation. Out of those approaches that support product line engineering, those that support both commonality and variability (in contrast to approaches that only focus on commonalities such as certain domain engineering approaches like ODM) are optimal for our goal as common and variable information entities are needed to support domain engineering.

Possible values: not product line related, partially related, commonality only, variability only, commonality and variability.

When analyzing the approaches we found, we mainly focus on those approaches that are at least partially product line related or address commonality or variability. By restricting the approaches to those with the given classification values, we can identify exactly those approaches that are applicable for finding information that is useful for product line engineering.

Secondary Classification Dimensions

We also identified secondary classification dimensions that are subordinate to the primary dimension product line relation but are also useful for classifying existing approaches. These dimensions contribute to further classifying existing approaches according to their usefulness for the overall goal of the survey but they are only secondary in a way that these dimensions do not give an estimate of the usefulness of the approach for the goal but just provide a further classification of the approaches into subcategories. The secondary dimensions are:

- *Constructiveness.* This classification dimension describes if the approach is constructive, which means something is produced or modeled, or if the approach only describes how to decompose existing information, elicit knowledge or analyze existing documentation. If the approach is described as a process, an indicator for constructiveness can be whether there is an explicit output of the process. Approaches that are constructive are better for our goal than those that are less constructive because for the envisioned tasks, extraction of information from legacy systems in order to build a product line model, the construction of a new product line model has to be done.

Possible values: selecting (selecting available information as a model element), constructive (constructing model elements from basic information), including producing, modeling, analyzing (abstracting information into higher level elements).

- *Area.* This classification dimension describes the research area (as part of the research areas of Computer Science and Software Engineering) that the approach is a part of.

  Possible values: requirements engineering RE (being the common super-area of the following three areas), requirements elicitation/RElicit, requirements analysis/RA, requirements reuse/RR, domain modeling/DM (including product line engineering and domain engineering), reverse engineering/RevEng, information retrieval/IR, knowledge engineering/KE, documentation doc.

- *Metamodel.* This classification dimension describes the existence of an explicit underlying meta-model that describes basic elements of a documentation or what the models to be constructed/analyzed look like in general. With a metamodel it is generally possible to identify a match between the elements of a concrete documentation and the elements of a metamodel.

  Possible values: no, partially, yes.

- *Input Artifacts.* This classification dimension describes the artifacts that are analyzed or the basic documentation elements to be addressed by the approach. If the approach is described as a process, this is normally the input of the process. As the approaches analyzed are all related to software development, the artifacts addressed by the approach can be any textual artifact produced during the development lifecycle.

  Possible values: requirements (user), documentation, code, code comments, models, other.

- *Output Artifacts.* This classification dimension describes the artifacts that are the result of applying the approach. If the approach is described as a process, this is normally the output of the process. As the approaches analyzed are all related to software development, the artifacts addressed by the approach can be any textual artifact produced during the development life-cycle.

  Possible values: requirements (user), documentation, code, models, other.

- *Operationalization.* This classification dimension describes whether the approach is automatable/operationalizable and is described in such a way that support by a tool seems to be possible. This is of high importance for applying the approach in industrial applications as there is often a large amount of information available that should be analyzed.

  Possible values: no, partially, yes.

- *LifeCycle Orientation.* This classification dimension describes the consideration of legacy information. It analyzes whether the information from previously developed systems is integrated into a new development lifecycle (as is the case when introducing product line engineering in the presence of a legacy system) or whether the information analyzed will be integrated into the same lifecycle again (as is the case in a refactoring situation, when information like code should be improved). For approaches that explicitly consider product line engineering, it is also possible to address the instantiation of generic requirements built in domain engineering.

  Possible values: legacy, same lifecycle, domain engineering, application engineering.

The secondary dimensions provide a classification of the methods according to context factors and help decide on the relevance and usefulness of the methods for the research goal.

4.3.2 Classified Approaches

We identified about 30 approaches that could possibly be related to our research goal and classified them according to our classification scheme. Only nine of the approaches we analyzed had a product line relation. Here we only present in detail the classification of approaches that have a product line relation here (see Tab. 4.1); a complete classification can be found in [24]. Further approaches that we analyzed and classified and had no product line relation (e.g., [1,9,33,36,38,39,46]) nevertheless can be used to find useful techniques for analyzing information.

When following our classification scheme in analyzing our research goal, the ideal approach would have the following form:

- Product Line Relation: Commonality and Variability
- Constructiveness: Analyzing
- Area: irrelevant
- Meta-model: yes
- Input Artifacts: Documentation
- Output Artifacts: Text and Models
- Operationalization: yes
- Legacy: Legacy

Table 4.1. Classification of related work

	product line relation	construc- tiveness	area	meta- model	input arti- facts	output artifacts	operatio- nalization	life-cycle orientation
[14] Cybulski Reed	partially C	analysis	RR	no	req	classified req	yes	legacy
[17] Frakes et al. DARE-COTS	C+v	analysis	DA	no	doc	models	yes	same lc
[22] Hoppen- brouwers et al.	C	constr	DA	yes	doc	models	yes	legacy +same lc
[35] Mannion et al. 1999	C+v	select	RR, DA	yes	req	req	yes	de→ae
[34] Mannion et al. 1998	C+v	analysis	DA/RR	no	req	req	no	legacy
[43] ODM	C+v	constr	DA	no	systems	domain models	no	legacy
[52] Roseti, Werner	C+v	constr	DA	no	docs	conc models	no	legacy
[45] Stierna	C	analysis + constr	RR	no	req		yes	legacy
[49] von Knethen et al.	Partially C	select	RR	yes	req	req	no	legacy

As it can be seen from Tab. 4.1, there is no approach addressing commonality and variability that is general and constructive enough to serve as an approach for the elicitation of product line knowledge from documentation. So there is a need for a systematic approach to analyzing documentation for product line engineering. In the following sections, we describe an approach that has the right values in all classification dimensions.

4.4 Metamodel

In this section, we describe the metamodel that is the basis for our approach. In general, a metamodel is an information model for the information that can be expressed during modeling [18]. Our metamodel consists of different packages and is accompanied by extraction patterns that describe the transformation from one package to another.

4.4.1 Overview

The metamodel we introduce here describes the elements that can be found in documentation like user documentation, etc. The metamodel describes how to find relevant product line knowledge as well as typical product line artifacts in this documentation in different stages, described in four packages. The metamodel gives transformations between the two stages "documentation" and "product line artifact" by adding two conceptual stages, the requirements concept level, which describes general requirements concepts (as opposed to documentation artifacts that are notation-dependant realizations of requirements concepts), and the variability level, which describes the kinds of variabilities and commonalities that can be found in documentation. For each of those four stages, a model exists that we will describe in the following. We also describe the extraction patterns that provide transformations between the different packages of the model and thus can give guidance on how to find meaningful product line artifacts in user documentation.

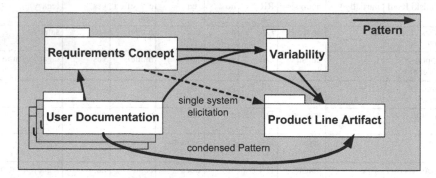

Fig. 4.3. Overview of the metamodel

The extraction model consists of four packages (see Fig. 4.3):

- A user documentation model describing the elements that are typically found in user documentations, manuals, and technical specifications (e.g., sections, glossaries, and lists).
- A requirements concept model describing concepts that are typically used in requirements specifications (e.g., roles, activities, functions) independent of the notation used.

- A variability concept model describing the principle commonality and variability concepts that can be found by comparing different documents and that are used for modeling.
- A product line artifact model describing elements of typical single system requirements specifications and product line models. These elements form a notation that is used to capture requirements (like Use Case elements, features or textual requirements). Those requirements can have, but do not need an explicit representation of variability.

The transition from one stage of the model to another stage is described by extraction patterns (specific rules-of-thumb or arguments derived from experience). The extraction patterns (Sect. 4.4.6) describe the transition between document elements and the other three parts of the metamodel. All arrows in the figure represent sets of extraction patterns. The extraction patterns from user documentation to product line artifacts ("condensed pattern" in Fig. 4.3) are of main interest when applying the approach. They give direct guidance on how to convert documentation elements into elements of a product line model or product line description. The other patterns give a transformation to or from the conceptual level. It is also possible to directly transform requirements concepts into requirements artifacts without searching for variabilities because the pattern sets are described independently. When we leave out the variabilities, we can also use the approach for requirements elicitation for single systems (see arrow "single system elicitation" in Fig. 4.3). All patterns have to relate explicitly to the model elements described in Figs. 4.4 and 4.5 so the models give a framework and basis for the extraction patterns.

4.4.2 User Documentation Model

Our user documentation model (see Fig. 4.4) describes the principal constituents of user documents. The document types that we analyze are user documentations or user manuals that describe the functions and usage of a system, and product descriptions that describe the features and technical details of a product. A document normally has a title, it often has a table of contents and a glossary, and it consists of several sections. A TOC entry normally corresponds to a heading in a section. A glossary consists of a list of terms that are described in paragraphs. A paragraph consists of sentences; it can also contain figures, tables, and formulas. A sentence is composed of phrases (language constructs consisting of a few words) and/or words. A phrase can also be a link (describing a reference to something inside or outside the document). Most elements of the user documentation model have attributes describing characteristics of this element (like highlighted for paragraphs and words, or numbered for lists); the attributes are not shown in the figure. This model describes the elements of a document on an adequate level for eliciting requirements concepts and finding product line artifacts.

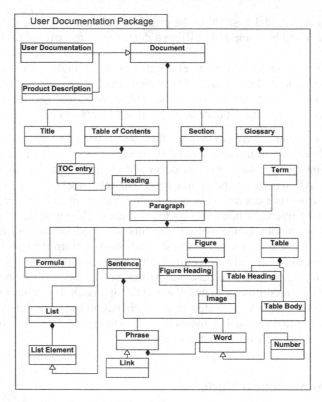

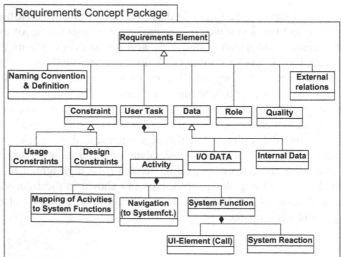

Fig. 4.4. User documentation model and requirements concept model

4.4.3 Requirements Concept Model

The requirements concept model (see Fig. 4.4) describes concepts that can be elicited from user documentation and that are normally realized or described by product line artifacts in requirements or product line specifications. The model describes the elements independent of a specific notation (like textual or Use Case representation). The most general requirements concept is a requirements element. A requirements element can be anything that is of value for a requirements specification. A requirements element can be a user task, a role, data, a naming convention, a constraint, or a relation to something in the environment of the system to be described. Data can either be I/O data or internal data; constraints can either be usage or design constraints. A user task that describes the high level task the user wants to perform with the help of the system can be decomposed into activities. Activities consist of navigation elements, system functions, and a mapping of the activities to functions.

4.4.4 Variability Model

A metamodel for modeling product lines has to support commonality and variability [41]. In the variability model, the variation aspects are described. In order to find different variability elements, the requirements elements (from the requirements concept model) found in different user documentations are compared. The variability model is a product line specific model as it describes commonality and variability between different products. Variabilities can normally be found by comparing different documents. Figure 4.5 shows the elements of the variability model. The metamodel contains the elements *commonality*, *alternative*, and *optional*. In general, it cannot be decided from scratch if elements that were found several times in different documents refer to a multiple selection, single selection or to a value reference. So, these three variability types are integrated into the one element *range*. The concrete variability type has to be determined during modeling and is not part of elicitation. Approaches on how to handle variability can be found in Chaps. 5–7.

4.4.5 Product Line Artifact Model

The fourth package of our conceptual extraction model is the product line artifact model (see Fig. 4.5). In this model, different elements of requirements specifications that can be used for single system modeling and for product line modeling during domain engineering are described. Unlike the requirements concept model, which describes the elements on a conceptual or semantic level, the product line artifact model describes requirements elements on a syntactic or notational level. In different kinds of requirements specifications, the same conceptual elements can be described with different notational elements, e.g., a role from the requirements concept model can be an actor in a Use Case description or a stakeholder description in a textual requirements specification.

As we also describe the application of our approach for product line modeling, we have to address variability, so we have integrated into our model a model of notation oriented

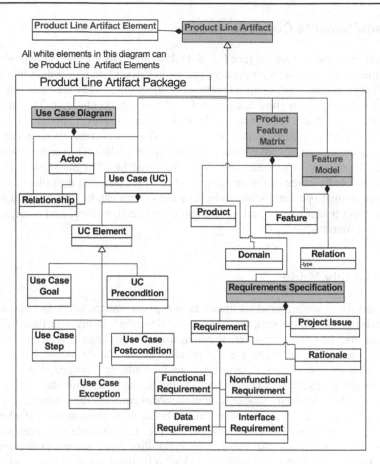

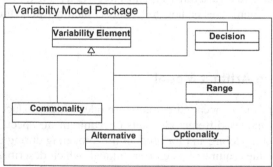

Fig. 4.5. Variability model and product line artifact model

variability here. As opposed to the model described in [41], which gives variability concepts, this model describes how variability can be documented in artifacts. The variability model we use here is the model described in [37]. This model describes generic product line assets. It is on the one hand specific enough to allow smooth transition of the artifacts into the other phases of the PuLSE Framework [6] but on the other hand it is also general enough to be valid and applicable for other product line engineering approaches like FAST [50] or the SEI approach [12]. Product line assets can be product line artifacts, describing the product line itself and decision models describing the constraints on the product line artifacts. Figure 4.5 shows the general structure of the metamodel for product line information. The grey boxes show the main artifacts, while the white boxes show their parts. A *ProductLineArtifact* is based on the model for general artifacts that consist of different representation elements (such as text, UML Models elements, Boxes). A *ProductLineArtifact* explicitly has to contain the concepts that make an artifact generic, like variation points or links to a decision model. In our model, product line artifacts can be use case diagrams, feature models, requirements specifications or product feature matrices. This is of course not a complete listing of all kinds of possible product line artifacts but only the artifacts that are used in the patterns. If new patterns are developed, the product line artifact package has to be extended with other artifacts.

In product line engineering, variability has to be made explicit in the product line artifacts. Different extensions (e.g., to UML Use Case diagrams or to textual Use Cases) exist that make the variability explicit and give support for the instantiation of requirements for application engineering. Some of these extensions use stereotypes or tags to describe variability, some extensions use extra elements to make variability explicit.

At the moment, we have specified different kinds of requirements notations: Use Cases, textual requirements specifications, and the product line specific notations: product feature matrix [42] and feature model [28]. Further requirements artifacts will be integrated into the product line artifact model. We added different representations here, as our general approach to product line modeling is customizable and highly depends on the requirements elements found in the organization that wants to do product line engineering. For performing product line engineering, we put variability elements on top of the existing notation and can thus keep the notation similar to the one used before. In our model, a Use Case diagram for example consists of Use Cases, actors and different relationships between the Use Cases and the actors. A textual Use Case (according to Cockburn [13]) consists of different elements like Use Case goal, precondition/post condition, Use Case exceptions, and the actual description of the Use Case, consisting of steps. Requirements specification can for example follow the IEEE Standard 830 [23]. A requirements specification is a textual document consisting of functional, nonfunctional, and data requirements, including project issues and rationales for the different requirements.

4.4.6 Extraction Patterns

As described in Sect. 4.3, requirements elements can be found in document elements of different forms. To allow a structured extraction, we developed a number of extraction patterns for different document elements and different requirements elements that describe a transition between document elements and the other three parts of the metamodel. In this section, we describe the template for the extraction patterns, showing some example patterns in this template form and giving a short description of all patterns.

Extraction Pattern Template

The extraction pattern template is used to store the patterns and describes the applicability of each pattern. The template consists of the following elements:

- *Name.* The *name* of the pattern and a unique number.
- *Short Description.* A *short description* of what the pattern should elicit.
- *Input.* The element that is converted into another element with the help of the extraction pattern. Input elements can be documentation model elements or requirements concept model elements (arrows in Fig. 4.3).
- *Output.* The type of the element that is the result of the extraction pattern. *Output* elements can be requirements concept model elements, variability model elements or product line artifact model elements (arrows in Fig. 4.3).
- *Recall.* The *recall* of a pattern describes its completeness. In Information Retrieval, the recall of a pattern is defined as the number of correct elements found by the extraction pattern divided by the number of correct output elements that can be found 3. In the template, the recall is given by a rough estimate of the correctness of the pattern. This estimate was determined experimentally (the determination is currently ongoing, so recall and precision do not yet exist for all patterns) and corrected by the authors. Possible values are "− −, −, o, +, ++."
- *Precision.* The *precision* of a pattern describes its correctness. In Information Retrieval, the precision of a pattern is defined as the number of correct elements found by the extraction pattern divided by the number of output elements found by the extraction pattern 3. In the template precision is given by a rough estimate, equally to recall. Possible values are "− −, −, o, +, ++."
- *Transition.* In the *transition* field the associated model of the input and output are given. Possible transitions are, e.g., "Documentation → Requirements Concept," "Documentation → Variability," or "Requirements Concept → Product Line."
- *Long Description.* In the *long description* field a longer description of the pattern including background information or rationale can be given.
- *Example.* In this field, an *example* of elements elicited with the pattern can be given.
- *Related Patterns.* This field gives the name and number of patterns that are somehow related to the described pattern (e.g., that generate the same or similar output).

Table 4.2 shows an example for a filled pattern.

Table 4.2. Template for pattern

name	1	heading-feature
short description		headings of sections or subsections typically contain features
input		heading
output		feature
recall		+
precision		++
transition		documentation → product line artifact
long description		as features describe functionalities that are of importance for the user, they are found at prominent places in the UD.
example		"Send SMS" as a heading of a mobile phone manual is a feature of the mobile phone
related patterns		–

List of Patterns

In this section we present the list of patterns. These patterns are the condensed pattern as it can be seen in Fig. 4.3, as the condensed pattern are normally used in the elicitation process. We do not give the complete template but only the short description and/or an explanation for the patterns:

Features
– Headings of sections or subsections typically contain features
– Features can be found in highlighted phrases (bold or italic font) or in extra paragraphs
– Technical descriptions or short descriptions of a system often contain lists of features

Use Cases
– Headings of sections or subsections typically contain names of Use Cases
– Phrases like "only by," "by using," "in the case of" can be markers for Use Case preconditions
– Use case preconditions and goals can typically be found in the beginning of a chapter
– Use case preconditions can be found before or within the description of a Use Case
– Phrases like "normally," "with the exception," "except" can mark Use Case extensions
– Numbered lists or bulleted lists are markers for an ordered processing of sequential steps and describe Use Case descriptions
– Sentences that describe interactions with the system in the form of "to do this…do that…" are Use Case descriptions
– Passive voice is typically a marker for system activity (e.g., "The volume of the radio is muted" = the system mutes the volume of the radio). These sentences can be used in the Use Case description.

Requirements
– Functional Requirements: User Interface and E/A Information and system functions
– Phrases like "press," "hold," "hold down," "press briefly," "select," "key in," "scroll," etc. mark a dialogue with the user interface or navigation elements

- The following phrases give hints for E/A elements: "type in," "enter," "transfer," etc.
- Activities or system functions are all those elements marked as features that contain a verb

Nonfunctional requirements
- Nonfunctional requirements cannot be found explicitly in user manuals, but hints to nonfunctional requirements and to qualities can be found
- Shortcuts are alternative usage scenarios and can therefore be a marker for a nonfunctional requirement like "the system shall be used in two alternative ways...."
- Adverbs and adjectives (longer, fast, quickly, etc.) can mark NFRs, especially if a phrase or sentence appears in the user manual once with the adverb, once without. (e.g., "to turn off the radio" and "to quickly turn off the radio")
- Technical data can give a clue to nonfunctional attributes of the system (e.g., size of the display, battery size, etc.)
- Numbers in the Use Case document can be hint for a nonfunctional requirement (why was exactly this number chosen?)

Project issues and usage constraints
- Project issues can be found in the beginning of a chapter. Project issues are related to usage constraints.
- Text passages that do not fit into the textual flow, that describe facts that do not fit to the rest of the description or that use words from another domain or from another subdomain of the system can be hints for project issues.

Commonalities and variabilities
- Arbitrary elements occurring only in one user manual probably are optional elements.
- Headings or subheadings that only occur in one of the documentations can be Use Cases that are wholly optional.
- Headings or subheadings that have slightly different names or headings or subheadings that have different names but are at the same place in the table of contents can be hints for alternative Use Cases.
- Phrases that differ in only one or a few words can be evidence for alternatives.
- If numerical values in the document differ they can be parametrical variabilities.
- Menu items that are described only in some of the documents can be hints for optional or alternative functionality (Use Cases or parts of Use Cases).

The patterns for features, use case elements, and requirements are used when analyzing one document; the commonality and variability patterns are used when comparing different documents. The patterns should not be seen as algorithms that always deliver a correct solution but rather as hints that can give a solution, but that can also be wrong in some cases.

New patterns can be derived from the metamodel by describing transitions from an element of one package to another (see Sect. 4.4.1). When building new patterns one has to make sure that the elements in the patterns are equal to existing metamodel elements (or the metamodel has to be extended).

4.4.7 Using the Metamodel

The metamodel can be used for the controlled transition of documentation elements to product line artifacts. The transition can either be performed directly (arrow "condensed extraction patterns" from user documentation to product line artifact in Fig. 4.3) or through the conceptual stages "requirements concept model" and "variability model." For the transition between the packages we have identified different extraction patterns. We will focus on the condensed patterns here. An example of such a condensed pattern is "an optional activity can be represented as an optional Use Case in a Use Case diagram."

Between all four parts of the model, extraction patterns can be defined to describe how elements are typically converted from one part of the model to another. A heading from the user documentation model can be a user task in the requirements concept model and can then be physically represented as a feature.

The metamodel serves as a basis and provides elements for the transitions. When analyzing documentation, we recommend to first use the patterns already defined (see "List of Patterns"). If an insufficient amount of information is found with the existing patterns, new patterns can be developed with the help of the metamodel. In order to develop a new pattern, the following steps should be followed:

- Shallowly analyze the documentation that you want to analyze: Which documentation elements from the user documentation model can be found in the documentation? Are there additional elements that are not described yet?
- Identify the requirements concepts that can be found in the new documentation elements or find additional requirements concepts.
- Identify the representation of variability in the documentation by comparing different documentations.
- Identify possible product line model elements in the documentation on the basis of examples.
- For each successful identification: Write a pattern describing the transition from one stage to the other and validate the pattern by applying it in your documentation.
- For each additional element of one of the four stages that you found: Extend the model with the new element, identify relations of the new element to the others.

By following these steps, the metamodel will be extended and further validated and new patterns can be found.

With the help of the new and existing transformations based on the metamodel, elements from user documentation can be integrated into product line models, describing the requirements on a product line.

4.5 Method

The process of analyzing a requirements document using information retrieval ideas [10] in a semiautomated process opens up the possibility to capitalize on the wealth of domain knowledge in existing systems considered for migration to next-generation systems. Converting these existing requirements into domain models can reduce cost and risk while reducing time-to-market. In this section, we describe the extraction method that is based on the metamodel and uses the patterns described in Sect. 4.4. This method guides product line engineers in finding the right documentation, in performing the analysis, and in preparing the results for further steps like scoping or model building.

4.5.1 Method Overview

CaVE is an approach enhanced with techniques for structured and controlled integration of user documentation of existing systems into the product line. With CaVE, common and variable features, Use Case elements, decisions and requirements can be elicited.

We restrict our description here to the extraction of Use Case elements. As existing systems are the basis for this approach, it can be seen as a reengineering approach for transferring user documentation into basic elements for product line Use Cases. The approach consists of the following phases (see Fig. 4.6):

- *Preparation.* The product line engineer prepares the user documentation and selects the appropriate extraction pattern
- *Search.* The product line engineer analyzes the documents with the selected extraction patterns and marks the elements found
- *Selection and change.* The selected elements are put together into partial product line artifacts and presented to the expert who can change elements and add additional information.

The first two steps of the approach can be performed by persons who just have a slight domain understanding, they do not have to be domain experts. The third step requires involvement of domain experts. We will now describe the three steps in more detail.

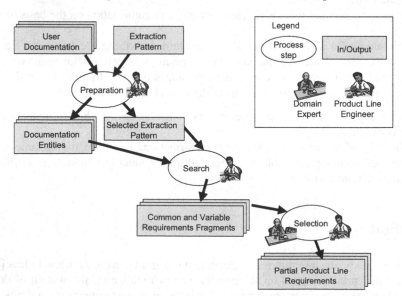

Fig. 4.6. An outline of the extraction approach

4.5.2 Preparation

Preparation consists of the five sub steps *collection, selection, division, browsing,* and *pattern selection*. During the collection step, the product line analyst collects all user documentations for the systems that should be integrated into the product line and for those systems that are related in order to have available all information that is needed. For analysis, all user documentations of existing systems in the domain should be considered. As parallel reading of more than one document requires divided attention and leads to lower performance [51], the number of documents to be read in parallel should be reduced to a minimum. So, if there are more than three systems in the selecting phase, the product line analyst selects three documents that cover the variety of systems to be compared (e.g., a documentation of a low-end system, a documentation of a high end system and a typical system) for an initial search in the documents. The other documents can be used for validation. After selecting the three typical documentations, the product line analyst divides them into manageable and comparable parts. Experience has shown that 3–10 pages (e.g. comparable sections) are a suitable size for the parts to compare. In the browsing step, for each of those manageable parts (or for a subset of those parts that includes typical sub-domains), the product line analyst browses through them in order to decide the amount of variability in them. There are two alternatives:

– If the documents differ in more than one third of the text, the product line analyst shall process them one after another in the second step and choose the biggest document as the document to start with the analysis.
– If the difference of the documents is less than one third of the text, the product line analyst shall compare the documents in parallel in the further steps.

The value of one third is a value we experienced to be suitable in the case studies.

In pattern selection, the patterns to be applied are selected. Generally, not all types of product line artifacts are needed, so only a subset of the complete pattern list is chosen. In some cases, e.g., during scoping, only features are needed, so only the patterns related to features are selected; sometimes only use case elements are needed. If several manuals can be compared, the variability related patterns are always selected.

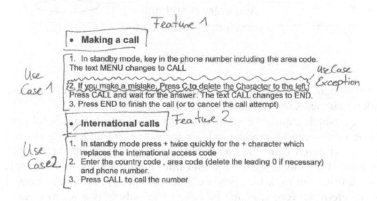

Fig. 4.7. Example of marked user documentation

4.5.3 Search

In the search step, the elements that should be identified when applying the approach are marked in the documents and tagged.

With the help of the subset of extraction patterns that were selected, which are not complete but help in finding a relevant part of the features, Use Case elements, other requirements, and variabilities, the user documents should be marked (e.g., with different colors for different Use Case elements and for variabilities).

Figure 4.7 shows how the elements can be marked. The boxes are potential features of the system; the two enumerations are Use Cases and there is a potential use case exception in one Use Case. There are two different ways to browse through the documents and mark the elements:

- *Pattern by Pattern.* When manually following the approach for the first time, it might be useful to concentrate on one pattern or a group of patterns (e.g., all pattern eliciting features or all patterns having similar input elements) browse through the document with those patterns in mind, and mark all elements that can be extracted with this one pattern or this group of patterns. Browsing through the documents is a bit time consuming, but doing it this way makes sure that all elements are marked.
- *Integrated.* When following the process for the second time, or if there are not so many elements to be marked, it is also possible to browse through the documents with all patterns at hand. This significantly shortens the time to search for elements, but one must be sure to have all applicable patterns in mind.

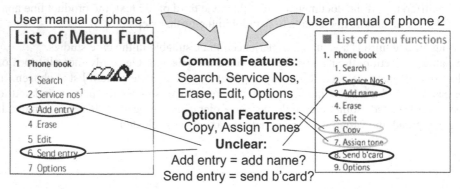

Fig. 4.8. Variability in documentation

Both ways have their advantages and disadvantages (like completeness, time), so both ways of marking elements are possible.

The elements, which should be sized from one word to at most 5–6 lines, that were identified to be useful can be marked only in the document and presented to the expert, but can also be extracted from the document and tagged with attributes containing the information needed for modeling the product line. Figure 4.8 shows how variability between documentations can look like. Some elements appear in both user manuals, they are common. Some elements (copy, assign tones) appear only in one user manual, they seem to be optional. For some elements it is unclear which variability type they have because it is not clear if they mean the same or not (add entry/add name, send entry/send bcard). The variability of those elements has to be further clarified in the selection step.

4.5.4 Selection

In the last step selection, the extracted and tagged elements have to be validated and changed by a domain expert. For instance, not all text excerpts marked as possible Use Case elements really are elements of a Use Case, not all elements marked as optional in the user documentation will really be optional in the new product line. So a domain expert has to judge whether the extracted elements should be used for modeling the product line Use Cases, features, etc. or not. In this step, the expert can change the "Use Case type" and "var type" in the tagged notation, extend or change the text of the element. The relations are used to make comparisons between the documents easier, to establish traceability to the source documents and, with tool-based selection, to support navigation in the elements and between the documentations.

With the help of the extracted document elements and the tables that contain the condensed information and the variability between documents, product line artifacts like product line Use Cases including variability (as, e.g., described in [27] or [20]) can be built. We already integrated the information found with our approach into use cases built in the PLUC notation (Product Line Use Cases) that is described in Chap. 11. Variability found in the documents when applying the CaVE approach is represented in tags and other extensions of use case elements. The integration is described in [15].

As the actual modeling is not part of the approach but only the extraction of candidates for models, we will not go into details for modeling here. Further details on modeling can be found in Chap. 11.

4.6 Validation of the Approach

In this section we describe the validation of the CaVE-approach in an experiment and in an industrial case study. The experiment gives evidence of the internal validity of the approach; the case study shows the external validity in practical application and shows the expert load reduction. We will give a detailed description of the experiment and the experimental results and will shortly describe the industrial case study. A detailed description of the case study as well as two additional, more explorative case studies that we performed in the action research phase of our research can be found in [24].

4.6.1 Industrial Case Study

The case study where we applied the CaVE approach was performed together with the Company SIEDA Gmbh, Kaiserslautern. The company "SIEDA – Systemhaus für intelligente EDV Anwendungen GmbH" was founded in Kaiserslautern in 1993 and has a staff of 14 employees at the moment.

The goal of the project, the case study was performed in was to derive an additional product from the existing products and, in parallel, to introduce product line concepts to their software systems. The new product should be a so-called light product to a low-end market.

Performing the Case Study

The current product line of planning systems for services in different shifts (roster system) of the Sieda GmbH consists of two large products (one for hospitals, one for fire departments) that are customized into a larger number of customer-specific products. A new, so-called "light product" with fewer features than the other products should be derived from the existing product line. In order to systematize the derivation of the new features, the CaVE Approach should be applied to derive the common and variable features of the existing systems, so a product-feature matrix [42] should be built. To build this matrix the staff from IESE in their roles as product line engineers used the CaVE approach and analyzed the user documentation of the two existing system. During the case study, we performed the following steps:

Preparation
The documentation of the two main products consisted of 28 pages each. As there were only two documentations and the amount of 2 * 28 pages is manageable for an analysis, the documents did not have to be split but could be analyzed in parallel and as a whole.

As the primary goal of the analysis activities was to find features, the patterns that extract features and the domains and subdomains the features can be found in, were selected from the set of patterns for the extraction. Also, the patterns that should find variability were selected for the analysis.

Search
The documentation was analyzed in parallel by the product line analyst with the help of the selected patterns. The analysis with the CaVE patterns produced 118 features, 11 domains and eight subdomains with their domain descriptions. The elements were marked in the documentation and after marking, collected in a preliminary product feature matrix. We also produced domain descriptions that describe what a domain is with the help of the documentation. For further description and examples for product feature matrix and domain descriptions see [24,25].

Selection
This preliminary product feature matrix (for an excerpt, see Tab. 4.3) which contained the features of two of the systems developed in the company (Orbis and Orbis Rettungsdienst), was presented to the domain experts (the lead architect and the CEO of the company) in order to

- Identify features that were extracted wrongly
- Identify additional features that were not found by the patterns
- Identify those features from the existing systems that should become part of the new light product

As a result of these activities, five of the existing features were identified as wrong or as duplicates and 17 additional features were found, so the final list consisted of 130 features. Later on, it was determined which of these features should be part of the Orbis light system (this step is not part of the CaVE Approach but can be seen as a modeling step). The domain descriptions did not have to be corrected at all.

Table 4.3. Excerpt of the product feature matrix in the case study

domains	subdomains	feature	values	product 1	product 2	product 3
system administration	general			X	X	
		support of different services	early, day, late, nightshift	X	X	
		stand-by		X	X	
	configuration			X	X	
		tariff-support		X		X
		support for free time		X	X	
....		......				

Validating the Case Study

In order to validate the case study we counted the correct and wrong features, domains and subdomains in the different stages of the case study. Furthermore we tracked the time needed to complete the different stages of the product feature matrix. With this quantitative data we are able calculate the correctness and completeness of the approach for this case study. Additionally, we developed a questionnaire to get qualitative data on expert opinion on the approach and to get qualitative measurement. To compute correctness and completeness according to the formulas for recall and precision of an information retrieval approach, we used the following formulas:

- *Completeness (Features, Domains)* =
  Number of correct (Features, Domains) identified by CaVE/
  Number of correct (Features, Domains) in the final product feature matrix
- *Correctness (Features, Domains)* =
  Number of correct (Features, Domains) identified by CaVE/
  Number of all (Features, Domains) identified by CaVE

With these formulas, we got the correctness and completeness values shown in Tab. 4.4 below:

At about 87% , the completeness is not as high as the correctness at 95.5%. With a correctness value of over 95% the results of the CaVE analysis are quite trustworthy but this data also shows that it is essential to have a selection step where the domain experts identify errors and find additional elements. This is fleshed out by the fact that in the analysis step, the non-experts could not identify wrong features or recognize duplicate features that had (slightly) different names.

In order to find out the value of the approach for the domain experts, we developed a questionnaire and let the two experts fill out the questionnaire after the selection step.

As we only have two experts in this case study and thus only two data points the results are, of course, not significant. But the results can give a trend in estimating if there is expert load reduction by using CaVE.

We asked the experts at how many hours they would assess the analysis; their estimate was 16 h. We compared the results with the actual time of the analysis. The total time for the analysis was 9.6 h. Of these 9.6 h, 3.3 h were expert hours and 6.3 h were non-expert (product line analyst) hours.

Table 4.4. Correctness and completeness of the approach

element	correctness of CaVE%	completeness of CaVE%
features	95.6	85.3
domains	100	100
subdomains	90.9	76.9
average	**95.5**	**87.4**

The analysis of the questionnaire showed that the value of the analysis to the experts (16 h for both experts) was even higher than the time for the whole analysis (9.6 h including expert and non-expert hours). This shows that in this case, there was a even a significant overall load reduction, not only an expert load reduction. When we compare the 16 h value of the analysis with the 3.3 h the experts actually spent with validating the results we have an expert load reduction of 12.6 h, which is a reduction of 78.8% (12.6 h/16 h) compared to the value estimated by the experts.

Overall, the case study was very successful. The correctness and completeness of the results could be validated as described and a significant expert load reduction could be shown. As there is no fixed value of correctness and completeness above which one can say that the approach produces "good" results, and since the correctness and completeness of an extraction approach influence each other a completeness of 87% and a correctness of 95% for such an extraction approach can be seen as highly acceptable values. As expert load reduction is the main goal of the approach the high correctness of the approach is a very important issue. The approach produced very few "false positives". The expert's time is not spent so much on deleting wrong results during the selection step but on finding new and innovative features.

4.6.2 Controlled Experiment

Performing the Experiment

In order to show the internal validity of the approach, we performed a controlled experiment where 45 students who did not know the approach before applied CaVE in controlled settings.

The experiment was applied at the University of Applied Science in Mannheim in the summer of 2003. The experiment design was a 2×2 non-related between subject design [5], so the students were randomly distributed into four groups (see Tab. 4.5). The goal of the experiment was to compare standard elicitation with CaVE. Standard elicitation, as it is normally done in projects, is done by browsing through documents and searching for elements. Two of the groups got a description of CaVE and of the patterns they should apply, and two other groups received a description of what features, use cases, requirements, and variabilities are and what they look like. Two groups first had to analyze the documentation of an information system (parts of the documentation for 3 variants of a word processor), two groups analyzed the documentation of an embedded system (parts of the documentation for three variants of a cell phone). Table 4.5 shows the distribution of

Table 4.5. Distribution of groups in the experiment

group	first run		second run	
1	standard elicit.	cell phone	CaVE	word proc.
2	CaVE	word proc.	standard elicit.	cell phone
3	standard elicit.	word proc.	CaVE	cell phone
4	CaVE	cell phone	standard elicit.	word proc.

groups in the two experiment runs that were performed. By making two runs with different distributions, the learning effect can be measured and the effect of the documentation can be excluded.

For each run, 1 h of time was allotted. During this time, the students had to understand the elicitation approach, browse through the documentation, and mark documentation elements they found when applying the approach in different colors. They also had to fill in a characterization questionnaire about their development know-how (e.g., in the area of product lines and information extraction) and, after each run, a questionnaire about their experiences when applying the approach.

After each run, the documentation and the questionnaires were collected. The results were compared with a reference solution (this reference was built by an experienced product line and requirements analyst who had no experience with the CaVE approach). All in all, about 5,000 different elements were marked in the documentation of the 45 students and about 4,000 of them were correct as compared to the reference.

Validating the Experiment

The goal of the experiment was, to show the completeness and correctness of the approach under controlled conditions. So, the marked elements and the correct elements were counted for each student and for each artifact type and accumulated afterwards. By using formulas for correctness and completeness similar to the ones described in the previous section, we arrived at the values that are shown in Tab. 4.6. The items that are better in each case are marked bold. The table shows that average correctness of the results is quite high, at 82 and 79%, respectively. The average correctness of the CaVE approach is higher than standard elicitation; the same holds for features options and alternatives. But for Use Case Elements and Requirements, the correctness of standard elicitation is better.

Table 4.6. Completeness and correctness of the experiment results

correctness	features	UC elem	requirem	options	alternatives	average
CaVE	**96.0%**	72.1%	51.8%	**79.2%**	**60.7%**	**82.2%**
standard	94.0%	**77.5%**	**62.7%**	43.3%	44.9%	79.4%

completeness	features	UC elem	requirem	options	alternatives	average
CaVE	**13.2%**	4.0%	**1.1%**	**3.0%**	**3.6%**	**5.3%**
standard	6.8%	**5.8%**	0.8%	0.8%	2.9%	4.1%

The average completeness of the CaVE results is also better at 5% compared to 4%, but the overall completeness is very low. This can follow from the fact that the participants did not have enough time to mark all documentations completely. More than 95% of the participants stated in the questionnaire that they did not have enough time for the analysis.

The results for features and variabilities are quite encouraging, more (in the case of options significantly more) and more correct elements could be found. But for Use Case Elements standard elicitation was better. For finding Use Case elements, CaVE should be improved, e.g., by looking for better patterns for use cases or by organizing the pattern list that was given to the students in a different way.

4.7 Conclusions and Future Research

In this chapter we have described an approach for the extraction of basic requirements items from legacy user manuals which can be used as information for product line engineering, especially for the early phases of scoping and product line modeling. The bases of the approach are a metamodel and a set of extraction patterns. The metamodel and the patterns described in Sect. 4.4 support the extraction process by giving concrete guidelines on how to identify items on a rather syntactical level, without having a deep domain understanding. At the moment, there exist about 30 patterns. This list of patterns will be extended in the future. We do not expect the list of patterns to be complete; there will always be new kinds of elements to find and new relations to discover. But it can be expected that a significant amount of product line model elements can be extracted from user documentation with the help of the process described within the approach and the patterns, although documents significantly differ with regard to layout, structure, and content.

The approach gives an extraction method that guides the extraction process. With the approach, different kinds of product line artifacts (like Features, Use Cases elements, functional and nonfunctional requirements) can be identified in user documentations by a non-expert and can later be approved and used for modeling by domain experts. The main advantage of this pattern based approach can be seen in the expert load reduction and therefore in the support of product line introduction in practice by avoiding the bottleneck of the workload of the domain experts.

In this chapter we have described the elements of the approach and its evaluation in a controlled experiment and a case study. Our general experiences are that the approach with its process steps and the patterns support the finding of relevant elements that can be used for modeling. In the industrial case study, with the help of the approach, more than 90% of a product feature matrix, an artifact that is often used in product line scoping [42], could be built.

In the future, more case studies are planned. The case studies should further demonstrate the applicability and usefulness of the approach in different situations.

Additionally, a tool is currently being developed to support the extraction process and to realize the patterns. Tool support can increase the efficiency of processing and the correctness of the results significantly for the techniques proposed and can further relieve domain experts and product line engineers. With a tool, models can be generated semi-automatically and thus efficiency and better traceability can be easily achieved.

As further work, we are currently about to extend the focus of our approach and integrate the approach into reengineering and architecture recovery methods [16] to broaden the information base that is used for building a product line architecture.

Acknowledgments

We want to thank Alessandro Fantechi, Stefania Gnesi and Giuseppe Lami for fruitful cooperation within the CAFÉ Project. We also thank Jaejoon Lee, Dirk Muthig, Clémentine Nebut, Timo Käkölä, and Sonnhild Namingha for valuable comments on the chapter and Klaus Schmid and Jörg Dörr for supporting this work.

This work was partially supported by the Eureka Σ!2023 Programme, ITEA (ip00004, Project CAFÉ; ip02009, Project FAMILIES).

References

1. Alexander, I., Kiedaisch, F.: Towards recyclable system requirements. Proceedings of the 9th IEEE International Conference on Engineering of Computer-Based Systems (ECBS 2002), 2002, pp 9–16
2. Ambriola, V., Gervasi, V.: Processing natural language requirements. In Proceedings of 13th IEEE Conference on Automated Software Engineering (IEEE, New York 1997) pp 36–45
3. Baeza-Yates, R., Ribeiro-Neto, B.: *Modern Information Retrieval* (Addison-Wesley, Reading, MA 1999)
4. Basili, V., Caldiera, G., Rombach, D.: The goal question metric approach. In: *Encyclopedia of Software Engineering*, ed by Marciniak, J.J. (Wiley, New York 1994)
5. Basili, V., Selby, R., Hutchens, D.: Experimentation in software engineering. IEEE Trans. Softw. Eng. **12**(7), 733–743 (1986)
6. Bayer, J., Flege, O., Knauber, P., Laqua, R., Muthig, D., Schmid, K., Widen, T., DeBaud, J.-M.: PuLSE: a methodology to develop software product lines. Proceedings of the 5th ACM SIGSOFT Symposium on Software Reusability (SSR'99) (ACM, New York 1999) pp 122–131
7. Bayer, J., Muthig, D., Widen, T.: Customizable domain analysis. Proceedings of the 1st International Symposium on Generative and Component-Based Software Engineering (GCSE'99), 1999, pp 178–194
8. Bayer, J., Girard, J.-F., Wuerthner, M., DeBaud, J.-M., Apel, M.: Transitioning legacy assets to a product line architecture. Proceedings of the 7th European Software Engineering Conference. Lecture Notes in Computer Science, vol 1687, 1999, pp 446–463
9. Becks, A., Köller, J.: Automatically structuring textual requirements scenarios. Proceedings of 14th IEEE Conference on Automated Software Engineering (IEEE, New York 1999) pp 271–274
10. Chastek, G., Donohoe, P., Kang, K., Thiel, S.: Product line analysis: a practical introduction. Technical report CMU/SEI-2001-TR-001 (Software Engineering Institute, Carnegie Mellon University 2001)
11. Chikofsky, E., Cross, J.H.: Reverse engineering and design recovery: a taxonomy. IEEE Softw. **7**(1), 13–17 (1990)
12. Clements, P.C., Northrop, L.: *Software Product Lines: Practices and Patterns* (Addison-Wesley, Reading, MA 2001)
13. Cockburn, A.: *Writing Effective Use Cases* (Addison-Wesley, Reading, MA 2001)
14. Cybulsky, J., Reed, K.: Requirements classification and reuse. Crossing domain boundaries. Proceedings of the International Conference on Software Reuse (ICSR-6). Lecture Notes in Computer Science, vol 1844, 2000, pp 190–210
15. Fantechi, A., Gnesi, S., John, I., Lami, G., Dörr, J.: Elicitation of use cases for product lines. International Workshop on Product Family Engineering (PFE5). Lecture Notes in Computer Science, vol 3014, 2004, pp 152–167
16. Forster, T., Ganesan, D., Girard, J.-F., Grund, M., John, I., Knodel, J.: Combination of requirements recovery and architecture recovery for existing systems. Deliverable of the FAMILIES project and IESE-report, 058.05/E (IESE, Fraunhofer 2005)
17. Frakes, W., Prieto-Diaz, R., Fox, C.: DARE-COTS: a domain analysis support tool. Proceedings of the 17th International Conference of the Chilean Computer Science Society (SCCC'97), 1997
18. Frankel, D.: *Model Driven Architecture* (OMG, New York 2003)

19. Gacek, C., Knauber, P., Schmid, K., Clements, P.: Successful software product line development in a small organization: a case study. IESE-report no. 013.01/E (IESE, Fraunhofer 2001)
20. Halmans, G., Pohl, K.: Communicating the variability of a software-product family to customers. J. Softw. Syst. Model. **2**(1), 15–36 (2003)
21. Hevner, A.R., March, S.T., Park, J., Ram, S.: Design science in information systems research. MIS Q. **28**(1), 75–105 (2004)
22. Hoppenbrouwers, J., van den Heuvel, W., Hoppenbrouwers, S., Weigand, H., Troyer, O.: The Grammalizer: a CASE Tool based on textual analysis. Unpublished paper, Submitted to Tools USA'99. http://infolab.uvt.nl/pub/hoppenbrouwersj-1999-43.pdf (1999)
23. IEEE-Std 830-1998: IEEE Guide to Software Requirements Specifications (IEEE, New York 1998)
24. John, I., Dörr, J., Schmid, K.: Building domain models based on legacy system descriptions. Deliverable of the CAFÉ project and IESE report 004/04/E (IESE, Fraunhofer 2004). http://www.iese.fhg.de/pdf_files/ iese-004_04.pdf
25. John, I., Kohler, K., Schmettow, M.: Use line – process description and case study. IESE report 074/04E (IESE, Fraunhofer 2004)
26. John, I., Muthig, D., Schmettow, M.: The state of the practice of systematic software development/product line development in Germany. IESE report 080/04E (IESE, Fraunhofer 2004)
27. John, I., Muthig, D.: Tailoring use cases for product line modeling. Proceedings of the International Workshop on Requirements Engineering for Product Lines (REPL'02), 2002, pp 26–32
28. Kang, K., Cohen, S., Hess, J., Novak, W., Peterson, S.: Feature-oriented domain analysis (FODA) feasibility study. Technical report, CMU/SEI-90-TR-21. (Software Engineering Institute, Carnegie Mellon University 1990)
29. Kasunic, M.: Synthesis: a reuse-based software development methodology, process guide, version 1.0. Technical report (Software Productivity Consortium Services Corporation 1992)
30. Knauber, P. et al: Applying product line concepts in small and medium-sized companies. IEEE Softw. **17**(5), 88–95 (2000)
31. Kuusela, J., Savolainen, J.: Requirement engineering for product families. Proceedings of the 22nd International Conference on Software Engineering (ICSE) (ACM, New York 2000) pp 61–69
32. Luisa, M. et al: Market research for requirements analysis using linguistic tools. Require. Eng. J. **9**(1), 40–56 (2004)
33. Maarek, Y.S., Berry, D.M.: The use of lexical affinities in requirements extraction. Proceedings of the 5th International Workshop on Software Specification and Design, Pittsburg, PA, 1989
34. Mannion, M. et al: Using viewpoints to define domain requirements. IEEE Softw. **15**(1), 95–102 (1998)
35. Mannion, M., Keepence, B., Kaindl, H., Wheadon, J.: Reusing single system requirements for application family requirements. Proceedings of the 21st International Conference on Software Engineering (ICSE'99) (ACM, New York 1999) pp 453–462
36. Melchisedech, R.: Investigation of requirements documents written in natural language. Require. Eng. **3**(2), 91–97 (1998)
37. Muthig, D.: A lightweight approach facilitating the incremental transition into software product line. PhD theses in Experimental Software Engineering (IRB, Fraunhofer 2002)
38. Nattoch Dag, J. et al: A feasibility study of automated support for similarity analysis of natural language requirements in market-driven development. Require. Eng. J. **7**(1), 20–33 (2002)
39. Rayson, P., Emmet, L., Garside, R., Sawyer, P.: The REVERE project. Proceedings of the International Conference on Applications of Natural Language to Information Systems (NLDB 2000), 2000, pp 288–300
40. Reason, P., Bradbury, H. (eds): *Handbook of Action Research* (Sage, Beverly Hills, CA 2001)
41. Schmid, K., John, I.: A customizable approach to full-life cycle variability management. Sci. Comput. Program. **53**(3) (2004)
42. Schmid, K.: Planning software reuse – a disciplined scoping approach for software product lines. PhD theses in Experimental Software Engineering (IRB, Fraunhofer 2003)
43. Software Technology for Adaptable, Reliable Systems (STARS): Organization Domain Modeling (ODM) Guidebook, Version 2.0 (1996)
44. Sommerville, I.: *Software Engineering* (Addison-Wesley, Reading, MA 2001)
45. Stierna, E.: Requirements reuse in support of the aviation mission planning system migration to the joint mission planning system. Masters thesis (Naval Postgraduate School, Monterey, CA 2000)
46. Tschaitschian, B., Wenzel, C., John, I. Tuning the quality of informal software requirements with KARAT. Proceedings of the 3rd International Workshop on Requirements Engineering: Foundations of Software Quality (REFSQ'97), 1997
47. van der Linden, F.: Software product families in Europe: the ESAPS and CAFÉ projects. IEEE Softw. **19**(4), 41–49 (2002)

48. Von der Maßen, T., Lichter, H.: Modeling variability by UML use case diagrams. Proceedings of the International Workshop on Requirements Engineering for Product Lines (REPL'02), 2002, pp 19–25
49. Von Knethen, A., Paech, B., Kiedaisch, F., Houdek, F. Systematic requirements recycling through abstraction and traceability. Proceedings of Joint International Requirements Engineering Conference (ACM, New York 2002) pp 512–519
50. Weiss, D., Lai, C.: *Software Product Line Engineering* (Addison-Wesley, Reading, MA 1999)
51. Wickens, C.-D.: Processing resources in attention. In: *Varieties of Attention*, ed by Parasuraman, R., Davies, R. (Academic, New York 1984) pp 63–101
52. Zopelari Roseti, M., Werner, C.: A knowledge acquisition systematic within the domain analysis context. Proceedings of the 2nd Ibero-American Workshop on Requirements Engineering, Buenos Aires, Argentina, 1999

5 Scenario-Based Application Requirements Engineering

S. Bühne, G. Halmans, K. Lauenroth, and K. Pohl

Abstract

In product line engineering, the application requirements engineers have to ensure both a high degree of reuse and the satisfaction of stakeholder needs. The vast number of possible variant combinations and the influences of the selection of one variant on different requirements models is a challenge for the consistent reuse of product line requirements. Only if the requirements engineers are aware of all product line capabilities (variabilities and commonalities), they are able to decide whether a stakeholder requirement can be satisfied by the product line or not. In this chapter we present a novel approach for the development of application requirements specifications. For this approach, we use an orthogonal variability model with associated requirements scenarios to support requirements engineers during the elicitation, negotiation, documentation, and validation of product line requirements. The presented approach tackles the existing challenges during application requirements engineering by the iterative use of the orthogonal variability model (abstract view) and the requirements scenarios (concrete view) of the product line.

5.1 Introduction

The goal of product line engineering is to develop applications based on predefined common and variable assets [11,34]. The development process in product line engineering is subdivided into the development of product line artifacts for reuse (*domain engineering*) and the development of individual applications with reuse (*application engineering*). Figure 5.1 shows the product line engineering framework of the FAMILIES project [5] with the respective activities in domain and application engineering.

5.1.1 Requirements Engineering within Product Line Engineering

In domain requirements engineering, common and variable requirements are defined for reuse in application requirements engineering. The identification and definition of requirements for reuse has been introduced in Chap. 4. This chapter focuses on application requirements engineering, where a multitude of application requirements specifications can be developed by reusing the requirements artifacts that were defined in domain engineering. If the application stakeholders have specific requirements that cannot be fulfilled by the product line (further called *application specific requirements*), either the existing product line requirements must be adapted, or new application requirements artifacts[1] have to be developed to satisfy the application stakeholder's needs. In this chapter, we use the term *application stakeholder* to refer to a role that represents customers, users, domain experts, IT experts, and other people who have an interest in the development of the application.

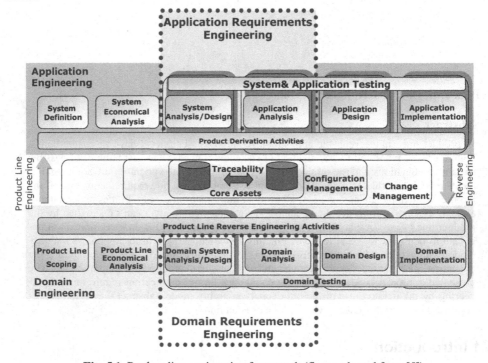

Fig. 5.1. Product line engineering framework (figure adapted from [5])

We differentiate among three major types of requirements: product line requirements, application requirements, and stakeholder requirements.

- *Product line requirements* are developed in domain engineering for being reused in application engineering.
- *Application requirements* are requirements that are defined for the application in the application's requirements specification. Application requirements can either be requirements that have been derived from product line requirements by reuse or can be requirements that are specific to the application under consideration (application specific requirements). *Application-specific requirements* result from differences that exist between stakeholder requirements and product line requirements. We call such differences *requirements deltas*.
- *Stakeholder requirements* are requirements that are elicited from the application stakeholders.

---

[1] The term *requirements artifact* is used to describe different types of requirements, e.g., goals, scenarios, functional requirements, quality requirements, etc. as well as parts of one artifact, such as steps or actors of a scenario.

5.1.2 Application Requirements Engineering

In single systems engineering, the requirements engineering process is traditionally described by the elicitation, negotiation, documentation, validation, and the management of requirements [13,30].

During *elicitation* the stakeholders, requirements, constraints, existing standards, and laws that have influence on the intended system have to be identified to establish a common understanding of the problem domain and the intended application. The *negotiation* task has to establish a common agreement about elicited requirements among all stakeholders (cf. [15]). During requirements *validation*, the elicited and documented requirements are analyzed and checked by the stakeholders to ensure that the right system will be built. The *documentation* of requirements is the task of writing down elicited requirements as well as negotiation and validation results. Requirements are documented using different (specification) languages to provide individual requirements views for the other tasks (e.g., negotiation) and finally to develop a requirements specification, which fulfills the quality attributes defined in the IEEE 830 standard [21]. Even if these tasks have a preferred order, they are not performed in a procedural order. Rather, they closely interact during requirements engineering. The *management* task is an administrative task in requirements engineering and has the goal to coordinate, schedule, and document the requirements engineering activities and changes [13].

Application requirements engineering (in software product line engineering) has the same intention as requirements engineering for single systems – the development of a requirements specification for an application. Additionally, application requirements engineering has to satisfy the goal of product line engineering, which is to develop applications by reusing predefined artifacts. Consequently, in application requirements engineering each requirements engineering task has to consider the goal of reusing product line requirements. Sommerville and Sawyer indicate that the reuse of requirements necessitates awareness of the reusable requirements, i.e., what is reusable (see [33], p. 63). Consequently, the requirements engineers in application engineering must be aware of the product line capabilities, i.e., they need to know all common and variable requirements that the product line offers.

Figure 5.2 presents the five tasks of application requirements engineering based on the previously identified tasks in requirements engineering. It furthermore illustrates the major inputs of application requirements engineering that originate from application stakeholders, domain engineering, and application design. The application stakeholders provide their *requirements, constraints, decisions,* etc. Domain requirements engineering provides the basic inputs for the efficient reuse, i.e., the *product line variability model* and the *product line requirements*. The application design process provides the estimated *change effort* to develop application specific requirements. The input from application design is optional and only provided, if a change effort estimation is requested from application requirements engineering. Figure 5.2 only shows the main information flows, thus there no information flows are shown from application requirements engineering to application design, domain engineering, or to the stakeholders. The output of the application requirements engineering process is the *application requirements specification*. This specification comprises all requirements that have been reused from the product line and all application specific requirements, which have been developed by considering the delta between requested stakeholder requirements and provided product line requirements.

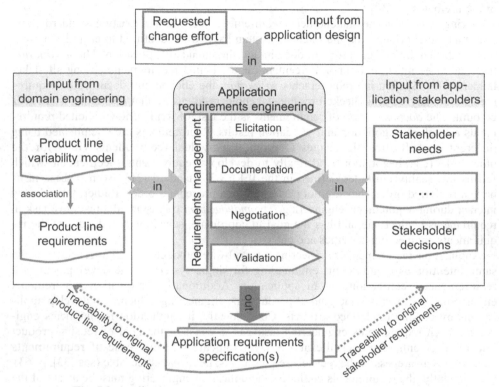

Fig. 5.2. Application requirements engineering process with its major inputs

5.1.3 Challenges During Application Requirements Engineering

In the following paragraphs, we briefly describe specific activities and challenges that the application requirements engineers have to deal with during application requirements engineering, to achieve the goal of a *high degree of reuse*.

Specific activities during *elicitation* are the elicitation of stakeholder requirements under consideration of product line requirements and the communication of product line capabilities (i.e., common and variable product line requirements) to the application stakeholders.

A specific activity during the *negotiation* of application requirements is establishing agreement with all stakeholders about application-specific requirements. That means agreement about: which product line requirements satisfy the application stakeholder's needs best; which derived product line requirements have to be adapted; and which requirements have to be developed from scratch. Furthermore, the change effort for the development of application specific requirements (considering the deltas) has to be estimated during the negotiation task to support trade-off decisions.

Specific activities during the *validation* of requirements are the validation whether application requirements satisfy the application stakeholder's intentions and the validation whether the composition and adaptation of application requirements is correct. Therefore, the validation has to check whether all defined dependencies between product line requirements have been considered, and whether these requirements are not in conflict with the stakeholder requirements. Finally, the validation has to check whether the developed application requirements specification leads to a valid application.

Specifics of the *documentation* task are the reuse of product line requirements and the consistent integration of application specific requirements into the application require-ments specification. Moreover, all reused product line requirements and all application specific requirements have to be made explicit for the subsequent development phases. During the documentation task, requirements engineers have to ensure that all selected requirements variants are documented for the application.

Specific activities during requirements *management* are the propagation and manage-ment of new or changed product line requirements. *Propagation* means the communica-tion of changed requirements and variants to all ongoing application requirements engineering processes and to all applications that are in use. *Management* means the maintenance of different versions of one variant resp. variation point to make sure which variant is provided by the "current release" of the product line.

The explicit representation of variability is a pre-requisite for tackling the specific chal-lenges of product line requirements engineering. To increase the awareness of the pro-vided product line capabilities, the requirements engineers and the involved stakeholders need to know:

– What is common and what is variable for an application?
– What can be or has to be selected for an application?
– What are the influences of the selection of one variant on other variants?
– What are the rationales for adapting product line requirements for the application?
– Which other application requirements are influenced by the adaptation?

5.1.4 Structure of the Chapter

The remainder of this chapter is structured as follows. In Sect. 5.2 we analyze the related work on application requirements engineering for product lines. In Sect. 5.3 we briefly introduce the orthogonal variability modeling approach and provide a small example. In Sect. 5.4 we describe the use and benefits of the orthogonal variability modeling approach in application requirements engineering. Illustrated by examples, we further show how the product line specific challenges in application requirements engineering can be tackled. Section 5.5 discusses the proposed approach and briefly reports on practical experiences. In Sect. 5.6 we summarize our work, list open issues, and sketch our future work in this field.

5.2 Related Work

Here we provide an overview of existing research, which focuses on application requirements engineering for product lines. In Sect. 5.2.1, we reflect on current research on the topic of requirements derivation, i.e., the development of an application requirements specification. In Sect. 5.2.2, we provide a brief overview of the research in the area of requirements reuse in product line engineering. Additional proposals focusing on the reuse of requirements in product line engineering can be found in [14]. In Sect. 5.2.3, we present our conclusions that can be drawn from the state of the art.

5.2.1 Requirements Derivation in Product Line Engineering

Weiss and Lai present a process for developing software families in [35]. The FAST process (Family-Oriented Abstraction, Specification and Translation) encompasses strategies for domain engineering and application engineering. FAST aims, for instance, at supporting rapid software production through application engineering and in systematizing the process of producing applications of the product line.

Weiss and Lai argue that "a key part of the application engineering environment is the application modeling language (AML) that is used to specify family members" ([35], p. 52). The AML of a product family is defined during domain engineering and serves as a basis for the product derivation process.

Weiss and Lai introduce the FAST PASTA (Process and Artifact State Transition Abstraction) model for defining product line development processes. Thus, the FAST PASTA model includes the application derivation process. It does not address the application requirements engineering facets in detail. Moreover, the model does not support trade-off decisions with regard to stakeholder-specific requirements. These trade-off decisions have to be performed if stakeholder requirements exist that cannot be satisfied by product line requirements alone. Therefore, these requirements lead to additional realization effort, and the stakeholders have to decide whether they insist on their specific requirements or not.

The key idea of the KobrA method lies in the incremental and recursive development of a component structure with generic components [1]. Atkinson et al. represent variability in a decision model. Each component description at each level of the component structure involves decision models that represent the variability of the particular generic component. The decision model of the root component is communicated to the customer. During the derivation of a product, the decision model of the root component is resolved by the decisions of the customer. The resolution of the decision model is then propagated to the next levels of the component structure. KobrA provides an approach to realize customer specific requirements that cannot be fulfilled by the product line. Although Atkinson et al. define a change management process they do not address the support for trade-off decisions.

Hotz, Krebs, and Wolter use, in their knowledge-based product derivation process, a configuration model that includes three different kinds of knowledge. The authors represent conceptual knowledge in domain objects, relations between domain objects, and constraints. In addition, they use procedural knowledge about the configuration process (e.g., backtracking strategies), and finally they introduce a so-called task specification that describes the application under consideration [19,20,37].

The main benefit of the proposed derivation process is the automatic selection of the platform artifacts that are related to the selected application features. This automatic selection makes it possible to handle the complexity of product line variability, which can be caused by a huge amount of variations.

In contrast to the approach that we propose in this chapter, the work of Hotz et al. does not focus on the special requirements engineering aspects (e.g., elicitation [20]). The description of their derivation process does not encompass the systematic detection and documentation of deltas between product line requirements artifacts and application requirements artifacts. Especially, their work does not address deltas that consider the product line variability. Application-specific requirements are always realized by integrating them into the platform and reusing them for the application under consideration.

Deelstra et al. describe different problems of product derivation that have been experienced in case studies [12]. The two main problems are the complexity of product line variability caused by a huge amount of variants and variation points as well as implicit properties, e.g., constraint dependencies between variants. Deelstra et al. describe a product derivation process that consists of two phases: During the first phase, an initial configuration is generated from the platform. In the second phase, the initial configuration is iteratively refined until the application fulfills the stakeholder requirements.

Deelstra et al. do not focus on requirements engineering in the application engineering process. They argue that it is necessary to address application-specific requirements, but they do not describe a solution for integrating application specific requirements.

Beuche describes the CONfiguration Support Library (CONSUL) in [4]. In this approach, the application domain (or product line) is represented by a feature model. Further, a component model is defined and the components are related to the features of the feature model using specific rules. The application is derived by selecting the appropriate features. Constraints of the feature selection are defined using OCL-constraints or Prolog.

The CONSUL approach provides support for product line engineering. Requirements and product line variability are represented by features. The approach does not focus on the application requirements engineering process. It is not described how application specific requirements can be integrated into the specification.

Lee et al. describe in their work on the Feature Oriented Reuse Method (FORM) for Elevator Control Systems, an application engineering process [23,27]. In this process, the feature model that has been defined during domain engineering is used to derive the application. The process encompasses the selection of appropriate features and components, the check of the model, the selection of the required architecture, and code generation. In their work, Lee et al. do not focus on application requirements engineering and they do not address application specific requirements. Adaptations of requirements are propagated to the platform; application-specific adaptations are not part of the described application engineering process.

In his book on software reuse, Karlsson defines a generic reuse development process [25]. The process encompasses the development for reuse and the development with reuse. Karlsson has identified several "with-reuse" specific activities that should be integrated into the classical software development life cycle. Such activities are, for instance, the retrieval, evaluation, and adaptation of pre-existing components. The process of reusing existing components is the same in all development phases (from the analysis phase to the test phase).

With regard to the analysis phase, Karlsson describes the "with-reuse" specific aspects to include the reuse of requirements; the reuse impact on the acquisition of domain knowledge; and the reuse impact on the object, dynamic, and functional modeling of the system.

Karlsson does not address the relation between variability and product line requirements. Moreover, in his work he focuses on the reuse and adaptation of components. The communication of variability to stakeholders or the use of scenarios for a detailed description of a variant is not addressed.

John and Muthig extend use case diagrams and textual use case descriptions to represent variability in requirements [22]. In [32], Schmidt and John extend different product line base models by the aspect of variability. They use a decision model and use cases with an integrated variability representation to derive an application. During application engineering, for each variant use case, whether the use case is part of the application or not is decided. The resulting use case diagram is the diagram of the application and serves as a basis for the application development. In the textual use case descriptions, the decisions of the decision model are integrated. In the instantiation of the use case description all variant text fragments are removed (depending on the decisions that are taken).

The work of John and Muthig shows how application use cases and application use case diagrams can be generated from the domain use case diagram. However, how application specific requirements are treated is not presented and, moreover, the specific tasks of an application requirements engineering process are not addressed.

5.2.2 Requirements Reuse in Product Line Engineering

The approach of Faulk aims at the development of a product line requirements specification [16]. This specification includes the variable requirements as well as the common requirements. In his contribution, Faulk describes the process that allows the development of an overall product line requirements specification.

Faulk argues that the product line requirements specification can be used to derive the specific application specification. In his paper, the derivation process itself is not described. Moreover, Faulk does not address the documentation of application specific requirements.

Mannion et al. present an approach for reusing requirements from a family of products [28]. The method MRAM (Method for Requirements Authoring and Management) defines how a product line requirements model can be built and how an application model can be derived from the product line requirements model. During the derivation of the application model, the product line variability is bound and variants or variations points are eliminated.

Mannion et al. focus on the product line requirements model and the derivation of application models. They describe how adaptations can be integrated into the product line requirements model, but do not address application specific requirements (that will not be integrated into the product line requirements model). Although Mannion et al. focus on product line requirements, they do not discuss the specific challenges of application requirements engineering.

Lam presents in his paper the FORE (Family Of REquirements) approach [26]. FORE aims at the definition of a generic product concept and the formalization of its requirements. One step of the FORE approach is the generation of the system (application generation) where the generic product requirements are used to produce the requirements for a specific system or product.

Lam discusses specific activities during system generation and focuses on the reuse of requirements. He also addresses changes to product line requirements caused by new customer requirements. In his approach, these new requirements will be integrated into the generic product concept. However, product (application)-specific requirements are not considered in his approach.

Cerón et al. [10] describe a metamodel for requirements engineering in product lines. With the metamodel they focus on the process improvement of requirements engineering using CMMI. In their paper they describe the necessity to support requirements engineering tasks for product lines. They argue that their model covers the evolution of requirements development activities from CMMI level 1–3. The metamodel furthermore captures a taxonomy for product line requirements. This requirements model or package describes the different types of requirements artifacts during system development and furthermore stresses the need of traceability between requirements artifacts. Cerón et al. give a short introduction to their tool ENAVER, which is based on the described metamodel.

The paper of Cerón et al. primarily focuses on the definition and explanation of the metamodel. It does not go into detail on the traditional requirements engineering activities during application requirements engineering. Moreover, the paper does not address application requirements that cannot be fulfilled by reusing system family requirements.

5.2.3 Summary of the Related Work

The discussions of the approaches described above point out that they do not address all the specific challenges and activities that are required for a comprehensive application requirements engineering process. Especially, the above approaches do not address the communication of product line variability in connection with product line requirements. Moreover, they do not offer a solution for handling application specific requirements (considering requirements deltas).

To provide comprehensive support for application requirements engineering and to tackle the identified product line specific challenges identified in Sect. 5.1.3, we introduce a derivation approach (Sect. 5.4) that is based on the concept of orthogonal variability modeling (Sect. 5.3).

5.3 The Orthogonal Variability Modeling Approach

The current state of the art reflects different ways of documenting and representing variability in requirements models. Chapter 6 describes different approaches that enhance modeling languages for the representation of variability in different product models. In our work we follow the idea of Bachmann et al. [2] of a uniform representation of variability across various activities in the product line engineering process.

In our work in the FAMILIES project [7] and in various other projects together with the automotive industry [6,8], we have developed an orthogonal variability modeling approach to document and manage the variability in different requirements artifacts. An orthogonal variability model (OVM) documents the variable aspects of a product line by specifying variation points and variants and possible interdependencies between these variation elements. Variants that are specified in an orthogonal variability model are related to the respective variable elements in the product line artifacts (e.g., use cases, parts of a state chart, or features of a feature model). The central idea of this approach is to consolidate the variability information from different requirements models to get an independent and consistent variability view of the product line.

The orthogonal variability modeling approach and the consolidated variability modeling approach (cf. Chap. 6) were developed in parallel and from different perspectives. The consolidated variability modeling approach was driven from architecture design whereas the orthogonal variability modeling approach was driven from (application) requirements engineering. Nevertheless, the resulting concepts of both research groups are quite similar, as we indicate below.

In this section we briefly introduce the basic intention of our *orthogonal variability modeling approach* (*OVM-A*) and introduce the notation of the variability model through an example. The orthogonal variability modeling approach serves as a basis for the application requirements engineering process. In Pohl et al. ([29], pp. 72–88), a detailed meta-model that defines the concepts of the OVM language and an in-depth introduction to the OVM approach are provided.

5.3.1 Overview of the OVM-A

As mentioned above, a product line variant is often reflected in elements of more than one requirements model. Therefore, a consolidated and consistent view of variability cannot be provided by the sole extension of single requirements models. The basic idea of orthogonal variability modeling is the explicit documentation of variability in one central model. This model represents the variability of the product line independent of the actual requirements models and can therefore be considered as being "orthogonal" to these models. The variability models of the OVM approach therefore provide an abstract and consistent view of the product line variability.

To avoid misinterpretations concerning the terminology that is proposed in Chap. 6, we briefly relate this terminology to ours. In comparison with the consolidated variability model, we distinguish between two types of variation elements, variation points and variants. We consider variation points as places in the model, where the application stakeholder can or has to select one of the provided variants. Variants themselves represent the abstract elements of the associated requirements artifacts that allow for the variation between different products. In the variability model one *variation point* can be associated with a set of variants. These *variants* are related by *variability dependencies* to the *variation point*. This dependency can be *mandatory*, *optional*, or an *alternative choice* with a defined range. Furthermore, *constraint dependencies* are used to express interdependencies between different variants, variation points, or even between variants and variation points. These constraint dependencies can be of the type *requires* or *excludes* (see notation elements in Fig. 5.3). The authors of the consolidated variability model use the term *variability constraint* when they talk about constraint dependencies. Variability dependencies are covered by transformers in the consolidated model. Finally, they use the term *variation model* instead of variability model as the document in which the variability information of the product line is documented.

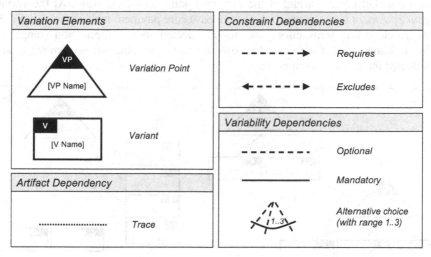

Fig. 5.3. Notation for orthogonal variability models

The variability models of the OVM-A allow the communication of what is variable (variation points), how it varies (variants), and how these variants are available for the application (variability and constraint dependencies). To express the variability in all corresponding *requirements artifacts*, each *variant* of the variability model can be associated to one or many requirements artifacts. For instance, the variant *"payment by credit card"* can be related to narrative scenario descriptions, sequence diagrams, entities of a data model, textual requirements, etc. to document variability in requirements ([29], pp. 89–113).

5.3.2 Variability Model for the E-Shop Example

To illustrate the OVM-A, we present a simple example of the variability for an e-shop product line. The e-shop product line provides the variability as represented by the variability model in Fig. 5.4.

The e-shop product line offers different variants for the *search item* functionality, which can be selected by the application stakeholder. The variant *search by name* is part of each application, because this variant is related through a mandatory relationship to the variation point. The three variants: *search by article number*, *search by article category*, and *search by article price,* are provided as a selection of which between one and three variants have to be selected (illustrated by the range 1..3). Furthermore, two advanced search variants are available at this variation point for an alternative selection: *search similar items*, and *provide search tips*, where at most one of the variants can be selected (represented by the range 0..1).

For the payment of items, different payment methods are selectable from the e-shop product line. Therefore, the variation point *payment by* offers the variants: *credit card*, *cash*, *e-cash*, and *transaction*. From these payment variants, at least one variant has to be selected (range 1..*n*). In addition to that, the payment method variant *e-cash* requires the SSL (secure socket layer) variant at the variation point *secure payment*. At the variation point *secure payment* exactly one of the provided secure payment mechanisms: *https*, *SSL*, *SET* (secure electronic transaction), has to be selected for an application (range 1..1). From this it follows that if the variant *e-cash* is selected no other *secure payment* variant can be selected for this variation point.

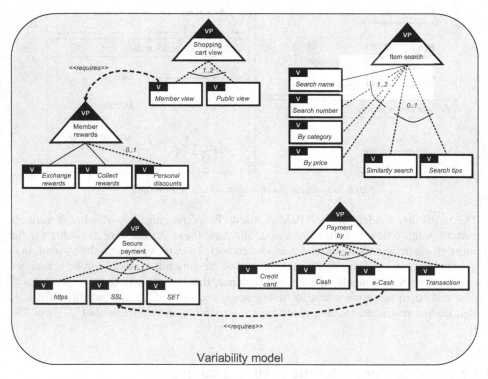

Fig. 5.4. Example: e-shop variability model

In this example, the e-shop product line furthermore provides a variation point *shopping cart view*, where the application stakeholders are able to select the variant *member view* of the cart, *public view* of the cart, or even both variants for the e-shop application. The variant *member view* provides an additional selection of variants for e-shop members. At the variation point *member rewards* the stakeholder is able to select the variants: *exchange rewards*, *collect rewards*, and *personal discounts*. For this variation point, both variants *exchange rewards* and *collect rewards* are mandatory and the variant *personal discounts* can be selected as an optional variant.

5.3.3 Relations Between the Variability Model and Product Line Scenarios

Each variant of the variability model (Fig. 5.4) is associated (through an artifact dependency [29], p. 82) to the corresponding requirements artifacts to express the variability in all affected requirements models.

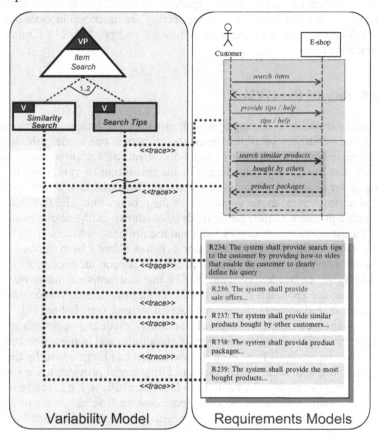

Fig. 5.5. Excerpt of the e-shop variability model with associated requirements

Figure 5.5 illustrates this association for an excerpt of two variants from the e-shop example (the artifact dependencies are identified by <<trace>>). In Fig. 5.5, the variant *search tips* is associated to the corresponding scenario (dark grey part of the sequence chart) and to the corresponding textual requirements description that belongs to the variant (*R234*). The variant *similarity search* is associated to the corresponding product line scenario (light grey part of the sequence chart) and to four textual requirements (*R236–R239*). Due to the association between requirements artifacts and variants, the variability in each requirements model can be represented and discussed in detail. In the example, the variants are associated to a bundle of messages in a sequence chart. The visualized variability in the sequence chart represents the difference between both variants in more detail. The variant *search tips* only provides the ordinary search for items and the request for help and guidance on how to search more effectively (dark grey part of the sequence chart). The variant *similarity search* also provides the ordinary search, but in addition to that, similar products can be offered by the system, such as packages with the product, most bought products, sale offers, etc. (light grey part of the sequence chart). Compared to the terminology of the consolidated variability model (Chap. 6), we use the term *requirements models* instead of base models, because we only focus on requirements engineering in this chapter.

The documentation of variability in requirements artifacts and the definition of variability for reuse in domain requirements engineering are described in more detail in ([29], pp. 89–113) (Variability in Requirements Artifacts), and pp. 193–216 (Domain Requirements Engineering).

5.3.4 Summary of the OVM-A

The orthogonal variability modeling approach provides a technique to document the existing product line variability of all requirements artifacts in one model, which represents a view on the variability. The variability model documents all variation points, variants, and dependencies that have to be considered for the resolution of variability in application engineering or for changes in domain engineering. The variability model provides a consolidated but abstract view to the variability of the product line. The fact that one variant can be reflected in many requirements models, as shown in the above example, can be handled by the association between variants and requirements artifacts.

The orthogonal variability modeling approach has already been applied in industrial projects with the automotive industry (see Sect. 5.5.1) to support the documentation of requirements variability of embedded systems [6]. In the automotive domain we furthermore demonstrated that the approach is capable of handling the documentation of product line variants that are shared among different product lines, resp. vehicle lines [8].

The key advantages of the orthogonal variability modeling approach are improved decision making, improved communication of variability, and improved traceability ([29], p. 74). The advantages result from both the views that can be provided by the orthogonal variability modeling approach. Where the variability model provides a view solely focusing on product line variability, the related product line artifacts, e.g., requirements provide a detailed description of the corresponding requirements. The use of the orthogonal variability modeling approach in application engineering is described in the following section.

5.4 Use of the Orthogonal Variability Modeling Approach During Application Requirements Engineering

In this section, we introduce our application requirements engineering approach [7] that is based on the orthogonal variability modeling approach from above. Our approach focuses on the product line specific aspects introduced in Sect. 5.1.2 that have to be considered during application requirements engineering. For the proposed application requirements engineering approach, we decided to use scenarios as requirements artifacts, which are considered as a well-established technique for communicating requirements in single systems engineering [3,9] and in product line engineering [18,22]. For the purpose of this contribution, scenarios are structured descriptions that document the usage of a system by means of textual templates or sequence diagrams. The proposed approach in Chap. 11 uses scenarios (resp. use case scenarios) to document and analyse product line requirements, and furthermore to develop test cases for a product line and their products. In our approach, we use scenarios to communicate the common and variable product line requirements to the application stakeholders.

Scenarios are combined with the variability model for specifying variability in scenarios. This combination enables requirements engineers to benefit from two different views that support the communication of product line variability on two levels of abstraction. Scenarios provide a *detailed view* of requirements in context of real-world settings [36]. Scenarios allow the communication of additional information about the system context, such as the environment, involved actors, goals, needed resources, etc. The variability model provides an *abstract view* of requirements variability and thus allows for a high-level communication of the product line capabilities (resp. variability) [2,5]. The iterative use of these two views is illustrated in Fig. 5.6).

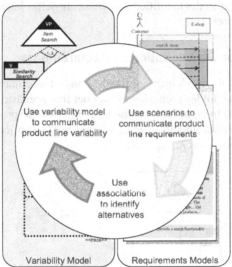

Fig. 5.6. Iterative use of abstract and detailed variability information

In the following sections we describe how the variability model and the associated scenarios support the development of an application requirements specification. For our proposed application requirements engineering approach, we only focus on the elicitation, negotiation, validation, and documentation of variable requirements for an application. The management of variable product line requirements is one major issue of a current research project [31].

5.4.1 Requirements Elicitation

The product line engineering specific part in elicitation is the consideration and identification of adequate product line requirements for reuse that fulfill one or more stakeholder requirements. The requirements engineers therefore have to be aware of the existing product line capabilities, and the valid combinations of variants for an application, i.e., which requirements can be selected and combined in one application. During elicitation, they have to map elicited application stakeholder requirements to existing product line requirements to ensure a high degree of reuse. During requirements elicitation, the requirements engineers therefore have to be aware of the provided product line capabilities to

- guide the elicitation process in the right direction to achieve a high degree of reuse;
- inspire the application stakeholders from a marketing perspective by stimulating their excitement needs or exciters, to provide some unexpected capabilities [24]; and to
- find adequate requirements variants that satisfy the application stakeholder's needs.

The outputs of this task are the elicited stakeholder requirements with the identified variants for reuse, as well as the identified requirements deltas between stakeholder requirements and product line scenarios.

Use of the OVM-A for the Elicitation of Requirements

The orthogonal variability modeling approach assists the communication of variability and the mapping of stakeholder scenarios to product line scenarios. During elicitation, the variability model is used to communicate the variability of the product line on a high level of abstraction to identify variants that are of interest to the application stakeholders (*identify variants for the application in* Fig. 5.7).

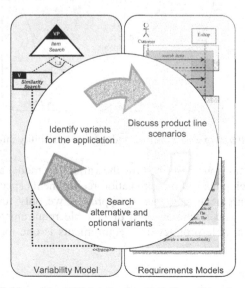

Fig. 5.7. Use of the OVM-A for the elicitation of requirements

Variants that are of interest to the stakeholders are discussed in detail by employing the associated scenarios (*discuss product line scenarios*). Furthermore, scenarios that fulfill the needs and satisfy the requirements of the stakeholders are selected during application requirements engineering. Thereby, the variability model supports searching adequate variants that are of interest to application stakeholders. It furthermore helps in inspiring the stakeholders during requirements elicitation.

Starting from scenarios, additional variants (alternatives or options) can be identified in the variability model by using the association between scenarios and variants (*search alternative and optional variants*). The identified variants can be communicated in detail by the associated product line scenarios, thus helping to identify the right variants for reuse (see iterative flow in Fig. 5.7). The iterative process during requirements elicitation supports the requirements engineers in identifying stakeholder requirements on different levels of abstraction and – as a result – helps developing a complete application requirements specification.

Example for the Elicitation Task

Figure 5.8 illustrates a small example for an elicitation task. The inputs and outputs for the elicitation task are represented by arrows. The arrow *product line capabilities* summarizes the documented information that is provided by domain engineering, i.e., the variability model and the scenarios.

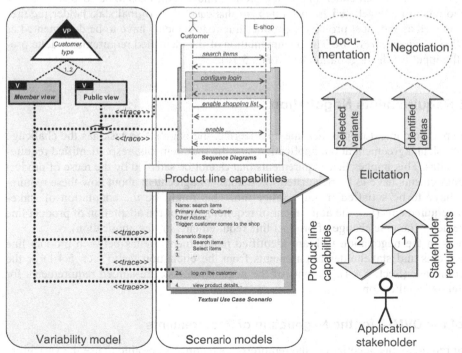

Fig. 5.8. Using the OVM-A to communicate product line variability

Arrow (1) represents the stakeholder requirements, constraints, etc. that are elicited from the application stakeholders. Arrow (2) represents the variability information of the product line that is communicated to the stakeholders during elicitation, i.e., the variation points, variants, dependencies, and the associated scenarios.

During elicitation, the requirements engineers use the variability model to communicate the variability of the product line. As illustrated in Fig. 5.8, two different variants can be selected at the variation point *shopping cart view,* namely variant *member view* and variant *public view.* This means that the application stakeholders are able to select either one or both variants at this variation point.

With the aid of the variability model, the requirements engineers furthermore are able to communicate the advantages of having the variant *member view* in comparison to only having the variant *public view.* As illustrated by the variability model in Fig. 5.4, the variant *member view* allows the additional selection of variants at the variation point *member rewards*: variants *exchange rewards*, *collect rewards*, and *personal discounts.*

The differences between both variants are communicated in detail by employing the associated product line scenarios. This communication enables the application stakeholder to select the best possible variants from the product line for the intended application. The selected variants during requirements elicitation are the basic input for the documentation task.

If some stakeholder requirements cannot be satisfied by the reuse of product line requirements, then these have to be documented to be analyzed and negotiated during requirements negotiation. If the stakeholder for instance requires the additional payment method '*pay by debit card,*' then either an existing product line scenario has to be adapted or a new scenario has to be developed from scratch. In this case, the original stakeholder requirements as well as the most promising product line requirements have to be documented as *identified requirements delta.* The documentation of the identified requirements delta provides the input for the negotiation task, (Fig. 5.10).

5.4.2 Requirements Negotiation

In the specific context of product line engineering, the negotiation task has the challenge to establish an agreement about application-specific requirements, resp. identified requirements deltas. This implies that requirements that cannot be satisfied by the reuse of product line requirements have to be negotiated to establish an agreement about how these requirements have to be satisfied in the application. This might be the adaptation of stakeholder requirements (i.e., the adjustment of requirements) or the adaptation of product line requirements (i.e., the change of product line requirements for the application).

Inputs of the negotiation task are identified requirements deltas between product line requirements and stakeholder requirements from the elicitation task (Sect. 5.4.1) or the validation task (Sect. 5.4.4). Outputs of the negotiation task are agreed requirements for the intended application.

Use of the OVM-A for the Negotiation of Requirements

During requirements negotiation, the requirements engineers are able to use the variability model and the scenarios as illustrated in Fig. 5.9. Product line scenarios are used to analyse the delta between a proposed product line scenario and a stakeholder scenario in detail (*establish agreement and analyse delta*). Moreover, product line scenarios can be used as mediator between different stakeholder views. For instance, the different stakeholder requirements concerning the search functionality for an application might be arbitrated by the discussion of reusable product line variants.

Starting from product line scenarios, the association between variants and scenarios can be used to seek for suitable alternatives (of the negotiated scenario) in the variability model (*search for alternatives*). To identify alternatives for the discussion, first the corresponding variation point of the variant is identified and then all variants of the variation point are discovered. By the association between scenarios and product line variants, each identified variant in the variability model can be analyzed in detail by employing the corresponding scenarios. This helps to evaluate if one variant satisfies the stakeholder requirements better than others.

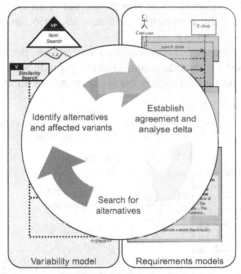

Fig. 5.9. Use of the OVM-A for the negotiation of requirements

Moreover, the variability model can be used to identify variants that will be affected by the adaptation of product line scenarios to satisfy stakeholder requirements (*identify alternatives and affected variants*). The identification of corresponding product line variants is essential for the adaptation of derived product line requirements in the application to assure that all affected requirements will be changed. Consequently, the iterative process during requirements negotiation enables the requirements engineers to establish agreement about application specific requirements, and furthermore, to identify deltas and change affects in detail (see circular flow in Fig. 5.9).

Example for the Negotiation Task

Figure 5.10 shows a small example of a possible negotiation task with its inputs and outputs. Arrow (1) represents the identified delta during requirements elicitation between the required stakeholder scenario (*Sz*) and the proposed product line scenario (*S7*). Arrow (2) represents the input from domain requirements engineering and includes the documentation of the capabilities of the product line. Arrow (3) represents the original stakeholder requirements (scenarios) and the trade-off decision. Arrow (4) represents the evaluation result for the adaptation of the product line scenario.

The requirements engineers use the *stakeholder scenarios*, the *proposed product line scenarios*, and the *identified delta* to analyse and negotiate possible solutions with the application stakeholders, Fig. 5.10. They use the *variability model* to search alternative variants and scenarios that satisfy the requirements of the application stakeholders.

In our example, the scenarios of variant *V1* and variant *V2* are discussed with the application stakeholders. Variant *V1* represents a scenario to *pay the selected goods by transaction*, and variant *V2* a scenario to *pay the selected goods before delivery* (prepayment). As depicted in Fig. 5.10, the application stakeholders request a payment by debit card (scenario *Sz*) for the application. Because no adequate product line scenario can be provided to satisfy the stakeholder requirements, either an existing product line scenario has to be adapted for the application or a new scenario has to be developed from scratch.

For the development of the application-specific requirements, the requirements engineers analyse the estimated effort for the adaptation of existing product line scenarios for the development of the new scenarios that satisfy the requirements of application stakeholders.

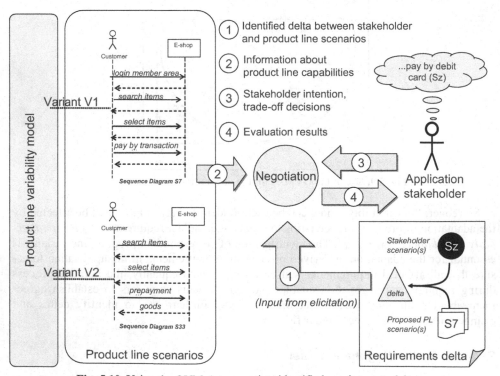

Fig. 5.10. Using the OVM-A to negotiate identified requirements deltas

To identify all affected product line scenarios, they use the existing trace information from the variability model. In fact the change of product line requirements for an application also influences the subsequent development phases. As a consequence, the estimated change effort for the realization is calculated in cooperation with application design. The requirements engineers finally provide the analyzed delta between product line and stakeholder requirements with the estimated adaptation effort to the application stakeholder (arrow (4)).

Based on the evaluation results, a trade-off decision on whether the stakeholder requirement has to be fulfilled by 100% or less is encompassed in cooperation with the involved stakeholders (arrow (3)). Hence, for the negotiation of requirements, it is essential that an agreement among all stakeholders be established for each application specific cific requirement and each trade-off decision (also see [17]).

5.4.3 Requirements Documentation

The goal of requirements documentation in product line engineering is to develop an application requirements specification with a high number of reused product line requirements. Therefore, during this task the requirements engineers develop a consistent and traceable application requirements specification of selected product line requirements and application specific requirements. Consistent documentation means that all dependencies between variants and variation points have been considered for reuse, and that all application specific requirements do not conflict with reused product line requirements. Traceable documentation means that all documented application requirements can be traced back to their origin, e.g., to stakeholder requirements or to product line requirements.

The initial inputs for this task come from requirements elicitation and negotiation. The elicitation task provides the original stakeholder requirements and the selected product line variants that have to be documented. The negotiation task provides application-specific requirements that have to be documented for the application. The intermediate requirements documents of the documentation task provide input for the negotiation, and validation of application requirements with the stakeholders. The final result of requirements documentation is the application requirements specification, which is composed of:

- *Reused requirements artifacts*, i.e., an application requirement is a 1:1 reuse of a product line requirement (common or variable requirement);
- *Adapted requirements artifacts*, i.e., an application requirement is a product line requirement that has been partially changed for the application;
- *New requirements artifacts*, i.e., an application requirement is developed from scratch and has no change influence to existing requirements;
- *Traceability* information between documented application requirements and their origin, i.e., to reused product line requirements and to stakeholder requirements.

Use of the OVM-A for the Documentation of Requirements

During requirements documentation, the requirements engineers are able to use the variability model and the scenario models for the reuse of product line requirements as illustrated in Fig. 5.11. The reuse of product line scenarios for the application requirements specification can be differentiated into the complete reuse of a scenario or the adaptation of a scenario (*reuse scenarios for the application*).

For each reused or adapted product line scenario, the existing dependencies to the variation point (variability dependencies) and to other variants and variation points (constraint dependencies) have to be checked for the development of a complete requirements specification, e.g., to identify mandatory or required variants. Only if all dependencies are considered during reuse, can a complete application requirements specification be developed. Therefore, the association between reused scenarios and corresponding variants is employed to identify the corresponding variants in the variability model (*identify all affected variants for the specification*).

The variability model is used to identify the variation points and dependencies of the corresponding variant to ensure that all necessary scenarios (especially requirements) are documented in the application requirements specification (*ensure completeness of reused variants*). This means that the scenarios of all variants that were selected explicitly (e.g., by the selection of optional and alternative variants) and were selected due to existing dependencies (e.g., mandatory variability dependency, or requires dependency) have to be documented in the application requirements specification. The requirements engineers use the defined dependencies between variants and scenarios to develop a complete application requirements specification. If, for instance, an optional variant at a variation point is selected that additionally provides a mandatory variant, then the scenarios of the mandatory variant have to be documented for the application requirements specification as well (e.g., the selection of the variant *personal discount* at the variation point *member rewards* demands the selection of the variants *exchange rewards* and *collect rewards*, see Fig. 5.4).

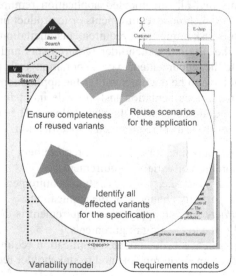

Fig. 5.11. Use of the OVM-A for the documentation of requirements

The iterative process during the documentation of requirements enables the requirements engineers to develop a complete and consistent requirements specification. Thereby, the variability model helps to ensure completeness of reused product line requirements and the associated requirements models help to ensure the correctness of reused requirements in the application requirements specification.

Example for the Documentation Task

In the following we continue our example and illustrate the general structure for the traceability between scenarios of the application and reused scenarios of the product line. We therefore differentiate three types of application scenarios:

- An application scenario is a reused product line scenario, reuse = 100%
- An application scenario is an adapted product line scenario, i.e., 1%< reuse <100%
- An application scenario is developed from scratch, i.e., reuse = 0%

During the documentation of requirements for the application, the requirements engineers have to document the origin of the application scenarios. Therefore, they differentiate between reused, adapted, and new scenarios for the application. Scenarios that have been reused by 100% from the product line are traced to the reused scenarios of the product line, e.g., scenarios S3 and S5 in Fig. 5.12. Further, a trace link (*fulfills link*) between the *application scenario* and the *original stakeholder scenario* shows that the reuse of the product line scenario fulfills the stakeholder scenario. As illustrated in Fig. 5.12, one product line scenario can fulfill one or many stakeholder scenarios, e.g., *S3 fulfills Sc AND Sa*, and vice versa.

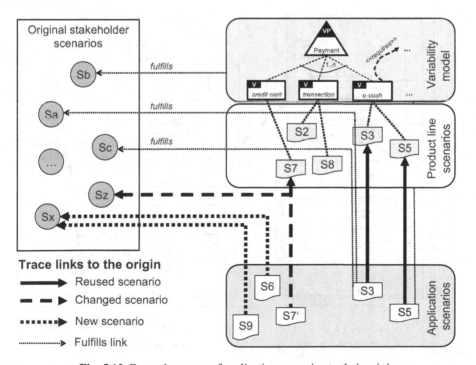

Fig. 5.12. Example: traces of application scenarios to their origin

Application scenarios that are adapted for an application have a trace link to the *original stakeholder scenario* and to the *original product line scenario*, e.g., scenario *S7'* has a trace link to the product line scenario *S7* and to the stakeholder scenario *Sz*. Application scenarios that are developed from scratch and do not influence any existing product line scenarios and are therefore only traced to the original stakeholder scenario, e.g., the application scenarios *S6* and *S9* have a trace link to the stakeholder scenario *Sx* (Fig. 5.12).

With the following example we focus on the adaptation of product line scenarios for an application and continue the example from requirements negotiation, Sect. 5.4.2 and Fig. 5.10. The input for application specific requirements is usually provided by the negotiation task. Figure 5.13 represents the adapted scenario (S7' *payment by debit card*) with its additional scenario steps for the application. To follow the naming convention, this scenario is called *application specific scenario*, because the derived product line scenario has been changed because of an identified delta for the application.

The explicit visualization of the adaptation is a pre-requisite for the validation task in requirements engineering and for the subsequent development phases. Therefore, the requirements engineers represent the changes of the reused product line scenario S7 *payment by transaction credit* in the application requirements model, Fig. 5.13. The changed or integrated steps, in the application specific scenario S7' *pay by debit card*, are highlighted in the scenario. Further, the scenario is related to both origins of the adaptation result. Trace link *(1)* represents the trace to the original product line scenario *S7 payment by credit card*. Trace link *(2)* represents the trace to the original stakeholder scenario *Sz payment by debit card* (see also Fig. 5.10) (negotiation of identified deltas).

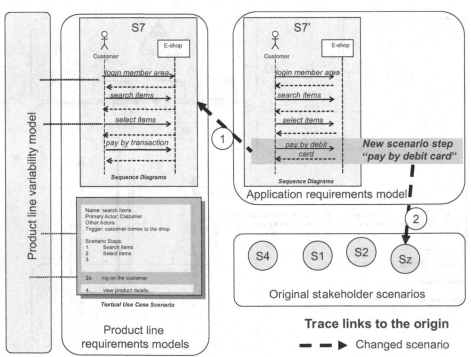

Fig. 5.13. Example: visualizing integrated requirements deltas

The explicit documentation of application specific requirements is essential for the subsequent development phases (e.g., testing) in order to identify which product line artifacts (e.g., test cases) have to be adapted and which ones can be reused as they are. Moreover, the documentation of both traces within the requirements specification is fundamental for the validation of the adaptation result together with the application stakeholders (Sect. 5.4.4).

5.4.4 Requirements Validation

The specific focus of the validation task in product line engineering is the validation of reused product line requirements and application specific requirements. On the one hand whether the reused product line requirements – as documented in the requirements specification – fulfill the stakeholder requirements has to be analyzed. This holds for both the directly selected variants and the indirectly selected variants, e.g., due to *requires* or *mandatory* dependencies. On the other hand, whether the application specific requirements satisfy the application stakeholder's needs has to be analyzed and if they are integrated completely and correctly in the application requirements specification.

The initial input for the validation task is the application requirements specification with all documented application requirements together with all the trace links to the original requirements, i.e., product line requirements and stakeholder requirements. The defined outputs of this task are either validated application requirements for the final requirements specification or identified requirements deltas that have to be further analyzed and discussed during requirements negotiation (Sect. 5.4.2).

Use of the OVM-A for the Validation of Requirements

During requirements validation, the requirements engineers benefit from the use of the variability model and the scenario models as illustrated in Fig. 5.14. With the variability model, the requirements engineer is able to validate if all constraint and variability dependencies – as defined in the variability model – are correctly observed by the reused requirements in the application requirements specification. For the validation of constraint dependencies whether the defined constraints for the corresponding variants – in the variability model – have been observed has to be checked. Therefore, for each *reused* variant it is made sure that all scenarios of *required* variants have been documented and that the scenarios of *excluded* variants have not been documented in the requirements specification. For the validation of variability dependencies it has to be checked if the resolution at one variation point is correct. That means that the selection of variants must not conflict with the defined variability dependencies and their ranges, e.g., the constraint imposed by the alternative choice of variants at a variation point with the range 1..1 is only satisfied, if exactly one variant of this variation point has been chosen (*validate dependencies of reused variants*).

To create an agreement on the documented application requirements, the requirements engineers use the traceability dependency between application and stakeholder requirements to validate if all reused product line scenarios and all application specific scenarios satisfy the application stakeholder's needs and if these are documented completely and correctly within the specification (*validate the satisfaction of application stakeholders*) (Fig. 5.15). To validate the completeness and correctness of the documented scenarios in the application requirements specification, the association between requirements models (e.g., scenarios) and the variability model (e.g., variants) is used to check if the existing dependencies in the variability model where observed (*validate completeness and correctness*).

If the application stakeholder's needs are satisfied with the documented application scenarios and if all dependencies of the variant have been complied with during the documentation task, then the application requirement is validated for the final requirements specification. Otherwise, the identified requirements deltas have to be documented and negotiated with the application stakeholders.

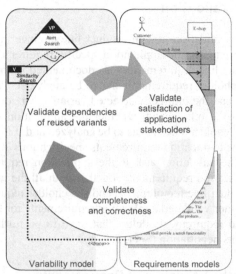

Fig. 5.14. Use of the OVM-A for requirements validation

Consequently, the iterative process during requirements validation enables the requirements engineers to develop complete and correct application requirements specifications that firstly satisfy all stakeholder requirements and secondly provide the foundation for the subsequent application engineering processes.

Example for the Validation Task

In the following we use the exemplary requirements specification of Fig. 5.12 as an input for the validation task. The validation of application requirements is assisted by the existing trace links between application scenarios and stakeholder scenarios, which are represented by the '*fulfills trace*' in Fig. 5.15. Based on the traceability information, the requirements engineers are able to validate each application scenario in cooperation with the application stakeholders. For example, they validate if scenarios S3 and S5 that are a 100% reuse of product line scenarios satisfy the original requirements of the application stakeholders. Moreover, they have to validate if the application specific scenarios, such as scenario S7' (adapted product line scenario) or scenario S9 (new scenario), are correctly adapted for the application and if these fully satisfy the requirements of the application stakeholders. Besides the validation whether one variant satisfies the application stakeholders, the requirements engineers have to validate if the reused and adapted scenarios are complete and if these do not conflict with each other. In the example, the reused application scenarios can be traced to the corresponding product line scenarios and in turn to the corresponding variants in the variability model. The requirements engineers use the variability model to analyse the valid requirements combinations for an application requirements specification.

The example illustrates the variation point *payment* with its alternative variants *credit card, transaction,* and *e-cash.* Moreover, the *requires* dependency indicates that the variant *e-cash* requires the selection of the variant (*SSL*) at the variation point *secure payment,* see also Fig. 5.4. Therefore, based on the information of the variability model, the requirements engineers validate if all variability and all constraint dependencies were correctly observed in the application requirements specification, and moreover, if the application stakeholders are aware of these dependencies. In the example, requirements engineers use the variability model to check if the requires dependency between the variant *e-cash* and the variant *SSL* is complied with, i.e., if the requirements that belong to the variant SSL have also been documented in the specification. Whether the alternative choice dependency between the variants at variation point *payment by* is correctly observed is validated by checking if at least the requirements of one variant are documented in the application requirements specification. Finally, the variability model is used to validate if the stakeholder is aware of the existing constraint dependencies and if the requested and excluded variants do not conflict with the stakeholder requirements.

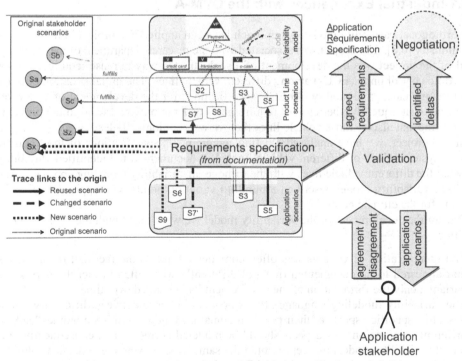

Fig. 5.15. Example: validation of scenarios with the application stakeholders

If, during validation, the requirements engineers realise that an application scenario does not satisfy the original stakeholder requirement, then the detected differences are documented as requirements deltas, to be additionally negotiated (Sect. 5.4.2). Otherwise, the agreed application requirement is documented as a final or validated requirement in the application requirements specification (ARS) (Fig. 5.15).

5.5 Discussion of the Proposed Approach

The proposed approach has been partially validated in industry. The orthogonal variability modeling approach (Sect. 5.3), or more precisely the orthogonal documentation of variability and the creation of dedicated views for different stakeholders, was applied in projects with the automotive industry, see Sect.5.5.1. The proposed combination of product line scenarios and the variability model for the development of an application requirements specification (Sect. 5.4) together with the proposed use of both models in each requirements engineering task has been validated by an existing example in the laboratory, see Sect. 5.5.2.

5.5.1 Industrial Experiences with the OVM-A

The orthogonal variability modeling approach has been applied in a project in the automotive industry [6,8]. The project was associated with the research department of the company. Goal of the project was the development of a sophisticated way to reuse requirements for electronic control units (ECUs) among different vehicle lines. The initial situation of reuse was to copy, paste, and modify old ECU specifications for the development of a new vehicle line. Consequently, the reuse of requirements was not only restricted to the previous vehicle line, but also to those vehicle lines that were technologically leading.

In the project, we have analysed existing requirements specifications of the "climate control system ECU" of different vehicle lines. We documented the identified variability between the different vehicle lines with the orthogonal variability modeling approach. The resulting variability model described around 40 variation points with approximately 150 variants for the climate control.

During the development of the variability model we were faced with the following difficulties:

- The identification of variants was often complicated due to the fact that requirements that appeared to be documented (named) differently were often in fact the very same variants; only the formulation of the requirement had changed over time.
- The variability modeling language allows people to choose between different ways of modeling specific aspects of their problem domain. In industry, this sometimes leads to different opinions on how aspects should be modeled correctly, and consequently, different variability models that represented the same aspects were created. As a solution, modeling guidelines have been defined for assisting the modelers in this respect.
- Identified requirements were not optional, mandatory, or alternative per se; rather their availability was often dependent on different vehicle properties, such as country type,

body type, engine type, etc. We therefore had to extend the orthogonal variability modeling approach (by extending the OVM's metamodel) to allow for a structured documentation of variability across vehicle lines (see [8]).

With the extended orthogonal variability modeling approach, we were able to document the commonalities and variability of the electronic control unit for the climate system in two different subclasses: First, the requirements that were common or variable for all vehicle lines, and second the requirements that were common or variable for a specific vehicle line only.

To support the reuse of requirements variants, we have developed a set of different reuse scenarios that fit to the different development strategies and projects in the company. In the project, we have defined specific scenarios that support the requirements engineers in finding reusable requirements by providing a name, the vehicle line, or the ECU. With the explicit definition of common and variable requirements for ECUs and their availability with respect to the vehicle line, we were able to provide support for the development of the requirements specification for an ECU of a new vehicle line.

With the use of the orthogonal variability modeling approach and the defined reuse scenarios, we have achieved the following:

- The variability of the ECU was explicitly defined for the strategic evolution as well as for the reuse of requirements for new product lines.
- The requirements engineers were able to identify in which vehicle lines a specific variant has been reused (important for call backs or other bug fixes).
- The requirements engineers were able to tell what is currently common to all ECUs (common requirements) and what is currently available for a specific ECU (variable requirements).
- The discussion between requirements engineers and product management about what shall be available for all vehicle lines or what shall be specific for one vehicle line was improved due to the explicit representation.
- Discussions were more focused, because people did not stick to specific realization requirements. With the variability model, they were able to discuss variants without being distracted by insignificant details.
- The reuse of requirements was much better supported than in the previous copy-paste-and-modify approach, and furthermore, the current situation (what is state of the practice, i.e., what is currently available in the context of climate control) was visible during any time of the project.
- The evolution of requirements artifacts (and variants) could be propagated much faster, because the knowledge about which vehicle lines use which variants was provided by the OVM.

With the OVM-A, we have been able to make the "hidden" knowledge of the experts (about which variants have to be or can be reused for a specific vehicle line) explicitly visible for all engineers in all development projects. For the documentation of variability and requirements, we have implemented the extended orthogonal variability metamodel in Telelogic DOORS. We have used the concept of modules to separate variability information from the requirements artifacts. For the realization, we differentiated between formal modules to document the variability information of the variability model with all variation elements and dependencies, and the formal modules to document the requirements for the ECUs. Finally, the assignment dependency between variants and the corresponding requirements artifacts was realized by trace links [8]. However, during the project we experienced that more sophisticated tool support is required to assist in (1) the definition of variability, (2) the maintenance of variability information, (3) consistency checking for all variability definitions across the product line sets, (4) the definition of advanced selective retrievals, and – last but not least – (5) the appropriate representation of variability for the different stakeholders that are involved in product line requirements engineering such as customers, users, domain experts, product managers, architects, or developers.

5.5.2 Experiences in a Laboratory Case Study

The proposed reuse approach is based on the results and experiences gained during the project with the automotive industry as has been depicted in the previous section. Based on the organization-specific reuse scenarios in the automotive context, we have developed a generic approach for the strategic reuse of requirements in application requirements engineering. We have evaluated this application requirements engineering process in a laboratory case study with an exemplary e-shop product line. The case study showed that the iterative use of the variability model and the scenario models enable requirements engineers to solve the product line specific challenges in application requirements engineering (Sect. 5.1.3).

By using the orthogonal variability modeling approach during *elicitation*, the requirements engineer is supported in the following ways:

- Product line requirements for the application can be selected by the communication of product line variability to the application stakeholders on different levels of abstraction. The variability model helps to identify appropriate variants on a high level of abstraction. The product line scenarios help to communicate and identify reusable product line requirements on a detailed level.
- The elicitation process can be guided to ensure a high degree of reuse by using the variability model for the explicit documentation of product line variability, and the association between variants and scenarios to identify all scenarios of one variant.
- Stakeholders can be triggered to ensure the completeness of the *specification* by the communication of what has to be selected (commonalities) and which decisions have to be made concerning the provided variability to develop a complete application requirements specification.

By using the orthogonal variability modeling approach during *negotiation*, the requirements engineer is supported in the following ways:

- Agreement about the reused product line scenarios can be established for the application requirements specification among all stakeholders by the communication of scenarios.
- Deltas can be evaluated as a basis to estimate change efforts. That means that the identification of changes in the scenario(s), and identification of transitive changes based on dependencies to other variants can be analyzed by the help of the variability model.

By using the orthogonal variability modeling approach during *documentation,* the requirements engineer is supported in the following ways:

– Reusing and adapting product line requirements for the application, under consideration of all existing dependencies, is supported by using the variability model to identify these dependencies.
– Developing a complete and consistent application requirements specification for reused product line scenarios is supported by the explicitly documented dependencies in the variability model and the association between variants and scenarios.

By using the orthogonal variability modeling approach during *validation,* the requirements engineer is supported in the following ways:

– Validating the completeness and correctness of the reused product line requirements and application-specific requirements is supported by the variability model.
– Validating if all application requirements (reused and application-specific requirements) satisfy the application stakeholder's needs is supported by the scenarios.

The proposed orthogonal variability modeling approach enables requirements engineers – together with the involved stakeholders – to identify what is common and what is variable in the product line, what can and what has to be selected at a certain variation point, what are the influences of the selection to other requirements variants, and finally what are the influences for the adaptation of a product line requirement for an application. The major benefits of this approach result from the orthogonal modeling of variability. The use of scenarios for the elicitation and discussion of requirements with the stakeholders is state of the practice nowadays. Consequently, the combination of both model views provides the expressed benefits of its application in application requirements engineering.

Although we have focused on scenarios in our approach, the approach can be extended to other requirements artifacts by employing the *artifact dependency* between a variant and its corresponding requirements artifacts (see Fig. 5.5). That means, similar to scenarios, all requirements artifacts, e.g., data, performance, usability, or security requirements, can be communicated to stakeholders.

5.5.3 Validation of the Approach

For the further validation of the proposed approach we have planned the following three steps: the development of tool support, a laboratory validation with an industrial example, and an industrial validation of the approach.

In a first step, a more sophisticated variability modeling tool (*VARMOD*) will be developed [31] to support the consistent definition and documentation of variability among requirements. This tool is aimed at resolving the shortcomings of traditional requirements management tools, as identified in [8]. With the focus on application requirements engineering, the tool shall furthermore assist the development of application specifications. Based on the experience with the tool development, we will achieve an additional proof of concept for the proposed approach. In the second step, the laboratory validation shall validate the scalability and applicability of the approach and the tool for real projects by applying the approach to data that has been provided by industrial partners. The results of the validation then will be presented and discussed with the industrial partners to improve the approach. Based on feedback and the experience gained with the case study, the approach – as well as the *VARMOD* tool – will be improved and extended. Based on these improved results, the third step is the validation in an industrial context to validate the applicability of our proposed orthogonal variability modeling approach as well as the *VARMOD* tool in real world projects.

5.6 Conclusions and Future Research

In this chapter, we have pointed out that requirements engineering for applications in product line engineering has to consider some specific aspects due to the fact that product line requirements should be reused in each application.

We have presented an approach for application requirements engineering that uses the input from domain requirements engineering (orthogonal variability model with associated requirements models) to develop an application requirements specification. The proposed approach enables the requirements engineer to solve a multitude of identified challenges during application requirements engineering (cf. Sect. 5.1.3), by iteratively employing the variability model and the product line scenarios. Moreover, the approach facilitates the consistent selection and documentation of variable requirements artifacts (e.g., scenarios). The introduced application engineering approach can be extended to facilitate the reuse of different requirements artifacts because of the flexibility of the underlying orthogonal variability modeling approach. Therefore, the approach also allows considering variability in performance, security, and other quality aspects of a product line.

In our future research, we have planned to focus on two major topics. One topic is the validation of our approach and the development of suitable tool support. The other topic is to establish a joint cooperation for harmonizing, extending, and standardizing the variability modeling approaches that have been suggested in this book (the consolidated variability modeling approach and our OVM approach), to benefit from the joint advantages of both approaches.

Acknowledgments

Numerous people have contributed to this work and putting it into practice. We therefore would like to thank our cooperation and project partners for the important and fruitful discussions during the project. We are also grateful to the reviewers of this chapter Øystein Haugen, Jason Mansell, Tor Erlend Fægri, Andreas Metzger, and Ernst Sikora as well as the editors of this book Timo Käkölä and Juan Carlos Dueñas for the helpful and sustainable comments and suggestions that substantially improved the quality of this work.

References

1. Atkinson, C., Bayer, J., Bunse, C., Kamsties, E., Laitenberger, O., Laqua, R., Muthig, D., Paech, B., Wüst, J., Zettel, J.: *Component-Based Product-Line Engineering with UML* (Addison-Wesley, Reading, MA 2002)
2. Bachmann, F., Goedicke, M., Leite, J., Nord, R., Pohl, K., Ramesh, B., Vilbig, A.: An International. WoMeta-Model for Representing Variability in Product Family Development, In: 5th International Workshop on Product Family Engineering (PFE-5), Siena, Italy, 2003, pp 66–80
3. Ben Achour, C. et al: Bridging the gap between users and requirements engineering: the scenario-based approach. Int. J. Comput. Syst. Sci. Eng. **14**(6), 379–405 (1999)
4. Beuche, D.: Composition and construction of embedded software families. PhD thesis (University of Marburg, Magdeburg, Germany 2003)
5. Böckle, G., Wittmann, M.: Catalogue of methods and processes for system-family engineering, Official Web site of the FAMILIES project. http://www.esi.es/Families/E1.4b-Method-Catalogue/ Start_SFE_Catalogue.htm. Cited 8 Aug 2005
6. Bühne, S., Lauenroth, K., Pohl, K.: Why is it not sufficient to model requirements variability with feature models? In: Proceedings of Workshop: Automotive Requirements Engineering (AURE04), co-located at RE04, Nanzan University, Nagoya, Japan, 2004, pp 5–12
7. Bühne, S., Halmans, G., Lauenroth, K., Pohl, K.: An extended and partially validated method to identify customer specific requirements for product family based applications, FAMILIES project, deliverable for task E2.2.2 (June 2004)
8. Bühne, S., Lauenroth, K., Pohl, K.: Modeling requirements variability across product lines. In: Proceedings of the 13th IEEE International Requirements Engineering Conference, Paris, France, ed by Atlee, J.M. (IEEE, New York 2005) pp 41–50
9. Carroll, J.: *Making Use: Scenario-Based Design of Human–Computer Interactions* (MIT, Cambridge, MA 2000)
10. Cerón, R., Dueñas, J.C., Serrano, E., Capilla, R.: A meta-model for requirements engineering in system family context for software process improvement using CMMI. In: 6th International Conference on Product Focused Software Process Improvement, Oulu, Finland, 13–18 June 2005, ed by Frank, B., Seija, K.S. Lecture Notes in Computer Science, vol 3547 (Springer, Berlin Heidelberg New York 2005)
11. Clements, P., Northrop, L.: Software Product Lines – Practices and Patterns. *Series in Software Engineering* (Addison-Wesley, Reading, MA 2001)
12. Deelstra, S., Sinnemaand, M., Bosch, J.: Experiences in software product families: problems and issues during product derivation. In: *Software Product Lines*, ed by Nord, R.L., Proceedings of the 3rd International Conference (SPLC 2004), Boston, USA. Lecture Notes in Computer Science, vol 3154 (Springer, Berlin Heidelberg New York 2004) pp 165–182
13. Dorfman, M., Thayer, R.H.: *Software Requirements Engineering* (IEEE Computer Society, Silver Spring, MD 1977)
14. International Workshop on Requirements Engineering for System Families: Position papers, ed by Dueñas, J.C., Schmid, K., allocated with ICSR8, July 2004, Madrid. Technical report (Universidad Politécnica de Madrid 2004)
15. Easterbrook, S., Chechik, M.: A framework for multi-valued reasoning over inconsistent viewpoints. In: Proceedings of International Conference on Software Engineering 2001 (ICSE 2001), 2001, pp 411–420
16. Faulk, S.R.: Product-line requirements specification (PRS): an approach and case study. In: Proceedings of the 5th IEEE International Symposium on Requirements Engineering, Toronto, Canada (IEEE, New York 2001) pp 48–55
17. Halmans, G., Pohl, K.: Considering product line assets when defining customer requirements. In: Proceedings of the International Workshop on Product line Engineering: The Early Steps: Planning, Modeling, and Managing (PLEES'01), Erfurt, Germany, 2001, pp 37–42
18. Halmans, G., Pohl, K.: Communicating the variability of a software-product line to customers. J. Softw. Syst. Model. (SoSyM) **2**: 15–36 (2003)
19. Hotz, L., Krebs, T.: Supporting the product derivation process with a knowledge-based approach. In: Proceedings of the International Workshop on Software Variability Management (SVM), co-located at ICSE 03, Portland, USA, 2003, pp 24–29
20. Hotz, L., Günter, A., Krebs, T.: A knowledge-based product derivation process and some ideas how to integrate product development. In: Proceedings of the Software Variability Management Workshop, Groningen, Netherlands, 2003, ed by Vangurp, J., Bosch, J., pp 136–140

21. IEEE: IEEE recommended practice for software requirements specifications, IEEE Standard 830-1998 (The Institute of Electrical and Electronics Engineers, New York 1998)
22. John, I., Muthig, D.: Tailoring use cases for product line modelling. In Proceedings of the International Workshop on Requirements Engineering for Product Lines 2002 (REPL'02), 2002, pp 26–32
23. Kang, K., Kim, S., Lee, J., Kim, K., Shin, E., Huh, M.: FORM: a feature-oriented reuse method with domain-specific reference architectures. Ann. Softw. Eng. **5**: 143–168 (1998)
24. Kano, N., Seraku, N., Takahashi, F., Tsuji, S.: Attractive quality and must be quality. In: *The Best on Quality*, ed by Hromi, J.D., vol 7(ASQ Quality, Milwaukee, WI 1996)
25. Karlsson, E.A.: *Software Reuse – A Holistic Approach* (Wiley, New York 1995)
26. Lam, W.: A case-study of requirements reuse through product families. Ann. Softw. Eng. **5**: 253–277 (1998)
27. Lee, K., Kang, K.C., Koh, E., Chae, W., Kim, B., Choi, B.W.: Domain-oriented engineering of elevator control software. In: *Software Product Lines, Experience and Research Directions*, ed by Donohoe, P., Proceedings of the First Software Product Line Conference (SPLC1), Denver, Colorado, vol 576 (Kluwer, Dordrecht 2000) pp 3–22
28. Mannion, M., Kaindl, H., Wheadon, J., Keepence, B.: Reusing single system requirements from application family requirements. In Proceedings of 21st International Conference on Software Engineering, Los Angeles, CA, USA, 16–22 May 1999, ICSE (IEEE Computer Society, Silver Spring, MD) pp 453–462
29. Pohl, K., Böckle, G., van der Linden, F.: *Software Product Line Engineering: Foundations, Principles, and Techniques* (Springer, Berlin Heidelberg New York 2005)
30. Pohl, K.: *Process-Centered Requirements Engineering* (Research Studies Press, Wiley, New York 1996)
31. Project Website of the DFG project VarMod-PRIME: variability modeling in process integrated modeling environments. http://www.sse.uni-essen.de/wms/en/index.php?go=139
32. Schmid, K., John, I.: Generic variability management and its application to product line modeling. In: Proceedings of the Software Variability Management Workshop, Groningen, Netherlands, ed by Van Gurp, J. Bosch, J., pp 13–18
33. Sommerville, I., Sawyer, P.: *Requirements Engineering – A Good Practice Guide* (Wiley, New York 2000)
34. van der Linden, F.: Software product lines in Europe: the ESAPS & CAFÉ projects. IEEE Softw. **19**(4), 41–49 (July/August 2002)
35. Weiss, D.M., Lai, C.T.R.: *Software Product-Line Engineering, A Family-Based Software Development Process* (Addison Wesley, Reading, MA 1999)
36. Weidenhaupt, K., Pohl, K., Jarke, M., Haumer, P.: Scenario usage in system development: a report on current practice. IEEE Softw. **15**(2), 34–45 (1998)
37. Wolter, K., Krebs, T., Hotz, L., Meijler, T.D.: Knowledge-based product derivation process. In: *Artificial Intelligence Applications and Innovations*, ed by Bramer, M., Devedzic, V., IFIP 18th World Computer Congress, TC12 1st International Conference on Artificial Intelligence Applications and Innovations (AIAI-2004) (Kluwer, Dordrecht 2004) pp 323–332

6 Consolidated Product Line Variability Modeling

J. Bayer, S. Gerard, Ø. Haugen, J. Mansell, B. Møller-Pedersen, J. Oldevik, P. Tessier, J.-P. Thibault, and T. Widen

Abstract

In this chapter we present an improved and simplified metamodel for product line variability. This model has been consolidated from diverse approaches in the earlier research projects ESAPS, CAFÉ and other existing work, supplied with recent research in FAMILIES. The consolidated metamodel aims to be the starting point for standardization. A standard will lay the grounds for commercial and open-source tool support. We present here a prototype tool based on the metamodel. To put the work in context, we present three different approaches for capturing variability: using standard languages (exemplified by UML 2.0), using annotations to standard languages, and using domain-specific languages. We use the same Watch example to present how variability is handled in all three approaches.

6.1 Introduction

During the past decade a number of methods and techniques for describing software product lines have been defined, e.g., FODA, FORM, Fusion and KobrA. In the ESAPS [11], CAFÉ [12] and FAMILIES projects, existing concepts and techniques were refined and new ones defined. The results were different overlapping approaches with diverse terminology, representation, etc. This diversity of concepts and approaches has dominated the product line engineering community which would benefit from a more unified approach that facilitates interoperability of tools and increased collaboration.

The work described in this chapter presents consolidated product line modeling. The consolidation is based on assessment of existing product line modeling concepts and techniques, attempting to converge towards a standard set of concepts for representing software product lines and product line variability. Our aim is to create a metamodel for variability that can be used for all different artifacts (both textual and graphical) across all product line engineering phases. A metamodel is a description of the abstract syntax of the proposed language constructs. A metamodel can also be understood as the model of the repository of a tool for the language. We associate semantics with the elements of the metamodel. We focus on conceptual and language issues of modeling variability rather than the process that would lead to the optimal variability description. We refer to Chap. 5 on the issues relating to the methodology for the variability modeling process.

In order to present variability modeling at large, we first present how variability is handled in standard languages. At the same time, we introduce our recurring example: a Watch. Then, we discuss at length variability modeling through annotations to standard languages and present a consolidated metamodel for that approach. Finally, we present how a (domain-) specific language can be applied to define variability modeling.

The three approaches to variability are distinguished mainly by how much new language is defined. But that is not the only property that differs between the approaches. Traditionally, product line researchers have concentrated on defining annotations to existing languages. This can be seen clearly by the review of existing research found in this chapter. These annotations are then input to a model transformation process that produces a system model in the standard language that was annotated. Variability in standard languages, on the other hand, needs no such preprocessing. The selection of the final system model is either done through modeling where the product line is defined as a framework or at runtime where the system itself creates the configuration based on online input. In the third approach, the (domain-) specific languages are in principle free to apply whatever techniques and mechanisms they want. In practice, we find that domain-specific languages copy constructs from standard languages, and may also apply model preprocessing.

The bulk of our work lies in defining a consolidated metamodel for annotations of variability. The need for a standard is apparent when we consider the huge diversity of concepts and techniques defined in methods and previous projects. The benefits of a standardized approach are many:

- A standard vocabulary that provides a common platform for discussing product line variability, thus facilitating communication and collaboration between people.
- A consolidated metamodel that can be the basis for a standard way of storing and exchanging models which describe product line variability, i.e., facilitating interoperability between product line engineering tools.
- A common foundation for defining (modeling) notations that support the modeling concepts.
- A basis for commercial or open source tool support for product line engineering.

The resulting harmonization we call the Consolidated Variability Metamodel. It is a metamodel that defines the nature of the concepts needed for variability modeling and how they are interrelated. As such, the concepts defined in the consolidated variability metamodel can also shed light on how variability is handled in standard languages and in domain-specific languages.

Agreeing on a single concrete notation supporting this metamodel has proved to be difficult, due to already established use of different tools and languages. We also want to be flexible with respect to specific notation. In order to support several notations for our consolidated model, we propose some different specific notation examples, which can be mapped to the metamodel.

The structure of this chapter is as follows:

- Section 6.2 shows how variability can be expressed in a number of ways also in standard modeling languages exemplified by UML 2.0 [24].
- Section 6.3 is the central core of our work, where we describe approaches to variability modeling based on annotations enhancing standard language descriptions. This section

presents the consolidated variability metamodel and shows how it can be used in anno-
tated modeling examples and by tools.
- Section 6.4 elaborates on how domain-specific languages can be used for modeling
  variability.
- Section 6.5 gives an evaluation of our consolidation efforts.
- Section 6.6 contains our conclusion and indicates a path forward.

6.2 Variability in Standard Languages Exemplified by UML 2.0

Throughout this chapter, we use a single example: a Watch. This section introduces the
example and shows how variability can be expressed in a standard language. We use
UML 2.0 as our example language, but in principle we could have applied the same
concepts to other graphical or textual languages provided they give support to the core
concepts that support the expression of variability: templates, plug-ins and specialization-
redefinition such as Java or SDL [17].

6.2.1 Introducing the Watch Product Line and its Description in UML 2.0

This section illustrates how mechanisms of UML 2.0 support variability. The product line
itself is represented by a class (Watch) and the features are represented by use cases, useful types, properties (attributes) and constraints. Furthermore, the product line may specify
a composite structure.

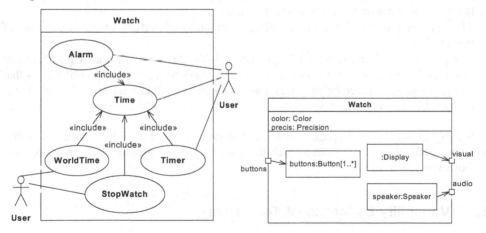

Fig. 6.1. Watch product line – functional and structural features

Figure 6.1 shows how the Watch product line has a set of functional features comprising timer, stopwatch, world time, and alarm capabilities in addition to the pure time capability. The composite structure shows that we want watches to have buttons, a display and
a speaker, and that a watch always will have a color and some precision.

Modeling the *architecture*, including possible variations, is considered essential for product line development.

As we have seen above, UML 2.0 permits the notion of composite structure of classes that covers the modeling of architectures. The class Watch (see Fig. 6.1) defines the general architecture of all watches. Each watch contains a number of *parts*: a number of Buttons, a number of Displays, and a number of Speakers. The watch interacts with the users through corresponding *ports*. Ports and parts are connected by means of *connectors*, and these specify potential communication.

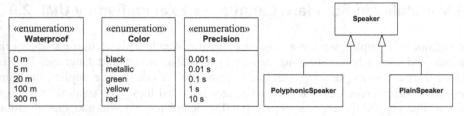

Fig. 6.2. Nonfunctional features and type hierarchy of one property

In Fig. 6.2 we define a set of enumeration types to describe potential nonfunctional features. All watches have color and precision, but we foresee also that watches may have waterproof capabilities. The small class hierarchy shows that speakers will come in different forms.

The composite class in Fig. 6.1. defines a framework in the sense that:

- It defines the architecture of a class of systems. This architecture defines the parts of the systems and how these parts may interact.
- The parts may have behavior that will be common to all systems made on the basis of this class.
- The parts are implicit elements of variation: in UML 2.0 the rule is that, e.g., a Speaker part may be any object that is either an object of class Speaker, an object of a class that is a subclass of Speaker, or an object that has an interface (here in terms of ports) that is compatible with the one of Speaker.

Simply by using the composite class mechanism of UML 2.0 we have seen above that we have defined both the general architecture of a line of products/systems and some obvious variations (on types of parts).

6.2.2 Variability by Means of Templates

Template parameters used for variation modeling are illustrated in Fig. 6.3. The type of the Speaker part is a type parameter.

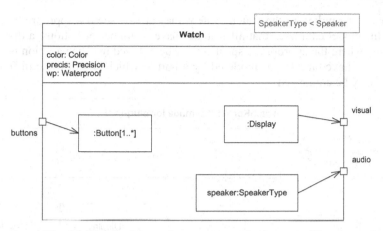

Fig. 6.3. Watch with template parameter for the type of Speaker

A watch with a plain speaker can be derived by binding SpeakerType to PlainSpeaker, see Fig. 6.4.

Watch with plain speaker:
Watch <SpeakerType -> PlainSpeaker>

Fig. 6.4. Binding the template parameter SpeakerType

This approach will benefit from the following UML 2.0 features of template parameters: it is possible to constrain a type parameter, either in terms of a type of which all actual types must be subtypes, or in terms of a signature (in terms of interfaces or ports) that all actual types must be compatible with. For the parameter SpeakerType in our example, we will be able to express that actual classes can only be Speaker and subclasses of Speaker or classes that have compatible sets of ports with the compatible provided and required interfaces.

As a curiosity, UML packages can also have template parameters. Other languages with template parameters only have these for classes, types and functions. The intended use of this is the following: suppose that all classes used in a specific domain have the same type of variation, then instead of giving all these classes the same kind of template parameter, the package defining these classes may have the parameter.

6.2.3 Variability by Plug-Ins (Component-Based Approach)

The plug-in approach is based upon the idea of isolating the variations in components which are external to the stable parts of the system, with well-defined interfaces that apply to all variant components. We use the term "plug-in" merely to mean that a component is fitted into a framework through an interface. The binding of such plug-ins may occur at design time as well as at runtime. Thus our term is somewhat broader than can be found in literature where plug-in is only used to mean a mechanism of post-delivery adaptation.

This approach applied to the watch system may at first seem inappropriate (Fig. 6.5). However, the model expresses that all watches have a number of buttons, a display and a speaker plug, where the appropriate speaker may be plugged in. The variation is what kind of speaker they have, and this is modeled by a port to which any of these different kinds of speakers may be connected.

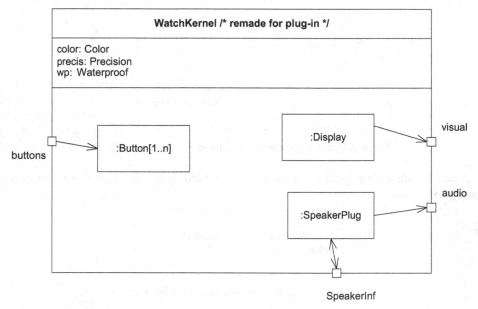

Fig. 6.5. Plug-ins by means of ports and connectors

Figure 6.6 specifies a watch with a plain speaker, simply by connecting a PlainSpeaker to the port of the watch kernel.

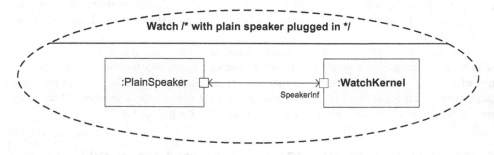

Fig. 6.6. Watch with plain speaker plugged in

The plug-in approach is directly supported by composite classes in UML 2.0. Plug-ins are modeled by parts (of a composite class or collaboration representing the complete system), connection points for plug-ins are modeled by ports, and plug-ins are connected by connectors. With the plug-in approach, it is straight forward to model the variant of either a plain or polyphonic speaker. The plug-in approach also covers the case where a brand new kind of speaker is introduced, as long as it adheres to the well-defined interfaces of the port. This means that all variants do not have to be foreseen when developing the product line.

6.2.4 Variability by Specialization and Redefinition

As we have seen above, specialization in itself may be used as a variation mechanism, in that each specialization of Watch represents a variation.

Specialization and overriding have been used in various approaches in order to express a particular system as a subclass of a class representing the whole product line, or in order to express variations. This is especially the case when making frameworks, where callbacks are represented by virtual methods that are overridden in subclasses as part of the specific use of the framework.

In order for this approach to cover variation on parts of the structure of a product line, it must be possible to override the *types* of the parts that may vary. This calls for virtual types (in line with virtual methods), i.e., types that may be redefined in subclasses. Different languages do this differently. In UML 2.0 all locally defined classes are by default redefinable, while other languages mark these as virtual classes.

In Fig. 6.7 the class SpeakerType is defined locally to the class "Watch" (and thereby redefinable), while the classes Button and Display are defined outside (but used to type parts of the Watch).

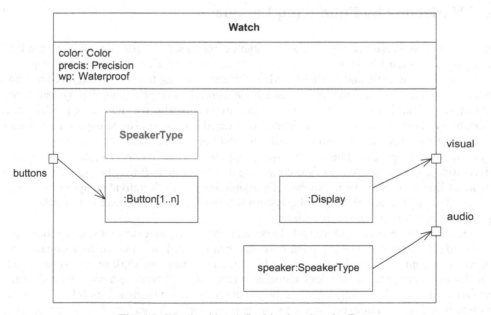

Fig. 6.7. Watch with redefinable class SpeakerType

It is therefore possible to redefine this local class in subclasses of Watch, as seen in Fig. 6.8.

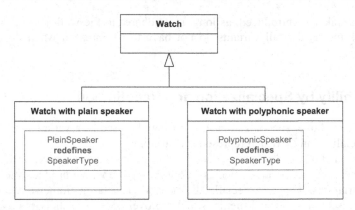

Fig. 6.8. Redefinitions of SpeakerType

Redefining the class SpeakerType in each of the two subclasses is enough. The whole composite structure of Watch is inherited. The only difference is that the type of one of the parts of this structure is redefined to be a part of a more specific type.

By its very nature, this mechanism covers the case with a new kind of speaker type that was not anticipated when the product line was defined: virtual classes can be redefined to any class that is a subclass of the virtual class itself.

6.3 Variability by Enhancing Languages

In Sect. 6.2 we presented how variability can be expressed in system models in standard languages. Standard languages, however, have not been developed to capture all types of variability consistently and explicitly. Also, different binding times of variability have not been considered. Typical binding times are for example, compile-time, deployment-time, startup-time, runtime. All but runtime variability are usually considered as product line variability. There is no technical evidence that variability must also be expressed through a pre-runtime phase, but it is undoubtedly the tradition that the derivation of the executing system from the product line is a two-stage approach – one phase of system description derivation and then one phase of executing the derived system. It may be argued that if the product line itself has a large number of possibilities, but each individual system is rather small, deriving the description of the system before runtime should lead to a smaller footprint and therefore improved efficiency.

Traditionally, product line models have been expressed by extensions, or annotations, to standard languages. These annotations can then be used in a model transformation to produce system models with less variability. In this section, we shall review some of the results of earlier projects and contributions in research, and propose a consolidated metamodel to describe how languages can be enhanced to accommodate variability. As mentioned in the introduction, our aim is to create a metamodel for variability that can be used for all different artifacts (both textual and graphical) across all product line engineering phases and therefore be a starting point for standardization and better commercial and open-source tool support.

We show how the Watch example may be expressed in two different variants of using the consolidated metamodel, and we show in detail the repositories, i.e., the object models corresponding to the metamodel. Finally, this section concludes with a presentation of a prototype tool based on the consolidated metamodel. This prototype tool has emerged through the FAMILIES project in parallel with the development of the metamodel to validate the concepts.

6.3.1 Earlier efforts

FODA, FORM and FAST. Much of the work on variation models stems from domain analysis methods. Feature-Oriented Domain Analysis (FODA) and the Family-Oriented Abstraction, Specification, and Translation (FAST) Commonality Analysis (CA) are two such methods that have provided input for the conceptual model of variability.

Feature-Oriented Domain Analysis (FODA) focuses on feature level commonality and variability [18,19]. Feature Oriented Reuse Method (FORM) extends this with some additional support for software design and implementation. However there is no consistent and coherent variability support throughout the lifecycle. Additionally, the model of variability is not explicitly stated or thoroughly described, but can be derived from the descriptions. Basically, the model for variability is that features can be variable. Features are marked as mandatory, optional or alternative (and then related to the alternatives). Also, composition rules can be declared for how features constrain other features. Additionally, text may be added to diagrams to capture additional variability. This is, however, neither systematic nor sufficient. FODA does have a particular notation for feature variability, which marks the features with either an open or a closed circle along the sub-feature or containment line to indicate optional or mandatory. Also alternatives are connected with arcs on their lines.

The Family-Oriented Abstraction, Specification, and Translation (FAST) Commonality Analysis (CA) is a text and table based domain analysis document [1]. The main part of the document is structured lists capturing the commonalities and variabilities separately. Each variability specification has a range of values. The range of values for all variabilities is captured in a table form list as the parameters of variation elements. This is what the Decision Model is based on. Variabilities are captured along with the range of possible choices and a default value. However, dependencies and constraints among variabilities are not explicitly captured. The CA output is used in the FAST process to create a domain-specific language.

PuLSE and KobrA. Product line software engineering aims at creating generic software assets that are reusable across a line of target products. PuLSE(tm) (Product Line Software Engineering) is a method for enabling the conception and deployment of product lines in a large variety of enterprise contexts [4].

The life cycle of a software product line in PuLSE is split into the following phases: initialization, product line infrastructure construction, usage, and evolution. In the initialization phase of PuLSE, the other phases and the technical components are tailored. Through this tailoring of the technical components, a customized version of the construction, usage, and evolution phases of PuLSE is created.

The principle dimensions of customization are the nature of the application domain, the organizational context, reuse aims and practices, as well as the project structure and available resources.

PuLSE provides technical components for the different deployment phases that contain the technical know-how needed to operationalize the product line development. The technical components are customizable to the respective context. Customization of PuLSE to the context where it will be applied ensures that the process and products are appropriate.

To introduce software product line engineering in software developing organizations, the products need to be extended to enable modeling of commonalities and variabilities. A systematic approach for extending single system models with the means to model commonalities and variabilities is described in [23]. The approach enables the extension of any given asset to be generic, i.e., to enable the explicit modeling of variability in that asset. The variability modeling is accompanied by decision models. This approach is also the basis for variability and decision modeling in the PuLSE approach and has been used as the basis for developing the conceptual model described in this section.

KobrA represents an object-oriented customization of the PuLSE method [2]. The infrastructure construction phase of PuLSE corresponds to KobrA's framework engineering activity, the infrastructure usage phase of PuLSE corresponds to KobrA's application engineering activity, and the product line evolution phase of PuLSE corresponds to the maintenance of the frameworks and applications [3].

UPM (Polytechnic University of Madrid) Notation. The UPM variation point identifies one or more locations at which variability will occur. Each variation point will be related to a decision. Once the decision is made, a set of variant elements will remain and others will be left apart. As a result, the variation point will have changed its state.

Tightly linked to the concept of variability, the decisions are part of the software product line. Therefore they are related to the models in the product line. In order to obtain specific products, decisions have to deal with variability, either in the requirement, or architectural or testing phases.

Variability is explicitly represented in the architecture through variation points. For UPM, each variation point is composed of one or more variants and it is formally defined by an algebraic expression. The expression denotes the relationships among elements, using as syntax operators those available in Boolean algebra. Expressions are composable, meaning that an expression can be created as a combination of others. The reference architecture obtained for a product line is a series of models in different views; each element in a model is labeled as a variable of the set of products in the product line.

The UPM notation belongs to the category of using UML extension mechanisms (stereotypes and tagged values) for representing variability. It does not represent variation elements explicitly as model elements, but marks all variable model elements [7,25].

Matthias Clauß work. Clauß [8] proposes a UML profile to model product line. Specifically, he defines UML extensions in order to express commonalities and variations in models when describing product lines. The work is focused on variability modeling of the structural aspects of a product line (i.e., mainly on class diagrams). The concept of variation proposed by this approach relies on the three following parts:

- The variation point is the location of the variability in a model. The UML element is also marked by the stereotype *«variationPoint»*.
- A variation point has a set of variants. A variant is a possible derivation for a variation point. This kind of element is marked by the stereotype *«variant»*.
- Relationships can exist between variants of different variation points. It is then possible to express dependencies between variable model elements. For instance if a variant needs to use another variant, a relationship stereotyped by *«requires»* may be modeled.

The *«variationPoint»* stereotype may be applied on model elements that are *GeneralizableElement* as defined in the UML metamodel. Consequently, classes, components, methods, collaborations and associations, can be stereotyped by either *«variationPoint»* or *«variant»*.

Moreover, it is also possible to model optional variation. A model element marked by the *«optional»* stereotype, signifies that it may be absent in a specific system model.

In the example depicted in Fig. 6.9, PaymentInfo is a local variation point with three possible variants: Building_Data; Delivery_Data; and CreditCard_Data. Contract is an optional element. That means that systems instantiated from this product line may or may not have Contract. Moreover, this class has a dependency with one of the attributes of PriceMethod. Consequently, a *«requires»* link is added between both optional elements.

Becker's variability model. Becker and others have also been working on defining a uniformly applicable model of variability [5,6]. Many of the ideas they discuss are similar to the mainstream, although the terminology is sometimes different and the model in the end looks different. In their model, they capture the various types of variability, dependencies and constraints between variabilities, and make a distinction between the variability (at the "specification level" in their terms) vs. capturing the variability points in the assets (at the "implementation level").

VTT and POLITEHNICA University of Bucharest. Another approach based on stereotypes is that of Dobrica and Niemelä of VTT and POLITEHNICA University of Bucharest [10]. This work was done to extend the Quality-driven Architecture Design and quality Analysis (QADA) method with support for variability. It is similar to other work with stereotypes, tagged values and OCL constraints, except that in their approach different variation mechanisms are used for different models/views instead of a uniform approach to handle all models and levels as we are striving to achieve. Also, variation is linked directly to a product instead of smaller decisions based on features or functionalities.

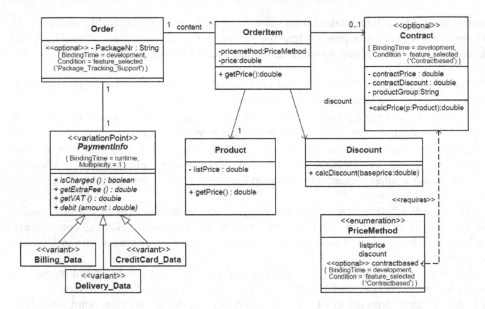

Fig. 6.9. Example of model using Matthias Clauß extensions for product line

Ziadi, Hélouët, Jézéquel: Towards a UML Profile for Software Product Lines. Ziadi et al. have suggested a profile of UML 2.0 for software product lines where they introduce a small set of stereotypes to define variability for classes as well as behavior (Interactions) [29]. They try to give this profile a precise semantics. One of the stereotypes is «optional» which describes that a given element may or may not be present in a product derived from the product line. The pair of stereotypes «variation» and «variant» work together. The «variation» stereotype defines the context for the «variant»s. For each «variation» one and only one of the «variant»s may be present in the product.

The paper refers to the distinction between runtime variability and development-time variability, and places itself in the latter group. This distinction is similar to the distinction in this chapter between applying standard language and enhanced, annotated descriptions.

The UML profile suggested is similar to the traditional "compiler directives" annotations in programming languages, also known as "pragmas." The UML profile is, however, well defined and gives adequate restrictions for the use of the constructs. This makes their approach better than simple "model pragmas."

From a semantic point of view, product lines defined through their UML profile do not lend themselves to analysis of the dynamic semantics before the variability has been bound. At that point, all the special stereotypes have vanished, and we are left with a derived product model in UML.

6.3.2 Consolidated Variability Metamodel

In this section we describe the metamodel of variability. The metamodel describes the elements that define a product line model and its resolution, i.e., instantiating a system model from the product line model. Conceptually, the product line model is constructed from a base modeling language with variabilities added. That is, any base model, such as UML models or feature models or Java descriptions or even structured text documents, can be extended to capture variability through the variability metamodel. A product line model is then given by a base model and a variation model.

Among modelers there is no complete agreement on what constitutes "one model" as opposed to "several interrelated models." Some modelers use the term "model" for what is described in a specific kind of diagram – such as the sequence diagram model, or the feature model. In this chapter, we generally use the term "model" to mean the full description of a given piece of reality regardless of which diagrams are used to describe it. Still we find that sometimes it is fruitful to distinguish between different models such as between the base model, the variation model and the resolution model even though they may apparently describe the same overall part of the world.

Our notion of a model and model elements also comprises structured textual descriptions. It is irrelevant for our approach whether the concrete syntax is graphical or textual. Furthermore, model elements may also consist of informal text, but then there is little we can do with them unless we provide further categorization.

Once a product line model exists, a resolution model can be made that defines the binding of variabilities to resolutions. This resolution model applied to the product line model yields a system model if all variabilities are bound. There can be multiple resolution models for a product line, each resulting in one system model or a partial instantiation of the product line.

The metamodel in Fig. 6.10 defines the concepts and their interrelationships more precisely. The watch example is used to illustrate some of the concepts.

The metamodel is captured in UML with classes representing concepts, and associations capturing the relations among concepts. Within the diagram descriptions, each element introduced in a diagram is defined.

The model is split into multiple diagrams, each diagram covering certain issues. The top-level diagram (Fig. 6.10) defines the core concepts. Central to this model is Model Element.

- *Base Model* is a model in any language (textual or graphical). For our purposes, we only consider the base model to consist of model elements.
- *Model Element* represents any kind of model asset in a model in a given modeling language. If UML is the modeling language, then Model Element is the element in the metamodel of UML with the same name. For example, a Model Element can be a feature from a feature diagram, or a class or a use case from UML, or a requirement name in a structured text document. Model Element will probably support composition (along with other kinds of relationships, e.g., associations and specialization between model elements), but this will be composition in a (base) model without any variation. Note also that Model Element is not defined by our metamodel, but considered already defined in the given modeling or programming language, while the other classes are defined here.

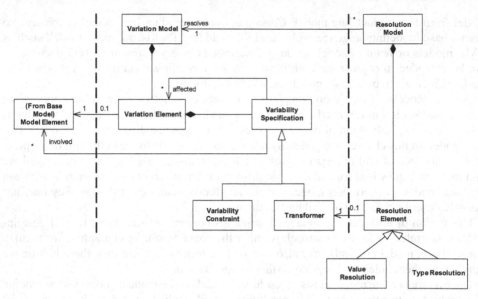

Fig. 6.10. Metamodel Core

A variation element refers to a model element, depicting the fact that for the purpose of this variation model, the referred model element is affected. This relationship has a zero-to-one cardinality, as not all model elements are affected by variability; common ones are not. However, variation elements only make sense as additions to base model elements. Variation elements only contain the information that the referenced model elements may be affected by variations.

– *Variation Model* is a collection of variation elements. The variation model keeps track of all the variation elements of the product line model.
– *Variation Element* represents something with variable nature. All model elements that are affected by the variability of this variation model are referred to by variation elements.

The information about how something can vary is captured by the variability specifications associated with a variation element.

– *Variability Specification* represents the actual variability of a variation element, such as optionality, required dependencies, etc. It has a range of further specializations (Fig. 6.11).

Variation Element owns a number of variability specifications. The variability specification is associated with the affected variation elements that may change based on the resolution and the involved model elements. At the top level, Variability Specification is specialized into two types of elements: Variability Constraint and Transformer.

- *Variability Constraint* represents constraints on valid resolutions and distinguishes between valid resolution models and invalid ones.
- *Transformers* have concrete transformations associated with them. When values are bound to transformers (from the Resolution Element), this defines the transformation of the variation model and the base model. Typically when a transformer is completely bound, the transformed total model (pair of base model and variation model) will not have any trace of this bound transformer. Instead the base model will have changed accordingly.

The other central part of the core model supports the resolution of variability that exists in a model. A set of resolution elements defines how a model with variability is bound.

- *Resolution Model* defines resolutions of variability for a product line model. It is a named collection of resolutions that reference variability specifications in a product line model. A resolution model represents a binding of variability specifications, which can be used to derive a new, more specific model. A resolution model that contains resolutions for all variability specifications of a model represents a derivation of a system model.
- *Resolution Element* is a model element that represents a binding of a variability specification, i.e., it represents a binding of variability. This is either a complete binding in which all variability is resolved, or a partial one in which some variability is still present. A resolution has a number of effects which represent the effects a resolution has on the model, such as narrowing a constraint or removing parts of the model. Resolution Element has two subtypes: Value Resolution and Type Resolution.
- *Value Resolution* represents resolutions that define a value for the variability. Most transformers are mapped to value resolutions. Examples for these will be presented later.
- *Type Resolution* represents resolutions for variabilities that are resolved with model elements. Type Alternative Transformer is the only transformer associated with this resolution. An example for this will be presented with the definition of Type Alternative Transformer.

There may be several resolution models pointing to the same variation model. For one resolution model, each transformer may be linked to zero or one resolution element. Not all transformers must be associated to resolution elements. Even in a completed product specification, some variability may be beyond the scope due to higher-level resolutions.

Variability Specification represents the variability present in a product line model. Certain kinds of variability commonly recur in product lines. These are captured in term of specializations of Variability Specification (Fig. 6.11).

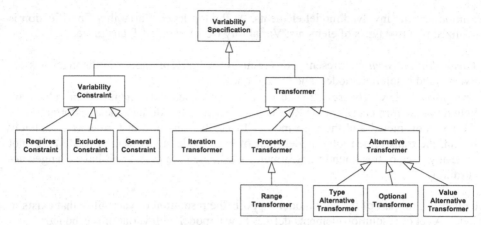

Fig. 6.11. Variability specification hierarchy

- *Property Transformer* represents variability bound by the type of a property, i.e., it requires a decision to be made regarding its value. The effect of a property transformer is to set the value for the model element in the base model that is affected by this transformer. The value is set to the value of the value resolution.
- *Range Transformer* is a special kind of property transformer, where the value of the property in question must be within a specific range of values. It can for example be an integer range defined for an integer attribute, or a string range defined for a string-type attribute. The effect of a range transformer is the same as that of a property transformer. That is to set the value for the model element in the variation model that is affected by this transformer. The value is set to the value of the value resolution.
- *Alternative Transformer* represents variability in terms of choices of values or elements (items). A set of possible items is referenced and the constraint defines minimum and maximum that can and must be selected (range_min and range_max). A resolution requires selection of at least *range_min* and at most *range_max* items.
- *Value Alternative Transformer* is a special kind of Alternative Transformer, where the selection of choices is a set of values. An example is a selection of values from an enumeration type, e.g., *select two of the values {red, green, blue, yellow, black}*. The effect is to set the value for the appropriate model element to the value of the value resolution.
- *Type Alternative Transformer* is a special kind of Alternative Transformer, where the selection of choices is other model elements, e.g., types, classes, features. The effect of a type alternative transformer is in some way to "keep" the model elements in the variation model that are referred to by the type resolution and remove the affected variation elements of the transformer that are not referenced. Alternatively, the model element that owns the type alternative transformer (through its variation element) may originally have no type. Then the effect is to bind the underlying model element to the selected elements represented by the type resolution.

- *Optional Transformer* is an Alternative Transformer where the possible choices of values are {range_min = 0, range_max = 1} regarding the inclusion of an item.
- *Iteration Transformer* represents a variability that repeats a variation element and its associated model element and all of its sub-elements in the base model hierarchy. The effect of the transformation is to duplicate the affected model element the number of times specified by the resolution value.
- *Requires Constraint* represents a constraint that indicates dependency between model elements, i.e., that the presence of one model element requires the presence of a set of other model elements.
- *Excludes Constraint* represents a constraint that indicates the reverse dependency between model elements; the fact that one model element is present may exclude the presence of another.
- *General Constraint* represents any constraints that are not possible to express through the specific constraints. It has a language and a specification property to allow constraint specification using different kinds of languages, e.g., OCL.

6.3.3 Variability Mechanisms Expressed by Annotations to UML

In Sect. 6.2, we showed how UML 2.0 can be applied to describe variability. In this section, we show how we can apply annotations to UML descriptions following the metamodel in Figs. 6.10 and 6.11.

A resolution model can be applied to a product line model yielding a system model. Thus the generality of an annotated product line model is somewhat different from the models applying only pure UML since a separate resolution (binding) process must be applied to the product line model before an executable model can be derived.

Our metamodel describes a repository for a UML-like language for product line modeling. We shall present two quite different syntactic approaches to the description of our product line specific concepts. One approach uses new symbols and resembles what is known in literature as a "Feature model" [9,18,19] This notation is not really annotation of some UML diagram, but rather a novel type of diagram that fits well together with other UML diagrams. The leaf nodes of the feature diagram are typically concepts from the UML model. The other approach is based on the more traditional UML stereotype approach. Neither of the two syntaxes gives detailed information about the procedure that leads to the resolution model. In general we shall assume that achieving the desired resolution model is the product of a separate strategy or decision process.

In Fig. 6.12 we see a feature model of the Watch product line. Here, we use a syntax which does not use special symbols, but rather applies text labels to the branches to indicate which of the meta-classes apply on that branch. Thus Fig. 6.12 may also very directly be seen as depicting the repository. The labels correspond to different subclasses of Variability Specification. The bold-faced nodes such as "Watch," "StopW" and "Buttons" represent variation elements. In a UML context the variation elements will typically be classes or behaviors of UML.

Each variability specification represents some kind of decision to make, but we do not imply any specific order in which to make those decisions. Since the variability specifications may be interdependent, e.g., described through a variability constraint, the feature model will transform itself incrementally as decisions are being made. In our model, there is interdependency between inclusion of Alarm and what kind of Buzzer can be chosen. If you have already chosen not to have a Buzzer, the option to choose Alarm is in fact prohibited. Conversely if you have chosen to include an Alarm, then the originally optional Buzzer choice must be transformed to being mandatory.

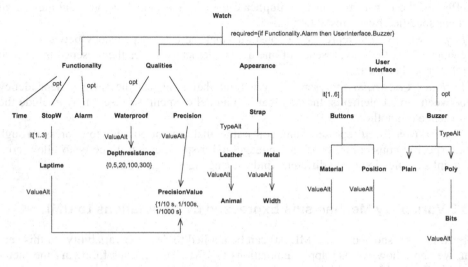

Fig. 6.12. Watch product line feature diagram

The feature diagram in Fig. 6.12 is too comprehensive to allow a closer look at how the metamodel relates to the feature diagram. We will therefore concentrate on showing the repository model relative to our variability concepts for a fragment of the total Watch model.

First, we assume that the feature diagram is described in a language of its own and that the model elements represent concepts of that Feature Language. Consequently, we have objects that are model elements of types such as Property, Feature and Feature Group.

We will consider a fragment of the User Interface shown in Fig. 6.13. The feature diagram in Fig. 6.13 is represented in a repository which may be depicted as an object model as in Fig. 6.14. We see that there is a very close correspondence between the feature diagram and the repository built on the metamodel.

Alternatively, we could describe this (fragment of the) Watch product line by annotations to UML. The idea is to start from something which is an incomplete (or over-specified) UML model of the Watch, and annotate it with stereotypes to describe the variabilities.

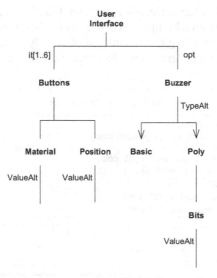

Fig. 6.13. Fragment of the Watch feature diagram

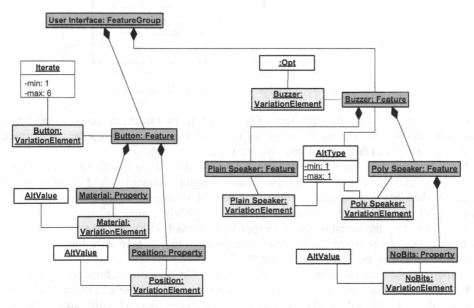

Fig. 6.14. Repository of a feature model based on a Feature Language

Let us again focus on the variabilities of the User Interface shown in the feature diagram. In Fig. 6.15, this is shown by the stereotype «it[1..6]» on the "buttons" Part and the «TypeAlt» in the "Buzzer" rectangle. The latter is obviously something that goes beyond pure UML, but described in a different way than previously in Sect. 6.3.3.

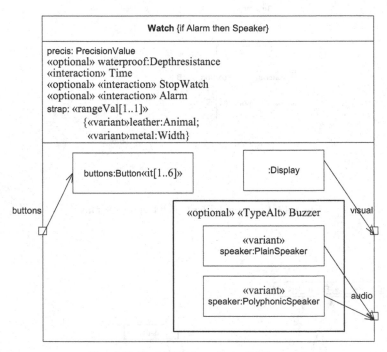

Fig. 6.15. Variability based on a UML model

In Fig. 6.16, we show the repository of the User Interface fragment based on the UML-annotated approach where the model elements are of kinds known from the UML (meta-model) such as Part (Property), Class and Attribute (Property).

If we compare the repositories of Figs. 6.14 and 6.16 we see that there are clear similarities, but that the base model of the Feature language contains the feature structure, while for the UML annotation version, the variabilities form the internal structure and the base model of UML model elements are not completely connected to each other, but rather attached to the variabilities. A proper UML model will only appear after all variabilities have been resolved. Notice that the repository in Fig. 6.16 only shows a fraction of what is described by stereotypes in Fig. 6.15.

Showing resolution is our next step in Fig. 6.17. We have not elaborated any concrete syntax for resolutions here, but only shown the resolutions in a table in order to illustrate how it could have been done. Again, the Feature language approach will look slightly different from the UML annotation one.

Notice that we have not resolved all variabilities. The detailed properties of each button have not been resolved, so we are still left with what should be called a product line model.

After having applied the resolutions, the repository in Fig. 6.18 emerges.

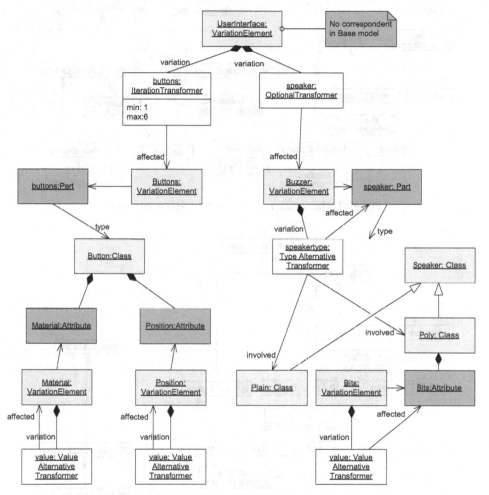

Fig. 6.16. Repository for UML-annotated model

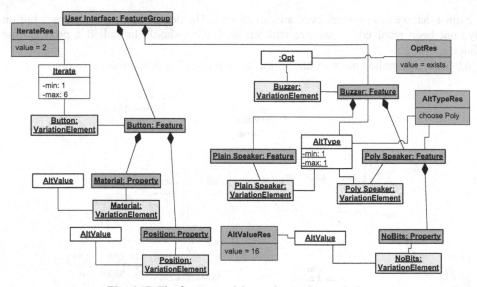

Fig. 6.17. The feature model repository with resolutions

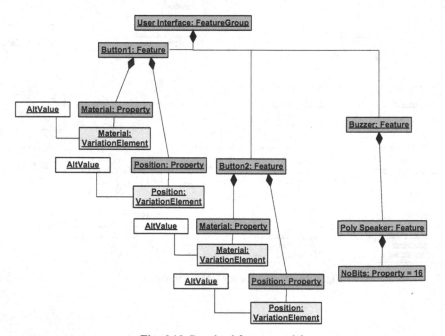

Fig. 6.18. Resolved feature model

We see that the resolution of the iteration has had an effect on iterating the unresolved variabilities, one for each button. On the other hand, the buzzer/speaker feature is completely resolved, and it is also possible to shortcut that part of the feature model by removing the Buzzer feature which now has outplayed its role.

Approaching this from the UML annotation side, we get the following resolution repository and resolved model for the buzzer/speaker side of the variabilities (Fig. 6.19).

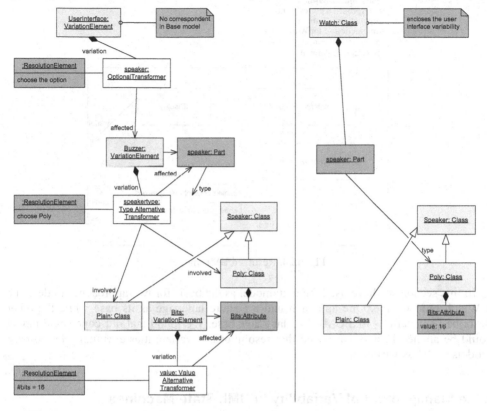

Fig. 6.19. Repository of UML-annotated model with resolutions, and the resolved model

The resolved UML model will eventually look like Fig. 6.20. We represent the resolution model of the UML annotated version in Tab. 6.1.

Table 6.1. Resolution Table representation for repository of Fig. 6.19

#	transformer	resolution values	effect
1	speaker: OptionalTransformer	option chosen	The optionality is removed, and the speaker part remains in the base model
2	speakertype: TypeAlternativeTransformer	choose Poly type for speaker	The dangling type-reference of the part "speaker" is set to reference the class Poly
3	value: ValueAlternativeTransformer	set to 16	The "bits" attribute of the "speaker" part is set to 16

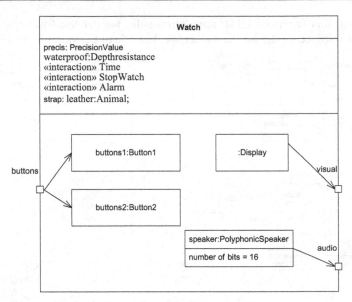

Fig. 6.20. Resolved UML model

In this section we have used the metamodel as the basis for two approaches to describe a Watch product line. One approach had a Feature language as its base while the other described annotations to a UML-like language base. We found that our conceptual model could be applied in both cases and that resolutions of variabilities eventually led to base models with less variability.

6.3.4 Management of Variability in UML State Machines

Until now, most efforts related to product line research have concentrated on the management of variability modeling of structural aspects. In the context of real time systems development, the behavior aspect is very important and so describing state-based models is crucial for efficient use of product line principles in the real-time engineering domain. The tool Accord|$_{UML}$-SyF [13,14] is an attempt to provide behavioral modeling features for product line design of real-time engineering applications. This section focuses on the improvement of variation modeling in behavior models, here state machines, and provides mechanisms to derive a state-machine based framework into various well-formed model instances of the product line.

The main issue that lies behind the derivation of a state-machine based framework is the ability to ensure that the derived specific state machine is well-formed. Consequently, it requires that the variation derivation process is structured in a way that eliminates models that are not well-formed. To reach this goal, we designed a specific theory which enables the determination of all possible well-formed framework derivations from a product line model containing state-machine based behavioral specification.

The research work proposed here is based on earlier proposals such as [8,18, 28]. During the design of a framework state machine, variation points can be specified in the same way as is usual in structural models. A variation point is a variation element referencing a simple model element that varies among specific products of a product line.

Behavior is specified by state machines that consist of nodes and transitions linking these. Behavioral variation points may then be either nodes or transitions. These variation points are constrained by using variability constraint or transformers as described in the metamodel (see Sect. 6.3.2). In Accord|$_{UML}$-SyF, a profile for product line modeling support was developed before the consolidated metamodel reached a stable version. Consequently, some concepts used in our approach are slightly different. Mainly, we introduced the concept of variation group that contains a set of variations, which is similar to the Transformer class.

Figure 6.21 depicts the product line model of a watch product line designed with Accord|$_{UML}$-SyF. The watch product line may be derived into either a simple watch, or a watch with alarm. The alarm of our system can be a beeper, a display or a display with a beeper. Note that the design of the system does not precisely define specific product specifications. Only possible functionalities are considered when designing the product line framework.

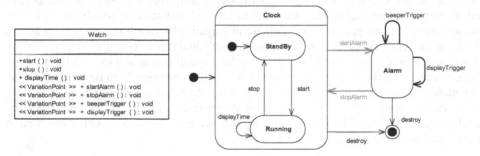

Fig. 6.21. Extract of the class and state machine diagrams of the watch product line

This system has several variation elements: *startAlarm()*, *stopAlarm()*, *beeperTrigger()* and *displayTrigger()* operations. Variations are dispatched into the following decisions definitions (Fig. 6.22):

- *AlarmVariationGroup* is an example of an optional transformer that has constraints *startAlarm* and *stopAlarm* services. When *AlarmVariationGroup* is set to true then both *startAlarm* and *stopAlarm* are likewise set to true, and when Alarm is set to False then both are set to False. This variation group is chosen when the developer wants the alarm functionality. A variation group corresponds to a variation element that does not reference a model element, but represents a group of variation elements.
- *TriggerVariationGroup* is a type alternative transformer with two possible resolutions: *beeperTrigger* and *displayTrigger*. When this option is chosen, the alarm of the resulting watch will contain exclusively a display and a beeper.

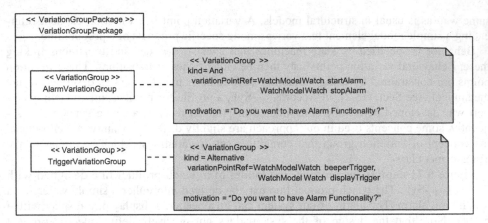

Fig. 6.22. Decision diagram for the watch product line model

In a model-based approach using the UML formalism, structural elements and behavioral elements are interdependent. In order to analyze and resolve possible conflicts in variation modeling, we propose an automatic propagation of variability constraints across the whole model. Thanks to this propagation mechanism, it is possible to evaluate the impact of structural variations on the state-machine specification and to calculate all possible derivations of the product line framework. It is then possible to detect derivations that construct an ill-formed state machine and finally to detect errors in the model or constraints on variations. Figure 6.23 shows an example of automatic derivation from the model specified in Fig. 6.21. In this case, four derivations of the state machine specified in the product line framework are possible.

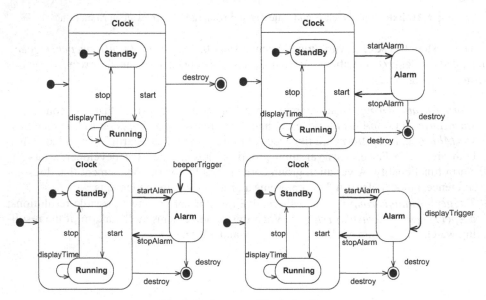

Fig. 6.23. Four possible derivations

6.3.5 Prototype Model Tool Integration

The different approaches to variability modeling have diversified its implementation in a few tools that support specific product lines, or general variability management concepts.

Nowadays end-users trying to develop their own product lines deal with variability modeling in different ways in order to achieve their own solutions. They do not mind the metamodels, notations or techniques within the tool (or tools) they are using to reach their objectives, but the way those topics are implemented in the tool will shape their approach to variability handling and its representation.

A consolidated metamodel for product line variability modeling will unify the tool solutions for its implementation in a common and comprehensive way, allowing the users to choose the tool that satisfies their needs, ensuring compatibility. If this is not possible for the actual results (file formats, graphical representations, notations, etc.), at least it should be possible on the level of conceptual representation of the variation model.

The impact of this metamodel will affect not only the modeling tools but also the variability resolution tools.

A tool supporting the decision model resolution must integrate, and interact with, those model elements at runtime to generate the appropriated transformation effect related to the selected value resolution (from the existing resolution elements) associated with the resolution of each variation element.

This behavior is clearly described by the consolidated metamodel and must be integrated into the tools. Any solution not developed under the definition of the resolution model will probably be incompatible with the consolidated model philosophy.

Metamodel implementation, V-Manage tool. V-Manage is a tool suite that provides full support for product line activities. Many of the issues addressed within the consolidated metamodel have been covered by the metamodel for variation models implemented within V-Manage. Moreover, the mechanism for resolving associations of model elements and variation elements based on the variation model ("Decision Model" in V-Manage terminology) is well defined in the tool.

With V-Manage, the user specifies a variation model and a resolution model, and provides the mechanism to specify product line models and produce concrete system models.

Not every concept of the metamodel is implemented in the tool; and the naming conventions and notations are different from the consolidated metamodel. V-Manage provides a good example of a particular solution for modeling variability that may evolve to adopt the consolidated metamodel and, at the same time, a good view of how a tool could integrate the variation model in a useful way for an end user.

This section will describe:

– V-Manage suite
– How the consolidated metamodel is supported by the tool
– Implementation and resolution of the example Watch product line following the definition and the UML 2.0 model described in this section

The V-Manage suite consists of three applications:

– V-Define to support the definition of variation models ("Decision Models" in V-Manage terminology) as well as the definition of the relationships (affected associations) between variation elements. It covers some of the variability specifications and extends it by a few proprietary ones.

- V-Resolve, to support the resolution of the model using the variation model and some specific components that contain the transformers, resolution elements and transformation effects for a specific product line.
- V-Implement to support the implementation of reusable components used on the resolution of the variation model for the production of a specific product.

These applications are interrelated, and this division in three different applications is related to the different sub-processes that conform to the software product line engineering process (domain engineering and application engineering) [40] and the different user roles that will use each application.

Domain engineering will use V-Define and V-Implement while application engineering will use V-Resolve.

The V-Define application is used to specify the variation model for a product line as a set of decisions representing the whole dimension of the variation of the product line. Decisions (representing variation elements and model elements) should be defined in such a way that they characterize univocally one system within the product line. V-Define is also used to establish some variability constraints and transformers between variation elements.

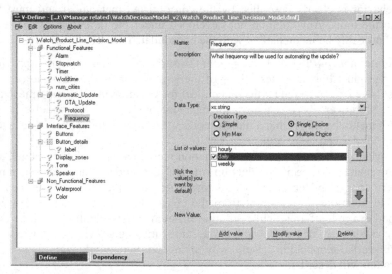

Fig. 6.24   An overview of the user interface of V-Define

Figure 6.24 provides an overview of the V-Define front-end. At the left side the tool provides a tree view representation of the variation model, and in the right side the information of each variation element being defined is shown for domain engineering to be able to define variation models. The tool provides a graphical interface to help relevant stakeholders understand the product line holistically.

The V-Resolve application is used to define a resolution model. This application is capable of dynamically adapting the resolution elements values and structure by processing the dependency rules. The dependency rules are the way V-manage defines variability constraints. The variability specifications affecting other variation elements (Decisions) are specified by using the V-Define. The resulting model from this tool is an Application Model (V-Manage concept), basically a variation model where every variation element has been resolved. It is a resolution model for a specific product.

For example, the processing of the dependency rules can:

– lock the variation elements values
– set predefined values to a variation element
– show or hide part of the variation model (as a type alternative transformer does)
– pre-assign the default value to some variation elements

By processing the dependency rules of the variation elements (Decisions), V-Resolve guides the user during the assignment of values from resolution elements for each variation element that is defined.

Figure 6.25. provides an overview of the V-Resolve front-end. At the left side the tool provides a tree view representation which aids in the resolution of the variation model and in the right side the information of each variation element being resolved is shown for application engineering to specify the system requirements.

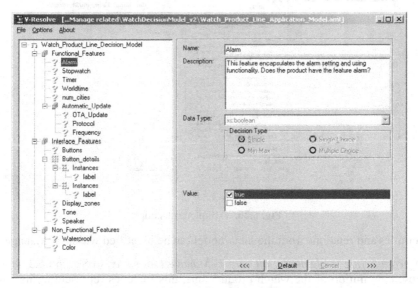

Fig. 6.25. An overview of the user interface of V-Resolve

The V-Manage suite groups the transformers, resolutions of transformation effects and Value Resolution actions within components named "Flexible Components" (FC). The FCs are executable components that produce a specific system model from a resolution model.

The V-Implement application allows the implementation of these FCs or architectures of FCs containing all the variation elements' variability specifications (variation points on V-Manage) that have to be solved in order to produce a product of the domain.

V-Implement provides:

- the implementation of independent FCs
- the specification of the binding, refinement, and final solving of the variability specifications and resolution elements
- the creation of FCs' architectures to establish the product line architecture.

Figure 6.26. provides a screenshot of V-implement. On the left side all the variation elements that a FC will handle are presented and can be dragged and dropped into the FC
implementation code. This enables the creation of different FCs conforming to a product
line architecture which handles all the variation elements within a variation model.

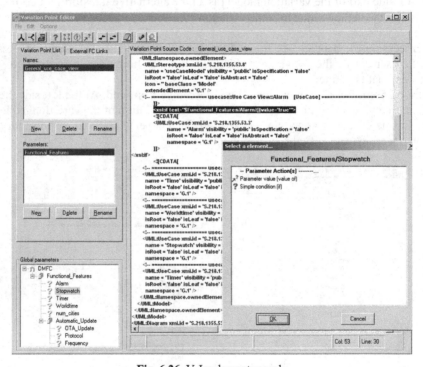

Fig. 6.26. V-Implement sample

Most entities and relations from the metamodel can be identified within V-Manage.

Watch product line implementation with V-Manage tool suite. In Section 6.3 we provide
a complete definition of the watch product line; this includes representing its UML 2.0
base models and variation models using the consolidated model for product line variability
modeling.

This section uses the V-Manage suite to implement the diagrams and to generate desired Watch products.

Following some of the guidelines for the product line-oriented software production
process [40] the domain engineer uses V-Define to specify the Watch variation model. In
V-Define, the variation model described in section 6.3 is treated as a tree-view of decisions (variation elements and model elements). The "dependency" area of V-Define
will allow the domain engineer to describe how the variation elements are affected by
transformers' effects and any other relations between the decisions and their effects.

V-Define will generate a complete variation model for the Watch product line that will be used as input for V-Implement (to generate the variability resolution mechanisms) and for V-Resolve (to generate the resolution model).

When the variation model has been defined, the next step is to construct the reusable assets that will be used to build the final systems. These reusable assets are called Flexible Components (FC) because they vary their execution according to the decisions made in the resolution model (Application Model on V-Manage terminology). Composed of a set of variability specifications, a FC is no more than an executable piece of code that produces parts or the entire final system. V-Implement is the tool for building the FCs.

Figure 6.27 provides an overview on how the V-Manage tool implements the UML models introduced in section 6.2 that represent the variation model for the Watch product line by means of a tree structure that captures the variation model and produces any product of the line by executing the underlying FC architecture and resolving variation elements.

With a simple drag-and-drop mechanism, variation elements (Decisions) from the variation model (Decision Model) are used as input to the FC creating variability specifications and sets of variation parameters that define exactly the behavior of each variability specification.

The domain engineer is the person using this tool. For the Watch product line, the domain engineer will create the FCs needed to generate the Watch products. These will manage the decisions specified by the Watch variation model such as "Alarm" and "Precision" and control, for example, when the Watch is waterproof, that the waterproof depth maximum is specified by the application engineer.

Finally, the application engineer will use V-Resolve to exploit the variability of the product line and produce the final applications. V-Resolve guides the application engineer while binding the variation elements, executing all the dependencies (due to value resolutions, type resolutions, iteration transformers, optional transformers, property transformers and alternative transformers), and checking the data types defined in the variation model. As a result, a resolution model is obtained.

The next step is to execute the pre-defined FCs with the resolution model to obtain the final assets.

A FC can be used to produce a graphical representation of the Watch features. Using a variation model generated with V-Define, we can launch V-Resolve to produce a resolution model with the resolutions *WorldTime* and *StopWatch* set as *"true"*. We execute the FC to obtain the resolved model 1 (see Fig. 6.28). If we take the same variation model and the same FC, but we set those variation elements to *"false"* in the resolution model (built using V-Resolve), the FC will produce the resolved model 2 (see Fig. 6.28).

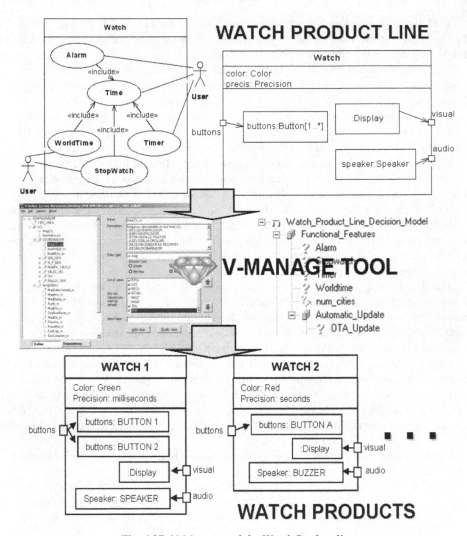

Fig. 6.27. V-Manage and the Watch Product line

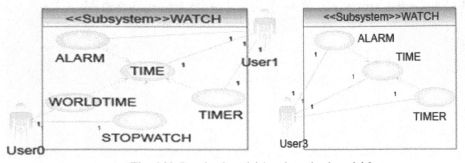

Fig. 6.28. Resolved model 1 and resolved model 2

Future of the tool with a consolidated metamodel. V-Manage confirms all the problems highlighted at the start of this section: every tool has its own notations and manages the variation models and variability in its own way, even when the "concepts" are equivalent or similar to those specified in the consolidated metamodel.

A standardized metamodel for product line variability modeling that unifies the representation of the variability (entities, relations, etc) will not only allow its standard representation using a language such as UML 2.0, but will harmonize the various approaches for tool development too.

This common modeling view will aid tool development and increase usability and interoperability. With the existence of a standard, it will be possible to graphically draw the variation elements and resolution models complying with the metamodel rules and restrictions (in UML 2.0 for example). The tools may then read or import those models, resolve them, and produce the desired results, facilitating model development (and the compatibility between different tools) and relieving tool developers from the hard work of implementing their own variability representations.

6.4 Domain-Specific Languages

In this section we apply domain-specific modeling (DSM) languages to demonstrate how the consolidated model of variability can be supported. We describe modeling support for the Watch product line and its variability space. We also demonstrate automatic product derivation – one of the main benefits the domain-specific languages approach offers for product lines (Kieburtz at al. 1996 [22], Tolvanen 2004 [26], Czarnecki 2004 [9]).

6.4.1 Similar Efforts: Software Factories

Software Factories became a layman's term in the IT-business at the end of 2004 when Microsoft helped launch a book by Jack Greenfield and Keith Short [15]. The book gives the methodology behind Microsoft's approach to DSL (domain-specific languages). The book defines a software factory as a configuration of languages, patterns, frameworks and tools that can be used to rapidly and cheaply produce an open-ended set of unique variants of an archetypical product.

The book does not intend to present new methods, but rather brings together many existing ones. Their aim is to bring the factory constituents together as a productive whole. The approach is driven effectively by the associated Microsoft tool that supports the methodology. This does ensure that the created languages are not only used for sketching but must define a path all the way to realization.

The book itself uses a large number of domain-specific languages. Most of the languages are intuitive, small, graphic languages similar to UML class diagrams. The book argues against UML as the solution to modeling, but it is probably the case that intuition has been well-prepared by the presence of UML in education.

6.4.2 Supporting Variability Directly in the Language

Modeling occurs always at two levels: type and instance levels. The type level denotes the language concepts, constructs and constraints that we use during modeling. The instance level refers to the actual design data. The same applies for expressing variability as we can express it both in instance data (i.e., in model) and directly in modeling constructs of the language itself (i.e., in metamodel).

A domain-specific modeling (DSM) language for a given product line allows us to address variation directly on the level of modeling language [26]. The DSM approach suggests that the variation within the product line should be managed with a well-focused modeling language specifically tailored to the product domain – in contrast to the traditional modeling languages that try to be as general as possible [15]. Accordingly, variation and decisions are not illustrated in models using naming conventions, stereotypes or additional constraint languages, but by using directly the product concept and its variation decisions [9] as model elements. The basic assumption is that it is more natural to specify variation directly using product variation terms, than in general-purpose feature concepts or in programming terms. For instance, if one variability point deals with the number of icons a single watch model can have, the modeling language directly has the concept of "Icon" and allows the number of icons applied to be described in an unambiguous way. The Icon is thus a concept of the language and the values chosen by the developer, e.g., Timer or Stopwatch icon, are instances. Similarly other concepts for describing watch product line variability would be Displays, Buttons, Alarms, Time units and so on.

Domain-specific modeling requires that product variation can be represented formally into a metamodel of a modeling language. Metamodel-based tools can then read these language (i.e., product line) specifications to implement the tool support [21]. Once defined, the DSM language sets the variation space for application engineers and ensures that the variation model is followed de facto. Setting variation space already at language level makes automatic variant generation, optimization, early error detection and correct reuse easier to achieve.

Describing static variability. The nature of variation (static or behavioral) and level of variation detail favors selecting computational models that can be represented with certain basic modeling languages. Pure static variability can be expressed in data models, while variation in sequencing requires some sort of flow model; state machines advocate state models, etc.

Figure 6.29 shows the example of specifying display structure for a given watch model. According to the variation model, each watch has one display consisting of a set of Icons, Time units, and Buttons. In the figure, the icons are in the process of being specified. Depending on the Decision Model, these selections could be implemented as an alternative decision (developer chooses among existing icons) or as a property decision (developer can create her own icons). Currently, the Icon selection is implemented as an alternative decision as illustrated by the selection list of Icons. Current Icon definition language could also be extended by an alternative representation decision. The language would allow choosing the way Icon is represented in the display, e.g., by letter A, by text Alarm, by certain bitmap, etc. Button definition is implemented as a property decision, since the developer can create new buttons and specify button labels.

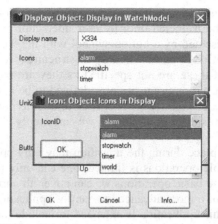

Fig. 6.29. Specifying the display structure for a given variant

In a similar manner, other static variation can be described using static modeling languages. These could be waterproof, precision and color definitions. This DSM language takes care of configuration of the product line as it guides the application engineer to choose among possible variations. It differs from the traditional configuration approaches by providing the means for generating complete code instead of plain configuration data. It also provides the design data to be referred to when describing behavioral variability and creating new functionality as described in the next section.

Describing behavioral variability. In most cases it is not possible to cover all variation within just one type of model and modeling language. Also in the watch product line, several variation points deal with behavioral functionality. Figure 6.30 shows the example of a modeling language for specifying a watch application. The model presents a simple application that displays and changes the current time.

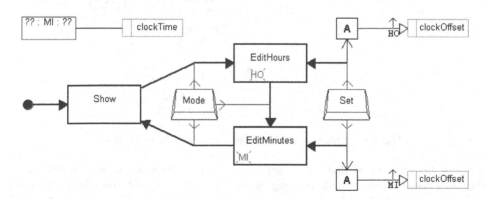

Fig. 6.30. State machine with watch domain extensions

In this case, state machines, typical computational models used with embedded software, are suitable for expressing behavioral variability. We can then enrich and narrow the semantics of the state machine to focus on the concepts and constraints of the watch product line. Basically, there are only two watch-specific extensions in our state machine. First, the transitions can be triggered only by user interaction when a certain button is pressed. Buttons are represented by a button symbol with the label in the middle. These buttons were already specified as part of the display structure (see Fig. 6.29). Also alarms can trigger transitions, but these are not specified as they are not suitable for the Time application. Other types of button usage are now defined to be outside the legal variation space, so it is not possible to press two buttons, or to double press, or to keep a button pressed longer. If such needs arise in the future, we can simply extend the set of possible button operations.

Second, actions taking place during the transition may only operate on time unit entities. Also the set of possible operations is limited: one can only roll the time units up to modify the time. With these basic operations we can cover all current needs of our watch product line (an example of a more advanced variant of application shown in Fig. 6.30 is presented in Fig. 6.31). This application is extended to include the possibility to subtract the time units and also to adjust the seconds.

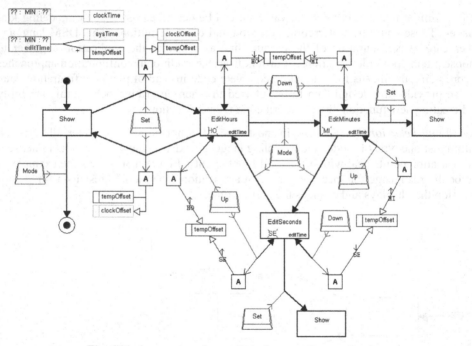

Fig. 6.31. A more complex variant of current time application

It must be emphasized that DSM languages allow the building of new functionality rather than just choosing and configuring existing functionality. For example, the variants specified in Figs. 6.30 and 6.31 are just two out of many possible variants and still further alternatives can be developed. For instance, the Time application that uses a special icon to emphasize editing mode could be another variant and a watch model for kids where time editing does not cover seconds yet another, and so on. If we make the Time application mandatory for every watch model, the possible variability could be handled (e.g., precision) purely in a static manner similar to what is shown in Fig. 6.29.

Resolutions and influence of design choices are specified via the metamodel. For instance, one watch application could be pure Stopwatch without Time or other applications. This would be a typical product targeted at coaches. As pure application selection among applications is not enough according to the watch variability space, modeling should also support behavioral configuration of watch applications. Figure 6.32 illustrates two different alternatives: one for specifying watch model with world time application for travelers and another with stopwatch for coaches. The latter one, illustrated on the right side, has one application only and the time units it shows on the Time display include milliseconds, seconds and minutes. Display functionality and usage of time units is illustrated at the top with the key and time unit value. Both models reuse applications, so individual applications like Time refer to the actual Time application specification, like the one illustrated in Fig. 6.31. The DSM language can also have rules for the model integration and reuse possibilities.

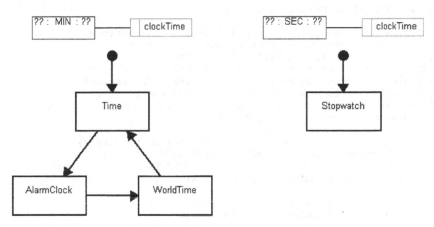

Fig. 6.32. Two alternative watch application configurations

6.4.3 Supporting Product Derivation Using Generators

In the previous section we described how variation could be handled from within the DSM language. We now move on to product derivation from the models described above, as some variation can be also incorporated into the generators.

The generator is a proper place for two kinds of variation. As each target platform or programming language requires, at least partially, a unique generator implementation, it is widely acceptable to handle the target variation within the generator. Another suitable way to use the generator for managing variability is to build higher-level primitives by combining low-level primitives during generation.

Listing 1 shows an example of Java code generated for the current time application. The product derivation is complete in as much as full code is generated from the model and manual rewriting of the code is not needed. This completeness is crucial for model-based product development – it has been the cornerstone of other successful shifts made with programming languages. Moreover, domain-specific models describing the application functionality in a code-independent manner enable use of the same models to generate code for multiple platforms. If the variability deals with implementation issues only, then only the generator is different, not the application designs. Therefore, for example, C code could be generated from the same design model, or different programming models could be used by the generator if this were part of the required variability.

```java
public class SimpleTime extends AbstractWatchApplication {
  //define unique numbers for each Action (a...) and DisplayFn (d...)
  static final int a22_1405  = +1; //+1+1
  static final int a22_2926  = +1+1; //+1
  static final int d22_977   = +1+1+1; //

  public SimpleTime(Master master) {
  super(master);
  // Transitions and their triggering buttons and actions
  // Arguments: From State, Button, Action, To State
  addTransition ("Start [Watch]", "", 0, "Show");
  addTransition ("Show", "Mode", 0, "EditHours");
  addTransition ("EditHours", "Set", a22_2926, "EditHours");
  addTransition ("EditHours", "Mode", 0, "EditMinutes");
  addTransition ("EditMinutes", "Set", a22_1405, "EditMinutes");
  addTransition ("EditMinutes", "Mode", 0, "Show");
  // What to display in each state
  // Arguments: State, blinking unit, central unit, DisplayFn
  addStateDisplay("Show", -1, METime.MINUTE, d22_977);
  addStateDisplay("EditHours", METime.HOUR_OF_DAY, METime.MINUTE, d22_977);
  addStateDisplay("EditMinutes", METime.MINUTE, METime.MINUTE, d22_977);
  };
  // Actions (return null) and DisplayFns (return time)
  public Object perform(int methodId)
  {
  switch (methodId) {
  case a22_2926:
  getclockOffset().roll(METime.HOUR_OF_DAY,true,displayTime());
  return null;
  case a22_1405:
  getclockOffset().roll(METime.MINUTE, true, displayTime());
  return null;
  case d22_977:
  return getclockTime();
  }
  return null;
  }
}
```

Listing 1. Java code generated for the current time application

6.4.4 Defining DSM Support

The benefits of high-level modeling and automated product derivation are not possible to achieve without creating the language and generators that fit with the product line. This is done during domain engineering. According to Weiss [27], the creation of DSM is cost-effective if there are more than three variants. This is the normal situation in most product lines.

Building a DSM for product lines is also proven to save development resources (see, e.g., Kieburtz et al. 1996 for USAF [22], Weiss & Lai 1999 for Lucent [27], Kelly & Tolvanen 2000 for Nokia [20]): Traditionally all developers work with the variation rules and map them to the implementation manually. There are big differences between developers. If experienced developers, who also perform domain engineering, define the modeling concepts and mapping to variation points, then others do not need to do it again. Similarly product derivation would be of better quality since we can expect that a code generator specified by an expert produces applications of higher quality than could be achieved by normal developers by hand.

6.5 Evaluation

There are no established criteria for evaluating approaches to product line modeling. Evaluation which emphasizes *variation* modeling would ignore how well the approach models *commonalities* between systems in a product line. Similarly, an emphasis on product line modeling would focus less on elementary issues from conventional *single systems* modeling, such as maintaining models or handling new and unforeseen features. A product line modeling approach that does not measure up favorably against the requirements of conventional system development approaches will not succeed.

In the following, we will evaluate our approach based upon a set of criteria that tries to cover both product line modeling and conventional system modeling issues.

6.5.1 Evaluation Criteria Relative to an Evaluation Reference Model

In order to evaluate product line modeling approaches, we present an evaluation reference model [16]. On a very general level, most product line approaches will have a distinction between the *generic* sphere and the *specific* sphere. In the generic sphere we have feature models and product line models, and within the specific sphere we have system models (Fig. 6.33). In addition to these models, we need to explain how the system model relates to the product line model. The relation – often described as a model transformation from the product line – is affected by feature selection. The process of transforming a generic product line model to a specific system model is called application engineering.

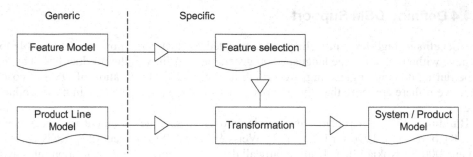

Fig. 6.33. Product Line and Application Engineering Reference Model

Given this general reference model, we may evaluate specific approaches by comparing this general model with the approaches and by answering the following questions on product line:

1. Does the approach enable proper documentation of the variations between the different product line members:

    – Is it possible to document variation, that is, is it possible to have models covering more than one system of the product line? Does the approach support the explicit documentation of points of variation?
    – Does the approach distinguish between different binding times for variabilities, that is does it distinguish between runtime variability and non-runtime variability?
    – Is it possible to see the variants in a product line model; the question here is whether the documentation enables people to understand the different variants in a product line model.

From requirements to modeling as part of (conventional) system development, we will get at least the following evaluation points:

2. Roundtrip engineering/model synchronization: what is the relation between product line model and system model? Is it a one-way transformation, or is it possible to add elements to the system model and have them reflected in the product line model?
3. Does the approach support iterative and incremental development, that is, are partially instantiated systems supported and can product line models be analyzed? How does the approach deal with unforeseen features?
4. Is it possible to track features: are features represented in the product line model, or are they represented in a separate feature model? Features are like requirements, and in ordinary system development it is important to track requirements.

6.5.2 Approaches

In this chapter, we have presented three main categories of variation modeling: through standard language, with annotations, and through specific language. We use this categorization as the starting point for our evaluation.

Variability in standard languages. This approach combines available mechanisms in a given language. Using frameworks and plug-ins, the domain concepts are represented by predefined classes/components in a standard language, and product lines are modeled either by frameworks or by composing predefined components with well-defined interfaces. System models are obtained by specializing or configuring a framework, or by composing specialized components.

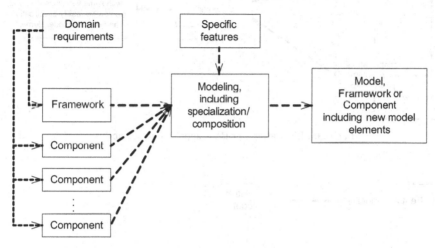

Fig. 6.34. Frameworks and plug-ins

The mechanism shown in Fig. 6.34 is typically augmented with the use of the following mechanisms:

- Generic type parameters
- Redefinition of virtual methods and types
- Templates

Variability through annotations. Figure 6.36 illustrates the Base-Variation-Resolution (BVR) approach. Besides the approach described in this chapter, the approaches proposed by Clauss [8], Ziadi et al. [28,29], as well as FODA and FORM [18,19] are Base-Variation-Resolution approaches.

The evaluation will be supplemented with a comparison with the Product-line-as-the-union-of-all-possible-systems (Fig. 6.37). This approach is characterized by having a product line model with variation-point model elements for all possible variations included. A product line-model is a model that is the union of all potential system models in which some elements are marked as variation points, and the specific system models are *generated*, i.e., there is no modeling involved in producing the system models. Examples for product-line-as-the-union-of-all-systems approaches are PuLSE [4] and KobrA [2], as well as the approaches proposed by UPM [7], Becker [5], and VTT [10].

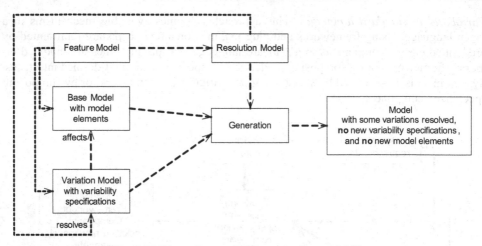

Fig. 6.35. Illustrating our BVR approach to variability

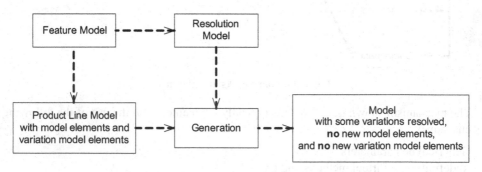

Fig. 6.36. Product-line-as-the-union-of-all-systems

Variability through a specific language. While general modeling languages represent domain concepts by means of classes/components, domain-specific languages express these as language constructs. There is thus really no product line model, but simply a (DSL) that includes the potential to make models that are guaranteed to adhere to the restrictions it is wise to have in a domain. In contrast to the approach above, there is no product line model, but rather a language specification (i.e., a metamodel). A product line is thereby the set of all systems that may be modeled with this language. Examples of the domain-specific language approach are FAST (compare Section 6.3) and MetaCase (see Section 6.4).

6.5.3 Evaluation Results

Evaluation with respect to product line engineering. A product line model, realized as a framework, covers a number of system models. The variants are, however, expressed

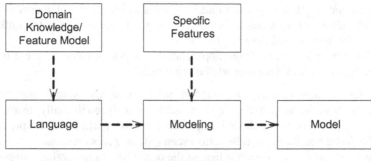

Fig. 6.37. DSLs

using traditional framework means. This means especially that variations can be modeled, but not in an explicit way. Consequently, the distinction between different binding times is not possible. The identification of the different variants in a product line model is also not possible in the framework/plug-in approach.

In the Base-Variation-Resolution approach, the possible variations and the resolutions are parts of different models of the model triplet (BVR). Therefore, variation can be documented explicitly. The distinction between runtime and non-runtime variability is supported as well. Since the variations and the resolutions are modeled separately, this approach also supports the identification of the different variants in a product line model.

The Product-line-as-the-union-of-all-possible-systems approach will have variation elements as part of the model, but typically the feature selection models are separate models. This approach does support the explicit modeling of variability and also the distinction between different binding times. The separation of information on the decisions and on the resolutions does not support the identification of the different variants directly. The benefit over the Base-Variation-Resolution approach is, however, that the product line model is not overloaded with resolution information. It is therefore also closer to the models used in single-system development.

In a domain-specific language, the possible variations are located in the language. The product line models (i.e., the models expressed in the domain-specific language) do not contain the points of variation in an explicit way.

6.5.4 Evaluation with Respect to Conventional Systems Engineering

Roundtrip engineering/model synchronization. In the Framework/plug-in approach, the system model is a separate model, but based upon specialization of a framework model and/or composition of components. It is thus no problem to add special elements in the specific system model.

In the Base-Variation-Resolution approach, the specific systems are not modeled explicitly, but rather generated. The resolutions are part of the system models, in the same way as the variability constraints are. There is no modeling involved, so round trip is an issue. It is a problem to add model elements to the specific system models since elements cannot be added to the resolution model, but have to be added to the resulting model.

For the Product-line-as-the-union-of-all-systems approach this is also an issue, as the system model is generated; this approach is a one-way transformation approach, from product line to system. It is possible to add system-specific model elements to generated system models. However, this has to be done with great care so as not to confuse model elements from the generic and the specific sphere.

For the Domain-Specific Language approach, this is not an issue, as there is really no product line, that is, each system is modeled separately.

Is the approach iterative and incremental? In order for an approach to support iterative and incremental development, it should be possible to analyze (formally, testing, reviewing, etc) product line models, it should be possible to have partial system (product) models, and it should be possible to handle unforeseen requirements/features.

The Framework/plug-in approach relies on the possibility of analyzing components and frameworks. Frameworks may form the basis for new frameworks, and components may be composed into new components, so both partial models and unforeseen features are supported.

In the Base-Variation-Resolution approach, a base model is not necessarily a model that may be analyzed; however, by applying a kind of default resolution model, one may generate a model that may be analyzed. Partial models may be generated; a model with some of the variability constraints resolved is a partial system model. Unforeseen features have to be handled by adding model elements for them to the generated system model.

In the Product-line-as-the-union-of-all-systems approach, the total set of products with all possible variations is modeled in one product line model. The resulting model contains information covering more than one system. The product line model can, therefore, not be analyzed using the same means of analysis as used in single-system development. Rather, additional analyses are necessary to analyze product line models that take into account the generic nature of the models. Another option is to first do application engineering and then use single-system analyses on the resulting system model. The generation nature of this approach does not support partial models, and unforeseen features either have to be put into (an updated version of) the product line or added as system-specific model elements.

For the Domain-Specific Language approach, as there are no product line models, they cannot be analyzed. However, properties of the domain-specific language can be analyzed. There is no notion of partial models. Unforeseen requirements are easily handled, unless they require new language constructs.

Unforeseen features come in two variants: features that belong to the product line and features that are required for a specific system. The Product-line-as-the-union-of-all-systems approach and the Base-Variation-Resolution treat these in the same way: as product line features, while the Framework/plug-in approach allows the addition of properties for specific systems. As indicated above, even with the Product-line-as-the-union-of-all-system approach, it is possible to add properties after the system model has been generated, but as mentioned above, this has to be done with great care. The Framework/plug-in approach may choose to let the unforeseen properties become properties of a new (specialized) product line model, instead of just of a specific system model.

The need for making a new domain-specific language for the purpose of supporting new features reveals the following challenges: can new constructs be added without corrupting existing constructs (are they orthogonal or are there any dependencies), can a domain-specific language be defined as a specialization of another (inheriting the semantics of the super language and adding what is needed for the new features)?

Feature Representation and Tracking. This aspect deals with the representation of features, which can be done either in the product line model or in a separate feature model.

The Framework/plug-in approach will have to have separate decision and resolution models, as the models are just specializations and compositions of existing frameworks and components.

The Base-Variation-Resolution approach is made so that the variation-model elements, the possible decisions (in terms of the variability constraints) and the resolutions are all part of the model triplets, and as such are easily tracked.

The Product-line-as-the-union-of-all-systems approach will have variation-point elements as part of the model, but typically the decision models and the feature selection models are separate models.

The Domain-Specific Language approach does not have any means for tracking features, except for tracking which languages constructs are being used.

Summary of Evaluation Results. The approach proposed in this chapter harmonizes and consolidates existing approaches to product line modeling. The proposed approach provides a standard vocabulary for discussing product line variability. The presented metamodel is a step towards a standard metamodel as a way for model exchange and storage. This metamodel can also be the basis for commercial tool support.

As shown above, the nature of the proposed approach satisfies most of the evaluation criteria covering product line engineering.

From a product line engineering perspective, a Base-Variation-Resolution approach makes explicit the variability in the product line models along with the possible variants that can be resolved from this model. It supports the distinction between runtime and non-runtime variability.

From a conventional system engineering perspective, a Base-Variation-Resolution approach also satisfies the criteria, which are roundtrip engineering and model synchronization, iteration and increment support, as well as the possibility to track features.

In contrast to other approaches that provide variation-constraints-resolution (the approaches published by Clauß as well as Ziadi et al.), the approach proposed in this chapter is more general and flexible, since it is not restricted to specific modeling constructs for modeling the relation between variability and variation, but uses the complete UML to express product line engineering concepts in the product line models.

6.6 Conclusions and Future Research

This chapter has described variability modeling in the broadest sense. We have presented a consolidated model for product line variability modeling and shown how it can be used and supported by tools. The consolidated metamodel is based on assessment and evaluation of existing approaches and techniques for product line variability modeling. Motivation for this work stemmed from the plethora of different approaches, uses and definitions of concepts within the product line community. The main drive was the clear benefits of standardizing a baseline for variability modeling, such as a common vocabulary, leveraged collaboration between people, and interoperability of tools.

The resulting metamodel defines the basis for variability modeling through a set of different kinds of variability that can be associated with model elements of a modeling language. It also relates these variabilities to resolutions through a resolution model, which defines the specific choices made from a variation model.

The consolidated model does not target the process used for resolving variabilities to create configurations or specific products. Rather, it opens for different kinds of processes to be integrated and to use the concepts defined. The model covers the most used variability concepts and also defines highly flexible and general mechanisms to define constraints. It also opens for future extensions in case specific domain requirements should appear. We have demonstrated the applicability of the conceptual model by using different notational techniques, and by presenting a prototype tool.

The results achieved here will be subject to further research and practical application in forthcoming research projects. Specifically, we will address the practical aspects of applying the conceptual model, both in terms of tool support and integration with product development and decision processes. We have shown the applicability of the consolidated metamodel on a rather small example. It would be advantageous also to perform an experiment on a much larger case with more intertwined and complex dependencies. The recursive structure of the metamodel indicates that it is reasonably scalable, but a case study would certainly produce valuable experience.

In the near future, we will look further into standardization of the conceptual model. We have initiated this topic within the Object Management Group (OMG) and will pursue this activity, hopefully towards a standardization process. We may also pursue a similar standardization activity within the ISO JTC1/SC7 (Software and System Engineering).

Acknowledgments

We gratefully acknowledge the extensive reviews of Stan Bühne, Günter Böckle, Juan Carlos Dueñas, Timo Käkölä, Janne Luoma, Mark Maier, Juha-Pekka Tolvanen, and Tewfik Ziadi that significantly improved the quality of this chapter.

References

1. Ardis M, Weiss D.: Defining Families: The Commonality Analysis. ICSE 97 Tutorial 4D (1997).
2. Atkinson C. Bayer J., Muthig D.: Component-Based Product Line Engineering: The KobrA Approach. In Proceedings of the First International Product Line Conference (SPLC1). Denver, Colorado, USA, (2000) 289-310.
3. Atkinson, C. Bayer, J. Bunse, C. Kamsties, E. Laitenberger, O. Laqua, R. Muthig, D. Paech, B. Wüst, J., Zettel J.: Component-based Product Line Engineering with UML. Addison-Wesley (2001).
4. Bayer, J., Flege, O., Knauber, P., Laqua, R., Muthig, D., Schmid, K., Widen, T., DeBaud, J.-M.: PuLSE: A methodology to develop software product lines. Proceedings of the Symposium on Software Reusability (SSR'99) (1999) 122-131.
5. Becker M, Geyer L, Gilbert A, Becker K.: Comprehensive Variability Modelling to Facilitate Efficient Variability Treatment, PFE 2001, (2001) 294-303.
6. Becker M.: Towards a General Model of Variability in Product Families. In Software Variability Management Workshop (2003) 19-27.

7. Cerón, R., J.L. Arciniegas, J.L. Ruiz, J.C. Dueñas, J. Bermejo, and R. Capilla. *Architectural Modelling in Product Family Context.* in *Software Architecture, First European Workshop, EWSA 2004.* St Andrews, UK, Springer LNCS 3047 (2004) 25-42.
8. Clauss, M.: Generic Modelling using UML extensions for variability. Presented at OOPSLA workshop 2001, Tampa Bay, Florida, USA (2001).
9. Czarnecki, K., Eisenecker, U.: *Generative Programming, Methods, Tools, and Applications*, Addison-Wesley. (2000).
10. Dobrica L, Niemelä E.: UML Notation Extension for Product Line Architectures Modelling. In Proceedings of International Workshop on Software Variability Management (SVM), ICSE'03 (2003) 8-13.
11. Engineering Software Architectures, Processes and Platforms for System-Families (ESAPS), Eureka 2034, ITEA project 99005, http://www.esi.es/esaps/.
12. From Concepts to Application in System-Family Engineering (CAFÉ), Eureka 2023, ITEA project ip00004, http://www.esi.es/Cafe/.
13. Gérard, S., Terrier, F., Tanguy Y.: Using the Model Paradigm for Real-Time Systems Development: ACCORD/UML. OOIS'02-MDSD. Montpellier: Springer LNCS 2426 (2002) 260-269.
14. Gérard, S., The ACCORD/UML methodology. Internal report CEA-List, Paris. (2003).
15. Greenfield, J., Short, K.: Software Factories: Assembling Applications with Patterns, Frameworks, Models & Tools, John Wiley & Sons (2004).
16. Haugen, O., Møller-Pedersen, B., Oldevik J.: Comparison of System Family Modeling Approaches. SPLC 2005. Rennes, France. Springer LNCS 3714 (2005) 102-112.
17. ITU, Recommendation Z.100, ITU Specification and Description Language. Reed, R. Editor., ITU-T: Geneva. (1999) 300p.
18. Kang, K., Cohen, S., Hess, J., Novak, W., Peterson: Feature-Oriented Domain Analysis (FODA) ASEI technical report: CMU/SEI-90-TR-21. (1990).
19. Kang, Lee, Lee, Kim.: Feature Oriented Product Line Software Engineering: Principles and Guidelines Book Chapter: Domain Oriented Systems Development – Practices and Perspectives, UK, Gordon Breach Science Publishers, (2002).
20. Kelly, S., Tolvanen, J.-P., Visual domain-specific modelling: Benefits and experiences of using meta-CASE tools, *International workshop on Model Engineering*, ECOOP 2000, (ed. Bezivin, J., Ernst, J.) (2000).
21. Kelly, S., Tools for Domain-Specific Modeling. Dr. Dobb's journal, September, (2004).
22. Kieburtz, R. et al.: A Software Engineering Experiment in Software Component Generation, Proceedings of 18th International Conference on Software Engineering, Berlin, IEEE Computer Society Press. (1996) 542-553.
23. Muthig D.: A Light-weight Approach Facilitating an Evolutionary Transition Towards Software Product Lines, Ph.D. Thesis, Fraunhofer IRB Verlag, (2002).
24. OMG Unified Modelling Language: Superstructure, Version 2.0, formal/05-07-04, OMG (2005).
25. Rioux, L., et al.: Style, structures and views for handling commonalities and variabilities. Eureka Σ! 2023 Programme, ITEA project 99005 (2001).
26. Tolvanen, J-.P.: Keeping it in the family, Application Development Advisor, July-August, 2002, 101 Communications (2002).
27. Weiss, D., Lai, C. T. R.: *Software Product-line Engineering*, Addison Wesley (1999).
28. Ziadi, T., Jézéquel, J.-M., Fondement, F.: Product line derivation with UML. Software Variability Management Workshop.. University of Groningen Department of Mathematics and Computing Science (2003).
29. Ziadi, T., Helouet, L., Jezequel, J.-M.: Towards a UML Profile for Software Product Lines. Fifth International Workshop on Product Family Engineering (PFE-05). Siena, Italy. LNCS 3014 (2003) 129-139.

Part 3: Product Line Architecture

Introduction

Part 3 deals with designing and leveraging product line reference architectures that incorporate product line commonality and variability. As requirements and architecture present, respectively, the problem view and the solution view and the variability addressed in the requirements needs to be designed in the variability in the architecture, Part 3 is closely related to product line modeling and requirements engineering discussed in Part 2.

It consists of four chapters:

Chapter 7. Dealing with Architectural Variation in Product Populations

Chapter 8. A Software Product Line Reference Architecture for Security

Chapter 9. Architecture Reasoning for Supporting Product Line Evolution: An Example on Security

Chapter 10. A Method for Predicting Reliability and Availability at the Architecture Level

The chapters of Part 3 identify numerous quality requirements such as variability, flexibility, evolvability, maintainability, security, availability, and reliability as the central drivers for designing product line reference architectures. Variability is considered as an especially important characteristic of software product line architectures that supports the description of common and variable elements pertaining both to solving functional requirements and to meeting the nonfunctional quality requirements.

The common architecture is a central asset of a product line. Variations in architecturally significant requirements between product line members often make it difficult to standardize architectural solutions across the product line, for example, when the scope of a product line expands due to repeated integration of new and/or legacy products or the product line is merged with other product lines.

In such product lines, often referred to as populations, the common architecture must allow for some degree of architectural variation. Chapter 7 proposes an approach to modeling architectural variation in product population reference architectures that to a large extent preserves the support for product derivation normally associated with more focused product lines, thus improving flexibility, evolvability, and maintainability of the reference architectures. The approach is validated by studying how it can be applied to improve the modeling of several real-life population architectures. It is aligned with the consolidated variability modeling approach (Chap. 6) but other modeling approaches such as those discussed in Chaps. 1 and 5 could be used as well.

Among the quality requirements for software product lines, security is a cross-cutting concern in software-intensive systems and should be subjected to careful architectural analysis and decision making. The requirements for cost-effective product line development complicate this task. Chapters 8 and 9 thus deal with security issues. Chapter 8 addresses two research questions:

1. Is it viable to represent architectural security knowledge in a reference architecture?
2. If so, is the reference architecture useful for designing product line architectures that effectively deal with security requirements?

Both questions are affirmed. The main contribution is a reference architecture that draws upon state-of-the-art techniques and practices from software product line architecture and information security and serves as a decision support framework for designing software product line architectures that effectively deal with security requirements. To validate the reference architecture, Chap. 8 presents experiences from using it at three distinct companies.

One of the most frequent problems in software product line engineering is supporting evolution. Guiding the evolution effectively requires the development and maintenance of architectural models. But the industry is increasingly relying on third party implementations of software platforms and components which may not be accompanied by architectural models. Adequate processes, methods, and techniques should thus be developed and adopted to support evolution holistically. Chapter 9 introduces a new process to support product line evolution with respect to nonfunctional security requirements. It is based on architectural conformance and recovery methods, techniques, and tools. It demonstrates and validates the process in the context of security requirements for distributed environments by analyzing the most important standards dealing with architectural security requirements, creating a security reference architecture for distributed environments (by drawing upon the results of Chap. 8), and utilizing the reference architecture to perform a complete conformance and recovery process for a specific system.

The demand of high reliability and availability of today's systems is considerable as an increasing number of complex systems are tightly embedded into our surroundings. These systems have to work as intended and when needed. Ideally, the problems in reliability and availability should be able to be analyzed prior to system implementation, when the fault corrections and modifications are relatively easy and cheap to perform and the right design decisions can still be taken. Chapter 10 presents a method for predicting reliability and availability at the architectural level. The Reliability and Availability Prediction (RAP) method defines how the reliability and availability requirements should be elicited, negotiated, and mapped to the reference architecture, how they should be represented in the architectural models, and how the architecture should be analyzed in order to validate whether or not the requirements are met. The method has been validated by simulating it in the reliability and availability prediction of a case example in a laboratory.

7 Dealing with Architectural Variation in Product Populations

S. Hallsteinsen, G. Schouten, G.J. Boot, and T.E. Fægri

Abstract

The common architecture is a central asset of a product line. In many cases, however, variations in requirements between product line members make it difficult to standardize architectural solutions across the product line. This typically occurs when the scope of a product line expands due to repeated integration of new and/or legacy products or when the product line is merged with other product lines. In such product lines, often referred to as populations, the variation in architecturally significant requirements may be difficult to accommodate in one common reference architecture. Therefore the common architecture must allow for some degree of architectural variation. In this chapter we propose an approach to modeling architectural variation in product population reference architectures that to a large extent preserves the support for product derivation normally associated with more focused product lines. We validate the proposed approach by studying how it can be applied to improve the modeling of several real-life population architectures.

7.1 Introduction

The common reference architecture is a central asset of any software product line. The benefits of and, indeed, the need for such an architecture have been proven many times [3,14,16]. It is particularly important in product lines that have not reached the level of maturity where variant derivation is only a matter of resolving explicit variation points, but also involve a significant amount of variant specific development. In such product lines the reference architecture plays a dominant role in guiding and constraining the variant specific development.

The design of the architecture is dictated by the architecturally significant requirements, which tend to be dominated by requirements relating to quality issues and constraints set by the anticipated execution environment [6], but also often include central functional requirements.

7.1.1 The Problem

In product lines with a fairly narrow scope there tends to be little variation in architecturally significant requirements, and the idea of a common architecture is unproblematic.

Often the product line consists of one application that is delivered in a number of variants and targets a focused domain. Even though functionality may vary considerably between variants, common architectural solutions are viable and very high degrees of reuse can be achieved. However, there are also product lines with much wider scope, typically containing several interoperating applications and also often spanning wider domains. In such product lines the architecturally significant requirements tend to exhibit considerable variation, and it may be necessary to allow for different architectural choices in different applications and application variants. In this chapter we refer to such wide scope product lines as *product populations*. This term was coined by van Ommering [27] when describing efforts to develop a product line that incorporates software for a wide range of consumer electronics products (TV sets, DVD players, etc.) that had earlier been produced on separate product lines.

Populations typically emerge as a result of evolution. A product line has to exist for long enough for the investment in the product line assets to be recovered, and therefore typically has to accommodate many changes and extensions during its lifetime that contribute to widening the scope and diversifying requirements. For example:

- Evolution of user needs in the domain or of underpinning technologies typically tends to widen the scope rather than just change it, since there are always users lagging behind in the adoption of new patterns of use or the acceptance of new technologies.
- The integration of additional products into a successful product line extends the scope of reuse of the product line assets and thereby increases the return on investment.
- The merging of existing product lines into a larger population might be fuelled by irreversible trends in the market or, for instance, simply by the acquisition of other companies.
- There might also be considerable benefit (e.g., lower development costs, a more common behavior or look and feel for end users) in introducing a new population architecture that over time substitutes the current set of products (which may incorporate outdated and hard-to-maintain technologies).

The forces driving the emergence of product populations are, therefore, not straightforward and are of a rather diverse nature. However, these are forces that tend to influence any successful product line and therefore we believe that, in general, product lines have a tendency to evolve towards populations and have to face variation in architecturally significant requirements.[1]

---

[1] Of course there are also numerous counter forces: For instance, the long term vision may not be clear, or the payback time may be too long to justify the investment; the existing organization may not be geared to a product-line approach because domain engineering activities and application engineering activities are not separated clearly. Another possible counterforce is a "not-invented-here" culture. Many software developers have a natural tendency to prefer to create the ultimate code from scratch themselves rather than to use someone else's not-so-perfect component.

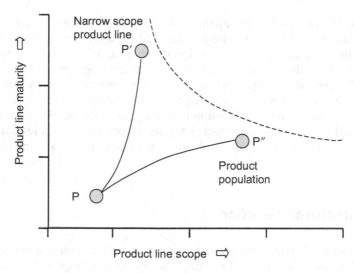

Fig. 7.1. Narrow scope product lines vs. populations

The concept of product population is illustrated in Fig. 7.1. The figure shows two alternative evolution paths for a product line with respect to maturity (expressed as the relative amount of product specific development typically needed to derive a new product) and scope. In path P–P' the scope has been kept narrow and the product line has evolved towards a high level of maturity where product engineering is solely a matter of selecting and configuring reusable product line assets. In the path P–P'' the scope has been gradually extended by the effect of the forces mentioned above, but this has been at the expense of maturity and there is still significant development effort required for product derivation. The dashed curve indicates that there is a limit to the level of maturity that is feasible because as the scope grows it becomes more and more difficult to achieve high levels of maturity

As mentioned above, populations often include several applications. These may be thought of as product lines within the population, in the sense that they are delivered in several variants that share similar quality requirements and therefore need the same architectural solutions. The maturity of such product lines within a population may be at a higher level than the maturity for the whole population. When we talk about product derivation in this chapter, we are primarily concerned with the derivation of new applications, and not the derivation of variants within such sub product lines.

7.1.2 Overview

In this chapter we investigate ways to deal with design conflicts in reference architectures for product populations caused by variation in architecturally significant requirements. We are particularly concerned with how well the approaches preserve the benefits of a common architecture and maintain adequate support for efficient variant derivation.

We propose an approach based on variation points that describes alternative specializations of the reference architecture, and compare this with other approaches described in the literature. We first discuss the merits of the various approaches analytically, and then seek to validate our claims by analyzing some real-life population architectures.

This chapter is organized as follows: Firstly, in Sect. 7.2, we explain more precisely what we mean by architectural variation and discuss existing approaches to dealing with it. Section 7.3 presents our approach to allow for architectural variation in product-line reference architectures. In Sect. 7.4 we seek to validate the proposed approach by analyzing experience with architectural variation in real-life product line architectures and how our approach could have been applied. Sect. 7.5 gives a brief overview of related work before we summarize the outcome of the analysis of the cases and draw some conclusions in Sect. 7.6.

7.2 Architectural Variation

Below we discuss in greater detail what we mean by architectural variation and what distinguishes this from other forms of variation that are typically captured as variation points in product lines. Furthermore, we discuss some approaches to dealing with architectural variation that are proposed in the literature.

7.2.1 The Nature of Architectural Variation

According to the IEEE 1471 standard [13] the architecture of a software system is "the fundamental organization of a system embodied in its components, their relationships to each other, and to the environment, and the principles guiding its design and evolution."

We will follow Pohl et al. [21] and use *structure* to denote the first aspect (the components and the relations between them), and *texture* to denote the second aspect (the principles guiding its design and evolution). The texture represents architectural design decisions that shape the structure and govern the design of components. They typically take the form of architectural styles, patterns and tactics as well as collaboration models for central functions of the systems. They tend to have a cross-cutting influence on the implementation and therefore are very difficult to change once the system has been implemented. Furthermore they tend to constrain the quality properties of systems built in accordance with the architecture.[2]

In product-line reference architectures a third important aspect is *variability*, i.e., rules governing the derivation of product variants with different properties from a common asset base.

---

[2] The term texture is also used by Jazayeri et al. [15] but they focus on the influence of common design principles in the form of recurring microstructure of components and does not mention the influence on the component structure itself.

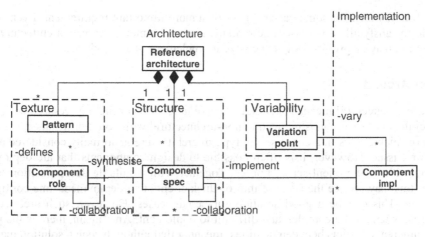

Fig. 7.2. Product-line reference architecture

Such rules typically take the form of *variation points* that specify points in the architecture where system properties are related to optional or alternative system elements of various sorts, for instance component implementations or configuration parameters of component implementations. This understanding of architecture is illustrated in Fig. 7.2.

In the model depicted in Fig. 7.2 variation only affects the implementation of the products. The architecture is common. The variation points allow for variation in the features of the products, but do not affect the architecture. This is often the case in narrow scope product lines. In populations one normally also has to accept variation in the architecture itself, both in the structure and in the texture.

7.2.2 Avoiding Architectural Variation

As should be clear from the discussion above, the allowance of architectural variation in a product line definitely complicates matters and it is therefore advisable to avoid it if possible. Fortunately, there are approaches that can make the architecture generic in one way or another with respect to an anticipated conflict without having to allow architectural variation.

Design for "Worst Case"

One may think that if the toughest requirements are allowed to shape the architecture, it will be satisfactory for all product variants. Indeed, in some cases this is true. For instance, if one product variant needs a short response time while a longer response time is acceptable for another, it is possible to accommodate this by designing for a short response time. However, there tend to be inherent conflicts between certain properties such that most solutions favor one at the expense of the other. In that case the design for worst-case approach may fail because it is impossible to design an architecture that satisfies all worst-case requirements at once. For instance, a short response time often comes at the expense of flexibility, which for some variants may be a more important requirement. Even if it is possible to satisfy all worst-case requirements in one common reference architecture, this architecture may be prohibitively expensive to implement in all products.

Design Around

There are architectural mechanisms that are able to absorb conflicting requirements, such that architectural variation is reduced to non-architectural variation. For instance, the issue of thin or thick clients in a client-server type of architecture is normally considered an architectural issue. However, it is often possible to design components that are deployable on either side of the client-server border. Together with a suitable decomposition of the system, this may reduce the issue of thin or thick clients to a deployment time configuration issue. This can be a good solution for certain cases. However, such architectural mechanisms tend to be complex and difficult to implement. And, again, there is the problem of inherent conflicts between qualities, meaning that although such a solution may absorb some conflicts it often introduces others, for instance with performance.

Modeling Architectural Variation

If variation in requirements is such that it cannot be accommodated within a variation-free architecture, variation has to be allowed for in the description of the reference architecture, which means we have an under-specified or under-constrained architecture [20]. In its simplest form a description of an under-specified architecture just leaves unspecified the points where the variation in requirements makes it impossible to standardize architectural decisions.

This approach has the drawback, however, that it compromises many of the benefits of a common reference architecture. Firstly, it postpones potentially difficult design decisions to application engineering and thus shifts the responsibility and the work onto the application engineers. Although much work may have been carried out during the design of the population reference architecture in identifying the conflict and analyzing possible solutions, this work will have been wasted if no common solution can be found. Secondly, there is the danger that the architecture may end up so underspecified that it offers few opportunities for supporting it with common reusable implemented components.

Several approaches to modeling under-specified product-line reference architectures have been proposed in the literature, with varying degrees of support for deriving product architectures.

Freely Composable Components

Attention has already been drawn to the strength of reusable components available off the shelf by Jacobson in [14]. New applications are simply created by selecting from a set of existing components and gluing them together "as they are." A familiar success in this area is the wealth of ActiveX controls (components) and Visual Basic (glue) to quickly generate graphical user interfaces, which have now completely taken over in Microsoft's .NET framework.

This idea has been elaborated by Van Ommering and Bosch [28]. They see composition as something that is complementary to variation: A composition means that two or more pieces of software that have been developed without direct knowledge of each other can be combined easily to create a working product. In their view, the way to create product populations is by using freely-composable components. The ideal software development process is agile. It is largely component-driven (bottom-up) and partly supported by a light-weight (top-down) architecture.

Although with this approach component specifications and interfaces are standardized, the ways components can be combined in products are only implicitly constrained by the restriction that interfaces must match. With cleverly designed component interfaces, this approach potentially gives a lot of freedom. However, it means that it may be a quite challenging task to find a composition of components that matches the given product requirements, and the architecture model contains no support for this task.

Van Ommering and Bosch are primarily concerned with the structural aspect of architecture and the flexibility with respect to structure that is achieved by such freely-composable components as those described above, which seem to assume a stable texture. If there is variation in the texture, it is more complex to achieve such composability. This is discussed in greater detail in the following sections.

Structural Variation Points

Thiel and Hein [24] have proposed a reference model for architectural variation as an extension to the reference model defined by the IEEE P1471 recommended practice for architectural description [13]. Their extension introduces architectural variation points as a means to explicitly model variation in product-line reference architectures. The essence of their proposal is illustrated in Fig. 7.3. An architectural variation point, according to their definition, allows the variation of structural elements, such as component and connection specifications, and the effect of the various options on product features to be expressed. Since this form of architectural variation point is restricted to structural elements of the architecture, we refer to them as structural variation points from now on.

Making variation explicit in the architecture in the form of structural variation points definitely improves the support for product derivation compared with just leaving the structure partly unspecified. However, if we have to deal with architectural decisions that cross-cut the structure backbone, the variability model may turn out to be very complex and difficult both to express and to use. This is because such an architectural decision will affect many structural elements in various ways, and there is no particular support in the model to express this, other than one variation point for each affected element.

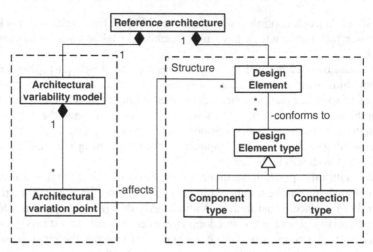

Fig. 7.3. Reference architecture with structural variation points

7.3 Textural Variation Points

Our approach to modeling architectural variation is a natural extension of the approaches discussed in the previous section. It also builds on the idea that components are major building blocks of products, and that architectural variation points can be used as a means to encode explicitly foreseen variations in the architecture and to provide decision support for specializing the architecture for a given set of product specific requirements. However, rather than focusing on the structure and the variation in structural elements, we focus on the texture and the variation in textural elements. The approach is based on the following three main elements:

– View of the texture as a pattern language with patterns as architectural building blocks.
– Use of variation points to make explicit the variation allowed in the composition of patterns between product architectures.
– Guidelines for the resolution of variation points based on knowledge of the effect of using a pattern in an architecture (i.e., the effect on quality properties of applications built according to this architecture).

A conceptual model for an architecture with encoded textural variability as described above is shown in Fig. 7.4. In the following we explain our approach in more detail. The ideas behind this approach were developed in the CAFÉ project [2,10,11] and further elaborated in the FAMILIES project.

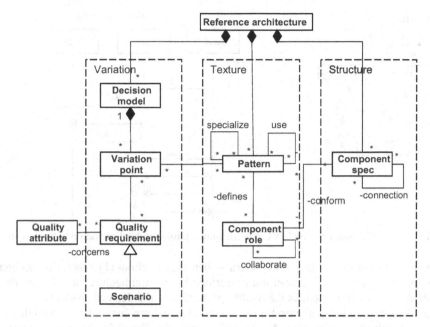

Fig. 7.4. Reference architecture with textural variation points

7.3.1 Patterns as Architecture Building Blocks

Patterns define solutions to recurring problems, which make them natural building blocks for architectures [5].[3] Moreover, established patterns often have known effects on quality attributes [1], making it possible to reason about the effect of choosing one pattern over another. A pattern language [23] is a collection of patterns that support the development of a class of systems, with relationships between the patterns that bind them together to form a whole. These relationships cover use (one pattern uses another pattern in its solution), specialization (one pattern is a specialization of another) and conflict (two patterns cannot be used together). In our approach the backbone of the architecture model is a pattern language encompassing recommended patterns and relevant relations between them.

We use the term "pattern" in a rather broad sense, meaning any problem solution pair recommended by the architecture. This means that the pattern language may contain both established patterns that are widely known and used throughout the software community, and "local" patterns that are specific to the product population. In the latter case, some may argue that this is not a proper use of the term "pattern," since we are talking about a local invention.

---

[3] In this chapter we do not distinguish between patterns and styles. We understand styles to be high-level patterns that have a strong overall organizing effect on a system.

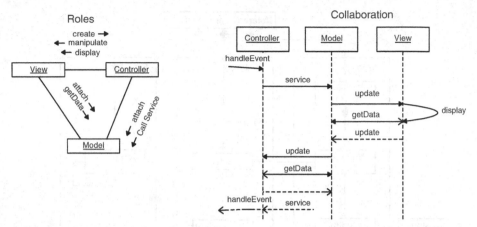

Fig. 7.5. Partial UML model for the MVC pattern showing roles and collaboration between roles

However, we prefer to use the term "pattern" when we talk about (1) a recurring problem within the product line and (2) a solution prescribed by the architecture, and the architect has an idea about how it influences the quality properties of the derived products.

Patterns define roles and collaboration between roles and are conveniently modeled using a sort of collaboration diagram. An example is given in Fig. 7.5. This shows a partial UML model for the MVC (Model View Controller) pattern. In a system designed and implemented using a set of patterns, these roles are fulfilled by component implementations. Normally, a component plays a role in more than one pattern.

Component specifications, which represent the components in the architecture, are defined by the synthesis of a set of roles from different patterns and possibly also collaboration models relating to the functionality of the system. In the example shown in Fig. 7.6, the patterns involved are the MVC pattern and the client-server pattern. The C1 component has the client role in the client-server pattern and the view role in the MVC pattern, and implements the presentation part of the user interface in one or more use-case-related scenarios that define the functionality provided by the system. Components C2 and C3 are synthesized from different role sets, as indicated in the figure.

7.3.2 Encoding Textural Variation

The patterns that make up the architecture are either mandatory, i.e., they must be used in every product belonging to the population, or their use is governed by one or more textural variation points. A textural variation point describes a variation in architecturally significant requirements and establishes relationships between variant requirements and patterns. Such a relationship means that the pattern helps to fulfill the requirement. A pattern may help to satisfy multiple requirements, and the ability to fulfill a requirement may be affected by multiple patterns.

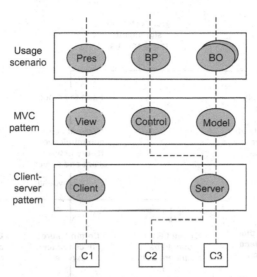

Fig. 7.6. Component specifications synthesized from roles defined by patterns

In this way the textural variation points make up a decision model that governs the derivation of product architectures that satisfy particular requirements.

There are two kinds of textural variation points: optional pattern variation points and alternative patterns variation points. An optional pattern is one that may or may not be adopted by a product architecture. An alternative patterns variation point encodes a choice between several patterns. The alternatives are typically patterns that in effect solve the same problem (often they are alternative specializations of a more abstract pattern), but in different ways and with different effects on the achievable quality attributes.

The ISO 9126 standard [9] serves as the basis for modeling requirements. This standard defines quality attributes and metrics for measuring them. The quality attributes defined in the standard are often too coarse-grained for our purpose and it is therefore permissible to break them down into more detailed ones. In addition, we recommend the use of scenarios, such as those used in scenario-based architecture assessment [6], to describe quality requirements. These scenarios are constructed as stimulus-response pairs, where the stimulus describes an event that may occur during the lifetime of a product, and the response describes how the product should respond to that event. In scenario based architecture assessment such scenarios has proven effective for reasoning about the properties of architectures.

Figure 7.7 shows an example decision model with both kinds of textural variation points. To the left it shows an example of an optional pattern variation point, which recommends using the model view controller patterns if there is a need to support variation in the user interface. To the right it shows an alternative patterns variation point that guides the choice between alternative specializations of the client-server pattern based on the requirements regarding how the system should react to communication failures in the client-server connection. If continued service is required in the event of a communication failure of the client server connection, the architecture should be based upon the self-reliant client pattern. If only partial service is required, the rich client pattern is recommended. If denial

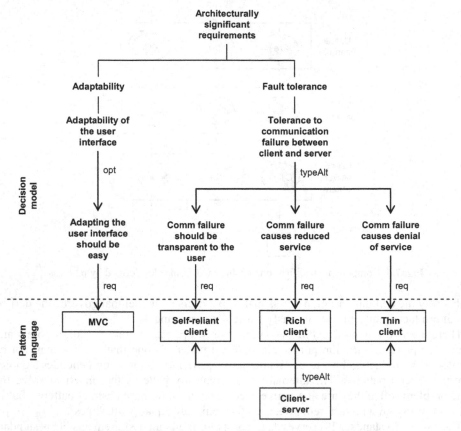

Fig. 7.7. Example of decision model with textural variation points

of service during the absence of communication is acceptable, the thin client pattern is preferred.

The representation of the decision model is based on the metamodel for variability modeling proposed in Chap. 6. The optional patterns variation points are represented by the Optional Transformer kind of Variability specification, while the alternative patterns variation points are represented by the Type Alternative kind of Variability Specification. The relationship between requirement variants and patterns are represented as Variability Constraints. This is indicated in Fig. 7.7 by text labels on the branches indicating the kind of metamodel concept represented by the branch.

7.3.3 Support for Product Architecture Design

An architecture modeled with textural variation points is also an under-specified architecture and further architectural design is needed to derive product architectures. However, the textural variation points serve as design guidelines that guide and simplify this task.

Use of the textural variation points to support the derivation of product architectures involves the following steps:

- Firstly, resolve the variation points according to the particular quality requirements of the application. For each optional pattern variation point, decide whether its requirement is relevant or not. For each alternative patterns variation point, select the alternative that best fits the needs of the product to be built.
- Then compose the texture of the product architecture from the mandatory patterns of the reference architecture and the patterns selected by the resolved variation points.
- Finally, select component specifications that match the product texture and connect them as dictated by the selected patterns. The roles a component is able to play are defined as part of its specification.

Since patterns normally affect more than one quality attribute, trade-off and/or conflict situations may occur. Prioritization of requirements may help to resolve such situations but in the worst case it may be necessary to renegotiate requirements. Use of the decision model during product specification will help to avoid conflicts.

7.3.4 Support for Reusable Component Design

As already explained above, in an architecture based on a pattern language the patterns define roles that the components have to play and the component structure is derived by the synthesis of a set of roles from different patterns and, in some cases, collaboration models relating to the functionality of the system.

The presence of textural variation points makes this more difficult because role sets that form natural components will typically include roles that are not always required. However, this difficulty may be overcome by using classic techniques for designing reusable components, such as generalization over the expected variation in responsibilities or introduction of configurability such that the component can be configured for different specializations of the architecture, or by providing alternative variants of the component.

Compared with just leaving the varying part of the pattern language out of the architecture, we believe that our approach has clear benefits for the identification and design of components that are reusable across the population, since it makes explicit the variation in responsibilities caused by architectural variation that the population components have to face.

7.4 Preliminary Validation

As a preliminary validation of our approach to dealing with architectural variability we have analysed experience with architectural variation in real-life product populations and the applicability of our approach. We have selected three architectures that have been developed to serve a population-like strategy for software development. One case is from Philips Applied Technologies, another from Philips Medical Systems and the third one is from DNV Software. For each architecture we briefly present key requirements and the chosen solutions. Then we discuss to what extent the population architecture does accommodate architectural variation, and finally how textural variation points could be used to model this variation and what benefits this could provide compared with the current approach.

7.4.1 Philips Equipment Control Platform

The Mechatronics department of Philips Applied Technologies develops a wide variety of positioning subsystems for professional equipment like wafer steppers, machines for placing components on PCBs, etc. A common factor in most of this equipment is the control of very accurate movements, often with nanometer accuracy. The equipment control platform is developed to capture domain knowledge and to speed up future development of control applications for mechatronic equipment. As such, it is based on the experiences and results of previously executed projects. The platform consists of meta-architectures and re-usable components, it provides a common infrastructure and tooling to aid development, and it defines a common way of working.

The Equipment Control Architecture

One of the basic principles of the equipment control platform is that all components have a generic interface that allows the development of EqCP services and facilities based on this generic interface. Once a (new) component has this generic interface, all the EqCP services and facilities automatically operate on/with this component. CORBA has been chosen as the middleware to provide the interoperability services and facilities. ACE [12] is used as the operating system abstraction layer and TAO [19] as the real-time implementation of CORBA.

A component built on top of ACE that provides the generic interface automatically operates within the platform infrastructure to give full freedom in composition of component structures. In this way the platform components can operate in every topology.

EqCP deals with variation points at two levels. The highest level is the meta-architecture, which is a template for families of architectures that can be instantiated by using it. The next level deals with variations within the meta-architecture, by configuring architectural variation points using strategies in a generic way. The strategies represent alternative solutions to the problem solved by the meta-architecture leading to different properties of the built product.

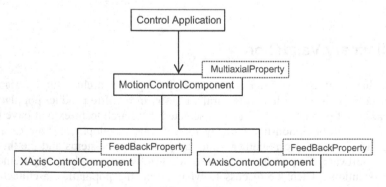

Fig. 7.8. Meta-architecture for motion control

A meta-architecture is described as a composition of EqCP components with a description of consistent interaction between the components. Meta-architectures are based on experiences and, as such, are a place to consolidate domain-specific knowledge and expertise. To illustrate the meta-architecture and strategy concepts, we provide two examples of their use for specializing the EqCP reference architecture for different products.

Example 1. The first example considers motion-control systems. Figure 7.8 shows a meta-architecture for a motion-control situation. The meta-architecture also encapsulates variation points within the architecture.

The UML template notation was used to denote a property that is part of the set of properties managed by a generic component. All components shown are in fact generic components. The motion-control component has strategies that determine how and if the movement of the axes is synchronized. The axes have strategies that determine how the position information is sent back to the motion controller. A possible instantiation of the meta-architecture is shown in Fig. 7.9.

The values of the properties determine that the motion-control component will synchronize the movements of the X- and Y-axes. The feedback property selects a strategy that will return the data by means of callbacks. Changing the architecture to use different mechanisms involves instantiating the architecture with different values for the properties.

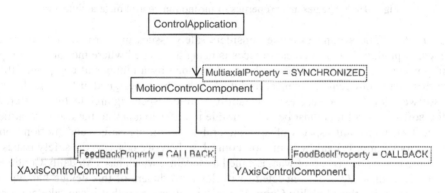

Fig. 7.9. Instantiated meta-architecture for motion-control

This implementation with the actual properties and strategies is shown in Fig. 7.10.

The same meta-architecture is used. Two versions of the MotionControl strategy are available: IndependentMultiAxial and SynchronizedMultiAxial. When a MoveTo command is given, the coordinates and trajectories of the individual movements are calculated. The first strategy sends these to the axis components and waits for their completion. The second strategy, however, also directs the axes components to send position data at regular intervals or to sample these (this is again a strategy). It will then continuously adjust and coordinate movements until the motion has finished. The meta-architecture for these two situations is the same. The only difference is the value of the property that selects the strategy.

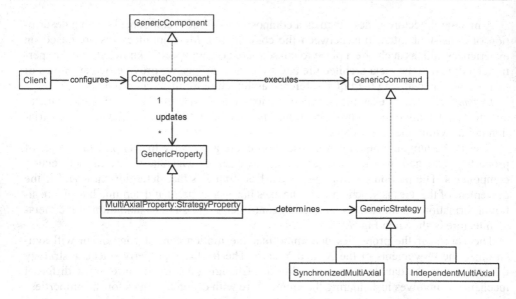

Fig. 7.10. Strategies and properties of the motion control meta-architecture

Example 2. The second example considers safety issues in a product line of medical devices. A product line of medical devices is being developed where motion control plays an important role. These devices are being developed by a number of companies that all have different architectures. A meta-architecture has been designed at both the hardware and software level to increase exchangeability, while respecting architectural differences. At the software level this must be configurable in order to adapt to the use in a particular device. Two important aspects of architectural variation are safety and motion control. The previous example dealt with motion control, so here we describe the safety issues.

The medical device is part of what is called a Modality, which has a Modality Controller to control all medical devices connected to it. Some producers of this device handle safety locally, and notify the Modality Controller of this situation so that it can take appropriate action, following a fully distributed approach. Other producers require a strictly hierarchical approach where the notification of an unsafe situation travels up to the root of the hierarchy, which then directs the medical device to take appropriate action. The device therefore gets its own notification back via the root of the hierarchy. A hierarchic approach and a distributed approach are clearly two different architectural approaches.

As in the case sketched above, the notification is a property in the meta-architecture as shown in Fig. 7.11.

If the value of the NotificationProperty is set to HIERARCHIC, a notification is sent to its immediate parent in the hierarchy. The safety strategy of the root component determines further actions. If the property is set to DISTRIBUTED, a notification is sent to all of those components that have registered to receive one. This could be both the local safety handler and the modality controller. If the property is set to LOCAL, the safety handler deals with the situation locally.

Discussion

The examples show two (parts of) meta-architectures that can be used as templates for the architecture to be defined by the product architect. Based on the specific requirements in question, the designer can select the appropriate meta-architecture for the system and specialize it with suitable strategies.

Although the two examples describe only parts of architectures, it is clear that they are architecturally different, yet solve a particular kind of problem for a large number of applications with a similar architecture. Experience with reusable mechatronic architectures at Philips Applied Technologies proves this point. The architecture proposed for a common patient table for the wide range of medical devices based on a meta-architecture has also been received with enthusiasm.

A meta-architecture bears many similarities to a textural variation point such as that presented in Sect. 7.3. It defines an abstract pattern in terms of a partial structure of roles and connections that can be specialized in different ways to satisfy different quality requirements by choosing a suitable set of strategies. More specifically, it corresponds to the alternative patterns class of textual variation points.

The aim is to develop reusable components that can be configured to work with the alternative specializations of the meta-architectures, in much the same way as discussed in Sect. 7.3.4. Up to this point, however, the reuse has relied on manual adaptation of components to a particular application. If meta-architectures and the configuration mechanism are used, architectures and components should remain intact, and variation points should be exposed only in separate strategies.

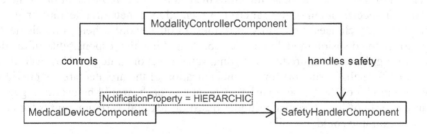

Fig. 7.11. Instantiated meta-architecture for safety control

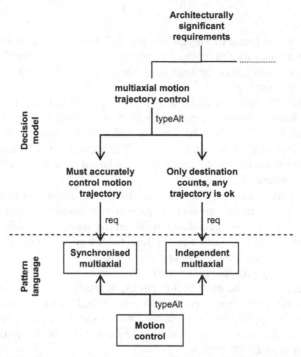

Fig. 7.12. Textural variation points applied to the EqCP architecture

In the current EqCP reference architecture there is no direct representation of the effect of a particular specialization of the pattern represented by a meta-architecture (in the form of a set of strategy choices) on quality attributes. In other words, there is no element that corresponds to the decision model in our approach, and it is the responsibility of the designer specializing the architecture to decide on a suitable set of strategies. However, it is anticipated that formalized support for the specialization of the architecture, as provided by the decision model of the textural variation point approach, would be useful. Figure 7.12 gives an example of how a decision model based on textural variation points for the motion control example could look like.

7.4.2 Composable Image Processor

Philips Medical Systems is a leading company that sells a wide range of medical scanning devices on the global market. These scanning devices rely on completely different image acquisition techniques (X-ray, ultrasound, magnetic resonance). In the past, each medical modality (i.e., type of body scanner) developed its own image processor product line, which was heavily based on dedicated hardware (ASICs). Nowadays, software is fast enough to replace the hardware solutions and, more importantly, many algorithms (like noise reduction) can be shared between applications.

Moreover, from a clinical point of view there is also a need, especially in today's interventional X-ray procedures, to combine information from different modalities in the examination room. Monitors in the examination room are no longer seen as modality-specific viewing devices. Instead, they are increasingly considered as a general display area to be used for all clinically relevant information that is available. The image processors of the near future are conceived as a population that must be able to cope with these requirements.

At Philips Medical Systems a highly flexible, open and composable image processing (IP) platform is currently being developed. It is capable of storing, processing and displaying all kinds of medical images almost in real time for the various modalities.[4]

IP Architecture

The system's basic architecture is sketched in Fig. 7.13. Depending on the type of body scanner (MRI, CT, Ultrasound or X-ray device) in which the IP platform is applied, specific graphs (coarse-grained composition) and nodes (fine-grained composition) are offered. A graph corresponds to a running video stream (see also [18]). Graphs are defined at design time and selected at runtime. They are triggered by user actions, e.g., "acquisition" means get images from the detector (i.e., a source), store them and send them through various enhancement nodes to the display(s), "replay" implicitly sets up a flow that streams images from disk to a given output device (i.e., a destination). Nodes live in graphs and may contain:

- Image enhancement software to improve image quality (e.g., reduce noise, increase contrast resolution).
- Reconstruction software that creates 3D volumes (made up of voxels) from a coherent set of 2D images (containing pixels).

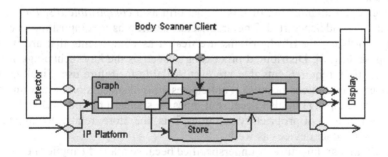

Fig. 7.13. Composable image processor connected to a body scanner. Instantiated connections and the image stream that corresponds to the selected graph are shown with bold lines

---

[4] Another related development project with a population scope has been launched at Philips Medical Systems. This focuses on providing components for building viewing applications (for each product line, i.e. type of body scanner) on top of this IP platform. From an architectural point of view this case is very similar. More extensive information on this case can be found in [26].

– Measurement software that retrieves numerical information from images, e.g., thickness of vessels.

The exact behavior of the nodes (in the selected graph) depends on its processing settings. They can be changed at runtime.

The concept of graphs and IP-nodes in this video streaming device allows for a wide variety in functionality. Since communication and administrative software for setting up and maintaining the flow is completely separate from the IP processing taking place inside a node, the system is very open for including new (as yet unknown) IP algorithms. It is just a matter of capturing the algorithm in a new node and embedding this node in the appropriate graphs.

In this project we are gradually moving towards a service-oriented architecture, in which "tasks" (not only IP, but also requests like "give me the current patient") are available on a network. The elements that make up the systems are conceived as services that can be discovered and assembled at runtime. They can be assessed using technology-agnostic protocols.

Another key element in the architecture consists of well-agreed and managed interfaces. They are the starting point for component decomposition. Implementations of the components (services) use the familiar object-oriented and component-based techniques.

Discussion

With this IP platform it is also possible to accommodate considerable variation in quality attributes. Computation-intensive nodes can be mapped to multiple CPUs by employing parallel processing techniques. This means that, in terms of pipeline latency and the number of images that can be handled per second, performance requirements have become scalable to a large degree.

We conceive the architecture of this IP platform as a *composable distributed open* architecture that is underspecified. The architecture is seen as a composition because both existing and forthcoming IP algorithms are treated as components that are in principle freely composable [28]. Distributed processing is seen as the key technology for dealing with hard real-time requirements that are even scalable for future use. Finally, the architecture is open to evolutions because it anticipates a rapid succession of new and better IP algorithms (see Chap. 1) but also because it relies on standard protocols (like UDP on Gigabit Ethernet) instead of proprietary solutions. It is, therefore, relatively easy to connect the IP platform to other devices as well.

We classify this architecture as underspecified because a lot of (implicit) expert knowledge is still required to determine the graphs that are needed in a specific end product from the set of requirements. At present, the architecture does not support this derivation process. More explicit coding rules are required in order to capture knowledge about order effects in processing and specific constraints that go with each application and modality. Textural variation points, as presented in this chapter, represent a viable solution for this.

We do not provide an illustrative example with textural variation points because the rules or patterns that lead to specific graphs constitute very sensitive information which has a major competitive impact. The main reason for this is that a graph "recipe" is strongly correlated with the overall image quality. What we can say about this in fairly general terms is the following:

– Types of graphs are associated with viewing protocols (defining what should be displayed and how the information is laid out over one or more display areas).[5]
– Obviously, graph construction depends heavily on and is strongly constrained by the available hardware. But other requirements, e.g., legal requirements, also affect the graph. For instance, exposure-like image acquisition should always end with both a display and a disk node because these images are required by law to be stored and archived for at least 10 years. For fluoroscopy imaging a display end-node is sufficient because it is not necessary to store these images. At present we do not have explicit patterns that capture all this knowledge; in practice we use "common sense" design rules to satisfy all the requirements.

7.4.3 The BRIX Platform

DNV Software is a company that delivers software aimed primarily at the marine, offshore and process industries. BRIX was originally developed as a common platform for a product line that targets the ship classification business. Now the DNV strategy is to establish BRIX as a common software platform for all DNV Software products, and second generation BRIX has been developed with this in mind (Fig. 7.14).

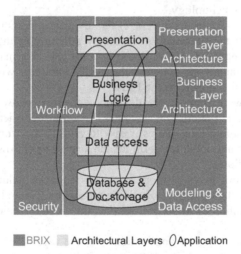

Fig. 7.14. The BRIX frameworks

---

[5] This is more or less comparable to the meta-architecture of the motion control strategy as described in Sect. 4.1 case.

This means that the scope of BRIX is very wide and that both avoidance and allowance of architectural variation has been necessary to accommodate the variation in requirements in a common architecture model.

BRIX Architecture

BRIX consists of a number of frameworks that can be combined in different ways in an application depending on the particular requirements. A framework is the solution to a particular architectural concern and may contain various elements like architecture patterns, reusable components, templates, guidelines and tools. The frameworks that make up BRIX can briefly be summarized as follows:

- The *Basis* framework contains prescribed, standardized design guidelines, services and patterns (examples: exception handling, transaction handling, application lock manager, façades, etc.).
- The *BRIX MDA (Modeling and Data Access)* framework provides data persistence and data sharing based on information models expressed in a variant of UML. The MDA framework also supports views on the data model that exposes only data relevant to an application, and supports caching of views.
- The *BLA (Business Layer Architecture)* framework supports flexibility with respect to deployment and client technology.
- The *PLA (Presentation Layer Architecture)* framework supports integration of different applications (tools) at the presentation layer. By adhering to these recommendations, the user interface components (controllers) of multiple tools may co-exist in a single solution. The PLA framework contains the BRIX explorer, which is a template for building applications that adhere to the PLA.
- The *Workflow* framework supports the development of workflow-oriented applications. It defines an architecture pattern that separates the workflow-oriented aspects of the application from the rest and thus makes it easy to modify the workflow. This pattern is supported by notation and tools for defining and storing workflows and a workflow engine to execute workflows.
- The *Security* framework gives support for access control. Included in the framework are services for authentication (i.e., obtaining reasonable certainty as to the identity of the actor) and specification of authorizations (i.e., the set of operations an actor is allowed to perform).
- The *Offline* framework supports applications that are capable of being used offline for shorter or longer periods and, in effect, provides mechanisms for replicating shared data on the client and for synchronizing with the central database. It is typically used together with the BLA to build applications that are capable of being used both online and offline.
- The *Rule* framework encapsulates engineering rules for use by applications. The assumption is that the rules, as a concept, might become useful across multiple systems. It does this by separating the logical rules from the front-end used to interact with them. In many respects, the rule framework is based on the same principal ideas as the workflow framework.

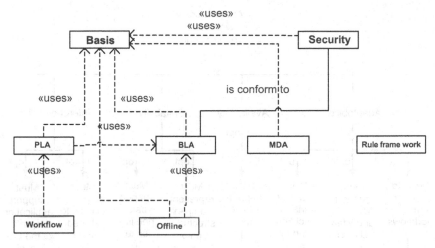

Fig. 7.15. The BRIX pattern language

The decision to include a particular framework in a product contributes to the definition of the application architecture by enforcing one or more patterns. It usually offers some reusable components or component templates, and in some cases tools as well. The documentation associated with the frameworks also provides guidelines about when to use the framework and its effect on the properties of the product to be built.

Discussion

The frameworks of BRIX propose patterns that may or may not be included in a product architecture. Thus, at the outset the BRIX architecture is specified primarily at the texture level. Structure is only indirectly specified through the patterns proposed by the BRIX frameworks and to a large extent it is left up to the product developers to determine this.

It is, therefore, quite natural to model the BRIX architecture as a pattern language as proposed by the textural variation point approach. An overview of a pattern language that describes the main patterns proposed by the BRIX frameworks is shown in Fig. 7.15.

Since use of the BRIX frameworks is not enforced, one may see each of them as a textural variation point of the optional pattern kind. A partial decision model is shown in Fig. 7.16. It was constructed partly on the basis of guidelines relating to the use of the frameworks found in the available documentation and partly on the basis of interviews with the developers and users of BRIX.

This model of BRIX represents the level of support for product architecture derivation that corresponds to what the BRIX platform offers. Each framework typically represents a fairly sophisticated architectural solution that is not needed by all products. A product development project that chooses not to include a framework is more or less on its own. It would improve the support for product derivation if the frameworks contributed more to providing alternative solutions.

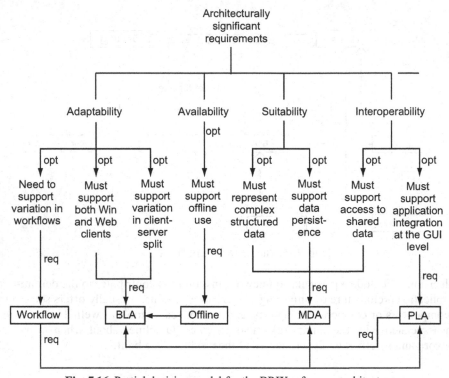

Fig. 7.16. Partial decision model for the BRIX reference architecture

Consider, for instance, the BLA framework that prescribes an architectural pattern that offers flexible deployment such that applications can be deployed with varying client richness and with varying client technology (Web or WIN). This means that an application developed in accordance with this pattern can be deployed with a wide range of client-server splits, ranging from a very thin Web client to a very rich Win client with data replication that will also work offline. A collaboration diagram for the central BLA pattern is shown in Fig. 7.17. The presentation layer accesses the business layer through a client facade component that may be connected to the business layer through different business façade components, depending on where the business layer is deployed. Together with business components that are deployable both on client and server machines, this gives the required flexibility.

One may see this pattern as an example of an architectural solution that "designs around" the variability in requirements that are normally architecturally significant. However, some products of DNVS do not need this flexibility and prefer to avoid the additional complexity and overhead associated with it. The alternatives are more traditional client-server patterns. Better support for the derivation of these products could be achieved by modeling the BLA and the alternatives as an alternative patterns variation point in a similar way as illustrated in Fig. 7.7.

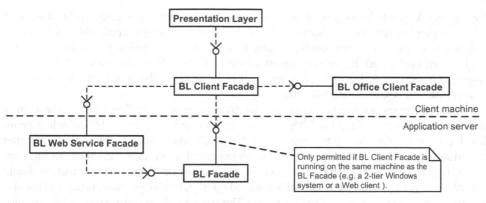

Fig. 7.17. Central pattern of the BRIX BLA Framework

One of the main products of DNVS is NAUTICUS, which supports the classification of ships. Another product is a system for ship owners that support the maintenance of ships throughout their lifecycle. There are also plans to launch variants of the latter system that support maintenance of other types for complex technical systems, such as offshore oil drilling and production platforms or industrial process plants. It is clear that these systems will have a lot in common and it is being considered to develop a domain-specific product line platform on top of BRIX for this class of systems, referred to as AIMS (Asset Integrated Management Systems). This platform will take the form of a set of components at the business layer.

This is an example of a product line within the population. It will share some BRIX frameworks with the rest of the population, and thus its reference architecture will be a specialization of the BRIX architecture with some variation points resolved. The domain specific business layer components will be developed according to the specialized architecture and will therefore not be reusable across the whole population.

7.5 Related Work

In addition to the work that we have built on and that have already been presented, there are several other works that are related to our research on architectural variability.

Research at SEI on ABASs [16] and later on the ADD method [1] is based on similar assumptions to ours, for example that certain quality properties can be associated with architectural patterns and that pattern like constructs (which they call mechanisms) are suited as building blocks for architectures. These ideas also underpin their work on architecture assessment techniques, such as ATAM and ARID [6].

The OOram method developed by T. Reenskaug et al. [22] advocates the use of role models and derivation of object specifications by role synthesis. This was the inspiration for our ideas on component roles and the derivation of component specifications based on role synthesis.

The issue of variability modeling has received much attention in product line engineering research, and several general approaches have been proposed capable of describing variation in any kind of development artifact. This issue is discussed extensively in several other chapters of this book. Chapters 5 and 6 propose generally applicable metamodels and notations for variability modeling and Chap. 1 uses a notation proposed by Ferber et al. [8] to model variability in different kinds of models. We chose to use the approach proposed by Chap. 6, but the other approaches mentioned above are also applicable in connection with textural variation points.

Although it does not use the term "architectural variation point" explicitly, a work that comes close to ours is the ADLARS architecture description language [4], which is being developed at the Queen's University of Belfast. ADLARS aims to be able to describe variation in a product-line reference architecture caused by variation in cross-cutting concerns. To this end, they introduce the concept of interaction theme. An interaction theme describes a collaboration between roles focused on a particular purpose, often a particular feature to be supported by the product line. The roles of themes are assigned to components, and components may be configured to support different role sets, depending on the features present in a given product. Complementary work by the same group [17] also describes tool support based on weaving techniques to automatically configure components to comply with a given set of interaction themes. The use of interaction themes in ADLARS is very similar to the way we use patterns in our approach.

Scenario-based architecting described in Chap. 1 focuses on creating a product line architecture that not only fits now, but is also future-proof (to some extent of course). Since the future cannot be predicted precisely, a number of reasonable scenarios that describe possible changes for the domain or business (in a wide sense) in question is developed. Each scenario represents a point in the variation space. These scenarios are related to the variation in models of the architecture in order to come up with an architecture that is "open in time." Variation modeling is carried out in different views that typically cover the range from customer wishes at one end to technological realizations at the other end. In this way the entire variation space is covered.

This approach to architecting recognizes the need to foresee architectural variation and to model it in order to support future evolution of the architecture. Textural variation points could serve as a complementary technique to this end.

7.6 Conclusions and Future Research

We have argued that in product populations there is often significant variation in architecturally-significant requirements, and that therefore significant variation in architecture between products must be allowed. This sets challenges for the design of the common reference architecture that has to balance the need for openness to variation against the need to provide platform and product developers with a firm architectural basis. We have proposed a solution based on architectural variation points where the unit of variation is the patterns that make up the texture of the architecture. We claim that this approach is more powerful than existing approaches to architectural variation, like just leaving architectural decisions open or associating variation points with structural elements of the architecture.

The reason for this is twofold. Firstly, textural elements are associated more directly with the architectural decisions that have to vary between products and therefore simplify the specialization of the architecture. Secondly, the texture model is a good basis both for platform developers to develop components that are configurable for different specializations of the architecture, and for product developers to structure the product-specific parts of products.

To justify this claim we have analyzed three existing population reference architectures and tried to investigate the applicability of our approach. We found that all three architectures required a degree of architectural variation in which our approach could be expected to be beneficial. In one case we found that the representation of the architecture actually included a concept very similar to a textural variation point. In another case we found that the representation of the architecture was indeed texture centric and contained textural variation points, although these variation points were not modeled explicitly in the way we propose, but instead were embedded in the documentation. In the third case the architecture was clearly under-specified, but without any particular support for specialization. However, it was recognized that some form of guidelines for specializing the architecture during product derivation would be useful.

This analysis has convinced us that textural variation points is a useful technique to model architectures that need to be open to variation in architectural choices but still provide comprehensive support for product derivation and relieve the product developers as much as possible from architecting. However, further research is required to provide better evidence for this claim. In particular we need experience from real life application of the approach.

Acknowledgments

The work reported here has been carried out in the context of the CAFÉ,[6] FAMILIES,[7] DAIM and Familier[8] projects. The collaboration with both academic and industrial partners in these projects has provided valuable inspiration and feedback to our work. We are especially grateful to Frank van der Linden, Anne Immonen, Isabel John, Timo Käkölä and Juan Carlos Dueñas whose comments to earlier drafts of this chapter have been of great help, and to Bjørn Egil Hansen, who was the primary contact with the BRIX team in DNV.

---

[6] ITEA project ip00004, CAFÉ [25].
[7] ITEA project ip02009, FAMILIES.
[8] DAIM and Familier are Norwegian projects led by ICT-Norway and partially funded by the Norwegian research council [7].

272   S. Hallsteinsen et al.

References

1. Bass, L., Klein, M., Bachmann, F.: Quality attribute design primitives and the attribute driven design method. In: *Software Product-Family Engineering*, ed by van der Linden, F., 4th International Workshop, PFE 2001, Bibao, Spain. Lecture Notes in Computer Science, vol 2290 (Springer, Berlin Heidelberg New York 2001) pp 169–188
2. Bayer, J.: Design for quality. In: *Software Product-Family Engineering*, ed by van der Linden, F., 5th International Workshop, PFE 2003, Siena, Italy. Lecture Notes in Computer Science, vol 3014 (Springer, Berlin Heidelberg New York 2003) pp 370–380
3. Bosch, J.: *Design and Use of Software Architectures – Adopting and Evolving a Product-Line Approach* (Addison-Wesley, Reading, MA 2000)
4. Brown, T.J., Spence, I.T.A., Kilpatrick, P.: A relational architecture description language for software families. In: *Software Product-Family Engineering*, ed by van der Linden, F., 5th International Workshop, PFE 2003, Siena, Italy. Lecture Notes in Computer Science, vol 3014 (Springer, Berlin Heidelberg New York 2003) pp 282–295
5. Buschmann, F., Meunier, R., Rohnert, H., Sommerlad, P., Stal, M.: *Pattern-Oriented Software Architecture – A system of Patterns* (Wiley, New York 1996)
6. Clements, P., Kazman, R., Klein, M.: *Evaluating Software Architectures: Methods and Case Studies* (Addison-Wesley, Reading, MA 2002)
7. DAIM: *Software Engineering Handbook*. http://www.ikt-norge.no (ICT, Norway, Oslo 2003)
8. Ferber, S., Haag, J., Savolainen, J.: Feature interaction and dependencies: modeling features for reengineering a legacy product line. In: *Software Product Lines*, ed by Chastek, G.J., 2nd International Conference, SPLC2, San Diego, CA, 19–22 August 2002. Lecture Notes in Computer Science, vol 2379 (Springer, Berlin Heidelberg New York 2002) pp 235–256
9. ISO: International Standard ISO/IEC 9126. Information technology – software product evaluation – quality characteristics and guidelines for their use (International Organization for Standardization, International Electrotechnical Commission, Geneva 1991)
10. Hallsteinsen, S., Swane, E.: Handling the diversity of networked devices by means of a product family approach. In: *Software Product-Family Engineering*, ed by van der Linden, F., 4th International Workshop, PFE 2001, Bilbao, Spain. Lecture Notes in Computer Science, vol 2290 (Springer, Berlin Heidelberg New York 2001) pp 264–281
11. Hallsteinsen, S., Fægri, T.E., Syrstad, M.: Patterns in product family architecture design. In: *Software Product-Family Engineering*, ed by van der Linden, F., 5th International Workshop, PFE 2003, Siena, Italy. Lecture Notes in Computer Science, vol 3014 (Springer, Berlin Heidelberg New York 2003) pp 261–268
12. Huston, S.D., Johnson, J.C.E., Syy, U.: *The ACE Programmer's Guide: Practical Design Patterns for Network and Systems Programming* (2003)
13. IEEE: IEEE Recommended practice for architectural description of software-intensive systems, IEEE Standard P1471 (IEEE Architecture Working Group 2000)
14. Jacobson, I., Griss, M., Jonsson, P.: *Software Reuse* (Addison-Wesley, Reading, MA 2000)
15. Jazayeri, M., Ran, A., van der Linden, F.: *Software Architecture for Product Families: Principles and Practice* (Addison-Wesley, Reading, MA 2000)
16. Klein, M., Kazman, R.: Attribute-based architectural styles. SEI technical report, CMU/SEI-99-TR-022 (SEI, Pittsburg 1999)
17. McRitchie, I., Brown, T.J., Spence, I.T.A.: Managing component variability within embedded software product lines. In: *Software Product-Family Engineering*, ed by van der Linden, F., 5th International Workshop, PFE 2003, Siena, Italy. Lecture Notes in Computer Science, vol 3014 (Springer, Berlin Heidelberg New York 2003) pp 98–110
18. Microsoft Directs how, part of DirectX. http://www.gdcl.co.uk/dshow.htm
19. OCI TAO Developers Guide version 1.3a (Part number 530-01)
20. Perry, D.E.: Generic architecture description for product lines. In: *Development an Evolution of Software Architectures for Product Families*, ed by van der Linden, F., 2nd International ESPRIT ARES Workshop, Las Palmas de Gran Canaria, Spain. Lecture Notes in Computer Science, vol 1429 (Springer, Berlin Heidelberg New York 1998) pp 51–56
21. Pohl, K., Böckle, G., van der Linden, F.: *Software Product Line Engineering – Foundations, Principles, and Techniques* (Springer, Berlin Heidelberg New York 2005)
22. Reenskaug, T., Wold, P., Lehne, O.A.: *Working with Objects – The Ooram Software Engineering Method* (Manning, Greenwich 1996)

23. Schmidt, D., Stal, M., Rohnert, H., Buschmann, F.: *Pattern-Oriented Software Architecture Volume 2 – Patterns for Concurrent and Networked Objects* (Wiley, New York 2001)

24. Thiel, S., Hein, A.: Systematic integration of variability into product line architecture design. In: *Software Product Lines*, ed by Chastek, G.J., 2nd International Conference, SPLC 2, San Diego, CA, USA, 19–22 August 2002. Lecture Notes in Computer Science, vol 2379 (Springer, Berlin Heidelberg New York 2002) pp 130–153

25. van der Linden, F.: Software product families in Europe: the ESAPS and CAFÉ projects. IEEE Softw. **19**(4), 41–49 (2002)

26. van der Linden, F., Schmid K., Rommes, E.: Software Product Lines in Action: The Best Industrial Practice in Product Line Engineering. Springer 2007 (forthcoming)

27. Van Ommering, R.: Building product populations with software components. Proceedings – International Conference on Software Engineering (IEEE Computer Society, Silver Spring, MD 2002) pp 255–265

28. Van Ommering, R., Bosch, J.: Widening the scope of software product lines – from variation to composition. In: *Software Product Lines*, ed by Chastek, G.J., 2nd International Conference, SPLC 2, San Diego, CA, USA, 19–22 August 2002. Lecture Notes in Computer Science, vol 2379 (Springer, Berlin Heidelberg New York 2002) pp 328–351

8 A Software Product Line Reference Architecture for Security

T.E. Fægri and S. Hallsteinsen

Abstract.
Security is a cross-cutting concern in software intensive systems and should consequently be subject to careful architectural analysis and decision making. The requirements for cost-effective product line development complicate this task. Two central research questions are addressed in this chapter (1) Is it viable to represent architectural security knowledge in a reference architecture? (2) If so, is such a reference architecture useful for security architecture design in software product lines? Initial evidence suggests that both questions can be affirmed. The main contribution of this chapter is a reference architecture that draws upon state-of-the-art techniques and practices from software product line engineering and information security and constitutes a decision support framework for security architecture design in software product lines. To validate the reference architecture, the chapter also presents our experiences from using it at three distinct companies.

8.1 Introduction

Increasingly, security related requirements constitute a significant portion of the total set of requirements for many software systems. Arguably, the most important aspect contributing to this trend is the seemingly continually growing demand for more open and flexible IT systems. Terms such as "the real-time enterprise," "software infrastructures," "service oriented architectures" and "composite software applications" proliferate in the corporate IT arena and denote information systems that support cross-application integration, cross-company transactions and end-user access through a range of channels, including the Internet. For product oriented companies these trends are important too, because most applications will in some form interact with other applications. Although this is a natural consequence of the desire to improve the operational efficiency and reduce the need for manual work, application integration and Internet access make critical assets vulnerable to many threats. For most product oriented companies, requirements for security are likely to be as varied as for any other quality. Thus it can be expected that companies will want to supply variants of the same product to satisfy the variability in product requirements.

The architecture of a software system is important for the system's ability to satisfy its requirements [2–4, 8, 14, 25, 39]. In other words, if the architecture is carefully designed the resulting system has a better chance of meeting its expectations. Constructing software systems of any significant size or complexity requires considerations to the architecture.

By architecture we mean its conceptual organization in components, connectors and the relations between them. This is an abstract view of the software system that allows us to reason about high level aspects such as security, performance, maintainability, deployment, and functionality without having to consider all the details.

The art of creating architectures is normally performed by people with lots of experience in the particular domain of the application. Experience creates valuable knowledge. In an effort to manage this knowledge, the software architecture community has created the architectural pattern concept. Architectural patterns are working principles that have proven useful in architectural design and have been documented so that others can reuse the knowledge. We argue that through careful management of this knowledge, for example in terms of architectural patterns, software architectures can be created more effectively and with a higher probability of achieving the desired qualities. However, the existence of architectural patterns is not enough to facilitate the construction of good architectures. No set of patterns will create an architecture that is optimal for all stated requirements. We must also capture and reason upon the various effects of these patterns. After all, architectural design is all about making sound tradeoffs. Architectural patterns, accompanied with knowledge of their effects, help us in making good design decisions.

Making these tradeoffs effectively becomes even more important in a context where a company wants to deliver multiple product variants to the market. While seeking to minimize the global cost of producing those products, the variability in quality requirements will favor a systematic approach to architectural design where variation among member products can be precisely managed. We build upon the large volume of research and experience within the area of Software Product Lines (SPL). SPL is an approach to software development that seeks to optimize productivity by assisting strategic reuse of software assets [34]. SPL incorporates methodologies for capturing and planning for variations among a group of products.

Security is a quality aspect of software systems that must be addressed by the architecture. It is a cross-cutting concern that is affected by a wide range of architectural decisions. For example, a software system that is constructed using third party components needs to have an architecture that is able to contain potentially malicious components within security boundaries. Simultaneously, the software architect is normally forced to balance this concern against a number of other, potentially conflicting concerns. The reference architecture presented here supports the software architect in the SPL approach. We treat security requirements as a natural source of variability among the product members. In order to capture and manage knowledge related to security architectural design we propose a reference architecture for software product line engineering. It is in essence a knowledge repository with a structure to support architectural design. It consists of

1. a quality model representing and organizing our vocabulary for security requirements,
2. a decision model constituted by the scenarios that represent the security requirements for the application to be designed
3. a security architecture language prescribing architectural solutions to the security requirements.

The structure of the remaining part of this contribution is as follows: Section 8.2 discusses the construction of software architectures facing security requirements. Section 8.3

describes the main theoretical framework for the reference architecture through conceptual models. Sections 8.4–8.6 constitute the reference architecture documenting the quality model, the decision model and the security architecture language, respectively. Section 8.7 elaborates upon how to use the reference architecture and Sect. 8.8 describes our experiences with using the reference architecture in practice. Section 8.9 presents work that is related to ours. Section 8.10 presents concluding comments.

8.2 Security Architecture Design

Software architecture is concerned with the overall structure of software systems. We generally adhere to the IEEE 1471 definition: "The fundamental organization of a system embodied in its components, their relationships to each other, and to the environment, and the principles guiding its design and evolution." p.3 in [27]. Thus, architectural design deals with making high level decisions regarding the overall organization of the software system. As most successful systems can be expected to have a long lifespan, the efforts required to maintain the system are a key concern.

The architecture of a software system has a great impact on its ability to satisfy its requirements. Conversely, making changes to the architecture of an already existing system can be very expensive. Furthermore, ensuring that the software system is able to remain compliant with its quality requirements is just as important [6]. Thus, the architecture becomes a critical asset for the organization. Therefore the architecture should undergo a thorough design and evaluation process.

Most software products have many stakeholders with different roles who want to influence the business drivers and the quality requirements set for the final system. One challenge in this work is to specify quality requirements in a way that makes them clear and testable. The software architect must carefully search for architectural constructions that promise to address the requirements in the best possible way. While designing the architecture, tradeoffs should be made explicitly to support an open design process involving the relevant stakeholders. Architecture design is not a simple task, neither is it a task that lends itself easily to automation.

8.2.1 Encoding Architectural Knowledge

As mentioned in the introduction, architectural design is a knowledge intensive art that depends heavily upon experience. In order to encode and reuse this knowledge, the software architecture community has created the concepts architectural tactics and architectural patterns. They are all documented, reusable architectural solutions that promise to address specific concerns in software architectures. They are, essentially, representations of knowledge of how particular problems can be solved [51].

As the number of solutions increases, so does the need to see relationships between them. Therefore, it is useful to put these architectural solutions into a system. Architecture solutions occur in widely different contexts, but they may nevertheless have a lot of similar characteristics. Also, architectural solutions occur at different levels of abstraction. Some are merely tactics in the solution space; others are very specific – prescribing components, interactions and roles. Generally we can say that architectural tactics are less specific than architecture patterns, but it is not possible to draw distinct borders between them. Architecture solutions form a continuum, where the level of abstraction is a viable dimension for considering them.

A reference architecture is a guideline for the design of architectures within a given domain, i.e., it is a recommendation for how to build a particular kind of system. One can say that a reference architecture is the architecture of a set of architectures. Typically, the main rationale for constructing reference architectures is the desire to capture, represent and share knowledge about what the requirements for certain types of systems are and how to build the systems, thus helping to standardize types of architectures. In the described reference architecture, we have systematized architectural solutions for security requirements. We call this system the security architecture language (see Sect. 8.6).

8.2.2 Security Design

Security design draws upon a large body of knowledge. Security has been a concern for computer system designers almost from the outset; the early systems were often used in sensitive military applications. Security then became a mainstream requirement with the advent of multi-user computers in the late 1960s when commercial use triggered concerns of malicious behavior from other users [17]. Since then, security has seen an increasing popularity. In the last years, as the attention to Internet based computing has exploded, security has again been a top priority in many fora.

Security deals with protecting assets and making sure that they remain valuable to their owner. In order to accomplish that, we must determine the relevant threats towards the assets, i.e., construct a risk assessment profile. Only after having gathered a good understanding of the threats facing the system can we make good decisions for what countermeasures we should introduce. The security submodel of the reference architecture (see Sect. 8.3) describes the conceptual model for how to create the risk assessment profile.

Security design introduces costs in terms of security technology, implementation and maintenance of security policies and effects on other quality attributes of the final software system (the latter aspect will be discussed in the next section). A key benefit of the risk assessment profile is that it provides support for deciding which investments in security should be made and which assets should be protected [24]. However, the task of determining *how* the assets should be protected must also be done.

It should be noted that this reference architecture only deals with the aspects of security that can be addressed through software. This might be called "logical security." Other aspects of security, such as the design of physical countermeasures or barriers (this could be called "physical security"), are not covered by this reference architecture.

8.2.3 Security Architecture

As previously mentioned, architectural design involves making sound tradeoffs between design alternatives in order to achieve sufficient product quality [3, 4]. We base this work upon using architectural solutions (in the form of architectural tactics and patterns) as building blocks for software architectures, as previously described in [26], but also advocated by others, e.g., [2, 3, 39]. A principal idea is that each solution is associated with a set of effects on the quality attributes. By having an understanding of the effects from each architectural solution we can more easily reason about the total effects of all the architectural solutions used in the actual architecture under consideration. It should be noted that we do not aim at building a formally precise machine for determining the sum of effects from a set of architectural solutions. This is a hard problem due to the lack of precise metrics, the large amount of tacit knowledge going into architectural design and the complexity of dependencies between different decisions in the many layers of abstractions in a final system [13].

The security architecture language (Sect. 8.6) defines our solution space. These solutions are *countermeasures* that we can use in order to protect against damage to assets. These countermeasures represent knowledge about how to deal with various security threats, described by many previous efforts [5, 45, 48, 52, 54, 59].

Security architectural design is confronted with the same challenges as architectural design in general; certain tradeoffs must be made between important quality attributes. Usability, performance, etc. are frequently in conflict with security [23, 44, 53, 55, 57, 58, 61]. In situations like that, it is important to have a clear understanding of the tradeoffs which have been made [3, 14]. Through the systematic approach to architectural design presented here, we hope to make these tradeoffs more explicit. Subsequently, it will become easier to design architectures that maintain the interests of all stakeholders.

8.2.4 Security Architecture for Software Product Lines

For various reasons, it may be beneficial for an organization to deliver multiple products with overlapping capabilities to its markets. If overlapping capabilities are implemented in a controlled way, using the same assets, we call such a set of products a product line. Product lines bring the additional challenge of managing variability among similar products in a cost-efficient manner. The field of Software Product Lines (SPL) addresses these concerns, and has produced a large body of knowledge [7, 15, 34]. The presented reference architecture builds upon these ideas while applying them in a security-focused setting.

To reduce cost, an organization will typically strive to introduce a certain level of standardization of the architecture between the product line members [26]. This can be at different levels, for example in terms of technical platforms, prescribed frameworks, general quality requirements or recommended architectural solutions. In order to accommodate standardization, the product architect must first consider the implications of the already prescribed requirements and architectural solutions.

Already prescribed quality requirements must be reconciled with the product requirements. Architectural solutions identified as contributors towards the quality requirements of the product must be reviewed and aligned with already standardized solutions.

8.3 Conceptual Model of the Reference Architecture

This section presents a conceptual model (or view) of the reference architecture. The conceptual model illustrates the reference architecture at a high level of abstraction by showing how the central concepts relate to each other. Also, the concepts and their relationships are explained.

The term reference architecture was introduced in Sect. 8.2. For organizations building software product lines, reference architectures play an even more important role because they are an appropriate tool for the capture of standardized requirements and guidelines within the product line. The reference architecture *is* the product line architecture.

Inspired by the same rationale, we have built a reference architecture for security. It consists of three submodels:

1. A *security submodel* that supports the development of a risk assessment profile for the assets covered by the system. The risk assessment profile assists the software architect in deciding what requirements should be set for the system and their internal priorities. The risk assessment profile is also helpful in the process of determining the most appropriate countermeasures
2. An *architecture submodel* that incorporates architectural solutions which promise to address security related requirements
3. A *decision support submodel* that supports capturing, specifying and reasoning about requirements for the product line members. Requirements are formulated as scenarios representing variation points. One scenario represents one variation point. A variation point will normally represent multiple variants. Now, in the presented reference architecture, not all of the scenarios contain multiple variants. In the development of the guidelines, we decided it was useful to capture this security architecture design knowledge despite the lack of direct variability aspects.

Together, these three submodels give the software architect an integrated environment for architectural security design.

Figure 8.1 illustrates a conceptual model of the reference architecture. It shows the three submodels with their core concepts and their inter-relationships. The decomposition into three submodels supports its extensibility. Also, our architectural solutions are organized in a taxonomy of tactics and patterns. New tactics and patterns may be added to the existing ones in order to represent other architectural solutions. In practice, many organizations develop or refine their own architectural solutions. However, the adopting company must be able to associate impacts on quality attributes with the architectural solution.

The following sections discuss the conceptual model in more detail.

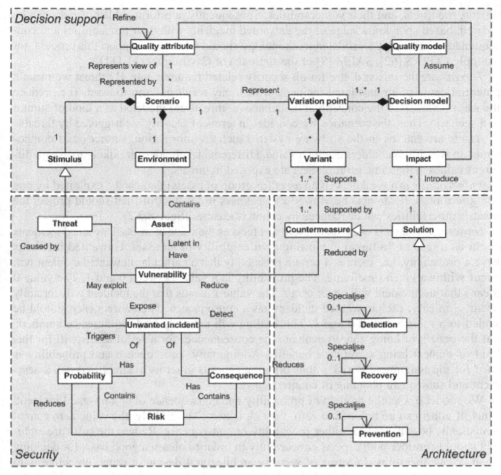

Fig. 8.1. Conceptual model of reference architecture

8.3.1 Security Submodel

The security submodel deals with risk assessment. Core concepts include threat, asset, vulnerability, unwanted incident and risk. Supplementary concepts include probability and consequence.

Arguably, the main objective for any efforts related to security is managing and mitigating risk. This might have significant economical impacts. Return of investment in security efforts must therefore be carefully evaluated [1, 11, 24]. In a product line context, this is even more important. To achieve strategic reuse one depends more heavily on careful planning and design [10].

The proposed reference architecture is not, however, intended to be a tool for risk assessment. Although it does cover the central topics for a risk assessment and provides core support for these activities, the application software architect should carefully consider the threats, the assets, and their vulnerabilities. Subsequently, a prioritized list of risks can be created, based upon knowledge of the unwanted incidents with their probabilities and consequences. Preferably, a validated methodology should be used to support this process, for example CORAS [62], SAEM [9] or the approach of Cavusoglu et al. [11].

Threats are the raison d'être for all security related requirements. By threat we mean a potential cause of an unwanted incident, which may result in harm to assets (i.e., reduce the asset's value). In the conceptual model above, threats are modeled as a kind of stimuli to a scenario. Thus, the scenarios we consider in terms of security are triggered by threats.

Assets are entities in the software system, such as information, services and components, to which stakeholders assign a value. Different stakeholders are likely to assign different values to the same asset. Assets are exposed to threats.

Vulnerability is a weakness of an asset (or group of assets) that can be exploited by one or more threats. It can also be viewed as weakness in the controls that should protect the asset. Vulnerabilities can be reduced by countermeasures (Sect. 8.3.2).

Unwanted incident is one kind of event that reduces the value of assets. Unwanted incidents occur as a result of a threat exploiting a vulnerability of an asset. Unwanted incidents have a probability, i.e., there is a certain probability that a particular unwanted incident will occur within a given timeframe. The probability is a value between 0 and 1. The value 0 means that the incident will never occur. The value 1 means that the incident will certainly occur. Similarly, each unwanted incident has a consequence. The consequence should be scaled to a value between 0 and 1. This scaling will naturally lead to imprecise numbers, but the benefit of being able to evaluate the consequences for a set of assets will for this kind of context bring significant benefits. Additionally, consequence and probability is used for the assignment of risk – thus bringing benefits in terms of simplified risk assessment and subsequent planning of countermeasures.

We model *risk* as the product of probability and consequence of an unwanted incident. Thus, if either can be reduced to zero, the risk is zero. More likely, the value zero cannot realistically be achieved for either probability or consequence. Rather, the software architect should consider both aspects concurrently in order to obtain a good basis for deciding upon countermeasures. In terms of security architectural design, a prime objective is to construct systems that carefully balance the risk with the economical impact of implementing the countermeasures.

8.3.2 Architecture Submodel

Within the submodel architecture we have located the concepts that are related to the architectural design of the application. These concepts include countermeasure, solution, detection, prevention and recovery.

A *countermeasure* is some kind of action, normally associated with some form of security control (an artifact), which seeks to reduce the vulnerability of an asset (or group of assets). A variant, as discussed in Sect. 8.3.3, is supported by one or more countermeasures. The meaning of this is that a variant is distinct within the variation point if the set of countermeasures is unique among the variants. An asset might be protected by multiple countermeasures, and the mapping of the countermeasure(s) to the architecture model is done to give the best possible effect for the asset in question.

A *solution* is an architectural decision that is used to achieve a quality attribute response. Beneath this definition we include both architectural tactics and patterns. An architectural tactic is a means of satisfying a quality-attribute-response measure by manipulating some aspect of a quality attribute model through architectural design decisions [3]. Tactics are means, principles, techniques, or mechanisms that facilitate the achievement of certain qualities in architecture. Similar to patterns, tactics capture a way to achieve a certain quality requirement, but are not concrete enough to be used directly and hence have to be instantiated as patterns. Examples of tactics for the quality attribute "reliability" are redundancy and exceptions. Tactics may be specializations of another tactic. At some level of specialization, the tactic becomes a pattern – i.e., a concrete solution to a problem. Referring to Fig. 8.1 above, architectural tactics are a kind of solution that promises to contribute to the wanted response from the scenario (i.e., maintain some of the security qualities discussed in Sect. 8.4). Unwanted incidents have two important properties: a probability and a consequence. We use this interpretation of unwanted incidents to identify three generic security tactics: detection, prevention and recovery (the latter two directly addressing probability and consequence).

These high level tactics are useful for the application designer in order to facilitate reasoning about general approaches to solving the security requirements. However, similar to high level qualities, they have very weak prescriptive power. We need specialized solutions. Figure 8.2 illustrates the high level part of our solutions taxonomy (the security architecture language is illustrated in Fig. 8.6).

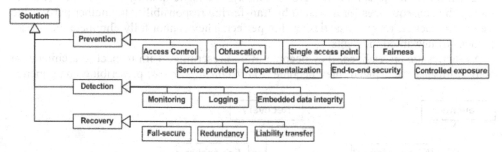

Fig. 8.2. High level solutions hierarchy

Prevention. Prevention tactics are used to reduce the probability of unwanted incidents. Figure 8.2 shows eight different specializations of this tactic that can be used in order to accomplish this, possibly in combination. *Access control* is the implementation of authorization, i.e., the process of ensuring that only designated actors are permitted to perform certain actions on the asset. *Service provider* includes approaches that delegate the implementation of preventive measures to external entities. *Obfuscation* means to re-arrange information in order to make it less intelligible. Cryptography is an example of obfuscation. *Compartmentalization* involves creating multiple security barriers and thereby reducing the probability that an attack endangers the whole system. *Single access* point is exactly the opposite of compartmentalization; it involves centralizing access to the system. The rationale is that it is easier to implement one access point correctly. *End-to-end security* means to ensure security over the whole information chain. For many complex IT systems, this tactic is of key importance as the number of part systems increases. *Fairness* denotes tactics that seek to prevent a single threat agent from taking over the system. Finally, *controlled exposure* is similar to obfuscation but includes mechanisms that actively partition information into a visible and an invisible part. Common for all prevention tactics is that they do not eliminate the probability of unwanted incidents. Rather, they reduce this probability to a certain level.

Detection. Detection means to determine that something is happening or has happened. It does not affect the system's direct resistance towards an attack. However, the detection tactic can have a great value in many system environments. For example, it may enable continuous improvement of system security. By examining unwanted incidents that have happened, the system can be tuned to counter these kinds of incidents in the future. *Monitoring* and *logging* are two kinds of detection tactics. Monitoring has some kind of active aspect, for example a process that continuously checks for changes or unwanted patterns in the usage of a system. Logging, on the other hand, is primarily a passive arrangement. An example might be the logging of certain events to a file. At some undefined point in time, the log might be inspected. *Embedded data integrity* implies that extra information is added to the original data which can be used to verify tampering.

Recovery. Recovery is the last main group of tactics. It seeks to address security concerns by reducing the consequence (or negative impact) of incidents. Three subgroups of recovery tactics are illustrated. *Fail-secure* is the tactic of designing the system so that in the case of unplanned events it will fail to a secure state, a state in which the system cannot be further jeopardized. *Redundancy* is the tactic of employing multiple, somewhat independently working components with similar functional capabilities in order to withstand certain failures in the component group. Finally, the tactic *liability transfer* involves reducing the consequences for a system by transferring responsibility to another party. Like prevention tactics, recovery tactics are not perfect. They cannot fully eliminate the consequences of unwanted incidents.

As tactics are specialized, they become more prescriptive with respect to architectural design. Further specialized, they become *architectural patterns*, prescribing components,

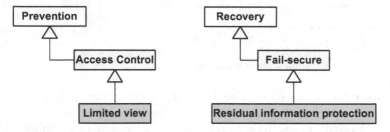

Fig. 8.3. Example specialization

component specifications, component collaborations and component roles. Figure 8.3 illustrates how two patterns (limited view and residual information protection) implement two specialized tactics (access control and fail-secure, respectively). These two are examples from the security architecture language depicted in Fig. 8.6.

Patterns are filled with a gray background in order to illustrate that they are more prescriptive than tactics.

Limited view implies that the user can only see information, menus or options for which he is authorized. That is, access control is performed before information is presented. The opposite approach, called full view with error, implies that access control is performed at a later stage, for example upon trying to execute a menu choice or view detailed information for an item.

Residual information protection involves making sure that no information is left available after a system crash or unexpected application termination. In this way the tactic of secure failure is maintained.

8.3.3 Decision Support Submodel

Within the decision support submodel we group concepts that deal with representing, organizing and reasoning about requirements. It is generic in the sense that it can equally well support other software qualities (e.g., generic ISO 9126 qualities).

The *quality model* represents and organizes our vocabulary for security requirements in a common, easy to use structure. Within a product line, there will be variations in the quality requirements between the different products. The ISO model says the following about security: "Attributes of software that bear on its ability to prevent unauthorized access, whether accidental or deliberate, to programs or data." This definition is clearly too generic to support requirement specifications for software architectures, a view that is also supported by Jung et al. [30]. The quality model we have developed for security is a specialization of the general ISO 9126 model for software qualities [29]. The detailed quality model is presented in Sect. 8.4.

The quality model is broken down into *quality attributes*, each of which is a characteristic of a software product. Quality attributes can be refined, meaning that they have one or more subcharacteristics. Further, quality attributes may influence each other, through the *impact* of architectural solutions.

We use *scenarios* to represent (views of) quality attributes. They consist of the three main elements: environment, stimulus and response.

All scenarios have an *environment*, i.e., a context that may include aspects such as system elements (i.e., assets), actors and processes.

Secondly, the scenario has a *stimulus*. The stimulus is used to model the activation of the scenario, i.e., what triggers the architecture's reaction to a security related concern. Generically, the stimulus may take different forms. In relation to security, a stimulus is something that may compromise the security of the system under evaluation. Thus, we model threat as a kind of stimulus.

Lastly, the scenario has a (set of) *response(s)* that are the *variants*. The response is used to model the architecture's reaction to the stimulus. Openness in the architecture is represented as multiple responses within the same scenario, i.e., some quality aspect that can vary and that has to be resolved by the software architect. The variation point includes a description of the achieved effect on the quality attribute represented by the scenario and a (set of) architectural solution(s) that promise to address that quality attribute. Each response details the architectural solution used to achieve it and other known effects of this architectural decision. Typically, an architectural decision will have impacts on other nonsecurity related quality attributes. The application architect must determine how to prioritize these.

Quality attribute: Confidentiality → Withstand attacks in a group of cooperating applications

Environment: Application a_c provides a set of services that makes sensitive information available to other collaborating applications over the Internet.

Stimuli	Response	Resolution
An application a_m attempts to invoke services from application a_c without the required authorizations.	The architecture prevents a_m from accessing nonauthorized services from a_c.	V. 1
	The architecture allows a_m access to the services, but all accesses are logged. This facilitates recovery.	V. 2

Scenario resolution:

Ref.	Approach	Architectural solution
V. 1	The architecture requires that a_m is both authenticated and authorized before being allowed access to the services.	Prevention. Access control. (Component) authentication. Authorization.
V. 2	The architecture acknowledges that availability of information may be more critical than preventing access to it. However, by logging all accesses to the information, liability is put on the application a_m.	Recovery. Liability transfer. Digital certificates. Auditing.

Each alternative solution included in the variation point is denoted a *variant*. Variants implement the architectural solutions indicated in the scenario.

Typically, an architectural decision affects more than one quality attribute. For example, the same architectural pattern can improve performance but cause an increase in complexity and a reduction of maintainability. We denote this phenomenon *impact*. Impacts are summarized for each architectural solution.

Lastly, the *decision model* is the collection of scenarios. The software architect must first determine the quality requirements that apply to the application to be designed. Then, the scenarios representing these quality requirements must be identified. These scenarios will then constitute the decision model for that application. Subsequently, for each applicable scenario, the variation point is resolved in light of the particular requirements of the application. The decision model is presented in detail in Sect. 8.5.

An example scenario, representing a certain aspect of confidentiality (maintaining confidentiality in an application integration setting) is given above. In this example, the scenario has two distinct responses – representing two alternative ways to affect the quality attribute. One is to prevent the incident from occurring, i.e., reduce its probability through access control. The other is to reduce the consequence of the incident by transferring liability. Each of the two variants is subsequently described in more detail in the scenario resolution part. The tactics and patterns that will help the architect in reaching the desired effect by resolving the variation point are documented in the column "Architectural solution."

The scenario is presented in two main parts. The main part, on the top, contains the environment, stimuli and response. The second part describes how the response can be accomplished. This scenario encompasses two different architectural decisions; (V.1) is to reduce the probability of a security breach or (V.2) is to reduce the consequences.

The scenarios included in this reference architecture have been developed by extracting security requirements from a number of companies, refining them to conform to our scenario structure and then collectively reviewed in order to extract generic architectural knowledge. Additionally, security literature has been utilized to support and extend this knowledge [21, 22, 28, 47, 54].

8.4 Quality Model

This section describes our quality model. It is used to represent and organize our vocabulary for security requirements The quality model assumed in the reference architecture is a specialization of the general ISO 9126 model for software qualities [29] (Fig. 8.4).

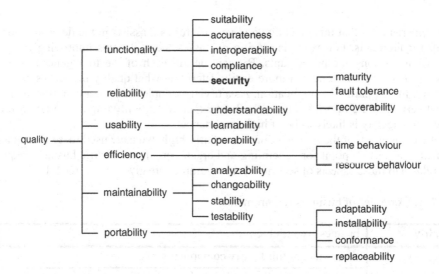

Fig. 8.4. The ISO9126 quality model for software systems

Although useful at an overall level, the quality "security" from ISO 9126 is too vague to be useful in requirements engineering. Furthermore, Jung et al. show that security as a subcharacteristic of "functionality" is problematic [30]. By defining security using more concrete terms, this problem can be reduced. To precisely capture and support reasoning about security requirements, security is broken down into the four intermediate level security quality attributes *integrity, confidentiality, availability* and *accountability*. Figure 8.5 illustrates the specialization relationship.

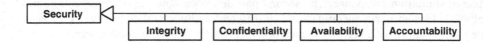

Fig. 8.5. Security quality breakdown

We understand with these four attributes the following:

1. Integrity: The property that assets have not been altered or destroyed in an unauthorized manner
2. Confidentiality: The property that assets are not made available or disclosed to unauthorized actors
3. Availability: The property of an asset being accessible and usable upon demand by an authorized actor
4. Accountability: The property that ensures that the actions of an actor may be traced uniquely to that actor

Our experience is that this breakdown is very useful as it assists in the determination of security requirements. For example, during risk assessment, it helps improving common understanding among the participants. By considering each of the four generic security quality attributes in turn, one can more easily determine what quality properties are relevant or not for the particular application. As a trivial example, in the context of an application that serves public information via the Internet, confidentiality might be a low priority quality, but integrity is likely to be of high importance.

As the complexity of the security domain is fairly high, we have used these four quality attributes as a starting point for generating and organizing more specific business requirements related to those aspects of security. Some examples are given in the Tb. 8.1.

Table 8.1. Examples of business requirements

quality	business requirement
integrity	secure use of third party components
	protection against unauthorized manipulation in user's application
confidentiality	withstand attacks in a group of collaborating applications
	maintaining security on shared computers
availability	protection against service disruptions
accountability	prevent false impersonation

For each business requirement there are multiple scenarios exemplifying the requirement. The scenarios are documented in the decision model (presented in Sect. 8.5).

Although we do not discuss the requirement specification process in more detail here, we assume that the application designer is supported by a risk assessment of the system. In security engineering, precise requirements can only be made after assessing the risks pertaining to the assets encompassed by the system. Broadly speaking, risks are events that can jeopardize the security qualities. It is important that the risk assessment is done at a suitable level of detail so as to give a good understanding of which assets are worth protecting and the level of risk that each of these assets is exposed to. This creates the basic decision framework for the application designer when determining the security qualities that shall apply for the application.

8.5 Decision Model

The process of building software architectures involves making well-considered design decisions that are highly sensitive to problem domain knowledge. This section contains a decision model for software architectures where security requirements must be addressed. The model has been developed in cooperation with four industrial partners. 1–2 representatives from each company participated in 2–5 one-day meetings discussing and capturing current practices. Roughly 150 man-hours were used on this activity. Additionally, material from security literature was used to aid the model's development. In order to reduce redundancy, literature is primarily cited in the security architecture language (Sect. 8.6), where the architectural solutions providing support to the scenarios have been described.

The structure of the decision model follows the conceptual reference architecture illustrated in Fig. 8.1; for each scenario, an environment describes the overall context, e.g. the considered assets and the kind of applications that might be applicable for the scenario. Subsequently, the stimulus illustrates the threat towards the assets.

Now, there might be different approaches to resolving a scenario. These are essentially variants within the product line architecture. Different architectural solutions illustrate design approaches that address the threat. Many variants thus refer to multiple architectural solutions (the numbers refer to the solutions presented in the security architecture language, the topic of Sect. 8.6). However, each response brings its own effects in terms of how the risks are affected and effects on other quality attributes.

8.5.1 Integrity

In the context of security, integrity is the property of information that it has not been manipulated by unauthorized actors. Integrity may be threatened wherever information is stored, transmitted or used. We have identified three relevant classes of environments within the scope of this quality model (a) third party components, (b) dynamic security boundaries, and (c) unauthorized manipulation in user's application.

Using Externally Developed Components Securely

The use of third party components (COTS or open source components) is an attractive approach to reduce cost of developing software. However, the approach brings significant challenges with respect to security. For example, it is difficult to determine whether a third party component contains dangerous code or not. Third party components cannot, without additional efforts, be trusted to the same degree as internally developed components. For the distrustful, a third party component has the same security characteristics as a virus. In real life however, most third party components will include some kind of insurance.

Scenario I.1 – Third Party Components

Environment: A software system includes components developed outside the company. Such components cannot always be trusted to the same degree as components developed within the company. Incurred threats include Trojan horse attacks and espionage [35].

Stimuli	Response	Resolution
A third party component attempts to modify information it is not authorized to modify.	The architecture prevents the attempt by restricting third party components' freedom, thus reducing the consequence of the attack.	V.1
	The architecture prevents the attempt by enforcing traditional access control policies for third party components.	V.2
	The architecture reduces the consequence of the attack by imposing liability onto the third party component's supplier.	V.3

Scenario resolution:

Ref.	Approach	Arch. Solution
V.1	The architecture reduces the freedom of execution of third party components. Third party components are not allowed to execute potentially dangerous actions.	Pattern 27: Sandbox. Pattern 21: Multi Barrier Security. Pattern 17: Layering.
V.2	Third party components' information access is protected by access control and unauthorized manipulation of information is prevented.	Pattern 3: Authentication. Pattern 6: Authorization.
V.3	As the third party components are verified by the supplier, the supplier can be more easily held responsible for the components' behavior.	Pattern 12: Code Signing.

Maintaining Integrity in Mobile Systems with Dynamic Security Boundaries

Occasionally, the security boundary of information changes over time. This introduces additional requirements with respect to the security architecture.

Scenario I.2 – Tampered Information During Mobile/Offline Usage

Environment: Support for disconnected clients complicates security. One must ensure that the extended system boundary is accounted for by the security architecture. There is a potential for loading the client or server with information that is not valid, e.g., it might have been tampered with.

Stimuli	Response	Resolution
A threat agent may compromise a mobile device and may subsequently cause manipulated information to be transferred to the server system.	The architecture detects maliciously manipulated information.	V.1
	The architecture prevents information from being maliciously compromised.	V.2

Scenario resolution:

Ref.	Approach	Arch. Solution
V.1	Integrity check in the information enables the detection of the maliciously manipulated information and may be used to prevent it from being accepted.	Pattern 12: Code Signing. Pattern 19: Message Authentication Codes.
V.2	The mobile device prevents successful attacks from threat agents.	Pattern 3: Authentication. Pattern 8: Biometric Authentication.

Scenario I.3 – Tampered Code Mobile/Offline Usage

Environment: Mobile clients get their code installed from the central server. In case the server is compromised, there is a potential for loading the client with code that is not valid, e.g., it might have been tampered with.

Stimuli	Response	Resolution
A threat agent has compromised the application server and thereby threatens to provide the client device with potentially dangerous code.	The architecture prevents maliciously manipulated code from being accepted by the client device.	V.1

Scenario resolution:

Ref.	Approach	Arch. Solution
V.1	Code on the server is protected by authenticity measures. Any integrity violations are detected by the client.	Pattern 12: Code Signing.

Maintaining a Defense Against Unauthorized Manipulation in User's Application

Information is, and should be, easily available in the user's application. However, ease of access constitutes a security risk in its own right.

Scenario I.4 – User Leaves Computer for some Time

Environment: A computer is left unattended for some time leaving it exposed to unwanted incidents.

Stimuli	Response	Resolution
A threat agent attempts to exploit a computer that has been left unattended by its user.	The architecture prevents any incidents by locking the application after a certain elapsed time, requiring the user to log in afterwards.	V.1

Scenario resolution:

Ref.	Approach	Arch Solution
V.1	The architecture enables the locking of the application after a certain period of inactivity.	Pattern 31: Timeout. Pattern 3: Authentication.

Scenario I.5 – Application Used on Exposed Device

Environment: An organization may gain significant benefits by enabling mobile workers to use corporate applications while being on the move. However, the use of mobile computers in noncontrolled physical environments may give rise to additional risks towards integrity of information.

Stimuli	Response	Resolution
A threat agent has gained physical access to the mobile computer.	The architecture helps in detecting the attack and providing timely alarms to the user.	V.1
	The architecture helps prevent unwanted incidents by strengthening user authentication procedures when the application is used in a hostile environment.	V.2
	The architecture reduces the consequence of unwanted incidents by reducing the amount of information stored on the mobile computer.	V.3
	The architecture reduces the consequence of unwanted incidents by limiting the information access rights when the application is used in a hostile environment.	V.4

Scenario resolution:

Ref.	Approach	Arch. Solution
V.1	The architecture contains surveillance functionality that detects hostile behavior.	Pattern 16: IDS (Intrusion Detection System). Pattern 1: Anomaly Detection.
V.2	The architecture supports the implementation of contextual security policies by which requirements on authentication can be adjusted.	Pattern 4: Authentication Levels.
V.3	The architecture minimizes the amount of information stored on the mobile computer.	Pattern 30: Thin Client. Pattern 25: Residual Information *Protection*.
V.4	The architecture supports the implementation of contextual security policies by which authorization levels are adjusted depending on the physical environment.	Pattern 14: Contextual Authorization.

Scenario I.6 – Information Access Rights not reflected in Application

Environment: During the development of applications, there is a continuous danger that the correct authorizations are not reflected in the application.

Stimuli	Response	Resolution
Security sensitive application code is being written or maintained.	Accidental errors, causing breaches in the integrity of the information, are prevented in the application code.	V.1
	The developer is provided with instruments to reduce the likelihood of not reflecting the correct authorizations.	V.2

Scenario resolution:

Ref.	Approach	Arch. Solution
V.1	Access rights are encapsulated with the information thus reducing the risk of writing erroneous application code.	Pattern 18: Limited View.
V.2	The architecture assists the application developer in maintaining the integrity of information. The architecture prescribes a common security resolving functional component.	Pattern 24: Reference Monitor. Pattern 28: Sentry.

8.5.2 Confidentiality

Confidentiality is the ability of a system to restrict access to information to authorized users only.

Withstanding Attacks in a Group of Cooperating Applications

In systems composed of multiple cooperating applications, a certain level of trust must be present. However, it is important to determine the implications and possible actions that should be the result of potential breaches of this trust [48].

Scenario C.1 – Application Integration

Environment: Application a_c provides a set of services that makes sensitive information available to other applications over the Internet.

Stimuli	Response	Resolution
An application a_m attempts to invoke services from application a_c without proper authorizations.	The architecture prevents a_m from accessing nonauthorized services from a_c.	V.1
	The architecture allows a_m access to the services, but all accesses are logged. The consequences for a_c are therefore reduced.	V.2

Scenario resolution:

Ref.	Approach	Arch. solution
V.1	The architecture requires that a_m is both authenticated and authorized before being allowed access to the services.	Pattern 3: Authentication. Pattern 6: Authorization.
V.2	The architecture acknowledges that availability of information may be more critical than preventing access to it. However, by logging all accesses to the information, liability is put on the application a_m	Pattern 3: Authentication. Pattern 2: Auditing. Pattern 15: Digital Signatures.

Maintaining Security on Shared Computers

The benefit of being able to use your applications despite being without a private computer might be justified in certain circumstances. However, the requirement to maintain the confidentiality of information is severely stressed when the computer used to access the application is shared with other people who may constitute potential threat agents.

Scenario C.2 – Secure Use on Non-private Computers

Environment: After a service has been used from public Internet access computers, there may be traces of information left on the machines that can cause confidentiality violations. This is a serious threat to confidentiality, as systems and applications may crash, which could prevent full application control of the data/code loaded onto the computer. Further, the administrative routines for the computer could prevent the user from manually ensuring that traces of service usage have been cleaned up.

Stimuli	Response	Resolution
A user accesses a corporate application from an untrusted computer. A threat agent subsequently gains control of the computer.	The architecture eliminates the storage of potentially vulnerable information on the untrusted computer.	V.1
	The architecture protects all information stored on the untrusted computer.	V.2
	The architecture forbids access to particularly sensitive information while using public computers.	V.3

Scenario resolution:

Ref.	Approach	Arch. Solution
V.1	Information is not persistently stored on the client computer, it is only viewed. The central server maintains all information.	Pattern 13: Cookie. Pattern 30: Thin Client.
V.2	All information that is stored, either temporarily or permanently is protected and only readable by authorized actors.	Pattern 11: Cryptography (of all sensitive data in memory and persistent storage). Pattern 25: Residual Information *Protection.*
V.3	When an application is used on untrusted computers, only certain, nonsensitive information is available.	Pattern 14: Contextual Authorization

8.5.3 Availability

Availability is a system's ability to provide service for a given percentage of the time. Understandably, a system that is unable to provide service may cause great disadvantages for its stakeholders. Reducing the availability of a service may of course be in the interest of a threat agent. Thus, it is critical that availability is included as part of a security quality. We choose to discuss availability in terms of the timeliness of services.

At a high level, there are two principal causes for reduced service timeliness (a) the service proper or (b) the service access path (i.e., networks and associated infrastructure).

For a client however, it is impossible to distinguish between the two. We also address the problems of hardware sabotage, i.e., attacks that cause physical damage to hardware.

Avoiding Service Disruptions

A threat agent may gain significant benefits from disrupting a service. Depending on the potential negative business impact, the software architecture should support instruments to reduce the likelihood or reduce the consequence of such attempts.

Scenario Av.1 – Malicious Third Party Components

Environment: When using a third party component in a solution, there is a threat that the component may attempt to cause service disruption.

Stimuli	Response	Resolution
A third party component attempts to cause service disruption.	The architecture prevents the component from disrupting the service.	V.1
	The architecture reduces the consequence of unwanted incidents caused by the component.	V.2

Scenario resolution:

Ref.	Approach	Arch. solution
V.1	The third party component is prevented from doing certain operations that may cause disruptions of the service.	Pattern 27: Sandbox. Pattern 21: Multi Barrier Security.
V.2	The component causes disruption at one server, but redundancy ensures that the service is quickly restored (note: measures need to be taken to ensure that the same incident does not occur at the redundant server).	Pattern 10: Clustering. Pattern 20: Mirror Sites.

Scenario Av.2 – Denial of Service Attacks

Environment: A threat agent may establish Denial of Service Attacks towards a service provider. Many sophisticated attacks, such as Distributed Denial of Service Attacks, may be difficult to distinguish from the load caused by high popularity among a high number of clients.

Stimuli	Response	Resolution
A DoS attack is established against the system.	The architecture reduces the consequence of the unwanted incident.	V.1
	The unwanted incident is detected and causes system administrators, etc. to be warned.	V.2

Scenario resolution:

Ref.	Approach	Arch. solution
V.1	The architecture reduces the impact of DoS attacks by invoking load balancing techniques that prevent the system from halting completely.	Pattern 26: Resource Throttling, Pattern 7: Bandwidth Throttling.
V.2	The architecture enables the detection of the attack.	Pattern 16: IDS (Intrusion Detection System). Pattern 1: Anomaly Detection.

Scenario Av.3 – Denial of Service Attacks Towards a User

Environment: As a security measure, an actor's account may be protected by a maximum number of failed authentication attempts. After this, the account is disabled for some time to prevent misuse. A threat agent may exploit this fact, and establish Denial of Service Attacks towards a single (or group of) user(s).

Stimuli	Response	Resolution
A threat agent establishes a DoS attack against a user of the system by attempting to login several times, thus exceeding the user's allowed number of failed login attempts.	The exposure of the login ID is reduced.	V.1
	Login IDs are not explicitly open for attack.	V.2

Scenario resolution:

Ref.	Approach	Arch. solution
V.1	The attack is not prevented, but the architecture should reduce the exposure of users' login IDs to minimize the chance of such attacks.	Pattern 18: Limited *View*.
V.2	The architecture supports the use of smartcards for authentication, optionally combined with biometric authentication, which do not expose login IDs to attackers. Alternatively, password authentication may be the last mechanism in a combination.	Pattern 3: Authentication. Pattern 8: Biometric Authentication.

8.5.4 Accountability

Accountability is the obligation or willingness to accept responsibility for one's actions. That is, accountability enables us to place trust in actors and have reasonable expectations about actors behaving according to their responsibilities.[1]

There are two key objectives related to accountability (a) making sure that the actor is identified correctly and (b) making sure that the identified actor cannot deny having performed certain actions. The text below contains scenarios that address the first of these two objectives. Scenarios representing the second objective have been omitted due to space limitations, but are typically resolved using some form of digital signature (see Pattern 15: Digital Signatures).

Preventing False Impersonation

An actor (e.g., a person or a component) should not be able to use the identity of another actor in a false manner.[2] If the attack is successful, the actor may subsequently endanger the confidentiality, integrity and availability of a target system's assets.

Scenario Ac.1 – User Authentication

Environment: Internally, most software systems need the ability to represent actors with their identity. In order to ensure a suitable level of trust in the identity the actor must be authenticated.

Stimuli	Response	Resolution
A threat agent attempts to impersonate an application by guessing valid username and password combinations.	The architecture prevents unwanted incidents by enforcing better policies for usernames and passwords, making it much more difficult to guess them.	V.1
	The architecture detects the attack and activates an alarm to administrative personnel.	V.2
	The architecture prevents that simply guessing a valid user ID and password combination is enough to breach the authentication procedure.	V.3

---

[1] Accountability includes a range of other issues also, of course. In order to enforce this quality, involved actors must have a common framework to deal with representations, negotiations, legal principles and resolution mechanisms. The framework should be maintained by an independent governing authority.

[2] Note that impersonation is a commonly used phenomenon in distributed systems because it allows a component to act on behalf of a user or another component.

Scenario resolution:

Ref.	Approach	Arch. Solution
V.1	The architecture reduces the likelihood of successfully guessing valid usernames and passwords.	Pattern 5: Authentication Policy. Pattern 22: Password.
V.2	The architecture detects the attack through monitoring functionality and reports the attack to a security team.	Pattern 16: IDS (Intrusion Detection System).
V.3	The architecture enables the use of a combination of different authentication mechanisms, for example biometric authentication.	Pattern 8: Biometric Authentication.

Scenario Ac.2 – Integration of Authentication Systems

Environment: Useful software systems are long lived. Such systems are thus more likely to face a requirement to be integrated with other systems. Application integration is a complex problem area which also raises concerns about security. Each application may have a separate security architecture dealing with authentication. Integration of these authentication mechanisms, for example by using single sign-on technologies (see Pattern 29: Single Sign-On), is a benefit for efficiency and operability, but might cause potentials for unwanted incidents in the form of more extensive attacks. Once inside, all systems comprising the solution may be compromised.

Stimuli	Response	Resolution
A threat agent has established an attack to impersonate an integrated authentication infrastructure.	The architecture reduces the consequence of the false impersonation attack.	V.1
	The architecture supports detection of the false impersonation attack.	V.2
	The architecture prevents the false impersonation attack.	V.3

Scenario resolution:

Ref.	Approach	Arch. solutions
V.1	The architecture enables the implementation of flexible security policies, for example including multiple authentication levels. There might be good reasons to implement policies that include extra authentication procedures for specific, highly critical tasks, even if the actor has already signed in successfully in the integrated authentication infrastructure.	Pattern 4: Authentication Levels. Pattern 14: Contextual Authorization.

| V.2 | The architecture detects that an actor has impersonated the system by observing unusual behavior by the actor. | Pattern 16: IDS (Intrusion Detection System). Pattern 1: Anomaly Detection. |
| V.3 | The architecture enforces the use of stronger authentication mechanisms that are judged to be strong enough for all systems participating in the solution. | Pattern 8: Biometric Authentication. |

8.6 Security Architecture Language

One way to structure architectural solutions is according to the kind of tactics they specialize or implement. In the context of security, we have identified and structured a number of architectural solutions. We have structured them according to the three high-level tactics detection, prevention and recovery. We cannot claim that this structure is the only one which is useful because architectural solutions will also address requirements other than security. However, the security architecture language presented here enables application architects dealing with those kinds of requirements to effectively identify tactics and patterns that address particular requirements related to security. The term "language" is discussed in the Chap. 7.

Architectural solutions are not described to a great level of detail. That would be outside the scope of this work. However, we provide references to further documentation. We also document significant impacts on nonsecurity related quality attributes, such as complexity and performance, for each pattern.

8.6.1 Tactics

This section discusses architectural tactics, general solutions adhered to in software architecture. Although this chapter only focuses upon the solutions used to ensure security qualities, such solutions apply to most architectural elements. Architectural solutions are essentially structured knowledge, helping software architects to think in terms of solutions for recurring problems.

We introduced architectural solutions in Sect. 8.3. Tactics can be structured in hierarchies where high-level tactics form the basis for more specialized tactics. At some level of specialization, the tactic is so refined that it takes the form of a pattern.

In this section, we describe three high-level security tactics; prevention, detection and recovery. Below these three, we identify subcategories of tactics. Figure 8.2 illustrates the conceptual hierarchy of security tactics that we discuss in this section. The intention of the figure is to show how we consider the relations between the tactics.

Prevention

Prevention is the tactic of creating barriers that potential enemies cannot circumvent. There will never be fully secure systems, so prevention tactics aim at reducing the probability of successful attacks.

Access control. Access control is the tactic of controlling which actors are allowed to operate upon assets.

Service provider. The tactic of using autonomous, possibly external entities to perform some predefined function on behalf of other actors. Examples might be validators that inspect certain data according to given rules.

Obfuscation. Obfuscation is the tactic of making data difficult to understand, thus increasing the cost of an adversary to interpret the data. This can for example be accomplished by applying cryptographic techniques.

Compartmentalization. The compartmentalization tactic means dividing a system into sections, so that breaking into one section does not enable direct access to the others. This tactic is useful to prevent attacks from damaging the whole system.

Single access point. This tactic is the opposite of the compartmentalization tactic. The single access point tactic is based upon the assumption that it is easier to build *one* good security barrier than multiple ones.

Fairness. The tactic of maintaining fairness involves balancing the consumption of resources fairly according to the current availability. The fairness tactic is a key to reduce the effects of Denial-of-Service attacks for example.

Controlled exposure. Complexity found in many software systems motivates the use of architectural tactics that reduce the risk of revealing information to nonauthorized actors. This tactic states that information is not exposed unnecessarily.

End-to-end security. End-to-end security is the tactic of ensuring that the whole channel between any two actors involved in service exchange is secured. The main rationale is that it simplifies security management. The tactic makes it more difficult to establish man-in-the-middle attacks, and it reduces the likelihood of weak points in the communication chain between two partners.

Detection

Detection is a key tactic in security for determining that the system is under attack. If enemy attacks are detected, they can be countered or knowledge about the attack may be used in the process of improving a system's security. The sophistication of attacks will increase. Therefore, it is crucial to be able to learn from attacks and adapt to an evolving threat landscape. Worth noting is that detecting anomalies is inherently difficult – even the best detection methods will always have false positives or false negatives, or both.

Monitoring. By monitoring, we mean inspecting certain parameters periodically. The monitoring tactic is useful for detecting security attacks as it enables rapid detection of attacks.

Logging. The tactic of logging implies that data are collected for inspection later.

Embedded data integrity. This tactic involves associating extra information with the data in order to facilitate the detection of security breaches. Examples are message authentication codes, extra data added to verify the message's integrity and watermarking.

Recovery

As a high-level security tactic, recovery involves reducing the negative consequences of attacks. In some situations, it makes sense to accept that attacks are successful and rather spend efforts in reducing the consequence of those attacks.

Fail-secure. This tactic implies that in the event of a failure, the system should be left in a secure mode, e.g., without leaving assets unprotected. A main element of the fail-secure tactic is that it is automatic, i.e., the system itself is designed to implement this tactic. One example of this tactic might be the following: If an application or component fails, sensitive data should be left in a protected state. Another example: Avoiding too much detail in error messages; detailed error messages could help attackers to exploit vulnerabilities in the application/component. Detailed error information could instead be written to the audit log.

Redundancy. Redundancy is the tactic of using multiple components with similar functional capabilities in order to withstand certain failures in the component group.

Liability transfer. Liability transfer is the tactic of making someone else responsible for the potential damage.

In the figure below (Fig. 8.6), we illustrate the full taxonomy of architectural solutions. Solutions become more and more specialized towards the leaves of the tree. Thus, tactics are located at the top of the tree, while patterns occur further down. With consideration to the volume of this chapter, only the architectural patterns that are referred to by scenarios of the decision model in subchapter 5 are described. These are indicated with italics in the figure.

8.6.2 Patterns

The following sections briefly present the architectural patterns for security that are referenced by the scenarios in the decision model (marked using italics in Fig. 8.6). Most of the included patterns are nevertheless well documented in the literature [16, 21, 37, 38, 42, 47, 50, 54, 59]. Patterns are more prescriptive than tactics and are therefore described at a more technical level than the tactics. Patterns implement tactics. However, there is a continuum of specialization among architectural solutions. No line can be drawn that unambiguously distinguishes tactics from patterns. The classification presented here is therefore suggestive. Patterns are presented in alphabetical order.

Pattern 1: Anomaly Detection

Architectural solution: Detection → Monitoring → Intrusion Detection System (IDS)

Problem. Attacks via the network, e.g., the Internet, constitute a continuous threat to networked computers (similar to the problem addressed by IDS in general, see Pattern 16: IDS). A key challenge concerning guarding against these attacks is the difficulty in determining what constitutes an attack. It must be expected that threat agents will frequently change the way attacks are established.

Solution. Anomaly-based intrusion detection is a kind of intrusion detection pattern. In this pattern, behavior in the system is analyzed, and unusual behavior is regarded as an attack [37]. The claimed benefit is an increased ability to prevent newly created attacks.

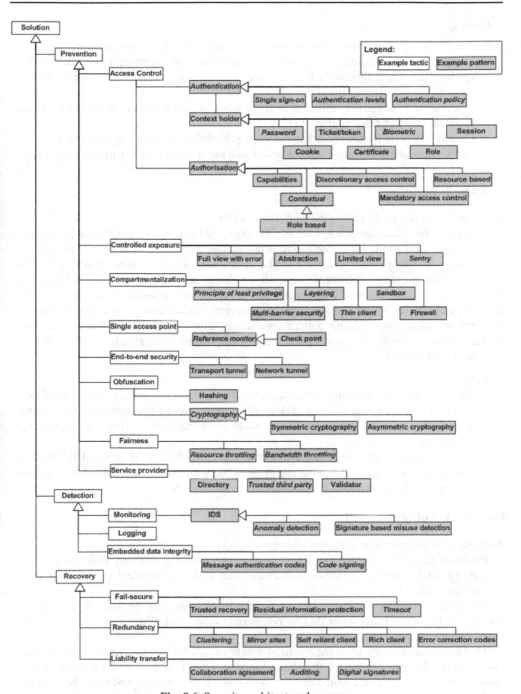

Fig. 8.6. Security architecture language

Impact.

1. Similar to signature based misuse detection IDS; anomaly detection incurs performance overheads, normally even heavier overheads than signature based misuse detection IDS. Their flexibility is also somewhat lower because it takes more effort to reconfigure the rules of the IDS.
2. Operability is negatively affected as these kinds of IDS have a tendency to generate large numbers of false alarms [11].
3. However, anomaly detection has a higher probability of detecting new kinds of attacks, because IDS of this kind are based on a more abstract set of trigger rules [37].

Pattern 2: Auditing

Architectural solution: Recovery → Liability transfer

Problem. Not all actors in a system can be expected to accept responsibility for the actions they have initiated. A mechanism to establish this responsibility is thus required.

Solution. Auditing builds evidence in the correlation of what subject was responsible for a particular event or set thereof. Normally, auditing depends on some kind of logging. These logs contain records of which actor performed certain actions in the system. Additionally, information related to the time of the event, certain communication parameters etc., are recorded. The auditing pattern means managing and using these logs in a controlled manner in order to support placement of responsibility in situations where this is necessary. See also [47].

Impact.

1. Auditing may involve sophisticated log analysis which in turn may have significant resource requirements causing delays for other current processing on the system. These delays may be somewhat alleviated by performing the analysis in low-priority processes.
2. Auditing may have a preventive effect in terms of security. If users of the system know that auditing mechanisms are in place, they might be discouraged from establishing attacks or trying to violate security in the system.

Pattern 3: Authentication

Architectural solution: Prevention → Access control

Problem. In order to implement access control, i.e., ensuring that only authorized actors are allowed to do certain operations, it is crucial that we know the identity of the actor we are dealing with.

Solution. Authentication helps to increase the probability that we allocate the correct identity to the actor. It achieves this by comparing some kind of extra evidence with the supplied identity from the actor.

There are many kinds of authentication solutions available, but there are three main categories (a) Knowledge-based, (b) object-based, or (c) ID-based (i.e., based upon something you know, something you have or some feature of yourself, respectively). Smartcards are able to support efficient and strong authentication [47], but require that the terminal or computer is equipped with a smartcard reader.

Authentication can be tailored to suit the security requirements of the application in various ways. That is, the probability of correct authentication is given by how authentication is implemented, for example using the length and alphabet of passwords as parameter (longer, more complex passwords are harder to guess). Please refer to [42] for a thorough discussion of the topic.

Impact.
1. Multiple aspects of security benefit from (and depend upon) authentication. Primarily, accountability cannot be attained without sufficiently strong authentication of the actor. Secondly, as access control depends upon authentication as a basic element, confidentiality and integrity will indirectly benefit.
2. Usability. Authentication must be done in a manner that is suitable for the environment in which the actor operates. Otherwise, usability will suffer. Usability is highly dependent on the choice of authentication solution (see above). Also, different user contexts will favor different authentication solutions. A range of usability design tactics that can assist in accommodating different authentication solutions can be found in [58].

Pattern 4: Authentication Levels

Architectural solution: Prevention → Access control → Authentication
Problem. For some applications, a single strength of authentication is inadequate. There might be different usage scenarios, caused by different user situations, which mandate differentiation.
Solution. Depending on the criticality of the asset to be secured, different strengths of authentication may be applied [16].

Impact.
1. In general, the same security benefits as for Pattern 3: Authentication apply. However, by differentiating the authentication levels, the security qualities will be improved as it simplifies authentication tasks for the user and thus may stimulate the use of better password routines, for example.
2. Operability will be negatively affected. Administration of different authentication levels requires good configuration practices and tools.
3. Usability will generally be positively affected. Users are able to do more with less hassle. Usability may also be negatively affected if the need for additional authentication procedures is not clearly motivated and communicated.

Pattern 5: Authentication Policy

Architectural solution: Prevention → Access control → Authentication
Problem. Many technologies, authentication technologies being no exception, do not give the promised benefits unless they are part of an overall policy for their use. The planned use of different authentication technologies should be coordinated and executed in order to achieve goals set by the organization.
Solution. An authentication policy can include multiple aspects, depending on the authentication technologies being used. Examples are (a) limited number of login attempts, (b) increasing delays between allowed login attempts, (c) password strength policies, and (d) invocation of different authentication levels (described above). See also [12].

Impact.
1. Given good tools for configuration and maintenance, operability is affected positively.
2. Accountability is highly dependent upon proper authentication of actors. Authentication policies can thus improve accountability.

Pattern 6: Authorization

Architectural solution: Prevention → Access control
Problem. Security implies that a certain level of control can be exercised with respect to which actors are allowed to perform operations in the system. In other words, we want to control which subjects are allowed to perform which operations on which objects. Implementing this kind of control function is nontrivial.
Solution. Managing relationships of the type (subject, operation, object) is called authorization management [50]. This is a complex problem area as its solution is heavily dependent upon many characteristics. Example characteristics that influence the solution are (a) the number of subjects compared to the number of objects, (b) the usage of the assets (i.e., the objects), and (c) the frequency of changes to the authorizations. Pattern 14: Contextual Authorization discusses a specialized alternative authorization regime. See [41, 44, 50, 55] for other variations of authorization schemes.

Impact.
1. The security qualities integrity and confidentiality can only be satisfied by a proper implementation of authorization.
2. Performance will be affected differently, according to the usage pattern.
3. Usability can be heavily affected through the choice of authorization regime.
4. Operability is significantly affected. Most important is to determine what changes most frequently: subjects, objects or the authorization operations themselves.

Pattern 7: Bandwidth Throttling

Architectural solution: Prevention → Fairness
Problem. Facing Denial of Service attacks, a system might easily be overloaded with traffic, causing the system to stop responding to any new requests, both from the network or local input sources. This might even make it difficult to perform necessary corrective adjustments to the configuration of the system.
Solution. By imposing limits to the bandwidth certain services on a server can consume, remaining services are left operative and responsive [18]. Certain systems, such as Microsoft's Windows Server System 2003, allow the configuration of such throttles for individual services. This way, for example the web server on a server machine can be throttled (see http://www.microsoft.com/windowsserver2003).

Impact.
1. It is very hard to distinguish legitimate traffic from malicious traffic. Thus, bandwidth throttling will be a suboptimal solution to the problem. Some of the available bandwidth will remain unused. Overall performance during periods of normal operation will be lower.

2. Operability is positively affected. Once established, the throttle requires little, if any, attention.

Pattern 8: Biometric Authentication

Architectural solution: Prevention → Access control → Authentication → Context holder

Problem. It may be critical to use features of the subject to determine the subject's identity.

Solution. Biometric authentication is based upon using human features to distinguish between different users. It is ID-based, meaning that it bears upon the uniqueness of the person's features to assist in safe authentication. See also [42].

Impact.
1. Biometry is recognized to give very high levels of confidence in authentication. Certain biometric features, such as the human iris, are very difficult to counterfeit. Thus, in situations where high correct authentication is critical, biometrics might be a good choice. Biometrics give good support against repudiation.
2. Biometry can be expensive to deploy; it normally requires additional equipment to what is supplied as standard.
3. Biometric authentication can be resource intensive due to inherent tradeoffs between precision and processing resources required [36].
4. Biometry has a strong influence on usability aspects; although they might be both positive and negative, depending on the equipment used and the operative support for the equipment [55].

Pattern 9: Certificate

Architectural solution: Prevention → Access control → Authentication → Context holder

Problem. In asymmetric cryptography, there is a need to manage public keys. Not only must they be stored and transmitted, but also their validity must be ensured.

Solution. A certificate is a digitally signed data structure that contains information about an actor (a subject, person or application) and the actor's public key [47]. Certificates are issued by trusted organizations called certification authorities (CAs) after the CA has verified the identity of the subject. The CA is a kind of trusted third party (see Pattern 32: Trusted Third Party).

Impact.
1. There are only minimal effects on quality attributes from the use of certificates per se. They are merely relatively simple data structures. However, most organizations want a certain degree of trust in the management of them. Thus, e.g., certificate management issuing, expiration management and trust management through CAs, etc. is more involved and is likely to affect quality attributes more. See Pattern 32: Trusted Third Party).

Pattern 10: Clustering

Architectural solution: Recovery → Redundancy

Problem. Single points of failure within a given system architecture must occasionally be eliminated in order to obtain the wanted availability.

Solution. Clustering is an established pattern to avoid single points of failure. Essentially, it means implementing a virtual server farm, so that two or more servers appear as a unified server resource. Clustering may be implemented at different levels in the system architecture, for example by replicating the communication links, the servers, the disks, etc. However, care must be taken to ensure that the redundancy is not broken unintentionally. Clustering may be used for multiple purposes, such as load-balancing or failover [39]. Failover means that a surviving server may completely take over the tasks of a failed server. Some clusters can support both kinds of functionality.

Impact.
1. Clustering solutions for certain server systems may allow for load balancing between the servers during normal operation (i.e., no failures). This will improve performance.
2. Operability is affected negatively. Clustering systems can be hard to maintain, and they do require a good overview of the working of the system. For example, certain applications may not work correctly in a clustered environment due to the risk of losing consistency.
3. Maintainability may be positively affected. Certain clustering technologies allow single machines in the cluster to be "taken out" of the cluster for maintenance, such as operating system upgrades and hardware component replacement. The remaining machine(s) respond to service requests in the meantime.

Pattern 11: Cryptography

Architectural solution: Prevention → Obfuscation

Problem. Often, information must be transmitted over media that is open to other, potentially malicious actors. Confidentiality should still be maintained.

Solution. Cryptography address the problem of maintaining confidentiality of information by scrambling the information into unintelligible data using secret keys [17]. There are two main categories of cryptography (a) symmetric and (b) asymmetric. The former requires that both originator and recipient know the key. The latter is based upon two keys, a private and a public key. The private key should remain known only to the owner while the public key can be shared with anybody. However, it is important that the association between the private and the public key remains protected (see discussion on certificates in Pattern 9: Certificate).

Impact.
1. Performance is affected strongly by the choice of cryptographic solution. Generally, there are two rules (1) Asymmetric cryptography is more computationally intensive than the symmetric counterpart. (2) Accessing encrypted information by guessing the key is more difficult as the length of the key increases. However, longer keys also increase the computational resources required to encrypt and decrypt the information.
2. Operability is highly affected, mostly negatively, by the use of cryptographic techniques. The challenge of managing keys, i.e., distributing them, is complex. See also the discussion of trusted third party in Pattern 32: Trusted Third Party.

Pattern 12: Code Signing

Architectural solution: Detection → Embedded data integrity

Problem. In many systems, there is a need to install additional code after activation. Additional code, sometimes originating via the network, must be trustworthy.

Solution. A digital checksum, computed from a code unit such as a component, is appended to the code unit. The digital checksum is computed by the owner of the code unit using some predefined scheme known also by the recipient of the code unit. With a certain probability, modifications to the code unit will result in a mismatch between the code unit and the checksum. The recipient, upon detecting this mismatch may decide how to proceed (e.g., reject running the code, run the code with reduced privileges, etc.) If no mismatch is detected, the checksum provides evidence that the code unit was developed by a given organization and that it has not been modified after leaving the developing organization.

Impact.
1. Code signing increases the complexity of communication. There must be a regime for agreeing on the code in the checksum.
2. Performance. If the granularity of the code unit becomes very small, or the frequency of importing new code units is very high, the signing and verification of the code may consume significant computing resources on both machines.
3. Code signing, given appropriate schemes for generating the code, gives very good protection against integrity violations. They also support nonrepudiation.

Pattern 13: Cookie

Architectural solution: Prevention → Access control → Authentication → Context holder

Problem. A server may need to manage stateless client sessions. The client should only maintain a minimum amount of state.

Solution. The cookie is a data item that stores certain information about a client's session (typically with a web server). The cookie enables the server to associate a series of client requests with the same client without adding significant overheads to the data transmissions [32].

Impact.
1. Installability (i.e., ease of deployment) is improved. Cookies support the notion of thin clients (see also thin clients discussed in Pattern 30: Thin Client).
2. Resource behavior, in particular scalability, is improved. The cookie is small and only adds a small amount to the volume of information that needs to be communicated between client and server.
3. Security, and confidentiality in particular, can be damaged by the use of cookies as they are normally transmitted in clear text as part of the HTTP protocol. Although the protocol does provide a suggestive security mechanism [32], it does not include functionality to encrypt or otherwise protect the cookie. Alternative mechanisms for this purpose have been proposed in [44].

Pattern 14: Contextual Authorization

Architectural solution: Prevention → Access control → Authorization

Problem. Certain application domains benefit from dynamic authorization policies in which changing parameters about the actor should be used to control authorizations.

Solution. Contextual authorization is a sophisticated form of authorization scheme. Contextual authorization implies that it is knowledge about the actor's current context (or situation) that defines the appropriate authorizations [50, 56]. Many aspects of the user's context can be relevant for determining the appropriate authorizations; examples include the current role, the environment of the user or other attributes [16, 41].

Impact.
1. Suitability is improved. The authorizations can more precisely reflect the real needs of the application.
2. Operability for the end-user is improved, as the authorizations better reflect the actual need. However, from an administrative point of view, operability becomes more elaborate and difficult, as there are more parameters and configurations to manage. The rule-based approach described in [16] might be a viable approach to keep the efforts manageable.
3. Performance is negatively affected because a more complex set of rules related to the actor's context must be processed before access is granted or denied to a particular (set of) object(s). Additionally, context information must somehow be gathered and managed by the system.

Pattern 15: Digital Signatures

Architectural solution: Recovery → Liability transfer

Problem. The recipient of a document may want to establish trust in that the claimed originator sent it, and that the document has not been modified after leaving the claimed originator.

Solution. A digital signature is a kind of watermark on a piece of information. An actor can sign an electronic document to increase the trust of the recipient in believing that the document originated from the claimed actor and that it is not tampered with. Digital signatures require asymmetric cryptography and use public and private keys. The signer uses his private key to encrypt a hash value generated from the document. The recipient will, by decrypting the hash value with the signer's public key, verify that the same hash value is generated from the received document. It is worth noting that digital signatures per se do not provide absolute guarantees, but rather function as evidence of the authenticity of the signed document [43].

Impact.
1. Digital signature is primarily an instrument to avoid repudiation and will therefore assist accountability.
2. The use of digital signatures will improve integrity. Forgery can be detected using digital signatures.
3. Operability may be negatively affected. In large user communities the management of public keys requires a good infrastructure (PKI).

4. Performance is negatively affected. The use of asymmetric cryptography is resource intensive. Similarly, the public key of the originator must be obtained before the signature can be verified. This will add extra time to the verification process.

Pattern 16: IDS (Intrusion Detection System)

Architectural solution: Detection → Monitoring

Problem. Attacks via the network, e.g., the Internet, constitute a continuous threat to networked computers. Implementing protection against spurious attacks via the network should not be the concern of applications – it should be dealt with at the systems (or framework) layer. Another part of the concern is to how to determine the difference between normal activity and attack.

Solution. An IDS addresses the problem by implementing functionality for monitoring activity [47]. A good IDS provides a high accuracy of detecting attacks while maintaining low false alarm rates.

There are two principal types of IDS, categorized by the strategy they use for detecting attacks (a) anomaly detection and (b) signature detection. Orthogonal to these strategies, they can be implemented as network-based or host-based IDS. A network-based IDS is mainly concerned with scanning the network traffic, while a host-based IDS targets traces on the different host machines (inspecting, e.g., log files on the host machine). See for example [37].

Impact.
1. Security in general will benefit from IDS because if attacks are detected, they may be prevented.
2. Operability is negatively affected. IDS, in particular by anomaly detection types which may require frequent updating of configuration settings.
3. Performance. Depending on the level of sophistication of detection, the IDS will consume a certain amount of computing resources on the host while scanning logs (in case of host based IDS) or network resources (in the case of network based IDS) for the monitoring of network traffic.

Pattern 17: Layering

Architectural solution: Prevention → Compartmentalization

Problem. Assuming that some attacks are successful, we want to limit the consequence of the attack.

Solution. Each security barrier an attacker must conquer adds to the resources the attacker must posses before being successful [47, 54]. Layering prescribes that the software architecture consist of a set of layers (or parts) which communicate through a well-defined set of interfaces. Although the interfaces are well-defined, this does not mean that an attacker has easy access to them. Note: Tiering is a more specific kind of layering, in which the layers are deployed with separate machines. Layering is not concerned with the physical deployment of the parts.

Impact.
1. Layering may benefit integrity and confidentiality. An attacker who is able to modify or read data used in one layer need not obtain the same capabilities over data in another layer of the architecture.
2. Layering is an implementation of the tactic separation of concerns (not part of this reference architecture) and is a benefit for maintainability.
3. Layering may benefit deployment. Although layering is not directly concerned with deployment, layers normally form natural process boundaries. Process boundaries can again be used to select deployment configurations.

Pattern 18: Limited View

Architectural solution: Prevention → Access control
Problem. The user should not be allowed to perform operations that from a security perspective are known to cause access violations (or "access denied" responses). This will only create a less operable system.
Solution. Reducing the exposure of information to a minimum is beneficial for operability. It is also good for security in general and confidentiality in particular. Limited view implements a solution to this challenge by not exposing any information that is not explicitly authorized to the actor [59]. Information in this context also includes application programming interfaces (APIs. Thus, by not being visible, the actor is not presented with functions that are not allowed while the risk of breaches to confidentiality is reduced. The pattern can be implemented by for example views in an SQL database or by GUI code.

Impact.
1. Operability is normally very positively affected. By implementing the limited view pattern, there is no need to implement custom data hiding functionality. Additionally, a positive effect of limited view is that the probability of error messages due to security violations is reduced.
2. Complexity of implementation and maintenance can be high.

Pattern 19: Message Authentication Codes

Architectural solution: Detection → Embedded data integrity
Problem. During data communication, data might become corrupted. There are many reasons for this; one is a malicious threat agent that establishes attacks to hinder communication between two actors by attempting to influence the data stream.
Solution. The solution is similar to code signing. Data integrity verification checksums are added to the source data. They are computed by the sender from the original data using some predefined scheme known to both sender and recipient [47]. With a certain probability, modifications to the original data will result in a mismatch between the received data and the checksums. The recipient, upon detecting this mismatch, can request a retransmission or trigger an incident response.

Impact.
1. For security, error detection codes increase the likelihood of detecting integrity breaches.
2. Performance. Computing checksums and adding these checksums to the data stream requires resources and consumes a certain amount of the available bandwidth on the channel. Further, depending on the frequency of retransmissions, predictability of communication latency is reduced.

Pattern 20: Mirror Sites

Architectural solution: Recovery → Redundancy

Problem. A threat agent, such as natural disasters like fires and floods, may set a whole set of machines out of service.

Solution. Redundant processing facilities can withstand this kind of threat. The mirror sites pattern defines a backup site that can take over normal operation if the master site becomes nonoperational. The correct operation of such disaster recovery sites depends not only on technical measures, but also on good and well executed manual procedures performed by on-site personnel [1].

Impact.
1. The cost of establishing mirror sites is high. To reduce the impact of the extra cost, applications may be run on both sites during normal operation thus making better use of the available resources. Further, failover procedures must be tested frequently to guarantee correctness.
2. A high degree of availability can be achieved. For certain kinds of environment this justifies the extra cost.
3. Operability becomes more complex. Procedures for failover, i.e., the actual procedure for switching from one failed server to another functioning server, must be properly and frequently tested.

Pattern 21: Multi Barrier Security

Architectural solution: Prevention → Compartmentalization

Problem. Complex systems should not be completely jeopardized due to single incidents.

Solution. By constructing multiple barriers for potential threat agents, the probability that the whole system is damaged will be reduced. The solution can be implemented using for example operating system processes as barriers. Multi barrier security is also known as defense in depth [45].

Impact.
1. Multiple barriers imply more administration and thus decreased operability. The system can also become more cumbersome to use for end users.
2. Multiple barriers may help to separate concerns, thus improving maintainability.
3. Multiple barriers may reduce performance.

Pattern 22: Password

Architectural solution: Prevention → Access control → Authentication → Context holder

Problem. Representing evidence for proving identity.

Solution. The password is a bit string (normally in the form of a character string) given to the actor by which the actor is later authenticated. Upon request, the actor supplies the password to the system which subsequently compares it with the password stored in the password database for that particular actor. Supplying the correct password is evidence that the actor is the one claimed.

In addition to this simple scheme, security policies directing the use of passwords, may involve rules for how to construct legal passwords, how often they should be changed and so on.

Impact.

1. A good high-entropy password that is kept secret gives very high confidence authentication. However, passwords do not give any support against repudiation because they can be shared or stolen [42]. That is, passwords can only partly support accountability.
2. Operability is likely to be challenged. Remembering passwords requires a certain mental effort. Long passwords are required to give appropriate protection against password cracking threats. Some environments make entering passwords difficult, for example small computers without proper keyboards. Further more, users can only remember a finite number of different passwords. As security policies enforce changing passwords frequently, user's mental capabilities are stressed.
3. Complexity is low, thus bringing benefits to maintainability.

Pattern 23: Principle of Least Privilege

Architectural solution: Prevention → Compartmentalization

Problem. In large scale software systems the number of actors and assets can be very high. This complicates the task of ensuring the security of assets. A key challenge is to keep the cost of maintaining security at a low level.

Solution. The pattern (consistently referred to as a principle in literature, but prescriptive enough to be called a pattern) states that anything that is not expressively permitted is denied. Essentially, it creates compartments of information accessible by certain actors only [53]. In practice, it means that unless there is an authorization for an actor to access a subject, the authorization request is denied.

Impact.

1. Usability (in particular operability) is likely to be negatively affected by this pattern. It is inherently difficult to predict in advance the assets needed by an actor to complete a set of tasks [61].
2. Confidentiality and integrity benefit greatly. The risk of gaining unauthorized access to an asset is reduced.

Pattern 24: Reference Monitor

Architectural solution: Prevention → Single access point

Problem. Having to administrate multiple security related mechanisms decreases operability. It may also be a threat to security itself, as the risk of making errors increases.

Solution. The reference monitor is a single access point for a range of security related requests. There is no other way to get to the resource. It is comparable to an interpreter with added security checking functionality [53]. Thus, if the reference monitor is implemented correctly, the risk of error is reduced. It simplifies the design of the architecture. Today, the reference monitor pattern is often implemented by operating systems [28].

Impact.

1. The reference monitor may become a performance bottleneck as all security related requests must be processed by the monitor. The problem could be alleviated somewhat by inline reference monitors, but only at the expense of increased complexity [33].
2. Maintainability is improved through separation of concerns. The reference monitor is a single functional module that handles all security related requests.
3. The enforcement of integrity and confidentiality is easier to verify, and is thus probably improved, because the reference monitor is the only functional module dealing with security requests.

Pattern 25: Residual Information Protection

Architectural solution: Recovery → Fail-secure

Problem. Upon unexpected termination of programs, data from that program may remain in storage and be available through malevolent allocation of that storage by a threat agent.

Solution. The pattern residual information protection seeks to prevent leakage of information from one instantiation of a type of object to another instantiation of that type of object [28]. For example, the approach taken in MULTICS, by only clearing residues when the storage area was explicitly re-assigned [49], does not give the appropriate protection.

At the basic level, residual information protection requires encryption of stored data (see the discussion on Pattern 11: Cryptography). To further increase the security, mechanisms for automatically deleting information upon failed login attempts or after a timeout can be applied.

Impact.

1. On small devices, for which this pattern might be especially useful, there are limited computing resources. Encryption functionality might incur significant performance overheads.

Pattern 26: Resource Throttling

Architectural solution: Prevention → Fairness

Problem. Certain types of unwanted incidents are caused by threat agents generating excessive load on critical system resources, thus rendering the system unresponsive to operative or administrative requests (also known as Denial of Service attacks).

Solution. One solution to the problem is to limit the amount of resources that can be allocated by certain services, for example web servers. Although a negative consequence of this is that the maximum workload that the system can sustain will now be lower than necessary. An implementation of the pattern has been described in [40].

Impact.

1. Performance, during normal operation is lower. Some resources are reserved.

Pattern 27: Sandbox

Architectural solution: Prevention → Compartmentalization

Problem. It might be beneficial to incorporate code in an application that has been developed by organizations for which a suitable level of trust cannot be established.

Solution. This pattern involves building a contained execution environment for potentially hostile code (and thus resembles a "sandbox"). Attempts to perform actions that are not permitted by the security policy for the execution environment are prevented. Within this execution environment, any code can run without the risk of endangering the system [47]. Examples of this pattern are, e.g., the Java Virtual Machine, the Common Language Runtime from Microsoft, and efforts at Hewlett Packard that extend the operating system [60].

Impact.
1. The sandbox introduces another level of indirection (i.e., the interpreter or reference monitor that governs requests for system resources). This adds a certain performance overhead.
2. In terms of security, both confidentiality and integrity are greatly improved by the sandbox pattern.
3. To provide a flexible platform for component execution, the sandbox must include flexible security policy management features. There are significant differences in the approaches prescribed by Sun's Java Virtual Machine and the Common Language Runtime from Microsoft [46]. These must be considered when determining the technical platform for the application.

Pattern 28: Sentry

Architectural solution: Prevention → Controlled exposure

Problem. It is desirable to simplify the programming model for application programmers. Rather than having to understand all sorts of authorization mechanisms they should be provided with a simple mechanism that would allow them to operate upon data that was already authorized for the subject.

Solution. The sentry pattern was observed during an architecture evaluation session and has not been published in other literature. However, the sentry is similar to the proxy described in [47], but it is different in the sense that it essentially encapsulates the implementation of authorization rules. The sentry is a kind of proxy for designated classes. It provides a security-amended interface that is identical to the underlying class. Use of the sentry is not enforced however, the programmers also have access to the underlying class, without the authorization checks built in.

Impact.
1. The sentry is a kind of proxy pattern, thus it does introduce extra overhead in processing by adding another level of indirection and most likely extra processing required for the authorization procedures. Having said that, the sentry also gives a very good potential for optimizing the determination of authorizations. Because the sentry instance is associated to only one object in the program, security parameters related to that object can be cached in the sentry, thus giving gains in terms of performance.
2. The sentry simplifies the programming model for the application programmer. Thus maintainability is improved.

Pattern 29: Single Sign On

Architectural solution: Prevention → Access control → Authentication

Problem. A very common problem in distributed systems is the burden felt by the users to remember a distinct password for any single system they want to use. Therefore, many users choose shorter passwords than recommended or even decide to write down passwords on paper notes.

Solution. The solution offered by this pattern is to integrate the authentication subsystems of multiple systems into a single, coherent whole [47]. Thus, by completing authentication via the single sign on solution, the actor is authenticated on all subsystems.

Impact.
1. The same security benefits as for Pattern 3: Authentication.
2. Reliability: The single sign on module constitutes a single point of failure. It therefore constitutes an attractive target for attacks such as Denial of Service attacks.
3. Performance: The single sign on module is responsible for all authentication requests for the subsystems. If not scaled appropriately, it may become a bottleneck.
4. Operability is increased: All administration can be performed through the same system.
5. Usability: Users will observe increased usability as they now need only a single authentication procedure.
6. Replaceability is hampered: Single sign on solutions typically require a certain amount of adaptation to the applications taking part.

Pattern 30: Thin Client

Architectural solution: Prevention → Compartmentalization

Problem. Certain environments are particularly vulnerable to attacks. Computers used in such environments should operate upon the least possible amount of assets, and seek to reduce the storage of assets locally.

Solution. The thin client pattern is a variant of the client server pattern [19]. One aspect of this pattern is that there is a physical boundary between the server and the client. In addition, the thin client pattern prescribes that only the minimal amount of processing and storage is done at the client (in contrast to thick- or self-reliant clients). Although there is a continuum between thin and thick clients, an example of a thin client would be a web-browser.

Impact.
1. Less information and code is stored on the client. This reduces the consequences if a threat agent is able to compromise the machine. Thus, integrity and confidentiality will be improved.
2. Time behavior is likely to be somewhat impaired. It may be difficult to achieve good responsiveness in a GUI which is heavily bound by the latency of the underlying network.
3. Installability is greatly improved by the thin client pattern. Clients are small, and require very little technical infrastructure on the client machine.

Pattern 31: Timeout

Architectural solution: Recovery → Fail-secure

Problem. In case a session is left open for an extended period of time, there is a chance that the actor forgot to close it. This creates a potential for unwanted incidents.

Solution. The timeout pattern automatically locks the session after a certain period of inactivity on a session [20]. The exact duration is determined by a timeout value, used in implementations of the pattern. The actor will have to re-establish the session if the lock has been triggered.

In practice, multiple variants of the timeout can be implemented. At the GUI level, a common approach is to lock the keyboard/screen after a period of inactivity. The user will then have to unlock the GUI in order to continue working. Typically, this is unlocked using a certain password. Another variant of the system lock is found at the communication session level. Upon establishing communication sessions, a timeout starts running. If the session is unused for the specified timeout period, the session will close and it will have to be re-established again.

Impact.
1. Operability is somewhat reduced. Depending on the timeout value of the timeout pattern, the actor can be forced to perform a number of unnecessary attempts to re-establish a session.
2. Complexity is negatively affected. Any actor interacting with a system that implements timeouts will have to consider the situation that a session expires and requires renewal.

Pattern 32: Trusted Third Party

Architectural solution: Prevention → Service provider

Problem. For transactions between two or more actors, a certain level of trust must be present in order to facilitate efficiency.

Solution. A solution to providing trust is a trusted third party (TTP). The TTP is a security authority or an associated agent that is trusted by the participating actors [47]. A TTP can support multiple services in a security architecture, for example authentication requests, authorization requests or issuing/revocation of certificates with public keys for digital signatures or code signing.

The TTP is a network entity which responds to requests from the trusting actors.

Impact.
1. The availability of the TTP is critically important for the actors. Thus, the reliability of both the network connectivity and the machine upon which it runs will have direct effects for the working of the cooperating actors.

8.7 Using the Reference Architecture

The reference architecture provides decision support for architecture derivation and evaluation in a product line context. It is intended to function as a tool for this purpose. Below we provide some guidance for its use.

8.7.1 Architecture Derivation

Each application will have specific quality requirements, these requirements must be accommodated in an application dependent quality model. The application dependent quality model is obtained by determining which quality attributes of the generic quality model are relevant, and then resolving the appropriate variation points in the scenarios using the application's specific quality requirements.

Using the variants suggested by the scenario, one should consider the architectural solutions referred to. Multiple solutions may help to satisfy the requirement; in that case one should select the solution (or solutions) that have the best total effect on the quality attributes. Priorities of the scenarios, determined for each product, may help to resolve such trade-off situations.

The architectural solutions selected here, together with any prescribed architectural solutions for the product line architecture, will constitute the architectural solutions preferred for the application architecture.

8.7.2 Architecture Evaluation

The requirements that an architecture should fulfill will vary over time. Thus, it makes sense to evaluate the architecture for potential gaps between the expectations and the quality attributes supported by the architecture.

The reference architecture is a tool that can support this process. Similar to the process for architecture derivation, the quality requirements that the architecture should fulfill must be determined first. By examining the quality model and the decision model embodied by this reference architecture, the scenarios that best represent the requirements can be selected and their variation points resolved. Then, the architectural solutions used in the actual architecture can be compared with the ones suggested by the scenarios. Divergences can then be used as a foundation for subsequent analyses of potential architectural changes.

8.7.3 Evolution of the Reference Architecture

Capturing valuable architectural design knowledge is an overall goal of the reference architecture. This is not a static activity. As new knowledge is collected in the organization it should be reflected in the reference architecture. The reference model accommodates this in several ways.

As previously noted, the decision model is based upon quality requirements formulated as scenarios, extracted, refined and generalized from business requirements relevant for the four companies contributing to the decision model (see Sect. 8.5). This approach has given us a useful starting point for the decision model, but the model should be maintained in order to provide maximum value to the organization using it. A significant advantage of the proposed decision model is its extensibility. New scenarios can be added, existing ones can be improved. Thus, the adopting company may tailor the model to internal knowledge and experience. An example of this is the adding of new responses to existing scenarios in order to increase variability in the application architecture.

The security architecture language has been developed by reviewing a large amount of security related sources. No claims can be made about its completeness or correctness however. Instead, it is a proposal that we have found useful in our work together with companies. As adopting companies gain knowledge of their own language, the proposed language can be extended, modified and maintained. For example, it is likely that companies use specializations of the described security architectural solutions. In that case, it will make sense to include also these in a revised language.

Hopefully, these efforts will help to ensure that the reference architecture remains an effective tool for the organization in its efforts to build better architectures. Similarly, it supports the management of this architectural knowledge within the organization.

8.8 Validation

There were two main questions we wanted to investigate through the development of this reference architecture: Firstly, is it viable to represent architectural security knowledge in a reference architecture? Secondly, and most important: Does the approach give value to a software company that wants to develop software architectures concerned with security?

By constructing such a reference architecture and subsequently describing it, we believe we have affirmed the first question. It has also been presented and discussed several times at various project meetings and the comments that were received have been used to revise and improve it.

To answer the second question we have used the reference architecture to guide architectural design and support architecture evaluation in three different software product companies. These three were also contributing to the construction of the reference architecture. The fourth company that contributed to the reference architecture did not participate in its validation. For reasons of confidentiality we denote them as A, B and C. Company A is a large international telecommunications solutions provider, companies B and C are medium sized software houses in the information systems domains. We did not have the resources available to do complete security architectural designs or reviews in any of the companies. Accepting this, we chose to focus on certain aspects of the various application architectures and selected a few particularly important capabilities in each. Here we cannot reveal all details of the security reviews but we'll provide examples from each of them.

Generally, for all the companies we observed a very positive attitude towards a systematic review of security architecture. During validation in company A we did not have the time to consider underlying threat and risk assessments, but for certain key assets we could do this in companies B and C. Although this should be done thoroughly, we learned from both B and C that this produced very valuable incitements for future development plans. Particularly the phase of determining what value an asset actually represented to the range of stakeholders generated intense discussions among the participants. Our belief is that even such rudimentary reasoning on this topic is forgotten in many companies.

8.8.1 The Quality Model

Our quality model, organizing security qualities into gradually more specialized quality attributes, proved to be a significant help in reviewing and specifying requirements. The main problem that the quality model addressed was confusion in terminology. As the hype around security has flourished it appears that the precision in what is really meant has been lost on the way. Many of the people we talked with confused qualities with technical solutions. As an example, authentication was often denoted as a quality attribute for a system. This is wrong. As we have explained, authentication is simply a means to achieve security qualities – primarily accountability. We believe that the quality model improves the communication among the stakeholders and increases the awareness of the wide range of security qualities that may be important for a software system. We also believe that it stimulates companies to perform more thorough threat assessments in order to further improve the security requirements engineering process.

While working with A we had to cope with a certain disagreement in terminology. It took some time before our model was accepted. However, we think it is crucial to take this seriously as a common vocabulary is critical for the work.

B worked with us over a longer period of time and we had a deeper cooperation with them. In fact, B provided significant input to our work in constructing the quality model. The input came through a range of inherent security concerns related to the release of a software platform for a new generation of web-based products. The quality model was reviewed and improved while working with them.

For C we considered security aspects related to a capability in their product to use e-mail as a communications channel to distribute highly sensitive business information to selected partner companies. Referring to the risk assessment we had done and going through the various elements of the quality model it was easy to conclude that confidentiality and accountability were the prime concerns. Integrity and availability was less important as the information exchange was one-way and there were minimal impacts stemming from moderate delays in the distribution.

8.8.2 The Decision Model

As expected, the decision model proved to benefit from contributions of business requirements originating in companies within different application domains. The existing scenarios were generic enough to cover the requirements in the companies, but one company felt that increased value would be obtained with more scenarios directly targeting technological infrastructure. To accommodate such needs, from this company and others, the decision model was designed to support evolution in the scenarios. New scenarios may be added in order to better capture the needs of particular organizations. It should be noted here that we had to concentrate our efforts at each of the companies. Thus, only the most highly prioritized scenario in each company was reviewed due to time and resource constraints.

Company A was particularly concerned about integrity aspects related to the use of third party components in large-scale distributed systems. Scenario I.1 was the primary reasoning framework for evaluating different architectural design alternatives. The different variants helped the company to determine the most appropriate architectural design, and through discussions of the impacts of the relevant architectural solutions the favored alternative was variant 3.

In B we also worked primarily with integrity. An important concern was to provide effective, yet easy to use abstractions for programmers that would assist in maintaining protection against unwanted modification of data. Scenario I.3 provided the reasoning framework for the architectural decisions. Further, B had concerns related to the potential exposure of corporate data while users were in a mobile context. We found that scenario

I.5 gave good architectural guidance in this case. Variants 3 and 4 were both relevant for further improvements of the architecture.

For C, the reference architecture did not provide applicable scenarios dealing with the particular problem of distributing information via e-mail. However, from the review of the architecture language, we had already selected a candidate architectural solution that we used to create a more detailed technical design.

8.8.3 The Security Architecture Language

The security architecture language was a good help for participating software architects that were searching for appropriate solutions in the security architectural design space. Of particular benefit was the clear structure and classification of solutions into detection, prevention and recovery. This triggered an exploratory review of the different solutions, which again were used to increase the accuracy in the resolved variation points in the scenarios.

In the case of A we concluded that the need to provide high performance and a minimum of added complexity in the administration of the solution motivated the use of tactics similar to the recommendation of variant 3 of scenario I.1, which is Pattern 12: Code Signing. In addition A wanted to explore open source components. In the platform, which is currently being implemented, open source components are investigated. It is not unreasonable however to compare the open source community with a code signing party.

Company B found, in accordance with the scenarios mentioned above, that a combination of thin clients and contextual authorization provided the most significant benefits in terms of integrity. A role-based security authorization scheme is currently under development for the new platform.

For C we determined that prevention was the most beneficial tactic. Since we were dealing with sensitive information, and the fact that even knowing that an actor is sending information to another named actor could be misused, the recovery tactic was abandoned. The detection tactic was also abandoned because we did not consider malicious attacks as the threat. Prevention tactics were investigated and the service provider solution was selected as the most promising candidate. We decided to examine the directory pattern in our further design (only illustrated in the reference architecture, see [47] for more information on the pattern). The idea behind using the service provider pattern was to make the selection process of e-mail addresses more secure, yet user friendly.

8.8.4 Summary

In summary, the reference architecture proved to be a good starting point for security architecture design. Naturally, as the reference architecture is a representation of knowledge at an abstract level it only provides general architectural design guidance and specialist domain knowledge must be used in the later design phases of actual architectures.

8.9 Related Work

Security has seen a formidable growth in interest during the last few years. A number of journals, conferences and other publications have been established to foster research in the field. Similarly in industry, security has been established as a key concern for those responsible for managing, buying or developing ICT systems. It appears reasonable to infer that with society's increasing dependence on ICT systems, the very same systems have become lucrative targets for persons with intentions to gain benefits through malevolent actions.

A key pillar of this work is the established relationship between quality attributes and architectural solutions. Work done at SEI on ABASs [31] and later within the ADD method [3] shows that quality properties can be associated with architectural tactics and patterns.

Risk assessments to the appropriate level of detail should be the foundation for any work related to the design of evaluation systems having to cope with security requirements. In [11], Cavusoglu et al. describe an evaluation framework that can be used in order to determine risks and also support the selection of appropriate security controls (artifacts related to countermeasures). They also bring up the need for architectural decision support in order to build architectures that provide the required level of security. The proposed reference architecture goes further into the architectural design aspects, by providing a more elaborate decision support framework – both in the area of security architecture language and in terms of a richer quality model. SAEM is a more pragmatic approach to the proposed reference architecture, focusing more on concrete risks and technologies than quality modeling and architectural design [9].

All professional activities related to security must be considered in terms of economical viability. The reference architecture presented here does not address this issue, but the reader should consult sources such as [24]. Consideration to economical justifications should precede the architectural design phase.

High level security tactics have been discussed by, e.g., Romanosky [48] although without any structured approach to their use or applicability. Such efforts are nevertheless useful as documentation of architectural solutions and effects. Further, a large amount of security design knowledge has been collected and made available through work in the security pattern community [5, 45, 48, 52, 54, 59]. This contribution does not attempt to repeat these efforts, but uses findings from that community in order to build increased credibility in the association of effects and architectural solutions. The language presented here makes numerous references to work from the pattern community. Further, by reviewing many of these efforts we have been able to determine important relationships between the architectural solutions.

Chapter 9 presents a framework for architectural evolution based on architectural recovery as a means to ensure alignment with nonfunctional requirements. The assumption is that these requirements are not properly addressed in currently available tools. While the reference architecture presented here is a conceptual model for quality driven architectural design, it does not go into the same level of detail with respect to the technologies. Neither does it address the problem of distributed service management.

8.10 Conclusions and Future Research

This chapter presented a reference architecture for security in product lines. It has enabled us to show that it is feasible to provide useful decision support, based upon architectural design knowledge, for companies developing product lines in which security is a quality requirement.

Software architectural design does still have similarities with an art form. And there is a significant amount of manual labor involved in making the appropriate tradeoffs of the design alternatives and subsequently determining the final detailed design. However, we believe that the proposed reference architecture can support those who need to embark on such tasks.

Reference architectures play two roles. One is to generalize and provide abstractions useful to a wide range of systems. The second role is to be a platform from which specific architectures can be instantiated. The presented reference architecture has been developed with generality as its primary objective. Our intention is that companies wanting to use it should adapt it to the specific needs of the product line in development. As part of our future research we will investigate the potential of specialization of the reference architecture for a specific product line.

Acknowledgments

The work presented here is the result of collaboration with – and kind assistance from – a number of people in the ITEA project FAMILIES and its Norwegian co-project FAMILIER (the latter sponsored by the Norwegian Research Council and led by ICT-Norway). Some deserve particular mention; Ivar Sandstad, Jens Glattetre from SuperOffice ASA, Frank Mikalsen from Finale, Miguel Ángel Oltra Rodríguez from Telvent, Frode Nergård from EDB Telesciences, Juha Savolainen from Nokia, Timo Käkölä from University of Jyväskylä, Eila Niemelä from VTT, and last, but not least, Juan Carlos Dueñas from The Technical University of Madrid provided valuable comments that helped shape this work. We would also like to thank our colleague Odd Nordland in SINTEF ICT for improving the language of the chapter.

References

1. Allen J, Gabbard D, and May C (2003) Outsourcing Managed Security Services In: Security improvement module, CMU/SEI-SIM-012. 2003, Carnegie Mellon, Software Engineering Institute: Pittsburg, PA.
2. Bachmann F, Bass L, and Klein M (2003) Deriving Architectural Tactics: A Step toward Methodical Architectural Design Technical report, CMU/SEI-2003-TR-004. 2003
3. Bass L, Clement P, and Klein M (2003) Software Architecture in Practice. 2 ed. Addison Wesley.
4. Bayer J (2003) Design for Quality. In: Linden FVd (ed) 5th Int'l Workshop on Product Family Engineering. Springer, Berlin Heidelberg New York
5. Blakley B and Heath C (2004) Security Design Patterns. The Open Group.
6. Bollinger T, Voas J, and Boasson M, *Persistent Software Attributes*. IEEE Software, 2004. **21**(6): p. 16-18.

7. Bosch J (2000) Design and Use of Software Architectures - Adopting and Evolving a Product-Line Approach. Addison-Wesley.
8. Bosch J and Molin P (1999) Software Architecture Design: Evaluation and Transformation. In: IEEE Conference and Workshop on Engineering of Computer-Based Systems. IEEE Computer Society Press. p. 4-10.
9. Butler SA (2002) Security Attribute Evaluation Method: A Cost-Benefit Approach. In: International conference on software engineering. ACM Press. p. 232-240.
10. Bühne S, Chastek G, Käkölä T, Knauber P, Northrop L, and Thiel S (2003) Exploring the Context of Product Line Adoption. In: Linden FVd (ed) 5th International workshop on Product Family Engineering. Springer, Berlin Heidelberg New York. p. 19-31.
11. Cavusoglu H, Mishra B, and Raghunathan S, *A Model for Evaluating It Security Investments.* Communications of the ACM, 2004. **47**(7): p. 87-92.
12. Chang S, Chen Q, and Hsu M (2003) Managing Security Policy in a Large Distributed Web Services Environment. In: 27th Annual International Computer Software and Applications Conference (COMPSAC'03). IEEE Computer Society Press. p. 610-621.
13. Chung L, Nixon BA, Yu E, and Mylopoulos J, eds. Non-Functional Requirements in Software Engineering (2000). The Kluwer International Series in Software Engineering, Basili V (ed). Kluwer Academic Publishers. 439pp.
14. Clements P, Kazman R, and Klein M (2002) Evaluating Software Architectures: Methods and Case Studies. Addison Wesley.
15. Clements P and Northrop L (2002) Software Product Lines: Practices and Patterns. The Sei Series in Software Engineering Addison Wesley.
16. Covingtony MJ, Fogla P, Zhan Z, and Ahamad M (2002) A Context-Aware Security Architecture for Emerging Applications. In: 18th Annual Computer Security Applications Conference (ACSAC'02). IEEE Computer Society. p. 249-258.
17. Denning DE and Denning PJ, *Data Security.* ACM Computing Surveys, 1979. **11**(3). p. 227-249.
18. Douligeris C and Mitrokotsa A, *Ddos Attacks and Defense Mechanisms: Classification and State-of-the-Art.* Computer Networks, 2004. **44**(5): p. 643-666.
19. Duchessi P and Chengalur-Smith I, *Client/Server Benefits, Problems, Best Practices.* Communications of the ACM, 1998. **41**(5): p. 87-94.
20. Eguiluz HR and Barbacci MR (2003) Interactions among Techniques Addressing Quality Attributes In: Technical report, CMU/SEI-2003-TR-003. 2003.
21. Fernandez EB and Pan R (2001) A Pattern Language for Security Models. In: PLoP 2001.
22. Firesmith DG (2003) Common Concepts Underlying Safety, Security, and Survivability Engineering Technical note, CMU/SEI-2003-TN-033. 2003, Software Engineering Institute, Carnegie Mellon University
23. Gates C and Slonim J (2003) Owner-Controlled Information. In: New security paradigms workshop. ACM Press. p. 103-111.
24. Gordon LA and Loeb MP, *The Economics of Information Security Investment.* ACM Transactions on information and system security, 2002. **5**(4): p. 438-457.
25. Hallsteinsen S, Fægri TE, and Syrstad M (2003) Patterns in Product Family Architecture Design. In: Linden FVd (ed) PFE-5. Springer Verlag. p. 261-268.
26. Hallsteinsen S, Fægri TE, and Syrstad M (2003) Patterns in Product Family Architecture Design. In: Linden FVd (ed) 5th International workshop on Product Family Engineering. Springer, Berlin Heidelberg New York. p. 261-268.
27. IEEE (2000) Ieee Standard No. 1471-2000: Recommended Practice for Architectural Description of Software-Intensive Systems. IEEE: http://shop.ieee.org/store/.
28. ISO/IEC (1999) 15408 Common Criteria for Information Technology Security Evaluation. v2.0 ed. Nat'l Inst. Standards and Technology Washington, DC.
29. ISO/IEC (1991) Fcd 9126-1.2: Information Technology - Software Product Quality. Part 1: Quality Model.
30. Jung H-W, Kim S-G, and Chung C-S, *Measuring Software Product Quality: A Survey of Iso/Iec 9126.* IEEE Software, 2004. **21**(5): p. 88-92.
31. Klein M and Kazman R (1999) Attribute-Based Architectural Styles. In: SEI Technical Report, CMU/SEI-99-TR-022. 1999.
32. Kristol D and Montulli L (2000) Http State Management Mechanism (Rfc2965). http://www.watersprings.org/pub/rfc/rfc2965.txt.

33. Landwehr CE, *Computer Security*. International Journal of Information Security, 2001. **1**(1): p. 3-13.
34. Linden Fvd, *Software Product Families in Europe: The Esaps and Café Projects*. IEEE Software, 2002. **19**(4): p. 41-49.
35. Lindqvist U and Jonsson E, *A Map of Security Risks Associated with Using Cots*, in *IEEE Computer*. 1998. p. 60-66.
36. Matyás V and Ríha Z, *Towards Reliable User Authentication through Biometrics*. IEEE Security & Privacy, 2003. **1**(3): p. 45-49.
37. McHugh J, *Intrusion and Intrusion Detection*. International Journal of Information Security, 2001. **1**(1). p. 14-35.
38. Microsoft (2002) Building Secure Asp.Net Applications. Microsoft: www.microsoft.com.
39. Microsoft (2003) Enterprise Solution Patterns Using Microsoft .Net. Microsoft Corp.: http://msdn. microsoft.com/library/default.asp?url=/library/en-us/dnpatterns/html/Esp.asp.
40. Min BJ, Kim SK, and Choi J-S (2003) Secure System Architecture Based on Dynamic Resource Reallocation. In: Chae K and Yung M (eds) Information Security Applications, 4th International Workshop, WISA 2003. Springer. p. 174-187.
41. Motta GHMB and Furuie SS, *A Contextual Role-Based Access Control Authorization Model for Electronic Patient Record*. IEEE Transactions on information technology in biomedicine, 2003. **7**(3): p. 202-207.
42. O'Gorman L, *Comparing Passwords, Tokens, and Biometrics for User Authentication*. Proceedings of the IEEE, 2003. **91**(12).
43. Oppliger R and Rytz R, *Digtal Evidence: Dream and Reality*. IEEE Security & Privacy, 2003: p. 44-48.
44. Park JS, Sandhu R, and Ahn G-J, *Role-Based Access Control on the Web*. ACM Transactions on information and system security, 2001. **4**(1): p. 37-71.
45. Peteanu R (2001) Best Practices for Secure Development. http://www.mkaz.com/ref/secure_webdev-3.0.pdf.
46. Probst S, Essmayr W, and Weippl E (2002) Reusable Components for Developing Security-Aware Applications. In: 18th Annual computer security applications conference (ACSAC'02). IEEE. p. 239-248.
47. Ramachandran J (2002) Designing Security Architecture Solutions. Wiley.
48. Romanosky S (2002) Enterprise Security Patterns. In: 7th European conference on pattern languages of programs (EuroPLoP). http://hillside.net/patterns/EuroPLoP2002/
49. Saltzer JH, *Protection and the Control of Information Sharing in Multics*. Communications of the ACM, 1974. **17**(7): p. 388-402.
50. Sandhu RS and Samarati P, *Access Control: Principle and Practice*. IEEE Communications Magazine, 1994. **32**(9): p. 40-48.
51. Schmidt DC and Buschmann F (2003) Patterns, Frameworks, and Middleware: Their Synergistic Relationships. In: International conference on software engineering. IEEE Computer Society. p. 694-704.
52. Schneider EA (1999) Security Architecture-Based System Design. In: New security paradigms workshop. ACM Press. p. 25-31.
53. Schneider FB, *Least Privilege and More*. IEEE Security & privacy, 2003: p. 55-59.
54. Shumacher M, ed. Security Engineering with Patterns: Origins, Theoretical Model, and New Applications (2003). Lecture Notes in Computer Science. Vol. 2754. Springer Verlag pp.
55. Smith SW, *Humans in the Loop: Human-Computer Interaction and Security*. IEEE Security & privacy, 2003. **1**(3): p. 75-79.
56. Ting TC (1993) Modeling Security Requirements for Applications. In: Conference on Object Oriented Programming Systems Languages and Applications. ACM Press. p. 305.
57. Viega J and Messier M, *Security Is Harder Than You Think*, in *ACM Queue*. 2004. p. 60-65.
58. Yee K-P (2002) User Interaction Design for Secure Systems. In: Fourth International Conference on Information and Communications Security. Springer Verlag. p. 278-290.
59. Yoder J and Barcalow J (1998) Architectural Patterns for Enabling Application Security. In: In Proceedings of the 4th Conference on Patterns Language of Programming (PLoP'97). p. 1-31.
60. Zhong Q and Edwards N, *Security Control for Cots Components*. IEEE computer, 1998. **31**(6): p. 67-73.
61. Zurko ME and Simon RT (1996) User-Centered Security. In: New Security Paradigms Workshop. ACM Press. p. 27-33.
62. Aagedal JØ, Braber Fd, Dimitrakos T, Gran BA, Raptis D, and Stølen K (2002) Model-Based Risk Assessment to Improve Enterprise Security. In: Sixth International Enterprise Distributed Object Computing Conference (EDOC'02). p. 51-62.

9 Architecture Reasoning for Supporting Product Line Evolution: An Example on Security [1]

J.L. Arciniegas, J.C. Dueñas, J.L. Ruiz, R. Cerón, J. Bermejo, and M.A. Oltra

Abstract

One of the most frequent problems in software engineering is supporting evolution. Guiding the evolution effectively requires the development and maintenance of architectural models. However the industry is increasingly relying on third-party implementations of software platforms and components, which may not be accompanied by architectural models. Product line engineering partially solves this problem using common concepts and artifacts and locating variation points. But adequate processes, methods, and techniques should be developed and adopted to holistically support evolution. In this chapter, we propose a new process to support product line evolution based on mature methods, techniques, and tools. The process involves architecture recovery and conformance methods and a set of techniques, and tools to support them. To demonstrate and validate the process, this chapter presents a case study dealing with nonfunctional security requirements in distributed environments, analyzes the most important standards dealing with architectural security requirements to create a reference architecture, performs a complete recovery and conformance process for an implementation of the OSGi standard (Oscar), and proposes ways to enhance the coverage of architectural security requirements of the OSGi standard and its implementations for distributed environments.

9.1 Introduction

One of the main results provided by the software product line (PL) engineering community is the recognition of software architecture as one of the foundations for the sofware engineering activities, including specific activities for domain and for application engineering.

---

[1] The work presented here has been developed in the projects FAMILIES and OSMOSE (Eureka 2023, ITEA ip00004 and ip02009), partially supported by the Spanish company Telvent and by the Spanish Ministry of Science and Technology, under reference TIC2002-10373-E. José L. Arciniegas and Rodrigo Cerón are visiting professors from Universidad del Cauca, Popayán, Cauca, Colombia. Rodrigo Cerón is sponsored by COLCIENCIAS – Colombia and AECI – Spain, and José L. Arciniegas' work is partially supported by the Ministry of Science and Technology, under reference TIC2002-04123-C03-01.

Since the seminal IST-ARES project [5], several improvements have taken place in the area of software architecture: the use of architectural modeling to manage variability and commonality [13]; the appearance of the Model Driven Architecture (MDA) [91] and the concepts of Computational Independent, Platform Independent, and Platform Specific Models; and the widespread use of architectural and design patterns [40] in the context of PL engineering [58], software reuse [57], and software components [116]. The main advantage of architecture-based software development is the capability for communication and analysis by using the architecture as a guide or roadmap for product(s) development (Chaps. 1 and 2) and for organizing concurrent development (Chap. 14).

Security has become one of the main drivers of the evolution of software systems, particularly of systems connected to networks such as Internet. What can be learnt from complex security-related problems is that there are no fixed, prepackaged solutions, because not all of the problems are known in advance. There is a need for evolution and, to keep it under control, the architecture must evolve. A practical view of architectural evolution, supported by after-deployment evolution, is provided by component-based systems where one of the component implementations is found unsafe (usually after a security attack). To solve such a problem, the evolution of the components of the system is performed in isolation so, in time, each of the system deployments can draw upon a different configuration based on the evolution of its components.

Managing architectural evolution effectively requires adequate knowledge of implemented systems. While the documentation of the systems and their architectures has improved as a result of the use of new technologies and standards such as MDA, organizations can seldom retain adequate knowledge without systematically leveraging architecture recovery and conformance activities and techniques to create up-to-date information about their rapidly evolving systems. This is especially the case with Open Source initiatives where the systems are seldom documented in adequate detail.

However, architecture recovery and conformance is an area where research has advanced at a relatively slow pace. This chapter addresses this area and describes a new kind of use of architectural models that reflects the current state of practice in some Open Source communities. The models enable:

1. An actual reflection of the system evolution and its current state by using architecture recovery techniques and patterns identification.
2. An improvement of the system, supporting preventive maintenance.
3. The identification of nonfunctional quality requirements described by quality models such as ISO-9126 [54] and the transformation of these requirements into design requirements.
4. The use of architectural conformance checking to compare the system architecture against reference architectures published by standardization bodies (understanding them in a broad sense).
5. A means to acquire from vendors or the open source community the detailed design, implementation, and testing of the components that best meet the reference architectures for the intended architecturally significant requirements [58].
6. A way to adapt the evolution of the system architecture to the evolution of reference architectures with respect to security requirements and to track the evolution of some specific components provided by third parties.
7. A vehicle to support the dynamic evolution of running systems after deployment and to keep their architectures updated.

The evolution of systems can thus be better managed by adopting techniques such as the identification of quality requirements, the conceptualization of architecturally significant requirements, the architecture recovery, the comparison of architectural models, and the evaluation of architectural conformance.

In this chapter, these techniques are described, analyzed, and integrated into an architecture-based reasoning process. The process will be applied in a case study about security. The case study deals with the adoption of a distributed services-based architecture composed of service platforms over which service implementations are deployed. The service platform implementation, that follows the OSGi (formerly Open Services Gateway initiative) standard [95], is an Open Source implementation that must offer security services as required by the standard. But several problems appear:

- The platform implementation is not fully conformant to the standard and the elements missing must be identified and implemented or adopted from third parties.
- The security services mandated by the standard may need to be extended if they are inadequate for some specific services or usage scenarios.

As a potential solution, the security requirements of these usage scenarios could be covered by any of the several security reference architectures proposed by standardization groups such as the Distributed Management Task Force (DMTF) [21] in the Common Information Model (CIM). But then

- The elements in the chosen security reference architecture must be checked against the security services in the OSGi standard
- The new security elements must be delegated in the system architecture to a well-defined space
- Implementations must be provided for the security reference architecture elements that are not present in the OSGi standard, and for the elements that are in the standard but not in the available implementation
- Required technologies for guaranteeing system security must be identified and adapted to the constraints of the target platform (OSGi)
- These new elements could be eventually chosen from Open Source communities

The rest of this chapter is composed of six sections. Section 9.2 recalls the product line architecture topics on which the subsequent sections will build upon. Section 9.3 presents a process for architecture recovery. Section 9.4 describes the architecture conformance checking process. Section 9.5 instantiates the processes to the architecture recovery and conformance checking of security aspects in distributed systems. Section 9.6 presents a case study to apply and validate the instantiated process in the context of a distributed software platform. Conclusions and future research issues are identified in Sect. 9.7.

9.2 Software Product Line Architecture

For many years, the software industry has been trying to achieve the development of software-intensive systems with a higher degree of reuse, cost reduction, and shortened time-to-market. Product line engineering is considered as one of the most successful approaches to achieve these objectives.

Software product lines are built on top of existing related software systems where the common artifacts among these systems are integrated in a common asset base. These assets are architectural artifacts used to design the reference architectures of resulting product lines [58].

The conceptual modeling of product lines has been studied extensively [8,19,32,45, 64,67,76,122,123]. The models provide a way of communication and a common vocabulary for the staff within an organization [2]. As a result, the assets for a PL include not only the software itself but also its models. For example, the Unified Modeling Language (UML) provides guidelines to modeling [73,93].

A conceptual model of product line environment is presented in [14]. The product line engineering framework of the FAMILIES project (Fig. 9.1) represents the major activities and methods operating on the core assets of a product line and allows the mapping of specific methods and supporting tools against a common reference. The place of the processes for architecture recovery and conformance is shown in the figure: horizontal arrows from application implementation to application design and from domain implementation to domain design correspond to architecture recovery activities (both in the domain and in the application engineering tracks). Architecture conformance (represented with a vertical arrow in Fig. 9.1) applies to application and domain architecture models. It can also be applied between any of the models and externally available reference architecture (in the example included in this chapter, the reference architecture provides the solution to specific security-related quality requirements). Architecture recovery and conformance are the processes described in this chapter.

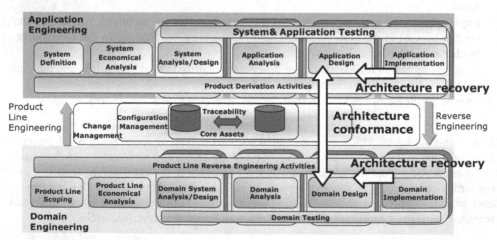

Fig. 9.1. FAMILIES Software product line engineering framework (adapted from [35])

Architectural artifacts (including both their common and variable parts) need to be identified. "Variability is what can be different among members of a collection (of problems, solutions, or products)" [31]. Variability can be managed at different stages: requirements description, architectural description, design documentation, source code, compiled code, linked code, and running code [6]. "Commonality is an assumption held uniformly across a given set of objects (S). Frequently, such assumptions are attributes with the same values for all elements of S" [19]. Commonality is relevant to identify a shared common problem (requirements and architecture commonality) and to select reusable components [8,16,19,31]. A particular way to handle the common parts in a product line is the usage of software platforms, which include component frameworks (the reader is referred to the definitions in the glossary of this book and [129]). The frameworks encapsulate parts of the domain design and their implementations offer parts of the domain implementations available for the creation of applications.

The variation point concept [8, 19] can be used to express variability in an explicit manner. A variation point identifies one or more locations at which variability will occur. Each variation point will be related to a decision. Once the decision is made, the chosen variants will remain and others will be eliminated; as a result, the variation point will have changed its state. This concept is known as "resolution."

Variability management is the main challenge an organization has to cope with in PLE. It gives a chance to gain flexibility in the products involved in the PL. As a consequence, variability modeling is an essential concern to build flexible PL Architectures (Part 2 in this book).

The decisions are part of the product line. Therefore they are related to the models in the PL. In order to obtain specific products, decisions need be taken to deal with variability and commonality in the requirements engineering, architectural design, implementation, testing, and deployment phases. The later the variability is resolved, the more flexible the PL is. Conflicts are a consequence of the variability in a PL; they have to be fixed to obtain coherent products. Different alternatives may lead to different conflicts, but there should be at least one solution for each conflict. The identified commonalities facilitate systematic reuse.

In this chapter, we explain how decisions about security impact the common domain design and implementation and how variation points can be identified and dealt with by finding applicable external reference architectures and comparing them with the common domain design and implementation.

Product lines are built from architectural artifacts taking into account the software product line architecture, also called reference architecture. There are several definitions in the literature about software architecture [41,52,88,98,108]. The best known are:

- A structure composed of components and rules characterizing the interaction of these components [41]
- The structure of components, their relationships, and the principles and guidelines governing their design and evolution over time [52]

The software architecture specifies the structure of the system under consideration. This structure can be complex, especially because several viewpoints are considered at the same time. The concept of architectural view tries to organize this large set of information about the system by partitioning it.

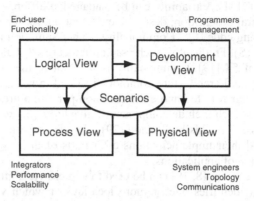

Fig. 9.2. "4+1" views of software architecture

Some of the most widely used models are reviewed in [73,93]. These models organize a description of a software architecture using views. Figure 9.2 shows 4+1 views of architecture. Each view addresses a specific set of concerns of different stakeholders. Architects capture their design decisions in four views and use the fifth view to illustrate and validate the decisions.

The architectural description is applicable to a variety of uses. For example, in [49] it is presented how the architecture description is used in a conformance process for a PL. The first four views (logical, development, process, and physical) are relevant in a conformance process. For each view, the set of used elements is defined (components, containers, and connectors), the relevant forms and patterns are captured, and the rationale and constraints are established, connecting the architecture to requirements. However, the key of evaluation is in the scenarios. Usually the conformance checking process is focused on one issue, for example, a quality requirement such as performance or security defined in ISO 9126 [54]. The scenarios define the issue taken into account in the architectural conformance process. This process is described in Sect. 9.4. Before proceeding to the actual conformance process, we review the current research into architecture recovery, one of the key pieces of the conformance process.

9.3 Architecture Recovery

An important part of checking architectural conformance relies on architectural recovery providing high-level views of the system or product line architecture by extracting and abstracting a subset of the software entities. Thus, architecture recovery pertains to the area of reverse engineering, which is defined in [15] as the process of analyzing a subject system to identify the system's components and their relationships, to create representations of the system in another form or at a higher level of abstraction, or to understand the program execution and the sequence in which it occurred [100,101]. In [72], reverse engineering activities are classified into three kinds of tasks:

- Extracting relevant information from system software, system experts, and system history
- Abstracting extracted information to a higher (design) level
- Presenting abstracted information in a developer-friendly way, taking into account the topic of interest

Reverse engineering has primarily focused on identifying and modeling the structure of a program by means of code examination in order to obtain both static and dynamic information. A complete description of the useful metrics, patterns, and methods supported by tools can be found in [65,114]. The advantage of using measurement in support of reverse engineering is that, in general, measurements are good indicators for important external behavioral attributes and could eventually be used for the assessment of quality requirements such as maintainability, reliability, reusability, usability, and performance [82,85].

Architecture recovery is a discipline within the reverse engineering domain aimed at developing methods for recovering the software architecture from an implemented system [66, 89,112]. Architecture recovery may proceed in a bottom-up or a combined (top-down + bottom-up) manner. Bottom-up approaches start with low-level knowledge (program sources, documentation, etc.) and provide abstraction techniques to recover a system's architecture [1,61,65,121]. Combined approaches start with high-level domain knowledge, produce a model of the domain knowledge and try to find instances of the model concepts in the system's implementation [9]. For instance, in complex systems, significant architectural information should be extracted first. As a result, another architectural model is obtained containing only the important software artifacts [27]. This is possible using architectural rules for model understanding and consistency checking [28]. Architecture recovery [30,38,65,66,89,112] has been used for:

- Reconstructing architecture descriptions for systems that are poorly documented or for which documentation is not available. Many systems have no documented architecture at all.
- Recovering the legacy of the system. Legacy systems are typically complex, with different levels of components based on different programming languages and development methods, and thus difficult to change. They have evolved over decades and passed through many developers.
- Understanding architectural dependencies.
- Analyzing and understanding the architecture of existing systems to enable modifications of the architecture to satisfy new requirements and eliminate software deficiencies.
- Re-engineering the system to a new desired architecture (system evolution).
- Identifying components (usable pieces) for reuse or for establishing an architecture-based software product line.
- Evaluating the conformance of the built architecture to the documented architecture. Architectures are often represented in such a way that the relationship between the representation and the actual system, particularly its source code, is unclear.

An important part of architecture recovery is understanding the architecture through software visualization [111], which provides a holistic overview of static [120] and dynamic [20,107,115] views. Static views describe associations and relationships among system components. Dynamic views are based on information from the analysis of recorded or monitored program execution, thus focusing on run-time analysis [48,81, 100,114]. In Fig. 9.2 four architectural views were identified, since a single view is rarely sufficient for understanding a software system.

9.3.1 Architecture Recovery Methods

Numerous recovery methods exist in the literature. This section focuses on those methods that have extensively guided our research. For example, Boucetta [9] presents a method composed of three main phases:

- Gathering the domain knowledge of the information system with the help of domain experts.
- Using software tools to automatically generate a preliminary system architecture from the source code.
- Refining the architecture by constructing a matrix linking the results of the first and the second step to establish the mappings between the domain knowledge and the initial architecture components.

Albeit similar, Kazman [66] divides the recovery process for large systems (such as product lines) into four phases:

- Extraction of static and dynamic domain knowledge using lexical analysis, parsing, and semantic analyzers.
- Database construction.
- Fusion of static and dynamic views.
- Architectural view composition to let users visualize, interact with, and interpret the system.

Krikhaar [72] describes a software architecture recovery method based on the Relation Partition Algebra that consists of sets, binary relations, "part-of" relations, and operations. It provides a sound formal foundation for the activity composed of four phases:

- Extracting the domain knowledge from source code, experts, and system history.
- Abstracting the extracted information to a higher design level.
- Presenting the abstracted information in a developer-friendly way, taking into account his or her current topic of interest.
- Improving the architecture of the existing system incrementally.

The approach proposed by Guo [46] relies on the definition of structures to be searched for (patterns). These structures are supposed to contain both domain and solution knowledge. The phases are:

- Developing a pattern recognition plan serving as a reference architecture.
- Extracting a model from source code.
- Detecting and evaluating pattern instances.
- Reconstructing and analyzing the architecture.

Riva [103] includes reorganization (also called refactoring) activities as part of the architecture recovery tasks:

- Experts define architectural concepts based on which the source code model is extracted.
- An architectural model is abstracted.
- Improvement plans for architecture documents are created.
- Architecture is analyzed.
- Source code is reorganized to reflect the improved architecture.

Sartipi [105] relies on an architectural description language for the execution of the architecture recovery activities:

- The software system is parsed into source code entities.
- The system architecture is extracted and analyzed by formulating an abstract pattern of the architecture in the form of an Architectural Query Language (AQL) query based on experts' domain knowledge, system document inspection, and/or source model analysis. AQL is used to describe the high-level abstraction of the system in terms of modules and interconnections.
- Unresolved source model entities can be distributed among the blocks of the architecture and the entities in the blocks can be selectively moved between the blocks based on overall closeness between the entities or user inspection.

The CELLEST project [115] presented a method for recovering user interfaces of legacy systems based on the code analysis of the system–user interaction [33]. The input of the reverse-engineering phase is a recorded trace of the user interaction with the legacy interface and the output is a state transition model specifying the unique legacy interface screens (states) and the possible commands (transitions) leading from one screen to another. CELLEST used a tool to support reverse engineering in terms of state-transition models. It consisted of the following phases:

- System–user interaction traces are un-intrusively collected by a middleware.
- The dynamic behavior of the system interface is reverse engineered in terms of the screens and the navigation it allows through them.
- Task–specific navigation paths are analyzed to extract a model of the task in terms of the interface navigation and the information exchange and an appropriate web-based interface is constructed by wrapping this navigation and enabling its execution through a standard web browser.

The method we describe here can be classified as an architecture recovery technique that considers the dynamic behavior in the recovery process.

9.3.2 Architecture Recovery Tools

Most of the aforementioned methods are performed manually [74]. For large systems and product lines, the manual application of these methods is tedious and error-prone and leads to poor results because of the amount and complexity of the information handled. Usually tools are needed to support the architecture recovery process to aid in the extraction, manipulation, and interpretation of architectural information. Several categories of tools are listed below:

– Manual-driven tools such as Portable Book Shelf (PBS) [38,119], Rigi [120], SHriMP [109,113], KLOCwork inSight Tool [70], and Bowman and Associated [11].
– Tools supporting query languages such as Dali [65], ARMIN [89], Architectural Recovery Tool (ART) [121], Rose/Architect [27,28], Architecture reconstruction method (ARM) [46], Riva [103], and Mitre [47] for writing patterns to automatically build aggregations.
– Tools supporting clustering and data mining, such as the tools proposed in the Software Architecture Reconstruction method (SAR) [72], Architecture recovery method [9], Data mining [105], Oblique lifting [12], and X-ray [80].
– Tools allowing architecture recovery from source code, in order to create class diagrams and, in some cases, activity diagrams automatically, such as the PBS toolkit [38, 119], Argo/UML, Poseidon for UML, Bauhaus [71], DIVOOR/CodeCrawler [23,77], Fujaba [84], Imagix4D, Visual Paradigm, and Eclipse/Omondo.
– Tools providing mechanisms for fine-grained inspection and verification of software by exposing the results of sophisticated whole-program analysis (see, for example, Jinsight [20,107], CodeSurfer [3], Columbus/CAN [37,124], CONCEPT [101,102], GSEE [36], Red Hat Source-Navigator, SniFF++ [68], and Scientific Toolworks).

9.3.3 The Process for Architecture Recovery

We present in Fig. 9.3 an architecture recovery method based on the previously cited methods [9,33,46,66,72,103,105,115]. The process is composed of five kinds of inputs, four activities, and three types of results.

The input data are composed by:

– *Available documentation*. This category includes a set of available specifications, design documents, implementation details, features, system architecture models, user manuals, etc.
– *Source code*.When source code is fully available (e.g., the open source software), relevant architectural information can be extracted from it. In some domains this is the key source of information.
– *Run-time information*. There are tools and techniques for recording the traces of the system in runtime. These data hold behavioral information.
– *Patterns*. Usually the systems have been created using well-known architectural patterns [40]. The recovery process thus needs to discover which patterns (if any) were used. These patterns behave as model templates that can be searched for in the preliminary architecture.

- *Experts' information*: Expert knowledge is needed in analyzing software architectures. Experts can associate patterns with some structures, recognize architectural assets and often provide domain level knowledge. For open source initiatives this information can be found in recorded email discussions.

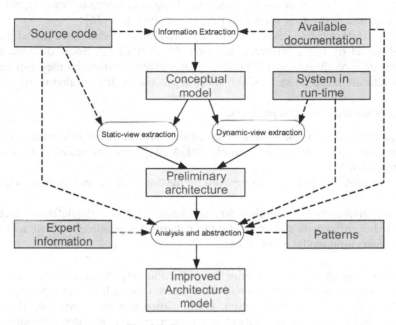

Fig. 9.3. Recovery process

The following activities must be performed:

- *Information extraction*. It takes as inputs the Available documentation and the Source code, and tries to produce a Conceptual model. The activity can be aided with experts [103] or capturing information from user documentation (Chap. 4 and [62]) by using techniques such as gathering knowledge [9], development of specific pattern recognition plans [46], lexical analysis [65,66], parsing [105], program slicing using algorithms to discover the contributions of specific code fragments to the architecture, or finding clusters of elements with a strong relationship [47,65]. The visualization of the available information can be done with specific graphical models, such as the treemap or the hyperbolic tree [75].
- *Static-view extraction*. It is the most common process in re-engineering. The architectural static view (i.e., classes and relationships) is obtained from source code as described in Sect. 9.3.1. This model is complemented with information from the already available Conceptual model [103]. Usually the static-view is composed of logical and physical views [73]. The most common technique is based on the relational and compositional abstraction: taking detailed relationships or detailed components and grouping them into higher-level relationships and classes [29].

– *Dynamic-view extraction.* The architectural dynamic view is obtained by capturing the traces from system-user, system-environment or intra-system interactions [115]. It corresponds with the process view [73], and can be represented with activity, sequence, use case, state chart, finite state machine, time-sequence, and other interaction diagrams. The most common techniques to produce them include logging function calls, collecting system traces (optimally in an un-intrusive way [115]), and analyzing trace dependencies by observing the lines of code on the running software system [26].

– *Analysis and abstraction.* Experts refine the preliminary architecture model into an improved model by using reference patterns [46,72,103,105]. Some of these reference patterns are directly related to specific quality characteristics, so they can be used to produce the architectural view with respect to specific quality requirements.

The process generates several products:

– *Conceptual model.* It is the system meta-architecture composed of domain concepts and relationships among them. For example, MDA [92] calls this model Conceptual Information Model.

– *Preliminary architecture.* It is composed by the "raw" static and dynamic views of the system.

– *Improved architecture.* The preliminary architecture rarely is the definitive architecture. With the help of experts and application of patterns it is possible to obtain a better structured architectural model of the system.

Especially in product line engineering it is of central importance to have an explicit and good reference architecture. Additionally, the process for architecture recovery is the first step to be taken when the architectural conformance process is enacted. Thus, starting from the available information – often the source code – it is possible to produce a highly abstract view of the system structure with respect to the topic of interest. This process will be illustrated by applying it to the analysis of architectural conformance of distributed systems with respect to security. Before we describe this case study, the architectural conformance process is introduced in Sect. 9.4.

9.4 Architectural Conformance

Conformance checking (or simply conformance, from now on) is the process to determine whether an asset developed for a specific domain meets a recognized standard for the domain. Traditionally, conformance has been associated with testing: conformance testing of an application includes the testing activities to demonstrate that the application complies with a certain standard. So, the standard behaves as the reference element to compare with. Several software architecture standards have appeared in the last years. For example, MDA [39,69,91,97] was created to solve integration and portability problems between models. MDA proposes a process to map a PIM (Platform Independent Model) to a PSM (Platform Specific Model) and vice versa in different levels of abstraction. Two implementations of a PIM will share a common conceptual design, although they may utilize incompatible technologies or incompatible mappings to the same technology. However, there is neither a process for assessing conformance between the implemented code and the PSM model nor for checking if a mapping can be found between a PSM and a PIM.

This section presents an architectural conformance process for detecting the differences and similarities between software product line implementations and standards. The process is clearly motivated by industrial needs: there is a large amount of software from third parties (including Open Source implementations) for which the source code is available but the architecture is not. Therefore, it is difficult with the current mechanisms to verify whether this software conforms to a given specification or standard before its integration into a full system. In other words, there is no means for assessing architectural conformance, only for testing conformance. The process thus applies the proposed architecture recovery process in the context of architectural conformance.

The process could be applied in a product line scenario to check if a given application design conforms to the domain design (Fig. 9.1). It could also be applied between the reference architecture of the product line and (parts of) an external reference architecture. The case study we present in this chapter performs this conformance process between the domain design (containing most of the common parts of the product line) and an external reference architecture for security. This chapter regards the external reference architecture as a standard when it is public and has been agreed upon by third parties.

The results of the architecture conformance activities are used, for example, in the maintenance phase for analyzing the system evolution. In [25,106] rules are presented to compare consistency between models. Conformance evaluation can be enacted at several development phases. In [83] a technique is proposed for comparing artifacts by summarizing where one artifact (such as a design) is consistent with and where it is inconsistent with another artifact. Despite the practical relevance of the architecture conformance process, there are few scientific works in this area.

For example, the Common Criteria (CC) (ISO/IEC 15408) present a methodology for evaluating the Information Technology Security [17] that will be taken as the basis of the case study of this chapter. However, the CC does not propose a conformance checking process, but only the security elements that must be present in a secure system. The SARA project [88] developed a guide and a reference model for software architecture review and assessment processes against domain experts knowledge, but as the processes did not formalize this knowledge, they did not address conformance.

Figure 9.4 presents the process for conformance assessment extracting ideas from [17, 49, 88]. The process is preceded by a phase where the objectives and focus for it are defined based on the needs of the relevant stakeholders and the desired requirements (in the figure, the set of requirements, including the nonfunctional ones, have been labeled "QoS," Quality of Service). Then, two parallel activities should be performed. From the Open Source implementation (or the available implementation), the set of Significant Implemented Assets (SIA) should be identified using the architecture recovery process. A Significant Standard Asset (SSA) should be abstracted from appropriate standards such as reference architectures. We have defined SIA and SSA as sets of assets that are important, respectively, for the implemented and the standard architectures with respect to the defined focus.

The key of the conformance process is the specification of qualities. A system's software architecture strongly influences the system's ability to support quality attributes such as modifiability, performance, and security [65]. Focusing on only one relevant point (quality) allows better analysis and reasoning about the architecture. Thus, the conformance process needs SIA and SSA to identify and compare differences and similarities.

While there are several tools supporting the architecture recovery process, there are only few for architecture conformance. It is expected that in the near future, tools supporting automatic management of architectural models can be used to support the conformance activities. A review of the state of the art in modeling tools, especially those close to the MDA initiative, can be found in Chap. 16. But until the tools reach industrial strength, architectural conformance must be performed manually.

There have been some proposals of methods for architectural reasoning that could eventually be used for architectural conformance such as: ontology-based algorithms that allow the search of common artifacts within the architecture [92], or measurements of similarities in quality requirements by using internal or external metrics [55].

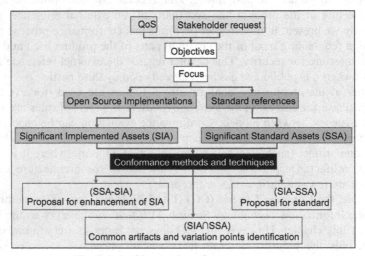

Fig. 9.4. Architectural conformance process

The conformance process yields three relevant results:

- The proposal for enhancement of SIA (SSA-SIA). As a product of the comparison between SSA and SIA, new requirements are identified for improving the implemented architecture.
- The proposal for enhancement of the standard (SIA-SSA). As a product of the comparison between SIA and SSA, some areas of improvement may be found in the standard; it is a frequent case when implemented technology goes beyond the scope of the standard.
- Identified common artifacts and variation points (SIA ∩ SSA). The common artifacts are identified and variation points are located. Variation points are the elements that present a certain degree of similarity, and also significant differences with respect to certain criteria used for comparison. This is the main result of the conformance process because it reveals how good the implementation is with respect to the standard.

Several situations may arise when the process has been performed based on the identified common artifacts and variation points:

- The system fulfils completely the standard. This is the most unusual situation.
- The system fulfils parts of the standard. This is the most common situation.
- The system takes the standard as a reference but the implementation includes several adaptations. Such variations of the standard may result in working solutions but they will be difficult to reuse or integrate.
- The system implementation goes beyond the standard when the standard is found inadequate.
- The system implementation is totally different from the standard.

These results may help to take strategic decisions about the intended evolution of the system or the product line.

9.5 Conformance and Recovery with Respect to Security

This section studies the domain of distributed systems developed in Open Source initiatives to provide services through the Internet. This domain is subjected to numerous security-related threats and vulnerabilities such as attacks. Security solutions are thus needed. Chapter 8 focuses on security-driven product line architecture design and product architecture derivation. However, the perspective of architecture recovery taken in this chapter necessitates an opposite direction from application engineering to domain engineering (Fig. 9.1) and thus does not enable us to fully leverage the reference architecture. This section therefore develops another reference model from the perspective of architecture recovery and compares it with an external reference architecture for security.

This section instantiates the architectural conformance model (Fig. 9.4), considering security as the quality attribute of interest. The stakeholders directly or indirectly interested in and setting the objectives for the conformance and recovery process include the system's clients, end users, maintainers, component distributors, developers, evaluators, architects, accreditors, sponsors, auditors, administrators, owners, consumers, and operators.

This section and the following one study the security-related standards and specifications for the conformance process. The security-related quality criteria and the objectives of stakeholders establish the requirements that the evaluated systems need to fulfill. The objective of the conformance process is to measure to what extent the evaluated systems satisfy the security requirements. The focus of the conformance process is a set of countermeasures that can be deployed in the evaluated systems to prevent, detect, and recover from activities that may compromise the security of the systems.

In this chapter, several security-related standards and specifications have been considered to define a complete reference architecture for security in distributed systems. These are:

- DMTF [21] has defined a Common Information Model (CIM) for security protection and detection technologies, which may include devices and services to classify security information, attacks, and responses. This emerging standard addresses firewalls, intrusion detection, vulnerability assessment, and antivirus functionalities. The goal is to ease the manageability of heterogeneous security systems within an enterprise or service provider environment.

- CC [88] states that "security is concerned with the protection of assets from threats, where threats are categorized as the potential for abuse of protected assets. All categories of threats should be considered; but in the domain of security greater attention is given to those threats that are related to malicious or other human activities."
- The Object Management Group (OMG) [90] states that "security protects an information system from unauthorized attempts to access information or interfere with its operation. It is concerned with: Confidentiality, Integrity, Accountability and Availability."
- The World Wide Web Consortium (W3C) [125] concentrates on Web security defined as "a complex topic, encompassing computer system security, network security, authentication services, message validation, personal privacy issues, and cryptography."
- The Internet Engineering Task Force (IETF) [51] has defined security protocols and infrastructure to help solving some Internet problems: limit data disclosure to the intended set, monitor communications to catch terrorists, keep data from being corrupted, destroy computers with pirated content, track down bad guys, and communicate anonymously.

Figure 9.5 is a UML profile proposal for CIM [21,22], where concepts are defined and mapped to UML diagrams. The security requirements support accessing services, components, and resources. The CIM Security model is not complete, but it does provide commonly needed classes from which vendor products may derive their specific information models.

The objective of the CIM User/Security Model is to provide a set of relationships among the various representations of users, their credentials, the managed elements that represent the resources, and the resource managers involved in system user administration. The model adds to the pre-existing set of requirements fulfilled by the CIM Core Model by introducing a "top" object class called ManagedElement. The introduction of ManagedElement and the associations that reference it provide a foundation for the linkages between the User/Security Model and the ManagedSystemElement derived classes that represent system components and resources.

OMG has proposed a security specification [90] detailing how secure services should be dealt with in distributed systems. It defines several concepts and proposes some tactics for solving classical security problems. OMG has introduced the Credentials, a key concept visible to the application after authentication, for setting or obtaining privileges and capabilities for access control. It is available to service implementers.

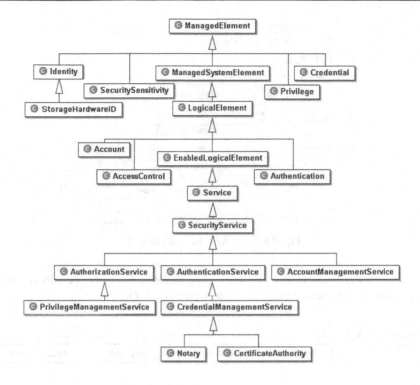

Fig. 9.5. CIM User/Security model

The model (Fig. 9.6) is an excerpt of CC [53] that sets up concepts such as Owner (who imposes a Countermeasure) and Asset (information, components, service, or application), Entity (user or organization), and their relationships. The CC includes more concepts related with security, such as Identity (a representation uniquely identifying an authorized user), Policy (a set of rules that regulate how assets are managed, protected, and distributed within a system), Role (a predefined set of rules establishing the allowed interactions between a user and the system), and Domain (security). In addition, the CC model identifies the Authorization, Authentication, and Accounting countermeasures [50,99,110].

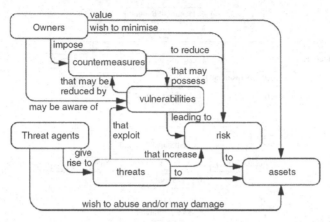

Fig. 9.6. Security conceptual model

The objective of the conformance and recovery process is to verify the adherence to the following security qualities as stated in Chap. 8 (see Fig. 9.7):

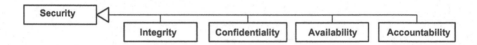

Fig. 9.7. Security requirements for distributed systems

- *Integrity*. Information is modified only by users who have the right to do so and only in authorized ways. It is transferred only between intended users and in intended ways.
- *Confidentiality*. The information is disclosed only to users authorized to access it.
- *Availability*. The usage of the system and the information cannot be maliciously denied from authorized users.
- *Accountability*. The users are accountable for their security-relevant actions. A particular case of this is nonrepudiation, where responsibility for an action cannot be denied.

Complementary security requirements posed by initiatives such as Web Services [126], Java Security [118], and other sources [18,43,78,117] include the administration of security information. For example, defining and setting a specific security policy is needed to guarantee the quality requirements of the system.

9.5.1 Countermeasures

Countermeasures need to be deployed to prevent, detect, and recover from activities that may compromise security. For distributed systems, the main countermeasures are those related with identity and communication (Fig. 9.8). Identity countermeasures deal with the access control to the system resources. The most relevant requirements dealing with access control can be met by the following countermeasures [50,53,56,99,110,128]:

- *Authorization.* Deciding whether a principal (human users and objects) can access an object (resource) normally using the identity (defined in terms of credentials) and/or other privilege attributes (such as role, groups, security clearance), and the control attributes of the target object (stating which principal or principals with which attributes which attributes can access it).
- *Authentication.* Verification that principals operating under their own rights are who they claim to be. Credentials can be used for verification purposes.
- *Accounting.* The Open Systems Interconnection (OSI) Management Framework defines accounting as a process of collecting, interpreting, and reporting costing and charging-oriented information on service usage. This process is divided into the following sub-processes: metering, pricing, charging, and billing. However, the term *accounting* will be used here as a synonym of only metering, which is the process of measuring and collecting resource usage information related to a single customer's service utilization. A part of accounting is security auditing to make users accountable for their security-related actions. It is normally the human user who should be accountable. Auditing mechanisms should identify the users correctly even after chains of calls through many objects.

Distributed systems are characterized by the usage of a network providing communication channels. The channels must guarantee certain quality requirements (e.g., message confidentiality and integrity) that, if breached, can compromise the security of the system in a distributed environment. The most relevant requirements dealing with communications can be met by the following countermeasures:

- *Security of communication between objects.* This requires trust to be established between the client and the target of the interaction, which may require authentication of clients to targets and targets to clients. It also requires integrity protection and (optionally) confidentiality protection of messages in transit between objects.
- *Encryption.* An algorithm is used to scramble data, thus making it unreadable to everyone except the recipient. Encryption is often used by e-commerce sites to secure financial data.

9.5.2 Specification of the Security Agent

The available security reference models are neither complete on their own nor absolutely incompatible. After a detailed study (which could also be considered a conformance process) we conclude that the most complete model was CIM, proposed by DMTF; the scope and coverage of this model in its security part was far wider than those of the other models. However, the CIM model is insufficient for applying the architectural conformance process to meet the security requirements for distributed systems. We have thus

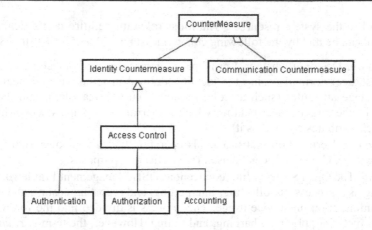

Fig. 9.8. Countermeasures in distributed systems

merged the concepts appearing in the aforementioned models and, in some cases (such as the concept of "firewall"), we have added others. The result of the merging and enhancement process is the "security agent" reference model. For further details, we refer the reader to the case study implemented in the OSMOSE project [96].

The security agent contains the architectural elements dealing with Access Control and Communication Countermeasures grouped in two main subsystems based on the concepts identified in the Common Criteria model. Each of the elements pertaining to these two subsystems will be called "services."

The Access Control Countermeasures come from the CIM model and provide several kinds of services, examples of which are given below.

1. Authentication Services
   - Credential Management Service manages activities related to the credentials assigned to clients (users or applications) within the system. The activities include: validate a credential to a client, renew a credential by means of managing the relationships with the certification authority, and evaluate a certificate.
   - Authentication Rule Check Service verifies the identity of a client trying to access or use a resource within the system.
   - StorageHardwareIDManagement Service manages the identity of hardware devices. This identity must be authenticated in order to guarantee the safety of the platform.

2. Authorization Services
   - Identity Access Service manages identities (e.g., User, Component) that are allowed to access the resources.
   - Privilege Management Service deals with setting the policy for authorization purposes. The policies can be defined for identities in terms of privileges in order to grant restricted or unrestricted permissions for accessing available resources on the system.

3.   Account Management Services
   –   Nonrepudiation Credentials provide evidence of application actions in a form that cannot be repudiated later; they support the accountability quality requirements. Nonrepudiation is a property achieved through cryptographic methods, which prevents an individual or entity from denying having performed a particular action related to data (such as mechanisms for nonrejection of authority -origin- for proof of obligation, intent, or commitment; or for proof of ownership) [79].
   –   Auditing Decision assists in the detection of actual or attempted security violations. This is achieved by recording details of security relevant events on the system. The term *audit* refers to a chronological record of system activities to enable the reconstruction and examination of the sequence of events and/or changes in an event [127].
   –   Auditing Channel is used to write audit records on a certain location, where the evidence of security-related events can be checked.
   –   Account functionality provides a log service and a service tracker in order to record relevant events on the system.

The Communication Countermeasures are divided into the following services:

1.   Firewall is composed of a set of related programs located at a network gateway server that protect the resources of a private network from users from other networks. How this firewall functionality is provided, will depend on the implemented solution within the target platform. For instance, a firewall provided over the operating system of the platform could implement the solution. Firewalls are frequently used to prevent unauthorized Internet users from accessing intranets and other private networks connected to the Internet. All messages entering or leaving the intranet pass through the firewall examining the messages and blocking those that do not meet the specified security criteria [127].
2.   Remote access lets users access the platform resources remotely (at the cost of slower data transfer speeds [127]).
3.   Communication encryption deals with the confidentiality of remote communications. This service encrypts data to ensure confidentiality among extremes and decrypts them for presentation to the client.
4.   Communication signing proofs the message origin. Communications can be signed with the credentials of the sender.
5.   Message Integrity ensures the integrity of a message received from a remote client. Integrity message criteria must be defined.

9.6   The Case Study on Security for Distributed Systems

This section details the conformance process using a case study about an implementation of the OSGi standard [94]. OSGi has defined a set of open-standard software application interfaces (APIs) for building open-services gateways, including residential gateways. This standard has been implemented for connecting the next generation of smart consumer and business appliances with Internet-based services [42]. Being the core of the residential gateways (and increasingly being adopted by embedded systems providers and network operators), it is essential to ensure or to enhance the security characteristics of the available implementations of the OSGi standard.

Using product line terms, the OSGi standard defines a specific type of component framework in which the plugged-in components offer one or several services registering them into the framework. The framework enables the run-time management and control of these service components. Implementations of this standard have been used as the basic component framework for several product lines in different domains requiring communication capabilities. The variability in these product lines is produced at three levels: the set of services running on the framework and their configuration (coarse-grain variability), the variation points in each of these services (fine-grain variability), and the (few) variations in the component framework itself. As will be shown later, the variation points inside the component framework are not really significant. On the other hand, one of the goals of the component framework is to provide support for nonfunctional requirements such as security. The higher support the component framework is able to provide to these non-functional requirements, the better reuse levels can be obtained. This is one of the main objectives for the product line strategy.

Figure 9.9 presents the conformance process for the case study. Two conformance levels will be considered:

– The conformance between the OSGi standard and the open source implementation Oscar [94] in order to detect inadequacies in the implementation with respect to the standard.
– The conformance between the OSGi standard and the security-related specifications (CIM, OMG, and CC) in order to develop recommendations to improve the level of support of these security specifications by the OSGi standard.

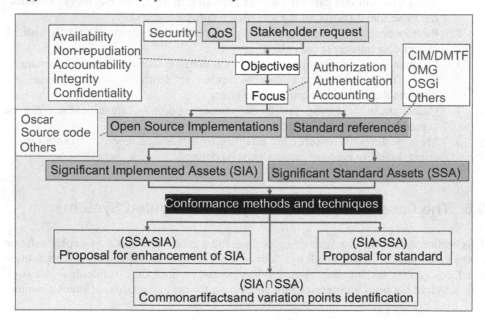

Fig. 9.9. Architectural conformance process with respect to security

Another important result is the identification of the missing elements in the OSGi standard that, once implemented, may leverage the OSGi system to comply with the security levels described by the main standards in the field. The OSGi-based product lines will probably evolve into the direction of the standard. By identifying these elements, the evolutions can thus be supported.

9.6.1 Conformance Between Oscar and the OSGi Standard

Oscar [94] implements most of the functionality in the OSGi standard [95], although it is not completely compliant with the standard yet. The eventual goal is to provide all standard services. At the time of the execution of the experiments we are describing, Oscar was found stable for deployment on controlled experiments and was being used by open source projects. Different open source products have been derived from the common platform such as Gravity, a dynamic component-oriented application framework for service-oriented applications [44]; Beanome, a component layer on top of the OSGi framework [7]; Exymen, an universal cross platform multimedia editor [34]; and JBones, an automatic tool for dynamic deployment [59].

Unfortunately, Oscar's architecture is not completely documented. An architecture recovery process should thus be performed to make the product line architecture explicit, address further evolution, and check Oscar's architectural conformance with respect to the OSGi standard. The recovery process shown in Fig. 9.3 was applied to the Oscar implementation as follows.

Input data for the recovery process:

- *Available documentation and source code.* Oscar's source code and documentation were available in [94,95]. The input documentation included the OSGi standard; instructions for installing, running, and using Oscar; the history of changes made to the source code; a simple OSGi tutorial; a description of the security requirements of Oscar; several descriptions of the included bundles; a description of the Oscar shell service bundle; a brief document discussing Oscar's design issues, by its author; and a description of Oscar's implementation.
- *System in run time.* The Oscar framework was installed, run, and tested over a PC having an Intel Pentium 4 CPU 2.8-Ghz processor and 1.0 GB of RAM with Linux Debian version 2.4.22.
- *Patterns.* In the OSGi standard, a tentative reference architecture is presented. It will be considered as the reference architecture. The main patterns we found to be used are: a service registry (using it is a characteristic of the now-called "Services Oriented Architectures"), the observer and the state pattern.

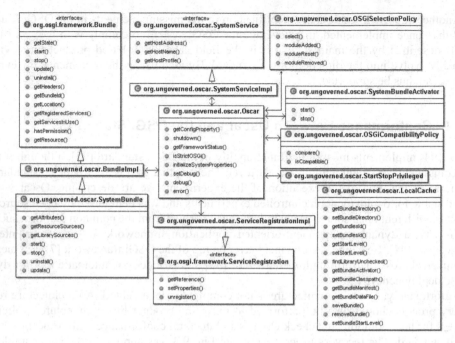

Fig. 9.10. Recovered Oscar framework core

The recovery process included the following activities:

– *Information extraction.* Although Oscar is not 100% compliant with the OSGi standard, the reference architecture was directly obtained from the standard. The structure of the source code was checked, proving that Oscar implementation is in agreement with the standard.
– *Static-view extraction.* The full class diagrams were recovered using the Eclipse/ Omondo tools [24]. The core of the Oscar framework is shown in Fig. 9.10. The diagrams are not yet related to the security requirements. Techniques defined in Sect. 9.3.1 were used to group the most relevant classes.
– *Dynamic-view extraction.* A metamodel about the roles and interactions among the entities is directly defined in the OSGi standard that could be understood as an external schema for the dynamic view. A specific business model should be defined taking into account the security requirements, where the Oscar implementation supports the service

platform component and the rest of the components can be implemented using other technologies [4,10,51,60,86,104,125]. The experiments for the extraction of dynamic runtime information from the inner part of the Oscar framework were unsuccessful due to the amount of instrumentation required to get this internal information about the framework execution.

– *Analysis and abstraction*. The architecture (Fig. 9.11) was obtained by taking into account the OSGi standard as well as the security requirements.

The results of the recovery process were:

– *The conceptual model* is detailed in the OSGi standard [95] and no new elements were defined.
– *The preliminary architecture*. Figure 9.10 shows the OSGi core. Figure 9.11 presents a class diagram with the most relevant classes and interfaces related to security requirements (authorization, user, roles, and groups).
– *The improved architecture model*. OSGi can be seen as a set of services and utilities. OSGi is supported by a basic core (Framework) extended with Java components [118]. Figure 9.12 shows the static architecture organized by services and utilities considering only the packages related to the security requirements.

Figure 9.12 shows the results of the application of the conformance process between the Oscar implementation and the OSGi standard. The Significant Implemented Assets (SIA) are depicted following a color schema: the Oscar implementation appears in dark-gray color, the third party implementations included in the Oscar distribution in white-gray color, and packages unimplemented by Oscar (version 1.0.0) in white. The results of the conformance process were:

– *Proposal for enhancement of Oscar (SSA-SIA)*. The basic framework is fully implemented. The following services need to be implemented to obtain a holistic security architecture (by adapting or reusing components from other OSGi implementations or source code services): device, wireadmin, useradmin, and log; permissionadmin and provisioning were missed.
– *Proposal for OSGi standard (SIA-SSA)*. No inadequacies were found.
– *Commonality and variation point identification (SIA ∩ SSA)*. A common artifact, the basic framework, and the following services and utilities were found: startlevel, url, packageadmin, and tracker. No variation points were detected.

Oscar thus partially fulfills the standard. In the future, Oscar should become closer to the standard by including the missing services.

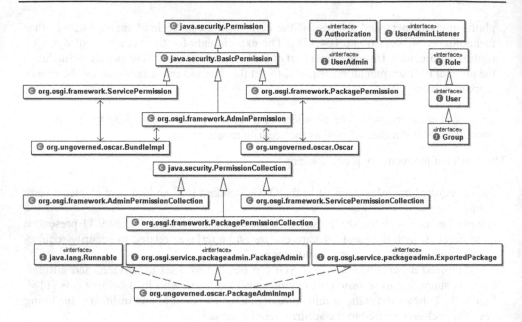

Fig. 9.11. Preliminary security Oscar architecture

9.6.2   Conformance Between the OSGi and the CIM Standard

CIM is the most general available standard for security. Consequently, the conformance process will be done taking into account the security part of CIM. The dynamic conformance is not included in this analysis because we are comparing standards, not implementations, and the behavior is thus not available (it could be created using a specific scenario). The conformance process is conducted at a high level of abstraction and the results are generic, independent of implementations. The results of the conformance mance process are:

1. *Proposal for enhancement of the OSGi standard (SSA-SIA).* Based on the analysis of the difference between CIM and OSGi, requirements for enhancing the conceptual model and the static architecture of OSGi are identified (Tab. 9.1). In the conceptual model the following additional elements are required:

   – *OrganizationalEntity* is a type of ManagedElement that represents an Organization or an OrgUnit (a part of an organization) with a defined structure.
   – *UserAccess* is a special type of UserEntity that relates the user account to its credential.

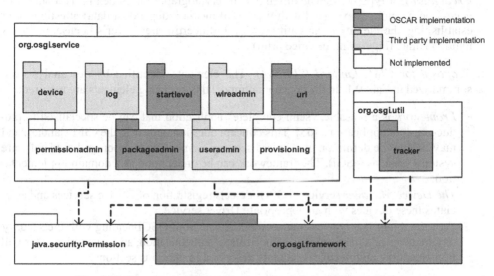

Fig. 9.12. Security architecture analyzed and abstracted from Oscar

- *Notary* is a service for credential management used in the authentication service.
- *AdminDomain* describes the system domain (context).
- *AccountManagementService* is a security service managing accounting on the system.

In the static architecture the following additional components are required:

- *Certificate authority* is a service for credential management used in authentication service. It can operate by accessing a trusted third-party organization that issues digital certificates used to create digital signatures and public–private key pairs (unsigned public key and public key certificate). The Certificate Authority guarantees that the individual granted the unique certificate is who he or she claims to be.

– *Credential* is a type of ManagedElement. In cryptography, a credential is a subset of access permissions (developed with the use of media-independent data) attesting to, or establishing, the identity of an entity (e.g., a birth certificate, driver's license, mother's maiden name, fingerprint, or voice print).

2. *Proposal for CIM standard (SIA-SSA).* The elements identified by our analysis are summarized in Tab. 9.1. In the conceptual model the following elements are required:

– *Framework* is a reusable, "semi-complete" application that can be specialized to produce custom applications [63]. This concept does not appear in the CIM standard and may help in the definition of standard security elements in component-based software systems (such as OSGi). The framework can be understood as a domain implementation.
– *The Device Manager* service in OSGi detects registration of Device services and associates these devices with an appropriate Driver service.
– *Security Agent* is a type of Management Agent from OSGi dealing with the security requirements of a platform, i.e., authorization, authentication, and accounting. This will implement the architectural elements described in previous sections.

Table 9.1. Extracted elements from conformance process between the OSGi and CIM standards

	conceptual model	additional element in static architecture
SSA-SIA	OrganizationalEntity UserAccess Notary AdminDomain AccountManagementService	Certificate Credential
SIA-SSA	Framework Device Manager Security Agent	Provisioning service StartLevel service WireAdmin service

In the static architecture the following components are required:

- *Provisioning service* is registered with the Framework and provides information about the initial provisioning of services.
- *StartLevel service* allows the Management Agent to manage the start level assigned to each bundle and the active start level of the Framework.
- *WireAdmin service* is used by user interfaces or management programs to control the connections between available services in the OSGi Services Platform.

3. *Commonality and variation points identification (SIA ∩ SSA).* Common concepts, common artifacts, and variation points are summarized in Tab. 9.2.
   - *Common concepts* are listed in Tab. 9.3. They are not exact matches, but the concepts can be considered equivalent because each of them has been defined [21,95] and the definitions have little differences.
   - *Common artifacts* are listed in Tab. 9.2. There are slight differences in their definitions.
   - *Variation points* in Tab. 9.2 include the concepts that appear in both standards but are defined differently. The criteria for comparison are based on the semantics of each concept. The differences in the definitions of the concepts suggest that they are elaborated in different ways and at least two interpretations appear for each concept. If the evolution of the OSGi framework followed the CIM standard, the variation points would eventually become common artifacts.

Table 9.2. Commonalities and variation points between the OSGi and CIM standards

	common concepts	common artifacts		variation points
SIA ∩ SSA	see Table 9.3	Privilege Identity Organization Resource Policy SettingData UserAdmin	PackageAdmin Device PermissionAdmin Log Tracker URL	Device Collection AuthenticationService AuthenticationRule Account

Figures 9.13–9.15 sum up the main results of the conformance process. The extra-functionalities of the security CIM are shown in dark-gray color. They are not supported by the OSGi standard. In a real scenario, they could be required and they could be supported by a third party, for example using Web Service Security [126]. The extra-functionalities of the OSGi standard are shown in white-gray color. They are specific for

Table 9.3. Commonalities between (the security part of) CIM and OSGi

CIM – DMTF	OSGi
ManagedElement	Bundle
ManagedSystemElement	Resource
System	Package
Service	Service
Network Protocol : IPSec	Network Protocol : IPSec
PhysicalElement LocalDevice	Device
Location	Bundle location
Collection	Collection : Identity or Role
Group	Group
UserEntity	User
Settingdata	ServiceRegistration
Identity	Identity
Policy	Policy
Role	Role
CertificateAuthority Notary	CertificateAuthority: Kerberos v5 Server
AuthenticationService	UserAdminService PermissionAdminService ConfigurationAdminService
AuthenticationRule	− AdminPermission − ServicePermission − PackagePermission (Supported on java.security.Permission)
Credential	Credential : KerberosTicket
AuthorizationService	UserAdminService
PrivilegeManagementService	PermissionAdmin
Privilege	Permission
SecuritySensitivity	Properties
Account	LogService State ServiceTracker

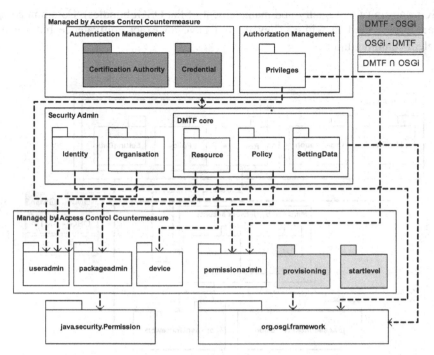

Fig. 9.13. Conformance OSGi-CIM with respect to Access Control Countermeasures

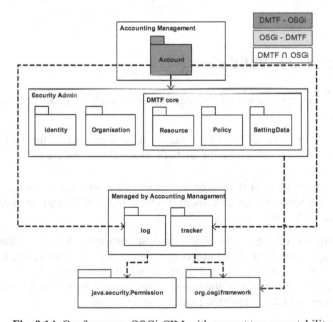

Fig. 9.14. Conformance OSGi-CIM with respect to accountability

the OSGi domain (e.g., registry and management of the OSGi bundles). Common components are represented in white. They do not have an exact equivalence but we have found clear commonalities.

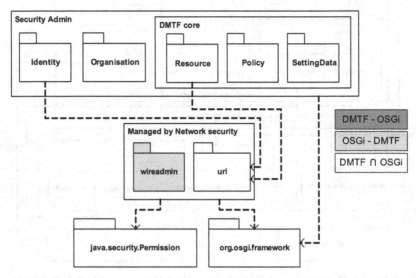

Fig. 9.15. Conformance OSGi-CIM with respect to communication security

9.7   Security Model Validation

Two examples of the application of the conformance analysis process have been conducted and described:

- The conformance analysis of the OSGi standard with respect to the DMTF standard identified proposals for enhancement of both the OSGi standard (SSA-SIA) and the DMTF standard (SIA-SSA).
- The conformance analysis of the Oscar implementation with respect to the OSGi standard identified proposals for enhancement of Oscar (SSA-SIA) and commonalities and variation points (SIA ∩ SSA).

These two examples of the conformance analysis process act as case studies for the validation of the approach to architecture conformance. There is, however, one step further in the validation: conducting a case study in which the proposals for enhancement could be applied for the evolution of the product lines using OSGi-based implementations as component frameworks and validated in a practical manner.

Thus, this second validation technique relies on the development of a prototype or a proof-of-concept operative system. To simulate the evolution of one of these product lines, we built two prototypes. The first one regards a distributed system that uses OSGi compliant platforms without any security enhancements and is thus exposed to security vulnerabilities. The second is the same distributed system, but now the OSGi platforms (and other supporting elements in this scenario) have been enhanced with components that implement the security agent described in Sect. 9.5.2. This second system should be able to resist the security attacks.

Taking into account the manpower effort required to validate holistically the results of the analysis, we focused our validation by defining a scenario to have the following objectives:

- The identification of the required supporting components for Oscar in order to guarantee a set of security requirements for the system in the scenario (e.g. permissionadmin, useradmin, etc.) and the development of the components when an implementation is not available.
- The validation of a set of functionalities identified by the Security Agent. The proposed Security Agent covers a wide scope of security requirements of a distributed system. The Security Agent model can be seen as a set of variation points representing each of the required functionalities. The most important variation points will be validated by using the scenario.

Figure 9.16 presents an overview of the validation process having the following steps:

1. Determination of the generic scenario providing its description, the required infrastructure, the (security) threats that can appear, and countermeasures to deal with the threats.
2. In order to focus the scope of the scenario for the validation, a set of criteria must be established. The proposed criteria are focused on the security requirements and countermeasures that must be validated within the scenario.
3. The inputs from previous steps indicate the variation points of the Security Agent determining the support components of Oscar needed in the system validation.
4. The implementation technologies represent again variation points: elements that may vary in the PL and for each of which a decision must be taken. Examples of these are the type of credentials: certificates, name, etc.; or the encryption protocol: RSA, DES, PGP, etc.).
5. Then the experiments for checking the system behavior in front of security attack are performed.

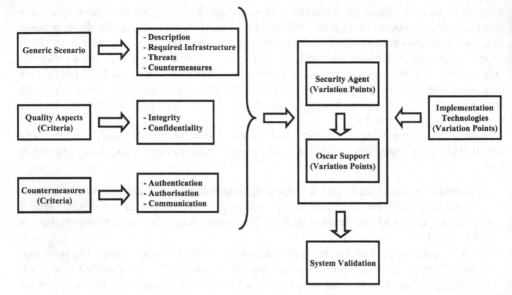

Fig. 9.16. Process followed for the validation

Recalling the definition that appears in the glossary of the book, a variation point is "a representation of a variability subject within a development artifact enriched by contextual information." In this validation process, several variation points appear in different points of the distributed system security requirements and system architecture: security requirements such as identification, authentication, authorization, accounting, and cryptography; alternative solutions such as standards, technologies, and ad hoc solutions; levels of security; domain-specific and application-specific functional variation points; and hardware variations. The elements in the architecture that deal with security requirements are covered by the Oscar platform and the security agent. The security-related variation points are associated with the services of the security agent.

9.7.1 Generic Scenario

The generic scenario for validation pertains to the domain of distributed systems. There are several services platforms connected to Internet for the deployment of services in the home environment and a system manager that controls the services and platforms. The services gateways are composed of PC-like computers over which the Oscar implementation runs. Obviously, these elements are prone to be attacked. The scenario also specifies a typical operation:

- A System Manager deploys a new service component (bundle) on a remote platform (Service Gateway).

– Deployment is made through Internet meaning that there are several security critical requirements such as user authentication and authorization and channel authentication that must be taken into account.

Data encryption at application level is required to ensure confidential communication through Internet and message signing is required to provide authentication and message integrity. There are many security threats the scenario must face:

– Message spoofing or identity supersede: Spoofing is defined as "getting one computer on a network to pretend to have the identity of another computer, usually one with special access privileges, so as to obtain access to the other computers on the network." In this scenario, spoofing happens when someone tries to send a request message to the Service Gateway with the credentials of the System Manager to achieve the authentication as System Manager on the Service Gateway.
– Message sniffing: The System Manager credentials can be obtained from message request sent through Internet. A malicious attack can be performed against the Service Gateway by using these credentials to supersede the System Manager identity.
– Platform damage: A deployment request message is sent to the Service Gateway, containing information for deploying a malicious component over it. The malicious component can be considered a Trojan Horse.
– Exploit information from platform: A malicious component deployed on the platform can retrieve, damage, or change information stored on the Service Gateway.

Based on the analysis of these security threats, the following countermeasures have been deemed necessary:

– System Manager authentication: A proof of the data origin must be provided in the request message, including the credentials of the System Manager. The credentials are verified by means of the "Authentication Rule Checker Service", which will allow proofing the identity of the System Manager, thus validating its authentication on the Service Gateway. The "Remote Access" service must obtain the credentials of the System Manager and provide them to the "Authentication Rule Checker Service."
– System Manager authorization: The credentials of the System Manager are also used for authorization purposes. They are provided to the "Identity Access" in order to validate the assigned privileges of the System Manager within the Service Gateway. If the System Manager has the appropriate privileges, the Service Gateway will do the requested operation.
– Validation of the integrity of the message: The integrity of the message must be guaranteed by means of the inclusion of the System Manager's signature and the time stamp information in the request message sent to the Service Gateway. The "Message Integrity" must check that both signature and time stamp are valid together.
– Administration privileges on the system to allow installation: The "Identity Access" must check that the System Manager has the required privileges for achieving the requested deployment service of the Service Gateway. The System Manager privileges are set in the "User Admin Service." The System Manager requires Admin Permission in order to deploy a component on the Gateway.

– Confidentiality of the message: The System Manager encrypts the request message with a encryption algorithm. The "Communication Encryption" service must decrypt the message. In order to achieve this, the Service Gateway must have the required information to decrypt the request message.

Chapter 8 defines a holistic set of tactics to support countermeasures dealing with security requirements. Figure 9.17 shows the subset of the tactics the security agent should provide in the validation scenario (as gray boxes).

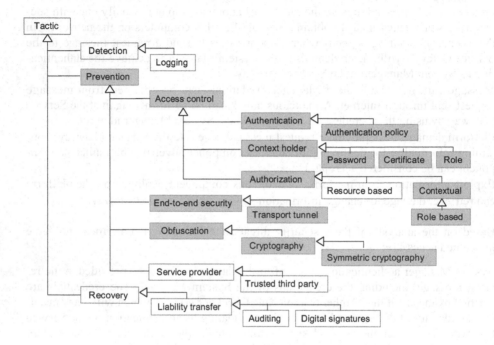

Fig. 9.17. Tactics from Chap. 8 required in the validation scenario

9.7.2 Criteria

The criteria for validation are based on the security requirements and countermeasures that, in conjunction with the information provided in the scenario, indicate the guidelines for designing the Security Agent and determine the support components to be deployed over Oscar.

However, not all security requirements (see Fig. 9.7) are covered. The scenario only takes into account Integrity and Confidentiality requirements. In consequence, only Authentication, Authorization, and Communication countermeasures have been validated. Other countermeasures will be validated in future work.

The Security Agent functionality is decomposed in the following services that support the countermeasures (see Fig. 9.18):

- *Communication Encryption* (from Communication Countermeasures) encrypts data for ensuring the confidentiality among communication ends and decrypts data for presenting them to the client.
- *Remote Access* (from Communication Countermeasures) represents the functionality for accessing the platform resources remotely.
- *Message Integrity* (from Communication Countermeasures) deals with the integrity of a received message from a remote client. The criteria for checking the integrity of messages must be defined and implemented by this service.
- *Identity Access* (from Access Control Countermeasures: Authorization Services) is related to the management of the identities that are granted to access the platform (e.g., User, Component) and permission validation. This functionality is the part of the system that can use the interfaces provided by UserAdmin Service of the OSGi.
- *Permission Bundle Management* (from Access Control Countermeasures: Authorization Services) deals with the relationships of the OSGi specified service "Permission Admin Service" in terms of accessing its capabilities.
- *Policy Rule Checker Service* (from Access Control Countermeasures: Authorization Services) deals with activities related to the validation of the established policy in concordance with the defined policy rules.
- *Authentication Rule Checker* (from Access Control Countermeasures: Authentication Services) deals with the verification of the identity of a client that tries to access or use a resource within the system.

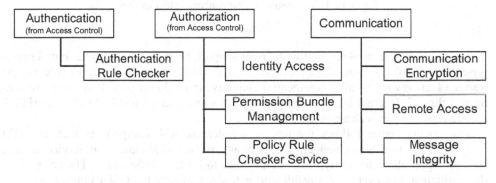

Fig. 9.18. Security agent services

Several similarities have been found in Figs. 9.8, 9.17, and 9.18. Figure 9.8 represents the most general classification of countermeasures, whereas Fig. 9.17 shows the countermeasures that must be implemented into the security agent functionality to be covered in the validation scenario. Figure 9.18 describes the set of services the Security Agent should offer to support these countermeasures.

9.7.3 Implementation Technologies

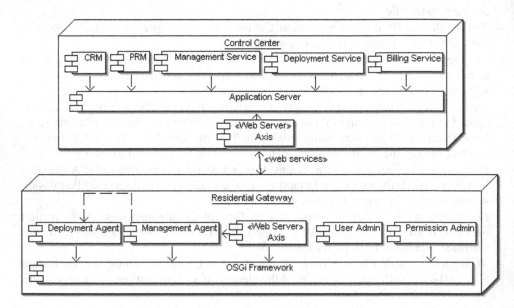

Fig. 9.19. Basic Scenario. Component deployment view

The scenario was implemented with Oscar support. Figure 9.19 shows the initial proto-type, including the System Manager (also called Control Center) in the upper side and the Service Gateway (also called Residential Gateway) in the lower part. Both parts are connected through Internet by leveraging the application-level protocol SOAP over HTTP, characteristic of the Web Services.

The control center follows the typical architecture with components such as CRM (Customer Relationships Management), Billing Service, and Management Service running over an Application Server (typically conformant to J2EE specifications). The key part for the validation, however, is the residential gateway that runs the OSGi Framework, over which there are services such as the User Admin Service and Permission Admin Service (these two are basic Oscar components). There are also services that offer a Web Service front-end of the gateway to the control center: the Axis bundle; a deployment agent (JBones is an open source implementation of it); and a "dummy" bundle to be installed (only to demonstrate scenario validation, so no special functionality must be provided). The residential gateway running the OSGi framework represents the common part of the domain implementation under study. As different services are put running on top, different application architectures are obtained.

9.7.4 System Validation

The first part of the validation implemented the scenario without security elements (see Fig. 9.19) and used tool support trying to detect threats to which it could be exposed. The implemented system was analyzed with three available security-testing tools: Nessus, NeWT Security Scanner, and Retina network security scanner. The analysis had the following results:

1. Checking the control center and service middleware (ports 9080 and 80) with Nessus resulted in two warnings and 15 notes.
2. Checking the navigation service and file remote access with NeWT security scanner resulted in a warning.
3. Checking the whole system with Retina network security scanner detected no additional security risks.

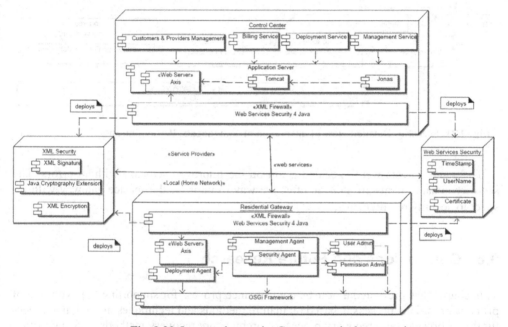

Fig. 9.20. Improved scenario. Component deployment view

Since vulnerabilities were detected, countermeasures were needed to deal with them. Then, the scenario was improved adding the security elements described in the previous sections. Once the countermeasures were implemented and the additional components added to the initial distributed system, the system described in Fig. 9.20 was obtained. The main differences correspond to the added elements: XML security and Web Services security [87] for the communication countermeasures and the XML Firewall and the Security Agent as parts of the OSGi Management Agent.

Bundle permissions can be managed remotely through a Web Services support bundle (Axis + WS-Security). With Axis support, a communication channel can be established between the Control Center and the Service Gateway (using SOAP over HTTP). To guarantee integrity and confidentiality of the communications over Internet, WS-Security is required. Technologies required for encryption and signing of SOAP messages include XML Encryption and XML Signature.

The Permission Bundle Management interacts with the OSGi specified Permission Admin Service to manage bundle permissions. Permissions are used for authorizing new bundles deployed on the Service Platform at run time. Permissions are stored in a Security Policy File containing information in a format that can be interpreted by the Secrity Manager included with the Java Virtual Machine and responsible for checking the policy defined for the system. Figure 9.21 presents a detailed view of relationships among components of the Service Platform.

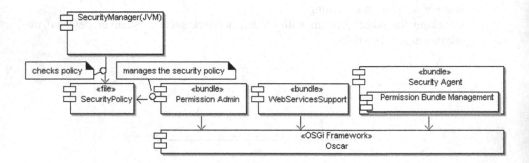

Fig. 9.21. Scenario. Detailed view of interaction of components. Permission Bundle Management

The security tests were executed again on the improved scenario without errors. The security enhancements are thus an effective way to improve the service gateway with respect to security requirements.

9.8 Conclusions and Future Research

This chapter has presented a holistic conformance process for supporting the evolution of product lines. This process is based on mature methods and techniques involving architectural conformance and recovery processes, architecture recovery methods, and supporting techniques and tools. Architecture conformance is a mechanism to evaluate and to check implementations and architectural models against a given standard. The main contributions of the proposed conformance process are:

- The identification of inadequacies, new requirements, and improvements to current implementations.
- The identification of recommendations to improve standards.

- The identification of commonalities and variation points for elements in product line architectures dealing with specific nonfunctional requirements (such as security).

The recovery process described in this chapter is a key part of the architectural conformance process when implemented solutions are poorly documented. It is a complex abstraction process making the product line architecture easier to understand and supporting the evolution and derivation of future products. Evolution in software engineering, as recognized by experts, is still an exceptionally hard problem; the processes described here may help in the exploration of paths of evolution of product lines. In particular, these processes may contribute to improve the support that product line reference architectures offer to specific architecturally significant requirements defined by standardization bodies.

The proposed architecture recovery process leverages existing methods by integrating their best practices into a common process that takes into account both static and dynamic system information and domain knowledge and crystallizes the architecture in the desired degree of detail through three increasingly detailed levels.

A complete conformance process case study has been presented in this chapter with two abstraction levels (implementation level and standards level). The study defined strategies and possible solutions for security-related requirements using standards, and applied them to a component framework that constitutes the basis of the domain design and implementation in several product lines of distributed systems. The following results were obtained:

- A complete conformance process was performed between the Oscar implementation and the OSGi standard with respect to security requirements.
- New security requirements were identified for the Oscar implementation in order to provide a full compliance implementation with respect to the OSGi standard.
- A complete conformance process was performed between the OSGi standard and the security part of CIM with respect to security requirements.
- New security requirements were identified for the OSGi standard in order to provide a full and trusted standard for security requirements with respect to the CIM standard.
- New security requirements were identified and integrated into the CIM standard in order to provide a full and trusted standard for security requirements. A security model called "Security Agent" was proposed to improve the CIM model based on other standards such as OMG and CC. It was particularly adapted to the domain of distributed systems.
- The Security Agent was validated with a real scenario covering security requirements. The scenario presented is a full system meeting the security requirements and implemented using distributed systems technologies such as Oscar, WS-Security, and XML Security.

The architecture recovery and conformance processes and their validation have been applied to the OSGi standard and its implementation that have then been used in the validation scenario. Services gateways – also called services platforms – are typical results of domain engineering. By exemplifying how to apply architectural reasoning to such domain assets, we propose and validate a method for guiding the evolutions of the product lines built using these platforms with respect to security requirements. Future research is needed to validate the generalizability of the method in the context of other types of product lines and with respect to other nonfunctional quality attributes.

Acknowledgments

We are grateful to Timo Käkölä, whose extensive reviews and feedback led us to rewrite this chapter resulting in very significant improvements in the scientific quality of the chapter, and also to the reviewers Tor Erlend Faegri, Svein Hallsteinsen, Félix Cuadrado and Isabel John, and to the members of the FAMILIES project who helped us in dealing with security issues.

References

1. Abowd, G., Goel, A., Jerding, D., McCracken, M., Moore, M., Murdock, W., Potts, C., Rugaber, S., Wills, L.: MORALE: mission oriented architectural legacy evolution. Proceedings of the International Conference on Software Maintenance'97, Bari, Italy, 29 September–3 October 1997
2. Alonso, A., León, G., Dueñas, J.C., de la Puente, J.A.: Framework for documenting design decisions in product families development. Proceedings of the 3rd IEEE International Conference on Engineering of Complex Computer Systems (IEEE Computer Society, Silver Spring, MD 1997)
3. Anderson, P. et al: Design and implementation of a fine-grained software inspection tool. IEEE Trans. Softw. Eng. **29**(8) (August 2003)
4. Apache community: http://www.apache.org
5. ARES Project: Architectural reasoning for embedded systems. ESPRIT 20477, 1995–1998. http://www.infosys.tuwien.ac.at/staff/hg/projects/ARES/
6. Bachmann, F., Bass, L.: Managing Variability in Software Architectures (2003)
7. Beanome: http://www-adele.imag.fr/~cervante/projects.html
8. Bosch, J.: *Design and Use of Software Architectures -- Adapting and Evolving a Product Line Approach* (ACM/Addison-Wesley, New York/Reading, MA 2000)
9. Boucetta, S., Hadjami Ben Ghezala, H., Kamoun, F.: Architectural recovery and evolution of large legacy systems. Proceedings of IWPSE99 International Workshop on the Principles of Software Evolution, Japan, 16–17 July 1999
10. Bouncy Castle: http://www.bouncycastle.org/
11. Bowman, T., Holt, R.C., Brewster, N.V.: Linux as a case study: its extracted software architecture. Proceedings of the 21st International Conference on Software Engineering, Los Angeles, CA, 16–22 May, 1999 (ACM, New York 1999) pp 555–563
12. Bril, R.J., Feijs, L., Glas, A., Krikhaar, R.L., Winter, T.: Hiding expressed using relation algebra with mul-tirelations-oblique lifting and lowering for unbalanced systems. Proceedings of the 4th European Workshop on Software Maintenance and Reengineering, 29 February–3 March 2000 (2000)
13. CAFÉ ITEA Project: From concepts to application in system family engineering (CAFÉ) is a project under Eureka 2023 programme, ip00004, 2001–2003. http://www.esi.es/Cafe/
14. Cerón, R., Arciniegas, J., Ruiz, J., Dueñas, J., Bermejo, J., Capilla, R.: Architectural modelling in product family context. 1st European Workshop on Software Architecture, EWSA 2004, St. Andrews, UK, 21–22 May 2004. Lecture Notes in Computer Science, vol 3047 (Springer, Berlin Heidelberg New York 2004)
15. Chikofsky, E., Cross, J.: Reverse engineering and design recovery: A taxonomy. IEEE Software pp. 13–17, January 1990
16. Clements, P., Northrop, L.: *Software Product Lines: Practices and Patterns* (Addison-Wesley, Reading, MA, 2001)
17. Common criteria for information technology security evaluation, Part 1: Introduction and general model, version 2.2. http://www.commoncriteriaportal.org/ (2004)
18. Controlled access protection profile, version 1.d, Information Systems Security Organisation (National Security Agency (NSA), 9800 Savage Road, Fort George G. Meade, MD 20755-6000 October 1999)
19. Coplien, J., Hoffman, D., Weiss, D.: Commonality and variability in software engineering. IEEE Softw. (November 1998)
20. De Pauw, W., Mitchell, N., Robillard, M., Sevitsky, G., Srinivasan, H.: Driveby analysis of running programs. Proceedings for Workshop on Software Visualization, International Conference on Software Engineering, Toronto, 12–13 May 2001

21. DMTF: CIM Core Specification 2.9, CIM User schema 2.9 and CIM Network specification 2.9 (UML diagrams). http://www.dmtf.org (2004)
22. DMTF: CIM User and Security Model White Paper (2003)
23. Ducasse, S., Lanza, M., Bertuli, R.: High-level polymetrics views of condensed run-time information. Proceedings of the 8th European Conference on Software Maintenance and Reengineering (IEEE Computer Society, Silver Spring, MD 2004) pp 309–318
24. Eclipse/Omondo: http://www.omondo.com/
25. Egyed, A.: Consistent adaptation and evolution of class diagrams during refinement. Proceedings of the 7th International Conference on Fundamental Approaches to Software Engineering (FASE), Barcelona, Spain, March 2004
26. Egyed, A.: A scenario-driven approach to trace dependency analysis. IEEE Trans. Softw. Eng. **29**(2) (February 2003)
27. Egyed, A., Kruchten, P.: Rose/architecture: a tool to visualize architecture. HICSS 1999. 32nd Annual Hawaii International Conference on System Sciences (HICSS-32), 5–8 January 1999
28. Egyed, A.: Automated abstraction of class diagrams. ACM Trans. Softw. Eng. Meth. **11**(4), 449–491 (2002)
29. Egyed, A.: Compositional and relational reasoning during class abstraction. Proceedings of the 6th International Conference on the Unified Modeling Language (UML), San Francisco, USA, October 2003
30. Eixelsberger, W., Ogris, M., Gall, H., Bellay, B.: Software architecture recovery of a program family. Proceedings of the International Conference on Software Engineering, Kyoto, Japan, April 1998, pp 508–511
31. El Kaim, W.: System family software architecture glossary, ESAPS, definition and description of system families. http://www.esi.es/esaps (December 2000)
32. El Kaim, W.: Managing variability in the LCAT SPLIT/Daisy model. 1st Software Product Line Conference, Colorado, 2000
33. El-Ramly, M., Iglinski, P., Stroulia, E., Sorenson, P., Matichuk, B.: Modeling the system–user dialog using interaction traces. Proceedings of the 8th Working Conference on Reverse Engineering, 2–5 October 2001
34. Exymen: http://www.exymen.org
35. FAMILIES ITEA project: FAct-based maturity through institutionalisation lessons-learned and involved exploration of system-family engineering. Eureka 2023 programme, ip02009. 2003–2005. Catalogue of Methods and Processes for System-Family Engineering, ed by by Böckle, G., Wittmann, M. Official Web Site of the FAMILIES Project: http://www.esi.es/Families/E1.4b-Method-Catalogue/Start_SFE_Catalogue.htm
36. Favre, J.: A new approach to software exploration: backpacking with GSEE. European Conference on Software Maintenance and Reengineering (CSMR'2002) (2002)
37. Ferenc, R., Beszedes, A., Tarkiainen, M., Gyimothy, T.: Columbus – reverse engineering tool and schema for C++. Proceedings of the International Conference Software Maintenance, 3–6 October 2002
38. Finnigan, P. et al: The portable bookshelf. IBM Syst. J. **36**(4) 564–593 (November 1997)
39. Flater, D.: *Impact of Model-Driven Standards* (National Institute of Standards and Technology 2001)
40. Gamma, E., Helm, R., Johnson, R., Vlissides, J.: *Design Patterns, Elements of Reusable Object-Oriented Software* (Addison-Wesley, Reading, MA 1994)
41. Garlan, D., Shaw, M.: An introduction to software architecture. In: *Advances in Software Engineering and Knowledge Engineering*, ed by Ambriola, V., Tortora, G. (World Scientific, Singapore 1993) pp 1–39
42. Gong, L.: A software architecture for open service gateways. Embedded systems. IEEE Internet Comput. (January–February 2001)
43. Graff, M., van Wyk, K.: *Secure Coding, Principles and practices* (O'Reilly, USA 2003)
44. Gravity: http://gravity.sourceforge.net/
45. Griss, M.: Implementing product-line features by composing component aspects. Proceedings of 1st International Software Product Line Conference, August 2000
46. Guo, G., Atlee, J., Kazman, R.: A software architecture reconstruction method. Proceedings of the 1st Working IFIP Conference on Software Architecture (WICSA1), San Antonio, Texas, 22–24 February 1999, pp 225–243
47. Harris, D.R., Reubenstein, H.B., Yeh, A.S.: Recognizers for extracting architectural features from source code. Proceedings of the 2nd Working Conference on Reverse Engineering (1995)
48. Harrold, M.J. Testing: a roadmap. In: *The Future of Software Engineering*, ed by Finkelstein, A. Proceedings of ACM ICSE 2000 Conference, 2000, pp 61–72
49. IEEE: Recommended practice for architectural description of software-intensive systems (September 2000)
50. IETF Working Group: AAA, authentication, authorization and accounting. http://www.ietf.org/html.charters/aaa-charter.html
51. IETF: Internet engineering task force. http://www.ietf.org

52. Institute of Electrical and Electronics Engineers: IEEE Std 1471-2000 (IEEE Computer Society, Silver Spring, MD)
53. ISO 7498-4: Information processing systems – open systems interconnection – basic reference model – Part 4: management framework, Geneva, 1989
54. ISO 9126: Software product evaluation: quality characteristics and guidelines for their use. ISO/IEC 9126. (ISO, Geneva, Switzerland 1991)
55. ISO/IEC JTC1/SC7/WG6 N461: Information technology – software product quality – Part 1: quality model, Part 2: external metrics, Part 3: internal metrics, Part 4: quality in use metrics. ISO/IEC 9126 (November 1999)
56. ISO/IEC: Information technology – security techniques – entity authentication mechanisms; Part 1: general model. Technical report ISO/IEC 9798-1, 2nd edn (International Organization for Standardization, Genève, Switzerland 1991)
57. Jacobson, I., Griss, M., Jonsson, P.: *Software Reuse, Architecture, Process and Organization for Business Success* (Addison-Wesley, Reading, MA 1997)
58. Jazayeri, M., Ran, A., van der Linden, F.: *Software Architecture for Product Families* (Addison-Wesley, Reading, MA 2000)
59. JBones: Java-Based OSGi Native dEployment System. http://jbones.forge.os4os.org/
60. JCP: Java Community Process. http://www.jcp.org
61. Jerding, D., Rugaber, S.: Using visualization for architectural localization and extraction. Proceedings of the 4th Working Conference on Reverse Engineering, Amsterdam, the Netherlands, 6–8 October 1997 (IEEE Computer Society, Silver Spring, MD) pp 56–65
62. John, I., Dörr, J.: Elicitation of requirements from user documentation. 9th International Workshop on Requirements Engineering: Foundation for Software Quality, Refsq'03, Klagenfurt/Velden, Austria, 16–17 June 2003
63. Johnson, R., Foote, B.: Designing reusable classes. J. Object Oriented Program. SIGS **1**(5) (June/July 1988)
64. Kang, K., Cohen, S., Hess, J., Novak, W., Peterson, A.: Feature-oriented domain analysis (FODA) feasibility study. Technical report, CMU/SEI-90-TR21 (November 1990)
65. Kazman, R., Jeromy, S.: Playing detective: reconstructing software architecture from available evidence. Technical report, CMU/SEI-97-TR-010 (Software Engineering Institute, Carnegie Mellon University, Pittsburgh October 1997)
66. Kazman, R., O'Brien, L., Verhoef, C.: Architecture reconstruction guidelines, 2nd edn, CMU/SEI-2002-TR-034
67. Keepence, B., Mannion, M.: Using patterns to model variability in product families. IEEE Softw. (July 1999)
68. Klaus, M.: Simplifying code comprehension for legacy code reuse. Wind River Systems. Embedded Dev. J. (April 2002)
69. Kleppe, A., Warmer, J., Bast, W.: *MDA Explained: The Model Driven Architecture™: Practice and Promise* (Addison-Wesley, Reading, MA 2003)
70. KLOCwork insight: http://www.klocwork.com/Accelerator.htm
71. Koschke, R., Simon, D.: Hierarchical reflexion models. In: Proceedings of the Working Conference on Reverse Engineering (IEEE Computer Society , Silver Spring, MD 2003)
72. Krikhaar, R.: Software architecture reconstruction, Ph.D. thesis (University of Amsterdam 1999)
73. Krutchen, P.: *The Rational Development Process: An Introduction* (Addison-Wesley, Reading, MA 1999)
74. Laine, P.: The role of software architecture in solving fundamental problems in object-oriented development of large embedded systems. Proceedings of the Working IEEE/IFIP Conference on Software Architecture, Amsterdam, The Netherlands, 28–31 August 2001, pp 14--23
75. Lamping, J., Rao, R., Pirolli, P.: A Focus+Context technique based on hyperbolic geometry for visualizing large hierarchies. In: Proceedings of the ACM Conference on Human Factor in Computing Systems, Denver, 1995
76. Lane, T.G.: Studying software architecture through design spaces and rules. Technical report, CMU/ SEI-90-TR-18 (Software Engineering Institute 1990)
77. Lanza, M.: CodeCrawler-lessons learned in building a software visualization tool. Proceedings of the 7th European Conference on Software Maintenance and Reengineering, 26--28 March 2003 (2003)
78. Linux Security Administrator's Guide, v0.98, 22 August 1998. http://www.nic.com/~dave/Security AdminGuide/SecurityAdminGuide.html
79. McCullagh, A., Caelli, W.: Non-repudiation in the digital environment. First Monday **5**(8). Available at http://www.firstmonday.org/issues/issue5_8/mccullagh/index.html (2000)
80. Mendonça, N., Kramer, J.: Architecture recovery for distributed systems. SWARM Forum at the Eight Working Conference on Reverse Engineering, Stuttgart, Germany, October 2001

81. Muccini, H. et al: Using software architecture for code testing. IEEE Trans. Softw. Eng. **30**(3) (March 2004)
82. Munson, J., Khoshgoftaar, T.: Measuring dynamic program complexity. IEEE Softw. 48–55 (November 1992)
83. Murphy, G. et al: Software reflexion models: bridging the gap between design and implementation. IEEE TSE **27**(4), 364–380 (April 2001)
84. Niere, J.: Recovering design elements in large software systems. Proceedings of the 6th Workshop Software Reengineering (WSR), Bad Honnef, Germany, May 2004
85. Nikora, A.P., Munson, J.C.: Understanding the nature of software evolution. Software maintenance, 2003, ICSM 2003. Proceedings of the International Conference, 22–26 September 2003
86. OASIS consortium: http://www.oasis-open.org
87. OASIS Web Services Security TC: http://www.oasis-open.org/committees/tc_home.php?wg_abbrev=wss
88. Obbink, J.H., Kruchten, K.W., Postma, H., Ran, A., Dominick, L., Kazman, R., Hilliard, R., Tracz, W., Kahane, E.: Software architecture review and assessment (SARA) report, version 1.0 (February 2002)
89. O'Brien, L., Stoermer, C., Verhoef, C.: Software architecture reconstruction: practice needs and current approaches, CMU/SEI-2002-TR-024 ADA407795 (2002)
90. OMG: Security Service Specification Version 1.8 (March 2002)
91. OMG: Model driven architecture (MDA) Architecture board ORMSC (9 July 2001)
92. OMG: Ontology definition Metamodel. Request for proposal (18 August 2003)
93. OMG: Unified modeling language specification. Object Management Group. Version 1.5 (March 2003)
94. Oscar: An OSGi framework implementation. http://oscar-osgi.sourceforge.net/
95. OSGi Service Platform, Release 3. http://www.osgi.org/ (March 2003)
96. OSMOSE: Open source middleware for open systems in Europe. http://www.itea-osmose.org (2003–2005)
97. Oya, M.: MDA and system design. Presentation at "MDA Information Day" during the OMG technical meeting (April 2002)
98. Perry, D.E., Wolf, A.L.: Foundations for the study of software architecture. ACM SIGSOFT Softw. Eng. Notes **17**: 40–52 (October 1992)
99. Pras, A. et al: Internet accounting. IEEE Commun. Mag. (May 2001)
100. Rilling, J., Lizotte, M.: Position paper: challenges in visualizing and reconstructing architectural views. 2nd IEEE International Workshop on Visualizing Software for Understanding and Analysis, Amsterdam, the Netherlands, 22 September 2003 (IEEE Computer Society, Silver Spring, MD 2003)
101. Rilling, J., Li, H.F., Goswami, D.: Predicate-based dynamic slicing of message passing programs source code analysis and manipulation, 2002. Proceedings of 2nd IEEE International Workshop, 1 October 2002
102. Rilling, J., Seffah, A., Bouthlier, C.: The CONCEPT project – applying source code analysis to reduce information complexity of static and dynamic visualization techniques. Visualizing Software for Understanding and Analysis, 2002. Proceedings of 1st International Workshop, 26 June 2002
103. Riva, C.: Reverse architecting: an industrial experience report. Proceedings of the 7th Working Conference on Reverse Engineering, Brisbane, Australia, 23–25 November 2000, pp 42–50
104. Shin, S.: Secure Web services. JavaWorld (2003)
105. Sartipi, K., Kontogiannis, K.: A graph pattern matching approach to software architecture recovery. Proceedings of the IEEE International Conference on Software Maintenance (ICSM 2001), Florence, Italy, 7–9 November 2001, pp 408–419
106. Selonen, P., Xu, J.: Validation UML models against architectural profiles. ESEC/FSE'03, Helsinki, Finland, 1–5 September 2003
107. Sevitsky, G., de Pauw, W., Konuru, R.: An information exploration tool for performance analysis of Java programs. Technology of Object-Oriented Languages and Systems, 2001. TOOLS 38. Proceedings, 12–14 March 2001
108. Shaw, M., Garlan D.: *Software Architecture: Perspectives on an Emerging Discipline* (Prentice-Hall, Englewood Cliffs, NJ 1996)
109. SHriMP Views: http://www.thechiselgroup.org/
110. Sovio, S., Asokan, N., Nyberg, K.: Defining Authorization Domains Using Virtual Devices (2003)
111. Stasko, J., Domingue, J., Brown, M.H., Price, B.A. (eds) *Software Visualization – Programming as a Multimedia Experience* (MIT 1998)
112. Stoermer, C., O'Brien, L., Verhoef, C.: Practice patterns for architecture reconstruction. Working Conference on Reverse Engineering, Richmond, VA, USA, 29 October–1 November 2002
113. Storey, M.-A., Best, C., Michaud, J.: SHriMP views: an interactive and customizable environment for software exploration. Proceedings of International Workshop on Program Comprehension (IWPC'2001), May 2001

114. Stroulia, E., Systä, T.: Dynamic analysis for reverse engineering and program understanding. *Applied Computing Reviews Spring 2002* (ACM, New York 2002)
115. Stroulia, E., El-Ramly, M., Inglinski, P., Sorenson, P.: User interface reverse engineering in support of interface migration to the Web. Automat. Softw. Eng. **3**(1), 271–301 (2003)
116. Szyperski, C.: *Component Software -- Beyond Object-Oriented Programming* (Addison-Wesley, Reading, MA, 1998)
117. Technology Roadmap on Software Intensive Systems: The Vision of ITEA (SOFTEC Project); ITEA Office (March 2001)
118. The Java Security Architecture for JDK 1.2. Version 1.0, Sun Microsystems, October 1998. http://java.sun.com/products/jdk/1.4/docs/guide/security/spec/securityspec.doc.html
119. The Portable Bookshelf: http://swag.uwaterloo.ca/pbs/
120. The Rigi Tool: http://www.rigi.csc.uvic.ca/
121. Tonella, P., Fiutem, R., Antoniol, G.: Augmenting pattern-based architectural recovery with flow analysis: Mosaic – a case study. Proceedings of the Working Conference on Reverse Engineering (IEEE, New York 1996)
122. van der Linden, F. (ed) *Development and Evolution of Software Architectures for Product Families*. Proceedings of the 2nd International ESPRIT ARES workshop, Las Palmas de Gran Canaria, Spain, 1998. Lecture Notes in Computer Science, vol 1429 (Springer, Berlin Heidelberg New York 1998)
123. van der Linden, F.: Software product families in Europe: the ESAPS & CAFÉ projects. IEEE Softw. (July 2002)
124. Vidacs, L., Beszedes, A., Ferenc, R.: Columbus schema for C/C++ preprocessing software maintenance and reengineering, 2004, CSMR 2004. Proceedings of the 8th European Conference, 24–26 March 2004
125. W3C: World Wide Web Consortium. http://www.w3.org/Security/
126. Web Services and SOA; D.K. Barry Mk (2004)
127. WebOpedia: Online dictionary available in http://www.webopedia.com/
128. Whittaker, J.: Why secure applications are difficult to write. IEEE Security Privacy (2003)
129. Wijnstra, J.G.: Component frameworks for a medical imaging product family. In: *Software Architectures for Product Families*, International Workshop IW-SAPF-3. Lecture Notes in Computer Science, vol 1951 (Springer, Berlin Heidelberg New York 2000)

10 A Method for Predicting Reliability and Availability at the Architecture Level

A. Immonen

Abstract

The demand of high reliability and availability of today's systems is considerable as an increasing amount of complicated systems are tightly embedded into our surroundings. These systems have to work as intended and must provide services when needed. The problems in reliability and availability should be able to be analyzed prior to system implementation, when the fault corrections and modifications are easier and cheaper to perform and the design decisions can still be affected. The contribution of this chapter is a method for predicting reliability and availability at the architectural level. The Reliability and Availability Prediction (RAP) method defines how the reliability and availability requirements should be negotiated and mapped to the architecture, how they should be represented in the architectural models, and how the architecture should be analyzed in order to validate whether or not the requirements are met. The method has been validated by simulating it in the reliability and availability prediction of a case example in a laboratory.

10.1 Introduction

In the near future, systems will be more complicated and more tightly embedded into our surroundings. We use these systems in our everyday life, for example, when playing games, shopping from home, handling money transactions or relying on alarm systems. Problems or faults in these systems can cause extensive damage, including, for example, financial losses and even threaten lives. Therefore, it is extremely important that these systems are of high quality, i.e., they work as they are intended to work and provide services whenever we would like to use them.

Many systems today are developed based on the product line engineering paradigm. A software product line is a set of products sharing common features and architecture, but which also have product-specific features [1,6,30]. The system family concept is equivalent to a product line, signifying a family of software-specific systems [58]. Product line engineering (PLE) is about increasing productivity and shortening time-to-market in software system development using existing artifacts and knowledge. Within product lines, quality issues are extremely important because weakness in quality can cause problems throughout the life cycle of a line. Faults and "poor" design decisions can cause extensive and long-term problems affecting all of the members of a line. Due to the required faultless and ready-to-use qualities of today's systems, the demand of high reliability and availability (R&A) is considerable.

There are several definitions for reliability and availability. ISO/IEC 9126-1 [28] defines reliability as the capability of the software system to maintain a specified level of performance when used under specified conditions. According to that, reliability is mixed with performance, and availability is one of the sub-characteristics of reliability. According to [3], reliability is the ability of the system to continue operating over time, and availability measures the proportion of time that the system is up and running. In this study, reliability is understood to be related to the probability of failure. Therefore, reliability is the probability of failure-free operation of a software system for a specified period of time in a specified environment [52]. Availability is closely related to reliability, being the probability of a software system or a service to be available when needed. For example, high reliability is required to guarantee the correctness of sensitive information in data transmission, and the high availability of a service is a necessity when calling for help in an emergency situation.

Problems in reliability and availability of systems are typically detected after system implementation, when corrections are difficult and modifications are time intensive. The traditional R&A analysis is based on measuring existing systems, and it expresses R&A using measures such as mean time to failure (MTTF), mean time to repair (MTTR), mean time between failures (MTBF), and the failure rate. Traditional analysis has been an independent task performed after system implementation, and it is usually performed by an independent analyst. Thus, it is time consuming and expensive. To achieve the benefits of PLE, such as faster time-to-market, high quality of products and large-scale productivity gains, the reliability and availability of the systems should be able to be analyzed prior to system implementation. In that way, the R&A problems can be solved easier at the architecture level. Also, the effects of the design decisions can be detected beforehand, in which they can still be affected.

Software architecture is the first asset that describes the product line as a whole. Several proposals have been made to predict reliability and availability already at the architecture level from UML (Unified Modeling Language) models, such as [12,37,52]. However, none of them are applicable or sufficient for today's complex systems. The earlier proposals do not take account of several possible requirement sources and how these affect design decisions. Furthermore, they do not define how to move systematically from R&A requirements to architecture, and how to trace requirements to architectural decisions and vice versa. The product line concept is not included in the existing approaches; the proposals do not consider the variability of systems at any level. Also, the proposed prediction methods typically require additional design work, such as supplemental analysis models.

The R&A prediction of today's systems is challenging, resulting from their complexity, large-scale requirements and often the distribution. Due to the complicated nature of today's systems and the shortcomings of the existing prediction methods, a new method is required to predict R&A of the systems from architectural models. The R&A prediction is not just about analyzing, it also requires that the entire system development approach must be refined, starting from the gathering of the requirements. All of the R&A requirement sources should be identified and the requirements should be negotiated in a way that the best possible requirement set can be identified. For each requirements set, several candidate architectural solutions, i.e., styles, can be identified, each of which support the R&A requirements differently. An architectural style is determined by a set of component types, a topological layout of the components, semantic constraints and connectors, and a description of the pattern of data and control interaction among the components [3,11, 18,33]. The careful consideration and selection of an architectural style is a requisite in order to meet the R&A requirements. The predictive analysis method should help to validate, prior to the implementation, whether or not the R&A requirements are met in the architecture. This predictive analysis should be able to be performed for each candidate architectural solution and the candidate that meets the requirements best can subsequently be selected. However, the analysis from the architecture is only possible if the architecture is represented in a way that enables analysis [30]. Therefore, the architectural modeling and analysis are closely related.

The PLE approach requires not only investments and organizational commitment, but also the use of special development methods and techniques. This chapter introduces the RAP (Reliability and Availability Prediction) method that assists in requirement engineering, architecture modeling and R&A analysis from the architectural models, providing the capability to ensure, prior to system implementation, that the requirements are met. The RAP method was designed in a manner that took into account the major shortcomings of the existing prediction methods, therefore, filling the gap from requirements engineering to analysis and providing the required tool and notation extensions, techniques and guidelines for R&A prediction at the architecture level. For the PLE approach, the RAP method provides a systematic way to predict and thus ensure the reliability and availability of the line and its members.

In the next section, a short literature survey is given as a background for R&A prediction. Section 10.3 provides an overview of the RAP method, briefly introducing its main phases. Section 10.4 introduces the case example, a distribution platform for a product line including three members, which is used to validate the RAP method. The RAP method consists of three separate phases. Sections 10.5–10.7 describe these phases and the validation of the method based on an experimental evaluation using a case example. Section 10.8 consists of a discussion and the identified requirements for future development. Finally, Sect. 10.9 concludes this work.

10.2 A Literature Survey of Applicable Methods and Techniques for R&A Prediction

A predictive R&A analysis method requires considerations for requirement engineering, architecture design and architecture analysis. There are several methods and techniques for all of these phases. This section briefly discusses the most promising approaches from the R&A prediction viewpoint. The most suitable approaches are further applied in the RAP method.

10.2.1 Requirement Engineering

Several requirements engineering methods have been suggested in order to acquire the requirements for the software and to lead them to most suitable architectural solutions, such as Procurement-Oriented Requirements Engineering (PORE) [44]. None of them consider the different requirement sources, the influences of the sources on the final requirements or the product line related aspects.

The i* framework [8] helps to detect where the quality requirements originate and what kind of negotiations should take place, and thereby can be used to depict the relationships among different types of stakeholders. The reasoning regarding the different quality concern leads to the most appropriate architectural design decision to be used in a particular context. The NFR (nonfunctional requirements) framework [9] refines and extends the i* framework. The NFR framework aims to refine the quality requirements, consider different design alternatives, perform tradeoff analyses and evaluate the degree to which the requirements are satisfied. The NFR framework utilizes nonfunctional requirements to drive the overall design process. It assists in acquiring and accessing the required knowledge of the domain and system. The framework identifies the particular NFRs for the domain and the possible design alternatives ("operationalizations") for meeting requirements. It also detects the interdependencies among NFRs and operationalizations, and assists in the selection of the architectural style among operationalization alternatives.

The CBSP (Component-Bus-System-Property) method [22] aims to reconcile the requirements and architectures using intermediate models. The intermediate model is used as a bridge while refining and transforming the requirements to architectural elements. The method defines five steps from the requirement selection to making trade-off choices of architectural elements and styles. Each requirement is assessed for its relevance to the system architecture's components, connectors and topology of the system.

Different sets of quality concerns can be transformed by architecture design into different architectural decisions. Together the NFR framework and CBSP method can be used to define, among other things, how the R&A requirements lead to different architectural decisions. This is valuable for R&A prediction. These two approaches are primarily aimed at a one-of-a-kind system development, but they can also be easily applied to PLE.

10.2.2 Architecture Design

One of the main pitfalls of the traditional software design methods has been that they do not integrate quality considerations into design. Therefore, the fact is that the architecture is not usually described in a way that assists in R&A prediction. Some design approaches have been proposed that emphasize quality attributes. QADA®[1] (Quality-driven Architecture Design and quality Analysis methodology) uses quality requirements as a driving force when selecting software structures [40,51]. It describes the architecture on two abstraction levels: conceptual and concrete. The conceptual level means delayed design decisions concerning, for example, functionality. Concrete level refines the conceptual designs in more detailed descriptions. The conceptual and concrete levels consist of four viewpoints: structural, behavioral, deployment and development. The structural viewpoint describes the compositional structure of the system, whereas the behavioral viewpoint concerns the behavioral aspects of the architecture. The deployment viewpoint allocates the components to various computing environments. Finally, the development viewpoint

---

[1] ® Registered trademark of VTT Technical Research Centre of Finland, http://virtual.vtt.fi/qada.

presents the components, their relationships to each other and the actors responsible for their development. The architectural views are also the basis of several design methods, such as in [24,29,36]. However, none of them are suitable as such for product lines and for systems where requirements come from various stakeholders of the domain [51].

The Model-Driven Architecture (MDA) approach separates the platform-independent and platform-specific concepts [17,43]. MDA enables one to specify an architecture for a system independently of the platform that supports it, specify alternative platforms for the system, choose a particular platform for the system and transform the system specification into one for a particular platform [43]. QADA supports MDA by enabling the separation of platform independent and platform specific models. The conceptual abstraction level of QADA is entirely platform independent. The concrete level, however, can also be described platform independently, if needed, until the development view finally maps the views to the technologies provided as the assets in repository. The mapping of the abstraction levels of QADA to MDA is described in more detail in [39]. QADA is especially intended for a product line context and its different abstraction levels and viewpoints enable strict and extensive descriptions of the architecture. Therefore, QADA seems to be the most suitable design method to be used in R&A prediction.

The mapping from the quality requirements to architecture design can be performed through architectural styles and patterns. Architectural styles employ qualitative reasoning in order to motivate when, and under what conditions they should be used. An architectural pattern provides a solution for a particular problem and is thus a realization of a style or styles. A design pattern commonly describes a recurring structure of communicating components that solves a general design problem within a particular context [7]. There is still a considerable lack of architectural styles and patterns that emphasize reliability and availability. The effect of architectural patterns on quality attributes is discussed in several studies, such as [6,7,14,54]. However, only one style, the Simplex ABAS (Attribute Based Architectural Style) [33], seems to focus on software reliability. The Simplex ABAS uses redundancy to increase reliability and tolerate faults, which is inadequate and expensive. The master-slave design pattern is one of the rare patterns that supports fault tolerance, parallel computation and computational accuracy [7]. In this pattern, the tasks are divided and delegated to several independent, but semantically identical, slave components and the final result is computed from these slaves return. Therefore, this kind of pattern is only useful for computational systems. Several styles and patterns, however, provide minor benefits for achieving R&A, for example, by providing monitoring and timer mechanisms. Still, the lack of R&A related architectural styles and patterns seems to be one of the major problem areas in modeling reliable and available systems.

To represent R&A in architectural models, an extension to the design notations is required. UML is a standard and widely accepted modeling language [46,49]. The UML standard can be extended by specific profiles to support certain quality aspects. A profile according to [46] is: "a stereotyped package that contains model elements that have been customized for a specific domain or purpose by extending the meta model using stereotypes, tagged definitions, and constraints." Some profiles for modeling quality attributes in architecture have been suggested, such as a UML profile for Schedulability, Performance and Time [47] and a UML profile for modeling the Quality-of-Service and Fault Tolerance [48]. In addition, a UML profile is defined in order to explicitly represent variation and to indicate the locations for which change is allowed [13]. Although there is no profile that could be used as such or applied for R&A modeling, a means exists to support reliability in design following the principles of MDA [53]. The approach exploits the standard UML and the profiles that have already been created, such as the profile for Schedulability, Performance and Time and the UML Profile for EJB [21], and tends to achieve reliability in such a way that it can be specified in the early stages of software architecture design in a platform-independent way. The concept of profiles is suitable for the context of reliability and availability. The R&A properties could be represented in architecture with the help of a profile tailored especially for these two quality attributes. The guidelines in [53] provide a good starting point for this.

10.2.3 R&A Analysis

R&A analysis can be quantitative and qualitative. Quantitative analysis methods tend to combine the architecture behavior with the failure behavior. These methods apply computational methods and calculate, for example, the probability of failure. Qualitative analysis methods rely on the developer's experience and documented design rationale, and they analyze architectural decisions. The analysis methods can also be roughly divided into measurement-based and model-based methods. The measurement-based methods are used for the assessment of the fielded system, and also for the prognostication of systems tested in the laboratory. Model-based methods analyze the reliability of composite software based on the architecture. The model-based quantitative and qualitative analysis methods are the most interesting from the R&A prediction viewpoint because of the architecture centricity.

Methods that use quantitative techniques have been adopted over a longer period of time than qualitative ones. There are several model-based quantitative analysis approaches that address architecture as a composition of logically independent components. These approaches can be classified into analysis methods of three different approaches: state-based, path-based and additive models [20]. The state-based models calculate the component reliabilities and composition reliabilities with the help of the architecture and its behavior and failure behavior. The architectural behavior is modeled as probabilities of the transfer of control between components. The representation techniques of state-based methods are typically the Markov chains. The path-based models compute the reliability of composite software based on the possible execution paths of the system. The representation and modeling technique are the execution graphs, and the combinations of architectural behavior with failure behavior are carried out experimentally. The additive models address the failure intensity of composite software, and therefore are not architecture based. They model the failure intensities with mathematical algorithms, and the system failure intensity can be calculated as the sum of component failure intensities. Examples of model-based quantitative analysis methods are [16,35,52,60]. The state-based and path-based models especially appear to be the most suitable for R&A prediction; however, none of them can be used as such. The diverse analysis methods do not have much in common; they even have different definitions for the basic concepts, such as reliability and architecture. From the R&A prediction viewpoint, the methods described in [52,60] would be the most beneficial, because they analyze the reliability of both components and architecture, also comprising the reliabilities of the connections between components. The assumptions of these methods are that the dynamic behavior of the composite system, as well as the failure behavior of individual components and component interactions are all known.

The qualitative analysis methods can be failure-oriented, analyzing how a software can fail, or they can be based on heuristics, such as the Scenario-Based Architecture Analysis Method (SAAM) [31] and the Architecture Trade-off Analysis Method (ATAM) [32]. ATAM has been especially used for reliability analysis. The purpose of ATAM is to facilitate the selection of an architecture that best supports the quality requirements for all of the stakeholders, with minimal risk and minimal cost. It uses concepts from the decision-making theory, such as the identification of value functions, prioritization and ranking (i.e., weighting) of goals and risks.

10.3 Overview of the RAP Method

The RAP method is an integral part of QADA methodology [40,45,51], specializing its activities in R&A related aspects. QADA bases on the following principles:

– Software product line engineering
– Quality-driven architecture design
– Quality evaluation based on architectural models
– Reuse of existing artifacts and knowledge

In the RAP method, PLE means capturing and mapping the R&A requirements to the product line and system architecture. Quality-driven architecture design is about mapping R&A requirements to architectural views and representing the R&A properties in the architectural models. Quality evaluation consists of the R&A analysis of the product line and system architecture. The RAP method also exploits the existing design knowledge, such as documentation patterns and architectural styles and patterns.

The abstraction levels of QADA enable the separation of the concepts of the required and provided R&A. Required R&A corresponds with the R&A requirements, i.e., what the system has to support. The required R&A is described in the conceptual abstraction level, as mapping the R&A requirements to the conceptual architecture. Provided R&A, however, stands for the R&A that the system implements or offers. This, in turn, is described in the concrete abstraction level when describing the R&A that the concrete architectural elements provide.

The RAP method consists of three main phases (Fig. 10.1). The phases can be applied separately to a product line and its members, as well as to individual systems. Within the lines, the R&A prediction is typically first performed line-specific, after which the prediction concentrates on a line member. Each phase includes several steps, which in turn consists of a set of activities. The phases are:

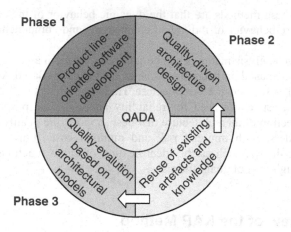

Fig. 10.1. Phases of the RAP method

1. Phase; defining reliability and availability goals, includes five steps
   - Identify stakeholders and their concerns
   - Refine R&A requirements
   - Map R&A requirements to functionality
     (a) Map common requirements to common, line-specific functionality
     (b) Map system-specific requirements to system-specific functionality
   - Select architectural styles and patterns and perform a trade-off analysis
   - Define criteria for a R&A evaluation
2. Phase; representing the reliability and availability in architectural models, includes three steps
   - Represent required R&A in architectural models (separating the line- and system-specific R&A)
   - Map the conceptual architecture to concrete architecture
   - Represent provided R&A in architectural models
3. Phase; R&A evaluation, includes three main steps with different activities. The steps are first used to evaluate line-specific architecture, and subsequently the system-specific architecture
   - Quantitative analysis
     (a) Estimate the reliabilities of the components
     (b) Estimate the R&A of the software system
     (c) Estimate the R&A of the system in its deployment environment
   - Qualitative analysis
     (a) Implement the (bi-directional) requirements tracking and analyze how the R&A requirements are met in the architecture
     (b) Identify potential problems caused by the unfulfilled requirements
   - Decision making based on the analysis

The three phases of the RAP method are described in more detail in Sects. 10.5–10.7. Each section also includes the validation of the phase and the steps with the help of a case example described in the following section.

10.4 Introduction of a Case Example

The validation of the RAP method corresponds to the experimental design evaluation method introduced in [23]. The RAP method is validated by using it to predict the R&A of the case example; a product line that consists of three members. The purpose of this section is to briefly introduce the case example.

DiSep is a distribution platform for a software product line that is formed by executing units in a networked environment. The DiSep platform was first introduced in [40], and ever since has been used as a case study in a number of studies. The platform embodies a service architecture [2,4]; thereby providing a variety of services for its users. The services of the platform are mobile, enabling spontaneous networking. The DiSep platform is used for two or more subsystems that run applications on top of the platform. The hardware of the system, the portable computational devices, are described by means of distributed computing units. Each computing unit, i.e., deployment node, is a platform for various services. The combination of services in different deployment nodes may vary. The platform services can be mandatory, alternative or optional. The platform consists of services of four different domains: *service user interface, system services, basic services* and *communication services*. Computing units, i.e., nodes, join the network spontaneously. They listen to the multicast signals of the network and register themselves to the network using the system services of the node where these services are active. After registration, the services of the network are available through this node, and the services of this node are also available for other users of the network.

The platform services are accessible for user applications through the system service user interfaces. The user interface services are described in Tab. 10.1.

Table 10.1. The user interface services of the DiSep distribution platform

service	responsibility
application service user	enables the use of application services through a directory service interface; enables the application to search for suitable services and to fetch a service proxy
application service provider	enables one to provide application services through a directory service interface; enables applications to create an appropriate service proxy, to register the service proxy to a directory service and to unregister the service proxy from the directory service
lease user	enables users to (re)negotiate for a lease with the provider of the desired service
lease grantor	enables users to grant lease(s) of provided service(s)
transaction manager	enables users to make a request to execute a transaction
transaction participant	enables users to participate in a transaction

System services provide services that are not autonomous, but are activated by the autonomous parts of the platform. System services are mandatory for each node, but they are active only in one node at a time. The services of the other nodes in the network use the system services of the node where they are active. The system services are described in Tab. 10.2.

Basic services provide services that operate autonomously. This domain consists of three sub-domains: controlling services (Activator and Service Allocator service), data management services (Data storage) and location services (Data distribution, Location service, Advertiser and Observer). These are described in Tab. 10.3.

Table 10.2. The system services of the DiSep platform

service	responsibility
lease service	utilizes the lease management between two independent units or other logical elements; accepts and hosts leases of lease grantors. Grants leases for users. Takes care of lease renewals for any leased system resource. Keeps track of lease renewals for any shared and leased resource
directory service	provides a directory service interface to the distributed data storage (active directory service, common to all of the nodes). Registers and unregisters service proxies, keeps track of registered services, searches for requested services and sends a requested proxy for the user. Provides a directory service interface to enable local services (i.e., services in the node) to register and unregister (passive directory service, i.e., local, inside node)
transaction service	performs and tracks transactions in order to reach synchronized operations between elements; prepares, starts, aborts and implements transactions

Table 10.3. The basic services of the DiSep platform

service	responsibility
activator service	monitors the state of the network and controls the system services Activates/deactivates system services of the node when needed
service allocator service	observes the execution, state and allocation of system services and notifies the Activator service about any problems
data storage	permanent data storage. Contains information about the available user services, registered users and allowed leases
data distribution	contributes to the operation of distributed data storage. Creates, maintains and tracks connections to other units in order to share data. Allows data to be stored in local resources. Negotiates about the copying, transferring or deleting data if necessary
location service	sends a notification signal regarding the existence of the node in the network after the given timeframe. Maintains the location map of the network. Sends a signal to the user services of its own node to start the registration when it is connected to the network for the first time. Announce the availability of the system services
advertising service	informs the active system service provider about the availability of the user services of its own node
observing service	routes messages from the network to listeners and forwards asynchronous messages. Routes outgoing messages to the network

Communication services provide messaging services that handle the communication between different units. The communication services are described in Tab. 10.4.

Table 10.4. Communication services of the DiSep platform

service	responsibility
synchronous mediator	creates and maintains connections with the other units, routes incoming and outgoing data
interpreter	encodes/decodes XML (eXtensive Markup Language) messages
asynchronous messaging	creates a mailbox through which the system services may communicate with each other in an asynchronous manner

Most of today's embedded software is based on a three-layer approach that consists of the application, middleware and infrastructure layers. Each of these layers has different stakeholders with different needs, and therefore different R&A requirements as well. The application layer is the closest to the end users of the system, whereas the infrastructure layer is closest to the hardware and is the most dependent of domain technology. The middleware layer is in-between, providing services to the application layer, based on the services provided to it by the infrastructure layer.

The members of the DiSep line can be included in the generic platform services domain [45]. The line includes variants, in this case "middleware systems," for three end user applications; a game, health care application and emergency intervention system. The game application is included in the entertainment category of end user services, and it is used by players across the network that would like to play that game. In order for the game developers to make the game beneficial, it should be readily available for the users and no communication breaks should occur. Reliability requirements are low in this case, because no significant damage can occur in error situations. The health care application is an information-centric application, which handles confidential medical information about patients. Information is read and updated by the medical workers. Because of the sensitive nature and significance of the information, the correctness and accuracy of the information is important. The third application, emergency intervention, is a critical end user service for emergency situations to be used by firemen, police and doctors. Reliability and availability are extremely important attributes of emergency intervention software, because human lives may depend on it.

To assist in the examination of the criticality of reliability and availability for a product line/system, the R&A levels will be defined. The three reliability and availability levels (R&A levels) are described in Tab. 10.5.

Table 10.5. R&A levels

R&A level	level description
level 1	high R&A: Includes systems in which R&A are critical. R&A problems may cause serious damage and danger, both financially and in relation to the safety of human lives. These types of systems are, for example, patient monitoring and fire alarms
level 2	medium R&A: Includes systems to which R&A are important, but not critical. R&A problems may cause small-scale damage. These systems include, for example, mobile shopping and banking
level 3	low R&A: Includes systems to which R&A are valuable, but not urgent. R&A problems do not cause serious damage, but mainly affect human satisfaction regarding the system or service. These types of systems include, for example, games and news

10.5 The First Phase: Defining Reliability and Availability Goals

The purpose of the first phase of the RAP method is to define the R&A goals. This means identifying and negotiating the requirements to find a satisfactory set of requirements that is subsequently brought further into the architecture design. All of the line members share a common product line architecture that provides the basis for the common functionality and quality properties. In addition, each line member embodies its own, system-specific, functionality and quality. Therefore, the product line architecture has to enable architectural variation to some extent. The UML extension approach introduced in [13] provides a profile that describes the variability modeling technique for architectural elements. Also, the approaches presented in Chapters 5–7 can be used to deal with architectural variation.

There may be different kinds of variations in quality among line members. First, there can be variability among different quality attributes. For example, for one member the reliability is important, but unimportant for other members. Second, there may be different priority levels in quality attributes. For example, for one member the reliability requirements are extremely high, whereas for another those requirements are at the lower level (see the R&A levels in Tab. 10.5).

In QADA, the requirements engineering is a generic activity common to all quality attributes. The first phase of the RAP method (see Fig. 10.1) extends this requirements engineering activity of QADA to support R&A concerns specifically. The following guidelines help to identify and refine common and system-specific R&A requirements, perform trade-off analysis, map the R&A requirements to the functional requirements, select an architectural style and define criteria for R&A evaluation.

10.5.1 Description of the Steps of the First Phase

Identifying Stakeholders and Their Concerns. Every new system has several stakeholders– i.e., persons involved in system development. Each stakeholder has his/her own interests regarding the system. Stakeholders can also be responsible for a set of activities, such as requirements specification, architecture design, coding or testing. The goals of the system stakeholders' must be in accordance with all of the interest groups of the product line.

According to [25], stakeholders related to the creation and use of architectural descriptions include the clients, users, architect, developers and evaluators. Bass et al. [3] define the players in a product line organization, that include marketers, customers, and managers that have a direct vision of the core assets group and the product production group of the product line. The interest groups of the line can be refined from these to include:

− Markets: the scope of the product line/system
− Business: economical goals and constraints
− Product line: common assets
− System: system-specific properties

The stakeholders in requirements engineering within a product line can be defined to include the following (Fig. 10.2):

- Markets: customers, end-users
- Business: marketing managers, product line owners
- Product line: product line architects, manager of reusable assets, domain experts
- System: system architects, developers, maintainers and other system development staff
- Other: developers of services/systems/applications that use the system/the part of the system

According to this classification, the stakeholders can be led to different business domains, such as performed in the context of the base station module development in [41].

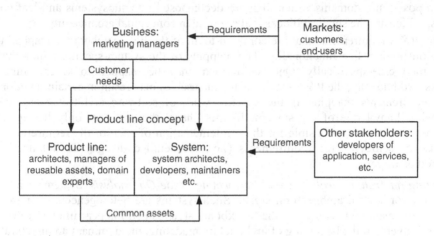

Fig. 10.2. Stakeholders in product line requirements engineering

The requirements of all the stakeholders must be identified and negotiated in order to achieve the final requirements for the system (i.e., the quality goals). In the RAP method, this is implemented applying the i* framework [8]. The i* framework traces the requirements to stakeholders and their dependency relationships, and therefore it is used to identify the stakeholders that have concerns regarding the system and their requirements, and to negotiate these requirements ensuring that all of the stakeholders are satisfied at least to a degree. The i* framework also helps to represent the variability in R&A between different product line members.

Refining Quality Requirements. After the R&A requirements are identified and negotiated, they must be refined to the final requirements of the product line (or the system) that are considered further in the architecture design. The R&A requirements should be expressed in a way that they can be measured. Unfortunately this is not always possible, because R&A requirements can result in certain structures or functionality (e.g., controlling or monitoring services). In that case, the requirements should at least be expressed in a way that they can later be verified in the architecture analysis.

The specification of the final R&A requirements is first performed line-specifically. After the specification of the product line requirements, the specification of requirements is then performed system-specifically. All of the requirements must be provided with the identification numbers. The id numbers of the product line requirements must be distinguished from the system-specific requirements. It is not always possible to implement all of the requirements, for example, due to time or money. Therefore, the importance of each requirement for the system must be defined. The importance is expressed using three classes: high, medium and low.

Mapping R&A Requirements to Functionality. According to QADA, the architecture of the system is first described at the conceptual level. The main functionality (i.e., "what the system does") can be considered as a main force of the conceptual design. The main functionality of the systems is divided into functional blocks. The entire product line is first decomposed into domains which then are decomposed into subsystems and leaf components, which are the smallest blocks that are used in conceptual architecture.

The R&A requirements that are common to all of the line members are mapped to the common product line functionality. The mapping of the system-specific requirements is performed case-specifically. One requirement may be mapped to several functional blocks. Additionally, the R&A requirements themselves may result in certain functionality. The requirements mapping is the specific work of software architects, and requires extensive knowledge of the system. In this phase, the architect only has to decide which services are responsible for the implementation of each of the requirements; the means for achieving the requirements (i.e., the detailed design) do not need to be defined as of yet.

Selecting an Architectural Style and Performing Trade-Off Analysis. Systems can be built from one or several architectural styles. Such systems are heterogeneous. For example, even if the main style is layered the blackboard style can still appear in one of the architectural layers. In the beginning of architecture modeling, the dominant architectural style must at least be selected. When the dominant style is decided upon, the other architectural styles and patterns can be selected for the smaller parts of the architecture where they may be beneficial. According to QADA, the architectural modeling is begun from conceptual architecture. In the conceptual structural view, the functionality (i.e., services or utilities) are organized according to the selected architectural style. The style should be selected carefully by examining how each candidate style can assist in achieving the requirements. The selection of the architectural style is first performed based on product line requirements. The system-specific requirements may sometimes result in different architectural styles. Typically at least the line members on the same R&A level have the same architectural style.

The different R&A requirements set should be transformed to the design decisions/ architectural styles and patterns in a pre-defined way. The different design alternatives can be searched for, for example, from a *style base* [45], that represents the mapping between the quality attributes and design decisions. The style base provides guidance for architects to see what kind of design alternatives there are. It is the responsibility of an architect to choose the best suitable styles and patterns. The choice of these styles and patterns is not necessarily final, but rather iterative, as more exact designs are made later. Furthermore, the style base can provide detailed design patterns. These are not, however, used until the concrete architecture level.

The R&A levels (see Tab. 10.5) of the systems define how important the achievement of the R&A requirements are to that specific system. For example, in the high R&A level, the reliability and availability of the system must be guaranteed using the best possible design techniques. The cost and effort of the design is normally higher in the case of high R&A level systems, whereas in the case of normal and low R&A level systems the simpler and inexpensive design techniques are used. Based on the literature, Tab. 10.6 provides an example of the use of styles and patterns to support reliability and availability. Although none of the styles, except Simplex ABAS, specially focus on software reliability, they still can provide some minor qualities that support R&A in a smaller context.

Table 10.6. Guidelines for making architectural decisions

R&A level	architectural style or pattern	design pattern/technique/means
level 1	Simplex ABAS style: redundancy in general master-slave pattern: fault tolerance, parallel computation, computational accuracy	fault tolerance: static redundancy (N-modular redundancy (NMR), error correcting codes) dynamic redundancy (reconfigurable NMR, backup sparing, recovery block)
level 2	event based styles: message manager element object oriented styles: independent (protected) entities implicit invocation style: system level fault handling	fault tolerance: passive redundancy (backup copy) fault treatment: error detection (e.g., duplication, error detecting codes, checksums), error handling, recovery block (back-up plan in error situations) facade design pattern: reduced complexity of interaction between subsystems observer design pattern: observing component proxy design pattern: data reliability
level 3	layered style: handling of lower level's errors by higher level black-board style: independent processing components, control component, good data availability	fault avoidance: use of reliable components and allocation requirements to several components fault treatment: error detection (e.g., error detecting codes, watch-doc timers), recovery of the failed component proxy design pattern: data reliability broker architectural pattern: disconnection of logical services from physical locations

There is always a risk that the R&A requirements will conflict with other quality requirements. This might even result in all of the important requirements not being met in the architecture. For example, redundancy is a means for achieving high reliability, but redundancy takes a lot of physical resources in which case reliability conflicts with performance. The purpose of the trade-off analysis is to guarantee the best requirements set considering all of the quality requirements. The NFR framework is one method for the negotiation of various conflicting quality attributes and evaluating the criticality of quality requirements [9]. The NFR framework is a process-oriented approach that treats quality requirements as soft-goals (i.e., the quality goals) to be achieved. Using the NFR framework, the requirements with the affected stakeholders can be renegotiated and a solution can be found that makes acceptable trade-offs for all of the stakeholders. One of the shortcomings of the NRF framework is, however, that the R&A support of the styles is defined based on the architect's knowledge and the literature. Thus, the style base is required to support the work of the architects.

In the RAP method, the NFR framework is used to detect which of the styles supports the product line requirements best. Also the system-specific requirements can be examined using the framework. A different architecture style can be selected for a member in case the style selected for the line does not support the system-specific requirements. The conflicting requirements can be handled using a domain specific correlation catalogue [9] introduced in Tab. 10.13. The conflicts are illustrated using the following types: *make, help, hurt* and *break*. *Make* represents the situation where the requirement is met in the architecture. *Help* provides partial positive support for meeting the requirement. *Break* means that the requirement is not met in the architecture, whereas *hurt* means that the architecture can in fact be considered to be used even if it does not satisfy the requirements. It is the duty of software architect to specialize the correlation rules using domain information. As a consequence of the trade-off analysis, the resulting problems of the analysis must be identified and solved.

Defining Criteria for R&A Evaluation. In PLE, the product line requirements are on the highest priority level. These requirements must be met in the architecture in any case. Thus, the R&A evaluation of the product line architecture is first performed at the high level product line requirements, after which at the medium level and finally the low level requirements. If the requirements common to all of members are met, the system-specific requirements can be evaluated starting from the requirements of high importance. Therefore, in the RAP method, the R&A evaluation criteria are categorized into four evaluation levels, see Tab. 10.7.

Table 10.7. R&A evaluation levels

evaluation level	evaluation criteria
level 1	product line R&A requirements
level 2	system-specific R&A requirements of high importance
level 3	system-specific R&A requirements of medium importance
level 4	system-specific R&A requirements of low importance

10.5.2 Applying the Steps to the Case Example

Step 1: Identifying Stakeholders and R&A Requirements. The stakeholders in the case of the DiSep product line are the following:

- Product line architect: common functional and quality requirements
- System architect: system-specific functional and quality requirements
- End users of the application that use the middleware: end user requirements
- End user application developer: application specific requirements, application interfaces

The i* framework [8] represents a graph called the Strategic Dependency model that enables the description of actors and their dependencies in organizational settings. Figure 10.3 describes the requirements definition using the framework for the three members; middleware for a game application (system 1), health care application (system 2) and emergency intervention application (system 3). Circles in the i* framework correspond to stakeholders, rectangles to the required functionality and ellipses to the R&A requirements. The arrows describe the dependencies. The line-specificity is highlighted in grey.

End users of the application that use the final middleware system are described on the left of Fig. 10.3. End users require an application, for which they also have R&A requirements. Application developers (in the middle of the figure) are responsible to ensure that the application fulfills the end user's requirements. The end user's requirements for the application may reflect indirect requirements for the middleware. Thus, the application developer requires a middleware system for the application and he/she also defines the R&A requirements for the middleware from the application point of view. Product line architect (in the middle of the figure) defines the functional and quality requirements (in this case; the R&A requirements) for the middleware that are common to all of the members. The system architects (on the right of the figure) take all of these requirements as inputs when designing the system architecture. He/she refines the stakeholders' requirements to the final R&A requirements.

The variation in R&A requirements of three members can be discovered in Fig. 10.3. From now on, this example concentrates on the description of the line-specific parts and, for simplicity, only one member. This still enables the identification of line-specific R&A, as well as variable, system-specific R&A.

Fig. 10.3. Variability in R&A requirements between product line members

Step 2: Refining the Quality Requirements. Table 10.8 represents the refined requirements from the product line architects viewpoint. Reliability related requirements are identified with an "R" and identification number as well as the availability requirements with an "A" and identification number. For each requirement the stakeholder is specified. The importance of the requirement is expressed using the "high, medium, and low" scale.

Table 10.8. The R&A requirements from the product line architect's point of view

req. ID	requirement description	stakeholder	importance
R2.1	middleware services are able to recover	product line architect	high
R5	data consistency is verified in every 5 seconds	product line architect	low
R6	data is replicated at least in 2 data storage	product line architect	medium
R7	data may not be lost in failure/error situations	product line architect	medium

The system-specific requirements for the middleware system for *emergency intervention application* are described in Tab. 10.9. The system identification symbol, S3 (i.e., system 3) is attached to the requirements' identification number to separate the different line members.

Table 10.9. The R&A requirements from the system architect's point of view

req. ID	requirement description	stakeholder	importance
A1-S3	the system service availability is 99%	end user of application	high
A2-S3	connections between nodes is ensured	end user of application	high
R1-S3	the probability of failure is not over 0.01	end user of application	high
R2.2-S3	recovery time of the middleware services is 3 seconds	end user of application	medium
R3-S3	number of lost messages must be 0	application developer	high
R4-S3	data must always be correct	application developer	high
R8-S3	back-up plan for fault situations	application developer	high
R9-S3	monitoring of service failing or booked up	application developer	high
A3-S3	the negotiation of service user and service provider should not take more than 0.1 seconds	application developer	medium
A4-S3	the great amount of users may not slow down the use of the service	application developer	medium

Step 3: Mapping R&A Requirements to Functionality. Figure 10.3 describes the variation in R&A requirements of the three members. The variation in functionality between the members is described in Tab. 10.10. According to Tab. 10.10, system 1, the middleware for game application, is a system with light functionality, whereas system 3, the middleware for emergency intervention application, has full functionality.

Table 10.11 describes the mapping of the line-specific R&A requirements to the conceptual components (i.e., services) of the product line architecture. The mapping of the system-specific requirements of the middleware system for emergency intervention application is described in Tab. 10.12. Thus, the responsible services for the requirements implementation are specified. In this phase, the architect does not have to decide how the requirements are implemented.

Table 10.10. Variability in functionality between line members

service category	variable services		system 1	system 2	system 3
communication	synchronous mediator		mandatory	mandatory	mandatory
services	asynchronous messaging		optional	optional	mandatory
	interpreter		mandatory	mandatory	mandatory
basic services	activator		mandatory	mandatory	mandatory
	service allocator service		–	optional	mandatory
	observer		mandatory	mandatory	mandatory
	advertiser		–	optional	mandatory
	data storage	local	–	alternative	mandatory
		remote	–		mandatory
	data distribution		mandatory	mandatory	mandatory
	location service		mandatory	mandatory	mandatory
system services	directory service		mandatory	mandatory	mandatory
	lease service		–	mandatory	mandatory
	transaction service		–	optional	mandatory
service user	lease user		mandatory	mandatory	mandatory
interface	lease grantor		mandatory	mandatory	mandatory
	transaction manager		optional	optional	mandatory
	transaction participant		–	optional	mandatory
	application service user		–	mandatory	mandatory
	application service provider		optional	mandatory	mandatory

Table 10.11. Mapping product line R&A requirements to functionality

R&A req.	corresponding service
R2.1	all of the involved basic, system and communication services
R5	data distribution
R6	data distribution, Location service
R7	data distribution

Step 4: Trade-Off Analysis and Selecting the Architectural Style. The NFR framework represents a graph called the soft-goal interdependency graph (SIG) that represents "soft-goals" (i.e., the nonfunctional requirement to be achieved) and the interdependencies among them. Figure 10.4 describes the graph including two attributes of the DiSep product line, reliability and performance, that are represented at the top of the graph. Two reliability requirements, service capability to recover and data replication are refined on a more accurate level. Service recovery can be backward, when the service rolls back its operations to an error-free state prior to the error occurrence, or forward when a new correct state is constructed from the state at the failure. Data replication can be replication for a local unit or remote unit. Performance is divided into space performance and time performance. The former means applying resources, such as secondary storage, and the latter means, for example, response time or throughput. The importance of the required property is described with + and – signs (three signs at maximum).

Table 10.12. Mapping system-specific R&A requirements to functionality

R&A req.	corresponding service
A1-S3	lease service, directory service, transaction service, service allocator service, location service, activator
A2-S3	synchronous mediator service, asynchronous messaging service
R1-S3	all basic, system and communication services
R2.2-S3	all basic, system and communication services
R3-S3	synchronous mediator service, asynchronous messaging service
R4-S3	synchronous mediator service, asynchronous messaging service, observer, interpreter, data distribution
R8-S3	data distribution, location service
R9-S3	service allocator service
A3-S3	service allocator service, location service
A4-S3	lease grantor, service allocator service

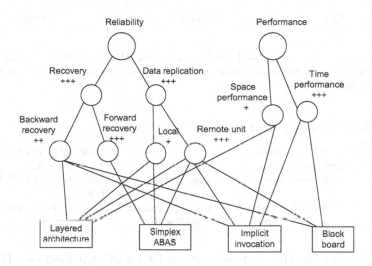

Fig. 10.4. Use of the NFR framework in style selection for the DiSep product line

As can be seen in Fig. 10.4, the data replication in the remote unit and forward recovery are very important reliability requirements for the DiSep product line. At the bottom of the graph the candidate architectural styles are identified and a line is drawn between a requirement and a style if the style supports the requirement. In the layered style, software is divided into horizontal layers where each layer provides a set of services to its higher levels [10]. The Simplex ABAS addresses the problem of how to take advantage of redundancy to increase reliability, and introduces the concepts of redundant components, acceptance tests and a decision and switch unit [33]. In the implicit invocation style, software is organized into components that generate events and a message manager that manages communication [3]. The blackboard style assumes a central data repository and a set of active components that use this repository. In this case, based merely on the reliability requirements, the Simplex ABAS would be the best architectural alternative. Time performance is an important requirement that is not met if Simplex ABAS is selected; therefore it can be said that performance conflicts with reliability.

Table 10.13 describes the trade-off resolving activity of the conflicting attributes. The estimation of the conflict types, i.e., make, help, hurt and break, is done based on the architect's knowledge about the different styles (in this case; based on the literature). Based on this trade-off analysis, the layered style is the best architectural choice and it is therefore selected.

Table 10.13. Resolving trade-offs using a correlation catalogue

goal style	reliability (backward recovery) ++	reliability (forward recovery) +++	reliability (data replication, local) +	reliability (data replication, remote) +++	performance (space) +	performance (time) +++
layered	helps	helps	helps	helps	helps	hurts
Simplex ABAS	breaks	makes	makes	helps	hurts	hurts
implicit invocation	helps	hurts	hurts	helps	helps	helps
black board	helps	breaks	breaks	helps	breaks	helps

Step 5: Defining Criteria for R&A Evaluation. Table 10.14 describes the mapping of the R&A requirements for the middleware system of the emergency intervention applications to the evaluation levels.

Table 10.14. Classification of reliability and availability requirements

evaluation level	evaluation criteria	corresponding requirement
level 1	product line-specific requirements	R2.1, R5, R6, R7
level 2	high level system-specific requirements	A1-S3, A2-S3, R1-S3, R3-S3, R4-S3, R8-S3, R9-S3
level 3	medium level system-specific requirements	R2.2-S3, A3-S3, A4-S3
level 4	low level system-specific requirements	–

Table 10.15 describes the evaluation criteria for the DiSep product line. These criteria are derived from the first evaluation level of Tab. 10.14; from the product line requirements.

Table 10.15. Criteria for evaluation of the DiSep product line

evaluation criteria	Req. ID	Importance	impacted architectural elements
service capability to recover	R2.1	medium	all basic, system and communication services
data consistency verification	R5	medium	data distribution
data loss prevented in error situations	R7	medium	data distribution
data replication	R6	low	data storage, data distribution, location service

10.6 The Second Phase: Representing Reliability and Availability in Architectural Models

The second phase of the RAP method (see Fig. 10.1) provides guidelines for how to model R&A in software architecture in a way that the R&A analysis can be performed directly from the architecture. The abstraction levels of QADA are used in R&A modeling in two ways. First, the required R&A of the system is described at the conceptual level, and second, the provided R&A of the system is described at the concrete level. Because reliability and availability are closely related, they are no longer separated at the architecture level. R&A appears in architectural models in two ways:

- R&A aspects, i.e., dimensions with values, are attached to architectural elements
- R&A requirements result in certain design decisions and functionality

To formally quantify different aspects of R&A, dimensions are needed to represent the metrics for the R&A aspects in architecture. These dimensions and their values respond to the tagged values of UML. Tagged values are pseudo attributes that can be assigned to UML model elements in the form of a pair "tag = value" [5,37]. The RAP method defines profiles for representing R&A aspects in architectural models using the tagged values, i.e., R&A dimensions and values. The required profile corresponds to the R&A requirements, and the provided profile is the R&A that the system offers. The dimensions here (Tab. 10.16) are applied partly from [34,48]; the rest of them are defined to support the needed R&A concepts identified in this study. The dimensions are mainly aimed at software and software components, but some of them are also applicable for hardware. One requirement can be distributed to several dimensions, and correspondingly, one dimension may include several requirements.

When the R&A requirements result in certain design decisions, such as structures or particular components, the design decision should be documented. Especially the qualitative analysis relies on documented design rationale. If the design rationale is documented and there is a mapping between each design decision and reliability and availability requirements, it can be verified that the requirements are met in the architecture level.

10.6.1 Description of the Steps of the Second Phase

Mapping Required R&A to Conceptual Architectural Elements. After the architectural style is selected at the conceptual architectural level, the R&A requirements are brought to the architectural models with the help of the required R&A profile that consists of dimensions that are defined in Tab. 10.16.

Table 10.16. Reliability and availability dimensions

dimension	value	description
MTTF	time	mean time to failure
fault treatment:	time, type,	prevents faults from being activated again. Error
error detection	technique/	detection helps avoiding catastrophic consequences
recovery	means	caused by errors. Recovery describes how the failed
repair		component is brought from the erroneous state to an error-free state
		repair defines how a failed component can be repaired
availability:	time, percentage,	the capability of being available when needed
service availability	means	
operation availability		
control		
Probability of failure	numeric value	estimated/known reliability
Control	means	control defines how to ensure avoidance of errors, faults and possible problems
Data:	percentage,	data reliability: the capability of data being available
Availability	means	when needed, being consistency, correct and integrate.
Consistency		The reliability of data transfer
Correctness		
Transfer reliability		
Integrity		
Fault tolerance:	number, time	fault tolerance is the capability of the system to
Max-number of faults		continue providing correct service even if a fault has
Redundancy		occurred

The requirements are first mapped to the dimensions, after which they are attached to architectural elements in the structural and deployment views. This means that the requirements are transformed to the required responsibilities of the architectural elements (i.e., the components and connectors). In architecture, the required R&A guides the design of concrete architecture and helps to make the design decisions. By mapping the R&A requirements to the system behavior in behavioral view, the requirements have an influence on the dynamic aspects of the system. The fourth view of QADA, i.e., the development view, is used in the RAP method only to organize the design work.

Structural view. The static relationships of the components are represented in the conceptual structural (and deployment) views. The structural view is used for the encapsulation of quality requirements as the responsibilities of components or restricted parts of architecture. The mapping of each R&A requirement to functionality was performed when defining the quality goals. This enabled the tracing of requirements to architecture. Now, vice versa, all of the related R&A requirements are defined for each architectural element. This enables bi-directional requirements tracing; from architecture to requirements. Using UML 2.0, the static structure of the system can be represented, for example, using a component diagram or composite structure diagram.

The conceptual architectural level defines the "required" properties, and therefore, the R&A requirements are attached to components and connectors with the help of a required R&A profile. Typically, in the required profile the exact means and techniques to implement the requirements are not yet defined, but the profile helps to define what is required from the system and its elements. The R&A requirements and design rationale are written inside the architectural elements (i.e., components/services and connectors).

Behavioral view. The behavioral view helps one to understand the dynamic aspects of the system. The view represents the dynamic relationships of components. According to QADA, the behavior of the system is described at the conceptual level as abstract descriptions of a collaboration that describe the interactions between components. The collaboration scenarios are derived from the functional responsibilities, but the quality requirements can also raise the functionality and collaboration between components. For example, fault tolerance can create a complicated collaboration scenario. The R&A requirements are mapped to these scenarios, or they can cause new scenarios. From the viewpoint of R&A prediction, the scenario modeling must begin from the scenarios that involve product line R&A requirements, continuing then according to the evaluation levels defined in Tab. 10.14.

When modeling the product line scenarios, the different usage profiles must be taken into account. Different tasks of the systems, i.e., use cases, can be employed in different ways in the case of different usage profiles. The idea behind the usage profiles is that different users (e.g., human or other services) can have different frequencies in implementing different use cases which will affect the overall frequency for each use case. In addition, the different users can have different ways to execute a use case. The different usage profiles have a great concern within the frequency of executing each component and each interaction between the components, and therefore they form a complex point of view when estimating system failure behavior. The different usage profiles must be identified and the system behavior must be described according to each of these profiles.

Deployment view. The conceptual deployment view allocates units of deployment to physical computing units. In the deployment diagram, components are described as deployment nodes or units of deployment with types, and relationships as is-allocated-to relationships. The required R&A is denoted by attaching requirements to nodes and relationships.

Development view. The conceptual development view does not itself assist in the R&A representation. The view helps to detect which component and services have to be developed, which can be found in the asset repository and the ones that have to be bought.

Mapping from Conceptual to the Concrete Architecture. When mapping the R&A requirements to the conceptual architecture, the results of the requirements are reflected in the concrete architecture. The traceability of the requirements to the conceptual architecture and the concrete architecture must be ensured. Conceptual components, i.e., services, are more logical modeling elements than concrete implementation components. Thus, one conceptual service may result in several concrete components, or one concrete component may contribute to the implementation of one or more conceptual services. The mapping between conceptual and concrete architecture must be documented to trace the R&A requirements to the concrete architectural level. Table 10.6 can be used again when considering design decisions and design patterns.

Mapping Provided R&A to Concrete Architectural Elements. The provided R&A means the R&A that the system offers, and can therefore signify the means and techniques for implementing the R&A requirements or, commonly, the numerical R&A values that the system elements provide. The concrete view is used in the R&A analysis and is therefore especially tailored to the needs of the analysis. The provided R&A are mapped to the R&A dimensions (described in Tab. 10.16) and are represented in the concrete architecture using the concrete structural and deployment views. In the architecture, the provided R&A guides the design of concrete components or represents the properties of the existing components (i.e., components in the asset repository or COTS components) that can be used. The behavioral view assists in the modeling of the behavior of the components and the systems. The development view refines the allocation that is defined in the conceptual development view to concrete components.

Structural view. The concrete structural view is used to describe the concrete components and interfaces needed for corresponding conceptual architecture. Therefore, the view decomposes the conceptual architecture into lower aggregation levels. The component diagram or composite structure diagram is used in order to describe the structure of the system. The provided R&A is attached to the architectural elements using the same dimensions as in conceptual levels. Due to the R&A analysis, it is important that at least the value for the probability of failure is attached for each component and connector. The probability of failure is a calculated value that provides a measure of reliability for a component or system. The value for the failure probability is between 0 and 1, because the value 0 stands for failure free operation. The provided means for achieving certain requirements are defined on the concrete level.

The concrete structural view also reveals the interfaces of the components. Interfaces must be described in a way that enables the estimation of the interoperability of components. Interoperability is the capability of the service to use the information exchanged with other services, and provide something new that has originated from it, and therefore the R&A of the interfaces can be estimated by examining the component interoperability. An example of an architectural level interface description is given in [27].

Behavioral view. In a concrete behavioral view, the state diagrams or message sequence diagrams can be used to describe the interactions between components. In RAP, the state diagrams are used to derive a model for calculating the probability of failure of a component. Therefore, for each new component, a state diagram must be defined to describe the internal states and state transition. The message sequence diagram is used to derive input messages for simulation-based R&A analysis. Also, the activity diagram is required to derive a model for the simulation. An activity diagram typically represents the operational workflows of a system. These models are described in more detail in Sect. 10.7.2 in the context of quantitative R&A analysis.

Deployment view. The concrete deployment view describes the concrete hardware and software components, the relationships between the hardware components, and the relationships between the software and hardware components. However, the RAP method concentrates only on software systems; therefore this portion is limited.

Development view. The concrete development view links the architectural views to the repository of common assets. Thus, the components that already exist can be linked to the concrete components that they realize.

10.6.2 Applying the Steps to the Case Example

Step 1: Mapping Required R&A to Conceptual Architectural Elements. Table 10.17 presents the related R&A requirements of each architectural element. The R&A requirements

Table 10.17. The related R&A requirements for architectural elements

service	product line requirement	system-specific requirements
lease service	R2.1	A1-S3, R1-S3, R2.2-S3
directory service	R2.1	A1-S3, R1-S3, R2.2-S3
transaction service	R2.1	A1-S3, R1-S3, R2.2-S3
activator	R2.1	A1-S3, R1-S3, R2.2-S3
service allocator service	R2.1	R1-S3, A1-S3, A3-S3, A4-S3, R9-S3, R2.2-S3
data storage	R2.1	R1-S3, R2.2-S3
data distribution	R2.1, R5, R6, R7	R1-S3, R2.2-S3, R4-S3, R8-S3
location service	R2.1, R6	R1-S3, A1-S3, R2.2-S3, A3-S3, R8-S3
advertiser	R2.1	R1-S3, R2.2-S3
observer	R2.1	R1-S3, R2.2-S3, R4-S3
synchronous mediator	R2.1	R1-S3, A2-S3, R2.2-S3, R3-S3, R4-S3
asynchronous messaging	R2.1	R1-S3, A2-S3, R2.2-S3, R3-S3, R4-S3
interpreter	R2.1	R1-S3, R2.2-S3, R4-S3
lease grantor	–	A4-S3

Table 10.18. Mapping R&A requirements to dimensions

req. ID	requirement description	related service	dimension & value
R9-S3	monitoring of service failing or booked up	service allocator service	availability: control (system services)
R5	data consistency is verified in every 5 seconds	data distribution	data: consistency = 5 seconds
R8-S3	back-up plan for fault situations	data distribution	fault tolerance: redundancy (data)
		location service	fault tolerance: redundancy (data)

are mapped to the R&A dimensions and thereafter represented in the structural view of the architecture. An example of the mapping is given in Tab. 10.18.

Figure 10.5 describes the conceptual structure of the *middleware of the emergency intervention applications*. The model (Fig. 10.5) illustrates the separation of product line R&A and variable, system-specific R&A. The middleware system embodies the layered architectural style, as it is divided into horizontal layers. The R&A requirements are written inside architectural elements. For visibility, they are shown in the model as notes. The grey colored highlights the product line requirements. When a note is attached to a domain, the requirements involve all of the services of the domain. The design rationale are written in the documentation fields of the elements and are readable when the element is double-clicked.

The end user applications; the game, health care and emergency intervention applications, have different requirements for the middleware and this has led to three variant middleware systems. In a connection of a certain middleware system, the different user profiles are not shown because the middleware services operate the same way no matter who the user is. When defining the product line scenarios, however, the different

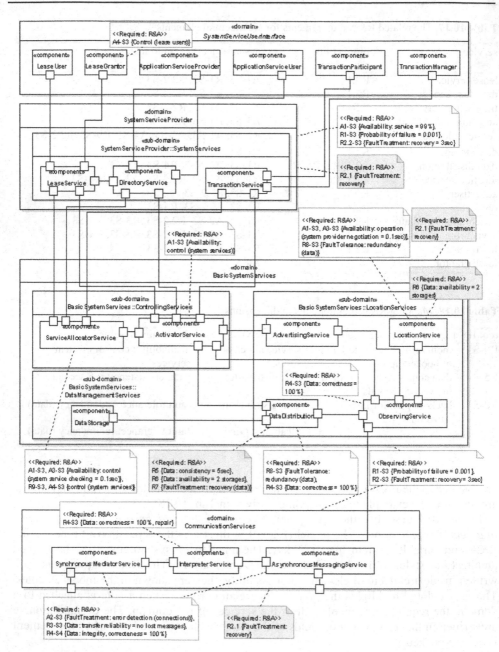

Fig. 10.5. Conceptual structural view with common and variable R&A requirements

scenarios are defined when the user is a game application or an emergency intervention application. Table 10.19 describes the R&A related scenarios for the product line.

Figure 10.6 describes a collaboration scenario of the middleware (Scenario 1 from Tab. 10.19). The Service Allocator service monitors the state of the Lease service and notifies the Activator service to deactivate the Lease service when the Lease service is jammed. The activator service informs the Location service to mark the system services of this particular node passive. After this, the Location service sends a normal beacon signal regarding the availability of this node. As the Location services of other nodes receive this signal, they notice that the active system service tag is missing from the signal. The node that is the first on the system service provider list activates the system services of its own.

Table 10.19. Example of R&A related product line collaboration scenarios

scenarios	R&A req.	services participating the scenario
1. Lease service is jammed, and continued in other unit	R2.1	service allocator service, lease service, activator service, location service, observing service
2. Directory service saves the data to the local database every 5 seconds wherefrom data is replicated every 5 seconds	R6, R7	directory service, data distribution, data storage, location service, observing service, synchronous mediator service
3. Data consistency and correctness is verified	R5, R6	data distribution, data storage, location service, observing service, synchronous mediator service

The deployment view is represented in Fig. 10.7. The basic and communication services are always active in each node, but the system services are active only in one node at a time. The user interface services are optional. The DiSep system consists of equal units that are networked spontaneously. This prevents the use of a centralized fault tolerance mechanism, such as a separate controlling and monitoring unit. The R&A requirements are especially directed to the communication between the nodes, and therefore, the requirements involve the network properties, or they result in design decisions in the end points of the connector. The requirements are the same for each connector because the nodes are equal. In the deployment view, nodes represent the hardware components.

All of the components of the system are to be developed from scratch, because no similar components exist in the repository.

Step 2: Mapping from the Conceptual to the Concrete Architecture. In the case of DiSep, the mapping from the conceptual architecture to the concrete architecture is straight-forward; one concrete component responds one conceptual component. As an example, the design rationale of the basic system service components are described in Tab. 10.20.

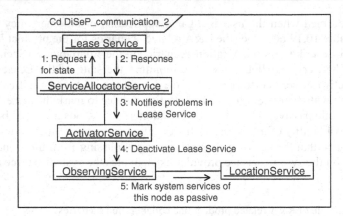

Fig. 10.6. Conceptual behavioral view: a description of a collaboration scenario

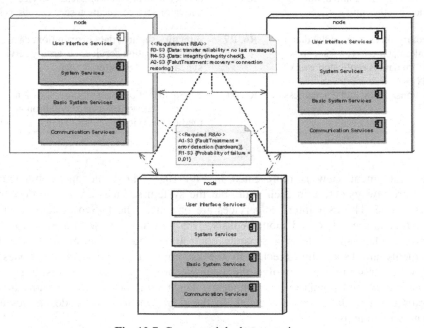

Fig. 10.7. Conceptual deployment view

Step 3: Mapping Provided R&A to Concrete Architectural Elements. Figure 10. 8 describes the concrete structure of the Basic Services domain. The system services and communication services domains are represented as packages. For simplicity, each of the domains are described in separate diagrams. The value for component's probability of failure is mandatory for the R&A analysis. If this value does not exist, e.g., in the case of a new component, it is estimated using the Markov chains model. The use of the Markov chains model is the first activity of the quantitative analysis when estimating the reliability of a component as an independent unit. The Markov chains model is further described in the next section.

Table 10.20. The design rationale of concrete components of basic system services

concrete element (component)	design rationale	R&A requirement
activator component	activates and deactivates system services. Enables the recovery of service execution in other unit	R2.1, A1-S3, R1-S3, R2-S3
service allocator component	monitors the system services. If the services fail or the response is too slow, informs the activator to switch the unit	R2.1, R1-S3, A1-S3, A3-S3, A4-S3, R2.2-S3, R9-S3
data storage	permanent data base (local)	R2.1, R1-S3, R2.2-S3
data distributor component	assists data storage. Keeps redundant data storages consistent and up-to-date	R2.1, R5, R6, R7, R1-S3, R2.2-S3, R4-S3, R8-S3
location service component	informs when the node is connected to the network and sends notification message about availability of node. Maintains the network map. Keeps a list of available system services in order of superiority (the active services are tagged). Announces the active system services. Notifies the Activator to activate system services when needed	R2.1, R6, R1-S3, A1-S3, R2.2-S3, A3-S3, R8-S3
advertising component	informs the active system services about the availability of user services of the node	R2.1, R1-S3, R2.2-S3
observing component	route incoming and outgoing messages	R2.1, R1-S3, R2.2-S3, R4-S3

The models of the behavioral view, i.e., the state diagram, the message sequence diagram and the simulation model derived from the activity diagram, are described in more detail in Sect. 10.7.2, because these are needed in the quantitative R&A analysis. The reliability analysis of hardware is a large research field and therefore out of the scope of this study. This study concentrates purely on the analysis of software product lines and therefore the provided R&A in the deployment view is not modeled. Moreover, because all of the components of the system are developed from scratch, no link to the repository of the common assets is needed.

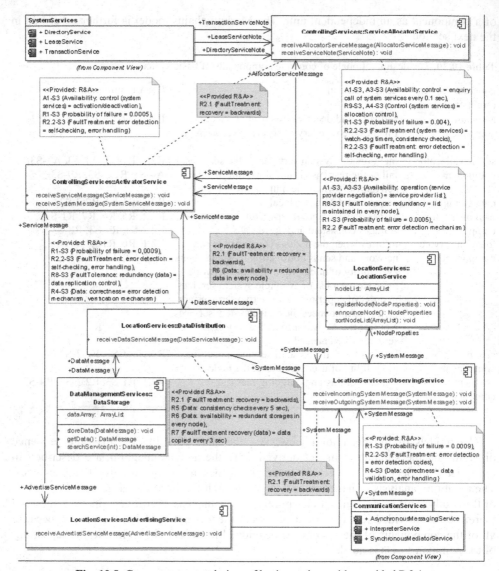

Fig. 10.8. Concrete structural view of basic services with provided R&A

10.7 The Third Phase: Evaluating Reliability and Availability

The third phase of the RAP method (see Fig. 10.1) is about analyzing the architecture to validate whether or not the R&A requirements are met. The R&A evaluation is performed using the quantitative and qualitative analyses. The quantitative R&A analysis compute the failure behavior of a system based on its structure in terms of composition (i.e., components and their interactions), the failure behavior of the components and the failure behavior of their interaction. This analysis requires that the structure of the system is known, both the static aspects represented by its components and the dynamic aspects represented by the frequency of executing each component and each interaction between components. The quantitative approach also assumes that the failure behavior of the components and component interactions are known. The possible fault tolerance mechanisms must also be taken into account when computing composed R&A values. From a computational point of view, the fault tolerance mechanisms will reduce the probability of the failure of the system. Qualitative analysis is complementary to the quantitative one and can be applied without knowing the failure behavior of components. The analysis consists of reasoning the design decisions (e.g., styles, fault tolerance and recovery mechanisms) and their support for the R&A requirements.

10.7.1 Description of the Steps of the Third Phase

Quantitative Analysis. Reliability and availability are execution qualities, and therefore they can be analyzed from the behavior of the system at run-time. Because the systems are not fielded yet, the simulation is needed to represent the execution of the system. The quantitative analysis consists of the state-based and the path-based analysis. Both of them result in the probability of the failure of the composite software, and they use architecture and failure behavior as inputs for the analysis.

The RAP method uses the state-based models to analyze component reliabilities. State-based models are usually represented by Markov chains that consist of the states, i.e., externally visible modes of operation that must be maintained, and the state transitions labeled with system inputs and transition probabilities. These kinds of models can be used even if the source code for the component is not available. The input of the methods is the software architecture and its behavior and its failure behavior. The failure behavior comprises the probabilities of the failure of components and transitions.

Path based models are used to analyze the reliability of the system with the help of the execution paths. In addition, the path-based analysis enables one to specify, with the help of the simulation, the reliability estimations of component. The path-based models consider all of the possible system execution paths with frequencies, and their computed reliabilities, as the basis of a reliability model. Paths are either extracted from component execution traces (i.e., real simulation), or identified during the system design phase (i.e., scenario-based simulation). The system level reliability is obtained from a weighted sum (based on usage frequencies) of path reliabilities.

The quantitative analysis of the RAP method consists of three activities (Fig. 10.9): The first activity is to estimate the component reliability, the second activity is to estimate software reliability based on the reliabilities of components, and the third is to estimate the reliability of the system reliability including the hardware components.

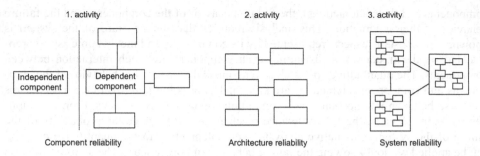

Fig. 10.9. The activities of quantitative analysis

The First Activity: Estimate Component and Connector Reliability. Independent component: A component is first considered as an independent unit, when separated from the architecture. We assume that components already exist or they need to be developed. Reliability values or failure rates of components are not likely known in the design phase. When using existing components (e.g., from the repository or third parties), the value of the failure behavior of components may already be known, based on previous execution of the components. Components should therefore be documented in a way that assists their quality estimation, such as [56]. The execution environment of a component affects its failure behavior, so the value for the failure behavior may be something else in a new environment. In the case of newly developed components, the values of failure and interaction behavior must be estimated prior to implementing these components. There are several techniques that have been proposed to estimate the reliability of components, such as [16,59]. These, however, base on existing components and the data attained through testing. The first activity includes the following tasks:

1. Estimate the probability of failure of the independent component. If the component is new, create a Markov chain model that represents both component failures and the usage of components between failures [57] and calculate the estimated probability of failure of a component. The Markov chain model is derived from the state diagram of a component by adding the failure state and probabilities of the state transitions [57]. By applying the Chapman-Kolmogorov equation [50], the static probabilities of states are calculated for each state of the components. The probability of failure of the component is defined as a probability of being in the failure state. For an existing component (in-house, COTS, OS), the value for the estimated probability of failure should be found from the component documentation.
2. Refine the achieved value with other factors that have an affect on R&A. There are several factors that have an influence on the reliability and availability of a component. The most common are described in Tab. 10.21. Each of these factors gives a share in the overall estimation of probability of failure. The estimation of these factors requires a comprehensive knowledge about the component (cf. qualitative analysis).
3. Estimate the probability of failure of the connectors. Estimate the reliability of connectors based on the type of connection (i.e., local/remote, wired/wireless, etc.).

Estimate the probability of the correct operation of components, i.e., interoperability of components through the connector. The concrete structural diagram and interface descriptions assist in interface evaluation.

4. Add the estimated reliability values to the concrete structural diagram. The estimated values must be added to the architectural models for R&A calculations.

Table 10.21. R&A related properties of a component

component property	description
size/estimate size	the lines of code or the estimated lines of code can be used to estimate fault occurrence in a component
(planned) implementation technology	compliers, machine instructions, the need of wrappers, the use of "safe languages," etc.
required processing time	how much the component requires physical resources and processing time. A resource and time consuming component is prone to hardware faults, and hardware availability affects on the service availability
third-party involvement	is the component third-party, open source or in-house. This determines if the documentation and code are available, the modifications allowed, test cases available, etc.
interfaces (provided, required)	the more interfaces the component has, the more possibilities there are for the component to fail to interact with other components
coverage of testing	how well the component has been tested; the coverage of testing and availability of test documentation
(planned) fault tolerance	does the component embody some fault tolerance technique to detect, mask and recovery from failures

Results: The estimated probability of failure (i.e., reliability) of independent components.

The First Activity: Estimate Component and Connector Reliability. Dependent component: Considering a component as a dependent unit, its reliability is affected by the surrounding components. In addition, the usage stresses components, and therefore, the usage of a component affects its reliability [16]. The more the component is used, the more likely its probability of failure increases. By predicting the R&A for each component separately, components with low R&A can easily be detected from the architecture and changed to more reliable ones.

The R&A estimation of components is performed by way of the system simulation that helps to detect how components are used in a system and how they communicate with each other. Simulation also helps to detect the critical components and the components with low R&A values. The simulation requires as inputs the message diagram and the simulation model. It also needs the values of the estimated probability of failure of the components for the calculations. This includes the following tasks:

1. Simulate the system. It is not always possible or rational to simulate the entire system. Therefore, the simulated part of the system must be defined
   - *Define the input messages for simulation.* The input messages are defined in the message sequence diagram, starting from the product line-specific messages. An input message represents an information container for simulation comprising data

objects involved in transactions between components. It is up to the architect to define the messages in a way that the simulation covers the system execution described in collaboration scenarios. Therefore, the messages are defined based on the collaboration scenarios. The order and density of messages must be tracked from the functional and R&A requirements. The architect also has to define the occurrence probability for each message and take that account in a message sequence diagram. The timeframe for the simulation must be comprehensive enough to cover the normal execution of the system and to reveal the most used execution paths and their frequencies. In the input message definition, the evaluation levels must be taken into account. The first round of the evaluation consists of product line requirements. An example of the product line scenarios was illustrated in Tab. 10.19. The messages that relate these requirements are used as first input for the simulation.

– *Build the simulation model.* The simulation model of the system is constructed based on the concrete structural diagram and the collaboration diagrams. The simulation model (see Fig. 10.12) is derived from the activity diagram, consisting of the object nodes, decision nodes and message flows between them. The decision nodes include the message handling and decision making unit. This enables the simulation of the actual system behavior. Simulation starts when a component receives an input message. For each input message, the simulation reveals a component sequence path.

– *Run the simulation.* The messages are given as inputs for the simulation. The simulation model is run through according to each message.

2. Based on the simulation, define and calculate
   – Execution paths of the system
   – Probability of each path execution
   – Frequency of each component execution in each path execution, and
   – Frequency of each connector execution in each path execution.

3. Calculate the probability of the failure of components in an execution path. The estimated probability of failure of a (independent) component is combined with the amount of the use of the component in a path execution. The result is the path-specific probability of failure of a component. The formula for the probability of the failure of component in the execution path is applied from [12].

4. Calculate the probability of failure of connectors in an execution path. The probability of failure of connectors is calculated in the same way as the components. The result is the path-specific probability of failure of a connector.

5. Calculate the probability of failure of components and connectors in all of the execution paths that they are involved in. Each path-specific probability of the failure of a component is multiplied with the probability of a path execution (i.e., weighted path-specific probability of failure). Finally these values are summarized. The probability of failure of connectors is calculated in the same way. The result is a refined reliability of each component and connector (in the entire system execution, i.e., in all of the execution paths).

6. Add the specified reliability values to concrete structural diagram for further calculations.

Results: The refined probability of failure of components, i.e., the probability of the failure of components in the surrounding environment. Probability of failure of connectors.

The Second Activity: Estimate Software System Reliability. After the component and connector reliabilities are defined, they are used to calculate the software system level reliability. The second activity includes the following tasks:

1. Compute the reliability of individual paths. The path reliability is the specified reliabilities of components and connectors involved in a path [19,35]. The result is the probability of failure of an execution path.
2. Calculate the software reliability. The reliability of the software is a weighted average of reliabilities of all the paths [55]. For each path, the probability of a path execution is multiplied with the probability of failure of a path. Finally, the probability of failure of each path is summarized.

Results: Probability of the failure (i.e., reliability) of the software.

The Third Activity: Estimate System Reliability (in Deployment Environment). The system consists of hardware and software. When deploying the software on deployment nodes, the entire system reliability can be estimated. The third activity includes the following tasks:

1. Determine the reliability of the hardware. Hardware components are represented as nodes. Define the reliability, availability and adequacy of hardware components, such as physical devices (i.e., computational resource having memory and processing capability). The reliability of the hardware components in the deployment environment can be determined from previous use (experiences) or testing.
2. Define the reliability of hardware/software component combination. Allocate the software components into nodes/devices and define the reliability for the combined hardware and software components.
3. Define the reliability of the network (between nodes). The reliability of the network is affected by network protocols, security, etc.

Results: The reliability of the entire system.

This study concentrates purely on the analysis of software product lines; therefore the third step is out of the scope of the analysis.

Qualitative Analysis. The qualitative analysis relies on documented design rationale that must be included or accompanied in the architectural models. If this is not the case, then the analysis relies heavily on the architects' tacit knowledge. By analyzing and reasoning about one architectural solution, the qualitative analysis provides assurance to the architect that the requirements have been addressed in the design. By analyzing different architectural solutions for the same requirements, the analysis provides an evaluation of the degree to which they address the requirements and it also allows to compare different architecture candidates and recommend one for the solution.

The process of qualitative analysis can be partly automated, for example, by automating the report generation. The main parts of the analysis still require a human analyzer. The qualitative analysis is about tracking the R&A requirements. The bi-directional requirements tracking means tracking the requirements to the architecture and the properties of the architecture to the requirements. The tracking is performed based on the requirement numbers that are associated to architectural elements using the required R&A and provided R&A profiles. The required R&A profile maps the requirements to the architecture at the conceptual level and the provided R&A profile describes how these requirements are taken into account at the concrete level. Therefore, the qualitative analysis verifies that each requirement has been taken into account in the architecture design. When analyzing the architecture and its components, the tracking is performed vice versa; from concrete architecture to the conceptual and furthermore to requirements.

Design rationale can be associated with individual components, with individual connections, and a set of components and their connections. The analyzer compares the design decisions with the R&A requirements and analyses how those requirements are met in the architecture. The analyzer also has to decide if the requirements are met sufficient enough, and to examine how to meet requirements better and how well all of these decisions work together. For comparing two different architectures, the qualitative analysis must be performed for each of the designs, and thereafter a numerical indicator for the coverage of requirements is used, but also human judgment regarding the proposed solutions has to be applied.

Fault tree analysis (FTA) is usually used in qualitative analysis to determine what are the points of the system that may cause system failure [15]. In the RAP method, the FTA is used to identify problems that may occur when certain R&A requirements are not met in the architecture. Thus, the FTA helps the architect to pay attention to the parts of the architecture that require an enhancement to meet the R&A requirements in this particular architecture, without changing the architectural style.

FTA introduces a fault tree that is a deductive, top-down method for analyzing and documenting the potential causes of system errors. The use of the fault tree involves specifying a top event to analyze, followed by identifying all of the associated elements in the system that could cause that top event to occur. Fault trees are generally performed graphically using a logical structure of AND/OR gates. The problem areas identified need to be analyzed separately in order to identify corrective actions to reduce or solve the problems.

Decision Making Based on the Analysis. If the result of the qualitative and/or quantitative R&A analysis reveals that the particular architecture is not sufficient enough for the reliability and availability requirements, the architect has two choices:

1. Keep the architecture and decrease the probability of the failure of components and their interactions. This can be performed by
   - Choosing components with higher reliability (if available)
   - Implementing higher reliable components by eliminating software defects in their implementation (by defect detection techniques, e.g., inspections and testing)
   - Deploying software on more reliable hardware
2. Change the architecture by
   - Using different architectural styles and patterns, and
   - Introducing new mechanisms, for example, for fault tolerance and fault treatment.

The RAP method enables that the reliability and availability analysis can be performed quickly and repeatedly for each architectural choice. The results of the analyses of different architectural choices must be evaluated against R&A evaluation criteria and against each other. Human analysis is required to decide which architectural alternative meets the requirements best.

10.7.2 Applying the Steps to the Case Example

Step 1: Quantitative Analysis. The values for probability of failure of components are estimated by the Markov chains model after which the simulation is executed to refine these values and to calculate the software reliability.

The First Activity: Estimate Component and Connector Reliability. Independent Component: The probability of failure of each component is calculated from the Markov chain model. Figure 10.10 describes the Markov chain model of the Location service component. The model is constructed from the state transition diagram by adding the failure state and probabilities of state transitions. These probabilities base on the architect's estimations and knowledge. The rounded rectangles describe the states where the component can be and the arrows describe the transitions between the states. The failure state describes a failure of a component and the occurrences of failure states are identified with failure events (transitions to the failure state).

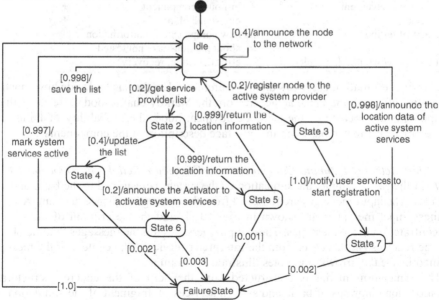

Fig. 10.10. Markov chain model of the location service

By applying the Chapman-Kolmogorov equation, the estimated probability of being in a state can be calculated for each state. The Location service consists of seven normal states and one failure state. Table 10.22 describes the probabilities of each states. Thus, the probability of failure for the Location service is 0.0005.

Table 10.22. Probabilities of states of Location service component

state 1	state 2	state 3	state 4	state 5	state 6	state 7	failure state
0.4543	0.1817	0.0909	0.0727	0.0727	0.0363	0.0909	0.0005

The achieved probability of failure of the component is evaluated together with the other properties of the component to achieve the total estimation for the reliability of the component. Table 10.23 shows the evaluation of the Location service component. Values for each property are examined component-specifically, after which it is estimated how these values affect the component R&A. The used extents are: affects positively (+), neutral (0) and affects negatively (–).

Table 10.23. R&A evaluation table of the Location service component

component property	value	effect on R&A
size/estimated size	small, about 400 LOC	+
implementation technology/planned implementation technology	Java	+
required (estimated) processing time	1 ns	0
third-party involvement	in-house component	+
interfaces	one standard interface	+
coverage of testing	new component, no information about previous use, not tested	–
fault tolerance/planned fault tolerance	error detection, recovery	+

The final estimation is always up to the architect. He/she has to decide how much these properties affect on the value achieved from the Markov chains model. Because all of the components are located in the same deployment node, the probability of failure of the connectors is estimated based on the interface description of the components.

The First Activity: Estimate Component and Connector Reliability. Dependent Component: In the case example, the simulation of the system is restricted to the basic and system services. The input messages are retrieved from the message sequence diagram. A fragment of these input messages are shown in Fig. 10.11, and the description of the simulation concentrates on these messages. These input messages are the messages that the observing service receives (in this case; from the interpreter service). The context of the messages is defined inside the arrows, and notes illustrate the examples.

The simulation model is constructed with the help of the concrete structural and collaboration diagrams of basic and system services. A fragment of the simulation model is shown in Fig. 10.12. The rectangles describe the object nodes (in this case; components), the diamond shapes describe the decision nodes and the arrows describe the message flows. The rounded rectangle describes the activity element, where the system can change the message (described in figure as a note).

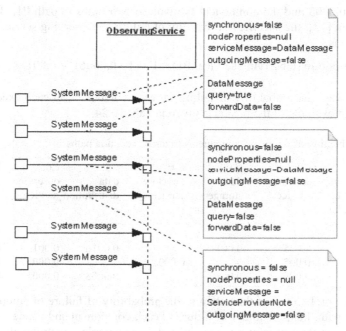

Fig. 10.11. Input messages for the system simulation

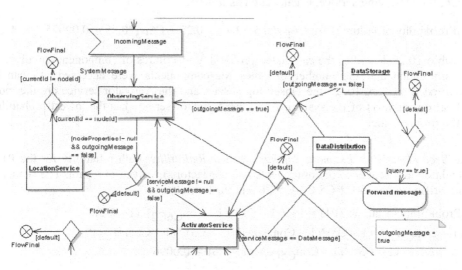

Fig. 10.12. A fragment of the simulation model

After the simulation has been run, the execution paths and their probabilities are defined. In addition, the density of a component and a connector execution is defined. For each component, the estimated reliability value (independent component) is specified with the value achieved from the simulation. The same is performed for the connector values. For example, the estimated probability of failure of the Observing service (as an independent component) is 0.0005 and the component is involved two times in path P1. By applying the formula from [12], the specified probability of failure of Observing service in an execution path (P1) is:

$$\text{Probability of failure (Observing service, P1)} = 1 - (1 - 0,0005)^2 = 0,001. \tag{1}$$

In the same way, the probability of failure for each component in each execution path is calculated. An example of the results is given in Tab. 10.24.

Table 10.24. Probability of failure of components in three execution paths

component	C1: application service provider	C2: activator service	C3: data storage	C4: directory service	C5: data distribution	C6: observing service	Path probability
Path							
P1	–	0.005	0.001	–	0.0016	0.001	0.5
P2	0.0011	0.005	–	0.0008	–	0.0005	0.25
P3	–	0.005	0.001	–	0.0008	0.0005	0.25

Basing on the probability of the path and the probability of failure of components and connectors in a path, the probability of failure of each component and connectors in all of the paths (i.e., in system execution) is calculated. For example, the probability of failure of C6, the Observing service, is calculated as follows:

$$\text{Probability of failure (C6): } C6_{p1}*0.5 + C6_{p2}*0.25 + C6_{p3}*0.25 = 0.00075. \tag{2}$$

Table 10.25 describes the calculated probability of failures of components involved in the simulation and the number of times the components were accessed. As can be observed from Tab. 10.25, the Observing service and the Activator service are the most critical components of the system. Also, the Activator service has the lowest probability of the failure value.

The Second Activity: Estimate Software System Reliability. Path reliability for the P1 is calculated as a sequence of components and connectors involved in a path. The sequence is identified to be C6-C2-C5-C3-C5-C6 and the formula is:

$$\text{Probability of failure (P1)} = 1 - ((1 - C6)*(1 - Con_{C6C2})*(1 - C2)* \tag{3}$$
$$(1 - Con_{C2C5})*(1 - C5)*(1 - Con_{C5C3})*(1 - C3)*(1 - Con_{C3C5})*$$
$$(1 - C5)*(1 - Con_{C5C6})*(1 - C6)) = 0.0096.$$

Table 10.25. Predicted probability of failure of components of the system

comp. ID	component	accessed	probability of failure
C1	application service provider	1	0.000275
C2	activator service	5	0.005
C3	data storage	3	0.00075
C4	directory service	1	0.000125
C5	data distribution	5	0.001
C6	observing service	8	0.00075

The sequence of the path P2 is C6-C2-C4-C1 and probability of failure is accordingly 0.0065. The sequence of the path P3 is C6-C2-C5-C3 and the probability is failure is 0.00347. Therefore, the probability of failure of the software system is calculated as:

$$\text{Probability of failure(system)} = \text{Probability of failure(P1)}*\text{Path probability(P1)} + \text{Probability of failure(P2)}*\text{Path probability(P2)} + \text{Probability of failure(P3)}*\text{Path probability(P3)} = 0.0073. \qquad (4)$$

The Third Activity: Estimate System Reliability (in Deployment Environment). The R&A analysis of the system including hardware has not been applied to the case example, because it has to be applied to the hardware selected to each product.

Step 2: Qualitative Analysis. The qualitative analysis is about bi-directional requirements tracking. Tables 10.26 and 10.27 illustrate the requirements tracking.

Table 10.26. Tracking the requirements to conceptual and concrete architecture

R&A requirement	conceptual level	concrete level
R5: data consistency is verified in every 5 seconds	*data distribution service* negotiates about data copies, transfers and deletions with other units	*data distribution component* includes a timer that starts data copying procedure every 5 seconds in the node of active system services
R6: data is replicated at least in 2 data storages	*data storage* is mandatory for each node. *Location service* of each node maintains location data independently	each node includes a data storage that is continuously updated by the *data distribution* component. *Location service* of each node maintains the list of system services independently

Table 10.27. Tracking from the architecture to requirements

concrete level	conceptual level	R&A requirement
data distribution component: Assists data storage. Control of redundant data.	*data distribution service*: Contributes to the operation of distributed data storage. Creates, maintains and tracks connections to other units in order to share data. Enables data to be stored in local resources. Negotiates about the copying, transferring or deleting the data if necessary	R2.1, R5, R6, R7, R1-S3, R2.2-S3, R4-S3, R8-S3
location component: Multicast signal sending and receiving. list of available system services.	*location service*: Informs about the existence of the node and services. Maintains network map. Keeps track of the available system services	R2.1, R6, R1-S3, A1-S3, R2.2-S3, A3-S3, R8-S3

The architect decides how well the requirements are met in the architecture. If the analysis reveals that certain requirements are not met in the architecture, the fault tree analysis is used to identify problems that may arise. Figure 10.13 describes an example of the fault tree analysis when it is detected that the requirement R5 is not met. The top event (the root) is the resulting problem of the unfulfilled requirement. The root is the fault in data replication, and the lower levels describe the problems that may result in the top fault event. The architect can use the tree to see the problem areas, pay attention to avoid the potential problems and fulfill the requirement in this architecture, without changing the architectural style.

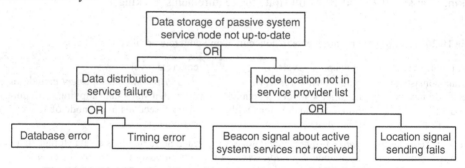

Fig. 10.13. Identification of a problem caused by an unfulfilled R&A requirement

Step 3: Decision Making. The quantitative analysis resulted to a numerical value for the probability of failure of the software system. This value was 0.0073. As the required probability of failure was 0.01 at the most, it can be concluded that the requirement R1-S3 is met in the architecture. The qualitative analysis revealed that all of the requirements have been taken into account in the architecture in a satisfactory manner. The architect can now decide to keep the architecture, but he/she must pay more attention to components with low probability of failure values, for example, by introducing new fault treatment mechanisms.

10.8 Discussion

The main idea of the RAP method is to compare different architectural solutions by predicting their reliability and availability. Several candidate architectural solutions can be identified for the defined requirements that implement these requirements in different ways. The RAP method can be used to validate which candidate supports the R&A requirements best. The phases and steps of the RAP method can be applied to the R&A prediction of a product line and individual systems.

The RAP method was developed especially for product lines, and therefore it supports PLE enabling the prediction of the reliability and availability of product line-specific parts separately from the system architecture. Thus, the product line requirements need to be evaluated only once, as long as the architectural style remains the same. The first phase of the RAP method enables the separation of product line and system-specific requirements and describing variability between members. It also assists in mapping the product line requirements to the product line architecture and the system-specific requirements to the system architecture. The different evaluation levels help to define the criteria for R&A evaluation. The second phase helps to represent the required and provided R&A in architectural models with the help of the R&A profiles. The phase helps to transform the R&A requirements to the required responsibilities of the architectural elements, which are then transformed to the provided R&A properties that the system expresses. Finally, the third phase helps evaluate R&A from the architectural models. The evaluation is performed according to evaluation levels, the first evaluation level especially concentrates on product line-specific parts.

The RAP method was validated by an experiment that simulated the use of the RAP method in the case of the DiSep product line. The phases of the RAP method were applied simultaneously to a product line and a product line member. However, the used frameworks, design and evaluation methods and techniques enabled the separation of product line and system-specific aspects. Because reliability and availability are execution qualities, the variable requirements involved the structural and behavioral aspects of the architecture. The R&A requirements typically led to some structures or functionalities. Therefore, variations in the R&A requirements between members may result in the different design decisions considering the architectural style, components and component collaborations. For example, for emergency services the high service availability and recovery were required and could be achieved by using an architectural solution that enabled the back-up service execution. For entertainment services (i.e., the game) the service availability needed only to be medium rate and thus could be ensured, for example, by modifying components to implement a recovery mechanism. Thus, the variable R&A requirements affected the entire architecture design of different members.

The validation of the RAP method revealed that the method supported each of the phases, i.e., requirements engineering, architecture modeling and R&A analysis, well and did not require much extra work from the architect. More so, it helped to organize the work of the architect and also helped him/her to concentrate on essential activities when engineering reliable and available systems. After the requirements engineering, the architect only had to map the R&A requirements to the architectural views and represent them in the architectural models using the R&A profiles, then he/she could make the design decisions and select means and techniques as usual. Therefore, the RAP method ensures that the requirements are actually taken into account when making the design decisions. In the evaluation phase, the required models for the analysis could be easily derived from the architectural models that the architect was required to define anyway. The RAP method guided specifically how to do the analysis.

The results achieved in R&A evaluation using the RAP method assisted and supported the software architect in making the decisions based on the evaluation. The results from the quantitative analysis helped to identify the critical components of the system execution that require special attention. Also, the results enabled one to see which components are low reliability and availability and should therefore be changed or improved. Furthermore, the architect was able to see the behavior of the system with the help of the execution paths and thus identify the possible bottlenecks of the system. The achieved probability of failure of the system can be used as numerical indicator when comparing the candidate architectures. The qualitative analysis can change the predicted values of the quantitative analysis. For example, the use of fault tolerance and fault treatment techniques positively effects the R&A values. Also, it is the responsibility of the architect to make a judgment on the appropriateness of each design decision. Thus, the architect has to provide estimations how much the capabilities of the system affect on the achieved R&A values.

To provide benefits in the system development, the R&A prediction should be able to be performed quickly, easily and cost-effectively for each candidate architecture. Therefore, tool support is required for the RAP method to automate and quicken the activities of the architect. A tool for the R&A prediction to support the RAP method has been defined in [26]. The tool – RAP tool – assists in representing R&A in architectural models and in R&A analysis. For R&A representation, a commercial architecture modeling tool was selected and extended with the needed R&A profiles. This tool had to support UML 2.0 [49] that provides enhanced architectural descriptions, supporting the required structural descriptions of the systems. Also, the tool had to support the views of QADA to enable the adequate architecture representation. In addition, the modeling tool had to be easily extensible and include open interfaces to enable the profile creation and interoperation with a separate R&A analysis tool. The developed R&A analysis tool supports the quantitative R&A analysis automating the simulation and R&A calculations. The tool support helps to achieve the numerical indicators. However, the evaluation of these results still requires a human analyzer.

To compare different architectural solutions, the modeled architecture should be able to be transformed from one style to another. Model transformation is about converting one model to another model of the same system [43]. The transformation process consists of identifying the quality attributes that are not fulfilled, identifying the locations where the attribute is inhibited, selecting the most appropriate transformation and performing the transformation [6]. The MDA support of the RAP method enables the platform independent architecture description, i.e., the conceptual architecture that is needed when transforming from a style to another. A technique has been defined for quality-driven architecture model transformation for software product lines [38] that can be applied within the RAP method when modeling candidate architectures. To allow for a fast model transformation, a tool support, such as introduced in [42], is required.

10.9 Conclusions and Future Research

The contribution of this chapter is the RAP method – a method for predicting reliability and availability from the architectural models. The RAP method is directed especially to product lines, but it can be applied to the individual systems as well. The R&A prediction requires changes to all of the system development phases from requirement engineering to architectural analysis. The RAP method consists of three phases: (1) Defining reliability and availability goals, (2) Representing reliability and availability in architectural models, and (3) R&A evaluation. Each phase includes a set of steps that further consist of activities.

The first phase of the RAP method describes how to identify the requirement sources, how to refine stakeholders' concerns to R&A requirements and how to negotiate the requirements to find the best possible set of requirements that is further brought to the architecture design. In addition, the phase guides how to map the R&A requirements to functionality and select the architectural styles and patterns. Finally, the phase helps to define criteria for R&A evaluation. The second phase guides how to map R&A requirements to architectural views and represent the R&A properties in the architectural models. The R&A properties are represented in the architecture with the required and provided R&A profiles. The required R&A guides the architecture design and helps to make the design decisions. The provided R&A represents the decided design decisions and thus provides the guidelines for the system implementation. Both profiles enable the tracking of requirements to architectural decisions and, vice versa. The third phase regards evaluating the R&A of the product line or systems from the architectural models. The evaluation consists of quantitative and qualitative analysis. The quantitative analysis produces the probability of failure at the component and architecture levels. The qualitative analysis is about tracking the requirements to examine how these are met in the architecture. The result of the RAP method is a predicted reliability and availability of the software system or product line.

The validation of the RAP method revealed that the RAP method is suitable in the context of PLE, enabling to predict the R&A of the product line and its members. The RAP method provides the techniques, methods and guidelines for R&A prediction at the architectural level. At this moment, the validation of the RAP method bases only on an experiment. More validation is required to refine the RAP method to be used systematically in PLE. The next phase is to use and apply the RAP method in industrial settings to see how suitable it is for the use of industrial software architects who have a strong experience with the architecture modeling and quality analysis. The use of the method in the context of real system engineering in industrial environments also helps to identify the future development needs and required improvements.

Some targets for future development and the required supporting concepts have already been identified during the development of the RAP method. It is still needed to have a controlled selection of architectural styles and patterns that promote reliability and availability in the architecture. At this moment the selection of architectural style is performed pretty much based on the architect's opinion and knowledge that typically base on the literature and experience. The RAP method provides a slight guideline for making design decisions (Table 10.6). A style base, such as introduced in [45], can formalize the style selection. The style base should connect each style with the quality attributes it promotes, and describe how and what level the quality attribute is promoted. At this moment rare styles and patterns support reliability and availability. Therefore, new styles and patterns are required that concentrate on these two quality attributes.

Acknowledgments

This work was carried out at VTT, the Technical Research Centre of Finland, within the ITEA project ip02009, FAMILIES, as part of the Eureka Σ! 2023 Programme. This work was guided and commented on by Eila Niemelä from VTT. Timo Käkölä from the University of Jyväskylä and Juan Carlos Dueñas from the Technical University of Madrid provided valuable comments.

References

1. America, P., Obbink, H., van Ommering, R., van der Linden, F.: CoPAM: a component-oriented platform architecting method family for product family engineering. In: *Software Product Lines, Experience and Research Directions*, ed by Donohoe, P., Proceedings of the 1st Software Product Lines Conference (Kluwer, Dordrecht 2000) pp 167–180
2. Barry, D.K.: *Web Services and Service-Oriented Architectures: The Savvy Manager's Guide* (Morgan Kaufmann, Los Altos, CA 2003)
3. Bass, L., Clements, P., Kazman, R.: *Software Architecture in Practice* (Addison-Wesley, Reading, MA 1998)
4. Bennett, K., Layzell, P.J., Budgen, D., Brereton, L., Munro, M.: Service-based software: the future of flexible software. In: Proceedings of the Asia-Pacific Software Engineering Conference (IEEE Computer Society, Los Alamitos, CA 2000) pp 214–221
5. Bondavalli, A., Majzik, I., Mura, I.: Automatic dependability analysis for supporting design decisions in UML. In: Proceedings of the 4th IEEE High Assurance System Engineering Symposium. (IEEE Computer Society, Los Alamitos, CA 1999) pp 64–71
6. Bosch, J.: *Design and Use of Software Architectures: Adopting and Evolving a Product-Line Approach* (Addison-Wesley, Reading, MA 2000)
7. Buschmann, F., Meunier, R., Rohnert, H., Sommerland, P., Stal, M.: *Pattern Oriented Software Architecture. A System of Patterns* (Wiley, New York 1996)
8. Chung, L., Gross, D., Yu, E.: Architectural design to meet stakeholders requirements. In: The 1st Working IFIP Conference on Software Architecture (Kluwer, Dordrecht 1999)
9. Chung, L., Nixon, B., Yu, E., Mylopoulos, J.: *Non-Functional Requirements in Software Engineering* (Kluwer, Dordrecht 2000)
10. Clements, P., Northrop, L.: *Software Product Lines: Practices and Patterns* (Addison-Wesley, Reading, MA 2002)
11. Clements, P., Kazman, R., Klein, M.: *Evaluating Software Architecture: Methods and Case Studies*, 1st edn (Addison-Wesley, Reading, MA 2002)
12. Cortellessa, V., Singh, H., Cukic, B.: Early reliability assessment of UML based software models. In: 3rd International Workshop on Software and Performance (Association for Computing Machinery 2002) pp 302–309
13. Dobrica, L., Niemelä, E.: Using UML notation extensions to model variability in product line architectures. In: ICSE, International workshop on Software Variability Management (2003) pp 8–13
14. Douglass, B.P.: *Doing Hard Time: Developing Real-Time Systems with UML, Objects, Frameworks, and Patterns* (Addison-Wesley, Reading, MA 1999)
15. Dugan, J.B.: Software system analysis using fault trees. In: *Handbook of Software Reliability Engineering*, ed by Lyu, M.R. (McGraw-Hill, New York 1995) pp 615–659
16. Everett, W.: Software component reliability analysis. In: IEEE Symposium on Application – Specific Systems and Software Engineering and Technology (IEEE Computer Society, Los Alamitos, CA 1999) pp 204–211
17. Frankel, D.: *Model Driven Architecture, Applying MDA to Enterprise Computing* (Wiley, New York 2003)
18. Garlan, D., Shaw, M.: An introduction to software architecture. In: *Advances in Software Engineering and Knowledge Engineering* (World Scientific, Singapore 1993) pp 1–39
19. Gokhale, S.S., Trivedi, K.S.: Dependency characterization in path-based approaches to architecture-based software reliability prediction. In: Proceedings of the IEEE Workshop on Application-Specific Software Engineering Technology, ASSET-98 (IEEE Computer Society, Los Alamitos, CA 1998) pp 86–89

20. Goseva-Popstojanova, K, Trivedi, K.S. Architecture-based approach to reliability assessment of software systems. Perform. Eval. **45**: 179–204 (2001)
21. Rational Software Corp.: UML Profile for EJB. In: *Public Review Draft JSR-000026*, ed by Greenfield, J. (2001)
22. Grünbacher, P., Egyed, A., Medvidovic, N.: Reconciling software requirements and architectures with intermediate models. Softw. Syst. Model. **3**: 235–253 (2003)
23. Hevner, A.R., March, S.T., Park, J., Ram, S.: Design science in information system research. MIS Q. **28**: 75–105 (2004)
24. Hofmeister, C., Nord, R., Soni, D.: *Applied Software Architecture* (Addison-Wesley, Reading, MA 1999)
25. IEEE: IEEE Std 1471-2000. Recommended Practice for Architectural Description of Software-Intensive Systems (Institute of Electrical and Electronics Engineers, New York 2000)
26. Immonen, A., Niskanen, A.: A tool for reliability and availability prediction. In: Proceedings of the 31st Euromicro Conference on Software Engineering and Advanced Applications (IEEE Computer Society, Los Alamitos, CA 2005) pp 416–423
27. Immonen, A., Holappa, J., Kallio, P., Kalaoja, J.: Towards interoperability of wireless services – a description model of service interfaces. In: Proceedings of the IADIS International Conference WWW/Internet 2004 (2004) pp 983–988
28. ISO/IEC: ISO/IEC 9126-1 International Standard: Software Engineering – Product Quality. Part 1: Quality Model (2001)
29. Jaaksi, A., Aalto, J.-M., Aalto, A., Vättö, K.: *Tried & True Object Development: Industry-Proven Approaches with UML* (Cambridge University Press, Cambridge 1999)
30. Jazayeri, M., Ran, A., van der Linden, F. *Software Architecture for Product Families* (Addison-Wesley, Reading, MA 2000)
31. Kazman, R., Abowd, G., Bass, L., Clements, P.: Scenario-based analysis of software architecture. IEEE Softw. 47–55 (1996)
32. Kazman, R., Klein, M., Barbacci, M., Longstaff, T., Lipson, H., Carriere, J.: The architecture tradeoff analysis method. In: The 4th IEEE International Conference on Engineering of Complex Computer Systems (IEEE Computer Society, Los Alamitos, CA 1998)
33. Klein, M., Kazman, R., Bass, L., Carriere, J., Barbacci, M., Lipson, H.: Attribute-based architecture styles. In: The 1st Working IFIP Conference on Software Architecture (Kluwer, Dordrecht 1999)
34. Koistinen, J.: Dimensions for reliability contracts in distributed object systems. Technical report HPL-97-119, October 3, Hewlett-Packard (1997)
35. Krishnamurthy, S., Mathur, A.P.: On the estimation of reliability of a software system using reliabilities of its components. In: Proceedings of the 8th International Symposium in Software Reliability Engineering (IEEE Computer Society, Los Alamitos, CA 1997) pp 146–155
36. Kruchten, P.: The 4+1 view model of architecture. IEEE Softw. **12**: 42–50 (1995)
37. Leangsuksun, C., Song, H., Shen, L.: Reliability modeling using UML. In: Proceedings of the International Conference on Software Engineering Research and Practice, vol 1 (CSREA, Athens, GA 2003) pp 259–262
38. Matinlassi, M.: Quality-driven software architecture model transformation. In: Proceedings of the 5th Working IEEE/IFIP Conference on Software Architecture (IEEE Computer Society, Los Alamitos, CA 2004)
39. Matinlassi, M., Kalaoja, J.: Requirements for Service Architecture Modeling in Workshop of Software Modeling Engineering of UML2002, Dresden, Germany (2002)
40. Matinlassi, M., Niemelä, E., Dobrica, L.: *Quality-Driven Architecture Design and Quality Analysis Method, A Revolutionary Initiation Approach to a Product Line Achitecture*, VTT Publication 456 (VTT Technical Research Centre of Finland, Espoo 2002)
41. Matinlassi, M., Pantsar-Syväniemi, S., Niemelä, E.: Towards service-oriented development in base station modules. In: *Service-Oriented Software System Engineering: Challenges and Practices*, ed by Zoran, S., Ajantha, D., vol 2 (Austrian Society for Cybernetic Studies, Vienna 2004) pp 440–444
42. Merilinna, J.: *A Tool for Quality-Driven Architecture Model Transformation.* VTT Publication 561 (VTT Technical Research Centre of Finland, Espoo 2005)
43. Miller, J., Mukerji, J.: MDA Guide, version 1.0.1 (Object Management Group 2003)
44. Ncube, C., Maiden, N.: COTS software selection: the need to make tradeoffs between system requirements, architectures and COTS/components. In: Proceedings of 2nd International COTS Workshop: Continuing Collaborations for Successful COTS Development, ICSE-2000, Limerick, Ireland (2000)
45. Niemelä, E., Kalaoja, J., Lago, P.: Towards an architectural knowledge base for wireless service engineering. IEEE Trans. Softw. Eng. **31**: 361–379 (2005)
46. Object Management Group: Unified modeling language (UML), version 1.5 (2002)
47. Object Management Group: UML profile for schedulability, performance, and time specification (2003)

48. Object Management Group: UML profile for modeling quality of service and fault tolerance characteristics and mechanisms. Revised submission (2003)
49. Object Management Group: Unified modeling language (UML), 2.0 Specification (2003)
50. Papoulis, A.: *Probability, Random Variables, and Stochastic Processes*, 2nd edn (McGraw-Hill, New York 1984)
51. Purhonen, A., Niemelä, E., Matinlassi, M.: Viewpoints of DSP software and service architectures. J. Syst. Softw. **69**: 57–73 (2004)
52. Reussner, R.H., Schmidt, H.W., Poernomo, I.H.: Reliability prediction for component-based software architectures. J. Syst. and Software **66**: 241–252 (2003)
53. Rodrigues, G.N., Roberts, G., Emmerich, W., Skene, J.: Reliability support for the model driven architecture. In: Proceedings of Workshop on Software Architecture for Dependable Systems, ICSE-2003 (2003) pp 7–12
54. Shaw, M., Garlan, D.: *Software Architecture: Perspectives on an Emerging Discipline* (Prentice-Hall, Englewood Cliffs, NJ 1996)
55. Shooman, M.: Structural models for software reliability prediction. In: Proceedings of the 2nd International Conference on Software Engineering (1976) pp 268–280
56. Taulavuori, A. Niemelä, E., Kallio, P.: Component documentation – a key issue in software product lines. Inform. Softw. Technol. **46**: 535–546 (2004)
57. Thomason, M.G., Whittaker, J.A.: Rare failure-state in a Markov chain model for software reliability. In: Proceedings of the 10th International Symposium on Software Reliability Engineering (IEEE Computer Society, Los Alamitos, CA 1999) pp 12–19
58. van der Linden, F.: Software product families in Europe: the ESAPS & CAFÉ projects. IEEE Softw. **19**: 41–49 (2002)
59. Voas, J.M.: Certifying off-the-shelf software components. Computer **31**: 53–59 (1998)
60. Yacoub, S., Cukic, B., Ammar, H.: Scenario-based reliability analysis of component-based software. In: Proceedings of the 10th International Symposium on Software Reliability Engineering (IEEE Computer Society, Los Alamitos, CA 1999) pp 22–31

Part 4: Product Line Testing

Introduction

Part 4 deals with product line modeling from the viewpoints of domain and application testing and explicitly links these processes with domain and application requirements engineering. It consists of three chapters:

    Chapter 11. Product Line Use Cases: Scenario-Based Specification and Testing of Requirements

    Chapter 12. System Testing of Product Lines: From Requirements to Test Cases

    Chapter 13. The ScenTED Method for Testing Software Product Lines

The chapters of Part 4 complement each other in many ways. Together they deal with both domain and application testing as well as the test stages from integration and system testing to the final acceptance testing of the completed system. They build upon well-known unit test techniques for components that are beyond the scope of this book. It should be noted that Chap. 14 in Part 5 also deals with testing but from a project coordination and management perspective slightly different from that of Part 4.

Use Cases can be employed in system requirements engineering to capture functional requirements from an external point of view. Chapter 11 defines extensions and modifycations of the Use Cases notation, called Product Line Use Cases (PLUCs), to describe commonalities and variabilities of a product line. PLUCs rely on natural language to deal with early analysis, whereas Chaps. 12 and 13 represent use cases using enhanced UML Sequence Diagrams in later stages of product line engineering.

In order to guarantee the conformance of the derived product with respect to the product line, the PLUC approach makes it possible to express in the requirements specification of the product line not only the possible variant characteristics that can differentiate products of the same line, but also which combinations of variant characteristics are "legal" and which are not. PLUCs are a good starting point for integration and system testing.

The derivation of test cases for product lines has so far received little attention. Traditional testing approaches cannot be directly applied on each product since, due to the potentially huge number of products, the testing task would be far too long and expensive. The cost of testing must be reduced by using common tests for the common parts of a product line. New testing methods are thus needed.

Chapter 11 outlines a simple methodology for this purpose, which relies on the early requirements specification expressed as PLUCs. Chapter 12 presents another approach based on the automation of the application system test generation. The system requirements of the product line are modeled using enhanced UML use cases, which are the basis for the test generation. Product-specific test objectives, test scenarios, and test cases are successively generated through an automated process. Functional variation points at requirement level are described to instantiate the behaviors specific to a chosen product. The test cases derived from product-specific behaviors are executed against the chosen product. The approach provides automated test generation for a new product and guided test generation support to validate the evolution of the product.

Chapter 13 presents the ScenTED (Scenario based TEst case Derivation) method to tackle the testing problem based on the systematic refinement of generic use case scenarios to generic system and integration test case scenarios. It includes activities in domain engineering for preserving the variability in the generic test artifacts as well as activities in application engineering for binding the variability of the test artifacts. In addition, the refinement of use case scenarios to test case scenarios enables the traceability between development artifacts and test artifacts.

In sum, the PLUC approach deals with abstract descriptions of test scenarios for acceptance testing to ensure that the completed application works according to the expectations of the targeted users. A refinement process from these descriptions to more concrete ones is needed for obtaining executable test cases for system and integration testing. Methods for system testing are found in Chaps. 12 and 13 and for integration testing in Chap. 13. Additionally, ScenTED complements the other two methods, for example, by preserving variability in test artifacts.

11 Product Line Use Cases: Scenario-Based Specification and Testing of Requirements

A. Bertolino, A. Fantechi, S. Gnesi, and G. Lami

Abstract

Use Cases can be employed in system requirements engineering to capture requirements from an external point of view. In product line modeling, commonalities and variabilities of a family of systems have to be described. To this purpose, we have defined extensions and modifications of the Use Cases notation, called Product Line Use Cases (PLUCs). In order to guarantee the conformance of the derived product with respect to the product line we add the capability of expressing constraints over the Product Use Cases that can be derived from a PLUC. Using this notation, it is possible to express in the requirements specification of the product line not only the possible variant characteristics that can differentiate products of the same line, but also which combinations of variant characteristics are "legal" and which are not. Testing is another activity in which PLUCs show their utility. Indeed, for a product belonging to a product line, testing is a crucial and expensive part of software development. Yet the derivation of test cases for product lines has so far received little attention. We outline a simple methodology for this purpose, which relies on the early requirements specification expressed as PLUCs.

11.1 Introduction

The development of industrial software systems may often benefit from the adoption of a development cycle based on the product line engineering approach [5,16]. This approach aims at lowering production costs by sharing an overall reference architecture and concepts of the products, but at the same time allowing them to differ with respect to particular product characteristics in order to, e.g., serve different markets. The production process in product lines is therefore organized with the purpose of maximizing the commonalities of the product line and minimizing the cost of variations [14].

In the first stage of a software project, that is, requirements specification, the information and knowledge of the system under construction is acquired. Chapter 4 addresses this point. When gathering and expressing requirements on a product line two different problems have to be addressed. On one side there is the problem of capturing both requirements common to all members of the product line and requirements valid only for a subset of products. On the other side there is the problem of specializing and instantiating the generic product line requirements into application requirements for a single product.

To deal with these problems, the relations between line and product requirements have to be handled by the adopted modeling approach, and the concepts of parameterization, specialization and generalization need to be supported by the modeling concepts. Product line requirements can be considered, in general, as composed of a constant and a variable part [1,17,25]. The constant part includes all those requirements that deal with features or functions common to all the products in the product line and, for this reason, do not need to be modified. The variable part represents those aspects that can be changed to differentiate a product from another.

Indeed, a product line can be seen as a set of products with common characteristics that link them together. While developing a product line it is possible to move from the line level (which represents those common features) to the product level (which represents the single product, with all its particular characteristics) by an instantiation process, and on the contrary from the product level to the line level by an abstraction process.

Use Cases [6] are an easy, natural way to express functional requirements of a system. Their popularity derives from the simplicity of their approach: a well structured, easy to understand document written in controlled natural language. Use Cases are widely used in modern industrial development, so it seems natural to try to find an effective way to combine them with the product line paradigm.

In this direction, we have previously proposed the notation of Product Line Use Cases (PLUC) [1,10], an extended version of Cockburn's Use Cases [7] aimed at expressing requirements of product lines. The well-known Cockburn's Use Cases allow the functional requirements of a system to be described, by imposing on requirements documents a specified structure, which separates the various cases in which the system can be used by external actors, and for each case defines scenarios of correct and incorrect usage. The PLUC notation adds variability to Cockburn's Use Cases, with the possibility of expressing variation points and optional parts.

In this chapter, we show how the PLUC notation can be exploited for two fundamental processes in product line engineering:

– The instantiation of a (legal) product from a product line at the early stage of requirements definition.
– The derivation of a scenario-based test plan for a product of a product line.

Moreover, in [10] it has been shown how PLUCs can also support the abstraction process for the definition of a product line from product instances.

The first issue is addressed by providing a PLUC with the capability to express constraints over the product-related Use Cases that can be derived from it. These constraints are expressed as Boolean conditions associated to the variation points. The information we add to PLUCs by means of such constraints provides on the one hand the ability of automatically checking whether a product-related Use Case is conformant to the product line requirements; on the other hand, the adoption of constraint-solving techniques may even allow for automatic generation of product-specific Use Cases from the line level Use Cases document.

The importance of the second issue we address in this chapter comes from the observation that testing takes a predominant amount of development resources and schedule. Therefore, also reuse of test assets is a crucial issue in production processes. And, in the same manner that a product line specification and design must tackle variability, the same need applies for testing. As evident from the discussion above, the phase in which the majority of variation points are introduced is the requirement specification phase. Accordingly, we believe that planning ahead for testing within the product line development must start from the requirements. Hence, we base the testing process of product lines back on the requirement specification, and in particular on the PLUC notation. We defined the PLUTO methodology to derive specific test cases for product lines, and to instantiate the line generic test plan into a suite of test scenarios for a specific product.

In Sect. 11.2, we present the proposed PLUC notation, with some examples of PLUC described using this notation; in Sect. 11.3 we show how to exploit the information of PLUC to support the derivation process of products conforming to the product line constraints. Section 11.4 discusses how PLUCs can be exploited to derive test cases. Section 11.5 presents related works, while Sect. 11.6 concludes the chapter.

11.2 PLUC Notation

Use cases are widely used in modern industrial development for early requirements elicitation and specification, so it seems natural to try to find an effective way to combine them with the product line paradigm.

A Use Case defines a goal-oriented set of interactions between external actors and the system under consideration. Actors are parties outside the system that interact with the system. An actor may be a class of users, roles users can play, or other systems. There are two kinds of actors: primary actors and secondary actors.

- A primary actor is one having a goal requiring the assistance of the system
- A secondary actor is one from which the system needs assistance

A Use Case is initiated by a primary actor to achieve a goal, and completes successfully when that goal is satisfied. It describes the sequence of interactions between actors and the system necessary to accomplish the task that will lead to the goal. Use Case descriptions also include possible extensions to this sequence, e.g., alternative sequences that may also satisfy the goal, as well as sequences that may lead to failure in completing the service in case of exceptional behavior, error handling, etc. The system is treated as a "black box"; thus, Use Cases capture who (actor) does what (interaction) with the system, for what purpose (goal), without dealing with system internals. A complete set of Use Cases specifies all the different ways to use the system, and therefore defines the whole required behavior of the system.

Generally, Use Case steps are written in an easy-to-understand, structured narrative using the vocabulary of the domain. An instance of a Use Case is a scenario, and represents a single path through the Use Case. Thus, there exists a scenario for the main flow through the Use Case, and as many other scenarios as the possible variations of flow through the Use Case (e.g., triggered by options, error conditions, security breaches, etc.). Scenarios may also be depicted in a graphical form using UML Sequence Diagrams.

Figure 11.1 shows the template of the Cockburn's Use Case taken from [7]. In this textual notation, the main flow is expressed, in the "Description" row, by an indexed sequence of natural language sentences, describing a sequence of actions of the system. Variations are expressed (in the "Extensions" row) as alternatives to the main flow, linked by their index to the point of the main flow from which they branch as a variation. This natural language form of Use Cases has been widely used in industrial practice to specify Use Cases, e.g., at Nokia [9].

USE CASE #	<the name is the goal as a short active verb phrase>	
Goal in Context	<a longer statement of the goal in context if needed>	
Scope & Level	<what system is being considered black box under design> <one of: Summary, Primary Task, Sub function>	
Preconditions	<what we expect is already the state of the world>	
Success End Condition	<the state of the world upon successful completion>	
Failed End Condition	<the state of the world if goal abandoned>	
Primary, Secondary Actors	<a role name or description for the primary actor>, <other systems relied upon to accomplish Use Case>	
Trigger	<the action upon the system that starts the Use Case>	
Description	**Step**	**Action**
	1	<put here the steps of the scenario from trigger to goal delivery, and any cleanup after>
	2	<...>
	3	
Extensions	**Step**	**Branching Action**
	1a	<condition causing branching> : <action or name of sub-Use Case>
Sub-Variations		**Branching Action**
	1	<list of variations>

Fig. 11.1. Use Cases template

In [1] we extended the classical Use Case definition given by Cockburn to product lines, adding variability to this formalism. The proposed extension is based on the inclusion of tags that indicate those parts of the product line requirements that need to be instantiated for a specific product in a product-specific document. For doing that, tags are included into the Use Case sections (main scenario, extensions, etc.) in order to identify and specify variations.

This extension is called PLUC, while Product-related Use Cases where all tags have been instantiated are called Product Use Cases (PUC).
The tags can be of three kinds:

– Alternative: They express the possibility to instantiate the requirement by selecting an instance among a predefined set of possible choices, each of them depending on the occurrence of a condition.

- Parametric: Their instantiation is connected to the actual value of a parameter in the requirements for the specific product.
- Optional: Their instantiation can be done by selecting indifferently among a set of values, which are optional features for a derived product.

The instantiation of these types of variabilities will lead to a set of different product-related Use Cases. Although mostly significant in scenario descriptions, tags can be inserted in each field of a Use Case, thus leading to variability of actors, preconditions, etc.

Two examples of a PLUC are provided in Figs. 11.2 and 11.3. These PLUCs apply to different mobile phones belonging to a same PL. We assume that the products differ at least for the set of games made available to the user and for the provision or not of WAP connectivity.

The example in Fig. 11.2 describes the behavior of the phones belonging to the product line when a game is played by the user, while the example in Fig. 11.3 describes the function of answering an incoming call.

PL USE CASE GamePlay

Goal: Play a game on a **[GP0]** Mobile Phone and record score
Scope: The **[GP0]** Mobile Phone
Level: Summary
Precondition: The **[GP0]** Mobile Phone is on
   Trigger: Function GAMES has been selected from the main menu
Primary actor: The Mobile Phone user
Secondary actors: The {**[GP0]** Mobile Phone} (the system)
                The Mobile Phone Company
Main success scenario
   1. The system displays the list of the {**[GP1]** available} games
   2. The user selects a game
   3. The user selects the difficulty level
   4. The user starts the game and plays it until completion
   5.The user records the score achieved {and **[GP2]** sends the
      score to Club XXX via WAP}

Extensions
   1a. No game is available:
      1a1. return to main menu
   3a. The user starts the game and plays it until an incoming call arrives. **See CallAnswer.**

Variations
GP0: Alternative:
       0. Model 0
       1. Model 1
       2. Model 2
GP1: Parametric
if **GP0**=0 then display msg "No game available"

      else if **GP0**=1 then Snake II or Space Impact

      else if **GP0**=2 then Snake II or Space Impact or Bumper.

GP2: Optional
   when **GP0**=2

Fig. 11.2. Example of a Use Case in the PLUC notation

As shown in the examples, the variation points within the Use Case are enclosed within curly brackets, and the tags are identified by proper labels ([GP*i*] for GamePlay PLUC in Fig. 11.2 and [CA*i*] for CallAnswer PLUC in Fig. 11.3). Moreover, the possible instantiations of the variable parts and the type of the variations are defined within an ad hoc Variations section within the PLUC.

A product line definition is given by a set of PLUCs describing the various (generic) requirements for all the derivable products.

When considering the repository of all Use Cases specified for a product line, it can happen that some scenarios in a PLUC depend on other scenarios in another PLUC. In other words, some functional requirements may span across several Use Cases, bypassing the modeling capabilities of the simple formalism of PLUCs seen so far. We refer to these requirements as *cross-cutting* features. We handle cross-cutting in a simple way: When a scenario in a PLUC interacts with a scenario in another PLUC, we introduce a textual note like "see PLUC name." This is for instance the meaning of the note "See CallAnswer" within the GamePlay PLUC of Fig. 11.2, i.e., if an incoming call arrives as the user is playing a game, the related steps to be undertaken can be found in the CallAnswer PLUC.

11.2.1 Specification of a PLUC

The specification of the tags into a PLUC is a critical step for making the PLUC approach effective in practice. The examples we have shown in Figs. 11.2 and 11.3 just refer to single use cases, each of which is intended to give all the possibilities foreseen within the product line for the particular function described by the use cases. The derivation of a product will amount to the instantiation to a given value of all the tags of all the PLUCs of the product line: However, not all the combinations of values will be feasible, or "legal," products. Some more information is needed at the level of the PLUC definition in order to set some constraints on the variability of the tag values. This requires a method to formalize the three kinds of tags described in Sect. 11.2 (Alternative, Optional, and Parametric), as a necessary preliminary step for the verification of the compliance of a PUC to the product line constraints. In fact, the constraints that characterize the products belonging to a product line can be expressed in terms of the relations among the different tags indicating the variation points, both belonging to a single PLUC, and belonging to several PLUCs (thus addressing cross-cutting features).

To express the variability tags of the PLUCs in a formal way we have to take into account all the possible situations that can arise during the writing of a PLUC, paying particular attention to the variable tags of the PLUC itself.

First of all, we have to define the formalism to be used for expressing those relationships:

1. A tag is a variable which can assume any value inside a domain (often it is a finite, explicitly enumerated domain). As already shown in the examples, for readability we denote tags with the abbreviation of the PLUC name and a number (e.g., CA0).

PL USE CASE CallAnswer
Goal: Answer an incoming call on a **[CA0]** Mobile Phone
Scope: The **[CA0]** Mobile Phone
Precondition: Signal is available; Mobile Phone is switched on
Trigger: Incoming call
Primary actor: The user
Secondary actors: The {**[CA0]** Mobile Phone} (the system)
                        The Mobile Phone Company
Main success scenario
         1.The user accepts the call by pressing the Accept button
         2. The system establishes the connection by following the {**[CA1]** appropriate} procedure.
Extensions
         1a. The call is not accepted:
                     1a.1. the user presses the Reject button
                     1a.2. scenario terminates
PL Variability Features
     CA0: Alternative:
         0. Model 0
         1. Model 1 **[CA2]**
         2. Model 2 **[CA2]**

     CA1: Parametric:
     case **CA0** of
     0: Procedure A:
     2.1 Connect Caller and callee
     1 or 2: if **CA2**= a then Procedure B
     2.1 Interrupt the game
     2.2 Connect Caller and callee
         else If **CA2**= b then Procedure C:
     2.1 Save current game status
     2.2 Interrupt the game
     2.3 Connect Caller and callee

     CA2: Alternative:
     a. games available, but if interrupted status is not saved
     b. games available, and if interrupted status is saved

Fig. 11.3. Another PLUC example

2. A tag predicate is a Boolean proposition asserting the value of a tag, such as (CA0 == 1), or an expression connecting such propositions using classical propositional connectives. We use the symbols "||" (the logical OR operator), "&&" (the logical AND operator) , "==" (the "equal to" logical operator), "=>" (the logical implication operator) and "~" (the logical NOT operator). We denote tag predicates with a name such as CA0_tag.

3. A tag predicate for a tag may include propositions about other tags, so to define relationships between the values of the tags. Moreover, other expressions can set constraints over the tag's values; such constraints can span over more than one PLUC.

Using this formalism we can describe the essential types of tags by a logical expression able to capture their meaning:

- *Alternative tag* indicates mutual exclusion, which means that during the instantiation process one and only one from a set of different values can be assigned to the tag. This type of relationship can be expressed with a logical Exclusive or.

- *Optional tag* represents a subset of a PLUC steps that can or cannot be present in an instantiated PUC, depending of the value of some other instantiated tag (i.e., if a mobile phone type contains game C, the PUC called "starting a game" will have a step "print GAME C on screen," otherwise this step will not be present in the PUC). The propositional connective that models this type of relationship is Implication.
- *Parametric tag* indicates that some subsets of PLUCs steps can be chosen so that at least one of them will be chosen for a specific PUC, but more than one is allowed to be chosen (i.e., there can be more than a way to start a game in a mobile phone interface, and at least one must be present). This relationship is modeled with a Logical or.

The two examples of PLUCs shown in Figs. 11.2 and 11.3 can be used to show the process to be followed to represent the tags indicating variability in a formal way using the formalism described above. For each of the variability tags in the two PLUCs we derive a logical expression:

GP0_tag (alternative): (GP0 == 1 XOR GP0 == 2 XOR GP0 == 0);

GP1_tag (parametric): ((GP0 == 0 && GP1 == "display msg "No game available"") || (GP0 == 1 && GP1 == "Snake II or Space Impact") ||(GP0 == 2 && GP1 == "Snake II or Space Impact or Bumper"));

GP2_tag (optional): (GP0 == 2 => GP0 == "and sends the score to Club XXX via WAP ") || ((GP0 == 1 || GP0 == 0) => (VGP2 == null));

CA0_tag (alternative): (CA0 == 1 XOR CA0 == 2 XOR CA0 == 0);

CA1_tag (parametric): (CA0 == 0 && CA1 == "procedure A") || ((CA0 == 1 || CA0 == 2) && CA2 == a && CA1 == "procedure B") || ((CA0 == 1 || CA0 == 2) && CA2 == b && CA1 == "procedure A");

CA2_tag (alternative): (CA2 == a XOR CA2 == b)

GP-CA-constraint: CA0_tag == GP0_tag

The last expression is actually a constraint that relates two PLUCs: In this case this constraint simply states that the first tag is actually common to the two PLUCs.

Due to the expressive power of propositional calculus, it is possible to define some more complex and structured relationships, which can be used to more easily describe some common situations we can find when we read through a PLUC. We have just considered those kinds of expressions that define the three types of tags we have identified. A deeper analysis of the needs of actual applications of PLUCs may enlighten the need for other types of tags that should be analogously formalized.

The constraints that define the borders and the characteristics of a product line and that must drive the specification of a PUC are expressed by means of the formalization of the tags as seen above. These tags may be considered as the way to represent the conditions to be satisfied in order to make a variability solution not contradictory with the product line characteristics.

In summary, a PLUC describes the general behavior which all products should yield during the accomplishment of a specific task: It acts like a template from which it is possible to derive single PUCs by the instantiation process of its tags, which can be of many different types.

11.3 PUC Derivation from PLUC

In this section we describe our approach to effectively verify the compliance of a PUC to the product line constraints. Our approach is in fact inherently conceived to handle closed product lines, where it is intended that application engineering does not change the requirement model. On the other hand, the verification of conformance during tag instantiation, following the principles described below, provides the application engineers with a means to detect those cases in which this could happen, and to identify the requirement parts that should be changed to allow for the design of the application outside the product line.

The process of instantiating tags consists of assigning an actual value to each variable appearing in the tag expressions of PLUCs we are interested in. The instantiation of the tags expressing the variabilities of the product line corresponds to the definition of the compulsory characteristics of the PUC we are deriving. In other words, the instantiation of the tags defines the requirements of a particular product belonging to the product line.

A possible instantiation of the tags of the two PLUCs in Figs. 11.2 and 11.3 is:

```
CA0 == GP0 == 1
CA1 == "procedure A"
CA2 == b
GP1 == "display msg "No game available""
GP2 == null
```

This instantiation produces two PUCs derived by the two given PLUCs. A PUC is compliant to the product line if, evaluating the tags expressions defining the constraints in the product line with the instantiation of variables given for that PLUC, all the tags are evaluated true. Otherwise, the PUC cannot be accepted as belonging to the product line: an inconsistent PUC has been identified. The expressions having value false indicates the points of the instantiation determining the non-compliance. Then it is simple to identify those instantiation to be modified to achieve the compliance to the product line constraints.

In the example the value of tag expressions of the PLUC with the actual values of the variables for the considered instantiation are:

```
CA0_tag: true
CA1_tag: true
CA2_tag: true
GP0_tag: true
GP1_tag: false
GP2_tag: true
```

This means that a PUC with the variabilities solved with the above values does not describe any valid product of the product line. In this case the lack of compliance is easily identified as the erroneous instantiation of GP1.

One of the main merits of the methodology we have described is the ease of inserting changes in product line requirements expressed by means of PLUCs. In fact, if a tag is modified, because of the parametric nature of the approach, the effects of the modification affect only its definition and not its individual occurrences over the PLUCs. Moreover, if some new tags have to be added, the effort for doing that is mainly concentrated on the corresponding formal definition, and, once the new tag formula has been defined, the updating of the product line requirements simply consists in the inclusion of the tag at the appropriate place of the affected PLUCs.

We note that our approach when used for the instantiation process (from product line to product) allows a designer to enforce closed PLs, i.e., it prevents the insertion of requirements which are not allowed. Then in this sense it is conceived for closed product lines. On the contrary, it is interesting to note how the described methodology can also be used for supporting the impact analysis of possible new variabilities on the existing (or planned) products belonging to the product line. When a new variable feature is to be added in the product line, it is of interest to evaluate its impact on the whole set of the products of the product line. In particular, for evaluating if the new variability will determine incompatibility with some of the existing or planned products of the product line, a preliminary verification can be made adopting the verification procedure shown above.

This approach is promising due to its simplicity and effectiveness for being implemented in an automatic way. In fact, it gives the advantage of an explicit identification of the variability points in a product line requirements specification by means of the tags.

This characteristic may strongly facilitate the application of our approach in the industry because it allows the use of automatic tools for the identification of variabilities. As an example, a tool can be built able to generate *all* the admissible PUCs from the PLUC, by assigning to tags all the combination of values admitted by the tool: This tool may be useful to explore the possibilities given by possible software products in a product line, before actually building them.

11.4 Using PLUCs for Derivation of Test Scenarios

We have addressed so far how PLUCs can help address variabilities and commonalities during the upfront stages of development, i.e., modeling and specification of Use Case scenarios. Commonalities and variabilities of course also affect test planning: In fact, when considering a line, a test plan consisting of a generic frame of test cases pertaining to the PL domain can be derived. In other terms, the line generic test plan includes a list of test cases that apply to the whole set of admissible products, plus other test cases which instead will vary for each specific product, depending on how the variants characteristics are instantiated. At the product level, then, a methodology should support testers in instantiating from the generic PL test frame the set of test cases relative to the specific product, inclusive of common and variable test features.

11.4.1 PLUTO: A Methodology to Derive Test Scenarios

PLUCs can provide a useful means for the above goal: Based on the PLUC formalism, we have developed a simple and intuitive methodology for the early derivation of test scenarios from the PL requirements specification, called PLUTO (Product Lines Use Case Test Optimization) [2].

The PLUTO methodology is inspired by the well-known Category Partition (CP) method [28], but expands it with the capability to handle PL variabilities and to instantiate test cases for a specific product. In the following we illustrate the CP method, and how this has been modified in PLUTO to handle PLUCs variabilities and commonalities. A remark is noteworthy: We generically speak in terms of "test cases," for readability. However, this is not compliant with the common meaning of a test case in the testing literature. A test case should consist of the precise specification of a test input, a sequence of events and the expected output. We deal rather with *abstract descriptions of test scenarios*: What we derive are not test cases, but scenarios of use that need to be tested for validating that the user requirements are satisfied. Being derived from the Use Cases description, which are high level and in natural language, both the input sequence and the expected behavior are provided at a quite high level of description (the same one in the considered scenario). A refinement process from these abstract descriptions to more concrete ones is needed for obtaining executable test cases. This is outside the scope of the current chapter, but a method for test case synthesis from test scenarios can for instance be found in Chap. 12. CP is a well-known and quite intuitive method proposed in the late eighties to derive functional tests from the specifications written in structured, semiformal language. CP provides a systematic, formalized approach to *partition testing* that is one standard functional testing methodology. Generally speaking, partition testing is based on the simple idea that the input domain is first divided into several equivalence classes (also called partitions, although to be true partitions these should be non-overlapping, which is rarely the case in practice); then one or few tests are selected from within each of the identified partitions, as representative of the behavior of the whole class.

CP is organized into a stepwise methodology. The first step is to analyze the system requirements to identify the functional units that will constitute the subjects of the test and can be considered separately. In the case of PLs the elementary units of analysis are naturally provided by the PLUCs.

Then, for each functional unit (here a PLUC), the tester identifies the environment conditions (the required system properties for a certain functional unit) and the parameters (the explicit inputs for the unit) that are relevant for testing purposes: these are called the *categories*.

For each category, the significant (from the tester's viewpoint) values that it can take are then selected, called the *choices*. A suite of test cases is finally obtained by taking all the possible combinations of choices for all the categories.

As the approach is based on structured, natural language requirements, the test derivation has to be done partially manually. In particular, the identification of relevant Categories and of the Choices to be tested is left to the tester's skill and judgment, and then this constitutes the most critical step of the approach. However, lexical and syntactical analyzers for natural language requirements [3,12] could be used to extract useful information to identify the relevant Categories. This could be augmented with pragmatic hints derived from the specific meaning of fields forming a Use Case. Moreover, this step has been empirically studied, leading to the identification of common mistakes made by testers and to the compilation of a relative checklist [4].

To prevent the construction of redundant, not meaningful, or even contradictory, combinations of choices, in CP the choices can be annotated with *constraints*, which can be of two types: either (i) properties or (ii) special conditions. In the first case, some properties are set for certain choices, and *selector* expressions related with them (in the form of simple *if* conditions) are associated with other choices: A choice marked with an *if* selector can then be combined only with those choices from other categories that fulfill the related property. The second type of constraints is useful to reduce the number of test cases: some markings, namely "error" and "single," are coupled to some choices. The choices marked with "error" and "single" refer to erroneous or special conditions, respectively, that we intend to test, but that need not to be combined with all possible choices. The list of all the choices identified for each category, with the possible addition of the constraints, forms a Test Specification. It is not yet a list of test cases, but it contains all the information necessary to instantiate them by unfolding the constraints.

A specific characteristic of test cases derived from Use Cases is the presence of several scenarios, i.e., the main success scenario and in addition the possible extensions. Of course all of them must be exercised during testing. Therefore a Test Specification derived from PLUCs will normally include a category "Scenarios," in which all the specified scenarios are listed as choices.

Finally, when considering PLs, the CP method described above must be adapted for dealing with the presence of the tags included in the PLUC to identify the PL variation points. However, this can be done in a quite intuitive way: We use the tags similarly to the original concept of CP constraints, i.e., in the Test Specification we associate to the corresponding choices the variability tags; then, in the process of test case derivation we match the tag values in such a way to establish the combinations that are significant with respect to a specific product. In particular, in case of:

- An alternative tag: the relevant feature is selected
- An optional tag: the corresponding feature is taken into account or not depending on whether it is present in the product
- A parametric tag: the feature corresponding to the pertinent value is taken

Note that actually parametric tags do not directly contribute to the task of identifying the test scenarios: In fact, they do not identify possible points of selection, but rather assign the appropriate values once some other related tags are fixed.

When dealing with PLUCs, to express the *selectors*, since these are here used to express relations over tag values, we continue to adopt the formalism of the logical expressions introduced in Sect. 11.3.1. Hence properties over categories in PLUTO are expressed as constraints over tags.

Conceptually, the suite of all potential test cases for a PL encompasses all those combinations of choices that are common throughout the product line and are given by those test cases that do not include variability tags. In addition to these, all the possible combinations of choices involving tags form a set of variable test cases. The complete set of mandatory and variables test cases, which would be obtained in this way, form the asset of test scenarios for the line.

In PLUTO we do not derive the list of all admissible PL test cases; rather we derive the PL Test Specification and leave it unfolded. The test cases are actually derived for a specific product after having instantiated the tags in each PLUC to the appropriate values.

More precisely, for each Test Specification relative to a PLUC, a different set of test cases will correspond to every specific product of the PL, depending on the tag values. We observe that this intermediate step of tag instantiation between the definition of the Test Specification and the derivation of the test sets is the means by which in PLUTO we tackle variability. For readers familiar with the CP test method, this is also what makes PLUTO basically different from the traditional CP. In the latter, only one set of test cases directly correspond to each Test Specification. In PLUTO, from each Test Specification several different sets of test cases can be instantiated, depending on the tag values.

Considering the testing process, the PLUTO approach addresses the stage of testing for validation of user requirements, i.e., it can be used to support Acceptance testing against the documented usage scenarios during application engineering to make certain that the application works according to the expectations of the targeted users. Such test cases are executed as Input/Output black box tests on the completed system. Along the application engineering process, they should be complemented with other test stages addressing unit and integration testing.

PLUTO could nicely be complemented with the ScenTED approach described in Chap. 13. Such an approach is conceived to derive application test cases for system and integration test levels. Moreover, unit test techniques should also be considered for components.

11.4.2 An Example

For illustration purposes, we now apply the PLUTO approach to the GamePlay PLUC in Fig. 11.2. As a first step, from an analysis of it we identify the following Categories: "Mobile Phone Model," "Games," "Difficulty Level," and "Club," plus of course "Scenarios," which is always present. These identify the relevant characteristics to be varied when testing the Mobile Phone system for validating the user requirements with respect to the functionality of playing games.

We proceed by partitioning these categories into the relevant choices, i.e., we single out for each of the categories the values that are the relevant cases to be considered in specific tests. As said, when applying the CP method to PLs, in general we will have that some of the choices will be available for all the products of the product line. On the other hand, some of the categories are specialized into choices that depend on the specific product considered. For instance, the category "Club," which relates to the capability to exchange the achieved game score with other Club affiliates, is relevant only for those models that support WAP connection. Hence it cannot be tested for any potential applications of the product line, but only for those supporting this feature. This is specified in the GamePlay PLUC by means of the GP2 optional tag. Hence, when the test cases are being derived, we make use of this tag similarly to the "constraint" formalism of the CP method. As shown in Fig. 11.4 we derive the two possible choices pertaining to the "Club" category, but we annotate them with an appropriate selector, which is a simple condition stating that these choices are of interest only when the tag GP0 takes value 2, i.e., the Mobile Phone is Model 2. The complete Test Specification is shown below in Fig. 11.4.

If we now applied to this Test Specification a generator that takes out all the possible combinations of choices, we would obtain a long list of test cases. This list would include all the potential test cases for all the products of the line relative to the PLUC under consideration. However, what is more interesting in our opinion is that we can instead derive directly a list of test cases for a specific product of interest. This is obtained easily by just instantiating the relative tags. So, for instance, if we are interested to test the Model 2 product of this line, we set the related optional tag to true (recall from Sect. 11.3.1 that this is modeled by Implication) and derive all and only the combinations that remain valid.

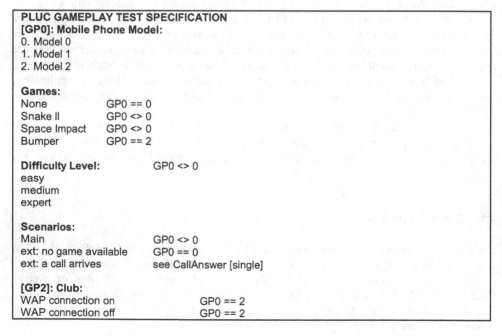

Fig. 11.4. Main test categories for the GamePlay PLUC

As an example, we list below in Fig. 11.5 some of the test cases that would be thus so obtained for different products, i.e., for different tag assignments. We show these as abstract descriptions and leave to the reader the obvious transformation of these into the corresponding functional test scenarios.

```
GP0 == 2
   Tj1:
   Mobile Phone Model: Model 2
   Games:  Snake II
   Difficulty Level:    easy
   Scenarios:           main
   Club:     WAP connection on


   Tj2:
   Mobile Phone Model: Model 2
   Games:  Bumper
   Difficulty Level:    expert
   Scenarios:           main
   Club:     WAP connection on


........


   Tk:
   Mobile Phone Model: Model 2
   Games:  Space Impact
   Difficulty Level:    medium
   Scenarios:           ext: a call arrives - see CallAnswer
```

Fig. 11.5. Some test scenarios

In Fig. 11.5 the test cases Tj1, Tj2 refer to a simpler situation in which the features in a PLUC do not depend on the features of another PLUC. Test Tk instead needs further consideration. It considers the choice "a call arrives" of the Scenarios category, which has a specific "See CallAnswer" annotation. This is an example of a cross-cutting feature, whose notion we have introduced in Sect. 11.2. We now see below how this can be handled in the PLUTO methodology.

11.4.3 Extending the Methodology

Referring to the example used so far, let us suppose that the Mobile Phone PL under consideration provides for some applications the capability to save the current status of a game being played in the case that an incoming call arrives. The user may answer or refuse the call. Then, after the communication is closed, the game can be resumed from the status in which it was interrupted.

This case depicts a cross-cutting feature arising from a functional dependency between the GamePlay PLUC and another Use Case, the CallAnswer PLUC, that describes the handling of incoming calls and that we have already presented in Fig. 11.3. Considering now the CallAnswer PLUC (independently from the GamePlay PLUC), we assume we have already derived a Test Specification by applying to it the PLUTO methodology, as shown in Fig. 11.6.

PLUC CALLANSWER TEST SPECIFICATION
[CA0]: Mobile Phone Model:

0. Model 0
1. Model 1
2. Model 2

Saving:
a. game status is not saved   CA0 <> 0
b. game status is saved   CA0 <> 0

Scenarios:
Main: Call is accepted
ext: Call is refused

Fig. 11.6. Main test categories for the CallAnswer PLUC

Similarly to what we have done for GamePlay, if we take all the potential combinations of choices in the CallAnswer Test Specification, in respect of the associated constraints, we would obtain the list of test scenarios relative to this PLUC. It is clear however that the PLUCs GamePlay and CallAnswer are related with respect to the possibility to interrupt and then retrieve a game play because a call arrives. To identify that a dependency exists, as said, when we elicited the Use Cases we have annotated the related scenario in the GamePlay PLUC with the note "See CallAnswer." Correspondingly, in the process of deriving the test cases from the GamePlay Test Specification (see Fig. 11.4) the case that a call arrives is contemplated in all those tests in which for the "Scenarios" category the choice "ext: a call arrives" is taken. In Fig. 11.5 the test case Tk for instance selects this choice (we report it again below):

Tk:
Mobile Phone Model: Model 2
Games: Space Impact
Difficulty Level: medium
Scenarios: ext: a call arrives - *see CallAnswer*

However, as described in the CallAnswer PLUC, when a call arrives several behaviors are possible. This test hence is not complete: It must be further refined into several related test cases, considering each of the possible combinations of choices offered in its turn by the CallAnswer Test Specification. Hence for example from the above Tk, considering the Test Specification relative to the CallAnswer PLUC (Fig. 11.6), we get at least four refined test cases as follows:

Tk-1:
Mobile Phone Model: Model 2
Games: Space Impact
Difficulty Level: medium
Scenarios: ext: a call arrives
          Saving: game status is not saved
          Scenarios: Call is accepted

Tk-2:
Mobile Phone Model: Model 2
Games: Space Impact
Difficulty Level: medium
Scenarios: ext: a call arrives
          Saving: game status is saved
          Scenarios: Call is accepted

Tk-3:
Mobile Phone Model: Model 2
Games: Space Impact
Difficulty Level: medium
Scenarios: ext: a call arrives
          Saving: game status is not saved
          Scenarios: Call is refused

Tk-4:
Mobile Phone Model: Model 2
Games: Space Impact
Difficulty Level: medium
Scenarios: ext: a call arrives
          Saving: game status is saved
          Scenarios: Call is refused

More in general, whenever a test specification includes a directive "See another PLUC," the derivation of test cases is made by combining the relevant choices from the two related PLUCs. Note that the annotation is made in the PLUC that triggers the test cases, in our example the GamePlay PLUC. Note also that in the GamePlay Test Specification we have marked the choice "ext: a call arrives" with the [single] constraint. As described above the common heuristic in the CP method is that special, unusual, or redundant conditions are not combined with all possible choices, and to recognize them, they are marked as [single]. This heuristic reduces the total number of test cases, while assuring that one frame will be anyhow created with the marked choice. As explained in [28] the decision to use a [single] marking is a judgment by the tester that the marked choice can be adequately tested with only one test case. It is an attempt to trade-off between exhaustive testing of combinations (which is unfeasible) against the pragmatic testing resource limitations. Accordingly, to reduce the number of test scenarios, we have decided not to test separately the arrival of a call together with all possible combinations of GamePlay choices (that are being tested already along the main scenario). Instead we select one representative combination (as the Tk example above) on the side of GamePlay, and from this we then derive as many tests as are the possible refinements when considering the CallAnswer Test Specification.

11.5 Related Work

The problem of the PL modeling and scoping has been approached following different approaches [13,15,29]. Our approach, aiming at introducing constraints on the variabilities inside PLUCs, is based on the proposal by Mannion [24] that addresses general product line model requirements: He presents a way to describe the relationships between product line requirements in order to formally analyze them and to extract information about the internal consistency of the requirements (i.e., they provide a valid template for at least one single product) and of the single products derived from the product line model (i.e., they satisfy all constraints of product line requirements).

We adopt a similar approach and we apply it to the PLUCs, by transforming the described relationships between PL requirements into relationships between PLUC tags and between different PLUCs, and we also extend the set of basic relationships with some composed new ones. The fact that we define a specific notation within which to embed such constraints and relationships provides the product line engineering with a more concrete technique, which can be supported by automatic tools as well.

Chapter 15 exploits UML diagrams and their transformation to address product derivation. The fact that we base our product derivation approach on Use Cases (instead of UML statechart diagrams) means that we focus on the early stages of the development process, that is, requirement elicitation. Addressing product derivation at an early stage has the advantage of early detection of problems and early derivation of test cases, as shown in Sect. 11.4, advantage paid in terms of a higher level of abstraction.

For what concerns the field of product line testing, we quickly overview related work, for the purpose of identifying relevant differences and commonalities with our ongoing research. For the first time, a whole workshop has been devoted to PL testing at SPLC 2004 [11], recognizing the urgent need for testing to keep pace with PLE development productivity gains. Some papers presented in that workshop [20,23,30] are particularly interesting because they address the problem of test cases generation starting from the PL variability.

In [22] test-related activities in a product line organization are described. Test-related activities are organized into a test process that is purposely designed to take advantage of the economies of scope and scale that are present in a product line organization. These activities are sequenced and scheduled so that a test activity expands on the testing practice area described by Clements and Northrop [5]. Here we present a test case derivation strategy for PLs described starting from a very general description like the Use Cases are. We can say therefore that the main difference between [22] and [5] and our work stays in the focus, which is there on the process while here is on the methodology. A mutual influence between these two directions of work would certainly be desirable and beneficial. In [18] the authors propose that variability is introduced in the domain-level test cases corresponding to the variabilities present in the Use Cases and that application specific test cases are then derived from them. The derivation strategy depends on how the variability is expressed, and different approaches, including Abstraction, Parameterization, Segmentation, Fragmentation, and Instantiation are overviewed. It is envisaged that a combination of these approaches needs to be used. The approach is still preliminary and details are missing, in particular it is not clear to what extent it can be automated. However, the idea of combining several derivation approaches is interesting and our approach could probably be incorporated in this general framework as one of the derivation strategies (in particular the Parameterization one). In [27] an approach to expressing test requirements and to formally validate them in a UML-based development process which takes into account PL specificities is presented. Behavioral test patterns (i.e., the test requirements) are built as combinations of use-case scenarios, these scenarios being product-independent and therefore constituting reusable PL assets. The difference between this approach and ours is that from a methodological point of view they propose a whole process from early modeling of requirements to test cases starting from UML specifications, whereas we instead exploit the description of a PL given in natural language and work at the early analysis stages. Perhaps the two approaches could be considered in combination, as addressing different concerns of the PL life cycle. Product line testing is also addressed in RITA [19], an environment under development at the University of Helsinki. RITA is orthogonal to our work, in that it is specifically designed for framework and framelet-based PLs, and does not assist the generation of test cases from requirements. Instead, assuming that the test cases are supplied in input, the environment is conceived for supporting test scripting, execution, result evaluation and more in general for helping with the test process management activities. Different from ours finally are some recent approaches that attack the testing problem based on the product line software architectures. Indeed, the increased use of product line architectures in today's software development poses several challenges for existing testing techniques. In [26] those challenges are discussed as well as the opportunities for addressing them. The Component+ architecture [8] defines instead standardized test interfaces that minimize the effort needed to verify the components by extending software components with configurations.

11.6 Conclusions and Future Research

We have presented the PLUC notation for the description of product lines requirements and shown how this notation allows several kinds of analysis to be performed over such documents, which are extremely useful in the development of products of a software product line. We have concentrated in this chapter over the analysis of PLUCs to derive Product Use Cases and to derive test cases for a product line and its products. In [10] we have applied PLUCs in the process of product line elicitation, that is, how to define a line of products by generalization of some similar products.

In order to support our belief that PLUCs can meet industrial expectations for a notation which is at the same time rigorous and easy to understand, we plan to validate the methodology through extensive industrial case studies. Another important direction we are currently working on is the development of a suite of tools that can support both product derivation from a line and test case derivation for the products of a line.

Moreover, PLUCs could complement the graphical and intuitive but abstract notation of UML Use Cases. Defining a UML profile for PLUCs in order to include variabilities in the diagrams and to associate them with the textual, more detailed descriptions using our notation could be a step toward a standardized version of PLUCs. When we have completed the validation of our methodology, we will thus initiate the international standardization process for PLUCs, facilitating wide industrial adoption and application of the PLUC notation.

Acknowledgments

This work was partially supported by the Eureka Σ!2023 Programme, ITEA (ip00004, Project CAFÉ). We wish to thank in particular Alessandro Maccari from NOKIA, Isabel John from IESE, and Emiliano Nesti from University of Florence for their contributions on the research activity summarized in this chapter. The reviews of Erwin Engelsma, Erik Kamsties, Timo Käkölä, Antti Tevanlinna, and Tewfik Ziadi significantly improved the quality of this chapter.

References

1. Bertolino, A., Fantechi, A., Gnesi, S., Lami, G., Maccari, A.: Use case description of requirements for product lines, REPL'02, Essen, Germany (September 2002)
2. Bertolino, A., Gnesi, S.: Use case-based testing of product lines. Proceedings of ESEC/FSE 2003 (ACM, New York) pp 355–358
3. Cascini, G., Fantechi, A., Spinicci, E.: Natural language processing of patents and technical documentation. Proceedings of DAS 2004, 6th IAPR International Workshop on Document Analysis Systems, Firenze, Italy, September 2004. Lecture Notes in Computer Science, vol 3163 (Springer, Berlin Heidelberg New York 2004)
4. Chen, T.Y. et al: On the identification of categories and choices for specification-based test case generation. Inform. Softw. Technol. **46**: 887–898 (2004)
5. Clements, P.C., Northrop, L.: Software Product Lines: Practices and Patterns. *SEI Series in Software Engineering* (Addison-Wesley, Reading, MA August 2001)
6. Cockburn, A.: Structuring use cases with goals. J. Object-Oriented Program. Sept–Oct 1997 (part I) and Nov–Dec 1997 (part II)
7. Cockburn, A., *Writing Effective Use Cases* (Addison-Wesley, Reading, MA 2001)
8. Component+, "D4 – BIT Case studies". http://www.component-plus.org (October 2002)
9. Fantechi, A., Gnesi, S., Lami, G., Maccari, A.: Linguistic techniques for use cases analysis. Proceedings of the IEEE Joint International Requirements Engineering Conference – RE02, Essen, Germany, 9–13 September 2002
10. Fantechi, A., Gnesi, S., John, I., Lami, G., Dörr, J.: Elicitation of use cases for product lines. 5th International Workshop on Product Family Engineering, PFE-5, Siena, 4–6 November 2003. Lecture Notes in Computer Science, vol 3014 (Springer, Berlin Heidelberg New York 2004)
11. Geppert, B., Krueger, C., Li, J.J. (eds): Proceedings of SPLiT 2004, International Workshop on Software Product Line Testing, co-located with SPLC 2004, Boston, MA, USA, August 2004, Avaya Labs Research Tech. Rep. series ALR-2004-031. http://www.research.avayalabs.com/techreport.html
12. Gnesi, S. et al: An automatic tool for the analysis of natural language requirements. Int. J. Comput. Syst. Sci. Eng. **20**(1), 53–62 (2005)
13. van Gurp, J., Bosch, J., Svahnberg, M.: On the notion of variability in software product lines. Proceedings of the Working IEEE/IFIP Conference on Software Architecture (WICSA 2001), pp 45–54
14. Halmans, G., Pohl, K.: *Communicating the Variability of a Software-Product Family to Customers Journal of Software and Systems Modeling* (Springer, Berlin Heidelberg New York 2003)
15. Jaring, M., Bosch, J.: Representing variability in software product lines: a case study. In: *Software Product Lines*, ed by Chastek, G.J., 2nd International Conference, SPLC 2, San Diego, CA, USA, 19–22 August 2002. Lecture Notes in Computer Science, vol 2379, pp 15–36
16. Jazayeri, M., Ran, A., van der Linden, F.: *Software Architecture for Product Families: Principles and Practice* (Addison-Wesley, Reading, MA 1998)
17. John, I., Muthig, D.: Tailoring use cases for product line modeling, REPL'02, Essen, Germany (September 2002)

18. Kamsties, E., Pohl, K., Reis, S., Reuys, A.: Testing variabilities in use case model. 5th International Workshop on Product Family Engineering, Siena, November 2003
19. Kauppinen, R., Taina, J.: RITA environment for testing framework-based software product lines. Proceedings of the 8th Symposium on Programming Languages and Software Tools (SPLST'2003), Kuopio, Finland, June 2003 (University of Kuopio 2003) pp 58–69
20. Knauber, P., Schneider, J.: Tracing variability from implementation to test using aspect-oriented programming. International Workshop on Software Product Lines Testing, Boston, MA, 31 August 2004
21. van der Linden, F.: Software product families in Europe: the ESAPS & CAFÉ projects. IEEE Software (July/August 2002)
22. MacGregor, J.D.: Testing a software product line. Technical report, CMU/SEI-2001-TR-022
23. MacGregor, J.D., Sodhani, P., Madhavapeddi, S.: Testing variability in a software product line. International Workshop on Software Product Lines Testing, Boston, MA, 31 August 2004
24. Mannion, M., Camara, J.: Theorem proving for product line model verification. 5th International Workshop on Product Family Engineering, PFE-5, Siena, 4–6 November 2003. Lecture Notes in Computer Science, vol 3014 (Springer, Berlin Heidelberg New York 2004)
25. von der Massen, S., Lichter, H.: Modeling variability by UML use case diagram. International Workshop on Requirements Engineering for Product Line (REPL'02), Avaya Labs Technical Report, ALR-2002-033 (September 2002)
26. Muccini, H., van der Hoek, A.: Towards testing product line architectures. Electron. Notes Theor. Comput. Sci. 82(6) (2003)
27. Nebut, C., Pickin, S., Le Traon, Y., Jézéquel, J.-M.: Reusable test requirements for UML-modeled product line, REPL'02, Essen, Germany, Avaya Labs technical report, ALR-2002-033 (September 2002)
28. Ostrand, T.J., Balcer, M.J.: The category partition method for specifying and generating functional tests. ACM Commun. 31(6), 676–686 (June 1988)
29. Schmid, K.: A comprehensive product line scoping approach and its validation. 24th International Conference on Software Engineering, Orlando, FL, 2002
30. Stephenson, Z., Zhan, Y., Clark, J., McDermid, J.: Test data generation for product lines – a mutation testing approach. International Workshop on Software Product Lines Testing, Boston, MA, 31 August 2004

12 System Testing of Product Lines: From Requirements to Test Cases

C. Nebut, Y. Le Traon, and J.-M. Jezequel

Abstract

Product line processes still lack support for testing end-product functions by taking advantage of the specific features of a product line (commonality and variabilities). Indeed, classical testing approaches cannot be directly applied on each product since, due to the potentially huge number of products, the testing task would be far too long and expensive. There is thus a need for testing methods, adapted to the product line context, that allow reducing the testing cost. The approach we present is based on the automation of the generation of application system tests, for any chosen product, from the system requirements of a product line. These PL requirements are modeled using enhanced UML use cases which are the basis for the test generation. Product-specific test objectives, test scenarios, and test cases are successively generated through an automated process. The key idea of the approach is to describe functional variation points at requirement level to automatically generate the behaviors specific to any chosen product. With such a strategy, the designer may apply any method to produce the domain models of the product line and then instantiate a given product: the test cases derived from product-specific behaviors are executed against the chosen end product to check that the expected functionalities have been correctly implemented. The approach is adaptive and provides automated test generation for a new product as well as guided test generation support to validate the evolution of a given product.

12.1 Introduction

Product lines elaboration and design brings up a large number of novel issues, testing methods being one among them [2,14,19,20,22,23,26]. While the elicitation of product line requirements is known as crucial task for the elaborated design, product requirements are seldom used for driving the functional testing task. However, the end product is expected to satisfy its requirements: testing is the classical way to obtain confidence in a given product with respect to its requirements. There is thus a need of adapted techniques to assist this test generation from requirement in a PL context. Like any kind of software, product lines obviously require several types of software tests. In particular, unit testing has to be performed independently on each asset, integration testing techniques can be used to assemble the assets to obtain a product, and system testing ensures that the end product has the required features. We here focus on system and functional testing. One of the specific issues related to PL testing concerns the way a testing technique deals with the creation of new products and the evolution of existing products. In this chapter, we present the automation as a relevant way for dealing with these issues.

Testing a PL is all the more tedious since the common and the shared variant requirements have to be tested for each instantiated product. Indeed, the same piece of functional test code, derived from a requirement, cannot be reused exactly: for instance, in an object-oriented product line, the objects addressed to realize a given functionality may be different from one product to another, due to the crossing of different variation points. For example, the initialization sequence leading to the testing of a particular point may be totally different from one product to another. So, for testing a given function common to all products, specific test cases may have to be written for each specific product. As a result, manually writing the tests cases for all the products is not conceivable, since it is far too expensive. Automating the test generation appears as a possible way to deal with these cost and time-to-market issues.

Many approaches already exist to automatically generate tests from the requirements of a "classical" software (e.g., [4,9,24]), but they have to be adapted in order to deal with the variability expressed in product line requirements. To benefit from the product line approach, there is a need for specifying the requirements of a product line and then deriving automatically the test cases. That means to solve several problems (1) How to express the product line requirements (and in particular the variability)? (2) How to generate tests from them? (3) Is it possible to generate test cases that can directly be applied by a test driver?

Our approach is a proposal to answer those questions. Our idea is to express the requirements using enhanced Unified Modeling Language (UML) [28] use cases or to transform the requirements into enhanced UML use cases. The UML use cases are enhanced in order to express commonality and variability, and enhanced with parameters and with contracts. Those use cases are also supposed to be documented by scenarios. Use cases and scenarios are combined to generate test objectives that are refined into test scenarios (a test scenario is a potentially abstract and incomplete representation of a test case). Then product-specific test synthesis is achieved to obtain test cases.

Two main approaches already exist to test PL from the use cases (see Chaps. 11 and 13 and [2,14]), that are complementary more than in opposition to ours. Though they have the same purpose of automating the testing task, the approach proposed here differs from the one proposed in Chap. 11 in the sense that this latter approach is data driven since it is an adaptation of the category-partition method, while ours is behavior driven. Our approach is also complementary to the ScenTED approach (Chap. 13) which is a systematic approach to derive test scenarios for product lines. It tackles in particular the issue of the test artifacts reuse. In Sect. 12.7.4, we explain how our approach could be coupled with those two approaches.

The rest of this chapter is organized as follows. Section 12.2 proposes an overview of the approach and presents an illustrative example. Section 12.3 details our requirement model, i.e., an enhanced use case model. Section 12.4 presents the simulation mechanism of the use cases. The simulation is used to generate test objectives, as detailed in Sect. 12.5. Section 12.6 explains how test cases can be derived from the test objectives, using test scenarios and behavioral test patterns to guide the test synthesis tools. Section 12.7 provides experiments and discusses our approach, in particular with respect to related work. Section 12.8 concludes.

12.2 Overview of the Approach

This section gives an overview of the proposed approach, which is summarized in Fig. 12.1. Each step of this approach will be detailed in a particular section in the following of the chapter. This section ends with the presentation of an illustrative example that is used all over this chapter.

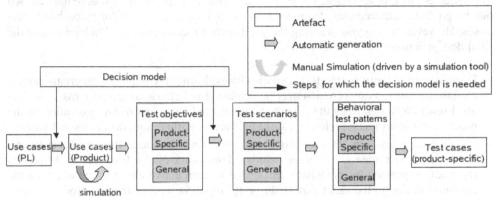

Fig. 12.1. Overview of the test case generation

12.2.1 From the Product Line Requirements to Product-Specific Requirements

Use cases are an easy and natural way to express system functional requirements. They are widely used in industry, probably since the underlying approach is simple and just consists in producing a structured document in natural language, for example following the Cockburn schema [7]. Thus we have based our approach on requirements written in the form of UML use cases. To be used as first input of an automated test generation process, UML use cases need to be formalized and specialized for the product line context. The formalization we propose first consists in making explicit the conceptual objects at business level that are implicit in the use cases; this leads to dealing with parameterized use cases. Use cases formalization implies the expression of the constraints linking them: use cases usually depend upon one another. The constraints are expressed locally on each use case using contracts, i.e., preconditions and postconditions, written in a dedicated use case constraint language (based on first-order logic).

The specification of the variation points in the use cases is also supported, allowing describing which parts are common to the product line, and which depend on a variation point.

From the knowledge of a decision model and the use cases describing the requirements of a product line, the product-specific requirements for each product can be automatically deduced. So, the strategy proposed is to go from the requirements expressed for the product line to the specific requirements that apply to a product; and then for every product the test case derivation method is (re)applied to its specific requirements. The test technique is thus functional/black box and does not include any specific tactic to deal with

PL typical variability and commonalities at design level. So, the force of the approach is to describe functional variation points at requirement level to automatically generate, based on the decision model, behaviors specific to any chosen product. Then, the designer may apply any method to produce the domain models of the product line and then instantiate a given product: the test cases derived from product-specific behaviors are executed against the end product to check whether the expected functionalities have been correctly implemented. In this approach, we do not take into account the design activities carried out to go from requirements down to domain applications, except for traceability purposes. However, we suggest bridging the gap between requirement level behaviors and the final design in two steps:

- Deriving test objectives into test scenarios by exploiting the sequence diagrams associated to use cases. Test scenarios may be combined in behavioral test patterns. A behavioral test pattern describes the expected and rejected behaviors of one execution of the product, but in an incomplete way, since the very specific design details are not known.
- By applying a test synthesis tool to generate the final test cases from each behavioral test pattern. The idea is to use a detailed description of the final design behaviors (typically expressed by statecharts associated to each active class) to extract from the end-product design the exact expected/rejected inputs/outputs of the end-product corresponding to a test scenario.

So, the "pattern," i.e., the skeleton of the product-specific test scenario is expressed using only requirement and analysis views while the final test cases are extracted from the final detailed design, without care of the intermediate refinement steps. As is explained in the following, the use of a test synthesis tool is not currently possible, mainly because of traceability and design incompleteness issues and also due to tools limitations. However, if a model-driven approach is adopted, these limitations are to be overcome.

Taking an opposite solution – but for testing purposes – to the general tendency in PL engineering, where a topmost important feature is reuse and factorization, every time a variation is introduced, all test cases for a newly instantiated product are automatically derived again. We believe this is the most efficient way to update dynamically the test cases for a product. An improvement of the approach, which is beyond the scope of this chapter, would be to identify among those derived, the test cases which are affected by the newly introduced variations.

12.2.2 Simulating Product-Specific Requirements

Once the product-specific requirements have been expressed using an enhanced use case definition, they can be simulated. The simulation process allows the requirement analyst to check whether the requirements are correct, which is of prime importance. Indeed, it is necessary to get trust in the requirements correctness before building the derived artifacts (such as system tests and analysis documents). Simulation is also the basis for the test objectives generation.

12.2.3 Generation of the Test Objectives

The simulation model is based on a transition system deduced from the use case description, and especially from the contracts. Not only does simulation allow the requirements analyst to ensure that her requirements are correct (from her point of view), but it also makes the test generation possible. We define a set of test criteria based on the simulation model to generate interesting paths of the simulation model, called test objectives. Such test objectives are obtained in the form of sequences of use cases with actual parameters.

12.2.4 Generation of the Test Scenarios

The generated test objectives are high-level tests that have to be progressively refined into test cases. A first step of this refinement consists in transforming the test objectives into test scenarios, using the sequence diagrams attached to each use case. A test scenario is a sequence diagram representing a test case, but in which there can be missing messages.

12.2.5 Behavioral Test Patterns and Synthesis of Test Cases

To transform the test scenarios into test cases, we propose to use synthesis tools. Test synthesis tools are originally used for testing telecommunication and distributed software. From a final design which describes precisely the expected product behaviors (using statecharts), a test synthesis tool automatically extracts the exact test cases which are the refinements of a test scenario. In our approach, the test synthesis tools are guided with particular test purposes called behavioral test patterns, and derived from the test scenarios.

12.2.6 An Illustrative Example of Product Line

The illustrative example that will be used all over the presentation of the method is a virtual meeting system offering simplified web conference services. The same system has been implemented in Java, Eiffel, and C# languages. It is used in the advanced courses of the University of Rennes. The whole system contains more than 80 classes but a simplified version is presented here with few variants for the sake of readability (only functional variants appear since we address functional testing). The case study is complete enough to illustrate our method. The virtual meeting server PL (VMPL) permits several different kinds of work meetings to be organized on a distributed platform. When connected to the server, a user can enter or exit a meeting, speak, or plan new meetings. Each meeting has a manager. The manager is the participant who has planned the meeting and set its main parameters (such as its name, its agenda, etc.). Each meeting may also have a moderator, designated by the meeting manager. The moderator gives the floor to a participant who has been asked to speak. Before opening a meeting, he or she may decide that it is to be recorded in a log file. The log file will be sent to the moderator after the closing of the meeting. Three types of meetings exist:

- Standard meetings where the current speaker is designated by a moderator (nominated by the organizer of the meeting). In order to speak, a participant has to ask for the floor, then be designated as the current speaker by the moderator. The speaker can speak as long as he or she wants; he or she can decide to stop speaking by sending a particular message, on reception of which the moderator can designate another speaker.
- Democratic meetings which are like standard meeting except that the moderator is a FIFO robot (the first client to ask for permission to speak is the first to speak).
- Private meetings which are standard meetings with access limited to a certain set of users.

We define our PL describing the variation points and products (the commonalities corresponding to the basic functionalities of a virtual meeting server, as described above). For the sake of simplicity, we only present 5 variation points in our product line:

- The limitation or lack thereof upon the number of participants to three.
- The type of available meetings; possible instantiations correspond to a selection of 1, 2, or all of the 3 types of possible meetings.
- The presence or absence of a facility enabling the moderator to ask for the meeting to be recorded.
- The languages supported by the server (possible languages being English, Spanish, French).
- The presence or absence of a supervisor of the whole system, able to spy and log it.

The other variation points which are not described here concern the presence of a translator, the operating system (OS) on which the software must run, various interfaces – from textual to graphical, network interface etc. Testing all the possible products independently is inescapable. In our case, this would mean testing $2*7*2*7*2*3*2 = 2352$ products (considering 3 OS and 2 GUIs), since the meetings can be limited or not (2 combinations), there can be 1, 2 or 3 types of meeting available among 3 types (7 combinations), the meetings can be recorded or not (2 combinations), there can be up to 3 languages supported (7 combinations), the system can be spied or not, there are 3 kinds of OS (3 combinations) and 2 GUIs (2 combinations). In order to simplify the presentation, in this chapter we only consider 3 products (a demonstration edition, a personal edition, and an enterprise edition). However, this does not in any way reflect a restriction on the method. The characteristics of the 3 products are given in the following Tab. 12.1.

Table 12.1. Variation points and products

edition	demonstration	personal	enterprise
meeting limitation	true	True	false
meeting types	{std}	{std, democ, priv}	{std, democ, priv}
recording	false	False	true
language	{En}	{En}	{En, Fr, Sp}
supervisor	False	False	true

12.3 An Enhanced Use Case Model for Product

Use cases are good entry points for test generation [3,4,9,24], and several proposals exist to adapt use cases to the product line context [1,5,10,11,13]. We detail in this section the use case model that is the foundation of our test generation process.

12.3.1 Enhancing Use Cases with Parameters and Contracts

Use case parameters. We consider parameterized use cases; parameters allow to determine the inputs of the use case (denoted UC in the following). For example, the use case *enter* is parameterized by the entering participant, and the entered meeting. It is expressed as follows:

UC enter (u:participant, m:meeting).

Parameters can be either actors (like the participant u in the UC *enter*) or main concepts of the application (like the meeting m in our example). Those main concepts will probably be reified in the design process and are pointed out as business entities in the requirements analysis. All types are enumerated types, they are only needed for the simulation.

Use case contracts. Use cases are also enhanced with contracts that can be statically evaluated. This approach is inspired by Meyer's Design-By-Contract method [21]. The declarative definition of such contracts expressions forces the requirement analyst to be precise and rigorous in the semantics given to each use case, being at the same time flexible and easy to maintain and to modify: writing contracts is quite an easy task as soon as the use cases are well defined.

To write contracts that can be evaluated, we propose a Use case Constraints Language (UCL), based on first-order logic. The constraint language recommended by the UML is the OCL [27]; nevertheless, we believe that the OCL is not suitable for requirements phases. Indeed, the OCL has a syntax difficult to understand and requires a specific learning. We have thus defined the UCL, however it can be seen as a subset of the OCL, with syntactic sugar in order to have an easy-to-handle language. The UCL provides a rigorous model as a response to proposals such as the Catalysis approach [8], which suggests enhancing use cases with pre and post conditions, like any other action.

The UC contracts are first-order logical expressions on predicates. A predicate has a name, and a (potentially empty) set of typed formal parameters (those parameters are a subset of the use cases parameters). The predicates are used to describe facts (on actors state, on main concepts states, or on roles) in the system. The predicates names are semantically rich: in this way, the predicates are easy to write and to understand. In order for the contracts to be fully understandable, the semantics of each predicate has to be made explicit, so as to avoid any ambiguity in the predicate's meaning. As an illustration, here are two examples of predicates with their semantics:

- Created(m) is a predicate which is true when the meeting m is created and false otherwise.
- Manager(u, m) is a predicate which is true when the participant u is the manager of the meeting m and false otherwise.

Since classical boolean logic is used, a predicate is either true or false, but never undefined.

The precondition expression is the guard of the use case execution, and the postcondition expresses the new values of the predicates after the execution of the use case. The operators are the classical ones of boolean logic: the conjunction (and), the disjunction (or) and the negation (not). The implication (*implies*) is used to condition a new assertion with an expression. It allows specifying conditional contracts. Quantifiers (forall and exists) are also used in order to increase the expressive power of the contracts.

We also defined enumerated properties, for example, *meetingType* can be defined as an enumerated property. For the simulation, the various possible values of *meetingType* will be required (for example: *standard*, *democratic*, and *private*).

An example of such contracts is given below, for the use cases *open* and *close*.

Examples of Enhanced Use Cases

```
UC open(u:participant;m:meeting)
pre created(m) and moderator(u,m) and not closed(m) and not
opened(m) and connected(u)
post opened(m)

UC close(u:participant; m:meeting)
pre opened(m) and moderator(u,m)
post not opened(m) and closed(m)
and forall(v:participant)not entered(v,m) and not asked(v,m)
and not speaker(v,m)
```

12.3.2 Expressing Variability at the Use Case Level

The objective is to provide ways to specify which parts of the requirements depend on a particular variant, i.e., to document variability in use case models. The coarsest granularity level to define variability is the use case itself. A use case can be specific to the presence of certain variants, as for example the use case *Record*, which is only present in the products owning the recording facility.

Variability can also occur at the parameters level. In our example, for some products the use case *Open* owns a parameter representing the moderator of the meeting, and in the others, for which only democratic meetings can be planned, the use case *Open* does not own such a parameter.

The contracts may also depend on some variants. For example, in the case of limited meetings, the use case *enter* will have a precondition checking that the meeting is not already full.

Thus, to specify the variability, we have defined tags (in fact UML tagged values) for the following model elements: contracts, parameters, and use cases. Those tags are a way to specify which variants the model elements depend on. If a tag is attached to a given model element *e*, then *e* is taken into account only for the product selected by this tag, i.e., the product owning one of the variants specified in the tag. By default, a model element *e* with no tag is taken into account for all the products. The format of those tags is:

VP{variant_list}, where *VP* is a variation point name and *variant_list* is a list of instantiations of the variation point.

For example, in our virtual meeting product line, the tagged value *recording{true}* selects the product owning a recording facility, i.e., the enterprise edition, and the tagged value *language{En}* selects the products handling the English language, i.e., all the products. Several contracts of the same type can thus be added to the same element, if they are differently tagged. When several preconditions (resp. post-conditions) are selected for a same product, they are conjuncted.

An example of contracts is given below: the use case *Enter* requires the entering participant *u* to be connected and the entered meeting *m* to be opened. For a private meeting, *u* must be authorized in *m*, and for limited meetings, there must be strictly less than 3 participants already entered in *m*.

Example of Variability in an Enhanced Use Case

```
UC enter(u:participant; m:mtg)
pre connected(u) and opened(m)
pre priv(m) implies authorized(u,m) {VPMeetingType(priv)}
pre not exists (u,v,w:participant) entered(u,m) and entered(v,m)
and entered(w,m) and u/=v and v/=w and w/=u {VPLimitation(true)}
post entered(u,m)
```

From a set of use cases with contracts for a product line, and using the decision model (i.e., characteristics of each product given in terms of variants), a set of use cases with contracts can be automatically built for each product, following the Algorithm 1.

```
algorithm extractRequirementsForAProduct
param p: the product
result : requirements R(p) for p

for each use case uc in the PL requirements
  if no tag t is present for uc or p.satisfies(t)
  then
     add uc to R(p)
  end
end
for each use case uc in R(p)
  for each precondition pre in uc
    if a tag t is present for pre and not p.satisfies(t)
    then
       remove pre
    end
  end
  for each postcondition post in uc
    if a tag t is present for post and not p.satisfies(t)
    then
       remove post
    end
  end
  for each parameter param in uc
    if a tag t is present for param and not p.satisfies(t)
    then
       remove param
```

```
      end
    end
  end
return R(p)
```

Algorithm 1. Algorithm to extract the requirements of a product from the product line requirements

12.4 Simulating the Use Cases

In this section, we explain how the enhanced use cases can be simulated for a chosen product, the simulation being the basis of our test generation process.

12.4.1 The Simulation Model

The simulation model is made of:

- Use cases enhanced with parameters and contracts
- The enumeration of all the instances of objects present in the system
- An initial state

Declaring the objects of the system allows to instantiate the use cases: an instantiated use case is a use case whose formal parameters have been replaced by actual parameters. As an example, in the virtual meeting, suppose that we declared 2 participants *p1* and *p2*, and a meeting named *m1*. The instantiated use cases of *plan(p:participant,m:meeting)* are *plan(p1,m1)* and *plan(p2,m1)*. In the following, we call instantiated use cases (resp. predicates) the set of use cases (resp. predicates) obtained by replacing their sets of formal parameters by all the possible combinations of their possible specific values.

To begin the simulation, we need an initial state and a simulation state. The simulation state is the current valuation of all the instantiated predicates of the system. In our implementation, the state is represented by a set of true instantiated predicates. The initial state is thus given in terms of instantiated predicates that are valuated to true at the beginning of the simulation. An instantiated use case can be executed or not executed from a given simulation state, depending on its precondition: it can be executed if its precondition is implied by the current state of the simulator. To determine the effects of the execution of an instantiated use case, we use its postcondition: to obtain the new current state, we modify the current state so that the postcondition becomes true. The simulator allows the requirement analyst to visualize at each step of the simulation which actions are valid, i.e., which use cases can be applied with which parameters. The requirement analyst can thus choose one of those actions, which will be simulated, leading the simulation system in a new state.

The benefits of such a simulation are obvious: the requirement analyst can check that the specified product has globally the same behavior like the one he or she had on mind. The simulator also permits to verify properties on the system. For example, one can check that it is not possible to be in a meeting if not connected to the server.

12.4.2 Exhaustive Simulation and Building of a Behavioral Graph

The exhaustive simulation leads to build a behavioral graph. We defined such a graph as a particular labeled transition system called UCTS (Use case Transition System). A UCTS is defined by the quadruple $M = (Q; q_0, A, \rightarrow)$, where:

- Q is a finite nonempty set of states, each state being defined as a set of instantiated predicates
- q_0 is the initial state
- A is the alphabet of actions, an action being an instantiated use case
- $\rightarrow \subseteq Q \times A \times Q$ is the transition function

A state of the UCTS represents the state of the system (in terms of value of predicates) at different stages of execution. A transition, labeled with an instantiated use case, represents the execution of an instantiated use case. A path in the UCTS is thus a valid sequence of instantiated use cases. A partial UCTS obtained for the demonstration edition is given in Fig. 12.2. Due to its finite set of states (itself due to the finite number of combinations of predicates), the UCTS is itself finite. Its maximal size in the worst case is 2^n, where n is the number of instantiated predicates present in the system. In practice, this maximal size is never reached, since all the potential states are not reachable. However, in case of combinatorial explosion of the number of states, the graph is not built exhaustively, but only partially using on-the-fly generation.

For example, in the virtual meeting, if the instantiated predicate $Entered(p1,m1)$ is true (meaning that the participant $p1$ has entered the meeting $m1$), then necessarily the instantiated predicate $opened(m1)$ is also true (meaning that the meeting $m1$ is opened). As a consequence, all the potential states for which $entered(p1,m1)$ is true and $opened(m1)$ is false are not reachable, and thus the actual size of the UCTS is smaller than the maximal size. For the demonstration edition with 3 participants and one meeting, there are 21 instantiated predicates (in fact 9 predicates were used to describe the requirements, which are instantiated into 21 instantiated predicates) and the UCTS has 1616 states whereas its theoretical maximal size is $2^{21} = 2\ 097\ 152$ states.

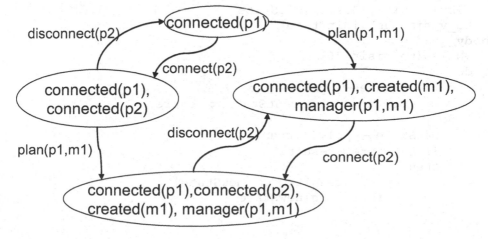

Fig. 12.2. An example of a partial UCTS

12.4.3 Simulating Each Product

The first step to build a UCTS for each specific product is to extract the requirements for each product from the PL requirements. This is simply done by parsing the variation notes in the requirements, and using a decision model, following algorithm 1. Then, for each product-specific requirement, algorithm 2 is applied to build the UCTS. Upon initialization, the initial state is deduced from the initial true predicates. Then the algorithm successively tries to apply each instantiated use case. Applying a use case is possible when its precondition is true with respect to the set of true predicates contained in the current state's label and leads to create an edge from the current state to the state representing the system after the postcondition is applied. The algorithm stops when all the reachable states are explored.

The simulation of the use case model for each product is the basis of the test generation process. The first step of this test generation process is detailed in the next section.

12.5 Test Objectives

In this section, we explain how test objectives can be generated using the simulation model. Test objectives can be seen as application test specification. We first formalize the notion of valid sequence of instantiated use cases and then we define test objectives from the notion of UCTS.

```
algorithm buildUCTS
param initState: STATE ; useCases : SET[ACTION]
var
  result : UCTS
  to_visit : STACK[STATE]
  currentState : STATE
  newState : STATE
init
  result.initialState initState
  to_visit.push(initState)
body
  while (to_visit`"0)
  do
    currentState←to_visit.pop
    ∀ uc ∈useCases | currentState ⇒ uc.pre
    do
      newState← apply(currentState, uc)
      if newState ∉result.Q
      then
          result.Q result.Q ∪ {newState}
          to_visit.push(newState)
```

```
      fi
      result.→←result.→∪{(currentState,uc,newState)}
    done
  done
end
```

Algorithm 2. Algorithm producing the UCTS

Valid sequence of instantiated use cases. A sequence S of instantiated use cases is said to be valid with respect to a system of enhanced use cases UCS if and only if there exists, in the UCTS corresponding to UCS, a path whose sequence of labels is identical to S. A path in the UCTS is here defined as the classical notion of path in a graph.

Test objective. A test objective (TO) is defined here as a valid sequence of instantiated use cases beginning with the root of the UCTS (i.e., the initial state).

Test objectives set consistency with an UCTS. A set of test objectives is said to be consistent with an UCTS iff each TO exercises a path of the UCTS.

When extracting test objectives, we aim at minimizing cost by generating:

- A small number of test objectives. Since a test objective has to be treated (either manually or automatically) to obtain a test case, too many test objectives would lead to having a large test cost.
- Small test objectives, since we believe that they are more understandable than larger ones (the size of a test objective being given in terms of the number of instantiated predicates composing it). For example, when built with a breadth-first algorithm, the height of the UCTS for demonstration edition is 10. We thus believe that the size of the test objectives should be smaller than 10.

In other words, we want to obtain a small number of efficient test objectives, instead of a large number of redundant test objectives. A test objective is redundant with respect to a set S of test objectives if it does not improve the global efficiency of S. The efficiency of the tests is measured here in terms of code coverage.

The two constraints (cost minimization and test efficiency) seem contradictory, but the experimental studies showed that the two criteria defined in the following satisfy these constraints [24]. The efficiency of a test objective can be measured using various criteria (code covered by the corresponding test case, coverage of control graphs, etc.). In [24] and in Sect. 12.7, we have used the code coverage.

All Instantiated Use Cases criterion. (AIUC) A test objective set TOS satisfies the all instantiated use cases coverage criterion for a given use case transition system iff each instantiated use case of the system is exercised by at least one TO from TOS. An instantiated use case is said to exercise a test objective TO iff it is included in it.

All Precondition Terms criterion. (APT) A test objective set TOS satisfies the All Precondition terms criterion for a contracts system iff each use case is exercised in as many different ways as there are predicates combinations to make its precondition true. A use case can be applied when its precondition is true; this precondition being a logical expression on predicates, there are several valuations of the predicates which makes it true (as an example, if a precondition is a or b, 3 valuations makes it true: (true, true), (true, false), and (false, true). The criterion APT will select sequences of use cases so that each use case is applied with all the possible valuations of the expression precondition = true.

These two criteria are not related by a theoretical subsume relationship. To illustrate the APT criterion, suppose that a use case $U(x{:}X,y{:}Y)$ has the precondition: $p(x)$ or $q(x,y)$. Then the APT criterion selects 3 states in the UCTS ($x1$ being an instance of type X and $y1$ being an instance of type Y):

- One for which the instantiated predicate $p(\text{x1})$ is true and the instantiated predicate $q(x1,y1)$ is false
- One for which the instantiated predicate $q(x1,y1)$ is true and the instantiated predicate $p(x1)$ is false
- One for which both instantiated predicates $p(x1)$ and $q(x1,y1)$ are true

Then a path will be chosen to reach each state, from the initial state of the UCTS. Those 3 paths satisfy the APT criterion.

Other criteria can be used, such as covering all the vertices or all the edges of the UCTS, but they lead either to inefficient tests (all the vertices) or to a very large number of tests (all the transitions) [24].

The two criteria are implemented with a breadth-first search of the UCTS. Such a technique ensures that the obtained TOs are consistent with the considered UCTS. The choice of a breadth-first visit is made in order to obtain smaller TOs: small tests are more meaningful and understandable than larger ones.

As an example, let us consider again the UCTS of Fig. 11.2, for which we assume that {connected(p1)} is the initial state. When applying the AIUC criterion, we will try to exercise the instantiated use case disconnect(p2). For that, if we adopt a deep-first search algorithm, we obtain the path [connect(p2), plan(p1,m1), disconnect(p2)] (the size is 3). If we apply a breadth-first search, we will first visit all the successors of the initial node (i.e., {connected(p1), connected(p2)} and {connected(p1), created(m1), manager(p1,m1)}) then explore the successors of those 2 nodes. The path that will then be found is: [connect(p2), disconnect(p2)] (the size is 2).

Robustness Testing

The tests generated as described above exercise the application into a nominal way since only expected behaviors are produced from requirements. The system robustness may also be tested since the application should detect the execution of nonexpected use cases in a given test sequence. To generate such robustness tests from enhanced UCs, the contracts must be detailed enough so that all the unspecified behaviors are considered incorrect: as soon as the requirements are precise enough, the generated UCTS can be used as an oracle for robustness tests.

The principle is to generate paths that lead to an invalid application of a use case. The idea is thus to exercise correctly the system and then make a nonspecified action. The execution of such a robustness test must lead to a specific treatment (e.g., emitting an error message, raising an exception). If not, a robustness weakness has been detected.

The criterion we use to generate robustness paths with the UCTS is quite similar to the *All Precondition Terms* one: for each use case, it looks for all the shortest paths leading to each of the possible valuations that violate its precondition. This criterion is illustrated in Fig. 12.3.

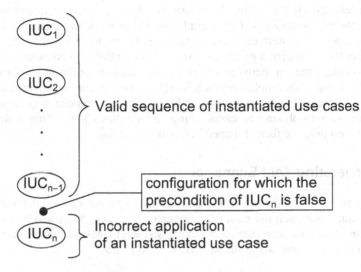

Fig. 12.3. Robustness test objectives

Robustness criterion. A test objective set TOS satisfies the robustness criterion for a contracts system iff each use case is exercised in as many different ways as there are predicates combinations to make its precondition false.

The robustness tests test the defensive code of the application, which is not tested with the functional tests previously generated. By joining the two sets of tests, not only will we test that the application does what it should (according to the requirements) but also that it does not do what it should not.

Specific and General Test Objectives

At this stage, when the sets of test objectives have been generated for each product, the various test objectives are parsed, in order to detect which test objectives are common to the product line, and which test objectives are specific to a given product.

Test Objectives versus Test Cases

In general, the test objectives generated as described above are not executable test cases. Indeed, they are sequence of instantiated use cases and have no links with the implementation of the system. In particular, they do not take into account the interface that the system uses to offer the described services. The following section proposes a method to generate application test cases from test objectives.

12.6 Test Case Generation

Generating test cases that can directly be launched by a test driver requires more information than only the use cases and their contracts. Other modeling elements are needed to make precise the exact interface of the system, i.e., the protocol between the users and the system under test to realize a given use case. In this section, we propose to use particular scenarios to bridge the gap between test objectives (that are at the requirement level) and test cases (that are at the implementation level).We first generate application test scenarios, that are scenarios the tester wants to exhibit. Then we propose to complete those test scenarios in order to obtain test cases, using test synthesis tools. This is done using an intermediate test purpose format named *Behavioral test pattern*.

12.6.1 Generating Test Scenarios

Test scenarios are derived from test objectives using the scenarios attached to each use case: we assume that each use case is documented by its contracts and by system scenarios. We assume that those scenarios are expressed with UML sequence diagrams. Examples of sequence diagrams are given in Figs. 12.4 and 12.5.

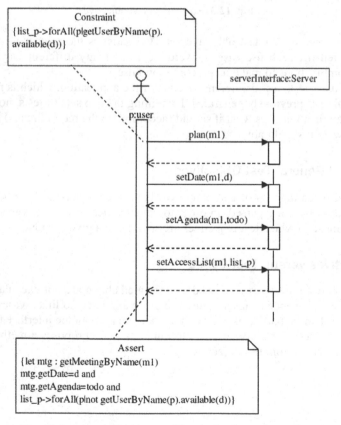

Fig. 12.4. A nominal sequence diagram for the use case plan

Using sequence diagrams. The use of sequence diagrams is interesting for three main reasons:

1. First, sequence diagrams are a way to improve the verdict preciseness. The test objectives built with the contracts method do not embed a precise oracle. The oracle embedded is just the expectation:
   - Of a noninterrupted execution for the functional test objectives
   - Either of an error or of a warning for the robustness test objectives
   Such verdicts are limited since they check neither the system outputs consistency nor any property of the system state. Sequence diagrams are of a lower level of abstraction than the use cases, thus they can embed more precise oracles.
2. Second, sequence diagrams allow to obtain test scenarios from which a code generator can generate the test cases. The test objectives generated are far from the messages exchanged during the test, since they just consist of sequences of parameterized cases. The communication protocols are unknown at this stage. The sequence diagrams attached to the use cases allow us to bridge part of the gap between the test objectives and the test cases, since they describe the expected exchanges of messages between the actors and the system.
3. Third, the scenarios and sequence diagrams are increasingly being used in industry in the early phases of requirements. The conclusion of the survey of industrial software projects [34] published in 1998 insists on the industrial need to base system tests on use cases and scenarios, and explains that most projects lack a systematic approach to define test cases based on scenarios. In [31] published in 2000, the authors still remark that in practice, scenarios from the analysis phase are seldom used to create concrete system test cases. The method presented here makes easier the use of scenarios in the validation phase.

Each of the sequence diagrams we deal with is attached to a use case and represents one of its nominal or exceptional scenarios. Nominal scenarios represent the basic ways to successfully exercise a use case. Exceptional scenarios represent ways to exercise a use case leading to a failure, the raise of an exception, or an error message: exceptional scenarios make the use case fail. The sequence diagrams are system level, in the sense that they only involve the system itself and the actors.

Those sequence diagrams may involve parameters: since they are attached to parameterized cases, it is quite natural to find in the sequence diagrams at least the same parameters as in its owner use case. The sequence diagrams contain more information than the use case, and thus they may own more detailed pre- and postconditions than the use case contracts. As a result, each of those sequence diagrams may own OCL constraints describing on which condition they can be exercised, and what are the consequences on the system.

One can wonder why the OCL is used instead of the UCL. The reason is that, at the use-case level, the contracts are high-level ones, and independent from the static models (class diagrams for example) that will be designed later in the development process. Thus for the use cases, the OCL is not well suited, that is why we defined the UCL. On the contrary, at the sequence diagrams level, we want to design contracts relying on the rest of the model (on static models for example).We thus need a language to navigate into a UML model, and the OCL is perfectly suited for that. In our context, the nominal scenarios will be used for functional testing and the exceptional ones will be used for robustness testing.

To sum up, the sequence diagrams we deal with are system level, they may involve parameters and they may own additional OCL contracts.

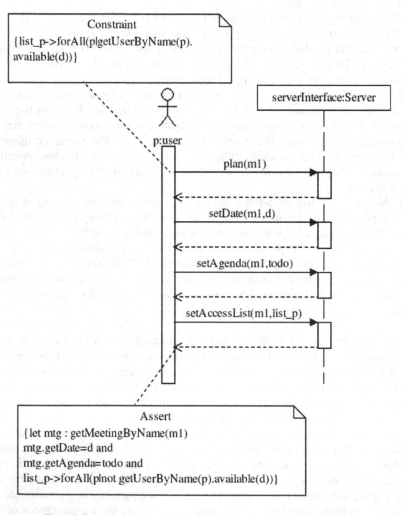

Fig. 12.5. An exceptional sequence diagram for the use case plan

Figures 12.4 and 12.5 provide a nominal and an exceptional scenario for the use case *plan* of the Virtual Meeting system. In the two scenarios, *d* and *list_p* are scenario parameters, which designate the date and the list of the invited participants of the meeting being planned, respectively. The nominal precondition is an OCL precondition that checks whether the invited participants are available at the meeting date. The nominal postcondition checks that the meeting has been planned with the correct parameters. The exceptional scenario checks that the participants are not available at the meeting date in its precondition, and that the meeting is not planned in its postcondition.

In the product line context, a given sequence diagram can be either common to the product line, or only to a given set of products, depending on the presence of a particular variant. We thus use the same notation as for the use cases to express the variability at the sequence diagram level (see Sect. 12.3.2). Future work will consist in using sequence diagrams directly modeling the variability, such as the sequence diagrams proposed in [35].

Building test scenarios. We propose to replace the instantiated use cases with instantiated scenarios in the test objectives. Sequences of scenarios are thus obtained, and scenario composition is applied on them to obtain a global system test scenario (strong sequential composition is used: strong sequential composition imposes that all the events of a scenario are executed before an event of the next scenario can be executed).

When an instantiated use case is replaced by a scenario, the scenario is partially instantiated using the effective parameters of the instantiated use case. As we already mentioned it, the scenario may also own other parameters; those parameters are not instantiated at this stage. A partially instantiated scenario is thus defined as a scenario whose formal parameters corresponding to the use case parameters are replaced by effective parameters. In the following, this instantiation is supposed to be achieved by the *inst* method.

To define precisely how test scenarios are built, we first introduce the following notations:

- We note $\{scn_{i,j}\}_{j \in 1..n}$ the set of n nominal scenarios attached to the use case uc_i, and $\{sce_{i,j}\}_{j \in 1..m}$ the set of m exceptional scenarios attached to the use case uc_i
- The strong sequential composition of scenarios is denoted by the symbol $\circ$.
- The Cartesian product on sets is denoted $\times$.

With those conventions, a test scenario is defined from a tuple of scenarios $(sc_1, ..., sc_n)$ as: $sc_1 \circ ... \circ sc_n$ (the strong sequential composition the tuple elements). The set of tuples defining a set of test scenarios $TS = \{ts_1, ..., ts_u\}$ obtained from a test objective $TO = [iuc_1...iuc_t]$ is denoted TS_{tuple}. The set TS_{tuple} is obtained applying a Cartesian product on sets of partially instantiated scenarios, as explained in the following definitions.

Functional nominal test scenarios. A nominal test objective $TO = [iuc_1...iuc_t]$ is transformed into the set of tuples TS_{tuple} defined by:

$$TS_{tuple} = \prod_{i=1}^{t} \{scn_{i,j}.inst(iuc_i)\}_{j \in 1,...,n}$$

$$= \{scn_1.j.inst(iuc_1)\}_{j \in 1,...,n} \times ... \times \{scn_t.j.inst(iuc_t)\}_{j \in 1,...,n}$$

Building the functional test scenarios can be seen as replacing one after the other each of the instantiated use cases of TO by each of its nominal scenarios. Once all the instantiated use cases have been replaced, then a tuple of sequence diagrams is obtained, and strong sequential composition is achieved to obtain a test scenario.

Functional robustness test scenarios. A robustness test objective $TO = [iuc_1...iuc_t]$ is transformed into the set of tuples TS_{tuple} defined by:

$$TS_{tuple} = \prod_{i=1}^{t-1} \left\{ scn_{i,j}.inst(iuc_i) \right\}_{j \in 1,\dots,n} \times \left\{ sce_{t,j} \right\}_{j \in 1,\dots,m}$$

$$= \left\{ scn_{1,j}.inst(iuc_1) \right\}_{j \in 1,\dots,n} \times \dots \times \left\{ scn_{t-1,j}.inst(iuc_{t-1}) \right\}_{j \in 1,\dots,n}$$

$$\times \left\{ sce_{t,j}.inst(iuc_t) \right\}_{j \in 1,\dots,m}$$

Building the robustness test scenarios can also be seen as replacing the instantiated use cases by its scenarios. The process to replace the $t-1$ first instantiated use cases is the same as for functional test scenarios. The last instantiated use case is each time replaced by one of its exceptional scenarios.

Some test objectives are general for the whole product line, and others are specific to products. During the replacement of the use cases by sequence diagrams, this is taken into account: for product-specific test objectives, only the sequence diagrams corresponding to the particular product have to be taken into account, thus producing specific test scenarios; while for general test objectives, all the scenarios have to be taken into account, thus producing either general test scenarios (when only general sequence diagrams have been used) or specific test scenarios.

The cartesian product of scenarios may lead to a very large number of tests if there are a large number of scenarios per use case. If the test launching is automatic, this is not a problem. If the number of tests has to be reduced, then another strategy has to be applied. Techniques such as the ones proposed in the tobias tool [15] can be used: in the tobias tool, _lters are proposed to reduce the combinatorial explosion of the number of tests generated by combining different test schemas. Filters applied at runtime allow not to run tests with a prefix that have already failed. Such a technique could be used with our approach.

Examples. To illustrate how the test scenarios are built, suppose that we want to generate the test scenarios corresponding to the functional test objective *[connect(p1), plan(p1,m1)]*. We suppose that the use case *connect* is documented by 2 nominal sequence diagrams:

- *SNconnect1* describing a participant asking to connect and then giving her address requested by the system
- *SNconnect2* describing a participant asking to connect giving her address
  and that the use case *plan* is documented by the 2 nominal sequence diagrams:
- *SNplan1* describing the planning of a meeting with a name, a date, and an agenda
- *SNplan2* describing the planning of a meeting with just a name and a date

Four functional test scenarios will then be generated: *(SNconnect1, SNplan1)*, *(SNconnect1, SNplan2)*, *(SNconnect2, SNplan1)*, and *(SNconnect2, SNplan2)*. All the combinations of scenarios are thus tested, for example, the one of Fig. 12.6 composing *SNconnect1* with *SNplan2*. In a general case, when the system under test is described by many scenarios, testing all possible combinations of scenarios may lead to a combinatorial explosion: another strategy may consist in executing each (nominal and exceptional) scenario at least once.

If we want to generate robustness test scenarios, only the exceptional sequence diagrams of the use case *plan* will be used. Suppose that we have 3 exceptional sequence diagrams *SEplan1*, *SEplan2*, and *SEplan3*, we will then generate 6 test scenarios composing the 2 nominal sequence diagrams of the use case *connect* with the 3 exceptional sequence diagrams of the use case *plan*.

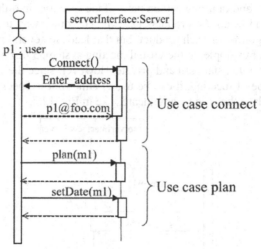

Fig. 12.6. An example of test scenario

Verdicts. The oracle embedded in the test scenarios is built from the OCL pre- and postconditions associated to the sequence diagrams. The test scenarios can emit 3 kinds of verdicts:

- The fail verdict is emitted when a postcondition is violated during the execution. The postconditions ensure that the system is in a correct state after the execution of a sequence diagram. If not, an error is detected.
- The pass verdict is emitted when the test scenario can be executed without error.
- The inconclusive verdict is emitted when a test scenario execution had to be aborted due to a violated precondition. An inconclusive verdict does not mean that an error is detected; it means that the test scenario could not be played. It should be possible to refine each test objective (except for the last use case of a robustness test objective) into a test scenario which satisfies all the preconditions. The fact a test scenario violates a precondition reveals a default in the test objective refinement, when use cases have been replaced by scenarios. An automated approach to generate test cases unhappily may generate such nonrelevant tests. Here we identify them with a distinct verdict, and a manual refinement of the associated test objective into a correct test scenario must be done.

12.6.2 Test Scenarios and Test Cases

The test scenarios may still be incomplete, depending on the sequence diagrams that have been used. The only case when a test scenario can directly be considered as an application test case occurs when the sequence diagrams used exactly contain the messages to exchange to realize the use case, only using the use case parameters, and without using wildcards (a wildcard is a symbol replacing any expression, the symbol * is often used, see Fig. 12.7).

In a product line, it is very useful to model the sequence diagrams documenting the use cases using parameters and omitting certain parts of the scenario, in order for them to be generic, and to correspond to all the products [25,26]. The other way to proceed is to design specific sequence diagrams for each product, but that leads to several problems: time, maintenance, and so on. For example, in the virtual meeting system, 3 different types of meetings can be planned: democratic, standard and private. However, since the way to plan a meeting is similar for each type of meeting, it can be useful either not to specify the type at all (like in Fig. 12.4) or to replace the type by a wildcard, like in Fig. 12.7.

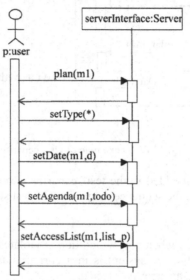

Fig. 12.7. An example of sequence diagram with wildcard

Thus the test scenarios built with the method described above still contain genericity marks: parameters, wildcards, or lack of certain messages or parameters. In the example of Fig. 4, the message setting the meeting type is missing, and in the example of the Fig. 12.7, only the type of the meeting is missing. In order to complete them, we propose to use test synthesis tools.

12.6.3 Test Synthesis Tools

The objective here is not to explain in detail the principles of the test synthesis tools, but to explain why and how they can be used to transform test scenarios into test cases. In short, the principle of the test synthesis tools (such as Agatha [16] or TGV [12]) is to explore the behavioral specification of a system, in order to derive tests from it. We have chosen to use the TGV tool since the exploration is driven by a test purpose: that means that the behavioral specification is parsed until a test case corresponding to the given test purpose is found.

The UMLAUT tool generates a simulation API from the UML model of a system. The way such an API can be built can be found in [29]. This simulation API can then be used by TGV. TGV also needs a test purpose, which has to be given in the form of a labeled transition system (LTS). From the simulation API and the LTS representing the test purpose, TGV builds on the _y the LTS representing the operational semantics of the system and stops this building task when a path in the built operational semantics satisfies the test objective. Such a path is considered to be a test case, and is transformed into a UML sequence diagram.

Ideally, it should be possible to use the test scenarios as test purpose (sequence diagrams can easily be transformed into labeled transition system), in order to obtain test cases using the TGV and UMLAUT tools. The problem with such an approach is the huge size of the LTS representing the operational semantics of each product. In practice, as soon as a real-sized system is studied, if the test purpose is not detailed enough, the part of the LTS that has to be built is far too huge. That is why we propose to use what we call *behavioral test patterns* to guide the test synthesis, instead of just test scenarios. As explained in the following, those behavioral test patterns can be generated from the use cases and the test scenarios.

12.6.4 Using Behavioral Test Patterns

A behavioral test pattern is a test purpose composed of 3 parts, each being given in the form of sequence diagrams:

- The specification of the behavior the test designer wants to test; such a scenario, also called .positive scenario., serves to select the scenarios of the specification which are relevant for the test case.
- The specification of the behaviors the test designer wants to avoid in the test; such scenarios, also called .negative scenarios., serve to eliminate the scenarios of the specification which are irrelevant for the test case.
- The specification of the behavior needed to place the system under test in a state in which the positive scenario can take place; such a scenario, also called .prefix scenario., serves to factorize the part of the positive scenario which may be common to several behavioral test patterns.

The behavioral test patterns are an efficient way to guide the test synthesis. The negative scenarios describe the behaviors which, though correct, are unwanted in the test. Several negative scenarios can be associated to the same behavioral test pattern. They serve to limit the exploration required by the synthesis algorithms in order to find a test case that fits the behavioral test pattern, thereby improving performance. From a pragmatic point of view, if several test executions fit the accept part of the behavioral test pattern, negative scenarios can be used to guide the synthesis tool to produce the most suitable test case. Guiding the tool may be done to help minimize the synthesized test case by excluding calls which are known to be superfluous for the purposes of the test. This reduction of "noise" is particularly useful in testing concurrent applications.

The prefix is a high-level representation of the initialization of the behavior to be tested. It describes the preamble part of the test case, i.e., the behavior previous to that described in the positive scenario. The prefix serves to guide the synthesis toward the production of a minimal preamble. Like the negative scenarios, the prefix can be constructed from the other use-case scenarios. Unlike a negative scenario, a prefix may be composed of a sequence of such scenarios. Building the prefix is therefore a process of selecting use-case scenarios and composing them.

To guide the test synthesis, behavioral test patterns are much more efficient than just test scenarios. The behavioral test patterns can automatically be generated from the use cases and the test scenarios, as explained in the following.

Generating behavioral test patterns. A test scenario corresponds to the prefix and the positive scenario of a behavioral test pattern. The test scenario is a composition of various sequence diagrams, the last one representing the positive scenario and the other ones representing the prefix.

The difficulty is thus to generate the negative scenarios. One criterion is to avoid behaviors involving objects which do not interact with the objects involved in the test objective. Suppose that we want to generate the negative scenarios of a behavioral test pattern from a functional test objective [iuc1,...,iucn]. All the instantiated exceptional scenarios of the system will be added as negative scenarios, as well as all the instantiated scenarios handling none of the object handled in the test objective [iuc1,...,iucn].

For example, let us come back to the example of Fig. 12.6. If we want to generate a behavioral test pattern corresponding to this test scenario, we will have as preamble the first part of the test scenario corresponding to the connection, then as positive scenario the second part concerning the planning. Concerning the negative scenarios, we will add all the instantiated scenarios which are not dealing with instances *p1* and *m1* (for example, the planning of *m2*), and all the exceptional scenarios of the other use cases of the system.

To sum up this section, from test objectives, test scenarios are generated using the scenarios attached to each use case. The use case scenarios may include genericity marks (such as parameters and wildcards), thus the test scenarios are still incomplete.

To complete the test scenarios, test synthesis tools can be applied. However, the test synthesis usually fails for large system when the synthesis is not guided by a very detailed test scenario. Thus we propose to guide the test synthesis using particular sets of scenarios called *behavioral test patterns*.

12.7 Results and Discussion

This section offers an experimental validation of the proposed approach: we give an overview of the tests synthesized for the 3 products of our PL example, then we study the efficiency of the tests generated for the demonstration edition. The link from the test scenarios to the test cases (using test synthesis tools and behavioral test patterns) is not yet integrated in our prototype tools, so the experiments we present here are based on the rest of the approach: from use cases to test scenarios.

12.7.1 Test Generated for the 3 Products

From the PL use cases enhanced with contracts, we derived one specific UCTS per product, and then we generated the test scenarios (TS). Statistics are given in Tab. 12.2 (demonstration, personal and enterprise edition are denoted DE, PE, and EE respectively). A study of those test scenarios reveals that common tests have been generated (corresponding to the commonalities of the PL), and specific tests have been generated for each product, due to the different combinations of variants in the products.

Table 12.2. Statistics on generated tests

edition	DE	PE	EE
# generated TS with AIUC	50	65	78
# generated TS with APT	15	18	21
# generated TS for robustness	65	110	128
average size of the tests	5	4	4

12.7.2 Study of the Generated Test Efficiency for Demonstration Edition

For the experimental validation, we used a Java implementation of the virtual meeting. The virtual meeting example has been built using a common modeling for the whole product line, making use of various well-known design patterns. To perform code coverage studies for the demonstration edition, we performed an ad hoc and manual analysis to distinguish the source code of the product line which was not executed by the demonstration edition, in order to obtain exact coverage figures, which only concerns the code involved in this product. For this given instance of product, around 20% of the code (in terms of executable lines of code) is specific to the product while the remaining is extracted from the common code. This proportion is the same for all of the products.

Moreover, we studied the code of the demonstration edition to evaluate which part of the code is possible to cover with a pure functional and system testing approach. Around 9% of the code is dead code. Nevertheless, this code is relevant: it consists of pertinent but unused accessors, which could be used in future evolutions of the system. Functional testing cannot deal with this code: it has to be tested during the unit test step. For the study presented below, we removed those 9% of dead code to focus on the efficiency of our tests on reachable code.

Around 26% of the code is robustness code: robustness with respect to the specification which asserts that only the required functions are present, and robustness with respect to the environment which asserts that the inputs coming from the environment are correct.

The results of the code coverage measures are given in Fig. 12.8. The APT (resp. AIUC) criterion covers 71% (resp. 60%) of the functional code. Note that since the AIUC criterion generates many more TC than the APT one, the APT criterion is more efficient in terms of covered statement per test scenario. Since our robustness tests stem from functional requirements, they cannot cover all the robustness code but they cover 100% of the robustness code with respect to requirements. The uncovered code concerns syntactic verification of the inputs treatment of network exceptions, these aspects are specific to the distributed platform. Globally, the robustness tests add a 10% code coverage to the functional tests. So, for the parts of code related to functional requirements, half of the robustness code and 98% of the functional one have been covered. The remaining uncovered code is specific to the platform or unused code ("dead code") dedicated to future PL evolution. This result is promising since it reveals that the functional code can be tested from test cases derived from requirement stages. The same kind of approach could be used to generate test cases dedicated to nonfunctional properties, such as security and real time.

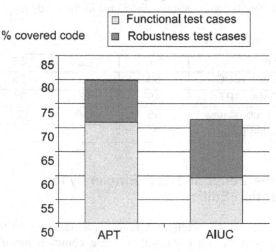

Fig. 12.8. Code coverage of the tests

The ratio between the number of robustness tests and the corresponding coverage is deceptive. Improving the robustness test efficiency would require defining more efficient test generation criteria and more detailed scenarios (however requiring such detailed diagrams from the designers has a heavy cost).

This study shows that the tests generated from the product requirements expressed at the PL level (and extracted for a specific product using a decision model) are relevant at the product code level, with the use of adequate criteria. However, to get higher confidence in these encouraging results, future work will consist in evaluating the approach with other case studies, and other efficiency criteria (code coverage is a weak criterion, better criteria are branch coverage or mutation score for example). Other experiments also showed that classical faults – using mutation analysis – manually injected in the products were detected by our tests. The approach has also been successfully applied on two systems components of last generation combat aircrafts (Mirage 2000-9 and Rafale), of mid-complexity (several thousands C++ KLOC). These real-case studies are not designed in a product-line context but reveal that approximately 80% of the functional requirements could be treated and used for test generation. This experience return shows the relevance of the approach for functional requirements, since the 20% nontreated requirements were related to detailed design features and did not describe services requirements.

12.7.3 Discussion on the Benefits and Limitations of the Approach

As several other approaches to test product lines (and in particular the approach presented in Chap. 11), we assume that a common requirement model is available. In Chap. 11, this requirement model is made of PLUCs (Product Lines Use Cases), while in our approach it is made of use cases with contracts, parameters, and sequence diagrams. Our approach is not dependent on the way UML models are obtained: they can be obtained using model transformations on a common model for the whole PL or manually built. In this sense, our approach fits into the overall process of product line engineering, since it only requires a common requirement engineering phase.

The automation of the approach can be discussed. Globally, to use our approach, a tester has to:

– Take the use cases, sequence diagrams, the decision model, and the UML model of the considered product
– Manually define the instances/objects the tests have to deal with (at the requirement level and at the code level)

The quality of the obtained tests strongly depends on the quality of the inputs, which come from the specification. This is a classical problem for testing, since tests are always generated to validate an implementation with respect to a specification. If the quality of the specification is low, test cases will only test a little part. Improving the quality of the input models is beyond the scope of this chapter. However, robustness test cases may help reveal lack of precision in the specification, since robustness test cases aim at exploring the bounds of the possible behaviors. This analysis is manual but may help identifying defaults in the specification. Concerning the artifacts the tester has to manipulate, if the inputs (mainly the use cases and the sequence diagrams) are detailed enough, the generated tests will be efficient enough, and the manual task of the tester will not be important: it will simply consist in the verdict analysis emitted by the tests. However, if those inputs are not detailed enough, some tests may be missing to satisfy a chosen coverage criteria. Classical unit testing must be done to complete the test. The main advantage of the approach is to get confidence in the end-product implementation with respect to the functional product requirements, even in the case these requirements are not complete enough to cover the whole code. A consequence of the approach is to identify – by measuring the actual test coverage obtained for requirement-based tests – the lack of precision in the requirements and analysis views.

Concerning the adequacy of the approach to the PL context, when new requirements are added, a brutal approach consists in regenerating automatically all the test cases.

However, the test generation tool allows a guided test cases generation. For instance, only tests cases that exercise the new added property, parameter, or use case can be generated. To ensure some regression testing, it is highly recommended to reapply the existing test cases when testing the newly added features. The approach is thus adaptable and allows both to generate again test cases and to generate test cases that exercise a chosen requirement. Thus, the process is either incremental for an underevolution product or allows a full-test generation when a new product is created. As explained in the case study, the approach does not allow nonfunctional test case generation from requirement. We believe that an analogous approach may be applied for some specific nonfunctional properties, such as execution time and security testing.

12.7.4 Related Work

The PL engineering now appears as a major issue in the field of software engineering; however, PL validation is not yet mature, and in particular PL testing is not studied enough in comparison with the large set of new issues implied by PL testing. However, judging by the test generation approaches briefly presented in the SPLIT workshop [32] (e.g., use of mutation techniques and formal methods), PL testing is undergoing a resurgence of interest.

The PL testing issues and challenges are described in [22]. They are also evoked in [18], which gives an overview of the product line testing. McGregor describes the whole PL testing process, in particular, all the different test artifacts that have to be produced are described, as well as the process from which they are produced and the related PL specificities. The main contribution concerning the testing process comes from references [6] and [33].

Concerning methodological and technical PL testing approaches, from our point of view the two main approaches are [2] and [14,30]. Details on those approaches can be found in Chaps. 11 and 13.

In Chap. 11, the authors have adapted the well-known Category-Partition (CP) method in their PLUTO approach. The CP method is applied at the use-case level, and more precisely at the PLUC level. The PLUCs mechanism to manage variability and ours are quite similar. However, the underlying testing method is different in the sense that the approach proposed in Chap. 11 focuses more on test data. We thus believe that for applications for which the handled data are more complex than the control, the PLUTO approach is better-suited than ours. On the contrary, for applications with complex control, our approach is better suited. As previously explained in this chapter, one of the weaknesses of our approach is that the test data have to be manually managed by the tester. We thus believe that our approach would benefit from a coupling with the PLUTO approach. The PLUTO approach could for example be used to generate adequate test data to feed our approach.

In Chap. 13, the authors propose a testing method relying on different test strategies, depending on the ways variability appears in the use cases. Four strategies are identified: abstraction, parameterization, segmentation, and fragmentation. The most adequate strategies are discussed depending on the type of variability that can appear in the event flow, the pre- and postconditions, the actors, and the relationships. This approach is systematic, but yet not automatic. Our approach would benefit from using parts of the ScenTED approach in several ways. A first obvious point is that we focus on functional system testing whereas ScenTED covers other kinds of testing such as integration testing. Second, ScenTED introduces an enhancement of activity diagrams such that activity diagrams can embed variability information. Such activity diagrams could be used in our approach instead of sequence diagrams, or (better) complementary to sequence diagrams.

12.8 Conclusions and Future Research

The testing task is known to be an important part of software development and usually suffers of time-to-market constraints leading to reduce the time dedicated to the validation of the system. The problem of the testing cost is all the more crucial in the product line context since it is not a single system that has to be validated, but several (and potentially a large number of) systems of the same product line. That is why the automation of the testing task is a challenging issue in the field of product line validation.

We have presented a complete chain for functional test cases derivation from the functional requirements of a product line. Avoiding testing all possible combinations of products (most of them being never instantiated in practice), the approach targets a given product in the product line, extracts its functional requirements using the decision model, and generates test cases from these requirements. Requirements, expressed by used cases, are improved by declarative information under the form of contracts as an anchor for further testability purposes and to express variability and commonality.

At requirement stage, the analyst may check the consistency of each product's requirements using the UCTS as a simulation platform. The test cases are generated in two steps: correct sequences of use cases are deduced from use case contracts and then scenarios are substituted to each use case to produce a test scenario that is finally transformed into a test case thanks to test synthesis tools. One of the principal objectives of this approach is the possibility to use it in an industrial context. For that, instead of pushing formal methods to the industry (one of the motto in this community) we proposed to work the other way round, i.e. starting from established practices and gently pushing them towards formally exploitable models. We concentrated here on widely accepted practices based the use of the UML to support an object-oriented development process. The industrial feasibility of the approach has been validated for a single product in the context of the Carroll project, with the industrial partner Thalès [17] and using academic case studies for the product-lines aspects.

In this context, the approach we presented partially automates the generation of product-specific system test cases from Use Cases, taking into account traceability problems between high-level views and concrete test case execution. Due to the automation, the approach is adaptable to several product-line evolution processes. Indeed, it supports full-test generation when a new product is added to the product line as well as partial generation of dedicated test cases when new features are added to an existing product.

Several future research directions can be explored to improve our approach. The first step consists of studying the different ways for users to enter the models of use case dependencies. As mentioned in the previous section, other approaches propose graphical notations and, in particular, UML activity diagrams to enter such models. It is thus worth studying precisely the exact expressiveness of the two languages (i.e., activity diagrams versus contracts) and detecting in which situations one language is better-suited than the other. Then, compatibility rules between the languages can be detected and transformations from one language to another can be envisioned. The second step is to focus on test data. Currently, our approach needs to be manually fed with the test data for the test generation and the simulation. Since the existing research work in the field principally aims at generating relevant test data for product line testing, future research can couple our approach with the existing work concerning test data generation and experiment the efficiency of the generated tests. Finally, our approach needs to be validated with real-world case studies.

Acknowledgments

We gratefully acknowledge the extensive reviews of Antonia Bertolino, Erik Kamsties, Timo Käkölä, Andreas Metzger, and Antti Tevanlinna, which significantly improved the quality of this chapter.

References

1. Bertolino, A., Fantechi, A., Gnesi, A., Lami, G., Maccari, A.: Use case description of requirements for product lines. In: Proceedings of the International Workshop on Requirements Engineering for Product Lines (2002) pp 12–19
2. Bertolino, A., Gnesi, S.: Use case-based testing of product lines. In: Proceedings of the 9th European Software Engineering Conference held jointly with 10th ACM SIGSOFT International Symposium on Foundations of Software Engineering (2003) pp 355–358
3. Binder, R.V.: *Testing Object-Oriented Systems* (Addison-Wesley, Reading, MA 2000) Chapter 8
4. Briand, L., Labiche, Y.: A UML-based approach to system testing. J. Softw. Syst. Model. 10–42 (2002)
5. Bühne, S., Halmans, G., Pohl, K.: Modelling dependencies between variation points in use case diagrams. In: Proceedings of the 9th International Workshop on Requirements Engineering: Foundation For Software Quality – REFSQ'03 (2003)
6. Clements, P., Northrop, L.: *Software Product Lines: Practices and Patterns* (Addison-Wesley, Reading, MA 2001)
7. Cockburn, A.: Structuring use cases with goals. J. Object-Oriented Program. 35–40 and 56–62 (Sept/Oct and Nov/Dec 1997)
8. D'Souza, D.F., Wills, A.C.: *Objects, Component, and Frameworks with UML: The Catalysis Approach, Chapter Interaction Models: Uses Cases, Actions, and Collaborations* (Addison-Wesley, Reading, MA 1999)
9. Fröhlich, P., Link, J.: Automated test case generation from dynamic models. In: Proceedings of the 14th European Conference on Object-Oriented Programming (ECOOP'00) (2000)
10. Gomaa, H., Shin, M.E.: Multiple-view meta-modeling of software product lines. In: Proceedings of the 8th International Conference on Engineering of Complex Computer Systems (2002) 238–246
11. Halmans, G., Pohl, K.: Communicating the variability of a software-product family to customers. Softw. Syst. Model. 2(1), 15–36 (2003)
12. Jard, C., Jéron, T.: TGV: theory, principles and algorithms. In: Proceedings of the 6th World Conference on Integrated Design and Process Technology (2002)
13. John, I., Muthig, D.: Product line modeling with generic use cases. In: Proceedings of SPLC2 Workshop on Techniques for Exploiting Commonality Through Variability Management (2002)
14. Kamsties, E., Pohl, K., Reis, S., Reuys, A.: Testing variabilities in use case models. In: Proceedings of the Fifth Workshop on Product Family Engineering. Lecture Notes in Computer Science, vol 3014 (Springer, Berlin Heidelberg New York 2003)
15. Ledru, Y., du Bousquet, L., Maury, O., Bontron, P.: Filtering tobias combinatorial test suites. In: Proceedings of ETAPS/FASE'04 – Fundamental Approaches to Software Engineering. Lecture Notes in Computer Science, vol 2984 (Springer, Berlin Heidelberg New York 2004)
16. Lugato, D. et al: Validation and automatic test generation on UML models: the AGATHA approach. Electron. Notes Theor. Comput. Sci. 66(2) (2002)
17. Lugato, D., Maraux, F., Le Traon, Y., Normand, V., Gallois, J.P., Dubois, H., Pierron, J.Y., Nebut, C.: Automated functional test case synthesis from Thales industrial requirements. In: Proceedings of the 10th IEEE Real-Time and Embedded Technology and Applications Symposium (2004)

18. McGregor, J.D.: Testing a software product line. Technical report, CMU/SEI (2001)
19. McGregor, J.D.: Building reusable test assets for a product line. In: Proceedings of the 7th International Conference on Software Reuse: Methods, Techniques, and Tools (Springer, Berlin Heidelberg New York 2002) pp 345–346
20. McGregor, J.D., Sykes, D.A.: *A Practical Guide to Testing Object-Oriented Software* (Addison-Wesley, Reading, MA 2001)
21. Meyer, B.: Applying design by contract. Computer **25**(10), 40–51 (1992)
22. Muccini, H., van der Hoek, A.: Towards testing product line architectures. In: Proceedings of the ETAPS03 Workshop "Test and Analysis of Component Based Systems" ("TACOS'03"), vol 82 (2003)
23. Nebut, C., Fleurey, F., Le Traon, Y., Jézéquel, J.M.: A requirement-based approach to test product families. In: Proceedings of the 5th Workshop on Product Families Engineering (PFE-05). Lecture Notes in Computer Science (Springer, Berlin Heidelberg New York 2003)
24. Nebut, C., Fleurey, F., Le Traon, Y., Jézéquel, J.M.: Requirements by contracts allow automated system testing. In: Proceedings of the 14th IEEE International Symposium on Software Reliability Engineering (ISSRE'03) (2003)
25. Nebut, C., Pickin, S., Le Traon, Y., Jézéquel, J.M.: Reusable test requirements for UML-modeled product lines. In: Proceedings of the Workshop REPL'02 (Requirements Engineering for Product Lines) (2002)
26. Nebut, C., Pickin, S., Le Traon, Y., Jézéquel, J.M.: Automated requirements-based generation of test cases for product families. In: Proceedings of the 18th IEEE International Conference on Automated Software Engineering (ASE'03) (2003)
27. OMG: OCL. http://www.omg.org/docs/ptc/03-08-08.pdf (2003)
28. OMG: Unified modeling language specification, version 2.0. http://www.omg.org/docs/formal/03-03-01.pdf (2004)
29. Pickin, S., Jard, C., Le Traon, Y., Jéron, T., Jézéquel, J.M., Le Guennec, A.: System test synthesis from UML models of distributed software. In: Proceedings of the 22nd Conference on Formal Techniques for Networked and Distributed Systems (FORTE'02), Houston, Texas (2002)
30. Reuys, A., Kamsties, E., Pohl, K., Reis, S.: Model-based system testing of software product families. In: Proceedings of the 17th Conference on Advanced Information Systems Engineering (CaiSE'05) (2005)
31. Ryser, J., Glinz, M.: Scent – a method employing scenarios to systematically derive test cases for system test. Technical report (Institut für Informatik, University of Zurich 2000)
32. Proceedings of the International Workshop on Software Product Line Testing (2004)
33. Tevanlinna, A. et al: Product family testing: a survey. SIGSOFT Softw. Eng. Notes **29**(2) (2004)
34. Weidenhaupt, K. et al: Scenario usage in system development: A report on current practice. IEEE Softw. (1998)
35. Ziadi, T., Hélouet, L., Jézéquel, J.M.: Behaviors generation from product lines requirements. In: Proceedings UML2004 Workshop on Software Architecture Description (2004)

13 The ScenTED Method for Testing Software Product Lines

A. Reuys, S. Reis, E. Kamsties, and K. Pohl

Abstract

In current practice, a significant problem of testing software product lines is the immense effort required. However, this effort can be reduced by applying the systematic reuse concepts of product line engineering to the reuse of test artifacts. Such a reuse is established by defining and preserving variability throughout generic test artifacts in domain engineering, and by reusing these generic test artifacts in application engineering to derive product-specific test case scenarios. In this contribution, the ScenTED method (*Scen*ario based *TE*st Case *D*erivation) is presented. The ScenTED method is based on the systematic refinement of generic use case scenarios to generic system and integration test case scenarios. The method includes activities in domain engineering for preserving the variability in the test artifacts as well as activities in application engineering for binding the variability of the generic test artifacts. In addition, the refinement of use case scenarios to test case scenarios enables the traceability between development artifacts and test artifacts.

13.1 Introduction

Testing in product line engineering has the same goal than testing in single system development. The goal is to uncover faults in the executable software modules. Although the individual applications of a software product line are derived from the core assets (cf. [17]), each application has to be tested individually, because the combination of common parts with different configurations of variants will lead to differing behaviors of the individual applications.

13.1.1 Strategies for Testing Product Lines

In product line engineering, artifacts for specific applications are derived from generic artifacts that have been developed in domain engineering. As a consequence, three different strategies for creating test cases for testing the derived applications can be identified [11,22]:

1. *Separate test case development.* In this strategy, test cases for each derived application are developed independently from each other (see Fig. 13.1). This strategy results in an extremely high test effort, because – without reuse – the same test effort as in single system development is required for each

application. Test cases for functionalities that are contained in several applications must be derived several times.

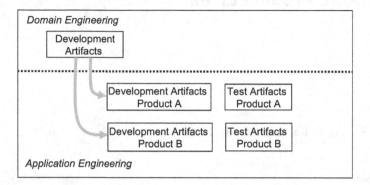

Fig. 13.1. Separate test case development

2. *Opportunistic reuse of existing test cases.* In this strategy, a first attempt is made for reusing application test cases. For the first application that is derived for a given product line, test cases are developed. As soon as a further application is derived from the product line, test cases of the first application can be reused for the new application (see Fig. 13.2). The main problem with this form of reuse is that it is not performed systematically. This means that there is no method that supports the tester in selecting reusable test cases. Functionalities of the new application might not have been tested completely if the selection of the test cases was carried out falsely, i.e., the test coverage of an application is not guaranteed.

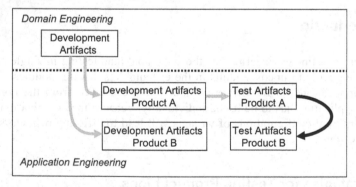

Fig. 13.2. Opportunistic reuse of existing test cases

3. *Design test cases for reuse.* This strategy follows the product line engineering principle *design for reuse* and enables the overall goals of shortening the time-to-market, reducing cost, and increasing quality (see Fig. 13.3). Testing is divided into two subprocesses. The partitioning takes place similar to the product line approach, which is classified into domain engineering and application engineering. In domain testing, reusable test artifacts are created.

In application testing, test cases for a specific application are derived on the basis of the generic test cases from domain engineering. The problem of this strategy is that initially, a set of domain test cases has to be developed. Therefore, the gain in effort when reusing these domain test cases has to be higher than the effort for developing these generic artifacts in the first place. Further, adequate techniques for describing generic test cases (by means of variability) have to exist.

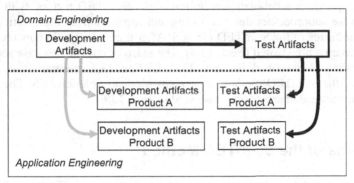

Fig. 13.3. Design test cases for reuse

Obviously, strategy (1) cannot be considered a serious approach for testing software product lines except in the cases where only very few applications are derived from the core assets. Equally, strategy (2) is not a suitable approach, because of the unsystematic reuse of test cases. Consequently, strategy (3) presents the most promising and efficient approach toward testing software product lines. A systematic approach for realizing strategy (3) is the ScenTED method that is presented throughout this chapter.

13.1.2 The ScenTED Method

The ScenTED method presents a solution for applying product line concepts to the testing process by providing detailed guidelines on how to create generic test artifacts in domain engineering and how to reuse these generic artifacts in application engineering. ScenTED supports the system test as well as the integration test of software product lines.

The method can be classified as a model-based testing approach [20]. Based on use cases and their scenarios, a test model is created. By employing the test model, test case scenarios for system and integration tests are derived systematically. This derivation is performed in such a way that the achievement of a specific coverage criterion can be guaranteed. The test model is represented by activity diagrams.

Traceability links are recorded between use cases, use case scenarios, architecture scenarios, and test case scenarios. This extensive form of traceability enables an effective change management.

Variability is preserved in the domain test artifacts to facilitate reuse. Test case scenarios can be derived from these domain test artifacts for each product line application, because all intended variants are reflected in the domain test case scenarios. If additional requirements should be realized, this has to be considered in application engineering. However, the decision, whether these additional requirements should be transferred to the reference model in domain engineering, is not the task of testing but that of requirements management.

13.1.3 Overview

This chapter provides a detailed description of the ScenTED method with its respective activities in the subprocesses domain testing and application testing. Section 13.2 briefly describes the basics of the ScenTED method. After that, we explain how reusable domain test case scenarios are created (Sect. 13.3). The reuse of domain test case scenarios in application testing is described in Sect. 13.4. Section 13.5 presents an overview of an evaluation of the ScenTED method at Siemens Medical Solutions HS. The contributions of this chapter are summarized and discussed in Sect. 13.6.

13.2 Basics of the ScenTED Method

The ScenTED method employs use cases and scenarios as test references, from which test cases are derived. In this section, we elaborate on the benefits of this use case-based approach and introduce the underlying information model of ScenTED.

13.2.1 Use Case Based Testing

Use cases represent the goal-oriented use of the system's functionality. The interactions of a potential user with the software system are described by the scenarios that are contained in the use cases [5]. Scenarios are particularly well suited for the derivation of test cases, because testing requires a description of interactions between users and the software system [3,4]. Moreover, as we already have shown in [8], use cases can be extended in such a form that variability can be suitably represented. Further, these extended use cases can be employed for supporting the communication between specialized experts and the customers.

Other approaches for testing product lines are also based on use cases, use case scenarios, and creation of domain test cases. Some of these approaches support the idea of extending the principle of proactive reuse to product line testing.

McGregor [13] and Geppert et al. [6] create reusable test cases during domain engineering. McGregor proposes to create reusable test cases by generalizing among the different variants. Application-specific test cases are derived by specialization, i.e., supplementing details about the chosen variant. The test cases are derived from natural language requirements. Geppert et al. assume that a set of applications already exist. That means, test cases are generalized from existing test cases. In contrast to ScenTED, both approaches are not model based.

Nebut et al. [15,16] also follow the idea of proactive reuse. They consider scenario fragments in domain engineering that are assembled to test case scenarios. However, there is no test model that guides the assembly of these fragments during domain engineering. Dependencies between use cases are specified in a use case transition graph, but test case scenarios are only derived for specific applications when the variability has already been bound. A detailed specification of this approach can be found in Chap. 12.

Hartmann et al. [9] use activity diagrams as a test model, which contain variability, but test cases are derived only in application engineering. Therefore, it is a model-based testing approach, but it does not consider the reuse of test cases. Bertolino and Gnesi [1, 2] do not use a test model, but a structured test specification that contains variability. Test cases are created for each application based on this specification.

In summary, the approaches of McGregor, Geppert et al., and Nebut support the idea of extending proactive reuse to product line testing. Hartmann et al. support the idea of model-based testing in product line engineering. However, there is no approach for product line testing up to now that combines proactive reuse with the benefits of model-based testing. The benefits of model-based testing like the systematic and repeatable creation of test cases, the early validation of the requirements, or the prerequisite for test automation as well as the pro-active reuse are realized by the ScenTED method.

13.2.2 Information Model of ScenTED

An information model is the general basis of the ScenTED method. The model describes the types of artifacts that are created and used by ScenTED (see Fig. 13.4). It is structured in four columns: requirements artifacts, architecture artifacts, test artifacts, and executable artifacts. The arrows between all artifacts represent traceability links. In the following paragraphs, the artifacts of the information model are briefly described.

- *Use Case.* A use case defines the high-level usage of the system's functionality in a given context, i.e., the application of the functionality of the system to achieve a particular goal of a user. By this, a requirement is enriched with a typical usage context (see [5]).
- *Use Case Scenario.* A use case scenario describes specific user–system interactions, which are instances of the use case's workflow. A scenario is either a success or an exception scenario. A scenario is one possible way to realize a use case goal (success scenario) or a flow of events that prevents the use case goal (exception scenario).
- *Architecture Configuration.* An architecture configuration defines a specific software architecture. It combines the specific components and connectors with complementary interfaces by defining allowed links between them.
- *Architecture Scenario.* An architecture scenario defines the specific architectural interaction sequences with respect to a given architecture configuration. An architecture scenario describes the interactions between components of the system and the user, as well as the interactions between the components themselves.
- *Test Case Design.* A test case design defines the functionality to be tested by a set of test cases, i.e., the scope of the associated test cases. Besides the functional test goal, the chosen quality attributes like correctness or performance are specified in the test case design. In addition, the test phase is indicated to which the associated test cases belong. Test phases that are maintained by ScenTED are system testing and integration testing.
- *Test Case Scenario.* A test case scenario defines the interactions that have to be executed to test a specific functionality. Depending on the associated test case design, a

test case scenario contains user–system interactions (system testing) or additional inter-actions between the system's components (integration testing).

- *Runtime System.* The run-time system consists of the implemented components of the architecture configuration. It includes additional information about the system environment, e.g., platform and hardware information.
- *Executable Test Case.* An executable test case contains specific test data (i.e., concrete input values and expected results) in addition to the test case scenario. For each executable test case, a set of verification points can be indicated. A verification point describes the place in the flow of the test case, in which an examination should take place.

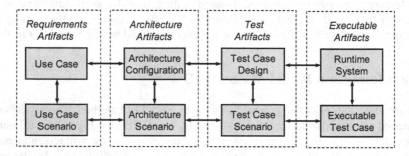

Fig. 13.4. Information model of ScenTED

13.3 ScenTED in Domain Engineering

In domain engineering, reusable test artifacts are developed with the ScenTED method. In this section, the method's activities for deriving generic system and integration test case scenarios in domain engineering are described together with the activities that are required for creating necessary intermediate artifacts. It should be noted that all domain artifacts contain variability.

13.3.1 Activities for System Testing

This section describes the activities of the ScenTED method that are executed to derive domain system test case scenarios. Figure 13.5 gives an overview of these activities, where these are represented by the numbered arrows. All other arrows represent traceability links.

ScenTED supports the development of system test case scenarios in domain testing through two activities:

DS1:   Development of Domain Use Case Scenarios
DS2:   Derivation of Domain System Test Case Scenarios

In the following sections both activities are described in detail. The activities are clarified on the basis of an abstract example.

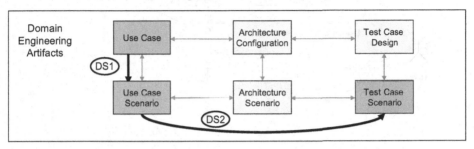

Fig. 13.5. Overview of the activities for deriving domain system test case scenarios

DS1: Development of Domain Use Case Scenarios

Domain use case scenarios are developed in the first activity DS1 of the ScenTED method. A use case contains the description of selected use case scenarios. However, other scenarios than the ones that have been described in the use case might be important for test case derivation. Therefore, a systematic creation of use case scenarios is necessary.

To accomplish such a systematic derivation, a model-based representation of the scenarios of a use case is necessary. The Unified Modeling Language (UML) provides sequence diagrams as a means to describe such scenarios [23]. These sequence diagrams can be used as a starting point to synthesize activity diagrams, which are a more comprehensive form of representing behavior. Consequently, these activity diagrams might have to be supplemented before they can be used for testing, e.g., if not all possible exceptions were modeled in the use case, the activity diagrams must be extended accordingly.

In ScenTED, activity diagrams are used to represent several use case scenarios in one comprehensive model (following the aforementioned synthesis approach). Therefore, variability of the use cases must be preserved in the activity diagrams to enable a later reuse of the domain use case scenarios. To model variability in activity diagrams, an extension of the representation of activity diagrams is necessary.

Representation of Variability in Activity Diagrams. The standard UML notation for activity diagrams does not provide means for explicitly modeling variability. Therefore, it is necessary to extend the activity diagram notation by the concept of variability to be able to use such models for the creation of domain test artifacts.

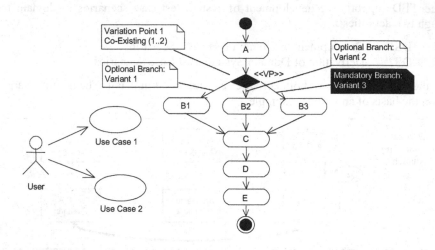

Fig. 13.6. Use case model and activity diagram including variability

A simple and abstract example of a use case model and a supplementing activity diagram is represented in Fig. 13.6. The activity diagram is a compact representation of all possible scenarios of Use Case 1. Variation points in activity diagrams are modeled as special decision points [21]. These variation points are identified by the stereotype <<VP>> (see Fig. 13.6). Additionally, the symbols of these special decision points are colored black. For the identification of the variation points their name is annotated by notes. By this means, a direct reference to the corresponding use case exists, which provides for traceability.

Variants that belong to a variation point can either be optional or mandatory ones. In this context, mandatory variants always have to be chosen if the associated variation point has to be considered for a specific application. If the variation point itself belongs to a variant that is not chosen for a specific application, the mandatory variant is also not part of this application. For deriving test case scenarios, this information is of utmost importance and therefore is also annotated by notes. A further relevant constraint on the selection of variants can be provided for each variation point. A variation point can describe that several variants from the possible (optional) variants can be selected (co-existing dependency), or that only one variant from the possible variants can be selected (alternative dependency). In the example in Fig. 13.6 at least one variant and up to two of the three possible variants can be selected.

Supplementation of Activity Diagrams with Additional Information. As it has been noted above, activity diagrams must be supplemented by additional information to derive the test case scenarios completely from the activity diagram. Most importantly, main scenarios, alternative scenarios, and exception scenarios must be reflected in the activity diagrams. Usually, not all existing exceptions are considered in activity diagrams. Depending on the intended purpose, activity diagrams are described on different levels of abstraction (starting with the activity diagrams that reflect the most important use case scenarios).

For test case scenario derivation, the diagrams must be modeled with the aforementioned detail.

In Fig. 13.7 such an activity diagram is shown, which is an extension of the one in Fig. 13.6. This activity diagram has been supplemented by considering one additional exception scenario and one additional alternative scenario. The additional exception scenario is caused by the additional end state after activity B3, the additional alternative scenario is caused by the additional activity F.

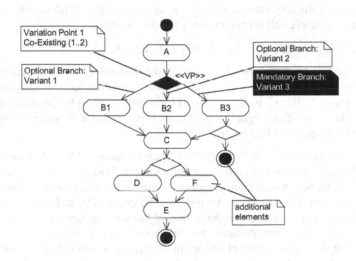

Fig. 13.7. Supplementation of activity diagram by considering additional scenarios

In this activity of the ScenTED method, the first explicit traceability information is generated. The traceability link between the use case and the supplemented activity diagram, which represents the use case scenarios, is called Link_DS1.

DS2: Derivation of Domain System Test Case Scenarios

The activity DS2 of the ScenTED method describes the derivation of domain test case scenarios for system testing from the domain use case scenarios that have been developed in activity DS1.

Definition of a Coverage Criterion. Based on the structure of the activity diagrams, a coverage criterion for the derivation of test case scenarios can be defined. Such a coverage criterion allows a tester to decide when a sufficient set of test case scenarios has been derived. A domain test case scenario corresponds to one possible path through the activity diagram. In the literature, coverage criteria for structural tests (initially developed for determining the coverage of source code) have been applied to use cases (e.g., see [24]). Well-known structural coverage criteria are the statement coverage criterion, the branch coverage criterion, and the path coverage criterion. Statement coverage is a poor criterion that does not imply a thorough test of the system. Path coverage on the contrary results in a thorough test, but achieves this thoroughness through a huge number of scenarios [14], which might prohibit its practical use.

In ScenTED, the branch coverage criterion is used as a coverage criterion that achieves a fairly thorough test (subsuming the statement coverage criterion) with a relatively moderate number of scenarios that have to be tested. To achieve full branch coverage, scenarios have to be derived in such a way that each possible branch of the activity diagram is covered by at least one scenario. In the example in Fig. 13.7, four scenarios are necessary to cover all possible branches. As a compact notation, scenarios can be represented by vectors that contain the sequence of actions (or scenario steps). With this notation, the following scenarios achieve full branch coverage in the example:

(A, B1, C, D, E), (A, B2, C, F, E), (A, B3, C, F, E), (A, B3)

However, the first two scenarios that contain the variants B1 and B2 become invalid if only variant B3 is realized in the application under consideration. Unfortunately, the remaining scenarios (A, B3, C, F, E) and (A, B3) do not cover all the branches of the activity diagram. Therefore, the original branch coverage criterion must be extended for the use within software product line engineering.

Technique for the Derivation of Domain Test Case Scenarios. The extension of the original branch coverage criterion has led to the following definition of the criterion: "For each application that can be derived from the domain artifacts, each branch of the activity diagrams where the variability has been bound must be covered by at least one test case scenario." To achieve this coverage, the derivation of domain test case scenarios is performed in two steps. In the first step, domain test case scenarios are derived in such a way that each branch that does not represent an optional variant is covered at least once. For all other branches placeholders are inserted. In the second step, the domain test case scenarios are supplemented by adding the optional variants of a variation point. All branches of all variants must be covered. If necessary, additional scenarios have to be developed.

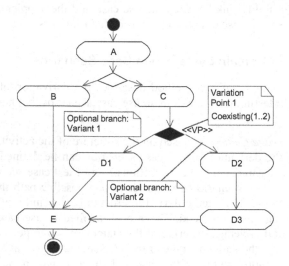

Fig. 13.8. Diagram including variability in only one branch of the control flow

The extended branch coverage criterion, which is achieved by this two-step technique, can be illustrated with the example in Fig. 13.8. The example shows the activity diagram for Use Case 2 (from Fig. 13.6). As it can be observed, the activity diagram contains one variation point in one of its branches. To reflect the occurrence of variation points within scenarios, the compact scenario notation from above is extended. Variation points are specified by sets. To the closing curly braces of each set, the identifier of the variation point is added as a subscript. Within these sets, the possible variants of the variation points are depicted by vectors that contain the actual activities (scenario steps) of the variant. Again, the closing brace of each vector is annotated with the respective name of the variant as a subscript.

Applying the first step to the example results in the following test case scenarios:

$$(A, B, E), (A, C, \{\}_{VP1}, E)$$

The first scenario represents a scenario without variability. It can be reused without any modification in the further activities of application testing. In the second scenario, the possible variants are represented by their variation point as a placeholder. After applying the second step, the following test case scenarios result:

$$(A, B, E), (A, C, \{(D1)_{V1}, (D2, D3)_{V2}\}_{VP1}, E)$$

The second test case scenario still contains variability, which has to be bound in application engineering to derive concrete test case scenarios.

If a decision point exists between the activities of a variant (e.g., assuming that in the above example, there was an additional decision point between D2 and D3 and a further branch to a hypothetical activity D4), additional test case scenarios have to be specified. These have to consider the different decisions that can be taken at the respective decision point.

Representation of Domain Test Case Scenarios by Sequence Diagrams. A more detailed representation of test case scenarios is necessary when pre- and postconditions of test cases should be described, and the expected test results should be annotated for the different steps of the scenario. We have chosen the UML's sequence diagram notation for this purpose.

To represent a test case scenario by a sequence diagram, two different possibilities for expressing variability in these diagrams exist: (1) segmentation and (2) fragmentation [10,12].

Using the *segmentation mechanism*, all possible variants of a test case scenario are represented in one single sequence diagram. The advantage of the segmentation mechanism is that each possible test case scenario for a specific application can be directly derived from such a "segmented" sequence diagram.

With the *fragmentation mechanism*, the domain test case scenario and its variability are described by more than one sequence diagram. In contrast to the segmentation mechanism, each possible variant is represented by exactly one sequence diagram. A disadvantage of this mechanism is that for deriving a test case scenario for a specific application, additional information is necessary. It is important to know, which fragments can be combined to a meaningful test case scenario. This information has to be described in separate documents. The advantage of the fragmentation mechanism is the possibility to reuse variants separately in different test case scenarios.

As a conclusion, both mechanisms can be useful when representing domain test case scenarios. Often, a combination of both mechanisms is appropriate. Different cases can be identified:

- In general, the segmentation mechanism is used, because test case scenarios for specific applications in application testing can be derived more easily and no additional information has to be documented.
- If a test case scenario includes too many possible variants, the fragmentation mechanism should be used. As the segmentation mechanism describes all possible variants in one single diagram, this diagram might become too complex or unreadable for many variants. The number of possible variants from which on the fragmentation mechanism should be used varied from project to project, as it depends on different influences, e.g., the number of interactions of a variant.
- The fragmentation mechanism should normally be used to specify the scenario steps that stem from pre- and postconditions of a domain use case scenario. The conditions are described by individual scenarios. Therefore, each one can easily be represented by a fragment, and thus the conditions can be reused for different test case scenarios.

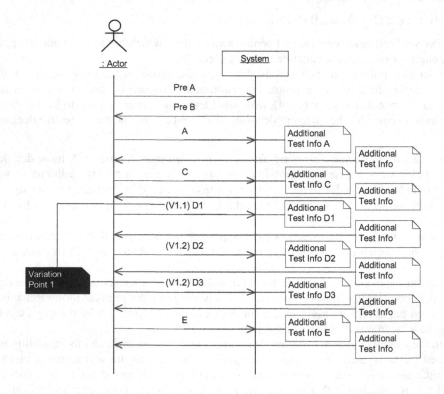

Fig. 13.9. Example of a domain test case scenario

Figure 13.9 shows an example of a test case scenario that is represented by a sequence diagram using the segmentation mechanism. Additional test information (e.g., expected results) is annotated by comments for each of the interactions. Accordingly, the variability within the sequence diagram is represented by annotations. The example contains the variation point and the two variants of the test case scenario (A, C, {(D1)$_{V1}$, (D2, D3)$_{V2}$}$_{VP1}$, E), which has been derived from the activity diagram in Fig. 13.8. All interactions of the two possible variants were transferred to the sequence diagram and in both cases marked by the name of the variant. A comment for the variation point identifies the variable part. The variation point enables the traceability to the associated use case, since the variation point is clearly identifiable by its name. The precondition is considered by two additional interactions Pre A and Pre B in the diagram.

The activity DS2 of the ScenTED method derives test case scenarios with the help of (1) the activity diagrams extended by variability aspects, (2) the extended branch coverage criterion, and (3) the associated two-stage coverage technique. These test case scenarios serve as a starting point for the further test case derivation for system testing of specific applications. The traceability link between domain use case scenarios and the domain test case scenarios is called Link_DS2.

13.3.2 Activities for Integration Testing

In this section, the activities of the ScenTED method that are performed for deriving domain integration test case scenarios are presented. These integration test activities are an extension of the activities of the above system test method. In these activities, interactions between components are considered in addition to the interactions between a user and the system. The component interactions are described in architecture scenarios, from which test case scenarios that contain component interactions are derived. The effects of different forms of integration strategies (i.e., how to incrementally construct sub-systems from smaller ones or components) and the additional variability that is contained in domain architecture models (e.g., the alternative choice of components for realizing a similar function) will be dealt with in future work.

Figure 13.10 shows an overview of ScenTED's integration test activities, which are:

DI1:   Development of Domain Architecture Scenarios
DI2:   Derivation of Domain Integration Test Case

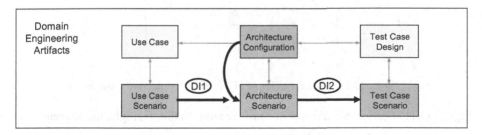

Fig. 13.10. Overview of the activities for deriving domain integration test case scenarios

DI1: Development of Domain Architecture Scenarios

An architecture scenario describes the interactions between users and the system components as well as the interactions between the individual components. The domain architecture scenarios are derived by refining the interactions that have been defined in the domain use case scenarios and which have been created in the activity DS1 of the ScenTED method (see Sect. 13.3.1). Therefore, the components of the system have to be known. The required information is found in the architecture configuration (see Fig. 13.10).

Analogous to the derivation of domain test case scenarios in system testing, the ScenTED method considers variation points and variants in the domain use case scenarios when deriving domain architecture scenarios. This implies a further variability in scenarios as some components might only have to be considered if they take part in an interaction.

For the development of the domain architecture scenarios, the interactions of the domain use case scenarios and the component information from the architecture configuration are merged. At this point, the interactions between components have to be known. Therefore, the interactions that have been described in the domain use case scenarios are augmented by adding these additional interactions.

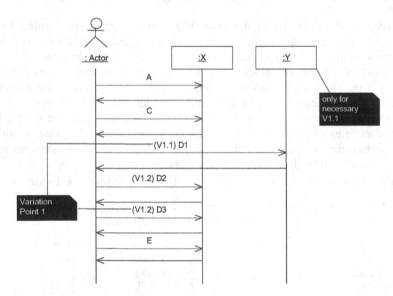

Fig. 13.11. Abstract example of a domain architecture scenario

Figure 13.11 shows a domain architecture scenario. In this example, the sequence

$$(A, C, \{(D1)_{V1}, (D2, D3)_{V2}\}_{VP1}, E)$$

is realized by components X and Y. Like domain system test case scenarios, sequence diagrams that include variability information are used for the representation of the domain integration test case scenarios (see Sect. 13.3.1). In the example, it can be observed that component Y is only necessary for variant 1.1 (as annotated by a respective comment).

The domain architecture scenarios that are developed in activity DI1 form the basis for the derivation of domain integration test case scenarios. In this step, two traceability links are generated. The first link connects the domain use case scenarios and the domain architecture scenarios and is called Link_DI1a. The second link that is created is called Link_DI1b and it connects the domain architecture configuration and the domain architecture scenarios. In this activity, two traceability links are recorded, because two artifacts have served as a starting point for developing architecture scenarios.

DI2: Derivation of Domain Integration Test Case Scenarios

Activity DI2 of the ScenTED method derives domain integration test case scenarios from domain architecture scenarios. The approach and the employed representations correspond to activity DS2 of the ScenTED method, in which domain system test case scenarios were derived (Sect. 13.3.1). The main difference lies in the additional consideration of the interactions between system components. The refinement that is performed by this activity again preserves the variation points by transferring them to the domain integration test case scenarios. Additional information and additional interactions for preconditions and postconditions of the use cases are supplemented. The traceability link that is generated in activity DI2 connects the domain architecture scenarios and the domain integration test case scenarios. It is called Link_DI2.

13.4 ScenTED in Application Engineering

Application testing has to ensure that the application derived from the product line fulfills the specified application requirements. On the one hand, the application requirements reflect the wishes (or needs) of the customers. On the other hand, these requirements must not violate the dependencies between variants and variation points defined in the domain requirements. The creation of application test cases is realized by considering these two aspects.

The efficiency of application testing can be improved if a structured reuse of former application test artifacts takes place. If a former application has bound a set of identical variants, some of test case scenarios that have already been derived for this application might be reused. The dependencies between the domain and application artifacts must be recorded to enable such a structured reuse. Based on these dependencies, a tester can identify reusable test artifacts and can incorporate them into the test set for the new application.

The goal of this section is to give advice on how to test applications that stem from a software product line. The application testing process can be separated into three activities that can be (and usually are) interwoven:

1. How to create application test case artifacts to test the functional correctness of the application (Sects. 13.4.1 and 13.4.2).
2. How to ensure that customer specific applications do not violate the dependencies defined during domain engineering (Sect. 13.4.3).

3.   How to make product-specific test artifacts reusable and how to systematically reuse them (Sect. 13.4.4).

The first activity describes how application test artifacts are derived from domain test
artifacts. To ensure the systematic reuse of these artifacts, a tester has to consider the relation between application-specific requirements and the specified variants in the domain
model. Three different cases of such a relation can be identified:

1.   The application-specific requirements represent a subset of the defined domain variants: The application requirements that are not part of the common
functionality are represented by variants. The domain artifacts that contain
the variants have to be determined first. The application use case scenarios
and application test case scenarios are generated based on the corresponding
domain artifacts.
2.   The customer requires specific adaptations of a use case: The domain artifacts are used as a basis and are then changed according to the specific customer requirements.
3.   Another case is that a customer requires new functionality in his application.
New application-specific use case scenarios and test case scenarios have to
be created in this case.

All of these tasks are performed in application system testing (AS) as well as in application integration testing (AI) (see Sects. 13.4.1 and 13.4.2).

13.4.1 Creating Application Test Artifacts for System Testing

For each of the three cases described above, different approaches for creating application
test case scenarios have to be chosen. These are (in the order of the above cases):

AS1: Create Application Test Case Scenarios by Reuse
AS2: Adapting Application System Testing Artifacts
AS3: Considering New Customer Requirements

AS1: Create Application Test Case Scenarios by Reuse

If the application-specific requirements represent a subset of the defined domain variants,
application test case scenarios can be created by reusing domain test case scenarios.
Four activities are performed in the ScenTED method to enable such a reuse process
(see Fig. 13.12):

AS1.1:   Identification of the domain use case scenarios
AS1.2:   Derivation of the application use case scenarios
AS1.3:   Identification of the domain test case scenarios
AS1.4:   Derivation of the application-specific test case scenarios

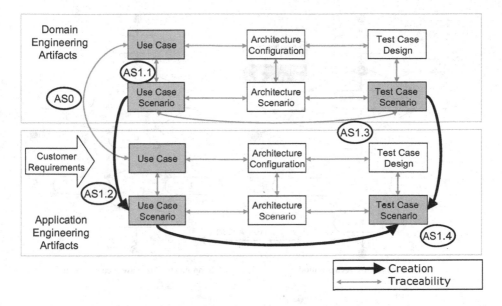

Fig. 13.12. Create application system test case scenarios by reuse

AS1.1: Identification of the Domain Use Case Scenarios. Based on the domain use cases, the corresponding domain use case scenarios can be identified. These were created during the first step of domain system testing (DS1) and are retrieved by following the traceability link Link_DS1.

As has been explained above, the domain use case scenarios are specified as activity diagrams. An example is shown in the right half of Fig. 13.6. This example presents domain use case scenarios, including a variation point with three variants. Two of the three variants may coexist, but one variant is mandatory. Not more than two of the three variants may be included in the application.

AS1.2: Derivation of the Application Use Case Scenarios. In this activity, the domain use case scenarios, more precisely the domain activity diagram, is refined for the desired application. The application use case scenario model is specified as an activity diagram and represents the application's functionality. The common activities that are described in the domain activity diagram do not have to be refined and are transferred into the application model without any changes. All variants must be examined whether they are part of the application or not. The variation point is transformed into a regular decision. Where the variants that are not needed are left out of the application model, the variants that have been selected for the application are added as regular activities.

In the example of Fig. 13.13, only the two variants B1 and B3 are chosen for the considered application, and therefore the application activity diagram is created accordingly (see right hand side of the figure).

During the activity AS1.2, the traceability link Link_AS1.2 between the domain activity diagram and the application activity diagram is created.

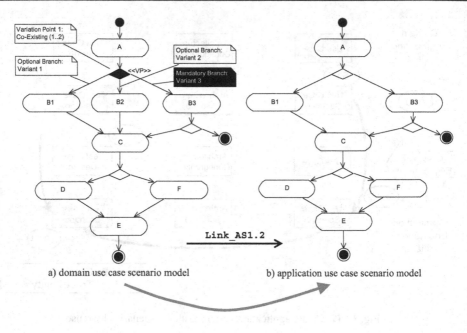

Fig. 13.13. From the domain to the application model – selection of variants

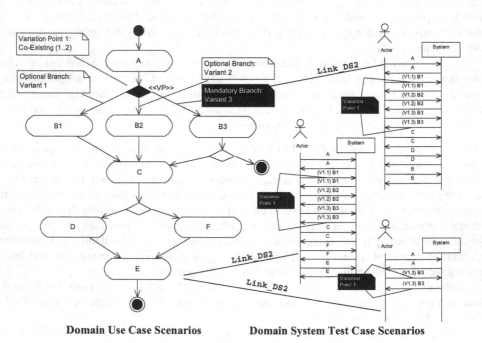

Domain Use Case Scenarios   **Domain System Test Case Scenarios**

Fig. 13.14. Domain use case scenarios and system test case scenarios

AS1.3: Identification of the Domain Test Case Scenarios. The domain test case scenarios have been derived from the domain activity diagram that represents the use case scenarios. Each domain activity diagram is related to *n* test case scenarios via the traceability link Link_DS2. This trace link can now be used to identify the domain test case scenarios.

In the example, three domain test case scenarios are produced for the domain use case scenarios (modeled by an activity diagram shown on the left-hand side of Fig. 13.14). The domain test case scenarios that preserve the variability are shown on the right-hand side of Fig. 13.14.

AS1.4: Derivation of Application Test Case Scenarios. The activity AS1.4 describes how the application-specific test case scenarios are assembled from the domain artifacts. The domain test case scenarios that have been retrieved in the previous activity are used as input. As the domain test case scenarios contain variability, this variability has to be bound to define the application-specific test case scenarios. This is done based on the information about which variants are desired by the customer. Only the variants that are desired by the customer are incorporated into the application test case scenarios. We have used the segmentation strategy to describe variability in the domain test case scenarios. Therefore, creating application test case scenarios from the domain artifacts is performed by removing all the variants that are not realized in the application.

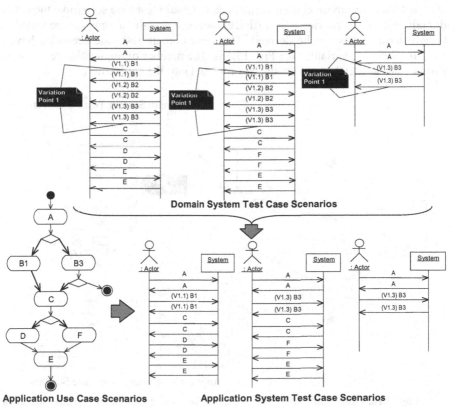

Fig. 13.15. Creating application test case scenarios

In Fig. 13.15, an example of this activity is shown. The variant B2 is deleted from the two domain test case scenarios (because it is not desired by the customer). Then, the two remaining variants are distributed over the three domain test case scenarios, e.g., B1 is kept in the first scenario, whereas B3 remains in the second and third scenarios. Consequently, the variability has successfully been bound in the application use case scenarios.

When the application test case scenarios are assembled from the domain test case scenarios, the question arises as to how many application test case scenarios have to be created, if we assume that there was only one variation point of which m variants had been realized and that there were n domain test case scenarios. With these assumptions, three different cases to cover all branches in the application test case scenarios can be identified:

- $n = m$: If there is an equal number of chosen variants and domain test case scenarios, then the variants are distributed over the test case scenarios. The number of application test case scenarios is also equal to the domain test case scenarios.
- $m < n$: If there are less variants than domain test case scenarios, the chosen variants may be used more than once in the test case scenarios. Each test case uses one of the realized variants and all realized variants are part of the test case scenarios. The number of application test case scenarios is equal to the number of domain test case scenarios.
- $m > n$: If there are more chosen variants than domain test case scenarios, the amount of domain test case scenarios is insufficient, because not all variants can be tested. Additional scenarios have to be derived. The same domain test case scenarios have to be used for different variants (see Fig. 13.16). The number of application test case scenarios is equal to the chosen variants incorporated into the application.

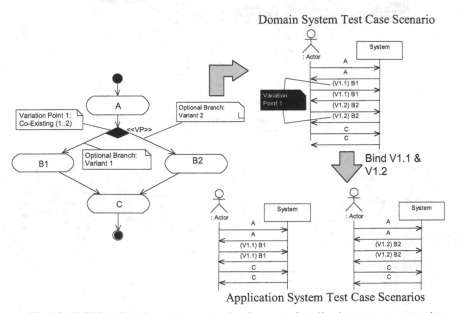

Fig. 13.16. Using domain test case scenarios for a set of application test case scenarios

If more than one variation point is contained within the diagrams, the determination of the required test cases is more complicated as the dependencies between the different kinds of variants (optional, mandatory, etc.) and the branch coverage criterion have to be considered.

The activities AS1.1–AS1.4 allow the derivation of application-specific test artifacts from previously created domain artifacts. However, this is not always the case, as a customer might wish to adapt the application to his specific needs (which are not matched by the existing domain artifacts).

AS2: Adapting Application System Testing Artifacts

As introduced earlier in this book, platform-based product line development (e.g., handy product line) and mass customization product lines (e.g., radiology systems for hospitals) exist. In the latter case, the customer may not only select variants from the domain model (which is hopefully most often the case to reduce effort), but also ask for specific changes to adapt the software to his specific needs. This change in requirements leads to changes in use cases and therefore requires adaptations of the test artifacts. One can distinguish between the following two basic forms of such changes:

– The customer adds functionality
– The customer deletes functionality

Another case, the modification of functionality, can be mapped to a respective sequence of adding and deletion of functionality. The aspect whether the change occurs in common or variant functionality and its implications to the use case model may be interesting. However, this is an advanced aspect, which should be dealt with in requirements engineering.

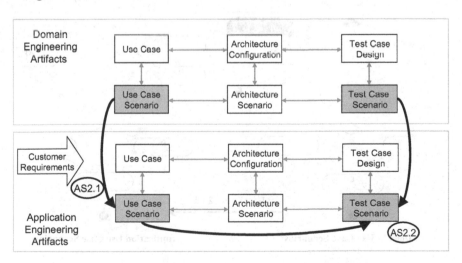

Fig. 13.17. Adapting application system test artifacts

For the following discussions, we use the example of a variant that has been enriched in its functionality. This fact is identified on the application use case level. The original domain use case is known. When the effected domain and application use cases are known, two activities are needed to incorporate the change into the test artifacts (see Fig. 13.17):

> AS2.1: Adaptation of the application use case scenarios
> AS2.2: Adaptation of the application test case scenarios

AS2.1: Adaptation to the Application Use Case Scenarios. The adaptation of application specific test cases requires the creation of application specific use case scenarios first.

The domain activity diagram that has been identified in step AS1.1 (see above) is retrieved as a template for the application use case scenarios. The chosen variants from the customer selection are incorporated as described in step AS1.2. The key activity in this activity is the adaptation to the activity diagram to reflect the desired changes in functionality. The place where the additional functionality has to be introduced into this model is identified and the required activities are inserted and deleted respectively. The dependency between the originating domain use case scenario model and the application model is recorded in a traceability link Link_AS2.1 for later use.

As an example (see Fig. 13.18), the customer selects the variants B1 and B3, but the functionality B1 shall be extended with the functionality BA. The result is an adapted set of application use case scenarios.

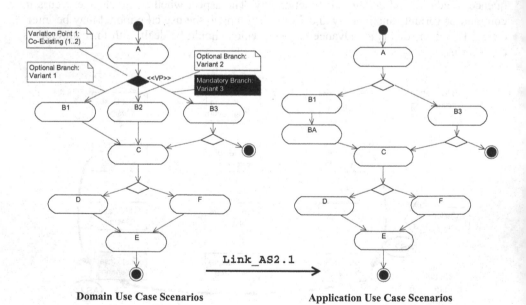

Domain Use Case Scenarios   **Application Use Case Scenarios**

Fig. 13.18. Changes in application specific control flow

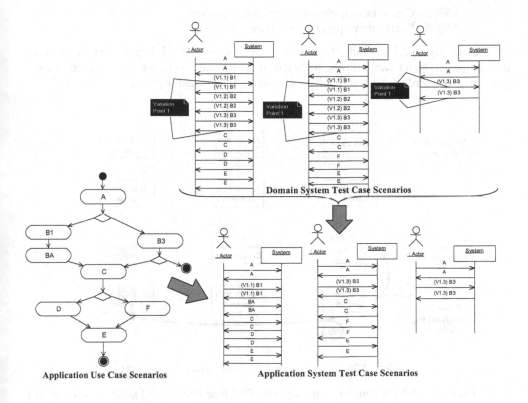

Fig. 13.19. Changes in application specific test case scenarios

AS2.2: Adaptation of the Application Test Case Scenarios. The application use case scenarios are used as templates for defining the application test case scenarios. The initial steps to create the application test case scenarios are identical to the steps that have been described for activities AS1.3 and AS1.4. However, after these steps, the application test case scenario is adapted, because the changed functionality has to be reflected in the scenarios.

Figure 13.19 shows an example of such an adaptation. The application-specific activity diagram is shown on the left-hand side of Fig. 13.19, the domain system test case scenarios (retrieved via the Link_DS2) are shown in the top of the figure. As has been explained, both models serve as input for creating the application-specific system test case scenarios. The application test case scenarios that contain the variant B1 are extended with the additional functionality BA.

AS3: Considering New Customer Requirements

Customers can add new requirements besides adapting existing ones. They can simply add new functionality by introducing new use cases. Consequently, the testing activities must support that. Two activities are necessary to derive application test case scenarios from "new" application use cases (see Fig. 13.20):

AS3.1:   Create new application use case scenarios
AS3.2:   Derive new application test case scenarios

The activity AS3.1 is similar to the activity DS1 (see Sect. 13.3.1). In fact, this activity is even easier, as no variability is included in the use cases. During this creation, the dependency is recorded. An activity diagram that must be tested is produced as result.

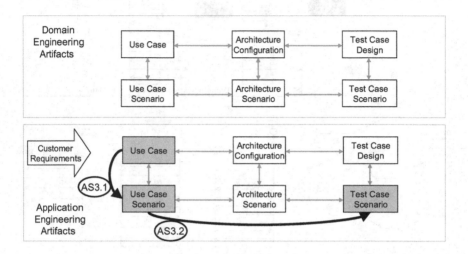

Fig. 13.20. Deriving new application system test artifacts

The activity AS3.2 is similar to the activity DS2 (see Sect. 13.3.1). Again, this activity is easier, because the traditional form of branch coverage can be applied.

Summarizing, this task consists of two previously described steps. If another customer requires the same enhancements, may be the created artifacts should be made reusable by transferring them to domain models. In this case additional activities are necessary. These activities are not part of this work.

13.4.2 Creating Application Test Artifacts for Integration Testing

For integration testing, we assume that the corresponding domain and application use case scenarios from system testing exist. The same constraints on the form of domain integration testing that have been explained in Sect. 13.3.2 accordingly hold for application integration testing.

Following the three different approaches for creating application test case scenarios in system testing, the following three approaches are possible in integration testing:

AI1: Creating Application Architecture Scenarios by Reuse
AI2: Adapting Application Integration Testing Artifacts
AI3: Considering New Customer Requirements

AI1: Creating Application Architecture Scenarios by Reuse

After the customer has selected the desired functionality, the affected domain architecture scenarios can be identified. Based upon these domain architecture scenarios, the application-specific architecture scenarios can be created. Four steps are needed to derive application-specific architecture scenarios from the domain architecture scenarios (see Fig. 13.21):

AI1.1:	Identification of domain architecture scenarios
AI1.2:	Derivation of the application architecture scenarios
AI1.3:	Identification of domain integration test case scenarios
AI1.4:	Derivation of the application integration test case scenarios

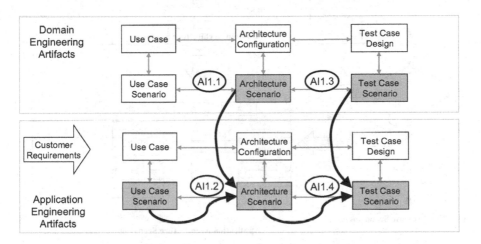

Fig. 13.21. Creating application integration test scenarios

AI1.1: Identification of Domain Architecture Scenarios. During the creation of the domain architecture scenarios in DI1 the traceability links Link_DI1 have been created. These links are used in this activity to retrieve the domain architecture scenarios for the respective domain use cases.

In the upper half of Fig. 13.22, the domain architecture scenarios for the previously shown domain use case scenarios are presented. Three domain architecture scenarios exist. Both contain variability and a component (Y) that is only needed when the variant B1 is used within the scenario.

AI1.2: Derivation of the Application Architecture Scenarios. In this activity (AI1.2) the application-specific architecture scenarios are created. Therefore, the application use case scenarios are required, which specify what must be included. The domain architecture scenarios are used as template to simplify the scenario creation. During this step, the variability in the domain architecture scenarios is removed.

Figure 13.22 shows the example for the derivation of architecture scenarios. The application requirement is that the two variants B1 and B3 are included. Three architecture scenarios are needed. Variant B1 requires component X, therefore three actors are involved in the first scenario. The variant B3 does not need this component. Therefore, it is not part of the second and third application test case scenarios.

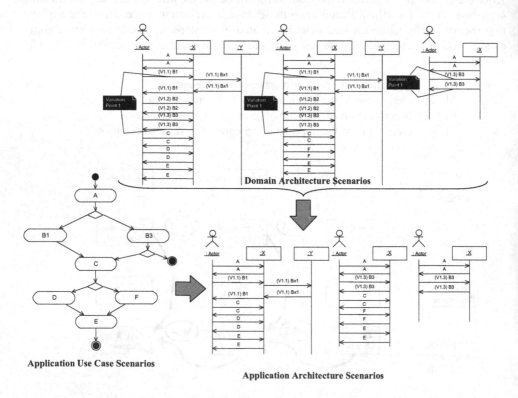

Fig. 13.22. Example for the derivation of application architecture scenarios

AI1.3: Identification of the Domain Integration Test Case Scenarios. The domain integration test case scenarios should be used as a template to create the application scenarios efficiently. Therefore, the domain integration test case scenarios must be retrieved. This can easily be achieved via the recorded trace links Link_DI2 that have been created during the domain engineering activity DI2 (see Sect. 13.3.2).

AI1.4: Derivation of the Application Integration Test Case Scenarios. The application architecture scenarios are refined to application integration test case scenarios. The domain integration test case scenarios that have been retrieved in the prior activities are used templates. Additional information is needed as described in activity DI2. This additional information is added and completes the application integration test case scenarios.

AI2: Adapting Application Integration Test Artifacts

This step assumes that the specified, additional functionality stemming from the customer can be added within the existing packages and classes. As this activity focuses on integration testing, no details will be given on how to change the architecture. Instead, it is assumed that the changes in architecture have been already incorporated. Furthermore, it is assumed that the changes have been propagated in the application use case scenarios.

Two steps remain for creating application-specific integration test case scenarios based on a customer-based change (see Fig. 13.23):

AI2.1:   Adapting the application architecture scenarios
AI2.2:   Adapting the application integration test case scenarios

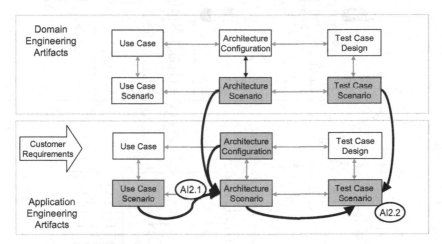

Fig. 13.23. Adapting application integration test artifacts

AI2.1: Adapting the Application Architecture Scenarios. The architecture scenarios have to be adapted according to the changes in use case scenarios and the architecture. One has to consider the following cases:

1.   The changes imply the deletion of steps in an architecture scenario
2.   The changes imply the addition of steps considering existing components
3.   The changes imply the addition of steps considering additional components
4.   The changes imply the change of components, as the functionality has been moved from one component to another

Ad 1: The deletion of scenario steps is quite trivial. As a result of this deletion, some components may not be required for the scenario anymore. These would have to be deleted also.

Ad 2: In this case, additional scenario steps have to be introduced. If there are new component interfaces involved, this information has to be elicited from the architects.

Ad 3: Similar to case 2), additional steps have to be incorporated. These steps involve at least one component that has previously not been considered in this architecture scenario.

Ad 4: This step can be reduced to cases 1 and 3. First, the steps for the moved functionality are deleted from the scenario. Second, the new component is included and connected with corresponding messages.

As an example for case 3, the additional functionality BA requires a component Z. This leads to the following application architecture scenario (see Fig. 13.24).

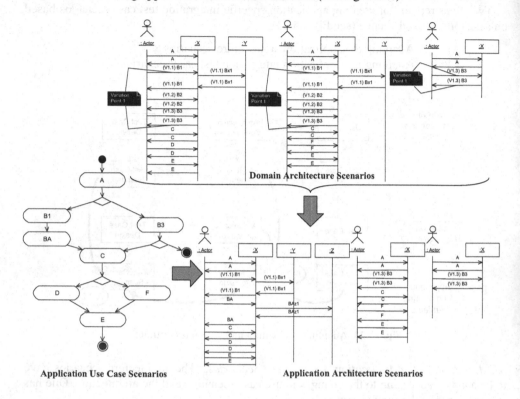

Fig. 13.24. Adaptation of the application architecture scenarios

AI2.2: Adapting the Application Integration Test Case Scenarios. The change in functionality must be propagated from the application architecture scenario into the application integration test case scenario. Therefore, one has to distinguish between the three cases described in the previous section, but as these have been considered in activity AI3.2, the changes in the application architecture scenarios have only to be propagated into the corresponding integration test case scenarios.

AI3: Considering New Customer Requirements

For the effects of new customer requirements, we consider the same assumption as in the previous section: The additional functionality can be incorporated in existing architecture elements. Furthermore, we assume that this adaptation in architecture has already been performed by the software architects.

The propagation of new customer requirements into the application integration tests artifacts consists of two activities (see Fig. 13.25).

AI3.1:   Creating new application architecture scenarios
AI3.2:   Derivation of application specific integration test case scenarios

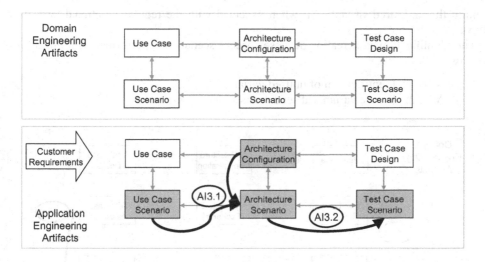

Fig. 13.25. Deriving new application integration test artifacts

The activity AI3.1 relates to the same cases that have been mentioned in activity AI1.2. The approach to create the application specific architecture scenarios is therefore identical to the above approach.

The activity AI3.2 is similar to the activity AI1.4. Its main contribution is to propagate the application-specific architecture scenarios into the application integration test case scenarios.

13.4.3 Ensure the Correct Binding

In addition to testing the functionality as has been described above, it has also to be tested, if the application does not contain more functionality than required and that no variability dependencies have been violated. The test approaches of the former sections have tested whether the specified application requirements have been correctly realized within the application. Now, we want to test whether an application does not contain more functionality than required.

Testing Excluded Variants

The domain artifacts of a product line contain all the functionality that has been identified as being relevant for the considered domain. However, the realized applications usually should contain a small portion of the whole functionality. From a company's perspective, the more functionality an application contains, the higher its price can be chosen (e.g., community editions of a software package vs. the developer editions). From the customers' point of view, only the desired functionally has to be paid and not the extra functionality that will never be used by them.

To evaluate if not too much functionality is contained within an application, additional tests are required within application testing. These are called *Variants Absence Tests (VAT)*. The special property of these tests is that VAT test cases are passed when the scenarios that contain the undesired variants fail when executed with the regular functional tests from above.

The identification and creation of these absence scenarios is performed as follows (also see Fig. 13.26):

VAT1:   Identification of unused variants
VAT2:   Derive variants absence tests

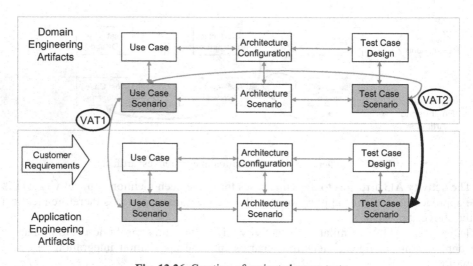

Fig. 13.26. Creation of variant absence tests

VAT1: Identification of Unused Variants. Based on the application use case model and the traceability link Link_AS1.2, one can identify the corresponding domain use case model. The domain use case model contains all variants of the product line. Therefore, the unused variants can easily be identified.

Revisiting the example from above, where the customer has chosen B1 and B3 out of three possible variants (see Fig. 13.27), the step VAT1 leads to the identification of variant B2.

VAT2: Derive Variant Absence Tests. The activity VAT2 aims at deriving one absence test for the variants that have not been selected. Therefore, the domain test case scenarios are retrieved via the traceability link Link_DS2. Based on these domain test case scenarios, one can derive the variant absence tests for the specific application.

Considering the example, a test case has to be created that includes the variant B2. The first domain system test case scenario is selected and the variant B2 is bound for the variant absence test. The result can be seen on the bottom right half of Fig. 13.27.

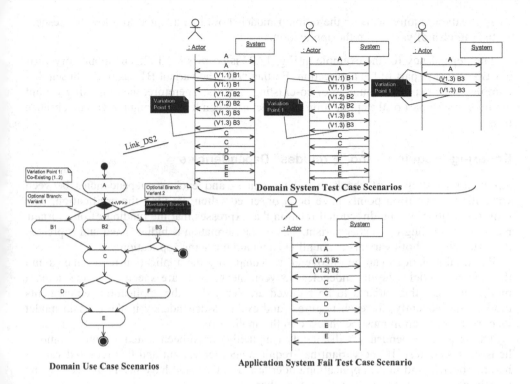

Fig. 13.27. Deriving fail test case scenarios

Ensuring "Co-Existing" and "Alternative" Dependencies

The dependencies between variation points and variants must be observed to reach at an application with correctly bound variability. The dependency between variation points and variants can be an alternative or a co-existing relation. Co-existing specifies a maximum number of variants that can be part of the application, whereas the alternative dependency limits the maximum number to one.

Checking that the maximum number of variants is not exceeded is performed by comparing the application requirements with the domain requirements. This is a form of review technique, because the two documents are compared and no execution of the application is required.

For a comprehensive assurance of quality, additional testing of the correct consideration of these dependencies can be performed with absence tests:

- If the maximum number of variants is not exceeded in the application requirements document, then the supernumerary variants must be part of the unused variants. This can be tested with the above variant absence test (VAT).
- If the maximum number of variants is exceeded, then the product derivation has not been performed correctly. In this case, either the product derivation has to correct the

application requirements or the domain model should be adapted to allow the respective number of variants in the application.

The dependency for the example in Fig. 13.27 is *co-existing* 1..2. The mandatory variant B3 is always part of the application. Furthermore, the variant B1 has been chosen that completes the maximum number of co-existing variants. Therefore, the remaining variant B2 must not be part of the application. This fact has been tested during the variant absence tests.

Ensuring "Requires" and "Excludes" Dependencies

Application testing must check that the requires- and excludes-dependencies between variants and variation points have been observed when deriving the application. The requires-relation is a unidirectional relation that expresses that the binding of one variant requires the binding of another variant. The excludes-relation is bidirectional and expresses that a binding of both variants is not allowed within the same application.

Potential violations can be uncovered by comparing the application requirements and the domain model. The dependencies between the variants are specified in the domain model, whereas the variants to be realized are defined in the application requirements model. Consequently, for each requires- and excludes-dependency in the domain model its correct observation must be checked in the application.

The requires-dependency will already (implicitly) have been tested within a comprehensive system test. If one variant had required another variant and this required variant had not been bound in the application under test, a fault would have been observed, as the variant cannot work correctly without the other.

In contrast to that, the excludes-dependency has to be tested explicitly. The reasons for the introduction of the dependency into the domain models may not have been stated explicitly (e.g., product management could have decided that two similar variants should never be offered in the same product). Therefore, binding both variants must not necessarily lead to a fault that could be detected by employing the above test approaches.

13.4.4 Reuse of Application Artifacts

So far, this chapter has shown how domain test case artifacts can be reused during application engineering for creating the desired application test artifacts. However, as this derivation still involves manual tasks (e.g., when the artifacts have to be modified to reflect customer-specific adaptations), one should also try to systematically reuse these application test artifacts.

Therefore, the goal is to provide an approach that allows one to identify identical application artifacts from an already developed application and reuse them during application engineering of the new application.

Coming back to our running example, three application test case scenarios have been created by employing activities AS1.1–AS1.4, and three scenarios have been created by performing the activities AS 2.1–AS2.2. As the reader can observe, two of the created scenarios are identical, namely the application test case scenarios containing the former variant C3.

Two activities are necessary to enable artifact reuse (also see Fig. 13.28):

    R1:   Prepare for application reuse
    R2:   Systematically reuse artifacts of former applications

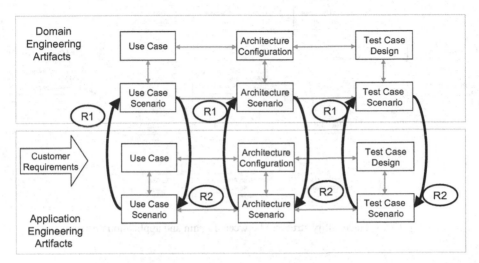

Fig. 13.28. Artifact reuse

Prepare for Application Reuse

All of the considered test artifacts, more precisely the application use case scenarios, the application architecture scenarios, and the application (system and integration) test case scenarios, should be stored in an *artifact base*. The dependencies between the artifacts must be recorded to enable the structured reuse. Trace links are used to record these dependencies as it has been explained in the above sections.

Figure 13.29 depicts the traceability structure between the domain and the application artifacts. During application testing, the domain variants are bound or domain artifacts are adapted. The information about this binding or adaptation has to be captured in the trace dependencies. Therefore, additional information is attached to each of these links to record what and how the adaptation has been performed. This is modeled in Fig. 13.29 by association classes *Use Case Scenario Adaptation*, *Architecture Scenario Adaptation*, and *Test Case Scenario Adaptation*, respectively.

For the application activity diagrams, that information includes the chosen variants, new activities, deleted activities, new transitions, and deleted transitions. This information is sufficient for describing the difference between the domain and application use case scenarios.

For the architecture scenarios and the test case scenarios, also the variant configuration, the new steps, and the deleted steps are recorded. With that information the application architecture scenarios and application test case scenarios and their originating domain artifacts can be identified unambiguously.

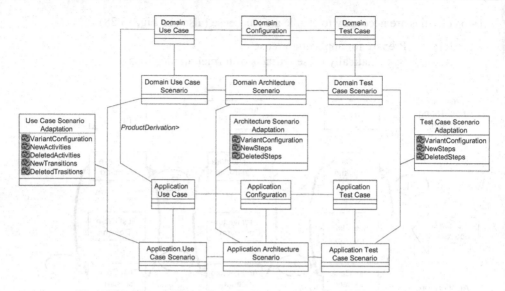

Fig. 13.29. Traceability structure between domain and application artifacts

Systematically Reuse Artifacts of Former Applications

The defined traceability structure can be used to retrieve similar application artifacts when needed. Usually, dependency links are stored in a database. Database requests can then be used to generate the information about similar or identical artifacts. Therefore, the previously described activities must be extended. Before an application artifact is generated, one would first search for an identical or similar artifact.

In activity AS1.2, it has to be checked if another application has been built that has used the same variant configuration. In this case, the attribute *VariantConfiguration* includes the same variants as for the application under consideration. It has to be checked if the available model is useable, e.g., one must ensure that there are no new activities or branches have been added or existing ones have been deleted.

Consequently, the same observation holds for AS1.4 considering the test case scenarios. Using the value of the attribute *VariantConfiguration* of the association class *Test Case Scenario Adaptation* it has to be verified that the same variants are implemented as in the intended application. Afterward, the other attributes can be inspected whether they are empty or adequate.

This procedure does not only work for variants within an application, but also for adapted artifacts. The step AS2.1 has to inspect the attributes *NewActivities, DeletedActivities, NewTransitions*, and *DeletedTransitions* if the adaptations are the same as for the intended application. Furthermore, the *VariantConfiguration* must be the same. The same adaptations and validations have to be made in activity AS2.2.

To summarize, this section has extended the activities within system application to allow for the reuse of application artifacts on top of reusing domain artifacts. In an analogous way, the activities of application integration testing are extended.

13.5 ScenTED at Siemens Medical Solutions – A Case Study

In this section, the partial validation of the ScenTED method at Siemens Medical Solutions HS IM is presented [18,19]. The validation is only shown in a shortened way. More detailed information is confidential.

First, the software product line development at Siemens Medical Solutions is briefly described. Then, the objectives of introducing the ScenTED method at Siemens Medical Solutions are depicted. Finally, the lessons that have been learned in the case study are presented.

13.5.1 Product Line Development at Siemens Medical Solutions HS

Siemens Medical Solutions HS IM develops software systems for workstations in the radiology domain. A typical clinical workflow includes the electronic assignment of a medical examination by the attending physician, the creation of patient images with the help of a so-called modality (e.g., an X-ray or CT scanner), and the diagnosis of the patient (see Fig. 13.30). The developed software systems support the registration and administration of patient and image data. The data are centrally stored on a server. Image processing is done on client workstations (the so-called workplaces), at which the diagnoses of the images are performed by radiologists.

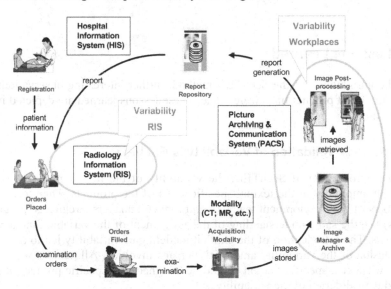

Fig. 13.30. Basic clinical workflow [7]

The variability of the product line concerns the workplaces as well as different RIS (Radiology Information System) alternatives. The focus of this case study is on the different workplaces. Several workplaces are developed based on the same development documents (requirements, architecture, and code). The workplaces have a varying functionality (possibilities of image editing) as well as variable nonfunctional properties (support of high-end and low-end hardware). This product line is a closed one, which means that all products that will ever be derived for this product line are known beforehand. To put it concretely, this means that Siemens Medical Solutions develops three different work-places based on common documents, architecture, and code.

13.5.2 Objectives of the ScenTED Introduction

ScenTED was introduced at Siemens Medical Solutions to achieve two objectives. First, ScenTED is supposed to support the handling of variability in requirements documents and test cases to allow for the systematic reuse of these artifacts. Second, an efficient traceability of use cases to test cases will be achieved by ScenTED, thus providing a con-sistent change management. Before the introduction of ScenTED, the derivation of test cases was based on textual specifications of the requirements. If requirements changed, there was no chance to identify the test cases that had to be customized without relying on the help of experts.

To evaluate the achievement of these two goals, two hypotheses have been formulated for this case study:

- *Hypothesis H1*: The ScenTED method supports the systematic reuse of test cases within product line development.
- *Hypothesis H2*: Test cases that are derived by the ScenTED method improve the trace-ability.

13.5.3 Lessons Learned

During the introduction of the ScenTED method, further interesting observations consid-ering the testing of product lines were made. These lessons learned are depicted in the fol-lowing sections.

Lesson 1: Early Validation of Variability is Enabled

Before the introduction of ScenTED, the variability of the radiology products was de-scribed only implicitly in the textual specifications of the products. Therefore, not all of the members of the development teams (e.g., product managers, architects, programmers, or testers) had the same understanding of the assignment of the variable functionalities to the products. The introduction of the explicit modeling of variability led to a much better comprehension of the variability among all persons involved. All persons were now able to check, whether a specific variant should be assigned to a specific product or not. This supported the validation of the variability.

Lesson 2: Developers Prefer the Product-Oriented Modeling of Variability

Techniques and methods usually have to be customized according to project specific objectives and the personal skills of the involved persons. During the application of ScenTED at Siemens Medical Solutions, the modeling of variability has been customized accordingly. For modeling the variability in activity diagrams (as has been introduced at the beginning of this chapter), variation points and possible variants were specified independent from any concrete product, i.e., depending on the desired functionality of the product, the required variants were determined in application requirements engineering. For ScenTED's application at Siemens, this process has been simplified by identifying the variants directly with the planned products. In the example in Fig. 13.31, the variants <<magicSyngo>>, <<mvNG>>, <<genericViewer>> directly relate to the products magicSyngo, mvNG, and generic Viewer, respectively (we have chosen a slightly different notation to make this modification of variability modeling visible). The involved persons are more adept to this way of variability modeling, because the names of the different products are part of their daily vocabulary and they can more easily associate functionality with the name of the product. What allows for this modification is the fact that the chosen product line is closed and all possible variants are known beforehand. If the result of the application of ScenTED is positive for only three well-known products, the results should be more positive if more than three products would be derived and the reuse rate is much higher. The effort to develop the domain test case scenarios would be the same and the benefit in reuse increases with every additional product. Therefore, no negative impact to the validation is expected.

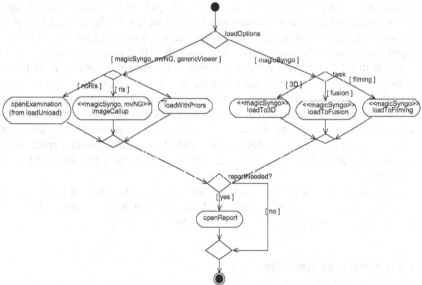

Fig. 13.31. Domain activity diagram (excerpt from [7])

Lesson 3: Reduction of the Test Effort by Preserving the Variability in the Test Case Scenarios

As has been noticed before, variability enables the reuse of test case scenarios. A direct measurement of the testing effort did not make sense in this case study, because of different reasons. One reason was that it is always difficult to generalize the results of the measurement of effort because of different knowledge of the involved persons and other constraints. The main reason was that the involved persons developed the scenarios in addition to their normal work. The measured effort would have been totally different to the real effort they needed. To still provide a feeling for the reduction in effort that was achieved, the number of test cases has been used as an evaluation criterion. Test case scenarios have been derived with the modified ScenTED method for seven use cases in the Siemens case study. Twenty seven domain test case scenarios based on these use cases have been developed. For the three different kinds of workplaces that are created by Siemens Medical Solutions, these test case scenarios were reused in the derivation of 63 application test case scenarios. These numbers already show that the reuse approach was a success, as on average, each domain test case was reused 2.3 times. In other words, to achieve a test effort reduction, the effort for the development of one domain test case scenario could have been more than twice as high as the effort of the development of one application test case scenario without reuse.

Lesson 4: A Hierarchical Storage of the Test Cases Supports Reuse

The storage of test cases in a suitable and hierarchical way can support the testing of multiple applications on the same basis. At Siemens Medical Solutions, the hierarchy – product – use case – test case scenario – test case – was realized in a test tool.

In the used test tool folders were created for each application. Under these folders other folders were arranged for the use cases which are realized by the respective application. The use case folders contain folders for the application use case scenarios. In each folder of the application use case scenarios, the application test cases are managed. The test cases differ in the different test case parameters. This hierarchy realizes the traceability. As soon as a use case has to be tested in a new product, the existing scenario folders of a prior product (same variability in this use case is assumed) are copied into the new product and use case folders of the test tool. The precondition for this is that the refinement from use cases to test cases is performed in a stepwise fashion and that the assignments of use cases to products are documented. If the product contains another variant, only common scenarios are used further on and the additional test cases are derived from the sequence diagram.

The storage of test cases in a hierarchical way supports the reuse of test cases, because for the test of a use case in a new product all test cases of another already tested product can easily be reused if the variability is bound in the same way.

13.5.4 Summary of Results

The systematic reuse of test cases (see Hypothesis H_1) is supported by the ScenTED method. In the case study the domain test cases were reused 2.3 times on average (see Lesson 3). Moreover, the hierarchical storage can support the reuse of application test cases for the test of a new application, if the same variability was bound (see Lesson 4).

ScenTED also improves the traceability (see Hypothesis H_2). The people who are involved in the case study modeled the variability by stereotypes of the different products (see Lesson 2). By this way of modeling and the refinement of use case to test case scenarios they associate functionality and requirements to test cases. The refinement of use cases to test cases is also a prerequisite for the hierarchical storage to reuse application test cases (see Lesson 4).

The application of ScenTED at Siemens Medical Solutions has found wide acceptance. The support for validating the variability, the product oriented modeling of variability, and especially the support of reuse was received most positively. The acceptance of the ScenTED method was evaluated through a questionnaire that was handed out to nine persons involved in the project. As a general result of the case study, the test engineers have suggested the ScenTED method to be applied in other departments at Siemens.

13.6 Conclusions and Future Research

Variability is the basic concept that is employed during software product line engineering. By using the concept of variability, generic artifacts are modeled during domain engineering, which are then reused during application engineering to derive concrete artifacts.

In this contribution, the ScenTED method has been introduced to systematically support such a systematic reuse for the purpose of system and integration testing of product line applications. ScenTED's activities that allow for developing reusable test artifacts in domain engineering as well as for reusing artifacts in application engineering have been described in detail. The conceptual basis of the ScenTED method is a scenario-based approach for describing requirements as well as test cases.

In domain engineering, domain use case scenarios are developed with ScenTED by creating or supplementing activity diagrams. The provided domain use case scenarios serve as starting point for deriving test case scenarios for system and integration testing by considering an extended branch coverage criterion. For the derivation of integration test case scenarios, the derivation of architecture scenarios from component interactions is an additional activity that is supported by ScenTED. These domain test case scenarios can then be reused during application engineering.

For application engineering, three product line specific issues have been covered by ScenTED:

1. *Structured reuse of test artifacts.* The domain test artifacts are reused in application engineering to derive test artifacts for testing the common functionality as well as application specific functionality. As most of the product line's functionality is common to all derived applications, a relatively high number of test artifacts can be reused. Specific functionality that is not common has to be reused in a structured way and not in an ad hoc fashion to achieve the product line engineering's goals of efficiency and time-to-market. Only if new functionality that has not been considered in the domain artifacts should be realized by an application, new artifacts have to be created. For this case, ScenTED supports the efficient derivation of such artifacts by a systematic selection and adaptation of existing domain artifacts.

2. *Considering dependencies.* For each application, it has to be ensured that the variability of the domain artifacts has been bound correctly. Dependencies that have been defined during domain engineering must be considered during product derivation, and it has to be ensured that these are correctly observed in the application. This also holds for variants that will not be part of

the application. Their absence must be tested, because the incorporation of such variants can lead to financial losses.

3. *Preparing application test artifact reuse.* Deriving application test artifacts still presents some effort. Therefore, reusing these application test artifacts for their reuse in future applications is a consequent continuation of the product line idea of design for reuse. It is therefore supported by ScenTED.

ScenTED has a high potential for automation. For example, the derivation of domain test case scenarios on the basis of the overall activity diagram can be performed automatically as well as the binding of variants to derive application test case scenarios.

Our current research plans include the extension of the ScenTED method in several directions:

First of all, new activities will be added to ScenTED that support the derivation of test inputs and expected results to extend the test case scenarios to form complete test cases.

In addition, adaptations of traditional integration strategies are evaluated in integration testing for reflecting product line specific aspects. A further extension that is planned for ScenTED's integration test approach is the consideration of additional variability in the domain architecture (e.g. alternative components) in the derivation of architecture scenarios.

Further, once an application test case has been identified as a reuse candidate, new activities for determining whether such a reused test case has to be executed again for the new application will be added to ScenTED. With such an addition, the redundant execution of tests can be eliminated, thus leading to a further reduction of test effort. Finally, nonfunctional (or quality) requirements will be dealt with in the future, and an analysis of the complexity of the ScenTED is planned.

Acknowledgments

We would like to thank the staff at Siemens Medical Solutions HS IM who contributed to the case study, especially Helmut Goetz, Frank Rometsch, Jürgen Neumann, Harald Lauritsch, and Josef Weingärtner. We would also like to thank Andreas Metzger for suggestions on improving the contribution. Moreover, we gratefully acknowledge the helpful comments from the reviewers Stefania Gnesi, Timo Käkölä, Patrick Tessier, and Antti Tevanlinna.

References

1. Bertolino, A., Gnesi, S.: PLUTO: a test methodology for product families. In: *Software Product-Family Engineering*, ed by van der Linden, F., 5th International Workshop, Siena, Italy, November 2003. Lecture Notes in Computer Science, vol 3014 (Springer, Berlin Heidelberg New York 2003) pp 181–197

2. Bertolino, A., Gnesi, S.: Use case-based testing of product lines. In: Proceedings of the 9th European Software Engineering Conference & 11th SIGSOFT Symposium on the Foundations of Software Engineering, ESEC/FSM, Helsinki, Finland, September 2003, ed by Inveradi, P. (ACM, New York 2003) pp 355–358

3. Binder, R.V.: *Testing Object-Oriented Systems – Models, Patterns, and Tools* (Addison-Wesley, Reading, MA 2000)

4. Briand, L., Labiche, Y.: A UML-based approach to system testing. J. Softw. Syst. Model. (SoSyM) **1**(1), 10–42 (2002)

5. Cockburn, A.: *Writing Effective Use Cases* (Addison-Wesley, Reading, MA 2001)

6. Geppert, B., Li, J., Rößler, F., Weiss, D.M.: Towards generating acceptance tests for product lines. In: *Software Reuse: Methods, Techniques, and Tools*, ed by Bosch, J., Krueger, C., 8th International Conference, ICSR 2004, Madrid, Spain, July 2004. Lecture Notes in Computer Science, vol 3107 (Springer, Berlin Heidelberg New York 2004) pp 35–48

7. Goetz, H., Kamsties, E., Neumann, J., Pohl, K., Reis, S., Reuys, A., Weingärtner, J.: Testing a product line of radiology systems at Siemens. In: Proceedings of the 5th Conference on Software Validation for Healthcare (CSVHC 2005), Düsseldorf, Germany (2005)

8. Halmans, G., Pohl, K.: Communicating the variability of a software product family to customers. J. Softw. Syst. Model. **2**(1), 15–36 (2003)

9. Hartmann, J., Vieira, M., Ruder, A.: UML-based approach for validating product lines. In: Proceedings of the International Workshop on Software Product Line Testing – SPLiT, Boston, USA, August 2004, ed by Geppert, B., Krueger, C., Li, J.J, Avaya labs technical report, ALR-2004-031 (2004) pp 58–64

10. Kamsties, E., Pohl, K., Reis, S., Reuys, A.: Testing variabilities in use case models. In: *Software Product-Family Engineering*, ed by van der Linden, F., 5th International Workshop, Siena, Italy, November 2003. Lecture Notes in Computer Science, vol 3014 (Springer, Berlin Heidelberg New York 2003) pp 6–18

11. Kamsties, E., Pohl, K., Reis, S., Reuys, A.: Anforderungsbasiertes Testen. In: *Software-Produktlinien – Methoden, Einführung und Praxis, dpunkt, Heidelberg* (in German), ed by Böckle, G., Knauber, P., Pohl, K., Schmid, K. (2004) Chapter 10, pp 119–136

12. Kamsties, E., Pohl, K., Reuys, A.: Supporting test case derivation in domain engineering. In: Proceedings of the 7th Biennial World Conference on Integrated Design and Process Technology, IDPT, Austin, USA, December 2003), ed by Ertas, A. et al, vol 2 (Society for Design and Process Science, USA 2003)

13. McGregor, J.D.: Testing a software product line. Technical report SEI, CMU/SEI-2001-TR-022 (Software Engineering Institute, Carnegie Mellon University, USA 2001)

14. Myers, G.J.: *The Art of Software Testing* (Wiley, New York 1979)

15. Nebut, C., Pickin, S., Le Traon, Y., Jezequel, J.-M.: Reusable test requirements for UML-modeled product lines. In: Proceeding of the International Workshop on Requirements Engineering for Product Lines, Essen, Germany, September 2002, ed by Geppert, B., Schmid, K., Technical report, ALR-2002-033 (Avaya Labs, Basking Ridge 2002) pp 51–56

16. Nebut, C., Fleurey, F., Le Traon, Y., Jézéquel, J.-M.: A requirement-based approach to test product families. In: *Software Product-Family Engineering*, ed by van der Linden, F., 5th International Workshop, Siena, Italy, November 2003. Lecture Notes in Computer Science, vol 3014 (Springer, Berlin Heidelberg New York 2003) pp 198–210

17. Pohl, K., Böckle, G., van der Linden, F.: *Software Product Line Engineering – Foundations, Principles, and Techniques* (Springer, Berlin Heidelberg New York 2005)

18. Reuys, A., Götz, H., Neumann, J., Weingärtner, J.: Medizintechnik bei Siemens AG Medical Solutions HS IM. In: *Software-Produktlinien – Methoden, Einführung und Praxis, dpunkt, Heidelberg* (in German), ed by Böckle, G., Knauber, P., Pohl, K., Schmid, K. (2004), pp 247–260

19. Reuys, A., Kamsties, E., Pohl, K., Götz, H., Neumann, J., Weingärtner, J.: Testen von Software-Produktvarianten – Ein Erfahrungsbericht. In: Multikonferenz Wirtschaftsinformatik (in German), MKWI, Essen, March 2004, ed by Adelsberger, H.H., Eicker, S., Kremar, H., Pawlowski, J.M., Pohl, K., Rombach, D., Wulf, V., vol 1 (Akademische, Berlin 2004) pp 244–259

20. Reuys, A., Kamsties, E., Pohl, K., Reis, S.: Model-based system testing of software product families. In: Advanced Information Systems Engineering, CAiSE 2005, Porto, Portugal, June 2005, ed by Pastor, O., Falcao e Cunha, J. Lecture Notes in Computer Science, vol 3520 (Springer, Berlin Heidelberg New York 2005) pp 519–534

21. Reuys, A., Reis, S., Kamsties, E., Pohl, K.: Derivation of domain test scenarios from activity diagrams. In: Proceedings of the International Workshop on Product Line Engineering: The Early Steps: Planning, Modeling, and Managing, PLEES'03, Erfurt, Germany, September 2003, ed by Schmid, K., Geppert, B., IESE-report no. 139.03/E Fraunhofer IESE 2003, pp 35–41

22. Tevanlinna, A., Taina, J., Kauppinen, R. Product family testing – a survey. ACM SIGSOFT Softw. Eng. Notes **29**(2) (2004)

23. Unified Modeling Language Specification (OMG), Object Management Group Document. http://www. omg.org/docs/formal/03-03-01.pdf (2003)

24. Winter, M.: Qualitätssicherung für objektorientierte Software – Anforderungsermittlung und Test gegen die Anforderungsspezifikation (in German). Dissertation, FernUniversität Hagen, 1999

Part 5: Specific Product Line Engineering Issues

Introduction

Part 5 deals with specific product line engineering issues that deepen the coverage of testing discussed in Part 4 and model-based product line engineering discussed in Chap. 6. Most importantly, Part 5 probes the transition from the product line assets (i.e., the results of domain engineering) to actual products under the responsibility of application engineering. It consists of three chapters:

Chapter 14. Incremental Systems Integration within Multidisciplinary Product Line Engineering using Configuration Item Evolution Diagrams

Chapter 15. Software Product Line Engineering with the UML: Deriving Products

Chapter 16. Evaluation Framework for Model-Driven Product Line Engineering Tools

A product line is developed by a domain engineering organization that produces components so that an application engineering organization can integrate these components into a system. Configuration Management is used to keep track of the configurations and their variability. Chapter 13 addressed integration and testing of components. It assumed implicitly that components are available and of sufficiently high quality to be tested. In practice, this is often not the case as efficient development, integration and testing of components is difficult due to synchronization problems between the evolution and delivery of work products from various organizational units (including those related with mechanical or systems engineering). Chapter 14 explains how to control the evolution of components and organize their testing with the help of Configuration Item Evolution Diagrams (CIED). To shorten project throughput time, the CIED specifies the order in which components evolve and clarifies the relationships between the work products that form the components and the testing of those work products. Preliminary validation, comprising two case studies, objective data taken from management statistics, and interviews, shows the usefulness and applicability of the CIED in industrial settings.

Both the model-driven development (MDD) and the product line engineering approaches envisage efficient and effective product development. Chapters 15 and 16 deal with model-driven product line engineering. Chapter 15 recognizes that there is plenty of research on modeling variability but product derivation, a complete process of building products from the product line, has been investigated very little. While Chaps. 5 and 11 deal with deriving application requirements from product line requirements in the front-end of product line engineering and Chap. 6 discusses, among other issues, the derivation of complete products (including automatically generated program code) from models designed using domain-specific modeling languages, Chapter 15 studies the derivation of detailed UML designs from which program code could be generated and, specifically, the formalization of product derivation using UML model transformations. It presents model transformation algorithms to transform both static and behavioral aspects of the product line into a specific product and two simple case studies to illustrate the overall process from the modeling of the product line to the product derivation.

To succeed with model-driven product line engineering, tools are needed to support the communication, coordination, and collaboration of architects, engineers, and other stakeholders involved in tasks such as system modeling, variability modeling, model analysis, model transformation, system derivation, code generation, and model traceability. How to manage and automate these processes and tasks? No existing tool fully supports the model-driven product line engineering approach. However, there is an increasing number of emerging tools that support model-driven development and could eventually be used for model-driven product line engineering. It can thus be difficult to know what tool features to look for and what to expect. Chapter 16 relates traditional model-driven engineering to product line engineering and defines a general framework for evaluating tools in this area.

14 Incremental Systems Integration within Multidisciplinary Product Line Engineering Using Configuration Item Evolution Diagrams

E.S. Engelsma

Abstract

A Product Line is developed by a domain engineering organization that produces components, so that an application engineering organization can integrate these components into a system. The components consist of proprietary and commercially available hardware and software. Configuration Management is used to keep track of the various configurations and their variability. In practice, efficient development, integration and testing of components is difficult due to synchronization problems between the evolution and delivery of work products from the various disciplines. This chapter explains how to control the evolution of components and organize their testing. It introduces a Configuration Item Evolution Diagram (CIED) designed for this purpose. The CIED specifies the order in which components evolve and clarifies the relationships between the work products that form the components and the testing of those work products, so that project throughput time can be won. A preliminary validation of the CIED, comprising two case studies, objective data taken from management statistics, and interviews of three key people, shows the usefulness and applicability of the CIED in industrial settings.

14.1 Introduction

Projects that develop product lines comprising work products derived from different disciplines have to integrate those work products. Often, valuable time is lost in the course of the integration process. During initial integration, faults are found, the root causes of which have to be traced, which is a time-consuming process. Solving these root causes often entails discarding work that has been done and reworking what remains. This loss of time and effort is one reason why many projects end up being late and over budget, if indeed they get completed at all. Within an organization where product line engineering takes place, the situation becomes more complicated still, since the organization is dealing with a number of components that are re-used in various system configurations. While product line engineering allows for greater flexibility, it also adds to the complexity of managing and testing components.

The current chapter addresses the integration and testing problem by introducing a way of evolving, integrating and testing work products from various disciplines in a closely defined and controlled manner. This approach makes early integration and testing of partly completed products possible. To this end, the Configuration Item Evolution Diagram (CIED) is introduced. The CIED enables a project crew taken from different disciplines to synchronize their work products, render these work products testable and link their deliverables to test activities. The role of testing in the proposed approach is extended beyond just a final evaluation of achieved quality. It is also used to measure project progress in terms of objectively realized functionality during the development process. An additional function of testing is to provide rapid feedback to development, so that mistakes can be solved with a minimum loss of time. The idea of "testing while developing" is not new [3]. The extent to which testing is part of project progress measurement is a new practice.

In an organization that develops Product Lines, a distinction is drawn between domain engineering and application engineering [21]. Domain Engineering is the product line engineering process in which the commonality and the variability of a product line are defined and realized. Application Engineering is the product line engineering process in which the applications of the product line are built by reusing domain artifacts and exploiting the product line variability.

It is important for the domain engineering organization to be adept at the configuration management of their work products, both in finished form and in intermediate forms, for the following reasons:

- Application-specific environments may need an early prototype of a configuration for, e.g., application experiments or compatibility testing with existing products or end-user protocols.
- Early tests on designated items are used to verify intermediate work products and to get an early feedback on true project progress. In traditional project management, project progress is measured using indicators such as "which requirements have been met," "which reviews have been passed" and "what code has been generated." In the proposed approach, in addition over and above the classical measures, tests are used to evaluate which functions are actually working as specified. This measure is then used to assess project progress. This approach ensures far tighter project control than the classical measures, particularly in an incremental and multidisciplinary development environment.
- New insights are gained during development. New requirements may emerge, or technological changes may have to be implemented in cases where a project has a long throughput time (relative to technology cycles or market influences).
- The business environment may introduce unexpected changes, demanding a flexible response.

The testing of components that are developed in a domain engineering (DE) organization and reused in an application engineering (AE) organization is a major and recognizable issue. Chapter 13 addresses the issue of how components can be effectively tested in an organization that produces product lines by reusing test artifacts. It assumes implicitly that the development work products are:

- Available to be tested
- Of a sufficiently high quality to make testing a sensible activity to undertake in a real-world project

In practice, the availability of development work products at the right time, with the right intermediate functionality, the right performance and with the right quality level is by no means a given. It is precisely this type of unfounded optimism about the ease of integration that places projects at risk of falling into the "90% finished trap" described by Brooks [7]. Therefore, the tool of choice to check actual project progress (besides the usual quality measures in a project, like reviewed documentation and effort spent) is testing. Testing ensures that only the functionality that has been verified and validated (against the Product Requirements to be fulfilled in a certain increment) and that is found to be correct is declared ready and "transferable" to a customer, or to an archive where it is baselined. The defined and controlled evolution, integration and testing of these development work products will be addressed later in this chapter.

The proposed approach can be used to advantage in environments that are characterized by:

- An organization that uses an integrated design, creation and testing process
- The use of incremental development to make components

A less stringent condition is that there is a clear distinction between domain engineering and application engineering activities in the organization.

Configuration Management plays a large part in the definition of what is to be developed.

The proposed approach entails paying special attention to the following issues:

- Defining how the defined Configuration Items evolve over time
- Defining integration moments during development
- Synchronizing testing and work products
- Actively ensuring that the right people have access to the right information

The CIED has been used in the development of Medical Imaging Equipment at Philips Medical Systems. Comparisons between projects that were executed before the introduction of the CIED and after the introduction of the CIED brought to light the characteristics outlined below.

Projects that were run without using the CIED were characterized by the following:

- A high level of initial optimism regarding timing – the project was "right on track" until testing started
- No (extensive) testing during development of work products
- A high level of independence on the part of the various development disciplines
- A large number of faults, not discovered until after integration
- Integration and testing of the product took (almost) an order of magnitude longer than expected

- Because of this delay, total project time was over budget by more than a factor 2
- A high level of rework and frustration

The projects that used the CIED were characterized by the following:

- Less initial optimism regarding timing
- More time spent initially on making sure everything fitted across the disciplines
- More intermediate testing moments
- More automated regression testing
- Steady progress
- High level of cooperation across disciplines
- Rapid response to unforeseen circumstances
- First projects were over target by only 30% (compared to a factor of 2), and once experience had been gained, projects were within time and budget

Discussions with representatives from the automobile industry indicate that the kind of problems encountered when developing the software for a car (specifically fuel injection systems and cruise control) lend themselves to the approach outlined in this chapter.

Using the CIED is of particular interest to organizations that use product line engineering because:

- The CIED forms an ideal interface between domain engineering and application engineering when discussing delivery of prototypes for testing purposes.
- The CIED forms a very good means of communication when decisions about how to solve errors are needed that cross the boundary between domain engineering and application engineering.
- The CIED gives insight in what tests are performed at what level and therefore can be used in optimizing testing across the DE and AE activities.

14.2 Configuration Management and Problems with Integration

According to the American Software Technology Support Center, "software configuration management (SCM) is a discipline to manage the evolution of computer program products during all stages of development and sustainment" [16]. Similar definitions exist in [11,14,20,27].

Thinking in terms of management of configurations has been (and continues to be) extremely useful. From the point of view of a company that designs and creates functionality involving several development disciplines, a number of problems remain during integration. In standard Configuration Management practices, the following issues are ignored:

- How to define and evolve software content along with development in hardware Mechatronics

- How to integrate the products from these disciplines (during development using a "bottom-up" of functional integration approach)
- How to test the integrated intermediate products

A standard way of implementing software configuration management (SCM) is to address the version and configuration control of software (and documentation) files (including the tools that created these files). This is done by creating items whose content is controlled for version and configuration. These items are referred to as Configuration Items (C.I.). While a Configuration Item is an abstract entity, the implementation of a Configuration Item is always something tangible, like a printed circuit board or a cabinet or a software carrier. Common SCM practices limit themselves to the question of how the "containers" of a given technical (software) content can be identified, and do not address the issue of how to define the content of those containers. They address the names given to files, how version and configuration numbering is done, and what identification to give to base lines. SCM may describe a generic set of tests to be executed before files are allowed to enter the project software archive, but it does not deal with the content of the files managed in the system – only with the processes surrounding the handling of the files. SCM facilitates Incremental Development by introducing the base lining approach (i.e., freezing the content of C.I.s in time) which solves the problem of how to ensure that there is a stable (and tested!) base to work from for an increment. SCM also uses workspaces to allow different developers or groups of developers to work in parallel [2,15,27,28]. It follows that there is a need to evolve C.I.s in a predefined and controlled way, so they can be integrated and tested during development. Otherwise, it is impossible in practice to test in a sensible and effective incremental manner, avoiding the Big Bang strategy.

14.2.1 Extensions Needed for SCM

To evolve and integrate C.I.s in the way proposed, a configuration management system needs to fulfill a number of additional requirements:

1. Synchronize deliveries from the disciplines involved, including test environments and infra structure
2. Manage the knowledge required to create the work products
3. Adapt the order in which configuration items develop, are integrated and tested to new situations
4. Manage testability of work products, test environments and test tooling
5. Manage synchronization of development and integration over several projects
6. Manage personal accountability for work products and their quality

In projects that do not meet the requirements listed above, project delays are likely. These delays are caused by:

1. Misunderstandings, which lead to problems during the integration of components and hence take time to solve. This is further aggravated by the amount of design and coding work that has to be redone.

2. Items being tested that were not yet ready for testing. This wastes time, and requires the unexpected re-planning of test resources. Moreover, faulty information is generated, as problem reports are written and responded to that should never have been written in the first place, tying up developers' time.

The above problems can be overcome with the correct application of a CIED.

14.3 Solving the Problems by Using the Configuration Item Evolution Diagram (CIED)

The content of hardware, mechanical and software C.I.s evolves step by step over time in a controlled manner. In the following sections, an approach is presented that lays out a practical, feasible content for each step. It synchronizes the contents of the work products from the various disciplines involved in the project. It is assumed that hardware and mechanics use Configuration Management in the same way that software uses it.

The term "synchronizing" entails:

– Communicating about the contents of these steps
– Adjusting the contents of each step for each discipline, so that the needs of other disciplines are met
– Providing feedback about impact on related disciplines
– Providing feedback about the needs that various disciplines have that need to be met by other disciplines, and how these needs are addressed

The approach centers on the use of the Configuration Item Evolution Diagram, which diagrammatically depicts:

– The content of C.I.s as delivered by development
– The technical relationships that are valid within and between the C.I.s
– The integration activities that take place
– The test activities that take place
– The deliverables to customers

14.3.1 Requirements of the Proposed Solution

Requirements for the solution to the problem are as follows:

1. It must be compatible with standard Configuration Management practices as used in the company. Any changes must be implemented using proper change management techniques [23].
2. It must be independent of the discipline (HW, SW, Mechatronics) involved.
3. A set of supplier-customer relations between projects (at multiple sites, and between the DE AE boundaries) must be definable.

4. The relation between development work products and testing must be indicated.
5. It must be applicable in an incremental development environment.
6. Modeling at various levels of abstraction must be possible.
7. It must support multiple configurations.
8. It must help minimize test effort for multiple configurations.
9. It must be communicable.
10. The items in the model must be traceable to requirements, Project Test Plan, test designs, test reports, as described in the IEEE standards [12].
11. The model must only indicate relations between C.I.s that are technically or logically necessary.
12. The CIED must be usable as an input for planning sessions.
13. The model should not be seen as a replacement for architecture overviews as described in tools like Rational Rose and Doors. Whereas the architecture overview presents the overall system in a finished state, the CIED indicates in which order it is to be built and tested.
14. The model must be in line with object-oriented development techniques and object-oriented testing techniques. The use of results of internal tests carried out by the development groups can save time [18].

14.3.2 Symbols Used in the CIED

A diagram is created using symbols to represent the evolution of Configuration Items, so that the decisions regarding what to integrate and test can be visualized. It would be ideal to use UML for this, but we find that these modeling techniques are not yet mature enough for use in our environment. An extension to this effect for UML would be very welcome.

The constraints listed in Sect. 14.2 lead to the selection of symbols that are used to create this diagram. The concepts (and the symbols) that are introduced are the following:

– dependency indicator
– development activity
– validated-deliverable-to
– validated-deliverable-from
– test activity
– Integration activity

For reasons of scalability, the validated-deliverable-to and the validated-deliverable-from are each other's mirror image. A development activity results in a work product that adheres to a defined level of quality, coming from a (team of) developer(s), before it is integrated with other work products and then tested. How each development activity results in a work product is a discipline responsibility. This shows the first step in abstraction that is needed to make disciplines synchronize their activities. Each of the activities that lead to a "validated-deliverable-to" has a person responsible for its correctness, who can be approached if problems arise. The concepts listed in the bullet list above are described in more detail below.

Dependency Indicator

The dependency indicator links the symbols that are used. This indicator makes explicit the technical or logical necessity between work products. Although a time indication for planning purposes can (and should) be derived from it, the time aspect is not in itself made explicit by this Indicator. It is not meant to represent a timing dependency for subjects like project planning and resource assignment issues. This is because timing dependencies in a project also depend on a number of other factors, like the assignment of personnel and the availability of other development resources. While this issue must be addressed in the project, this can not be done until the technical requirements are clear. The assignment of project resources takes place later in the project, using more traditional methods like Gantt charts [17] and work sheets for individuals. The dependency indicator is depicted as an arrow (Fig. 14.1).

Fig. 14.1. Dependency indicator

The direction of this arrow is defined such that the tip indicates the client of a certain dependency and the start indicates the previous activity that the client is dependent upon.

Take as an example motor and mechanics assembly that needs software to control its movements. Successful integration requires the presence of the motor assembly, the relevant controlling hardware and at least some software. The dependency indicator indicates this "must." Once this "must" is known, project – timing relations and resource assignment can be worked out.

Development Activity

A development activity results in a work product from a monodisciplinary team within the project. A work product can be a C.I. in a defined state. The development team itself is supposed to have executed its discipline tests, like white box testing for a Software discipline. The team has applied all standard quality actions (code coverage, design reviews, etc.) needed to achieve a predefined quality level. If a product is the result of more than one team, this is always indicated by at least two Development Activities and an integration activity.

Depending on the likelihood of faults being made and how great the impact of a fault would be, the development activity may be directly linked to an integration activity or tested first by an independent team. The integration manager can decide on this and communicate his/her decision in the diagram. The likelihood of faults being made is influenced by both technical and nontechnical factors. Technical factors include the technology used and the complexity of the algorithms or decision structure in the software. Nontechnical factors include the maturity of the development team, the location and the level of competence and experience of the developers.

The development activity symbol is shown in Fig. 14.2.

Fig. 14.2. Development activity symbol

The symbol contains a reference to the functionality that has to be made and the team that will make it. The reference to the functionality includes a description of the level of functionality and the corresponding quality contributed by this development activity. The development activity also contains a reference to the C.I. (or set of C.I.s) to which it contributes. By using this symbol, the diagram helps to clarify what has been delivered for possible testing (or further integration), so that a clear definition emerges of what is going to be tested (or integrated). Examples of Development Activities are:

 — A prototype for an image sensor chip that gives images with substandard image quality.
 — A Sequencer[1] board that provides the hardware infrastructure to program all sequences to be generated.
 — A control board with only its HW communication layer working. In this context, a control board may also have an application layer that provides functions to a user, and several technical layers translating user input to device-specific instructions. The full product would be the result of the integration of HW, software drivers and application layers.
 — Part of a Feedback Control Loop with specified behavior, used to adapt (real-time) the precise characteristics of an X-ray beam to optimize image quality for a specific patient. The behavior of the Feedback Control Loop is based on knowledge about how X-ray behaves in a human body and knowledge of the transfer functions of the imaging subsystem and the X-ray generation system. The technical implementation of the Feedback Control Loop spans a number of C.I.s, as it measures data from the imaging subsystem as well as adapting the output parameters of the X-ray generation subsystem.

Validated-Deliverable-To

The validated-deliverable-to indicates that a work product has been validated and can be transferred to a higher level in the organization. The higher level may entail transferring from one project to another project or from the DE organization to the AE organization. It is used:

 — To define cross-border deliverables between domain engineering and application engineering groups.
 — To define cross-border deliverables between projects.

---

[1]A Sequencer is a device that controls the real-time synchronization of sequences (of State Changes) in other devices. It may react to synchronization signals that the devices return to it. The Sequencer referred to controls the X-ray imaging equipment.

The validated-deliverable-to is depicted in Fig. 14.3.

Fig. 14.3. Validated-deliverable-to

A validated-deliverable-to is usually a combination of software and hardware. It consists of a number of C.I.s (this number may be equal to 1) in a defined state, but not necessarily complete. A C.I. may be simulated. It provides the customer (i.e., the higher level project or application engineering group) with a defined set of functionality (with agreed nonfunctional requirements implemented) with a known and agreed level of quality. The end-functionality may be present but not yet guarded against user input errors, or only one type or algorithm may be selectable, or the processing speed may be lower than in the final product, and so on.

A validated-deliverable-to has

- An identification (for trace ability purposes)
- A person who is responsible
- A link to requirements that are implemented in this deliverable (using tagging)
- A link to a Validation Report (e.g., IEEE 829-1998 based)
- Some other meta-data (ownership)

It does not have a time or milestone associated with it. It defines the "what" (content in terms of realized functionality from a technical point of view), not the how or when. In terms of Configuration Management, this represents a C.I. (or set of C.I.s) in a particular state. The state indicates the functionality that is supported by a C.I., and the actual level of quality and performance involved. The C.I.s are considered here in terms of the tests needed to verify and validate the content of a C.I. From a software configuration management point of view, there will still be a list of files indicating which files comprise the used C.I.s at a particular time. Similarly, version control is also required for hardware.

Validated-Deliverable-From

The counterpart of the validated-deliverable-to is the lower-level validated-deliverable-from. The symbols used for these two concepts are the same. The validated-deliverable-from may be used to look at a project from a subcontractor's point of view or to look at DE products from an AE point of view. The way these symbols are connected to the rest of the diagram makes the distinction clear and unambiguous. In the case of the validated-deliverable-from, the dependency indicator emerges from its top, whereas in the case of the validated-deliverable-to, the dependency indicator enters at the bottom.

Test Activity

A test activity is the complete set of activities needed to test an integrated set of work products coming from a development activity, namely test preparation, test execution, test result reporting, and test incident reporting, plus retesting and regression testing. It is executed on a known and identified test base, by a more or less independent team of testers. The level of independence of the test team can be selected as appropriate to the phase of a project. In practice, if verification takes place while development is still in progress, it is more effective to have a high level of dependency between developers and testers, as this generates fast feedback loops. Exploratory testing is a good technique to use. The level of independence does not become a serious issue until a phase has been reached in which validation is more important than verification. Experience has shown that the more closely the proposed way of working with a CIED is followed, the better testers and developers are able to work together, exchanging valuable information. The level of cooperation may or may not be an issue, depending on the organization in which the CIED is introduced. Organizations determined to maintain a strict division between development and testing (as suggested by TMAP [22,26]) will struggle to reap the benefits of the CIED. The integration model discussed in this chapter is used in a development organization where a high level of integration and cooperation exists between developers and testers.

The symbol used to represent the test activity is shown in Fig. 14.4.

Fig. 14.4. Test activity

The symbol contains a reference to the items that must be tested, and to the test designs and test cases used to execute it. It also holds:

– A reference to test reports that are to be produced
– A reference for test incident reports when the testing is actually executed
– The person or group responsible for test execution

As the activities for testing and the type of test design used are indicated in the Project Test Plan, a reference to the relevant chapter in the test plan is the most practical. Our experience is that at the time of writing the Project Test Plan, detailed knowledge about a certain item may not be precise enough to give the level of detail needed to derive test designs. This will often be the case in large-scale projects. This problem can be addressed in one of two ways:

– Work incrementally on new versions of the Project Test Plan
– Write a detailed test plan per increment, referred to as an Increment Test Plan

The right choice depends on the organizations' ability to work with incremental documents and the level of abstraction that is preferred for the Project Test Plan. Both options have their strengths and weaknesses. What matters most is that a decision regarding the approach to be taken is made, deployed and adhered to throughout the running project.

On the basis of the outcome of the test execution, the project manager or management can decide whether the project is ready to proceed to the next integration phase or whether rework is needed. The results of the tests provide the project manager with early objective feedback about the achieved functionality and quality of the product, thereby all but eliminating the "90% finished" syndrome. [7]

The term "objective" (above) means that tests have been designed using existing test design techniques and have been reviewed by a body made up of both testers and designers to give impartial and correct information about the status of a given tested functionality.

Resource usage is an issue at this point. As not all eventual functionality will be running on a processor at the time an increment is tested, a process may actually be taking too much time. However, as it can use a greater amount of processor time than in the end situation, this may not be evident from the tests (the same is true for memory usage and other types of resources). Testing at this stage must also make sure that no more than the allotted resources are actually used.

Integration Activity

An integration activity is the work needed to integrate several deliverables. These deliverables may be:

- The output from a previous integration activity
- The output from a previous test activity
- The output from a validated-deliverable
- The output from a development activity

Its symbol is shown in Fig. 14.5.

Fig. 14.5. Integration activity

The symbol refers to the person responsible for the integration activities (building a software archive, setting up a test environment, organizing the hardware and software needed) and the functionality that is to be realized in this particular integration activity. It acts as a summation point for the deliverables that are now about to "see" each other for the first time. The work in practice consists of:

- Integrating HW and SW
- Making sure archives are in order
- Making sure a test system is in a fit state to be used

- Ensuring that testers are competent to carry out the testing activities that are to follow
- Ensuring that test interfaces are supplied
- Ensuring that scripting languages are available (where automated testing is used)
- Making sure that regression test sets are available or defined

14.3.3 How the CIED Should be Used in Practice

This section addresses how the symbols described above are used to create a CIED in a real organization. In order to introduce this approach successfully, the organization must have a certain level of maturity. In other words, it must have a clearly described and deployed development process, based on, e.g., IEEE Standards for software development [25].

In addition, the role of Integration Manager must be filled in. The Integration Manager defines the CIED, makes sure that testability requirements are generated for the design and acts as Test Manager. He/she writes the test plans and test reports, and may have daily operational responsibility over the test engineers. The last point is not essential – daily operational leadership can also be delegated to the leaders of a development team.

Although the CIED approach can be used within the context of many different Software development lifecycle models, it has by nature more in common with rapid development models than with the traditional waterfall development model. See [13] for an extensive discussion of the various development models. It is questionable whether an organization that works strictly in accordance with the waterfall model will have the mindset needed to use the CIED. This has not been researched.

The starting situation is that a set of main product requirements is available in (nearly) completed form. An overall architecture or system design is also available. The minimum prerequisite is that the requirements and overall architecture must be in a form in which the experts can make reasonable technical assumptions based on those requirements. It is also assumed that the product is not completely new. The subject matter is fairly well understood and something similar to the present functionality has been made before, though the technological implementation may be completely new and new functionality may have been added. The above assumption is made because this is the only situation in which the CIED has been used in practice.

The first goal is to get the different disciplines to give their input in a group session to enhance common understanding. This process is layered, in that the work starts at a high level of abstraction, with individuals able to operate at this level. One person, assuming the role of integration manager, will moderate the meeting and create and distribute the resulting integration diagrams. Also present are an architect, several designers from the various disciplines and a test expert. As moderator, the integration manager will invite the people, make sure that a common goal is defined and generally fulfill all the standard tasks of a moderator [9]. The architect shows an initial version of the integration diagram that he has drawn up beforehand in cooperation with the integration manager. This is then adapted according to remarks made by the various designers and the test expert. Ideally, these changes are made "real time" using a setup with a beamer once those present have agreed that an amendment is valid. The precise way of reaching agreements will have been outlined in advance by the moderator. Where questions or objections are raised that cannot be immediately answered, it may be necessary to assign "homework," in which case the moderator has to decide whether the meeting should be postponed or whether it is advantageous to continue.

Questions and remarks can be made about the following subjects:

– The ground for certain decisions
– Particular behavior at an interface, including possible "side effects"
– The definition of side effects and preconditions
– How a behavior can be tested at this point

All questions and solutions are written down, preferably by a secretary. After a small number of these sessions, a development and integration strategy will have been developed.

The second goal is for the project manager to define the project milestones, based on the above development and integration strategy. The project manager defines tasks and assigns people (or subgroups) to those tasks. He may also draw up more precise planning, as well as analyzing and addressing risks.

The third goal is to use the diagrams to create common understanding of all relevant issues for the engineers. The resulting diagrams are deployed in the project organization. This is done in small groups, where an overview is given to the engineers so that they understand their position within the project, and where more attention is given to the details that matter to these particular engineers. This enables engineers to gain a rapid overview of where their contribution fits in the whole picture and what its importance is to the overall project progress. More detailed discussions will then take place within development subgroups.

The fourth goal is to define, clarify and create insight into the subject matter for testers. They can then design their tests and have a means of knowing when which tests can be meaningfully run.

14.3.4 Simple Examples of a CIED

In this section, a number of simple combinations of the elements of an integration diagram are shown and their meanings are discussed. The examples are imaginary (though based on a realistic technical background) and are used simply to provide the reader with a "taste" of a CIED. See Fig. 14.6.

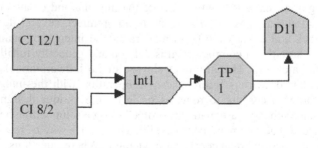

Fig. 14.6. A simple example of a CIED

Figure 14.6 depicts how two development activities are delivered for integration. A number indicates the Configuration Item to which these development activities contribute. CI 12 has version 1 and CI 8 has version 2. A separate document (a configuration plan) describes what this version of a C.I. contains. In practice, any agreed way of coding and referencing C.I.s that is found useful can be applied. The two development products are integrated. A separate plan describes which actions and test models are needed for this integration action, identified by Int 1. Section 3.5 describes the management of the documents that are produced. After integration, a working software archive according to predefined acceptance criteria is transferred to the test phase TP 1. The integration manager specifies beforehand which type of tests will be run in TP1, having analyzed the risks involved and the necessary test-depth. These tests are designed by the verification engineers and reviewed by peers and a designer before being applied. Following successful completion of the test phase, the product is validated for customer use (indicated by D1). Incident reports have been solved during this phase. The customer receives the product plus a transferal document as outlined in step D1 (D = delivery). This example leads to the introduction of an integration as input for another integration (see Fig. 11.7).

In this case, there is no external team that tests Int 2 before delivery to Int 3. The C.I.s 1, 5, 8, 12 and 14 with their respective versions are integrated, once initial steps (Int 1 and Int 2 plus TP 1) have been taken to ensure a good enough quality to start TP 2. The validated-deliverable-from is then introduced (VDF21). This may be a software package from a subcontractor. Validation has taken place, so in this diagram no further testing is done prior to integration.

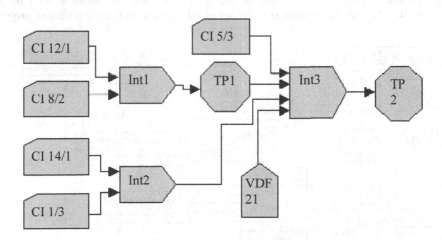

Fig. 14.7. Integration as input for another integration

Additional remarks about the diagram (Fig. 14.7):

1. The outcome of balancing the risk for project throughput time against the effort of additional testing of CI 5/3 has resulted in the decision that it can be transferred directly to Int 3. A number of reasons may have influenced this decision
   - Version 2 of CI 5 may have been thoroughly tested, with only very small changes implemented in version 3
   - The internal testing carried out by the group that produces CI 5 may have been considered sufficient
   - It may be prohibitively expensive, for whatever reason, to test CI 5 stand-alone

   If testing is not carried out because of prohibitive expense, there is a risk for the organization, and it may be wise to review the architecture or research cheaper test possibilities.
2. Similar remarks apply to the outcome of Int 2.
3. One of the added values of the CIED is that it makes the decisions taken visible. The more transparent nature of the decisions means that they can be challenged and adapted if needed.

14.3.5 Linking Test Documentation to Design Documentation

At this point, the question arises as to how the test documents are managed and made accessible to the staff in the project. The purpose of this chapter is to provide the answer. Figure 14.8 shows an overview of the documents that are of immediate interest for the testing activities. These documents are a subset of all documents used in an entire project.

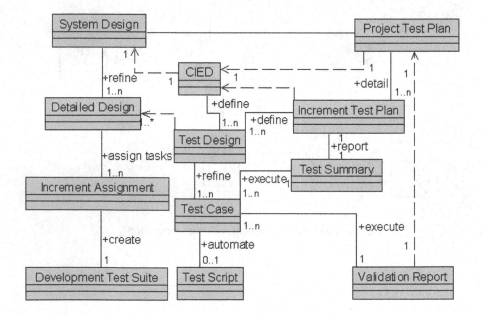

Fig. 14.8. Document overview

Below is a description of each of the documents depicted in Fig. 14.8.

- System Design: A Document that describes the System Design at the highest level of abstraction. It describes how the requirements are to be implemented at a global level.
- CIED: This is the Integration Diagram. This diagram is heavily influenced by the System Design Document. It gives feedback to the System Design Document, for instance to make sure part deliveries are testable.
- The detailed design per increment and per C.I. gives the design details required for implementation.
- The Increment Assignments details the development activities that are to be undertaken to develop the current increment, and assigns these activities to specific people. Part of the Increment Assignments defines the relationship between the work products that are created for the current increment and the configuration of the final system, as described in the Configuration Management Plan (not depicted).
- The Development Test Suite is the set of test cases (usually based on a white box approach) that is developed, maintained and executed by development staff themselves. Test engineers may be consulted on the definition of these suites.
- The Increment Test Plan is a detailed version of the Project Test Plan, which is relevant for the current increment. Details are added that were not known at the time of writing the Project Test Plan.
- Test Design Documents describe the important values (or actions) that the system must be exercised with, based on a formal test design technique ([4] introduces the subject of formal test techniques).
- Test Cases describe step by step the actions that must be taken to enter the values or take the actions as described in the Test Designs.
- Test Scripts are the automated versions of the Test Cases.
- The Test Summary is a summary of the findings as a result of testing an increment.
- The Validation Report gives the results of the validation tests that were executed and advices about release or otherwise of a product.

The relations between the documents are as follows:

The System Design Document serves as input for determining the CIED. While the CIED is being made, remarks will be made that reflect upon the System Design Document. The System Designer updates the System Design Document accordingly. In practice, Requirements also come under test scrutiny. As Test Designs are made before the CIED is used, the question arises as to whether Requirements are testable in principle. In practice, the verifiability of Requirements is essential from the moment they are drawn up. This means that requirement engineers have to be taught the basics of testing theory and need to cooperate with verification engineers.

The detailed designs are derived from the System Design Document, and use the CIED to ensure that the correct decisions are made regarding what should be implemented in what increment. Once the detailed design is good enough to start assigning tasks, development tasks are defined and assigned to people. Development groups themselves make the development test suites to test the work product they make.

The Project Test Plan derives its information from the System Design Document and other relevant sources. It describes the strategy for testing the work products, gives an overview of the work involved and lists the resources required. When adaptations to the design are needed, these are implemented into the System Design Document. The newly acquired details are added per increment to form the increment test plan for the increment in question. In this increment test plan, the link is made to the Test Activities within the CIED. The CIED is updated to show in which increment an activity takes place.

Test Designs are derived from the specific Test Activities as described in the Increment Test Plan. Test cases and scripts can therefore be derived from Test Designs. Test results arising from test execution are described in the reporting documents.

Project staff can access the documents via an intranet application, where documents are categorized in accordance with FDA[2] criteria for health and safety critical systems. A strict document control mechanism is in place to ensure that versions are correct and up to date.

14.3.6 A Practical Example of Using a CIED

This section gives an example of how the CIED is used for a simple imaging system (generic and simplified, based on a number of real systems). The purpose is to make the abstract diagrams used so far more accessible, and to show a relation to the Configuration Plan. The system consists of:

1. A sensor (to detect X-rays).
2. A control system to optimize the settings of the sensor.
   - Mechanical shutters that regulate the amount of X-ray that is incident upon the detector
   - A focusing mechanism for the detector
   - Setting the resolution of the detector
3. A control system to control system timing
   - To synchronize the detector system with the X-ray bursts, which may last from a few milliseconds to several minutes
   - To synchronize data transfer to an Image Processing system
   - Other issues that are beyond the scope of this section
4. Communication with a Main Data Acquisition system. This Main Data Acquisition system informs the detector regarding the image resolution it has to acquire, how many images to expect, what type of calibration to use and a number of other technical settings.
5. An Image Processor System (with controls for setting required processing functions, filter parameters and controlled timing to synchronize with the detector).
6. A pipeline to streamline processed image data (in a standard format) to the outside world.

This example is based on commercial projects that have actually been completed using the CIED. A number of technical details that make this system quite complex to develop in

---

[2] The American Food & Drug Agency also verifies adherence to standards for Medical Systems.

the real world have been ignored. Figure 14.9 gives a static overview of the system and its decomposition into Configuration Items.

The division into Configuration Items makes visible which parts are implemented into hardware, indicated by the letters HW in front of the number (e.g., the Sensor Assembly, and the Iris motor assembly) and which are implemented into software.

This static overview can be used as a preparation for the logistics operations, such as selecting possible providers of the hardware and starting initial negotiations with them. A Configuration Item that implements a function that is high enough in the function hierarchy to be of interest to customers is given the letters CI S and a number (CI = Configuration Item, S = System). In a perfect world with the capacity available to build the C.I.s flawlessly in one go, the project would now essentially be ready.

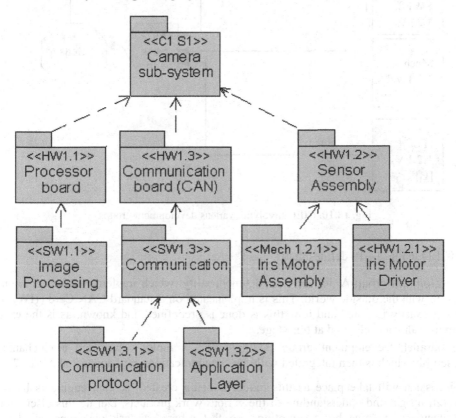

Fig. 14.9. Decomposition into Configuration Items

In practice, people make mistakes and have misunderstandings, and capacity is far from limitless, so not everything can be built perfectly in one go. Hence the need for incremental development and reviewing techniques. These can also be used to verify functionality that can be delivered to a customer. Because functions and C.I.s have a many-to-many relationship, C.I.s are sometimes needed in a form that is not necessarily a completed C.I. Hence the policy to integrate partly completed C.I.s. It must be made very clear to all project members which state C.I.s must reach before integration is possible.

Similarly, testers must know precisely what functions can be meaningfully tested. The diagram that emerges as a result of the discussion between Integration Manager and designers is shown in Fig. 14.10.

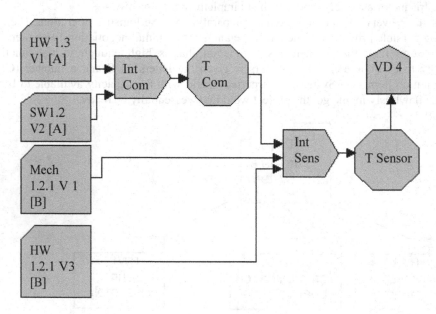

Fig. 14.10. CIED involving various development groups

The CIED in Fig. 14.10 defines that:

– Development group A delivers tested functionality, which implements the communication with the outside world. This is implemented on a standard CAN Card (HW1.3). What exactly is tested and how this is done is predefined and known, as is the exact functionality as delivered at this stage.
– In parallel, Development group B implements a motor driver and a mechanical assembly which is then integrated with the communications card and tested in MT 2.

Discussion will take place as this model is being created, so that engineers have a thorough insight and understanding of the various work products. During this discussion, each designer explains his assumptions, so that others can ask questions, challenge assumptions and verify whether they can actually do what is being required of them. This is especially helpful in the case of testing, as it means that test interfaces and test services can be predefined. It should be clear that this does not lessen the need for clear requirements. However, requirements can only be clear and unambiguous if there is a commonly understood context. The discussions held while making these diagrams create much of the needed context that facilitates true understanding.

It would take more steps than depicted above to model the entire set of activities needed to create this subsystem. But the above serves as a good illustration, and one which the reader might like to complete. A preliminary question would be whether HW 1.2.1 and Mech 1.2.1 really do not need a separate test before linking them with the rest of the system. That choice may have been made because it is difficult to test these two without having the communication layer running. The point is that once you have the diagram in front of you, you start asking questions that would probably not have been asked otherwise.

The diagram in Fig. 14.10 shows the following: A group (group A) is identified that is responsible for integrating the communication functionality. The integration manager who is responsible for the Test Activities (T Com) is involved at this point to:

- Verify that the requirements are testable
- Make sure he understands the functionality
- Prepare the testing activities (possibly adding requirements for a script editor or other test tooling)
- Design test cases
- Make sure by asking penetrating questions that the developers understand what is expected of them (this task can be assigned to a designer)

At this point, the designers of the various work products can clarify how they intend the functions they have designed to be used. For example, the mechanics people can tell the software developers about overshoot, speed requirements, mechanical response times and other technical aspects.

After T Com has been completed, we trust that the communication has been correctly implemented so the commands can now be issued to exercise the agreed functionality. For this trust to be warranted a high level of test process maturity in the organization is necessary. This agreed functionality is laid down in the Increment Design Specifications, and the precise types of tests are described in the Increment Test Plan. Specific examples of test subjects that may be described in the Increment Test Plan at this point are:

- All communication commands have been correctly transferred to the Sensor Assembly (HW 1.2)
- The mechanical shutter can be moved from fully open to fully closed, but not (yet) to intermediate positions
- Image Resolution parameters have been correctly transferred to the Sensor Assembly. The Sensor Assembly is not yet reacting to these parameters

This list would be longer in practice.

At T Sensor, tests can be run on positioning accuracy, reliability of repositioning, performance, mechanical wear and so on, in an environment that imitates the true working conditions (using user profiling for example, [19]) to determine how the equipment will be used. The above tests all are related to functionality that is created, but in the medical world additional operating constraints are imposed by Federal Agencies. These constraints are related to safety (hazard of electrical shock, parts falling out, EMC). The tests carried out to make sure these constraints are satisfied are referred to as "approbation." At this point, a test prototype may be defined to be used to execute all actions related to running the approbation tests. The entire system is gradually built up by continuing along this path.

It should be clear by now how the initial requirements as outlined in Sect. 14.2.1 are met. These requirements are to make it possible to carry out combined evolution of work products and to synchronize integration and testing activities. The CIED as such is not what really matters – what is important is the mutual understanding that is the result of all the relevant disciplines having joined forces to build the CIED and then depict it correctly in the model for future reference. This approach enables the parties involved to gain a clear insight into the complexity of a certain function beforehand. As s result, risks can be better identified and mitigated by, e.g., testing or paying special attention to these risks in the design phase.

14.3.7 Configuration Item Cycle Times

One result of the above course of action is that the developers of C.I.s may work with different cycle times. It can also lead to the project having several types of cycles, i.e.,

- Release management
- Increment delivery
- Work product promotion
- Archive building
- Document release

A release is a completed set of functionality, delivered to the customer. It is meant to be stable for some length of time. As such, it is the end deliverable of a project, which makes its cycle equal to the project cycle.

The increment delivery is the longest cycle within the project. It is the cycle in which increments (a set of related functionality that is of some use to a customer) are released during the project. In the case of medical systems products, typical cycle times are measured in months.

Work product promotion is the cycle in which a software module is created by a developer in his own environment, released by him to his own group, tested and released to the project. The duration of this cycle is measured in weeks.

The archive building cycle is a potentially short cycle. It may even be as short as twice a day, though in medical equipment every two days or weekly is more usual. This is the cycle in which all promoted modules are built into a new archive.

Documents are under strict change control. The cycle therefore starts with initial conception and moves via draft and reviews to a final state. The documents in question may be design documents, project control documents, test plan documents, etc.

The CIED has considerable impact on work product promotion planning and execution, and on the quality of built archives. Experience shows that the CIED tends to speed up cycles, until they arrive at an optimum point at which no further project throughput time is won by making the cycles even faster. Each C.I. has its own specific cycle length, thanks to the insight that the CIED creates into what is needed.

14.4 A Preliminary Validation of the Proposed Solution

A preliminary validation process has been carried out, comprising two case studies, objective data taken from management statistics, and interviews with three people who played key roles in the projects.

14.4.1 Comparing Two Case Studies to Illustrate the Usefulness of the CIED

Two case studies are described, the first one using traditional project management techniques only. The second project adds the CIED approach into the existing project management practices. The purpose of these studies is to clarify the difference it makes to a project when the CIED approach is adopted. The projects were not defined in order to show the viability of the CIED concept. Both projects were real-life projects set up to create actual products.

Project A: Using Traditional Project Management Techniques Only

The need for the CIED started to become apparent early in the 1990s, during the implementation of a project to develop a device called a collimator. A collimator is a mechatronical device that limits, shapes and spectrally filters an X-ray beam. This beam can be aimed at those parts of a patient that actually need to be imaged with the required X-ray spectrum, so that a certain contrast in the patient image can be created. The device contains material that can spectrally filter or block an X-ray beam. This material can be moved about quickly enough to adapt the shape of the X-ray beam in real time. As a result of the X-ray imaging equipment moving about the patient, the actual image as projected onto the patient changes if no action is taken to collimate the X-ray Beam. An extremely high availability and reliability of the function is required.

The project was started in the traditional way, using designs, work breakdowns, GANTT charts and other standard project management practices. This led to a number of monodisciplinary building blocks being defined for the various disciplines (mechanics, motor control, analogue hardware, digital hardware, communication layers and software control). The people involved then went their own way, building their deliverables as specified in the Design Documents and carrying out the tasks as defined in the Gantt chart. Each of the disciplines was reporting progress to the project manager, and the expectation was that the project would finish on time and within budget.

But towards what should have been almost the end of the project, cracks started to appear:

- Due to the required reliability of the system, the mechanical engineers required a set of test models for checking some aspects of their design that were critical for reliability. These could only be meaningfully tested if they were tested in a way that closely resembled actual use. To this end, they needed some software and a driver as used in the actual product. The software department had not planned the specific software needed to do this until much later. Since changing the order of development would adversely influence their throughput time, the software department was not willing to supply the required software functionality for the test. The mechanical engineers just built some test models using a form of Automated Test Equipment that exercised the mechanics in a nonuser specific way and hoped for the best. The project manager was not informed.

– The people from the software department were unaware of a certain number of characteristics and behaviors of the hardware they were controlling, despite all the traditional interface specifications and designs having been made and reviewed. For example, the mechanical system had some overshoot, before returning and finding its intended position. Under certain conditions, this led to damage being caused to the hardware after a fairly large number of repetitions of the movement under those special conditions. Nobody had identified the problem.

When the cause of the damage (overshoot) was established, the software department studied more closely the way the motors should be controlled, and came up with a newly adapted algorithm. However, at the same time the mechanics people had found that some of their constructions (which could now be tested as the software was available) were not reliable enough. So they changed the mechanical subsystem. When the new software became available, the newly developed algorithm was unsuitable for the new situation. At that point, tempers began to flare.

Many similar cases started to appear. Taken on their own, they were not terribly difficult to solve. But each change influenced the products of another team at design level. This started a domino effect throughout all disciplines, and people started blaming each other. It was not long before the project manager was forced to admit he had lost control.

This situation is by no means unique. There are numerous examples of company projects where something similar has happened. Richard Feynman's book *The Pleasure of Finding Things Out* contains an excellent chapter about the Space Shuttle Challenger accident [8].

One question that may be raised is why it takes people so long to see that something is going wrong. The answer lies in psychology and people's capacity to live in cognitive dissonance. The early tests as proposed by the CIED force people to relinquish this stance much faster than traditional ways of working.

Management accepted that it was correct to conclude that the project was out of control. Sessions were held with the aim of finding the root causes and formulating approaches to solve them. Coaching was needed to put a stop to unhelpful blame games. Below are a number of the root causes relevant to this subsection:

1. Changes affecting other disciplines were implemented without consultation
   – In most instances, nobody had realized that the change would impact another discipline.
   – People did not have the knowledge to judge how their changes would influence other disciplines. The hardware disciplines did not have the knowledge to ask the software group the right questions. The result was that everyone remained in the dark until harsh reality clarified the situation.
2. Changes in the different disciplines were not synchronized. This resulted in combinations of hardware and software that temporarily failed to function upon integration. People started to search for faults that were not caused by design or coding

mistakes. Synchronizing the software and hardware solved a number of problems that had caused severe loss of time. Synchronizing was a tedious job, and would have happened automatically anyway at the next software archive built. This made people feel they were chasing windmills and had a negative impact on motivation.

Management made it clear that it was only interested in a completely finished product, with the right level of functionality and reliability. Starting from this basis, sessions were organized, during which the different disciplines came together to discuss a certain building block and how it worked from their point of view. A working method was soon established that made sure people knew and understood the requirements and their and others' contributions towards fulfilling these requirements. It must be clarified that the requirements had all been written down and reviewed. They were accessible to everyone in the project. These group discussions made the subject really come alive. Now, everybody was working towards the same project goal that had been defined at the beginning of the week. They kept to the agreement even if it meant additional work for their own discipline. They soon found that in order to get things going and establish clear communication, it was helpful to draw diagrams. This was the start of the CIED. In popular parlance these diagrams were called the "rocket model." Now that the project goal was clear, common communication could be established and work could be synchronized. The product was completed rapidly. People from the various disciplines enjoyed working together and started to appreciate each other. The collimator is now a successful product.

Project B: Using CIED from the Start

The aim of the project discussed in this subsection was to develop a new concept for X-ray detection. The sensor technology was completely new, and a number of issues were not fully clear when the project was started. The product consisted of the new X-ray detector, digital hardware to control the detector and Image Processing Algorithms to adapt for detector characteristics. When this project started, the CIED had already been introduced to testers and project managers, following the successful launch of the CIED in the collimator project discussed previously. The project manager believed in the CIED, and appointed a person to act as integration manager with the specific task (among others) of creating a CIED that was supported by the development and test crew. The integration manager started by holding a number of meetings with the chief designer and the senior verification engineer about how best to establish the order of building the device and identifying high risk areas (defined as "we do not know precisely how this should be done as there is no experience with this technology"). Based on these initial discussions, a first CIED was made. When this was presented to more members of the development staff, it met with some resistance. To start with, people from various disciplines claimed that the discussions were robbing them of time they could put to better use developing their own (monodisciplinary) products. However, the project manager was quick to pick up the signals, and got his team together to impress upon them how important he considered the CIED to be. At the second discussion with the development team, people were more involved and started expressing the problems they saw at certain integration moments. It also became clear how much extra effort was going to be put into making test activities for part deliveries possible. Tough discussions followed. Meanwhile, however, the verification engineer (who was a specialist both in software and testing) had already started to cooperate with a few software developers. He had carried out tests that showed shortcomings that were easy to solve at the time they were found but would have been very time-consuming to solve at a later stage. Developers started seeing that the net result of the extra effort of making testing possible and the time advantage it gave them in solving mistakes more quickly was positive. Another characteristic that started to emerge was that in the discussion surrounding the so-called calibrations,[3] certain issues had not been thought about by anyone. And though this meant that much more work had to be done than anticipated, staff also realized that if they had discovered these issues in the final testing phase there would have been even more work. As things stood, the design could be adapted to solve these issues with the least possible effort. The first integration took less time than predicted, as there were fewer complicated problems than had been anticipated. Thereafter, testers and developers intensified their cooperation. Faults were detected within 1 or 2 days, so solving them went very quickly and without any negative feelings. Not everything went completely smoothly: There were some issues that nobody had thought about, but even then the CIED always made clear where the project as a whole was. For example, the suppliers of a printed circuit board made a change on one of the processor boards without making a notification. It should not have had an impact, but it did. The resulting problem was not easily solved, as extensive analysis was needed to find the way from the symptom to the root cause. But here again, the CIED came to the rescue. Firstly, the CIED made it possible to trace things back beyond a shadow of a doubt to a stage at which the problem did not yet arise, although it had been tested for. Secondly, the CIED was used to show what functionality could already be offered to the customer in a prototype to ensure that overall delay was minimal, despite the problems. There was no panic, there were no blame games – only a concerted effort to find the error and to deal with it in the best way possible. The clarity provided by the CIED meant that the project customer's point of view could easily be taken into account. In the end, the project delivered the complete, fully functional system, ahead of the agreed deadline.

14.4.2 Comparing the Two Projects

The first project went from initial optimism and enthusiasm to moments of deep despair when reality hit. The second project used the CIED to identify and address the tough issues head-on, the moment they were spotted. In the first project, every mishap came as an unwelcome surprise leading to internal discussions, turf battles and a lot of rework. In the second project, the few surprises that arose were quickly identified, acknowledged and solved in a cooperative manner. At no time did those involved in the second project feel they were out of control. These differences should not be attributed to the "mechanical" use of the CIED but to the mindset of interdisciplinary cooperation facilitated by the CIED and stimulated by the mindset and way of working that go with it.

At the beginning of a project, drawing up the CIED takes time and there is a risk of running into analysis-paralysis. When properly managed, the time it actually takes can be measured in a few man days, even for complicated products – time that is soon regained

---

[3] Measuring the various characteristics of the detector so they can be corrected for.

via improved communication and a reduction in the number of surprises encountered during integration.

14.4.3 Objective Evidence

Several projects to develop products have been carried out by Philips Medical Systems, and specifically by the X-ray development group. Most of these projects did not use the CIED, and can therefore be used for reference purposes. In a small number of projects (5), the CIED was defined and then refined following feedback. The CIED is now in use for all running projects. Projects the outcome of which form part of this study involved the development of a medical diagnostic imaging device consisting of millions of lines of code, developed at several different sites in the world across many disciplines, including digital hardware, software, mechatronics and domain-specific engineering skills. This project involved more than ten subprojects, each bigger than 70 man-years. Projects that used the CIED have been compared with projects that did not use it.

To illustrate practical advantages as experienced in real-life projects, objective evidence has been collected from project management statistics. These statistics relate to project planning information and project progress reports. The project progress reports are official reports from the project manager to the operational management of the Business Unit. The figures quoted are based on the money spent and the hours that staff have booked in an automated system. Graphs compare the time and money that was planned to be spent with the time and money actually spent. A project progress report is written each time a project move on to a different phase. A project starts at phase 0 and finishes at phase 6. For each phase transition, a "GO/NOGO" decision is taken by management, based on the evidence in the progress reports. The first few phases focus primarily on requirement analysis and architecting and overall-design issues. Later phases involve engineering and testing.

The following trends emerged from projects undertaken before the CIED was used:

- The first three phase transitions were met with a unanimous GO at the time that was planned for these transitions.
- The fourth phase transition also met with a GO, but usually slightly later, and with conditions attached.
- The fifth and sixth phase transitions were initially met with NOGO, after which the project started working overtime and other measures were taken. A much later GO was given.

Depending on the project, the time and effort taken to complete the project could be up to an order of magnitude more than originally planned, and a factor of 2–3 was not unusual.

The first few projects that used the CIED (introducing the concept) showed the following profile:

- The first two transitions were met with unanimous GO, on time.

- The third transition met with some difficulty, was usually a bit late and demanded the adaptation of the original project planning for the next phase transitions. This meant a small delay of about 20–30% on the original planning.
- The final phase transitions were then completed with a GO at the re-planned time.

The projects undertaken once the CIED had been "learned" showed the following profile:

- The first transition was on time, with a GO.
- The second transition became the critical point. Here, it was either decided to cancel the project or the transition got a GO and then the project was completed on time and within budget.

14.4.4 Qualitative Evidence from Interviews

A system designer; an integration manager and a project manager who have used the CIED in a number of real projects were interviewed. All three interviewees have worked both in a more "traditional" environment and with the CIED. Their position and experience also gives them a good overview of the projects and what they entail. This enables them to make practical comparisons between the two ways of working.

Focus points of interest in the interview were:

- What practical advantages do working with the CIED have, in your experience?
- How can this be demonstrated by your experience in the projects you have worked for?
- What indications do you have that the practical advantages you noted are actually due to the CIED?

The opinions of the interviewees can be used as supporting evidence of the practical relevance of using the CIED. Their opinions are detailed below. All interviews were conducted in Dutch, and the questions were posed in an open way, giving the interviewees as much scope as possible to express their own opinion using their own words.

Bas Wolfs is system-designer, involved with the design of a new generation of imaging subsystems for X-ray applications. His opinion is that using the CIED contributes to a holistic understanding of the issues, which in turn contributes to time-to-market. In his own words:

> The practical advantage of using the CIED is that it helps the developers enormously in gaining a true insight into the technical relationships within the increments. Reasoning is now based on an individual's position in the whole, rather than on his/her own little area. If we had not used this, the project would have reached completion a lot later. It was used not only by the system designer but by the whole team. It can be shown to work in relation to other projects that I have been in, because in the past integration of systems has always led to huge problems, whereas this time everything just fell in place. It was clear that the advantages were down to the CIED because we literally saw true understanding dawning as we were making these drawings. In fact this way of drawing relationships is essential for incremental development.

Andre Vermeulen is integration manager in a product group that deals with Image Processing. In his opinion, a holistic insight into technical relationships is created, which creates better opportunities to take a proactive approach to dealing with problems. Any unexpected issues that arise can also be dealt with more effectively. These factors lead to better project control. In his own words:

> The practical advantages are that you gain a true insight into the technical relationships and dependencies across the various development disciplines. You can see beforehand where you may run into problems, as the preconditions at each point are known, so you have the chance to do something about it ahead of time. Also, unexpected issues always pop up, and because now you always know exactly where you are, you are better equipped to deal with the unexpected. All in all, this creates a basis for much better project control and flexibility. The first project I worked for did not use this approach, and we often ran into problems because we did not know what was in the software archive, did not really know what to test and how to test it and we were running round trying to find the right things like proper documentation, or hardware, or some special software that we needed. But now, all deliverables are defined and related to the CIED - even design documents and test reports. Before we adopted this approach, we had a lot of arguments with customers. They wanted functions (in prototype models) that we could not yet supply, and we had great problems explaining why. Now it is much easier to see the relationships, and not only can we explain the issues better, we are also better able to make changes to meet our customers' wishes. The test activities that are defined serve as a entry for doing proper test design, using the IEEE standard. These things are clearly related to the CIED, because that is the backbone of our communication. We have also adapted its use to graphically display progress. Once a work product or integration phase has been tested and is correct (and complete), we make its symbols green and hang up a new version in the corridor. People are always looking at it when they come in and before they go home.

Frans van Grotel is the project manager for a new technology imaging system. In his opinion, the use of the CIED leads to a shorter time-to-market, because the project is better controlled, planning can be done more proactively, and response to unexpected situations is more rapid. He says:

> The advantages are that the CIED gives a very clear graphical overview of what you are doing in a project. Once the planning and the relations have been visualized, the developers become much more involved in discussing dependencies. The planning comes alive, and we now know where we stand at all times. Especially when things change because of outside influences, we can react quickly because we have a clear insight in relationships at all times. It is not a substitute for a Gantt chart. [28] It gives our customers and other projects that depend on us a very clear insight into what we will deliver, and gives them a basis for discussing planning and technical relations. The fact that test moments are clearly defined means that we also know what we have really achieved.
>
> We have introduced a color code to make clearly visible what has and has not been achieved. This brings the planning alive for all disciplines, leading to better-controlled and shorter development cycles. You can see that it really works because it is alive. It is such a powerful communication tool that we are finding many sorts of information being added to the original concept, such as types of documentation (like design documents and test documents and their state), an indication of the teams that are responsible (using color coding). We have added planning data that has been derived from the Gantt Chart, which clearly marks the "critical path." We apply a tag to a development work product as it is put into the software archive, and we provide a link to the daily build software archive in which the software for a work product is archived. During project progress meetings, we discuss these blocks to see if there are any items that we have missed or whether any new insights have been gained. The CIED is discussed on a weekly basis with all the different disciplines involved. The above should make it clear that the successes are actually due to the use of this approach. However, the CIED should not be seen as a complete substitute for a Gantt chart.

To sum up the findings that emerged from the interviews:

1. The CIED leads to a better holistic understanding for developers of technical relationships and their own roles.
2. The CIED leads to better understanding of project planning issues.
3. The CIED provides greater flexibility to deal with changes in the outside world and unforeseen problems.
4. The CIED provides excellent synchronization between project activities.
5. The CIED leads to shorter development cycles.
6. Insight in what has really been developed improves the efficiency of testing.
7. Because of the above, the CIED leads to better time-to-market times.

Table 14.1 gives an overview of the findings and whether the interviewees agree, according to the evidence contained in their interviews.

Table 14.1. Overview of agreement in evidence

finding	B Wolfs agrees	A Vermeulen agrees	F van Grotel agrees
better holistic understanding of project	yes	yes	yes
better insight into planning issues	yes	yes	yes
greater flexibility	no data	yes	yes
good synchronization	yes	yes	yes
shorter development cycles	no data	no data	yes
more efficient testing	no data	yes	yes
insight into what has really been developed	no data	yes	yes
better time-to-market	yes	yes	no data

14.5 Conclusions and Future Research

This chapter presented a model that adds those aspects to Configuration Management that would enable a company to manage content for a complicated multidisciplinary product and to predefine the evolution of content. The beneficial effects of the CIED and the associated approach can be summarized as follows:

– The CIED functions as a mental tool, creating clear understanding between the relevant designers, developers and testers regarding what is to be made and in which order, and especially why it is to be done in a given way.

- The CIED furnishes clear insight into how disciplines can help each other achieve the project goal.
- The technical and logical relationships between the various C.I.s are identified.
- Where test tooling and a test environment is required, the requirement is identified in advance, so that the design can be optimized to incorporate the tooling.
- Clear criteria are identified for each testing point, against which the work product is to be measured during testing, thus creating clarity and a practical sense of purpose among the developers.
- It is found in practice that the process of discussing the CIED brings to light a good many requirements that were not clear or interactions that no-one had thought of. This improves the inherent quality of the product, and simplifies the integration process.
- The increment work breakdown document defines how a C.I. (or set of C.I.s) grows and how functionality is mapped over C.I.s.

The integration diagram together with the associated approach is a simple and valuable tool for enhancing technical understanding and better managing the development and integration of C.I.s. In the real-life industrial environment for which this way of thinking was developed, it is impractical to expect to achieve the scientific rigidity that would be required of a proper completed theory. However, the following conclusions are supported by large-scale projects:

- Developers involved see the CIED as an excellent way of enhancing understanding of the subject matter.
- Project managers feel that their project is better defined (as evidenced by project throughput times).
- Testers have a better idea of what they can expect to be testing.
- Test interfaces and test methods can be defined beforehand.
- Group motivation to achieve a common goal is far higher, across the disciplines.

If an organization wants to adopt the use of CIED's, critical success factors are:

- An integrated product development and test environment
- A mature development and testing process
- Highly skilled testers
- A highly qualified integration manager
- Deployment of a near-perfect Configuration Management process
- As in all changes, initial management commitment
- A Project Manager who understands change management

The approach described here is the approach of a company that needs to make products and will therefore take anything that is "good enough" for their practical needs. This in itself does not invalidate the results, but the symbols and what they stand for have not been checked for orthogonality, nor have they been checked for completeness. A further area of interest may be to define a vocabulary that would enable mechatronics experts, hardware developers, domain specialists and software developers to work together. Further research would give this a more thorough scientific base, and possibly enable implementation in standards such as UML. It is not always the case that changes in a product can readily be modeled by the CIED. Take a change of operating system. An operating system provides a set of services that can be used and a complicated set of parameter settings, which in many cases influence each other. The task of working out how to model this in a CIED was too complicated in the time available for the real projects, due to the high number of parameters that had to be set and their interactions. How to group these parameters into some kind of equivalence classes that can then be modeled in the CIED may be an area for further research. Further study could also focus on the scientific rigidity of the concept of using the CIED. This would include working out where the limits of the applicability of the CIED lie and what they are.

Acknowledgments

I gratefully acknowledge the extensive reviews of Juan Carlos Dueñas, Tor Erlend Fægri, and Anne Immonen that significantly improved the quality of this chapter. Timo Käkölä diligently guided the numerous revisions of this chapter during a period of more than a year. I thank Philips Medical Systems for allowing me to spend considerable time researching for and writing the chapter and my colleagues for the information they willingly shared with me.

References

1. Alciatore, D.G., Histand, M.B.: *Introduction to Mechatronics and Measurement Systems* (McGraw-Hill, New York 2002)
2. Bachmann, F., Bass, L.: Symposium on software reusability, Toronto, Canada. http://www.sei.cmu.edu/plp/variability.pdf (18–20 May 2001)
3. Beck, K.: *Test-Driven Development* (Addison-Wesley, Reading, MA 2003)
4. Beizer, B.: *Black Box Testing* (Wiley, New York 1995)
5. Binder, B.: *Testing Object Oriented Systems* (Addison-Wesley, Reading, MA 2000)
6. Booch, G., Jacobson, I., Rumbaugh, J.: *The Unified Software Development Process* (Addison-Wesley, Reading, MA 2002)
7. Brooks Jr., F.P.: *The Mythical Man-Month*, Anniversary edn (Addison-Wesley, Reading, MA 1995)
8. Feynman, R.: *The Pleasure of Finding Things Out.* (The Perseus Books Group 1999)
9. Gilb, T., Graham, D.: *Software Inspection* (Addison-Wesley, Reading, MA 1993)
10. Gilb, T.: *Requirements Engineering* (Addison-Wesley, Reading, MA 2002)
11. IEEE Std 1042-1987: IEEE Guide to Software Configuration Management
12. IEEE Std 829-1998: IEEE Standard for Software Test Documentation
13. IEEE Std 1058-1998: IEEE Standard for Software Project Management Plans
14. IEEE Std 828-1998: IEEE Standard for Software Configuration Management Plans
15. Jonassen-Hass, A.M.: *Configuration Management Principles and Practice* (Addison-Wesley, Reading, MA 2003)
16. Jones, J., Hewitt, P., Lee, R., Smith, L., Sorenson, R.: Software configuration management technologies and applications, STSC (Software Technology Support Center), US Air Force report. http://www.stsc.hill.af.mil (May 1999)
17. Kerzner, H.: *Project Management, A Systems Approach to Planning Scheduling, and Controlling* (Wiley, New York 2003)
18. McGregor, J.D., Sykes, A.M.: *A Practical Guide to Testing Object Oriented Software* (Addison-Wesley, Reading, MA 2001)
19. Musa, J.: *Software Reliability Engineering* (McGraw-Hill, New York 1999)

20. Paulk, M., Mark, C. et al.: Key practices of the capability maturity model for software, version 1.1, Technical Report CMU/SEI-93-TR-25 (Software Engineering Institute, Carnegie Mellon University, Pittsburgh 1993)
21. Pohl, K., Böckle, G., van der Linden, F.: *Software Product Line Engineering* (Springer, Berlin Heidelberg New York 2005)
22. Pol, M., Teunissen, R., van Veenendaal, E.: *Software Testing: A Guide to the TMAP Approach* (Addison-Wesley, Reading, MA 2002)
23. Senge, P.: *The Dance of Change* (Doubleday, Broadway 1999)
24. Sommerville, I., Sawyer, P.: *Requirements Engineering* (Wiley, New York 1997)
25. Steve McConnell, S.: *Rapid Development* (Microsoft 1996)
26. Van Veenendaal, E., McMullan, J.: *Achieving Software Product Quality*, Chapter 12 (Tutein Nolthenius 1997)
27. White, B.A.: *Software Configuration Management Strategies and Rational Clearcase* (Addison-Wesley, Reading, MA 2000)
28. Wysocki, R.K., McGary, R.: *Effective Project Management: Traditional, Adaptive, Extreme*, 3rd edn (Wiley, New York 2003)

15 Software Product Line Engineering with the UML: Deriving Products

T. Ziadi and J.-M. Jézéquel

Abstract

Software product line engineering introduces two new dimensions into the traditional engineering of software-based systems: the variability modeling and the product derivation. The variability gathers characteristics that differ from one product to another, while the product derivation is defined as a complete process of building products from the product line. Software Product Line Engineering with the UML has received a lot of attention in recent years. However most of these works only concern variability modeling in UML static models and few works concern behavioral models. In addition, there is very little research on product derivation. This chapter investigates the product derivation in the context of the product line engineering with the UML. First, a set of extensions are proposed to model product line variability in two types of UML models: class diagrams (the static aspect) and sequence diagrams (the behavioral aspect). Then we formalize product derivation using a UML model transformation. An algorithm is given to derive a static model for a product and an algebraic approach is proposed to derive product-specific statecharts from the sequence diagrams of the product line. Two simple case studies are presented, based on a Mercure product line and the banking product line, to illustrate the overall process, from the modeling of the product line to the product derivation.

15.1 Introduction

Rather than describing a single software system, the model of a software product line (PL) describes the set of products in the same domain. This is done by distinguishing elements shared by all the products of the line, and elements that may vary from one product to another. Concepts of *commonality* and *variability* are, respectively, used to designate common and variable elements in a PL [39] Variability can concern two main aspects: *optionality* or *variation* [7,18]. An optional element only concerns some products and it can be omitted in others. Variation elements define alternatives (variants) to choose from. Beyond variability modeling, the *product derivation* process is defined as a complete process of constructing products from the software PL [12].

Unified modeling language (UML) [33] is an object-oriented notation for software system modeling. It proposes a set of models to specify several aspects of systems. Class diagrams are UML models that can be used to specify static aspects of systems, while sequence diagrams (SD) and statechart diagrams are examples of models describing behavioral aspects. Software PL Engineering with the UML has received a lot of attention in recent years [3,5,9,10,13,14,18,26,27,37,38]. Section 15.4 presents a study on these works and shows that the most of existing works only concern UML static models and few works concern behavioral models [3,14,17]. In addition, there is very little research on product derivation [3,13]. The product derivation support is a significant criterion for determining the utility for users of any PL approach. The approaches that only model variability in UML models without product derivation support have only a descriptive utility. This means that these approaches are only useful for PL architecture description.

In this work we defend the idea that any approach of PL engineering should go beyond the descriptive utility and propose supports for resolving the variability and obtaining product models. For this, we investigate the product derivation process in the context of PL engineering with the UML. We give an overview of PL design by first presenting structural variability involved in class diagrams, then how behavioral aspects may be designed using UML sequence diagrams. We then formalize product derivation as UML model transformations. First, a transformation algorithm is given to automatically derive the static product model from the PL model. Second, an algebraic approach is proposed to derive product-specific statecharts from PL sequence diagrams.

To present these design techniques, Sect. 15.2 focuses on static aspects of the PL design, its constraints, and its derivation process into specific products; this part also stresses the need to check derived products with respect to variability constraints. Next, Sect. 15.3 proposes an algebraic approach to derive product-specific statecharts from the SD of the PL. Here PL behaviors are specified as algebraic expressions on basic UML2.0 sequence diagrams, where variability is introduced by means of three new algebraic constructs. Our derivation approach is defined in two steps: We first define an algebraic way to derive product expressions from the PL expression and then statecharts are generated by transforming product SD given as an expression into a composition of statecharts. Section 15.4 discusses related work, and finally Sect. 15.5 draws some conclusions and perspectives.

15.2 Deriving Static Aspects

15.2.1 The Mercure Product Line

As a case study for describing static aspect derivation, we consider the Mercure PL, which is a line of Switched Multi-Megabit Data Service servers whose design and implementation have been described in [23,24]. It can abstractly be described as a communication software delivering, forwarding, and relaying messages from and to a set of network interfaces connected into heterogeneous distributed system. The Mercure PL must handle variants for five variation points: any number of specialized processors (Engines), network interface boards (NetDriver), levels of functionality (Manager), user interface

(GUI) and support for languages (Language). Figure 15.1 shows a feature diagram of the Mercure PL (we follow FODA notations [28]). The Mercure consists of Engine, Net Driver, Manager, GUI, and Language. The Mercure product may support one or more of Engine 1,..., Engine N, the selection being represented by FODA alternative features. In the same way, we define all NetDriver, Manager, GUI, and Language dimensions.

The FODA [28] notations allow us to specify dependency relationships, called *composition rules*, between domain features. FODA supports two types of composition rules: the "require" rule that expresses the presence implication of two or more features, and the "mutually exclusive" rule that captures the mutual exclusion constraint on feature combinations. A "require" rule is identified in the context of the Mercure PL: it specifies that the choice of the NetDriver1 implies the choice of the Engine1 (see Fig. 15.1).

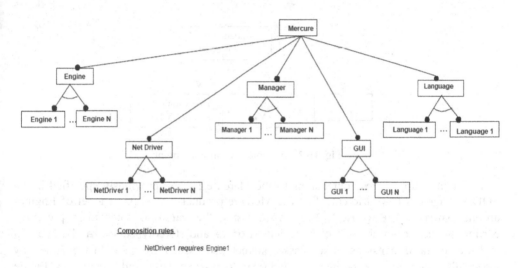

Composition rules

NetDriver1 *requires* Engine1

Fig. 15.1. The FODA diagram for the Mercure PL

15.2.2 PL Static Architecture as UML Class Diagrams

To describe the PL static architecture, we use UML class diagrams. In [42], we have proposed a UML profile for PL. This profile includes mechanisms to specify variability within two types of UML 2.0 diagrams: class diagrams and sequence diagrams. For class diagrams, we proposed to specify variability using two mechanisms:

- *Optionality.* Optionality in PL means that some features are optional for the PL members, i.e., they can be omitted in some products. To specify optionality in class diagrams, we introduced the <<optional>> stereotype. This stereotype can be applied to classes, packages, attributes, or operations [42].

– *Variation.* Inheritance in UML allows defining variability in class diagrams [2]. The idea is to define a variation point as an abstract class and variants as concrete subclasses. Each subclass defines the implementation of the abstract class in a specific way. However, this variability is only resolved at run time and it is not explicit in the model. To explicitly specify the variation in UML class diagram, we introduced two stereotypes <<variation>> and <<variant>> [42]. The <<variation>> stereotype is associated with the abstract class while <<variant>> is associated with subclasses. Each product can choose one or more subclasses [42]. Figure 15.2 shows an example of a variation point specified using the <<variation>> and <<variant>> stereotypes. Notice that the subclass A in Fig. 15.2 is not stereotyped <<variant>>; this means that this subclass is mandatory for all products.

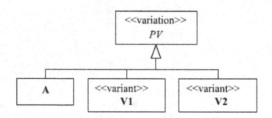

Fig. 15.2. Example of a variation point

Let us now apply these extensions to the Mercure PL. As previously specified in the FODA diagram of the Mercure PL, the Mercure product may support a set of Engines among Engine1, Engine2, EngineN. Using the variation mechanism presented earlier, we define an abstract class called Engine and stereotyped <<variation>> and the several dimensions as subclasses stereotyped <<variant>>. In the same way we specify other variation points: NetDriver, Manager, GUI, and Language. Figure 15.3 shows the UML class diagram of the Mercure PL. It basically says that a Mercure system is an instance of the Mercure class, aggregating an Engine (that encapsulates the work that Mercure has to do on a particular processor of the target distributed system), a collection of NetDrivers, a collection of Managers (that represent the range of functionalities available), and the GUI that encapsulates the user preference variability factor. A GUI has itself a collection of supported languages (see Fig. 15.3).

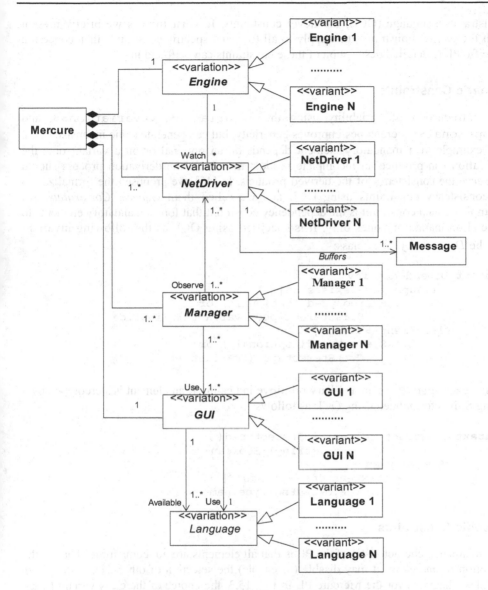

Fig. 15.3. The Mercure Product Line UML class diagram

15.2.3 Product Line Constraints

In addition to variability, the PL architecture is defined as a standard architecture with a set of constraints [4]. In this context, we have identified in [45] two types of PL constraints that guide the product derivation process. We proposed to define them as Object

Constraints Language (OCL) metalevel constraints. In what follows we briefly present both the generic constraints that apply to all PLs, and specific constraints that concern a specific PL (a detailed description of these constraints can be found in [45]).

Generic Constraints

The introduction of variability using the <<variant>>, <<variation>>, and <<optional>> stereotypes improves genericity, but can generate some inconsistencies. For example, if a mandatory element depends on an optional or on a variant one, the derivation can produce an incomplete product model. So the derivation process should *preserve* the consistency of the derived products. In [45], we proposed the formalization of consistency constraints using OCL and we called them *Generic Constraints*. An example of such constraint is the dependency constraint that forces mandatory elements to depend on mandatory ones only. It is specified using OCL as the following invariant for the *Dependency*[1] metaclass:

```
context Dependency inv:
      self.supplier->exists (S|
            S.isStereotyped('optional') or
                  S.isStereotyped('variant')) implies
      self.client->forAll ( C|
            C.isStereotyped('optional') or
                  C.isStereotyped('variant'))
```

isStereotyped(S) is an auxiliary primitive indicating if an element is stereotyped by a string S. It is formalized using OCL as follows:

```
context Construct::Class::isStereotyped(
                  s: string):Boolean;
      isStereotyped =
            self.extensions-> exists(E|
                  E.ownedEnd.type.name =s)
```

Specific Constraints

A fundamental characteristic of the PL is that all elements are not compatible. That is, the selection of one element may disable (or enable) the selection of others. For example in the class diagrams for the Mercure PL in Fig. 15.3, the choice of the class variant Net-Driver1 in the specific product needs the presence of the Engine1 variant. Another challenge for the product derivation is to *ensure* these dependencies in the derived products. In our work, these dependencies are called *Specific Constraints* and are also formal-

---

[1]A dependency in the UML specifies a require relationship between two or more elements. It is represented in the UML metamodel [33] by the metaclass *Dependency*; it represents the relationship between a set of suppliers and clients. An example of the UML Dependency is the "Usage," which appears when a package uses another one.

ized as OCL metalevel constraints [45]. The presence constraint in the Mercure PL is formalized as an invariant for the *Model* metaclass as follows:

```
context Model inv:
      self.presenceClass('NetDriver1') implies
      self.presenceClass('Engine1')
```

presenceClass(C) is an auxiliary operation indicating if a specific class called C is present in the model. It is formalized using OCL as follows:

```
context Model::presenceClass(C : Class) : Boolean;
  presenceClass =
      self.ownedMember->exists(el : NamedElement|
      (el.oclIsKindOf(Class) and cl.name = C.name) or
      (el.isKIndOf(Namespace) and el.presenceClass(C)))
```

15.2.4 From Product Line Models to Product Models

Deriving static aspects in PL consists in generating the UML class diagram of each product from the PL class diagram. As shown previously, the PL class diagram is defined by a set of variation points and to derive a product-specific class diagram, some decisions (or choices) associated with these variation points are needed. For example, each Mercure product could choose among the presence or absence of all variant classes. A mechanism is needed to capture the decisions that are made for a specific product. As in [3], we call this mechanism a *decision model*. In this section, we propose to use the *Abstract Factory* design pattern as a decision model associated with the PL class diagram. Then we propose an algorithm, based on models transformation, to derive product class diagrams. To illustrate this algorithm, we use three products in the Mercure PL: FullMercure, Custom-Mercure, and MiniMercure:

– *FullMercure* is the product that includes all NetDrivers, all Engines, all Managers, all GUIs, all Languages. Thus, all combinations can be dynamically bound.
– *CustomMercure* is a restricted product. It only supports two different network drivers : NetDriver1 and NetDriver2, one manager: Manager1, two GUIs: GUI1 and GUI2, two languages: Language1 and Language2.
– *MiniMercure* is the lightest product that only supports NetDriver1, Engine1, GUI1, Manager1, and Language1.

The Decision Model

The *Abstract Factory* is a creational design pattern [15]. It allows defining an interface for creating a line of related objects. In [25], one of the authors proposed the use of this pattern to refine product derivation at compilation time. Our aim in this section is to reuse again this pattern as a design of the PL decision model. Figure 15.4 shows the structure of our decision model applied to the Mercure PL. We use an abstract factory, called Mercure_Factory, to define an interface for creating variants of Mercure's five variation points. The abstract class `Mercure_Factory` defines five factory methods, one for each variation point. `new_gui()` for example is the factory method, which concerns the GUI variation point. These factory methods are abstractly defined in the class `Mercure_Factory` and given concrete implementation in its subclasses called *concrete factories*. We create one concrete factory for each product in the PL. `FullMercure`, `CustomMercure`, and `MiniMercure` in Fig. 15.4 are concrete factories for the Mercure PL. We propose to specify decisions related to each product using stereotypes applied to method factories. We use stereotypes to restrict the return type of factory methods to the possible one. For example, the `CustomMercure` product model includes only `GUI1` and `GUI2`. The Factory Method that corresponds to the GUI variation point is `new_gui()`, so we add two stereotypes <<GUI1>> and <<GUI2>> to this factory method (see Fig. 15.4).

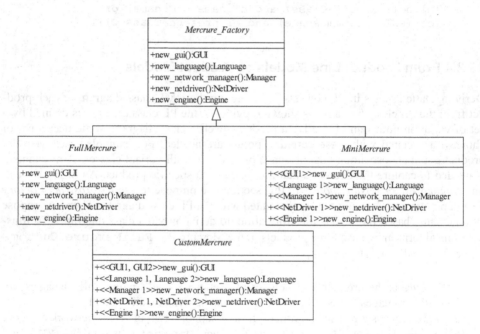

Fig. 15.4. The Abstract Factory as a decision model for the Mercure PL

Derivation

Now we have to tackle the automation of the derivation process exploiting the variation points and the decision model. The derivation algorithm we use to derive product models is described in Fig. 15.5. It takes as input the PL class diagram, and the concrete factory from the decision model and it generates as output the product class diagram. It is decomposed into three steps: selection of variant classes, model specialization, and model optimization. They are:

- *Step 1: Variant classes selection.* The first step consists of selecting variant classes using the concrete factory. For each factory method, we retrieve its stereotypes. These stereotypes define the names of the selected subclasses of the abstract class returned by the factory method. When the factory method does not define stereotypes (such as in the `FullMercure` concrete factory methods), all the subclasses of its return type are selected.
- *Step 2: Model specialization.* In this step, we remove all variants classes from the model that have not been selected in the first step. However, to preserve coherence, variant ancestors of selected variant elements are not removed.
- *Step 3: Model optimization.* Here we delete unused factories and optimize the inheritance. Inheritance optimization is applied when there is only one concrete class inheriting from an abstract one. In this case the abstract class is omitted and replaced by the concrete one.

---

algorithm: *DeriveProductModels()*

Input : PL_classDiagram: Model, aConcreteFactory: Class
Output : Product_classDiagram: Model
 – Step 1: Variant classes selection
selectedVariantsList:=∅;
for each factory method in aConcreteFactory do
   initiate definedVariantsList to
   significant stereotypes of the factory;
   if definiedVariantsList is empty then
     selectedVariantsList.add(all sub-classes of the returned type of the
     factory);
   else
     selectedVariantsList.add(definedVariantsList);
   end if
end for
–Step 2: Model specialization
for each variant class *C* in *PL_classDiagram* do
   if (the class name of C not in selectedVariantsList) and (names of all
   sub classes of C not in selectedVariantsList) then
       delete the class C from the PL_classDiagram;
   end if
end for
–Step 3: Model optimization
delete unused concrete factories;
optimize inheritance;
Product_classDiagram:= PL_classDiagram;
return Product_classDiagram;

Fig. 15.5. Static aspect derivation: the derivation algorithm

To achieve the implementation of the derivation algorithm, we have used the INRIA Model Transformation Language (MTL). Information about implementation and technical materials can be found at http://modelware.inria.fr/mtl. We have applied the derivation for the three Mercure products: `FullMercure`, `CustomMercure`, and `MiniMercure`. Figure 15.6 shows the `CustomMercure` model obtained by derivation from the Mercure model in Fig. 15.3.

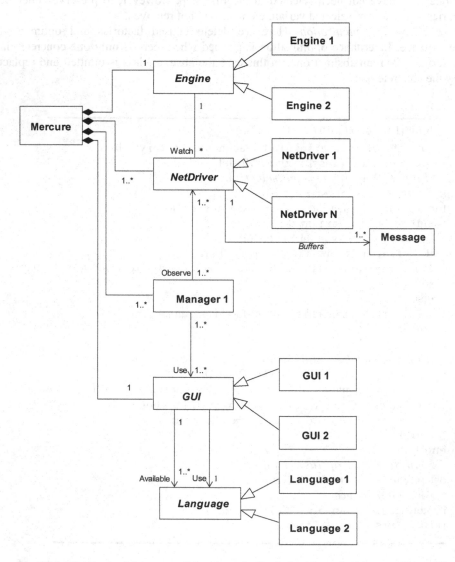

Fig. 15.6. The CustomMercure model, automatically derived from the Mercure PL model

Derivation vs. Constraints

The PL model should satisfy generic constraints before the derivation and the product model derived should satisfy specific constraints. The generic constraints represent the preconditions of the derivation algorithm while specific constraints represent the postconditions:

```
DeriveProductModels(PL_classDiagram:Model,
                    aConcreteFactory:Class)
    pre:  check Generic Constraints on PL classDiagram
    post: check Specific Constraints on the Product classDiagram
          result.
```

15.3 Deriving Behavioral Aspects

In addition to static aspect description, behavior modeling plays an important role in the traditional engineering of software-based systems; it is the basis for systematic approaches to requirements capture, specification, design and simulation, code generation, testing, and verification. Scenario languages such as UML2.0 SD are an example of formalisms for modeling behavior. They focus on the global interactions between actors and system components. To be useful in the PL context, SD should also allow for expression of variability. We show in this section how variability can be expressed in UML2.0 SD using UML stereotypes and tagged values. We take advantage of UML2.0 SD and their composition operators to specify PL SD as algebraic expressions extended by algebraic constructs for variability. Then we present an algebraic approach to derive the product behaviors from the PL SD. Before illustrating behavioral aspect derivation, we briefly present the banking product line (BPL) as an example, which is used throughout this section.

15.3.1 The Banking Product Line

In this section, we reuse the example of a BPL as described in [3]. It is a set of products providing simple functionalities to clerks in the banking domain. It provides four main functionalities:

- *Creation of accounts (F1).* Customers are able to open simple accounts but must do so with a minimum balance. Account can have an associated limit specifying to what extent a customer can overdraw money.
- *Money deposit on accounts (F2).* Customers can deposit an amount of money on their accounts.
- *Money withdrawal from accounts (F3).* Customers can withdraw money from their account. If the account has a limit, a customer can only withdraw money up to this limit. If not, he (or she) cannot withdraw beyond the current balance of the account.
- *Currency exchange calculation (F4).* The bank system can offer a functionality for exchange calculation. This particularly concerns currency exchange: euros, dollars, etc.

Variability in the BPL example concerns the support of overdrawing to a set limit, which is optional because some products do not allow the addition of limits on accounts. Currency exchange calculation is also an optional functionality and it is only supported by some products. Table. 15.1 shows four different product members of the BPL. The BS1 product for example supports limits on accounts and does not support exchange calculation while BS4 is a complete product with limits on accounts and exchange calculation support.

Table 15.1. The Banking PL members

product	limit support	exchange calculation
BS1	yes	no
BS2	no	no
BS3	no	yes
BS4	yes	yes

15.3.2 Product Line Behaviors as UML 2.0 Sequence Diagrams

UML2.0 Sequence Diagrams

UML2.0 SD [33] enhances the previous versions of scenarios proposed in UML1.x by introducing composition operators. A basic SD describes a finite number of interactions between a set of objects. The semantics of a basic SD is now based on partially ordered events (instead of ordered collections of messages as in UML1.x), which makes it easy to introduce concurrency and asynchronism, and allows the definition of more complex behaviors.

Figure 15.7 shows the basic SD related to the Banking PL. A UML2.0 SD is represented by a rectangular frame labeled by the keyword **sd** followed by the name of the SD. The SD Deposit for example shows interactions between Clerk, Bank, and Account to deposit an amount on a specific account. The vertical lines represent life lines for the given objects. Interactions between objects are shown as horizontal arrows called messages (like deposit). Each message is defined by two events: message emission and message reception, which induce an ordering between emission and reception. Events located on the same lifeline are ordered from top to down.

UML2.0 basic SD can be composed into composite SDs called *combined interactions* using a set of operators called *interaction operators* [33]. We only use three fundamental operators: **seq**, **alt**, and **loop**. The **seq** operator specifies a weak sequence[2] between the behaviors of two operand SDs. The **alt** operator defines a choice between a set of interaction operands. The **loop** operator specifies an iteration of the SD. For all these operators, each operand is either a basic or a combined SD. The combined SD BankPL in Fig. 15.8 shows how basic SDs for the BPL are related. It refers to the basic interactions

---

[2]UML2.0 [33] defines two operators, **seq** and **strict** to define weak and strict sequence, respectively. A weak sequence means that only events on the same lifeline in the first SD are executed before events on the same lifeline in the second SD. A strict sequencing means that all events in the first SD are executed before events in the second diagram.

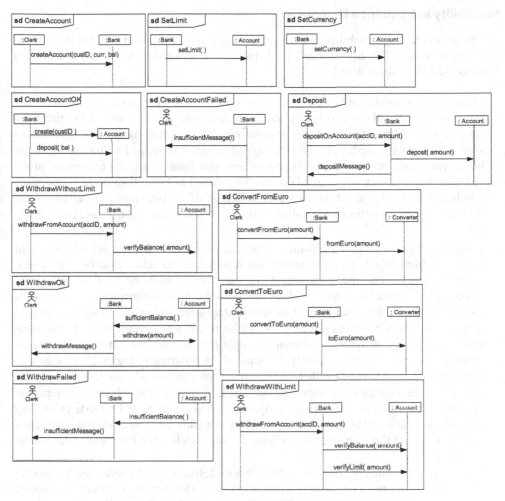

Fig. 15.7. UML2.0 sequence diagrams for the Banking PL

using the **ref** operator. BankPL specifies that there are five main alternative behaviors for requirements of BPL members (1) Account creation. (2) Deposit on account. (3) Withdraw from account (this last functionality is described using the combined SD WithdrawFromAccount). (4) Exchange calculation from euro and (5) Exchange calculation to euro. Following UML2.0 notations [33], combined SDs are defined by rectangles whose left corner is labeled by an operator (**alt**, **seq**, **loop**). Operands for sequence and alternative are separated by dashed horizontal lines. Sequential composition can also be implicitly given by the relative order of two frames in a diagram. For example, in the SD BankPL basic SD CreateAccountOk is referenced before SD SetLimit. This is equivalent to the expression CreateAccountOk **seq** SetLimit.

Variability in Sequence Diagrams

As shown in [42,43], variability can be specified in UML2.0 SD using simple stereotypes and tagged values. We briefly describe here these mechanisms; interested readers can refer to [42,43] for more details:

- *Optionality*. A combined SD can refer to an optional SD: interactions specified by this optional SD are only supported by some products and can be omitted in others. To specify optionality of an SD, we introduced the `<<optionalInteraction>>` stereotype and the `optionalPart` tagged value. The tagged value specifies the occurrence name of the optional SD (to differentiate among various occurrences of the optional SD, since an optional SD might be referred to more than once in the same combined SD). Figure 15.8a shows an example of a combined SD called `CDS1`, which refers to an optional SD called `SD1`. The tagged value `optionalPart` takes `SD1-occ1` as value.[3]

- *Variation*. This variability mechanism makes it possible to define a set of variants of behaviors from which a particular product would have to select exactly one variant. Using UML2.0 SDs, the variation of the behavior is modeled as a combined SD stereotyped `<<variation>>`, which refers to a set of subinteractions stereotyped `<<variant>>`. Each subinteraction specifies a variant behavior. As for the optional SD, a variation SD `<<variation>>` can be referred to several times in the same combined SD. To differentiate among multiple occurrences, we introduce the tagged value `variationPart` to specify the name of the occurrence. Figure 15.8b shows an example of a variation SD called `CSD2`, which refer to two SD variants `SD-v1` and `SD-v1`. Note that this variation mechanism is different from the **alt** interaction operator. The variation mechanism proposes a choice that must be made at product derivation time so that the derived product contains only one of the alternative behaviors, while the **alt** operator defines a choice made *after* the product derivation, i.e., at run time.

- *Virtuality*. The virtuality of an SD means that its behavior can be redefined by another SD or refinement associated with a specific product. This type of variability is inspired by an existing construction in MSC [22]. The behavior of the virtual SD will be *replaced* at product derivation time by the behavior of the refinement SD associated with the product. Virtuality is introduced by the stereotype `<<virtual>>` and the tagged value `virtualPart` indicating the occurrence of the virtual interaction. Figure 15.8c shows an example of a combined SD called `CSD3`, which refers to a virtual SD called `SD3`.

---

[3] We follow new notations of tagged values in UML2.0: a tagged value is now represented in UML2.0 as a note [33].

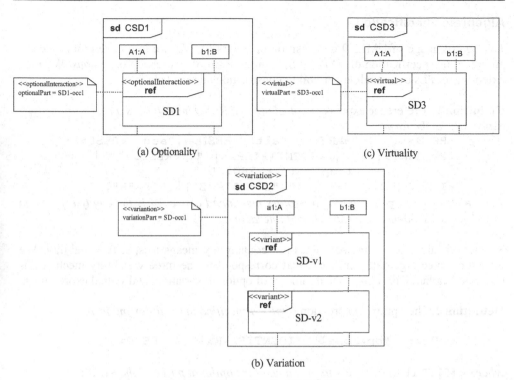

Fig. 15.8. Variability for UML2.0 SD

The combined SD in Fig. 15.9 `BankPL` illustrates two variability mechanisms: *optionality* and *variation*.

1. Since some products of the BPL do not support overdrawing, a stereotype `<<op-tionalInteraction>>` is added to the basic SD `SetLimit` and the tagged value `optionalPart` takes the value `settingLimit` (see the combined SD `AccountCreation` in Fig. 15.9). In addition, since exchange calculation is an optional functionality in the BPL, basic SD `SetCurrency`, `ConvertToEuro`, and `ConvertFromEuro` are defined as optional too (see the combined SD `AccountCreation` in Fig. 15.9).

2. There are two SD variants when withdrawing from an account: withdraw with balance and limit checking, and withdraw with balance checking only. The SD `Withdraw` is defined with the `<<variation>>` stereotype. The two SDs `WithdrawWithLimit` and `WithdrawWithoutLimit` are stereotyped `<<variant>>`. The tagged value `variation Part` takes withdraw `Account` as value (see the `WithdrawFrom Account` combined SD in Fig. 15.9).

Algebraic Specification

Taking advantage of UML2.0 composition operators for SD, we introduce in this section an algebraic specification of UML2.0 SDs in the form of *reference expressions*. We then extend it for PLs by including variability constructions defined above.

Definition 1. *A* reference expression *for SD (noted RESD hereafter) is an expression of the form:*

```
<RESD>::=<PRIMARY> ( "alt" <RESD> |"seq" <RESD>)*
<PRIMARY>::=E∅ | <IDENTIFIER> | "("<RESD>")" |
            "loop" "(" <RESD> ")"
<IDENTIFIER>::= (["a"-"z","A"-"Z"]|["0"-"9"])*
```

seq, **alt** *and* **loop** *are the SD operators mentioned above.* $E_\emptyset$ *is the empty expression that defines a sequence diagram without interaction.*

So far, this algebraic framework does not contain any means to specify variability. We introduce three algebraic constructs that correspond to the three variability mechanisms presented earlier. This allows the definition of optional, variation, and virtual expressions.

Definition 2. The optional expression *(OpE) is specified in the following form:*

```
OpE ::= "optional" <IDENTIFIER> "[" <RESD> "]"
```

where <IDENTIFIER> *refers to the name of the optional part and the* <RESD> *refers to its corresponding expression.*

An optional SD (i.e., an SD stereotyped <<optionalInteraction>>) can be specified by an optional expression. The tagged value optionalPart in the diagram specifies the name of the expression. For the BPL example, optionality of the interaction SetLimit is specified by the expression:

```
optional settingLimit [ SetLimit ]
```

Definition 3. A Variation expression (VaE) *is defined as follows:*

```
VaE::="variation" <IDENTIFIER> "[" <RESD> "," ( <RESD>)* "]"
```

For example, the variation interaction Withdraw in Fig. 15.9 encloses two interaction variants. It is specified algebraically as follows:

```
variation withdrawAccount [ WithdrawWithLimit,
                            WithdrawWithoutLimit ]
```

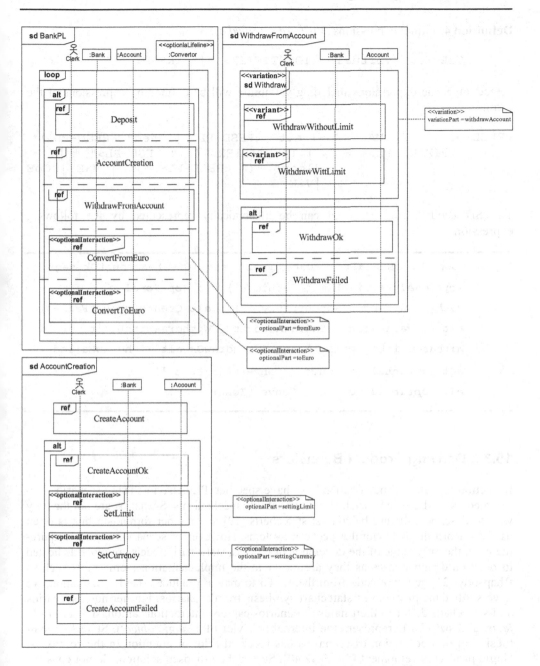

Fig. 15.9. The UML2.0 combined sequence diagram for the Banking PL

Definition 4. Virtual expressions *(ViE) are specified as:*

```
ViE ::= "virtual" <IDENTIFIER> "[" <RESD> "]"
```

Hence, algebraic expressions including variability will be defined by expressions of the form:

```
<RESD-PL>::=<PRIMARY-PL>("alt" <RESD-PL> | "seq" <RESD-PL>)*
    <PRIMARY-PL>::= E∅ |<IDENTIFIER> |"("<RESD-PL>")" |
                        "loop" "(" <RESD-PL> ")" | VaE | OpE
                        |ViE
```

The SD BankPL of Fig. 15.9 can be algebraically represented by the following expression:

E_{BPL} = **loop** (Deposit **alt** (CreateAccount **seq** (CreateAccountOk **seq**

   (*optional* settingLimit[SetLimit]) **seq** (*optional*

   settingCurrency [SetCurrency])))   **alt** CreateAccountFailed)

   alt ((*variation* withdrawAccount [WithdrawWithLimit,

   WithdrawWithoutLimit]) **seq** (WithdrawOk **alt** WithdrawFailed))

   alt (*optional* fromEuro [ConvertFromEuro])

   alt (*optional* toEuro [ConvertToEuro]))

15.3.3 Deriving Product Behaviors

In section "Algebraic specification," we have specified PL behaviors using scenarios represented as UML2.0 SD enriched with variability mechanisms. Scenarios are not the only way to describe software behaviors; statecharts [19] are another formalism that is often used to depict the behavioral aspects of systems. However, if scenarios capture requirements in the early stage of the development process, statechart models are more dedicated to detailed design phases as they are closer to the implementation (some tools such as Rhapsody [21] generate code from them). To formalize product behavior derivation, we have studied the problem of statechart synthesis from scenarios. Furthermore, scenarios and statecharts differ in their nature (scenarios capture interactions amongst a *set of objects*, and statecharts represent the internal behavior of a *single object*). Statechart synthesis out of a collection of scenarios has received a lot of attention in the context of single product development [29,30,32,40]. So far, the proposed solutions do not consider the PL aspects. In this section, we propose an algebraic approach to synthesize product statecharts from PL scenarios. Firstly, variability is resolved by deriving the RESD-PL into a set of RESDs, one for each product. Then statecharts are generated by transforming product scenarios given as an RESD into a composition of statecharts.

Step 1: Product Expressions Derivation

The first step toward product behavior derivation is to derive the corresponding product expressions from the RESD-PL. Decision resolutions for a specific product are defined in what we call an *Instance of decision model (IDM)*, which is defined as follows:

Definition 5. An Instance of Decision Model (noted hereafter IDM) for a product P is a set of pairs $(name_i, Res)$, $name_i$ designates a name of an optional, variation or virtual part in the RESD-PL and Res is its decision resolution related to the product P. Decision resolutions are defined as follows:

- The resolution of an optional part is either TRUE or FALSE.
- For a variation part with E_1, E_2, E_3.. as expression variants, the resolution is i if E_i is the selected expression.
- The resolution of a virtual part is a refinement expression E.

Table. 15.2 shows four Instances of Decision Model associated with the four products in the BPL. For example, IDM1 is the Instance of Decision Model associated with the product BS1, which supports limits on accounts and does not offer the currency exchange calculation functionality.

The derivation can be seen as a model specialization through abstract interpretation of a generic PL expression in the IDMi context, where IDMi is the Instance of Decision Model related to a specific product. For each variability mechanism, the interpretation in a specific context is quite straightforward:

1. Interpreting an optional expression means deciding on its presence or absence in the product expression. This is defined as:

$$[\![\text{optional name [E]}]\!]_{IDMi} = \begin{cases} E \text{ if } (name, TRUE) \in IDMi \\ \\ E_\emptyset \text{ if } (name, FALSE) \in IDMi \end{cases}$$

Note that the empty expression is a neutral element for the sequential and the alternative composition. It is also idempotent for the loop, i.e:

- E **seq** $E_\emptyset$ = E ; $E_\emptyset$ **seq** E = E
- E **alt** $E_\emptyset$ = E ; $E_\emptyset$ **alt** E = E
- **loop** $(E_\emptyset)$ = $E_\emptyset$

This allows us to replace a complete part of a RESD-PL by $E_\emptyset$ when this part should be removed.

2. Interpreting a variation expression means choosing one expression variant among its possible variants. This is defined as:

$[\![$`variation name [ E1, E2, ..] `$]\!]_{IDMi} = E_j$ if $(name,j) \in$ IDMi

3. Interpreting virtual expressions means replacing the virtual expression by another expression:

$[\![$`virtual name [ E ] `$]\!]_{IDMi} = E'$ if $(name,E') \in$ IDMi

Table 15.2. Instances of the decision model for the banking product line

product	instance of decision model (IDM)
BS1	IDM1 ={(settingLimit,TRUE),(settingCurrency, FALSE),(withdraw Account, 1),(fromEuro, FALSE), (toEuro, FALSE)}
BS2	IDM2 ={(settingLimit, FALSE), (settingCurrency, FALSE),(withdrawAccount, 2), (fromEuro, FALSE), (toEuro, FALSE)}
BS3	IDM3 ={(settingLimit, FALSE), (settingCurrency, FALSE), (withdrawAccount, 2), (fromEuro, TRUE), (toEuro, TRUE)}
BS4	IDM4 ={(settingLimit, TRUE),(settingCurrency, TRUE),(withdrawAccount, 1), (fromEuro, TRUE), (toEuro, TRUE)}

The BS2 product expression E_{BS2} is obtained by the interpretation of the E_{BPL} in the IDM2 context:

$$E_{BS2} = [\![E_{BPL}]\!]_{IDM2}.$$

The derivation of the four optional expressions and the variation expression in E_{BPL} is realized as follows :

$[\![$`optional settingLimit [ SetLimit]`$]\!]_{IDM2} = E_{\emptyset}$
$[\![$`optional settingCurrency [ SetCurrency]`$]\!]_{IDM2} = E_{\emptyset}$
$[\![$`optional toEuro [ ConvertToEuro]`$]\!]_{IDM2} = E_{\emptyset}$
$[\![$`optional fromEuro [ ConvertFromEuro]`$]\!]_{IDM2} = E_{\emptyset}$

$$\left[\!\!\left[\begin{array}{l} \text{variation withdrawAccount} \\ \quad \text{[WithdrawWithLimit, WithdrawWithoutLimit]} \end{array} \right]\!\!\right]_{IDM2} =$$
$$\text{WithdrawWithoutLimit}$$

The reference expression obtained for the BS2 is the expression E_{BS2} below. Since $E_\emptyset$ is a neutral element for **seq** and **alt**, $E_\emptyset$ is removed from the product expression:

E_{BS2} = **loop**(Deposit **alt** (CreateAccount **seq** (CreateAccountOk)
   alt CreateAccountFailed) **alt** (WithdrawWithoutLimit
   seq (WithdrawOk **alt** WithdrawFailed)))

The BS4 product, which provides overdrawing on accounts and exchange operations, will be characterized by the presence of SetLimit, SetCurrency, ConvertToEuro, and ConvertFromEuro SDs; and by the choice of WithdrawWithLimit SD. The product expression obtained for product BS4 is:

E_{BS4} = **loop**(Deposit **alt** (CreateAccount **seq** (CreateAccountOk
   seq (SetLimit **seq** SetCurrency)) **alt** CreateAccountFailed)
   alt (WithdrawWithLimit **seq** (WithdrawOk **alt**
       WithdrawFailed))
   alt (ConvertFromEuro)
   alt (ConvertToEuro)

Step 2: Statechart Synthesis

The derived product expressions are expressions without variability, i.e., expressions that only compose basic SDs by interaction operators: **alt**, **seq**, and **loop**. The second step of our derivation approach aims at generating statecharts for objects in each derived product. Product SD are translated into statecharts using the method proposed in [44]. We generate flat statecharts, i.e., statecharts without hierarchy. Figure 15.10 shows examples of flat statecharts, in which states represented by double circled states are called junction states. Junction states are introduced to formalize statechart composition [44]. Transitions are labeled e/a, where e is a triggering event and a is an action. $ST_\emptyset$ refers to an empty statechart, containing a single state, which is at the same time an initial and a junction state (see the $ST_\emptyset$ statechart in Fig. 15.10).

Statechart Operators

Our method for statechart synthesis is based on an algebraic framework for statechart composition. This framework is inspired by the algebraic composition of UML2.0 SD [44]. We have formalized three statechart operators: **seq$_s$**, **alt$_s$** and **loop$_s$** for the

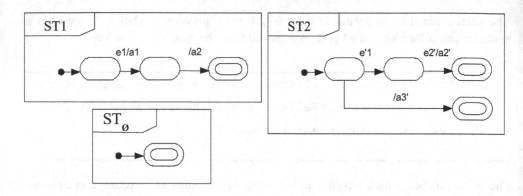

Fig. 15.10. Example of flat statecharts

sequencing, alternation, and the iteration of statecharts, respectively. In the rest of this section, we briefly describe these operators; the complete formalization can be found in [44]:

- *Sequence (seq$_s$)*. The sequential composition of two statecharts is a statechart that describes the behavior of the first operand *followed* by the behavior of the second one. Figure 15.11 shows the sequential composition of the ST1 and ST2.
- *Alternative (alt$_s$)*. The statechart resulting from the alternative composition describes a *choice* between the behaviors of its operands. See for example ST1 **alt$_s$** ST2 in Fig. 15.11.
- *Loop (loop$_s$)*. This operator defines *iteration* of a statechart. Figure 15.11 shows the iteration of the ST2.

As for sequence diagrams, we algebraically describe statechart composition with reference expressions.

Definition. 6. A reference expression *for statecharts (noted REST hereafter) is an expression of the form:*

```
<REST>::=<PRIMARY-REST> ( "alts" <REST> | "seqs" <REST>)*
    <PRIMARY-REST>::= STø | <IDENTIFIER> | "("<REST>")"
                        | " loops " "(" <REST> ")"
```

Synthesis Process

Using our algebraic framework for statecharts, translating product UML SD to statecharts is defined in two steps: synthesis from basic sequence diagrams and synthesis from combined SD. The next paragraphs describe these two steps.

Synthesis from basic sequence diagrams. In the first step of our synthesis method we generate statecharts from all basic SD in the PL. This step is based on an algorithm generating a statechart P(SD,O) depicting the behavior of each object O in each basic SD SD. We do not detail here the algorithm computing P(SD,O), which can be found in [44]. To summarize, this algorithm uses projections of SDs on object lifelines to generate the statecharts. Receptions in the SD become events in the statechart and emissions become actions. For a transition associated with a reception, the action part will be void, and for

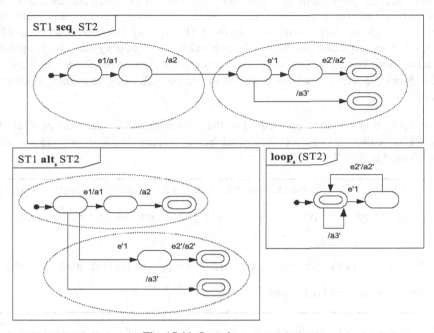

Fig. 15.11. Statechart operators

transitions associated with actions, the event part will be empty. The generated statechart contains a single junction state, which corresponds to the state reached when all events situated on an object lifeline have been executed. When an object does not participate in a basic SD, the algorithm generates an empty statechart. Figure 15.12 illustrates the synthesis of the statechart associated with the Bank object from the Deposit basic SD.

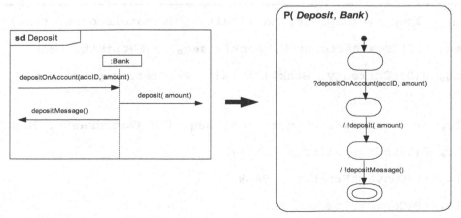

Fig. 15.12. Statechart synthesis from basic SD

Figure 15.13 shows the flat statecharts generated from the twelve basic SDs from Fig. 15.9 for the Bank object.

Synthesis from Combined Sequence Diagrams. Once we have obtained a collection of statecharts through projections of basic SDs, we now deal with combined SDs. Our method is based on the correspondence between interaction operators and statecharts operators and it allows constructing RESTs from RESDs [44]. For each object O, a REST is constructed by replacing in the RESD **seq**, **alt**, and **loop** by statecharts operators **seq$_s$**, **alt$_s$**, and **loop$_s$**, respectively, and each reference to an SD S by the statechart P(S,O) From the REST obtained, a statechart can be built using statechart composition operators.

Let us apply this construction method to the combined SD for the BS2 product. The Bank's REST, called REST$_{BS2}$ is described below. Figure 15.14 shows the statechart obtained from this REST.

REST$_{BS2}$ = **loop$_s$** (P(Deposit,Bank) **alt$_s$** (P(CreateAccount, Bank)

seq$_s$ (P(CreateAccountOk, Bank) **alt$_s$** P(CreateAccountFailed,

Bank)))

alt$_s$ (P(WithdrawWithoutLimit,Bank) **seq$_s$** (P(WithdrawOk,Bank)

alt$_s$ P(WithdrawFailed,Bank)))))

The same method can be applied for the BS4 product. Its reference expression E$_{BS4}$ is transformed into the statechart composition expression REST$_{BS4}$ defined below. Figure 15.15 shows the Bank statechart obtained from REST$_{BS4}$. Note that as BS2 and BS4 differ in the presence or the absence of an overdrawing limit and exchange operations, the synthesized statecharts differ in the transitions that concern these two functionalities. The differences between the statecharts obtained for product BS2 and BS4 are illustrated in Fig. 15.15 by gray zones.

E$_{BS4}$ = **loop$_s$** (P(Deposit, Bank) **alt$_s$** (P(CreateAccount, Bank)

seq$_s$ ((P(CreateAccountOk, Bank) **seq$_s$** P (SetLimit, Bank)

seq$_s$ P(SetCurrency, Bank)) **alt$_s$** P (CreateAccountFailed,

Bank)))

alt$_s$ (P(WithdrawWithLimit,Bank) **seq$_s$** ((P (WithdrawOk, Bank)

alt$_s$ P(WithdrawFailed, Bank)))

alt$_s$ (P(ConvertFromEuro, Bank))

alt$_s$ (P(ConvertToEuro, Bank)))

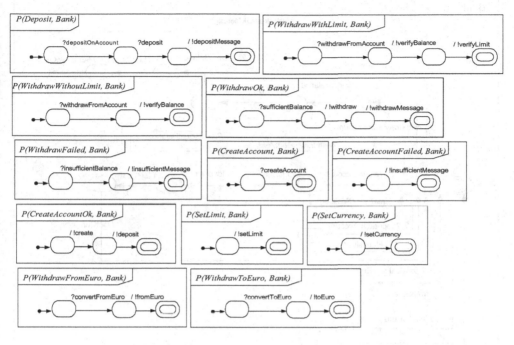

Fig. 15.13. Bank basic statecharts

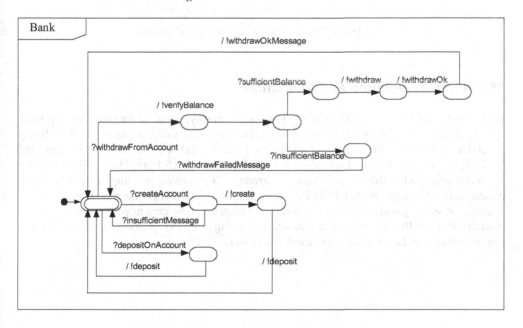

Fig. 15.14. The Bank statechart in the BS2 product

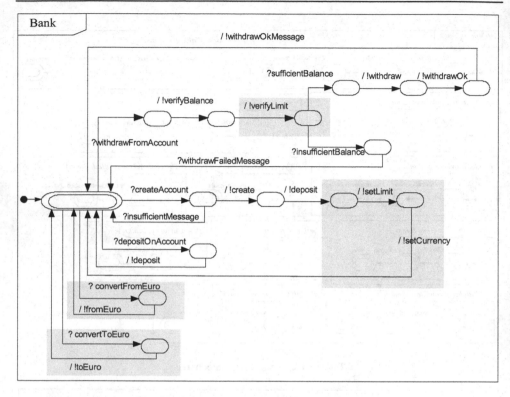

Fig. 15.15. The Bank statechart in the BS4 product

15.3.4 Implementation and Validation

In the context of the ITEA FAMILIES [1] project, a prototype tool of the proposed approach has been implemented in Java and is integrated into the Eclipse platform. It is freely available from http://modelware.inria.fr/plibs. UML2.0 SD with variability are specified in Eclipse, thanks to the Omondo case tool (see Fig. 15.16a) Then RESD-PL are automatically extracted from these diagrams. The prototype implements product expression derivations from RESD-PL according to a given IDM. Then a statechart for a specific object is generated from the derived expression. The generated statecharts can be visualized using the Omondo case tool again (see Fig. 15.16b). A complete description of the prototype can be found at http://modelware.inria.fr/plibs.

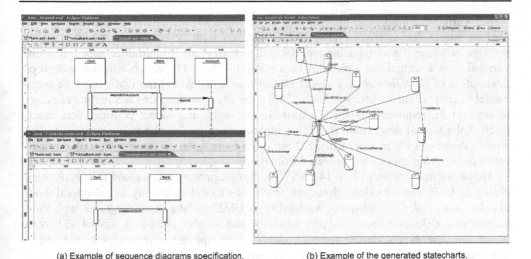

(a) Example of sequence diagrams specification.   (b) Example of the generated statecharts.

Fig. 15.16. Sequence diagrams and statechart visualization in the PLiBS prototype

We have used our approach for a complete BPL case study with 14 basic SDs. Table. 15.3 shows statistics (number of states and transitions) on the generated statecharts for the Bank object in each BPL member (these statistics show that the generated statechart for the Bank object differs from one product to another). We have also validated our approach on two case studies: The camera PL [42] and the auction PL [41]. As we noticed in Sect.15.3, some tools allow generating code from statecharts. We are currently studying code generation from the generated statecharts in our method using existing tools.

Table 15.3. States and transitions for the generated Bank statechart in the different products.

product	# states	# transitions
BS1	12	16
BS2	10	14
BS3	13	19
BS4	15	21

15.4 Related Work

Software PL Engineering with the UML has received a lot of attention in recent years. Table 15.4 summarizes existing work on PL engineering with the UML. Most of these works address variability modeling whereas only two works refer to the product derivation process.

For variability modeling, many works [5,17,18,26,37] are related to functional models (use cases). *Halmans et al.* [18] extend use cases with stereotypes to specify variability. Use cases are described using templates. *Bertolino et al.* [5] introduce tags to describe variability in a textual description of uses cases. In Chap. 11, readers can find a detailed description of *Bertolino et al.*'s work. *Maßen et al.* [37] extend the UML use case metamodel to support variability. *John et al.* [26] tailor use case diagrams and textual use cases to support PL requirements specification. In our work, we do not consider uses cases. Even if the textual description through templates, used by the previous works, is a good way to document PL requirements, SD are more operational and as shown with our approach detailed design can be generated from them.

There are many works [3,10,14,16,27,34,38] that propose extensions to specify variability in UML static models. However, few works model variability in behavioral models: *Gomaa et al.* [17] introduce variability in UML collaboration diagrams with three stereotypes <<kernel>>, <<optional>>, and <<variant>>. KobrA [3] introduces the stereotype <<variant>>, which can be applied to messages in SD and to statecharts. The KobrA's solution to specify variability in SD is difficult to use in practice. Indeed, if all messages in the same SD are optional, the user should specify all these messages with the stereotype <<variant>>. This can compromise the readability of the SD. On contrary, our <<optionalInteraction>> is applied to the complete SD. Flege [13,14] also introduces variability in UML statecharts. Note that all these works only concern UML1.x models.

While we formalized product derivation as UML model transformations, KobrA and Flege do not propose a means to implement derivation. *Cerón et al.* [8] propose two practices implementing the product architecture derivation. The main assumption in this proposition is: the PL is defined by an engineering assets repository and each product should choose components from this repository to obtain a product-specific architecture. *Haugen et al.* [20] also use UML2.0 SD to specify behaviors of systems. They introduce a new operator called **xatl** to distinguish between mandatory and potential behaviors. A potential behavior represents a variant of a mandatory behavior. This is close to our **variation** construct where interaction variants correspond to the potential behaviors.

In addition to these works, readers can find in Chap. 6 a complete study about Model Driven Engineering for Software PLs. The chapter also proposes a framework for modeling variability in PLs.

In Sect. 15.3, we have used statechart synthesis from scenarios to derive product-specific behaviors. There are many works on statechart synthesis; however these works only concern single product development (i.e., without consideration for variability). To our knowledge, there are no other works proposing statechart synthesis from software PL scenarios. The next paragraph describes existing works on statechart synthesis in the context of a single product development. There are works that synthesis statecharts from UML1.x, from Message Sequence Charts MSC [22] and from Live Sequence Charts [11].

Due to the poor expressive power of UML1.x SD, the proposed solutions for statechart synthesis [29,30,32,40] often use additional information or ad hoc assumptions for managing several scenarios. For example, *Whittle et al.* [40] enrich messages in SD with pre- and postconditions given in (Object Constraint Language) OCL, which refer to global state variables. State variables identify identical states throughout different scenarios and guide the synthesis process. Our approach does not use variables, and structures the state-charts and transitions based on information provided by lifeline orderings and SD opera-tors. *Koskimies et al.* [30] use the Biermann–Krishnaswamy algorithm [6], which infers programs from traces. This work establishes a correspondence between traces and scenar-ios and between programs and statecharts. In [29,32] it is also proposed to use interactive algorithms to generate statecharts from UML1.x sequences diagrams.

Several other approaches [31,35,36] study statechart synthesis from MSC [22], a scenario formalism similar to sequence diagrams. MSCs allow composition of basic scenarios (bMSCs) with High-Level Message Sequence Charts (HMSC). This composition mechanism is very close to that of current SDs in UML2.0 and our approach can be used to generate statecharts from MSCs.

Finally, Chap 13 also uses SD but it uses them to derive product-specific test cases from PL requirements and not for statechart synthesis.

Table 15.4. Existing works on PL engineering with the UML

	variability modeling			Product Derivation	
	functional aspects	**static aspects**	**behavior aspects**	**static aspects**	**behavior aspects**
Bertolino et al. [5]	X				
Halmans and Pohl [18]	X				
John and Muthig [26]	X				
Maßen and Lichter [37]	X				
Robak et al. [34]		X	X		
Clauß [9,10]		X			
Gomaa [16, 17]	X	X	X		
Flege [13, 14]		X	X	X	
KobrA [3]		X	X	X	X
SPLIT-Daisy [27]		X			
Webber [38]		X			

15.5 Conclusions and Future Research

In this chapter we have described PL design and derivation techniques building on advanced model transformation technology. Working at the level of UML design models, derivation of both static and behavior aspects was considered. For static aspect derivation, we started from a class diagram modeling the full PL along with a decision model given in the form of a set of concrete factories to build specialized UML models corresponding to the selected products. The challenge of such model manipulation is to be able to trans-form the model accessing its metalevel and ensuring the integrity of the derived model according to the PL-specific constraints.

For behavioral aspects derivation, we started from UML2.0 Sequence Diagrams extended with algebraic constructs to specify variability. We use interpretations of the algebraic expressions to resolve the variability and derive product expressions, which are ultimately transformed into a set of product-specific statecharts. The introduction of variability in behavioral models can be used to factorize common behavioral models in different products, and should then facilitate domain-engineering phases. However, some parts of the synthesis can be reused from one product to another, hence facilitating reuse during application engineering. As discussed in [44], statechart synthesis should be considered more as a step toward implementation rather than as a definitive bridge from user requirements to code.

In the context of the ITEA FAMILIES [1] project, prototype tools of the proposed app-roaches have been implemented. We used Model Transformation Language MTL and its related framework UMLAUT-NG for implementing the static aspect derivation. For behavioral aspects, a prototype tool has been implemented in Java and integrated into the Eclipse platform. We used our approach in several case studies; however we hope in the future to use it in an industrial context.

Acknowledgments

This work has been partially supported by the ITEA project ip02009, FAMILIES in the Eureka $\sum$! 2023 Program. We wish to thank Loïc Hélouët for many inspiring discussions. We also gratefully acknowledge the reviews of Stan Bühne, Juan Carlos Dueñas, Timo Käkölä, Kim Lauenroth, Jim Steel, and Patrick Tessier, which significantly improved the quality of this chapter.

References

1. FAMILIES project. http://www.esi.es/Families/ (2003)
2. Anastasopoulos, M., Gacek, C.: Implementing product line variabilities. Technical report, IESE report no. 089.00/E, version 1.0, IESE (November 2000)
3. Atkinson, C., Bayer, J., Bunse, C., Kamsties, E., Laitenberger, O., Laqua, R., Muthig, D., Paech, B., Wüst, J., Zettel, J.: *Component-Based Product Line Engineering with UML. Component Software Series* (Addison-Wesley, Reading, MA 2001)
4. Bass, L., Clements, P., Kazman, R.: *Software Architecture in Practices*, 1st edn (Addison-Wesley, Reading, MA 1998)
5. Bertolino, A., Fantechi, A., Gnesi, S., Lami, G., Maccari, A.: Use case description of requirements for product lines. In: International Workshop on Requirement Engineering for Product Line (REPL02), September 2002, pp 12–18
6. Biermann, A.-W., Krishnaswamy, R.: Constructing programs from example computations. IEEE Trans. Softw. Eng. **2**(3), 141–153 (September 1976)
7. Bosch, J., Florijn, G., Greefhorst, D., Kuusela, J., Obbink, H., Pohl, K.: Variability issues in software product lines. In: 4th Workshop Product Family Engineering (PFE4), 2001, pp 11–19
8. Cerón, R., Arciniegas, J.L., Ruiz, J.L., Dueñas, J.C., Bermejo, J., Capilla, R.: Architectural modelling in product family context. In: *EWSA*, ed by Oquendo, F., Warboys, B., Morrison, R. Lecture Notes in Computer Science, vol 3047 (Springer, Berlin Heidelberg New York 2004) pp 25–42
9. Clauß, M.: Generic modeling using UML extensions for variability. In: Workshop on Domain Specific Visual Languages at OOPSLA 2001, Tampa Bay, FL, USA, 2001
10. Clauß, M.: Modeling variability with UML. In: GCSE 2001 Young Researchers Workshop, 2001

11. Damm, W., Harel, D.: LSCs: breathing life into message sequence charts. Formal Meth. Syst. Des. **19**(1), 45–80 (2001)
12. Deelstra, S. et al: Product derivation in software product families: a case study. Syst. Softw. **74**(2), 173–194 (January 2004)
13. Flege, O.: System family architecture description using the UML. Technical report, IESE-report no. 092.00/E, IESE (December 2000)
14. Flege, O.: Using a decision model to support product line architecture modeling, evaluation, and instantiation. In: Proceedings of Product Line Architecture Work-shop. The 1st Software Product Line Conference (SPLC1), 2000, pp 15–20
15. Gamma, E., Helm, R., Johnson, R., Vlissides, J.: *Design Pattern Elements of Reusable Object-Oriented Software* (Addison-Wesley, Reading, MA 1995)
16. Gomaa, H.: Object oriented analysis and modeling for families of systems with UML. In: IEEE International Conference for Software Reuse (ICSR6), ed by Frakes, W.B., June 2000, pp 89–99
17. Gomaa, H.: Modeling software product lines with UML. In: International Workshop on Software Product Lines: Economics, Architectures, and Implications (SPLW2), ed by Knauber, P., Succi, G., 2001, pp 27–31
18. Halmans, G., Pohl, K.: Communicating the variability of a software-product family to customers. Softw. Syst. Model. **2**(1), 15–36 (2003)
19. Harel, D.: Statecharts: a visual formalism for complex systems. Sci. Comput. Program. **8**(3), 231–274 (1987)
20. Haugen, O., Stolen, K.: STAIRS-steps to analyze interactions with refinement semantics. In: UML Conference UML2003, October 2003, pp 388–402
21. I-Logix. Rhapsody. http://www.ilogix.com/
22. ITU-T. Z.120: Message Sequence Charts (MSC) (November 1999)
23. Jézéquel, J.-M.: *Object Oriented Software Engineering with Eiffel* (Addison-Wesley, Reading, MA 1996)
24. Jézéquel, J.-M.: Object-oriented design of real-time telecom systems. In: IEEE International Symposium on Object-Oriented Real-Time Distributed Computing, ISORC'98, Kyoto, Japan, April 1998
25. Jézéquel, J.-M.: Reifying configuration management for object-oriented software. In: Proceedings of the 20th International Conference on Software Engineering (IEEE Computer Society, Silver Spring, MD 1998) pp 240–249
26. John, I., Muthig, D.: Tailoring use cases for product line modeling. In: International Workshop on Requirement Engineering for Product Line (REPL02), September 2002, pp 26–32
27. El Kaim, W.: Managing variability in the LCAT SPLIT/Daisy. In: Proceedings of Product Line Architecture Workshop. The 1st Software Product Line Conference (SPLC1), 2000, pp 21–32
28. Kang, K., Cohen, S., Hess, J., Novak, W., Peterson S.: Feature-oriented domain analysis (FODA) feasibility study. Technical report, CMU/SEI-90-TR-21 (Software Engineering Institute November 1990)
29. Khriss, I., Elkoutbi, M., Keller, R.: Automating the synthesis of UML statechart diagrams from multiple collaboration diagrams. In: Proceedings of UML'98: Beyond the Notation, 1998, pp 115–126
30. Koskimies, K. et al: Automated support for modelling OO software. IEEE Softw. **15**: 87 94 (January 1998)
31. Krüger, I., Grosu, R., Scholz, P., Broy, M.: From MSCs to statecharts. In: *Distributed and Parallel Embedded Systems* (Kluwer, Dordrecht 1999) pp 61–71
32. Mäkinen, E., Systä, T.: MAS – an interactive synthesizer to support behavioural modeling. In: Proceeding of International Conference on Software Engineering (ICSE 2001) (2001)
33. Object Management Group (OMG): Unified modeling language specification version 2.0: superstructure. Technical report pct/03-08-02 (OMG 2003)
34. Robak, S. et al: Extending the UML for modeling variability for system families. Int. J. Appl. Math. Comput. Sci. **12**(2), 285–298 (2002)
35. Uchitel, S. et al: Synthesis of behavioral models from scenarios. IEEE Trans. Softw. Eng. **29**(2), 99–115 (February 2003)
36. Uchitel, S., Kramer, J.: A workbench for synthesising behaviour models from scenarios. In: Proceedings of International Conference on Software Engineering (ICSE 2001) (2001) pp 188–197
37. van der Maßen, T., Lichter, H.: Modeling variability by UML use case diagrams. In: International Workshop on Requirement Engineering for Product Line (REPL02), September 2002, pp 19–25
38. Webber, D.L.: The variation point model for software product lines. Ph.D. thesis (George Mason University, George Mason University, Fairfax, VA 2001)
39. Weiss, M.D., Robert Lai, C.T.: *Software Product-Line Engineering: A Family Based Software Development Process* (Addison-Wesley, Reading, MA 1999)
40. Whittle, J., Schumann, J.: Generating statechart designs from scenarios. In: Proceeding of International Conference on Software Engineering (ICSE 2000) (2000) pp 314–323
41. Ziadi, T., Hélouët, L., Jézéquel, J.M.: Moédélisation de lignes de produits en UML. In: Proceedings of LMO 2003, Langages et Modeles a Objets, Vannes, France, February 2003

42. Ziadi, T., Hélouët, L., Jézéquel, J.M.: Towards a UML profile for software product lines. In: Proceedings of the 5th International Workshop on Product Family Engineering (PFE-5). Lecture Notes in Computer Science, vol 3014 (Springer, Berlin Heidelberg New York 2003) pp 129–139
43. Ziadi, T., Hélouët, L., Jézéquel, J.M.: Modeling behaviors in product lines. In: Proceedings of REPL'02, Workshop on Requirements Engineering for Product Lines, Essen, Germany, September 2002
44. Ziadi, T., Hélouët, L.L., Jézéquel, J.M.: Revisiting statecharts synthesis with an algebraic approach. In International Conference on Software Engineering, ICSE'26, Edinburgh, Scotland, UK, May 2004, pp 242–251
45. Ziadi, T., Jézéquel, J.M., Fondement, F.: Product line derivation with UML. In: Proceedings of Software Variability Management Workshop (University of Groningen, Department of Mathematics and Computing Science February 2003)

16 Evaluation Framework for Model-Driven Product Line Engineering Tools

J. Oldevik, A. Solberg, Ø. Haugen, and B. Møller-Pedersen

Abstract

Both the model-driven development (MDD) approach and the product line engineering (PLE) approach envisage more efficient system development capable of delivering high-quality products by means of reuse, abstraction, configuration, and transformation. In order to succeed with model-driven product line engineering we need tools that support architects and engineers in tasks such as system modeling, variability modeling, model analysis, model transformation, system derivation, code generation, and model traceability.

Managing and automating these processes and tasks can be complex processes themselves. How to solve these complexities is a current topic of research. Unsurprisingly, no existing tool provides full support for an envisioned model-driven product line engineering approach. However, MDD and PLE are being paid a great deal of attention by the software development community, leading to an increasing number of tools emerging within this area. This is particularly the case for tools supporting Object Management Groups (OMG) envisioned model-driven engineering approach, Model Driven Architecture (MDA).

When exploring tool support for the evolving MDD and PLE disciplines, it can be difficult to know what features to look for and what to expect. This chapter relates traditional model-driven engineering to product line engineering and establishes a general framework for evaluation of tools in this area. The framework is defined in terms of desired characteristics, based on elicited requirements for model-driven product line engineering. It adheres to the general tool selection process described in the ISO 14102 standard. Some example MDD/PLE tools are evaluated using the framework to show its applicability and results.

16.1 Introduction

In product line engineering (PLE), the philosophy is to specify a general product line from which specific products can be derived or configured. The product line is specified at a higher abstraction level than the specific product, and it encompasses commonalities and variability [35]. Chapter 6 defines an approach toward a standard way of representing commonality and variability of product lines. Based on the product line, specific systems are derived by resolution of variability and abstractions. This task is often called *product derivation*. There exists a set of various techniques for performing product derivation, such as model transformation, code generation, and variability resolution. Examples are the approach described in Chap. 15, which looks at using UML for describing static and dynamic PL aspects and deriving products from these, and the approaches described in [1,2,17].

In model-driven system engineering, system development is performed in an integrated environment where models are the main instrument for development and integration. In model-driven development (MDD) processes, an extensive set of different interrelated models at different abstraction levels is developed. These models may range from business models, requirements models, and design models to deployment models and code. MDD envisions efficiency through modeling at different abstraction levels and automatic transformations between abstractions, including the generation of executable code. Thus, an advanced framework for MDD should provide well-structured support for modeling at different abstraction levels, traceability between model elements at different abstraction levels, model transformations, code generation and model synchronization.

MDD and PLE are currently being paid a great deal of attention by both academia and industry. A growing number of tools supporting MDD and PLE tasks are becoming available. In [4], Gartner predicts that model-driven service frameworks with architecture-based code generators will become as prevalent as traditional fourth-generation languages were in the 1990s. Furthermore, the Gartner Group recognizes portfolio management of product lines becoming a peak technology by 2004 [9].

MDD and PLE have similarities and differences, which in combination can provide mutual benefits. For instance, [14] suggests using PLE principles and techniques to define appropriate modeling concepts and thus obtaining proper scoping in an MDD environment, and using MDD principles to model the product line and derive systems. A combined approach has also been investigated in the FAMILIES [11] project [17,34]. Within testing, PLE and MDD share many of the needs. Chapters 11 and 12 show this in their applications of testing product line requirements.

Performing MDD and PLE tasks can be very complex, and tool support is essential to success. Since MDD and PLE are evolving and are relatively recent software system engineering disciplines, there are no well-established guidelines on how to evaluate and select proper MDD and PLE tools. In this chapter, we present an evaluation framework to support evaluation and selection of MDD and PLE tools.

The following sections justify, define, and exemplify the evaluation framework. Section 16.2 describes the relationships that exist between model-driven development and product line engineering. Section 16.3 elicits characteristics for tools and defines the evaluation framework. Section 16.4 shows an example of an evaluation of a selection of tools. Section 16.5 evaluates the tool evaluation framework and draws conclusions.

16.2 Combining Model-Driven Development and Product Line Engineering

Combining model-driven development (MDD) and product line engineering implies that the set of artifacts developed is based on models. In MDD, models are actively used in the development process, both as first-class artifacts and for producing documentation, code, etc.

The product line engineering approach brings concepts such as scoping, product line architecture, definition of domain concepts and components, variation, and product derivation into play [1,2,3,5,6,14]. A well-defined product line inherently specifies the scope of ones domain and defines the common architecture for the set of products in the product line. The variation spans the set of systems that may be derived. The product line approach aims to gain extensive reusability by generalizing a set of related products in a product line.

To combine MDD and product line engineering, it is necessary to specify the product line by models. Models can be specified using a standard modeling language such as Unified Modeling Language (UML). Another trend in MDD is to specify the models using Domain Specific Modeling (DSM) languages, for example using the MetaCase approach [24], Microsoft's software factory approach [14,24], or Xactium [38]. In UML, the profile mechanism [33] provides a means of defining DSM languages, for instance by defining stereotypes of domain specific concepts.

In addition to product specifications the model specifications typically describe the product line reference architecture, domain concepts, patterns, variability specifications, etc. By viewing product line derivation as a special case of model transformation [17], tools supporting MDD should in principle be able to support essential PLE tasks.

Many MDD and PLE approaches are based on component frameworks [8], in which abstractions, concepts, transformations, etc. are defined as part of the framework. The MDD/PLE combination can be implemented as a component framework, in which the product line defines the scope and MDD technologies, such as for instance UML and Meta Object Facility (MOF) [27], are used for specification of the framework. Model transformation technology may be used to perform model transformation and product derivation.

An example of a generic MDD framework that can be customized to support PLE is described in [36]. It provides tailoring to specific domains by means of UML profiles, reusable models, and patterns. UML profiles are used for defining domain concepts and reference architectures. Existing models are prepared for reuse if applicable. Patterns describe standard solutions of recurring problems within the domain. Using a product line to scope the domain, the framework will provide an environment of (a) domain concepts relevant for the actual product line, (b) the product line architecture, (c) common components and artifacts represented as reusable models at the product line level, and (d) variability mechanisms and variability that can be specified by patterns. Table 16.1 shows some parallels between activities of PLE and MDD.

Table 16.1. Parallels between the product line and MDD approaches

product line approach	model-driven development approach
scoping	elicitation of requirements
model of product line	high-level model of system
variability resolution and product derivation	model refinement and transformation
model of product	model of system
transformation of product model	transformation of system model
testing of product	testing of system
executable product	executable system

There are many overlaps between activities in PLE and traditional MDD approaches. The major difference is the reuse aspect of a single product line model, the scoping of this model, and the management of variability and commonality within it. The product line model is used for each production of new products. However, this is similar to the reuse of domain libraries (and models) in traditional development. Reuse is the main motivation for product lines. The main differentiating technical factor is the explicit usage of variability and variability resolution in the development process in PLE.

Variability resolution can be viewed as a kind of transformation process, or part of a transformation process, whereby decisions regarding variability in a Product Line Model are taken. The result is a new model, with less (or no) variability. The main difference between variability resolution and traditional MDD transformations is that the latter traditionally has no human interactions during the process.

Looking at the forthcoming standard transformation specification language in OMG, the Query/View/Transformation language (QVT) [30,32], human interactions during the model transformation are not allowed. However, provision of such interactions has been suggested in an evaluation report on QVT [15]. QVT is in the final stages of standardization at the time of writing. It defines a metamodel for transformations and concrete notations for expressing transformations. Two main parts are defined: a relational part that provides a declarative way of specifying and enforcing relationships between metamodels, and an operational part that offers imperative constructs for writing transformations in a procedural style. Another related process in OMG is the standardization of MOF Model to Text Transformations [29]. This process addresses the generation of text from MOF-based models, for example generating code or documentation from UML models. Standards such as these are likely to become key technologies in MDD and play important roles in model-driven product line engineering processes.

An example of a process in which a product line approach is combined with model-driven techniques is illustrated in Fig. 16.1. Here, it is assumed that the product line model is defined by a formal model, e.g., in UML. This model describes different aspects of the product line, such as business aspects, requirements, architecture, design, platform details, and the variability of the product line.

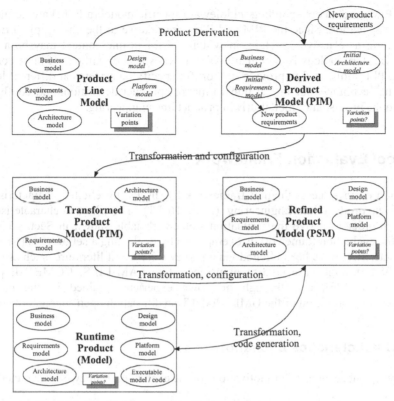

Fig. 16.1. Model-driven product line engineering – example process

When the process of developing a new system is initiated, it is based on a *product derivation* from the Product Line Model. This derivation and the model of the variability in the product line are the main factors that differentiate PLE and MDD. The variability defines a space of possible systems that can be derived. Once this process is completed and the Product Model has been defined, PLE can use the same techniques as traditional MDD.

During the development process, there may be *unresolved variabilities* from the original Product Line Model at different levels, which can be resolved at some point in the process. Consequently, a product line can be resolved, or configured, through a set of steps toward a more specific system.

Following the product derivation come phases that allow for system extension as well as refinement and configuration toward the final runtime system, starting with the Derived Product Model. Here, MDD techniques such as transformation and configuration may be used. New model elements, driven by new requirements, may be introduced on the way. In this kind of process, there may be any number of refinement steps toward different levels of model abstraction. In the example, the terms *platform-independent model* (PIM) and *platform-specific model* (PSM) are used to describe the abstractions.

The terms PIM and PSM are relative to some definition of the platform. For example, defining middleware as the platform (e.g., J2EE, CORBA and .Net), separation of platform-independent and platform-specific concerns occurs when a middleware-independent model (a PIM) and a corresponding middleware-specific model (a PSM) are defined for a particular application. Since the PIM and PSM are relative to the chosen platform, these concepts form a recursive structure, in which a PSM in one context may be a PIM in another. (This terminology is compliant with the MDA [31] definitions of these concepts.) MDD and PLE tools need to provide support for specifying systems at different levels of abstraction. Techniques for model transformation, product derivation, and configuration are keys to the provision of model-driven product line engineering.

16.3 Tool Evaluation Framework

This section defines the evaluation framework by discussing elicited characteristics for model-driven product line engineering (Sect. 16.3.1). The elicited characteristics are analyzed in order to derive the evaluation framework table shown in Sect. 16.3.2. The usage of the evaluation framework is exemplified by evaluating a set of tools (Sect. 16.4). The characteristics have been elicited via a survey of relevant literature, such as [1,2,5,8, 12,15,30,38], through case studies in projects like FAMILIES, COMBINE [7], and MODELWARE [26], and through our own experience gained in the course of development and provision of the UML Model Transformation open source tool [16,37].

16.3.1 Characteristics Elicitation

The following subsections offer motivation for the evaluation framework characteristics.

Support for MDD and PLE Mechanisms

Combining model-driven development (MDD) and product line engineering implies some prerequisites. First, it is required that the set of artifacts developed is in the form of models. Furthermore, model specifications of both the product line and the specific products need to be available. In MDD, the engineering process is driven by the set of prescribed models that need to be developed. Thus, tool support for modeling should be provided, and modeling languages such as UML should be supported.

Providing tailoring and configuration of the tool to better support a specific domain such as support for defining DSM languages (e.g., UML profiling) is important. In [10], several advantages of DSM languages over general purpose modeling languages are discussed. For instance, a DSM language raises the level of abstraction using constructs directly related to the application domain and provides notation close to practitioners' natural way of thinking.

In a combined MDD and PLE approach, the domain should be scoped by the product line. Variability specification and support for transformations and product derivation are other key mechanisms that ought to be in place.

Support for Standards

In many cases, it is important that a tool should support standards, as this caters for open architectures, easy integration, tool interoperability, and tool migration. For a business that is investing in model-driven tool technologies, this is important in order to avoid vendor locking.

The Object Management Group (OMG) is a major standardization organization in the MDD area. It operates through the promotion of MDA, which is based on standard modeling technologies such as the Unified Modeling Language (UML) [33], Meta Object Facility (MOF) [27], and XML Metadata Interchange (XMI) [28]. Ongoing standardization efforts like QVT and MOF Model to Text Transformation are also expected to be key technologies for realizing the MDA vision. These standards target languages for specifying model transformations and code generation, respectively.

MDD and PLE tools should provide mechanisms that support the separation of concerns, such as abstraction levels and views. Most graphical modeling languages provide a set of views through its set of diagram types (e.g., UML, which provides class diagram, interaction diagram, deployment diagram, etc.). Furthermore, the modeling language should support modeling of standardized viewpoints such as ISO RM-ODP [18], as well as any number of user-defined views. Also, features for modeling of PLE variability should be provided. General modeling languages like UML enable modeling of standardized and user-defined views. UML also support modeling of PLE variability to some extent, and UML profiles can be defined to extend the support for variability modeling [17,39].

Product Line Support

Currently, MDD does not address all aspects needed for product line engineering, such as specification and resolution of variability, which are key tasks for PLE.

In PLE, the timing for resolving variabilities may vary. For example, some variation elements may be resolved when deriving architecture models from business and requirements models, others when deriving detailed design models. When deriving implementations as executable code, some variabilities may still remain unresolved. These can be resolved at run time (*runtime variability*), for instance in order to gain context adaptation of the running system.

A tool should provide a flexible way of handling variability resolution. Variability should be permitted to be resolved at different stages in the development lifecycle, and also during run time.

Variation specifications may be inter-related. This may imply that a specific resolution of a variation may conflict with a set of possible resolutions of other specified variations. A resolution of a variation can depend on resolutions of a set of other variation specifications. Management of these kinds of dependences needs to be handled.

The consolidated meta-model for variability described in Chap. 6 provides valuable input for model-driven product line engineering, as it brings forward standard concepts for representing variability. It aims to provide a common basis for implementation by PLE tools.

Process Support

Process support is important in software engineering. Many general-purpose system development process frameworks are available and can be chosen in a combined MDD and PLE approach, for example the Rational Unified Process [22]. In addition to support MDD and PLE tasks, a model-driven product line engineering tool should enable integration and interoperability with standard tool portfolios used in software engineering processes.

In order to support a consistent development process, iterative and incremental development should be supported. In comparison with a waterfall-oriented process, iterative and incremental development caters better for change and for the fact that knowledge of the system and its purpose is typically evolving as it is developed. Iterative and incremental processes have become mainstream in the software engineering discipline, and tool chains used in software development should provide support for this paradigm. For MDD and PLE tools, this includes features such as:

- Support for roundtrip engineering
- Management of traces and relationships between models
- Management of change propagation between model abstraction levels without distorting model consistency

Model Transformation

Providing general refinements of abstract system specifications to more concrete specifications, and eventually to executable artifacts that meet expectations in terms of provided functionality and quality is a complex process.

Tools supporting a combined MDD and PLE approach should offer the capability to *specify* and *execute* transformations between models at different abstraction levels, as well as between models and implementation code. The standardization of model transformation technologies within OMG (QVT and the MOF model to text transformation) will coerce a new level of maturity in this field. Related aspects, such as *traceability support* in transformations and *bidirectionality*, will be of importance in many model transformation scenarios.

When performing model transformation and code generation it is essential to produce the desired results in terms of derived models and code. An important consideration in this respect is production of *expected functionality*; another key aspect is to deliver models and code that specify systems that will adhere to the required *quality* of the provided services. Thus, the specification and consideration of quality of service (QoS) when deriving product models are significant. Quality aspects such as usability, availability, performance, and security need to be managed throughout the system development process. For this reason, the support provided by tools in this respect needs to be evaluated.

Nonfunctional Properties

Nonfunctional tool properties will also be of importance for selecting the appropriate tool. Aspects such as tool pricing, availability, licensing, and maturity of the tool are important properties that affect decisions and the selection of tools. In [20], a more extensive set of nonfunctional properties is defined; subsets of these may be considered relevant dependent on the particular needs of the user.

16.3.2 Evaluation Characteristics

This section presents the evaluation characteristics for MDD tools in general and MDD tools that support PLE in particular. The previous section suggested a number of characteristics that were analyzed with the aim of identifying appropriate criteria within the evaluation framework.

The evaluation characteristics define a set of desired properties. The justification for each of them is indicated by a question, which needs to be answered during an evaluation. The output domain of permitted answers is defined for each question. Some questions have *Yes* or *No* as the output domain while others have a range of possible answers. An evaluation framework can hardly be complete, as is also argued in [23]. This framework includes common characteristics derived from a survey of relevant literature, case studies and own experience. However, the user can extend or modify the framework. For instance, more details of a characteristic can be explored by adding subcharacteristics with associated questions. Answers can be extended to include more options, and the weighting and criticality may be altered. Finally, characteristics can be added or removed by users. Each answer may also be accompanied by a more elaborate description of the specific issues concerning that feature of a tool. Table 16.2 shows the characteristics of the evaluation framework.

Table 16.2. Evaluation characteristics

CID x.y	characteristic	description/question	weight 1–5	critical Y/N
1	model specification	does the tool support specification of systems as graphical models? *{Yes/No}*	4	N
2	graphical notation for model transformation	does the tool support graphical specification of transformation? *{Yes/No}*	1	N
3	lexical notation for model transformation	does the tool support lexical specification of transformation? *{Yes/No}*	5	N
4	model-to-model transformation support	does the tool support model-to-model transformation? (e.g., from one UML model to another?) *{Yes/No}*	4	N
5	model-to-text transformation support	does the tool support model-to-text transformation, such as generation of source code? *{Yes/No}*	5	Y
6	support for model analysis	is there any support for model analysis? *{Yes/No}*	1	N
7	support for QoS management	is there any support for managing QoS during model specification and transformation? *{Yes/No}*	1	N

8	metamodel-based	is the tool based on explicit descriptions of the metamodels of source and target transformation? *{Yes/No}*	3	N
9	MOF integration	is the tool integrated with a MOF (or other metamodel-based repository)? *{Yes/No}*	4	N
10	XMI integration	is the tool integrated with XMI? *{Yes/No}* which version(s) of XMI is supported? *{list of versions}*	4	Y
11	based on UML	is the tool based on UML models as source and/or target models for transformation? *{Yes/No}*	2	N
12	UML specification	does the tool provide support for UML modeling *{Yes/No}*	4	N
13	UML tool integration	can the tool be integrated with existing UML tools? either directly, as active plug-ins in UML tools, or indirectly through model exchange via, e.g., XMI? *{Yes/No}or{names of the set of techniques}*	4	N
14	iterative and incremental transformation support	does the tool handle reapplication of transformation after model updates? *{Yes/No}*	3	N
15	bidirectional transformations	does the tool support bidirectional transformations? *{Yes/No}*	1	N
16	traceability	does the tool handle traceability of transformations, i.e., can it maintain traces of the source and targets of a transformation? *{Yes/No}*	4	N
17	product line variability modeling	is there support for modeling product line variability? *{Yes/No}*	4	N
18	product line variability Resolution	is there support for variability resolution? *{Yes/No}*	5	Y
19	DSM language support	is there support for defining domain-specific modeling languages (e.g., UML profiling) and DSM transformations? *{Yes (1)/DSM Transformations (0,5)/No.(0)}*	4	N
20	QoS variability	is there support for modeling and resolving QoS variability? *{Yes/No}*	3	N
21	decision process support	is there support for a decision process? *{Yes/No}*	5	N

22	maturity	what is the maturity of the tool? {Mature (0.7–1), medium(0.4–0.6), under development (0–0.3)}	2	N
23	usability	what is the usability level of the tool? is it *{Easy and intuitive (0.7–1), medium learning curve (0.4–0.6), steep learning curve (0–0.3)}*	1	N
24	availability and license	what is the license for the tool? *{Open source (1), freeware (0.4–0.9), commercial(0–0.3)}*	2	N
25	pricing	what is the pricing of the tool? *{the approximate pricing (0–0.9), N/A (1)}*	4	N

Characteristics 1–6 evaluate general support for MDD and to what extent a tool supports model specification and transformation. The *support for model analysis* characteristic will evaluate support for analysis and checking of model consistency, correctness, etc. Management of QoS during system specification and transformation is evaluated through characteristic 7. Flexibility and the extent to which the tool supports standards and enables easy integration and interoperability are the focus of characteristics 8–13. Supporting an iterative and incremental process model is evaluated through characteristics 14–16. Characteristics 17–21 are specifically tuned to supporting the specific requirements of product line engineering. General nonfunctional properties of the evaluated tool are the focus of characteristics 22–25. Many additional nonfunctional properties such as the extensive set presented in [20] may be relevant in particular cases. This framework only includes some of the important ones that will typically be considered. The user can add more nonfunctional properties if needed.

The Characteristic Identification (CID) field is used to number the characteristics for later reference. The numbering can be flat as shown in Table 16.2. The CID field can also be used to define a hierarchy of categories and characteristics. For instance, defining a category five named *Support for Product Line Techniques* would appear as shown in the table below.

5	support for product line specific techniques	
5.1	product line variability modeling	is there support for modeling product line variability? *{Yes/No}*
5.2	DSM language support	is there support for defining domain specific modeling languages (e.g., UML profiling) and DSM transformations? *{Yes (1)/DSM Transformations (0.5)/No(0)}*
5.3	product line variability resolution	is there support for variability resolution? *{Yes/No}*
5.4	decision process support	is there support for a decision process? *{Yes/No}*

This allows categories of characteristics to be summed separately. The CID field can also be used to add subcharacteristics using a similar technique. The weights and critical fields of the table are optional and are used to perform more advanced evaluations. The values assigned are used for the purpose of exemplification. The weight field is used to indicate how important a particular feature is for a particular user/domain. The weight function is used to cater for different users with various preferences and different problem categories requiring different types of support. The answers to the set of questions are normalized to a figure ranging from zero to one. For yes/no answers, *yes* can be normalized to 1 and *no* to 0. The weight may be a number from 1 to 5, and the final value of the characteristic is the product of weight and normalized value. If all features have the same importance, the weighting function is superfluous.

The *critical field* is used to indicate if a feature is critical. If the normalized answer appears to be 0 for a critical characteristic, the tool is not usable for the particular case. The evaluation framework characteristics in Table 16.2 define example instances of weights for each characteristic and set some of them to be critical [5,10,18].

In the following section, the evaluation framework is applied on a set of MDA-oriented tools.

16.4 Examples of Tool Evaluations

This section presents a selection of existing tools in the MDD/PLE area, examining their characteristics and seeing how they support the characteristics described in Sect. 16.3.2. The evaluations apply the weights for each characteristic and calculate the weighted score, which are summed up for each tool.

16.4.1 The Evaluated Tools

Since variability, domain concepts, and reference architectures can be specified in modeling languages like UML and product derivation can be viewed as a special case of model transformation [17], tools supporting MDD should in principle be able to support essential PLE tasks. Most of the relevant tools currently on the market are promoted as MDD tools. However, the evaluation framework explores the extent to which tools are able to support essential PLE tasks and to which they can be used in a model-based PLE approach.

The focus has been on evaluating a selection of tools, some of them commercial and some open-source based, which are positioned within the MDD arena and that focus on model transformation and code generation. In consequence, they should in principle support product derivation to some extent. Pure modeling tools such as traditional UML tools have not been evaluated, since we are interested in evaluating tools that provide support for the distinctive software engineering tasks that have appeared with the introduction of the MDD and PLE approaches, such as model transformation and system derivation.

The list below gives a brief overview of the tools evaluated:

- *Atlas Transformation Language* (ATL). An open-source MOF-based model transformation tool, which is part of the Eclipse GMT project (Sect. 16.4.3).
- *UML Model Transformation Tool* (UMT). An open-source UML/XMI-based tool for model transformation and code generation (Sect. 16.4.4).
- *ArcStyler*. A commercial MDA tool from Interactive Objects, which is bundled with the UML tool Magic Draw (Sect. 16.4.5).
- *XMF-Mosaic*. A commercial tool from Xactium, which provides a meta-programming environment (Sect. 16.4.6).

16.4.2 A Common Example

This chapter introduces a common example used in the evaluation of the tools – the watch example – a simple application representing a software wrist watch, described in terms of a UML-based feature model as shown in Fig. 16.2.

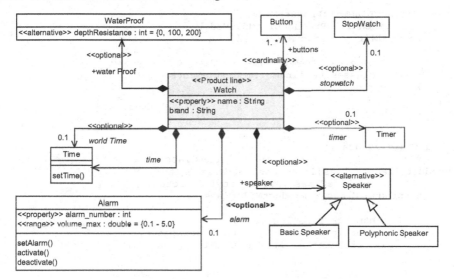

Fig. 16.2. The Watch example UML model

The Watch model represents a Watch product line (a general watch application), with a set of commonalities (such as the Time feature) and a set of variabilities (such as the Alarm and StopWatch feature). We recommend specifying a concrete domain example relevant for the particular product line, and using this actively when performing tool evaluation and selection. The watch example used here is defined in full detail in Chap. 6.

In the evaluation process, the Watch example has been used as a common basis for investigating tool characteristics. It has typically been used as an input model for testing transformation and product derivation capabilities, which has been valuable input for performing evaluation of the set of characteristics specified by the framework.

16.4.3 Atlas Transformation Language (ATL)

The Atlas Transformation Language (ATL) was developed by INRIA/University of Nantes as open source under the Eclipse (Generative Model Transformer GMT – http://www.eclipse.org/gmt) project. It is a hybrid language (a mix of declarative and imperative constructions) designed to express model-to-model transformations. ATL is similar to the QVT submission in terms of semantics, but differs in syntax. It is based on declarative rule definitions, which define mapping between source models and target models. The example below illustrates the ATL syntax in a transformation from a product line model to a product model, which could take as input, the Watch model.

```
module ProductLineDerivation;
create OUT:ProductMdl from IN:ProductLineMdl, IN2:VariabiliyMdl;

--
-- Product Line Model to Product Model rule
--
rule ProductLineMdl2ProductModel {
    from lineMdl : ProductLineMdl!Model
    to prodMdl : ProductMdl!Model
    (
            name <- lineMdl.name,
            classes <- lineMdl.modelElements
    )
}
--
-- Optional classes
--
rule ClassToClass {
    from                            lineClass :
ProductLineMdl!Class[lineClass.getVariability('Optional')
            and lineClass.variabilityIsSelected()]
    to productClass : ProductMdl!Class
    (
            name <- lineClass.name,
            description <- lineClass.description,
            attributes <- lineClass.attributes
    )
}
```

ATL provides no direct support for product line derivation. One possible way of supporting this would be to use a variability resolution metamodel as input for transformations together with the Product Line Model. The transformations could then use this combination of models to derive product models. The ATL code shown above illustrates this process. Two separate models are defined as input models; one defining the product line; the other the variability resolutions. Table 16.3 describes the characteristics of ATL.

Table 16.3. ATL characteristics

CID	characteristic	score/evaluation	weighted score
1	model specification	no. ATL cannot be used to specify models. It uses models as input for transformations and can generate new models	0
2	graphical notation for model transformation	no. ATL only provides lexical syntax for transformation	0
3	lexical notation for model transformation	yes. ATL lexical language, a declarative (hybrid) language	5
4	model-to-model transformation support	yes. ATL's main functional purpose is model-to-model transformation.	4
5	model-to-text transformation support	yes. Model-to-text transformation can be supported by streaming mechanisms of models to textual format.	5
6	support for model analysis	no. There is no direct support for model analysis. However, queries on models may be used to perform different analytical tasks	0
7	support for QoS management	no. There is no support for quality of service in ATL	0
8	metamodel-based	yes. ATL is based on MOF metamodels. It provides integration with several metamodel repository implementations	3
9	MOF integration	yes. ATL integrates with Netbeans Metadata Repository (MDR) and Eclipse Modeling Framework (EMF)	4
10	XMI integration	yes. ATL imports XMI files for metamodels and models, using support in underlying MOF/XMI frameworks, such as EMF	4
11	based on UML	yes. ATL supports transformation on UML models through MOF and XMI support	2
12	UML specification	no. There is no support for UML specification in ATL	0
13	UML tool integration	no. There is no direct integration with UML tools. There is indirect integration through MOF/XMI	0
14	iterative and incremental transformation support	no. There is no specific support for handling aspects such management of retransformations, reverse transformations, etc.	0
15	bidirectional transformations	no. There is no support for bidirection transformations	0
16	traceability	no. Traceability is not handled explicitly	0

17	product line variability modeling	no. There is no support for variability modeling in ATL	0
18	product line variability resolution	no. There is no support for variability resolution in ATL, but it may be supported through transformations based on input models that represent resolutions	1
19	DSM language support	the tool does not provide support for defining DSM languages. It provides support for transformations of DSM languages. E.g., transforming one DSM-based model to another DSM-based model	2
20	QoS variability	no. There is no support for variability of QoS aspects	0
21	decision process support	no. There is no support for handling a decision process. This would require human interaction during the transformation process	0
22	maturity	medium/underdevelopment	0.8
23	usability	steep learning curve	0.2
24	availability and license	open source (Eclipse Public License)	2
25	pricing	N/A	4

Summary. ATL provides a transformation language and tool that supports very general and flexible means of transforming between model abstractions defined by metamodels. It is open source, with an increasing user community, and currently under continuous development. However, it provides poor support for product line characteristics, such as the critical characteristic 18. The total weighted score using the defined weighting system is 37.

16.4.4 UML Model Transformation Tool (UMT)

UMT is an open-source tool for code generation from UML models [34,37]. It is based on reading UML models via XMI from different UML tools, such as Rational Rose, Together, ArgoUML, Poseidon, and Objecteering. Currently, it supports structural models (class) and activity models. It uses Java and XSLT as code generation/model transformation language and provides several example transformations toward EJB, WSDL, XML Schema, IDL, SQL, and more. The process of installing new transformations is quite simple.

UMT provides a graphical environment to install generators and run transformations on UML models. It uses a simplified XMI-like representation as the internal format, which is the structure used as input by transformations. There is no explicit basis in metamodels of target and source models. Transformations are thus based on ad hoc assumptions regarding input and output. It has support for a crude representation of profiles, which to some extent can be used to check model compliance. Figure 16.3 shows a snapshot of the UMT GUI after the product line model (the Watch model) has been loaded. The left field shows the model tree, with different model features and properties. The right field shows the variations and provides the user with resolution options.

In addition to code generation support, UMT supports variability resolution of UML product line models based on profiles and constraints on the source models. It provides a GUI that allows the user to resolve variabilities and generate configurations or products based on the decisions taken. Variability can be expressed within a UML model according to a simple UML profile. It supports selection of values (resolution of variability) and generation of new model configurations or concrete product models. Table 16.4 describes the characteristics of UMT.

Summary. UMT is an open-source, XMI-based tool tuned to code generation through XSLT or Java. It provides support for UML-based models, but not general MOF models. It provides support for product line variability based on a UML profile. Product line functionality is currently limited to using UML models that are according to a predefined UML profile. All the critical characteristics are supported. The total weighted score using the defined weighting system is 35.5.

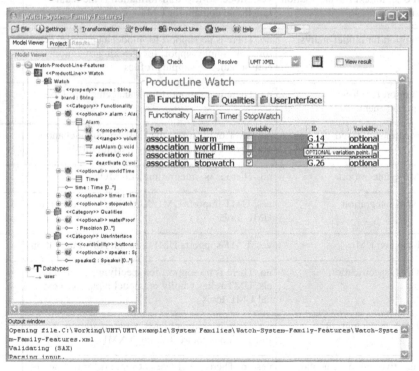

Fig. 16.3. UMT with variability resolution support

Table 16.4. UMT characteristics

CID	characteristic	score/evaluation	weighted score
1	model specification	no. There is no support for specifying models in UMT. It relies entirely on exported models from UML tools	0
2	graphical notation for model transformation	no. There is no graphical notation for model transformation	0
3	lexical notation for model transformation	yes. UMT uses XSLT and Java as transformation languages, with possibilities of extending to support other languages	5
4	model-to-model transformation support	no. There is no real support for model-to-model transformations. There is, however, possibility to generate "new" XMI models based on existing ones	0
5	model-to-text transformation support	yes. Model-to-text transformation is the main functional domain for UMT	5
6	support for model analysis	no. There is no support for model analysis, except for very simple support for checking of a model's conformance to simple profiles	0
7	support for QoS management	no. There is no support for management of QoS	0
8	metamodel-based	no. UMT only targets the UML metamodel and is not flexible with respect to changing this	0
9	MOF integration	no. There is no integration with MOF	0
10	XMI integration	yes. UMT imports UML/XMI files from different UML tools	4
11	based on UML	yes. UMT supports UML through XMI integration.	2
12	UML specification	no. There is no support for specifying UML models. UMT relies wholly on model input from external UML tools	0
13	UML tool integration	no. There is no direct UML tool integration. Integration is indirect through XMI	0
14	iterative and incremental transformation support	yes/no. There is lightweight support for regenerating code without overwriting previously generated and modified code	1

15	bidirectional transformations	no. There is no direct support for bidirectional transformation. However, there is some support for reverse engineering of code to XMI models	0
16	traceability	no. There is no support for traceability in UMT	0
17	product line variability modeling	no. There is no modeling support, but active support for loading UML models in which variability is specified	0
18	product line variability resolution	yes. There is support for resolution of variability specified in a UML model. This is supported for models that adhere to a product line profile, provided by a specialized tool for variability resolution.	5
19	DSM language support	the tool does not provide support for defining DSM languages. It provides support for transformations of DSM languages. E.g., transforming one DSM-based model to another DSM-based model	2
20	QoS variability	no. There is no support for QoS variability	0
21	decision process support	yes. A decision process is partly guided by the variability resolution part of the tool	4
22	maturity	medium	1
23	usability	medium learning curve	0.5
24	availability and license	open source (LGPL)	2
25	pricing	N/A	4

16.4.5 ArcStyler

ArcStyler is a commercial MDA tool bundled with the MagicDraw UML tool. ArcStyler is tuned to code generation, based on what are called MDA Cartridges, which have been developed in the MDA Cartridge Architecture – CARAT. A cartridge is essentially a specification and implementation of a transformation.

In ArcStyler, a set of predefined cartridges for common platforms is provided (e.g., J2EE, .NET). A user can also develop his own cartridges or adapt existing ones. A special model and code-based editing environment is provided for cartridge development.

Cartridges are designed partly on the basis of cartridge models, which specify the high-level structure of a cartridge in terms of artifacts and sets of artifacts. These specify which metamodel elements to work on. The details of cartridge transformations are implemented in Jython (previously JPython). Table 16.5 describes the characteristics for ArcStyler.

Table 16.5. ArcStyler characteristics

CID	characteristic	score/evaluation	weighted score
1	model specification	yes. Model specification is provided in a bundled UML environment (MagicDraw)	4
2	graphical notation for model transformation	yes. The overall structure of a cartridge is specified as a graphical model structure. The details of a transformation, however, are specified textually	1
3	lexical notation for model transformation	yes. The Jython language is used for lexical transformations	5
4	model-to-model transformation support	yes. There is some support for specifying and executing model-to-model transformations	4
5	model-to-text transformation support	yes. Generation of code is supported via the MDA Cartridges and the Jython language. This is the main functional area of ArcStyler	5
6	support for model analysis	no. There is no specific support for model analysis	0
7	support for QoS management	no. There is no specific support for QoS management	0
8	metamodel-based	yes. In some sense, ArcStyler is based on metamodels. The elements of a Cartridge use metamodel elements as input	3
9	MOF integration	no. There is no MOF integration	0
10	XMI integration	yes. The XMI capabilities provided by MagicDraw are supported	4
11	based on UML	yes. UML models from the bundled MagicDraw tool are the basis of generation	2
12	UML specification	yes, through the bundled UML tool	4
13	UML tool integration	yes. ArcStyler is bundled with MagicDraw. Integration with other UML tools is also possible through plug-ins	4
14	iterative and incremental transformation support	yes/no. Does not protect code areas in the built-in editor. Regeneration operates on the basis of commented tags. There is support for re-engineering through a Harvesting component	2

15	bidirectional transformations	no. There is no support for bidirectional transformation. However, there is support for harvesting code and regeneration	0
16	traceability	yes. Traces model elements to code using ID's in code comments	3
17	product line variability modeling	no. There is no support for variability modeling. However, this can be supported by applying a product line profile	0
18	product line variability resolution	no. There is no support for variability resolving	0
19	DSM language support	yes. Since it is bundled with MagicDraw, DSM language definitions can be specified using UML profiles	4
20	QoS variability	no. There is no support for QoS variability	0
21	decision process support	no. There is no support for a decision process in transformations	0
22	maturity	mature	1.6
23	usability	steep learning curve. Medium usability when just applying built-in cartridges. Cartridge development requires more time/has a quite steep learning curve	0.2
24	availability and license	commercial. Free "Community Architect Edition"	0.6
25	pricing	from €0 for the Community Edition to €9,800 for the full Architect Edition	0.4

Summary. The transformation capabilities of ArcStyler are powerful with respect to structuring, definition, and reuse of transformations. However, it is not possible to define points in a transformation where user decisions can control a transformation during progress. It thus seems difficult to support product line derivation using variation elements. The evaluation reveals a lack of support of critical characteristics [18]. The total weighted score using the defined weighting system is 47.8.

16.4.6 XMF-Mosaic

XMF-Mosaic has been developed by Xactium. It is a new tool, currently available in version 1.0. XMF-Mosaic provides a metaprogramming environment, which aims to offer freedom to program and model in *any* language with full support from graphical and textual editors.

The languages and tools that come with XMF-Mosaic provide general capabilities for language modeling. The tool is currently based on MDA standards such as MOF, OCL, and QVT.

XMF-Mosaic provides a modeling interface that is typically used to define the domain language (metamodel). It may also be used to model mappings. An example is shown in Fig. 16.4, which shows the definition of a simple interaction metamodel and a mapping to Corba Interfaces (the arrow symbol in the model). The source and target are specified using domain and range associations to the anchor concepts of the source and target for the specific transformation (*Lifeline* and *CORBAInterface* in Fig. 16.4).

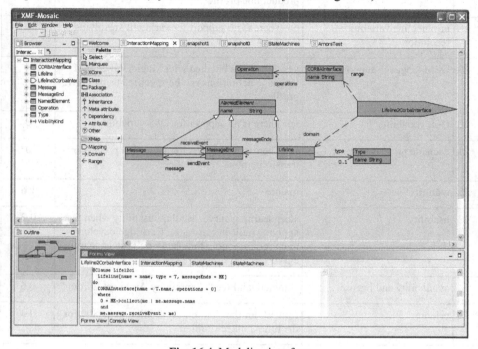

Fig. 16.4. Modeling interface

XMF-Mosaic provides support for the specification of model transformation through a language called XMap. XMap is defined using the XOCL language, a metaprogramming language for constructing languages and environments. It provides facilities for inspecting and controlling its own behavior and is the key technical feature that allows XMF-Mosaic to support tool development. The language is an imperative extension of OCL.

XMap is aligned with OMG's QVT language. An example of XOCL XMap syntax is as follows:

```
@Clause Lifel2ci
  Lifeline[name = name, type = T, messageEnds = ME]
do
  CORBAInterface[name = T.name, operations = O]
  where
    O = ME->collect(me | me.message.name
    and
    me.message.receiveEvent = me)
end
```

Since XMF-Mosaic is a framework with support for defining languages and environments and for building tools, and almost every technical criteria of our evaluation framework may be supported. *It just has to be built first.* However, the current version provides basic tools that support modeling and model transformations. The following evaluation is partly based on the provided tools and partly on the fact that characteristics may be developed as extensions. Table 16.6 describes the characteristics of XMF-Mosaic.

Table 16.6. XMF-Mosaic characteristics

CID	characteristic	score/evaluation	weighted score
1	model specification	yes. The tool supports specification of systems as graphical models by providing a subset of UML diagrams and notation	4
2	graphical notation for model transformation	yes. The downloadable version comes with limited graphical notation, which is combined with lexical notation (XMap) to make the specification complete	1
3	lexical notation for model transformation	yes. Lexical notation for model transformation is provided through XMap	5
4	model-to-model transformation support	yes	4
5	model-to-text transformation support	yes	5
6	support for model analysis	yes. Validity of models can be checked (i.e., whether they are according to their metamodel), both through an editor console and by building snapshots using the modeling interface. XWalk is an extension to XOCL, which provides facilities for efficiently running over large XCore object structures and evaluating their properties, for example running constraints or modifying data	1
7	support for QoS management	no. There is no explicit support for QoS management. However a QoS profile may be defined and used to specify QoS. These QoS profile concepts may also be used to derive QoS-aware transformation specifications	0
8	metamodel based	yes. It is based on XMF XCore, which is a MOF-like metakernel	3
9	MOF integration	yes	4

10	XMI integration	yes. XMF provides facilities for parsing and generating XML documents. High-level grammatical rules can be written, which state how a specific XML element pattern can be mapped to an XCore element or trigger the invocation an XOCL action. These rules can be used to generate a parser for a specific XML syntax	4
11	based on UML	yes. There is support for UML. It may support arbitrary modeling languages defined using XOCL. The downloadable version provides UML syntax	2
12	UML specification	yes. A subset of UML diagrams and notation is provided	2
13	UML tool integration	no. May use XMI. XMF-Mosaic supports sophisticated input and output facilities, which enable data to be streamed to and from files or other tools in a variety of different data formats	0
14	iterative and incremental transformation support	no. Process support, configuration management, etc. are not part of the XMF-Mosaic framework. XMF-Mosaic comes with the XSync language, which provides a high-level way of synchronizing data, where changes in one element cause changes to be automatically propagated to other elements	0
15	bidirectional transformations	yes. Languages for specifying bidirectional transformations may be defined using XOCL	1
16	traceability	no	0
17	product line variability modeling	yes. A product line variability modeling language may be defined	4
18	product line variability resolution	yes. Product line variability resolution mappings may be defined	5
19	DSM language support	yes. The tool provides support for defining DSM language through its metaprogramming environment and performs transformations based on these language definitions	4
20	QoS variability	no. There is no explicit support for QoS variability, but resolving functional types of QoS such as security and transaction control will be similar to defining and resolving functional variability	0
21	decision process support	no. There is no explicit support for a decision process	0

22	maturity	mature. XMF-Mosaic v1 was released in 2005	1.4
23	usability	medium learning curve	0.5
24	availability and license	commercial, free evaluation version	0.6
25	pricing	according to the web page XMF-Mosaic is competitively priced and includes 12 months' support and maintenance as standard. Discounts are available for bulk purchases and with consultancy-related packages. A significantly discounted noncommercial license (for students and academic departments) is also available	1.2

Summary. XMF-Mosaic is a very flexible tool, due to its meta-architecture providing functionality for defining relevant metamodels of the actual product line. This flexibility can appear as a problem as it lays the burden of defining metamodels on the user. However, some common metamodels and features come with the tool. Due to its flexibility, the tool can be configured to support many of the MDD and PLE tasks. The tool is model oriented, and both metamodels and transformations may be specified using models. The total weighted score using the defined weight system is 52.7.

16.5 Evaluation of the Framework

This section evaluates the work done, by analyzing the evaluation framework, the evaluated tools, and the applicability of the results. Then it compares the results with related works.

16.5.1 The Tool Evaluation Framework

The evaluation framework was derived from characteristics discussed in Sect. 16.3. The evaluation criteria are tuned to model-driven development tools in general with a specific focus on model transformation. The tool also includes important requirements for product line engineering, which are essential for supporting PLE in a model-driven context.

The resulting criteria are a mix of technical and practical aspects, which can act as a guide for selecting appropriate tools. The criteria alone do not allow for an easy comparison. In order to achieve this, the weight and critical properties must be defined and used in the evaluation. It is not fruitful to predefine these properties, since they will always be relative to specific domain needs. A set of domain experts should therefore define these prior to an evaluation.

16.5.2 The Tools Evaluated

The example evaluation is included to illustrate how the evaluation framework can be used. A set of state-of-the-art and advanced tools for model-driven development, both open source and commercial, are evaluated. The particular tools were included on the basis of their positioning as MDD tools, with a tuning to model transformation and code generation aspects. However, other tools could as well have been chosen. As part of the work, several additional tools were evaluated. These were mostly dedicated MDD tools, most of them lacking support for PLE, but providing different aspects of MDD functionality. The ones evaluated here were selected on the basis of their maturity and relevance as open source or commercial tools. Among the tools evaluated but not included in this chapter were the open source tools *MTL Engine, ModFact,* and *AndroMDA,* and the commercial tools *OptimalJ, Codagen Architect,* and *IQGen.*

This study has not included evaluations of dedicated UML tools. To a large extent, these also provide many aspects of MDD functionality, such as modeling and code generation. Traditionally, there has been little support for model transformation in this category of tools, and no direct support for PLE characteristics. At this time, however, we observe a growing degree of support for model transformation frameworks and even QVT in commercial UML tools. Examples are the latest Borland Together product, which implements the QVT specification, and the IBM Rational Software Architect (RSA), which implements a proprietary model transformation framework. Using built-in extension mechanisms in these tools, some support for PLE characteristics may be provided.

The evaluated Xactium tool is a representative of a DSM tool. This category of tools is characterized by their ability to support specification of domain specific languages. The language definition is then used to specify appropriate transformation specifications. In a PLE setting this is appealing, since specifying domain specific languages is an efficient mechanism for scoping product lines. Examples of other tools in this category are [24, 25].

The *V-Manage* tool suite from European Software Institute (ESI) has been described in Chap. 6. It provides an environment for defining and resolving variation models, and relating this to implementation of specific components. This tool has been excluded primarily because it is an in-house product not available to external purchasers.

16.5.3 Applicability of Results

The evaluation framework provides a baseline that can be used to evaluate and compare tools in order to make decisions when acquiring tools for model-driven product line engineering.

As shown above, the framework can be applied using selection guidelines and weights based on user requirements, which would leverage it for practical applications. It can also be integrated with existing case tool evaluation frameworks [20,23] for more holistic purposes. The evaluation examples show how different tools can be evaluated using the assigned weights. The resulting evaluation sum for a tool can be used to guide the final tool selection. A clear specification of the characteristics and the weighting is the key to a good evaluation.

This framework can be used in tool selection processes for model-driven product line tools, and will give the users a baseline, which can be modified based on their specific selection of characteristics. Such a selection would be more easily achieved if the framework characteristics have assigned weights and criticality.

16.5.4 Related Work

The ISO 14102 standard, guideline for the evaluation and selection of CASE tools [20], proposes a general standard for evaluation and selection. It defines a broad hierarchy of characteristics used to evaluate and select case tools in general. As pointed out in [23], there is a coverage problem with this standard; in any given case, it is not likely that the standard will cover all relevant characteristics; at the same time, it will probably include irrelevant characteristics.

This framework has a smaller scope and focuses only on evaluations of MDD- and PLE-type case tools. In line with experiences presented in [23], this framework is less extensive than that of ISO 14102, but it includes characteristics not listed there. Reference [23] also argues that the hierarchy presented in ISO 14102 can be a problem, since there is an agreed characteristic hierarchy, while most cases will need to deviate from this hierarchy. This framework provides a flat structure that can be defined as a hierarchy by the user. This is done by means of the identification number for categorization. (For example, the identification numbers of characteristics in category 1 is numbered $1[.x]*$, where x is a subnumber and $[.x]*$ implies zero or more subnumbers in order to build a multilevel hierarchy.) Other standards in the area such as [19,21] have similar problems to those of the ISO 14102 standard.

This framework can be seen as a specialization of ISO 14102, in which the domain of tools has been narrowed. Moreover, when using this framework, the evaluation and selection process as described in ISO 14102 can be used. ISO 14102 defines four major processes: Initiation Process, Structuring Process, Evaluation Process, and Selection Process.

In [13], the Gartner group suggests a list of recommendations when evaluating and selecting tools, including (1) do not worship one "hot" technology, (2) do not select tools before institutionalizing an application architecture and infrastructure, (3) do not acquire tools without an analysis/design tools acquisition strategy, (4) do not acquire too many or too few tools, (5) do not make deliberate trade-offs between application portability and optimization per platform, (6) always consider return on investment (ROI) and time-to-payback of analysis and design technologies, but extend the ROI model through end-user costs/benefits, (7) always try to select stable vendors with durable technology, (8) institute a modern, iterative methodology for analysis and design.

These characteristics are generally valid when evaluating and selecting many kinds of tools and are somewhat orthogonal and supplementary to guidelines like ISO 14102 and the framework presented here. One of the criteria (7), however, is in conflict with selecting open source technology, which is not always good advice. As this evaluation shows, open-source providers may provide software that supports pieces of model-driven product line processes, which may not even be supported by commercial tools.

16.6. Conclusions and Future Research

This chapter has offered an overview of model-driven development and product lines and has looked at how they can be integrated. We have described a framework, based on tool characteristics that can be used to evaluate and compare the suitability of MDD and PLE tools. We have also described a set of tools, which we have used as examples for evaluation, and applied the framework to these in specific evaluations.

When considering MDD and product lines in light of existing tools, it is clear that few tools available today provide specific functionality capable of supporting product line and MDD concepts out of the box. This is primarily due to lack of acknowledgment of the need for product line support from traditional MDD tool providers. Looking at the assessment of the range of tools used as input for this chapter, some tendencies can be seen: A growing number of tools support model-driven development in both modeling and transformation. Generally speaking, few of these specifically address PLE at present. However, the inherent flexibility of many tools permits extensions that may address this to be built. Looking ahead, we can expect more stability and more possibilities of providing such extensions. The increasing attention to domain-specific modeling (DSM) languages in the MDD area, e.g., [14,24,38] is promising seen from the PLE perspective. Defining domain-specific modeling languages can for instance be used to scope product lines and provide more efficient support for modeling domain specific concepts.

Product line engineering is currently the subject of much attention, as documented for instance in [5,9,35]. In [14], which describes the Microsoft *Software Factory* concept, PLE is predicted to be an important part of modern software engineering. This is confirmed by recent provisions in Microsoft's Visual Studio tool suite, such as the domain-specific language tools and the spec# language [24].

Our experience from projects such as COMBINE [7] and MODELWARE [24] is that well-defined scoping is essential for success with MDD. Using product line engineering techniques to provide proper scoping seems appropriate. For this reason, we believe that PLE techniques and mechanisms will be incorporated in future MDD tools. Initially, this will happen through suitable configuration and scoping mechanisms, then through the provision of product line-reusable assets and variability management. Support for more interactive transformation processes is also needed both for pure MDD [15], and in model-driven product line engineering approaches.

The market and focus for tools supporting different aspects of MDD are steadily growing, and the quality and functionality of such tools are improving. Influencing or initiating standards, e.g., for variability modeling, will improve the chances of achieving more tool support for PLE, through both open source and commercial tools.

The evaluation framework presented here provides a baseline for evaluating MDD and PLE tools. It can be extended or supplemented, for example with characteristics defined in ISO 14102 and tailored to the need of the specific domain, and as such would be applied to future tools.

Acknowledgments

We gratefully acknowledge the extensive reviews of Juan Carlos Dueñas, Alessandro Fantechi, Timo Käkölä, Janne Luoma, Juha-Pekka Tolvanen, and Tewfik Ziadi, which significantly improved the quality of this chapter.

References

1. Atkinson, C., Bayer, J., Bunse, C., Kamsties, E., Laitenberger, O., Lagua, R., Muthig, D., Peach, B., Wust, J., Zettel, J.: *Component-based Product Line Engineering with UML* (Kobra) (Addison-Wesley, Reading, MA 2001) ISBN 0-201-73791-4. http://www.iese.fhg.de/Kobra_Method/
2. Atlas Transformation Language (ATL) homepage. http://www.sciences.univ-nantes.fr/lina/atl. Cited 24 Nov 2005
3. Becker, M.: Towards a general model of variability in product families. In: Software Variability Management Workshop (SVM 2003). 25th International Conference on Software Engineering (ICSE, 2003)
4. Blechar, M.J., Driver, M.: Predicts 2004: MDSFs Offset J2EE Complexity, Gartner report, ID Number: SPA-21-5432
5. Bosch, J.: *Design & Use of Software Architectures – Adopting and Evolving a Product-Line Approach* (Addison-Wesley, Reading, MA 2000) ISBN 0-201-67494-7
6. Clauß, M.: Generic modeling using UML extensions for variability. In: Workshop Domain Specific Visual Languages, OOPSLA, USA, October 2001
7. COMponent-Based INteroperable Enterprise system development (COMBINE), ESPRIT V IST project no. 20893. http://www.opengroup.org/combine/. Cited 16 Nov 2005
8. Czarnecki, K., Helsen, S.: Classification of model transformation approaches. In: 2nd Workshop on Generative Techniques in the Context of Model-Driven Architecture, Conference on Object-Oriented Programming, Systems, Languages, and Applications 2003 (OOPSLA'03)
9. Duggan, J., Vecchio, D., Plummer, D.C., Driver, M., Natis Y.V., Hotle, M., Feiman, J., James, G.A., Sinur, J., Pezzini, M., Light, M., Blechar, M.J., Valdes, R., Lanowitz, T.: Hype Cycle for Application Development, 25 June 2004, Gartner report, ID Number: G00120914
10. Estublier, J., Vega, G., Ionita, A.D.: Composing domain-specific languages for wide-scope software engineering. In: MoDELS 2005 Conference, ed by Briand, L., Williams, C., ISBN3-540-29010-9, pp 69–83
11. FAct-based Maturity through Institutionalisation Lessons-learned and Involved Exploration of System-family engineering (FAMILIES), ITEA project ip02009, Eureka Σ!2023. http://www.esi.es/en/Projects/Families/. Cited 16 Nov 2005
12. Gardner, T., Griffin, C., Koehler, J., Hauser, R.: A review of OMG MOF 2.0 Query/Views/Transformations Submissions and Recommendations towards the final Standard, (MetaModeling for MDA Workshop Nov 2003. York, UK)
13. Gartner Group: Application Development Management – Enterprise Applications Development Tools – Evaluation and Selection, Strategic analysis report, Gartner Group, Sept 1996
14. Greenfield, J., Short, K., Cook, S., Kent, S., Crupi, J.: *Software Factories, Assembling Applications with Patterns, Models, Frameworks and Tools* (Wiley, New York 2004) ISBN 0-471-20284-3
15. Grønmo, R., Aagedal, J., Solberg, A., Belaunde, M., Rosenthal, P., Faugere, M., Ritter, T., Born, M.: Evaluation of the QVT Merge Language Proposal, MODELWARE project report, SINTEF report number STF90 A05046, ISBN 82-14-03659-3, OMG document ad/2005-03-05. http://www.omg.org/cgi-bin/doc?ad/05-03-05
16. Grønmo, R., Oldevik, J.: An empirical study of the UML Model Transformation Tool (UMT). In: The 1st International Conference on Interoperability of Enterprise Software and Applications (INTEROP-ESA), Geneva, Switzerland, Feb 2005
17. Haugen, Ø., Møller-Pedersen, B., Oldevik, J., Solberg, A.: An MDA-based framework for model-driven product derivation. In: The 8th IASTED International Conference on Software Engineering and Applications, ed by Hamza, M.H. (ACTA, Nov 2004) pp 709–714
18. International Standards Organization (ISO): ISO/IEC 10746-1:1998, Information technology – open distributed processing – reference model: overview (ISO RM-ODP), ISO/IEC 10746-1:1998 (ISO standard, 1998)
19. International Standards Organization (ISO): ISO/IEC 12119:1994, Information technology – software packages – quality requirements and testing (ISO Standard 1994)

20. International Standards Organisation (ISO): ISO 14102:1995, Information technology, guideline for the evaluation and selection of CASE tools, JTC 1/SC 7 (ISO Standard 1995)
21. International Standards Organization (ISO): ISO/IEC 25000:2005, Software engineering – software product quality requirements and evaluation (SQuaRE) (ISO Standard, 2005)
22. Jacobson, I., Booch, G., Rumbaugh, J.: *The Unified Software Development Process* (Addison-Wesley, Reading, MA 1999) ISBN 0-201-57169-2
23. Lundella, B., Lings, B.: Comments on ISO 14102: the standard for CASE-tool evaluation. Comput. Standards Interf. **24**(5), 381–382 (November 2002)
24. MetaCase Whitepaper: ABC to MetaCase Technoology. http://www.metacase.com/, © 2004 by MetaCase. Cited 26 Nov 2005
25. Microsoft Corporation: Visual Studio 2005 Team System Modeling Strategy and Faq, In: MSDN Library. http://msdn.microsoft.com/library/default.asp?url=/library/en-us/dnvs05/html/vstsmodel.asp. Cited 16 Nov 2005
26. MODELing Solutions for softWARE systems (MODELWARE), ESPRIT VI IST project no. 511731. http://www.modelware-ist.org. Cited 16 Nov 2005
27. Object Management Group (OMG): Meta Object Facility 2.0 (MOF), Meta Object Facility (MOF) 2.0 Core Specification, OMG document ptc/03-10-04. http://www.omg.org/cgi-bin/apps/doc?ptc/03-10-04.pdf. Cited 16 Nov 2005
28. Object Management Group (OMG): Meta Object Facility 2.0 XMI Mapping Specification, OMG document ptc/04-06-11. http://www.omg.org/cgi-bin/apps/doc?ptc/04-06-11.pdf . Cited 16 Nov 2005
29. Object Management Group (OMG): MOF model to text transformation language request for proposal, OMG document: ad/2004-04-07. http://www.omg.org/cgi-bin/doc?ad/04-04-07. Cited 16 Nov 2005
30. Object Management Group (OMG): MOF Query/Views/Transformations RFP, OMG document: ad/2002-04-10. http://www.omg.org/cgi-bin/doc?ad/02-04-10. Cited 16 Nov 2005
31. Object Management Group (OMG): OMG MDA Guide v1.0.1, OMG document omg/2003-06-01. http://www.omg.org/docs/omg/03-06-01.pdf. Cited 16 Nov 2005
32. Object Management Group (OMG): MOF QVT Final Adopted Specification, OMG Adopted Specification, OMG document number ptc/05-11-01 http://www.omg.org/cgi-bin/doc?ptc/05-11-01. Cited 9 April 2006
33. Object Management Group (OMG): Unified Modeling Language 2.0 (UML 2.0), UML 2.0 infrastructure final adopted specification. http://www.omg.org/cgi-bin/apps/doc?ptc/03-09-15.pdf. Cited 16 Nov 2005
34. Oldevik, J., Model transformation for system families prototype, FAMILIES consortium-wide deliverable, CWD4.3:2.3 version 1.0. http://www.esi.es/Families/. Cited 16 Nov 2005
35. Pohl, K., Böckle, G., van der Linden, F.: Software product line engineering – foundations, principles, and techniques (Springer, Berlin Heidelberg New York 2005) ISBN 3-540-24372-0
36. Solberg, A., Oldevik, J., Jensvoll, A.: A generic framework for defining domain-specific models. In: *UML and the Unified Process*, ed by Favre, L. (IRM, Hershey, 2003) pp 23–38
37. UML Model Transformation Tool (UMT). http://umt-qvt.sourceforge.net/. Cited 16 Nov 2005
38. Xactium Limited: Language Driven Development and XMF-Mosaic, Whitepaper. http://www.xactium.com (2005). Cited 24 Nov 2005
39. Ziadi, T., Hélouët, L., Jézéquel, J.M.: Towards a UML profile for software product lines. In: *Software Product-Family Engineering*, ed by van der Linden, F., 5th International Workshop, PFE 2003, Italy, Nov 2003. Lecture Notes in Computer Science, vol 3014 (Springer, Berlin Heidelberg, New York 2003) pp 129–139

Glossary

Annotations or, in UML 2.0 terms, stereotypes are used to describe extra language constructs for defining variability within the notations of the *base model* language.

Application Artifacts are the *development artifacts* of specific product line applications.

Application Design is the development of a single application architecture conforming to the *reference architecture*.

Application Engineering is the process in which the applications of the software product line are built by reusing *platform artifacts* and exploiting the variability of the product line.

Application Realization is the development of applications based on the *application architecture* and the set of *domain artifacts*.

Application Requirements Engineering is the sub-process of *application engineering* dealing with the communication of product line capabilities to the stakeholders, the elicitation of stakeholder requirements, and the creation of the application requirements specification.

Application Test Case captures the input specification, output specification, execution information, environment information, and fail-pass criterion for the application under test. It refers to the corresponding *application test case scenarios*.

Application Test Case Scenario specifies the interactions between internal and/or external actors of the application under test in terms of precise instructions for the tester.

Application Test Plan contains the specification of the resources, the test strategy, and the test case prioritization for the application. It specifies precisely the application test cases to be created and how variability is dealt with in the application test, e.g. which configuration mechanisms are used for the test cases.

Application Testing is the process of uncovering the evidence of defects in a software product line application.

Architecture, see *software architecture*.

Architectural Pattern is a specialized *architectural tactic* that may include prescribed components, component specifications, component collaborations and component roles.

Architectural Solution is a representation of knowledge of how particular problems can be solved in *software architecture*. Architectural solutions span a continuum from high-level *architectural tactics* to specialized *architectural patterns*.

Architectural Structure is the decomposition of a software system into parts and relationships.

Architectural Tactic is a means of satisfying a *quality-attribute-response measure* by manipulating some aspect of a quality attribute model through architectural design decisions. Architectural tactics are high-level architectural patterns.

Architectural Texture is the collection of common development rules for realizing the applications of a software product line.

Asset, see *development* artifact

Base Model is a model defined in a standard language such as UML 2.0 that consists of *model elements*.

Component is a unit of composition with contractually specified *component interfaces* and explicit context dependencies only; it can be deployed independently and is subject to composition by third parties.

Component Framework is a structure of *components*, or object classes, where *plug-in* components or object classes may be added at specified plug-in locations. To fit, each plug-in has to obey rules defined by the framework.

Component Interface provides a connector between *components*. A required interface of a component has to be connected to a provided interface of another one.

Composite Structure, a UML 2.0 term, denotes the *architectural structure* of parts of an object or system.

Consolidated Variability Metamodel defines the concepts of variability modeling and how the concepts are interrelated. The metamodel contains *base model*, *variation model*, and *resolution model*.

COTS is the acronym of "Commercial-off-the-shelf". This term subsumes *components* from different sources with different degrees of modification possibilities. Sources may vary from in-house, through nuances of non-developmental, to commercial.

Development Artifact is the output of a sub-process of *domain* or *application engineering*. Development artifacts encompass requirements, architecture, components, and tests.

Domain is an area of process or knowledge driven by business requirements and characterized by a set of concepts and terminology understood by stakeholders in that area. The problem domain and the solution domain are two kinds of domains.

Domain Artifacts are reusable *development artifacts* created in the sub-processes of *domain engineering*. Synonyms are *platform artifacts* and *product line artifacts*.

Domain Design is the development of a *reference architecture* for the complete software product line.

Domain Engineering is the process of *software product line engineering* in which the commonality and the variability of the product line are defined and realized.

Domain Realization is the development of the set of reusable *components* and interfaces within a given *reference architecture*.

Domain Requirements Engineering is the sub-process of *domain engineering* dealing with the identification of common and variable *requirements* and their documentation in reusable *requirements artifacts*.

Domain Specific Language is a (modeling) language designed for a particular domain. It expresses domain concepts as language constructs. A product line is the set of all systems that may be modeled with this language.

Domain Specific Modeling is the art of using a *domain specific language*.

Domain Test Case is a description of a single test flow that has to be performed to test a specific test item. A test case consists of a test case scenario, input data, the expected result, information about the execution, environmental needs, and fail-pass-criteria.

Domain Test Case Scenario A domain test case scenario is a variable sequence of interactions between variable internal and/or external actors of a system under test.

Domain Test Plan specifies the kind of results of the test planning activity. Additionally, it documents precisely the domain test cases to be created and how to deal with variability.

Domain Testing is the process of uncovering the evidence of defects in domain artifacts and creating reusable test artifacts for *application testing*.

DSL, see Domain Specific Language.

DSM, see Domain Specific Modeling.

Evolution denotes the changes performed to any *asset* or a set of them with respect to time, including expectations for future changes.

External Variability is variability of *domain artifacts* that is visible to customers; see also *internal variability*.

Feature is an end-user visible characteristic of a system.

Feature Model is a description of a *variation model* (often in a specific non-standard language).

Goal is an objective the system under consideration should achieve.

Internal Variability is variability of *domain artifacts* that is hidden from customers; see also *external variability*.

Mass Customization is the large-scale production of goods tailored to individual customers' needs.

Metamodel is a model which describes a language with which models can be expressed. A metamodel can also be understood as the model of the repository of a tool for the modeling language.

Model Element represents any kind of a model asset in a model in a given modeling language. It is a constituent of a *base* model.

Orthogonal Variability Model describes the *variation points* and *variants* and their relationships in a model that is separate from other software models. Links are defined to relate the orthogonal variability model to artifacts of these other models (or *base models*).

Platform Artifacts, see *domain artifacts*.

Plug-in denotes a component fitted into a *component framework* through an explicit interface (in UML 2.0, through a port).

Product Line Artifacts, see *domain artifacts*.

Product Line Model is an instantiation of the *consolidated variability metamodel* for one specific product line. Specific products may be derived from the product line model by instantiating the related *resolution model*.

Product Management is the process of controlling the development, production and marketing of the software product line and its applications.

Quality-attribute-response Measure denotes a quantifiable impact on a quality attribute.

Redefinition is the mechanism to override definitions of properties in a *specialization*.

Reference Architecture is a core *software architecture* that captures the high level design of a software product line.

Requirement: (1) A condition or capability needed by a user to solve a problem or achieve an objective. (2) A condition or capability that must be met or possessed by a system or system component to satisfy a contract, standard, specification, or other formally imposed document. (3) A documented representation of a condition or capability as in (1) or (2) [IEEE Std 610.12-1990].

Requirements Artifacts are products of the requirements engineering process. They can be textual or model-based *requirements*.

Resolution Element is a constituent of a *resolution model* defining a particular binding of *transformers*.

Resolution Model defines resolutions of variability for a product line model. The resolutions reference *variability specifications*. A resolution model defines the particular bindings of variability in a *variation model*. A resolution model containing resolutions for all *variability specifications* of a product line model represents the derivation of a product model.

Scenario is a specific sequence of interactions between two or more actors illustrating the external behavior of these actors.

Security Architecture Language denotes a semantically rich vocabulary of architectural solutions that individually promise to address security quality *requirements*. The reference architecture containing the language adds a reasoning framework to support the construction of software architectures expressed in the language.

Software Architecture is the set of the main guiding development principles for one or more software applications. The principles are the solution for one or more architectural concerns dealing with quality. There are other, more instrumental, definitions in literature.

Software Platform is a set of software subsystems and interfaces that form a common structure from which a set of derivative products can be efficiently developed and produced.

Software Product Line is a set of software-intensive systems that share a common, managed set of features satisfying the specific needs of a particular market segment or mission and that are developed from a common set of *domain artifacts* in a prescribed way.

Software Product Line Engineering is a paradigm to develop (models of) software product lines and to produce software applications (software-intensive systems and software products) by resolving variability in *product line models*. It uses *software platforms* and enables *mass customization* through *domain engineering* and *application engineering*.

Software Product Line Engineering Framework is an abstract representation of the two core processes for *software product line engineering* and the *assets* produced.

Specialization denotes a relation between concepts indicating that a concept is more specialized than the other more general concept in the relation. In object orientation, the respective term is *inheritance*.

Subclass is a *specialization* of a class.

Template is a generic term used in languages such as C++ and UML 2.0 to denote the parameterization of types.

Transformer denotes a *variability specification* describing the change needed to the referred *model elements*. When a transformer is completely bound by a *resolution element*, the *base model* will change accordingly and the transformer is no longer needed in the model, see *variant*.

Use Case is a description of system behavior in terms of scenarios illustrating different ways to succeed or fail in attaining one or more *goals*.

Use Case Model captures the functional *requirements* of a system in terms of *use cases*.

Variability Constraint is a *variability specification* representing constraints on valid resolutions, see *variability dependency*.

Variability Dependency is a relationship between a *variation point* and a set of *variants* indicating that the *variation point* implies a decision about the *variants*.

Variability in Space is the existence of an artifact in different shapes at the same time.

Variability in Time is the existence of different versions of an artifact that are valid at different times.

Variability Object is a particular instance of a *variability subject*.

Variability Specification represents the variability of a *variation element*, such as optionality (the element is either included or not in the derived product), required dependencies etc. It has a range of further *specializations*.

Variability Subject is a variable item of the real world or a variable property of such an item.

Variant is a representation of a *variability object* within a *development artifact*.

Variation Element represents something with variable nature. It is a constituent of a *variation model*. The variation elements will refer to *model elements* of the *base model* pinpointing what *model elements* are affected by variation. Common *model elements* of a product line are not related to variation. Variation element is more general than a *variation point*.

Variation Model consists of *variation elements* and defines the properties of variation. It keeps track of all *variation elements* of the *product line model*.

Variation Point is a representation of a variability subject within a development artifact enriched by contextual information.

Index

Activity diagram, 44, 336, 398, 403, 408, 474, 475, 481, 483, 485-489, 491, 495, 497, 500-502, 511, 515, 517-519

Annotation. *See Variability by language enhancement, Variability using annotations/extensions*

Application, 161, 162, 163-172, 174, 175-188, 190, 191

architecture, 267, 319, 320, 330, 364, 615
scenario, 502-506, 511
artifact, 479, 493, 510-512. *See Artifact*
design, 163, 181, 330
engineering, XIII, XIV, 120-122, 127, 136, 143, 161-163, 166-168, 174, 186, 192, 204, 222, 233, 234, 238, 246, 250, 327, 330, 341, 424, 433, 437, 479-481, 483, 489, 493, 495, 499, 502, 503, 505, 507, 508, 510, 511, 517, 521, 523-526, 531, 532, 586
requirements engineer, XV, 126, 161, 164
requirements engineering, XV, 125, 126, 161, 163-170, 174, 175, 177, 190, 191, 192, 423, 515
requirements specification, 126, 161, 164-166, 175, 177, 181, 182, 185-188, 190, 191, 192, 493, 509
stakeholders, 126, 161-164, 172, 175-178, 180, 181, 185-188, 190, 191
system test, XVI, 423, 447, 494, 499, 502
test case, 437, 461, 467, 479, 480, 493, 512, 516, 518
test case scenario
integration test, 479, 481, 483, 484, 491-494, 502-507, 511, 512, 517, 518

system test, XVI, 481, 483-485, 487, 491-497, 499, 501, 502, 508, 510
testing, 423, 480, 482, 489, 490, 493, 507, 510, 511. *See Domain testing, Testing*
test plan. *See Test plan*
test scenario, 462
test specification, 458
use case scenario, 168, 494, 495, 498, 500-503, 505, 511, 516

Architecting method, 3-6, 15
Attribute Driven Design, 4
Bosch, 4, 13
Scenario-Based Architecting, 1, 5, 6, 11, 12, 14, 15, 49, 55, 57, 270
Visual Architecting Process, 4, 5, 10, 46

Architectural
model, VI, XIII, 244, 252, 327-329, 333, 335, 338, 340, 366, 373-380, 395, 407, 409, 417-419, 491
pattern, 248, 253, 266, 268, 269, 276, 277, 284, 286, 302, 336, 377, 386, 387, 410, 419
solution, 246, 266, 267, 268, 276-280, 285, 286, 289, 300, 302, 304-323, 374, 375, 409, 417, 418
structure, 10, 29, 47, 197, 198, 201, 202, 214, 218, 248, 249, 251, 252, 257, 261, 267, 271, 277, 331, 338, 376, 377, 386, 395, 396, 398, 399, 401, 402, 404, 405, 407, 408, 417, 418
style, 9, 40, 46, 248, 253, 374-377, 379, 380, 384, 386-388, 393-395, 399, 405, 410, 416-420
tactic, 277-279, 282, 283, 300, 301, 328
texture, 248, 249, 251, 252, 257, 267, 270, 271